READINGS IN

ACOUSTIC
PHONETICS

READINGS IN
ACOUSTIC
PHONETICS

Edited by Ilse Lehiste

THE M.I.T. PRESS

Massachusetts Institute of Technology
Cambridge, Massachusetts, and London, England

INTRODUCTION

This collection of articles is intended primarily for readers who come to acoustic phonetics with a background in general linguistics and articulatory phonetics. Meant to serve as a basic collection of references, the volume does not constitute a graded reader or a substitute for an introductory course in acoustic phonetics. A number of introductory textbooks are listed among the references at the end of this book, but I am convinced that acoustic phonetics should not be learned from books alone and that some laboratory experience is indispensable before one can really become an acoustic phonetician. Although the articles have been selected primarily with linguists in mind, I hope that the volume will be useful to anyone interested in acoustic phonetics and that it will contribute to the kind of overlap of knowledge between acoustic engineers, physicists, linguists, and speech scientists which makes successful cooperation between them possible.

The articles in this collection have been selected on the basis of several criteria, all of which could not be simultaneously satisfied. First of all, I have tried to present articles in which an original idea was formulated for the first time. In many cases, the idea has been developed further either by the author himself or by others who have followed the same line of investigation. Thus the articles do not represent the latest "state of the art"; in fact, some of them have been superseded by more recent work. But many notions that are now in the public domain were once formulated in an article for the first time, and it appeared to be the right thing to make available the articles in which this first formulation appeared.

A second criterion was based on whether the item was difficult to obtain. Anyone who has tried to teach acoustic phonetics to a class consisting mainly of linguists has heard the complaint that the references on the reading list are located in physics or engineering libraries where an intruding linguist is met with amused suspicion. Since the collection is, first of all, aimed at readers with a linguistic background, I have omitted articles that have appeared in reports of linguistic and phonetic congresses and articles that have been published in relatively recent issues of linguistic and phonetic journals.

A number of other restrictions had to be adopted for reasons of space and availability. Thus I have not included any part from a monograph or book (except for Chapter 3, which is, however, a complete chapter rather than an excerpt) ; a list of books, parts of which I would have liked to include, is given at the end of this text. Furthermore, most, if not all, selected articles deal with English. This is partly due to historical reasons: much of the recent work in acoustic phonetics has in fact been done by investigators for whom the English language was of paramount interest. Also, any attempt to cover a wider selection of languages would have extended the scope of the book to unmanageable proportions.

A further criterion was completeness of coverage in terms of subject matter. An attempt was made to include at least one article in each area in which acoustic phonetics has made important contributions. The articles are grouped under three headings. Part I contains articles dealing with acoustic theory of speech production and the techniques of acoustic analysis. Part II presents articles dealing with the acoustic structure of vowels, diphthongs, stop consonants, fricatives, nasals, laterals, trills, and glides, as well as prosodic features. Speech synthesis has provided an indispensable tool for testing the relevance of the results of acoustic analysis; Part III contains some basic articles describing speech synthesis as a research technique, as well as a few selected articles dealing with speech perception. Within each part, the articles have been arranged according to year of publication; articles that appeared in the same year have been alphabetized according to the name of the author.

The attempt to achieve completeness in coverage resulted in a tighter selection in some areas than in others; some readers will probably feel that certain stronger articles have been excluded, while some weaker articles have been included, or that an author is not represented by his most important article. I wish that it had been possible to include all articles of great and lasting merit; in a way, however, it is pleasing to know that our field has produced much more than can be condensed into a volume like this one.

The time appears to be right for a stocktaking in the field of acoustic phonetics. We seem to have reached a plateau, and the focus of research in experimental phonetics seems to have shifted — perhaps temporarily — to areas about which less is presently known. There is a renewed interest in articulatory phonetics, with electromyography as the most promising research technique, and a resurgence of interest is anticipated in studies of perception when more becomes known of the functions of the human brain. New and very interesting work in acoustic phonetics continues to be done, but in a very real sense we are witnessing the consolidation of the achievements of a generation of researchers — some representative papers of which are assembled in this collection.

I should like to thank all authors and publishers whose cooperation has made the compilation of this volume possible. Detailed references to sources from which the articles were reprinted are given at the beginning of each article and in the Contents.

Columbus, Ohio
March 2, 1967   ILSE LEHISTE

CONTENTS

PART I

Acoustic Theory
and Methods of Analysis

CHAPTER 1

Reprinted from THE JOURNAL OF THE ACOUSTICAL SOCIETY OF AMERICA, Vol. 17 (July 1946).

The Sound Spectrograph*

W. KOENIG, H. K. DUNN, AND L. Y. LACY

Bell Telephone Laboratories, Inc., New York, New York

(Received May 4, 1946)

The sound spectrograph is a wave analyzer which produces a permanent visual record showing the distribution of energy in both frequency and time. This paper describes the operation of this device, and shows the mechanical arrangements and the electrical circuits in a particular model. Some of the problems encountered in this type of analysis are discussed, particularly those arising from the necessity for handling and portraying a wide range of component levels in a complex wave such as speech. Spectrograms are shown for a wide variety of sounds, including voice sounds, animal and bird sounds, music, frequency modulations, and miscellaneous familiar sounds.

I. GENERAL

IN many fields of research it is necessary to analyze complex waves. If these waves are steady in time, the analysis presents no particular difficulties. If, however, the wave is complex in its frequency composition and also varies rapidly in time, the problem is very difficult. Numerous methods have been employed in the past to try to show changing energy-frequency distribution; several examples have appeared in the pages of this journal. Figure 1, for instance, shows a series of harmonic analyses of the successive periods of a vowel sound.[1] The dotted lines mark the regions of resonance which change continuously throughout the production of the sound. By performing this operation on a whole sentence, an effort was made, as shown in Fig. 2 taken from the same paper, to represent the time variations in the energy-frequency distributions. Here the frequencies of the various resonant regions are represented by the solid lines and their relative amplitudes are roughly indicated by the widths of the lines. The generation of this graph represented a formidable amount of time and labor.

Figure 3 shows another representation of a changing wave form.[2] This is an oscillogram of a series of 11 steady tones sent over a radio channel and received through a bank of narrow band filters whose outputs were commutated at the rate of $12\frac{1}{2}$ times per second. A slight gap was left between cycles, as marked at the bottom of

Fig. 3. The successive cycles show varying profiles, due to the fact that the frequency response of the radio channel was continually changed by selective fading. Similar pictures would have been obtained if a varying signal such as speech had been impressed on the bank of filters without

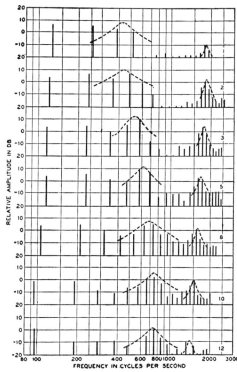

FIG. 1. Illustrating one method which has been used in the past to show how vocal resonances change with time. This is a series of harmonic analyses of successive periods of the vowel in the word "out."

* Paper presented before the meeting of the Acoustical Society of America, May 10, 1946, New York, New York.
[1] J. C. Steinberg, J. Acous. Soc. Am. 6, 16–24 (1934).
[2] R. K. Potter, Proc. I.R.E. 18, 581–648 (1930).

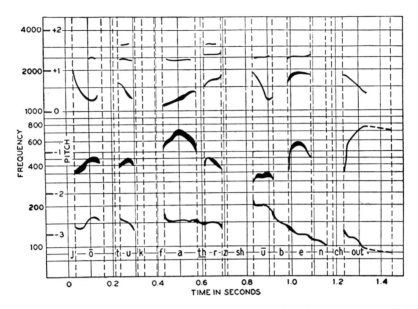

FIG. 2. A plot of the time variations of the vocal resonances in a short sentence, compiled from a series of analyses like those in Fig. 1.

the radio link. Instead of making oscillograms, however, the output was at that time displayed on a cathode-ray tube. The changing profiles of these patterns portrayed the changing energy frequency distribution in speech. An attempt was made to learn to recognize these word patterns, but with little success.

Figure 4 shows another device for portraying a complex wave.[3] Here a kind of three-dimensional model was developed by analyzing the amplitude of each harmonic component of a piano note as a function of time, plotting the results on cards, and cutting out the profiles.

Still another method is illustrated in Fig. 5. Here the frequency range was divided into ten bands[4] by means of band filters. The output of each band was rectified and recorded with a string oscillograph, so that each oscillogram shows the variation of amplitude with time. Despite the rather small number of bands, a kind of speech pattern can be discerned in this array of oscillograms.

Figure 6 shows this process carried further.

These are solid models built up of oscillograms of about 200 overlapping frequency bands, cut out in profile and stacked side by side. In the upper model only the high peaks in the speech are prominent. In the lower model the level differences among the various regions have been equalized by electrical compression which will be explained subsequently. Of particular interest in these models is the sharpness of the wave front which appears at the beginning of some of the words. It can be seen from these models that in speech the energy-frequency distribution is very complex and changes form rapidly with time.

The production of solid models, while useful for particular purposes, is hardly a practical method for everyday needs. Furthermore, it is difficult to portray the results usefully in a two-dimensional picture. If, however, we substitute for the third dimension in these models a system of varying shades of gray or black with the highest amplitudes represented by dark areas and the lowest amplitudes by light areas on a flat surface, then we have a method which can be rapid and convenient. This is the method of the sound spectrograph.

[3] O. H. Schuck and R. W. Young, J. Acous. Soc. Am. 15, 1–11 (1943).
[4] Homer Dudley, J. Acous. Soc. Am. 11, 169–177 (1939).

20

II. GENERAL PLAN AND FIRST MODEL OF
THE SOUND SPECTROGRAPH

Figure 7 shows in highly schematic fashion the basic method of the sound spectrograph, as originally proposed by Mr. R. K. Potter.[5] It is necessary, first, to have a means of recording the sound in such a form that it can be reproduced over and over. The means shown here is a magnetic tape, mounted on a rotating disk. In recording, some predistortion of the signal may be desirable and is therefore indicated in connection with the recording amplifier. With speech, for example, it has been found advantageous to raise the amplitude of the higher frequencies by about 6 db per octave in order to equalize the representation of the different energy regions.

Second, a means of analyzing must be provided. Most convenient is the heterodyne type of analyzer employing a fixed band pass filter, with a variable oscillator and modulator system by which any portion of the sound spectrum can be brought within the frequency range of the filter.

Finally, the output of the analyzer must be recorded in synchronism with the reproduced sound. The simplest method is by means of a drum, on the same shaft with the magnetic tape, carrying a recording medium which should be capable of showing gradations of density depending on the intensity of the analyzer output. Each time the drum revolves, the stylus which marks the paper is moved laterally a small distance, and the oscillator frequency is changed slightly. Thus a picture is built up which has time as one coordinate and frequency as the other, with intensity shown by the density or darkness of the record. It may be necessary or desirable to distort the amplitudes in the analyzer output, depending on the recording medium used and the use to be made of the spectrograms. This function is indicated in the figure by the compression in the last amplifier.

The first spectrograph set up in the laboratory differed in some particulars from the arrangement shown in Fig. 7. Instead of a recording drum on the same shaft with the magnetic tape, use was made of a machine built for radio fac-

[5] See introductory paper of this series.

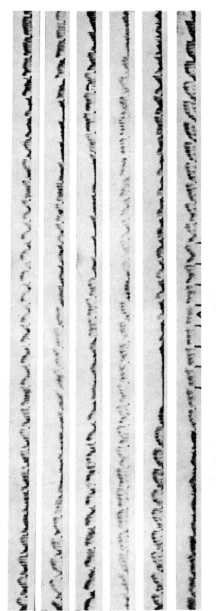

FIG. 3. Oscillogram of a series of 11 tones transmitted over a radio channel and received through narrow band filters whose outputs were repeatedly scanned with a commutator. A single cycle is included in the section marked A; here the circuit was momentarily almost flat; the other cycles show changing profiles due to the changing response of the circuit through selective fading.

21

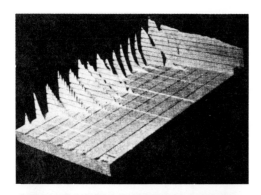

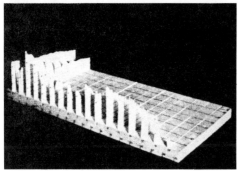

FIG. 4. Three-dimensional models portraying the amplitudes of the several harmonics of a piano note as functions of time.

simile reception, which happened to be available. This device had a cam-driven arm sweeping a stylus across a strip of conducting paper. The paper had a light-colored surface which became progressively darker as the current passing through it increased. Each sweep of the arm was started by a synchronizing signal which in this case came from a contact connected to the disk carrying the magnetic tape. The paper was automatically advanced 0.01 inch between sweeps. The machine had to be modified to the extent of slowing down the motion and providing a new cam to make the motion more uniform.

For the analyzing portion of the system, use was made of another piece of available equipment, namely an ERPI heterodyne analyzer. No mechanical connection was provided between the analyzer and the magnetic tape or the recording system, so the frequency had to be shifted by hand after each sweep of the recording arm. In the beginning, the output of the analyzer was rectified and a thyratron threshold arrangement was employed ahead of the recorder, so that it printed only when the analyzer output rose above a predetermined level, and there were no gradations in density. When it was found that intensity could be shown by the density or blackness of the record, the threshold was dispensed with; but because of the small range of currents required for printing the full density range of the paper, it was necessary to compress the sig-

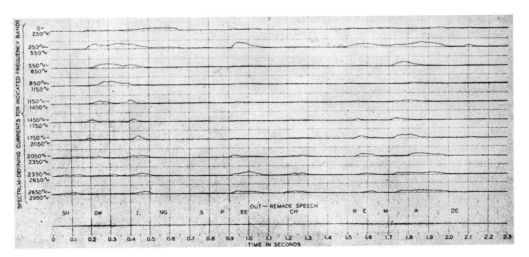

FIG. 5. Another method of illustrating the energy-frequency-time distribution in speech: a series of oscillograms of the rectified outputs of 10 band filters.

22

FIG. 6. A solid model built up of oscillograms, similar to those of Fig. 5, for 200 overlapping frequency bands. The words are "visual telephony for the deaf." The two models differ in the amount of amplitude compression.

nal. This was done with a sort of partial automatic volume control arrangement, and adjustments were made until a 35-db signal level range was covered, with what looked to the eye like even density steps on the paper for even db changes of level.

A sample spectrogram of speech made with this arrangement is shown in Fig. 8. The coordinates of time and frequency are indicated. The analyzing band width was 200 cycles, with the band being shifted (by hand) 50 cycles for each new sweep of the recording arm. The sentence shown is a familiar one, containing most of the vowel sounds. The most gratifying feature of these early spectrograms was the clear indication

of the almost continual shifting in frequency of the dark bars which represent the vocal resonances. It would take weeks or months of harmonic analysis from oscillograms to obtain the same information. Considerable consonant detail may be seen as well. Predistortion, to the extent of raising the higher frequencies by 6 db per octave, was used in making this spectrogram.

While pitch inflection is not shown in Fig. 8, it may be brought out by two methods. If the analyzing band is made narrow enough, the separate voice harmonics appear and their rise and fall with pitch can be seen. The other method is to permit the beats between harmonics in a wide band to register. producing characteristic

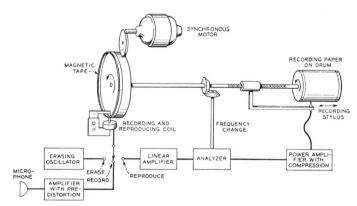

FIG. 7. Schematic representation of the basic method of the sound spectrograph. The sound is recorded on the loop of magnetic tape, and analyzed while repeatedly reproduced. The fluctuating analyzer output builds up a pattern of light and dark areas on the electrically sensitive paper.

23

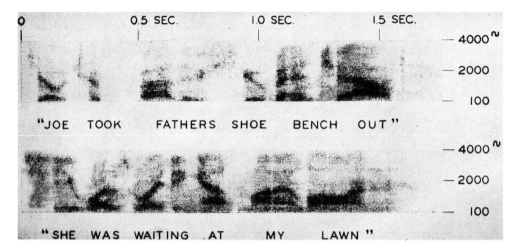

FIG. 8. Spectrograms made with the first laboratory model assembled from available equipment. The vocal resonances are clearly indicated. Further description of the features of spectrograms will be given in connection with subsequent illustrations.

striations vertically across the pattern. Both of these effects will be illustrated subsequently.

The work with this experimental equipment was carried out before our entry into the war. Because of its military interest it was given official rating as a war project and a self-contained model was developed which is described in the next section.

III. PRESENT MODEL

A photograph of the present model portable sound spectrograph is shown in Fig. 9 with the equipment set up as in operation. The recorder unit is at the right, the amplifier-analyzer is at the left with associated control circuits mounted on a panel attached above it, and the power supply is on the lower shelf of the table. The units are interconnected by means of flexible cords and connectors so they can be transported separately. This spectrograph, although basically the same as the early model described above, differs considerably in mechanical and operational details.

The recorder unit, which serves as the magnetic tape recorder as well as the spectrograph pattern recorder, is built around a modified commercial two-speed turntable of the type used for disk recording. The signals to be analyzed are recorded on a length of vicalloy magnetic tape $\frac{1}{4}$ inch wide and between 2 and 3 mils thick,

mounted against a shoulder in a step turned on the lower edge of the 13″ turntable platter. About

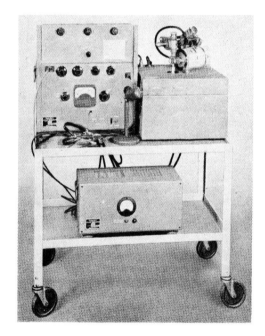

FIG. 9. The present model of the sound spectrograph, built in three parts for portability. The magnetic tape unit is in the right hand box, whose superstructure also carries the paper drum and stylus. The amplifiers, analyzer, etc., are in the left-hand box. The lower unit houses the regulated power supply.

24

one-third of the tape projects below the platter rim. Precise machining of the step is necessary to prevent eccentricity or wrinkling of the tape. The ends of the tape are sheared diagonally at about 45°, to a length which will provide a 2- or 3-mil butt joint when the tape is mounted. The joint is slanted so that the overhanging sharp pointed edge of the tape trails as the turntable rotates. When the tape is cut and mounted carefully, the joint is hardly noticeable in the patterns. The tape is held to the platter rim by a serving of heavy linen thread wrapped around the upper two-thirds of the tape and cemented in place by several coats of clear lacquer. The turntable is rim-driven by a synchronous motor through friction drive idlers at 25 r.p.m. for recording and 78 r.p.m. for analysis.

Two sets of magnetic pole pieces, one for recording (or reproducing) and another for erasing, are mounted on the bed of the machine so that the overhanging edge of the tape passes between their faces. The recording pole faces are about 40 mils square and are mounted with a pivot and spring so that their inside edges will just pass in a shearing fashion when the tape is removed. In order to insure good contact with the tape at the shearing edges, the pole faces are initially machined at a slight angle (2 or 3 degrees to the tape) to reduce the time for "running in" to a good fit. Very small misalignments of the pole

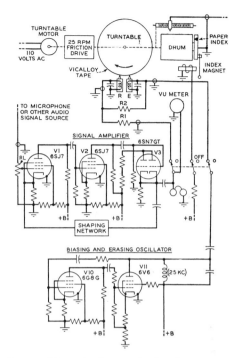

FIG. 11. Schematic diagram showing the spectrograph components arranged for recording a sample on the tape. The erasing and recording processes are continuous until stopped by the switch; the last 2.4 seconds of signal are then on the tape.

faces may cause a decided loss of high frequency response. As shown in Fig. 10, the erasing pole pieces are placed about one inch ahead of the recording pole pieces; their pole faces are slightly wider than the recording pole faces so that erasing will be effective even if there is a small relative misalignment of the two sets of pole pieces. Between the two sets of pole pieces may be seen a spreader with which they may be lifted out of contact with the tape for safety during shipment or handling of the turntable. An oil-saturated wick placed ahead of the pole pieces serves to clean and lubricate the tape as it rotates.

The superstructure mounted above the turntable (Fig. 9) serves as the spectrogram pattern recorder. In addition to the conventional cutting head carriage and lead screw, a 4″ diameter metal drum, mounted on a shaft parallel to and below the lead screw, is driven through 1:1 spiral gears from a vertical extension of the turntable shaft. A flexible stainless steel stylus about

RECORDING-REPRODUCING POLE PIECE, 40 MIL FACE   ERASING POLE PIECE 50 MIL FACE

FIG. 10. View with cover removed, showing the magnetic tape and the pole pieces. The butt joint in the tape is exaggerated in this picture.

25

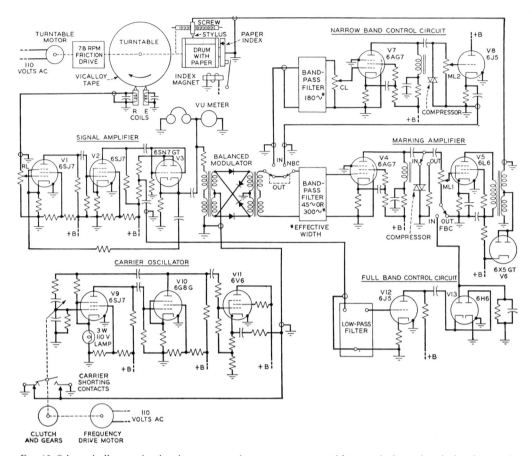

FIG. 12. Schematic diagram showing the spectrograph components arranged for reproducing and analyzing the recorded signal. The carrier oscillator is slowly swept through the frequency range while the signal is repeatedly reproduced and impressed on the modulator. The output of the band pass filter is amplified and marks the paper with a density corresponding to the instantaneous level. The control circuits govern the amplitude compression.

10 mils in diameter is mounted on an insulating block fastened to the cutting head carriage, which can be lowered to or raised from the recording position manually. An automatic paper index mounted on the drum shaft indicates the position for placing the lap in the facsimile paper so that the beginning of the sound sample recorded on the tape will coincide with the leading edge of the paper.

The schematic diagram in Fig. 11 shows the various elements of the spectrograph used in the recording condition. The signal amplifier and the biasing and erasing oscillator are in the amplifier-analyzer unit. The signal amplifier is used also for reproducing and the oscillator forms a part of the carrier oscillator for analysis of the recorded signals. Switch contacts for making the change from the "record" to the "reproduce" condition, however, are left out of the schematics to make them more straightforward.

A microphone or other signal source is connected to the amplifier input, and the recording level, which can be read on the VU meter, is adjusted by means of the RL potentiometer. Shaping networks are provided in the feedback circuit so that the relative levels of high and low frequencies in the signal may be changed if desired. The low impedance output of the amplifier is connected to the recording coil R through a high resistance $R1$ which gives essentially constant recording current for equal voltages over the frequency range of the input signal. Erasing current of 25 kc is supplied to the erase coil E by the biasing and erasing oscillator. Some of this current is also applied as a bias to the recording coil R through the resistor $R2$. Small tuning condensers across the recording and erasing coils raise the effective coil impedance at 25 kc but have little effect in the voice frequency range. These condensers also serve to reduce oscillator switching transients which otherwise tend to magnetize the tape so strongly that complete erasure is difficult.

The turntable and tape are driven at 25 r.p.m. which permits recording a sample of 2.4-second duration at a linear tape speed of approximately 16 inches per second. Continuous recording and erasing are effected as long as the switch is in the recording position. The erasing coil, since it is just ahead of the recording coil, erases signals which were recorded 2.4 seconds earlier. When the "record-reproduce" switch is thrown to the right, erasing and recording are simultaneously stopped, thereby capturing the last 2.4 seconds of signal on the loop of tape, after which it may be reproduced over and over.

The paper index magnet is energized in the recording position, and the paper index rotates frictionally with the drum until the index magnet armature engages a pin projecting on the side of the paper index, causing it to remain in a fixed position. When the index magnet is released at the end of a recorded sample, the paper index is free to rotate with the drum again. The paper index then indicates the position on the drum corresponding to the end of the sample recorded on the tape. Since the drum is directly geared to the turntable on which the tape is mounted, the above relationship will remain fixed and the facsimile paper can be placed on the drum so that the end of the paper coincides exactly with the end of the recorded sample. After a desired sample has been recorded, the turntable is stopped and a pre-cut sheet of electrically sensitive paper is secured to the drum by means of rolling springs.

The turntable is then speeded up to 78 r.p.m. by shifting idler pulleys in the friction drive. It should be pointed out that, although the signal sounds unnatural when speeded up approxi-mately 3 to 1 by this shift, its wave form is unaltered. The effect is merely to divide the reproducing time approximately by 3 and multiply all of the frequency components of the recorded signal by the same factor. This operation converts the original frequency range of approximately 100 to 3500 cycles to about 300 to 10,500 cycles. Since it is very difficult to vary a narrow band-pass filter over this range for analysis, a heterodyning process is used with a fixed band filter.

Figure 12 shows the various circuits of the spectrograph in the reproducing condition. Starting at the upper left of the diagram, the signal is picked up from the magnetic tape by the reproducing coil R. A small equalizing condenser in shunt resonates the coil at about 12,000 cycles to keep the high frequency response from falling off. This provides an over-all frequency response which is essentially flat when the sample has been recorded without pre-equalization.

The reproducing coil works into the RL potentiometer which is used to adjust the level of the reproduced signal to a suitable value. The three-stage feedback signal amplifier has a resistive feedback network to provide a flat frequency response with a voltage gain of about 100 times while reproducing.

The output of the signal amplifier is impressed on the balanced copper oxide modulator. Carrier is supplied to the modulator by the R-C carrier oscillator through the cathode follower amplifier stage $V11$. As the carrier frequency is slowly

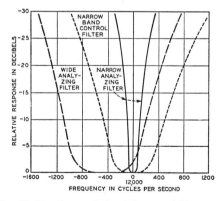

Fig. 13. The characteristics of the several filters used in the spectrograph. The effective band widths are less than those shown by a factor of 3:1, which is the speed-up ratio of reproducing *vs.* recording.

27

shifted by the frequency drive motor from approximately 22,500 cycles to 12,000 cycles, the lower sideband output of the modulator is swept slowly across the fixed band filter connected to its output. The normal sweep rate is such that the turntable makes approximately two hundred revolutions in the time required for the frequency to change from the highest to the lowest value. Since the stylus advances about 10 mils for each revolution of the turntable, the resulting spectrogram is approximately 2 inches wide for the 3500-cycle frequency range. The carrier shorting contacts, which are operated from a cam on the condenser drive shaft, switch the carrier current on and off to define the high and low frequency boundaries of the spectrograms.

Either of two filter widths may be slected by a switch which selects one of two values of mutual capacity between the anti-resonant sections of the band-pass filter. The characteristics of the two filters are shown in Fig. 13. It will be noted that the mid band frequency of the wide analyzing filter is lower than that of the narrow filter. With this particular filter structure, changing the pass band is accomplished by shifting the lower cut-off; the upper (theoretical) cut-off remains the same. These curves show the actual pass bands of the filters; the effective widths are about one third of the indicated widths, because the frequencies of the speeded-up reproduced signal are spread apart by a factor equal to the speed-up ratio, namely about 3:1. As pointed out previously this does not alter the wave shape of the signal but spreads out frequencies and reduces time, with a net effect of speeding up the analysis by a factor of three.

The output of the analyzing filter is impressed directly on a two-stage amplifier which has enough gain to raise the rather low voltage to a value sufficiently high to mark the facsimile paper. The output of the amplifier is not rectified, but is connected to the stylus through a step-up transformer having a turns ratio of about 1:2. Under some conditions a very high signal may reach the grid of the final marking amplifier stage. If the stylus is not lowered to load the amplifier, very high positive peak voltages tend to appear across the output transformer secondary. The biased diode (V6) is shunted across a portion of the high winding to limit the peak voltage to a value which will not damage the transformer insulation. When the stylus is on the paper, the normal range of marking voltages does not exceed the bias voltage and the diode has no effect. A rather small transformer with ordinary insulation will safely withstand the voltages with the diode protection.

In this connection it may be noted that the process of recording on the paper generates a considerable amount of smoke. A blower is therefore incorporated in the recorder unit to draw the smoke through a charcoal filter. The hinged plastic shield which may be seen in Fig. 9 directs the smoke into a slot in the top of the recorder box.

The marking range of the paper is limited to about 12 db. A 70-volt signal on the stylus will make a barely visible mark and about 300 volts will mark the paper full black at the linear paper speed of approximately 16 inches per second. Since for some applications it is desirable to show components of speech which cover a range of 30 or 40 db, it is necessary to apply a compressing action to the marking amplifier to reduce the signal range to the limited range of the facsimile paper. One kind of compressing action is secured by shunting across a high impedance point a non-linear compressing resistor (thyrite) whose voltage varies as the 3rd or 4th root of the current through it. This form of compression operates directly on the wave shape, and there is no time constant involved. It produces a rather uniform gradation of blackness on the recording paper over a 35 or 40 db range of signal intensity and brings out low level detail in the signal being analyzed. However, the compressing action when secured in this manner tends to degrade the frequency resolution of the filter. Better definition has been secured by the use of control circuits which accomplish compression in a different manner.

Two control circuits are provided as shown in Fig. 12. The narrow band control circuit is used with the narrow (45-cycle) analyzing filter and the full band control circuit is used ordinarily with the wide (300-cycle) filter. The narrow band control circuit is a series arrangement which may be switched in ahead of the 45-cycle analyzing filter. It includes a control filter whose characteristic is shown in Fig. 13. Its pass-band is

28

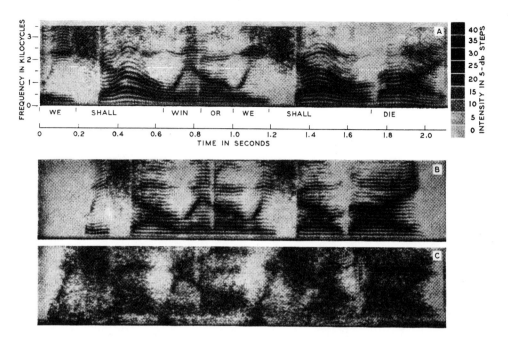

FIG. 14. Spectrograms of speech made on the present model, using a 45-cycle analyzing filter. These and subsequent illustrations have been trimmed and reduced. The originals are 12.5 inches long (for 2.4 seconds) and 2 inches high, recorded on pre-cut sheets 4.5 inches wide. Section (A) normal speech. (B) monotone. (C) whisper.

about 180 cycles (effective) surrounding the passband of the narrow analyzing filter. A compressor having the same characteristics as the one described above is inserted in the control circuit amplifier. Since the compressing action takes place ahead of the analyzing filter, the frequency resolution of the analyzing filter is not impaired as it is when the compressing action is placed after it. Compression at this point is permissible because the control filter passes such a narrow band that no important modulation products generated by the compressor fall in the passband of the analyzing filter. Various degrees of control can be obtained by changing the working level of the compressor by means of the gain controls provided.

The full band control circuit ordinarily but not necessarily used with the 300-cycle analyzing filter, is a shunt arrangement. The low pass filter passes the entire frequency spectrum of the signal which is then amplified and rectified with a time constant of 2 milliseconds. The filtered or smoothed d.c. output of the rectifier is applied

as a bias to the marking amplifier grid thereby controlling its gain. This arrangement serves to control the gain after the analyzing filter by the spectrum ahead of the filter. The direction of control is to reduce gain for higher spectrum energy.

The effect of these control circuits on the spectrograms will be illustrated in the next section.

Returning to the photograph Fig. 9, the location of the various items mentioned above is as follows. The panel attached above the amplifier-analyzer unit houses the control circuits, which were added relatively recently. The two left-hand dials regulate the degree of narrow band control, and the right-hand dial the degree of full band control. The switch on this panel selects the type of control—"full band," "narrow band," "compressor (in the marking amplifier) in" and "compressor out."

The main panel has two attenuators at the upper left, one for controlling the recording level, the other for the reproducing level, both levels

29

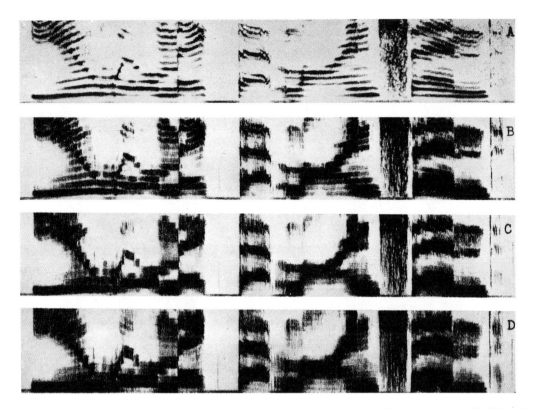

Fig. 15. Showing the effect of widening the analyzing filter, with a high pitched voice. The widths are 90, 180, 300, and 475 cycles in Sections (A) to (D), respectively. The words are "you will make that line send."

being read on the VU meter in the center. The next knob is the recording-reproducing switch, and the next the filter selecting switch. To the left of the VU meter is the predistortion selector, and to the right is the dial for resetting the carrier oscillator at the beginning of each pattern. This dial returns the rotating condenser plates to their starting position; a small motor inside the panel then drives them slowly back through a friction clutch.

Just below the VU meter is a gear shift lever by means of which the rate of frequency sweep can be changed so as to make the patterns 4 inches high instead of 2 inches. The two buttons at the bottom permit reading the carrier and marking voltages, respectively, on the meter.

The power supply unit provides filament and plate voltages to the rest of the equipment. It is highly regulated and operates at 280 volts from 110-volt a.c. power.

IV. SPECTROGRAMS OF SPEECH

Figure 14A shows one kind of spectrogram produced by the later models of the sound spectrograph. The well-known sentence which appears in this spectrogram has been used for testing and illustrative purposes because it contains monosyllabic words with a variety of resonance patterns. The frequency scale of the spectrogram is linear and covers 3500 cycles as shown by the scale at the left. The time scale is also linear and covers 2.4 seconds (in the illustrations the spectrograms have been trimmed at the ends). They have also been photographically reduced; in the originals the vertical height is 2 inches and the length is 12.5 inches, making the time scale slightly over 5 inches per second.

This spectrogram shows a great deal more detail than the ones in Fig. 8; it was made with a much narrower analyzing filter—about 45 cycles wide at the 3-db points. With this filter the

30

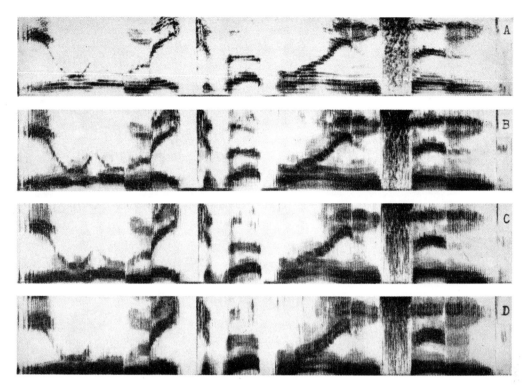

FIG. 16. Same as Fig. 15, but with low pitched voice.

individual harmonics of the voiced sounds can be clearly distinguished. The traces curve up and down as the pitch of the voice is varied in normal speech. The wider the spacing between harmonics, the higher the pitch at any particular instant. In the word "shall" for instance, the pitch first rose and then fell. If the words are spoken in a monotone, the harmonic traces remain level and equi-distant as shown in Section B of Fig. 14. If the words are spoken in a whisper, the spectrogram appears as in Section C. It will be noted that the distribution of dark and light areas is closely similar in all three spectrograms. These dark areas indicate the regions of maximum energy—in other words the vocal resonances. In the whispered words the vowels and consonants all have the same fuzzy texture with no harmonics present. The same texture appears in normal speech in unvoiced sounds such as the "sh" sounds in Section A.

These spectrograms were made with the compressor in the marking amplifier. The gradations of black produced by various signal intensities are shown in the upper right-hand corner. Since the last two steps are nearly alike in blackness, the range is somewhere between 35 and 40 db.

The effect of widening the analyzing filter can be seen in Fig. 15. These are spectrograms of a rather high pitched female voice. The filter used in Section A of Fig. 15 was twice as wide as that in the previous illustration, that is, 90 cycles. In Section B the filter width was 180 cycles, and the harmonics of this high pitched voice are still clearly resolved. In Sections C and D the filter widths were 300 and 475 cycles, respectively; with these wide filters the individual harmonics tend to merge and only the resonant areas can be clearly resolved. The first word in these illustrations shows clearly that the trend of the resonant areas may be opposite from that of the voice pitch. It is evident that the pitch is rising in this first word but the frequency of resonance is rapidly falling so that each harmonic in turn is reinforced momentarily,

31

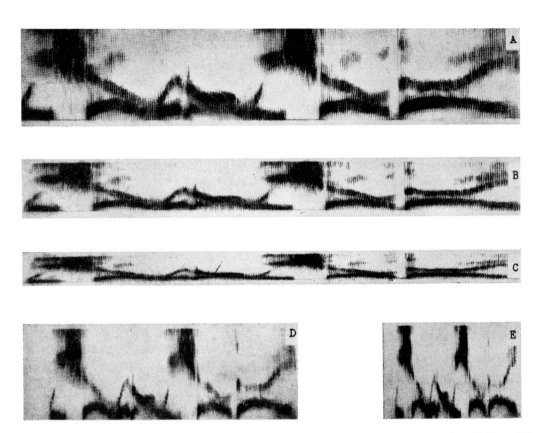

FIG. 17. Spectrograms illustrating various aspect ratios, using the 300-cycle analyzing filter. Section (A) "normal." (B) and (C) frequency dimension reduced by 2 and 4, respectively. (D) and (E) time dimension reduced by 2 and 4, respectively. The words are "We shall win or we shall die " identical sample in all spectrograms.

producing a step effect which is somewhat undesirable for visible speech purposes. With a lower pitched voice such as is illustrated in Fig. 16, the resonance areas tend to form smooth dark bands as soon as the filter becomes wide enough so as not to resolve the individual harmonics. The filter widths in this figure are the same as in Fig. 15. With most male voices a filter about 200 cycles wide would be adequate to smooth the resonance bands. A 300-cycle width has been adopted as a compromise, and is adequate for most voices.

In Fig. 16 it will be noted that there is a distinct pattern of vertical striations in the voiced sounds. This pattern is caused by the fact that more than one harmonic is passed by the analyzing filter. It is well known that two or more frequencies separated by equal intervals will produce beats at the interval frequency. In the case of speech, this frequency of course is the voice pitch. Each vertical striation represents the crest of a beat, and the separation between crests can be seen to vary as the pitch changes. In Fig. 15, where the pitch is very high, the vertical striations are so close together as to be barely distinguishable. Incidentally these vertical striations sometimes persist unbroken across the whole frequency range, which is probably due to the particular kind of phase relations resulting from the mechanism of phonation. Sometimes there are phase reversals in the striations, however; this subject would make an interesting study in itself and probably throw light on the voicing mechanism.

The time and frequency dimensions of spectrograms were originally chosen so as to give ade-

32

16

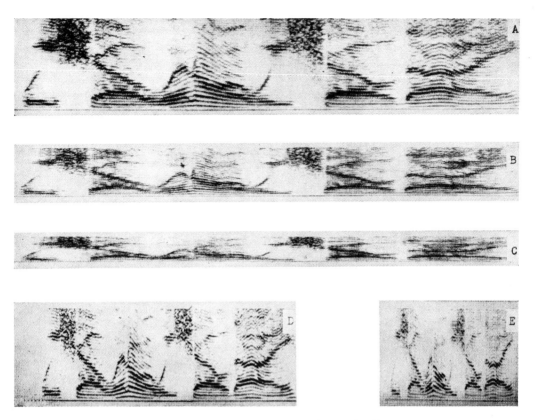

FIG. 18. Same as Fig. 17, but with 45-cycle analyzing filter.

quate resolution for a particular purpose. When the spectrograph was applied to visible speech, the question naturally arose whether some other choice of dimensions might not be more suitable. Figure 17 shows some spectrograms made to explore this question. The upper one (A) has the original aspect ratio, that is, the ratio of the frequency to the time dimensions. In (B) the frequency dimension has been cut in half by increasing the speed of the carrier oscillator sweep, leaving the time dimension the same as before. In (C) it has been reduced by a factor of 4. Changing the aspect ratio in this direction apparently does not contribute to the appearance or legibility of the patterns; rather, it tends to reduce the curvatures of the resonant traces and thereby make the different sounds less easily distinguishable. Spectrogram (D) was made with the opposite kind of change. Here the time dimension was cut in half by decreasing the di-

ameter of the paper drum, while the frequency dimension was left normal. In (E) the time dimension was reduced by a factor of 4. After a study of these and other samples, it was felt that while the aspect ratio originally chosen might not be an optimum, at least there would be no very great advantage in changing it.

Figure 18 shows the same series of spectrograms and the same speech material analyzed with the narrow filter. Here again there appears to be no particular virtue in changing the aspect ratio. In addition there is a distinct loss of detail when the frequency scale is reduced. The "normal" spectrogram is made up of 200 horizontal lines so close together that the frequency is shifted only about $\frac{1}{3}$ the width of the filter. Spectrograms (B) of Figs. 17 and 18 were made with only 100 lines and (C) with only 50. It is apparent from these illustrations that when the narrow analyzing filter is used the number of

33

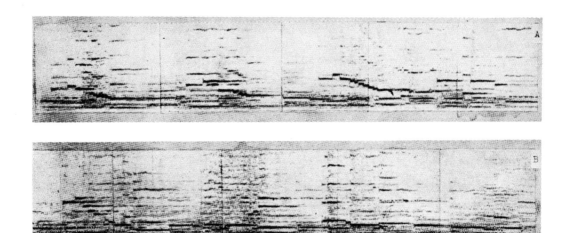

Fig. 19. A passage of piano music with reduced time dimension as in 18(E). This aspect ratio seems quite appropriate for music, though not for speech.

lines cannot be materially reduced, at least with low pitched voices, without loss of frequency detail.

In this connection it may be mentioned that while the normal aspect ratio appears to be nearly optimum for speech, it is not necessarily so for other applications. Figure 19, for instance, portrays a passage of piano music with the time dimension reduced by a factor of 4. With this aspect ratio the musical action is clearly indicated while speech, as shown in the previous illustrations, appears much too crowded in the time dimension. For other applications it has been found desirable to lengthen rather than shorten the time dimension.

Figure 20 illustrates in a somewhat different fashion the effect of changing the amount of frequency overlap in successive lines. Section (A) shows a normal spectrogram with the narrow filter and (B) shows the same sample with the same time and frequency scales; however in making spectrogram (B) three successive lines were made alike, and the frequency was then shifted by three times the normal amount. The effect is the same as though a stylus three times as wide as normal had been used with the lateral shift and the frequency shift also three times normal. The harmonics now appear to rise and fall stepwise rather than smoothly. With the wide filter, however, this process can be carried much further. Section (C) for instance shows the same material analyzed with the wide filter. Here each line has been repeated 4 times and it requires close inspection to distinguish this from a normal spectrogram. In Section (D) each line has been repeated 12 times. Obviously this has carried the process too far, but these illustrations show that if only a wide analyzing filter is of interest, considerable time could be saved by reducing the number of lines in the spectrograms and hence reducing the number of times the sample must be reproduced in the process of analyzing it. In the present spectrograph of course the analyzing time has been set by the requirements of the narrowest analyzing filter rather than the widest.

Figure 21 shows the need for some kind of compression in portraying speech sounds and illustrates the action of the full band control circuit mentioned in Section III. Spectrogram A shows the words "one, two, three, four, five, six" made without any compression except a certain amount of limiting action in the last power stage of the marking amplifier. The strongest consonants such as the "t" in "two" and the "s" in "six" can be seen in the spectrogram, but the weaker consonants such as the "f" in "four" and "five" are completely missing. Section B was made with the thyrite compressor in the marking amplifier. This spectrogram shows all the

34

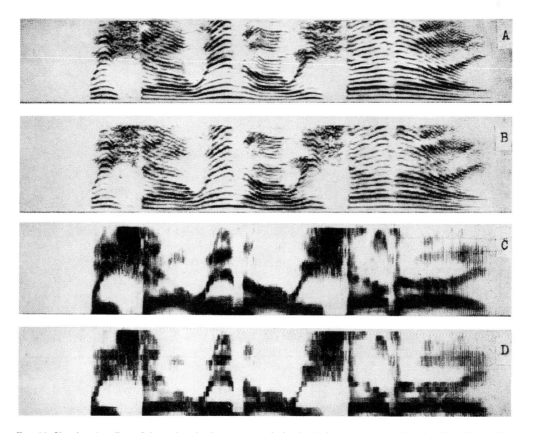

FIG. 20. Showing the effect of degrading the frequency resolution by laying down several identical lines, then shifting the frequency by a correspondingly greater amount to keep the normal frequency dimension. Section (A) normal spectrogram, (B), (C), and (D) 3, 4, and 12 repetitions, respectively.

consonants clearly. However, the low level portions of the vowel sounds are also brought out and the resonance bars are made fuzzy. For visible speech purposes it was desired that the consonants should show as clearly as they do in (B), and at the same time that the vowels should be portrayed as they are in (A). The full band control circuit accomplishes these purposes as illustrated in Section (C). Here the consonants show at least as clearly as they do in (B) and the vowel bars are resolved about as they are in A, with the low level material suppressed. The action of the full band control circuit, as discussed in the previous section, is to adjust the gain of the marking amplifier not according to the momentary output of the analyzing filter, but according to the energy in frequency bands other than the one being scanned at the moment. With

this arrangement sounds in which the energy is weak in all portions of the frequency range are amplified, but the low level portions of vowel sounds are suppressed.

Figure 22 illustrates the action of the narrow band control circuit, using the same words as Fig. 21. Again Section (A) was made without any compression except the limiting action of the last marking stage. Section (B) was made with the thyrite compressor. It is clear that a wider range of levels is covered in (B), which is desirable; however, the harmonics have become fuzzier and tend to merge together. Section (C) was made with the narrow band control circuit with a setting such as to show the same range of levels as appears in (B), but here the harmonic traces are much more clear-cut than in (B). The control can be set to bring out an even wider

35

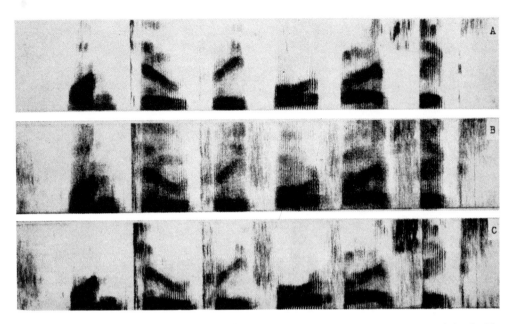

FIG. 21. Illustrating the need for amplitude compression and the action of the full band control circuit. The words are "one, two, three, four, five, six." Section (A) no compression. (B) compressor in the marking amplifier. (C) full band control.

range of levels, if desired, still leaving the harmonics clearly resolved. The action of this circuit is to adjust the over-all gain depending on the energy in the frequency regions immediately adjacent to the one being scanned. The gain is not raised when the analyzing filter happens to pass between two harmonics, but it is raised when the energy level is generally low.

V. OTHER APPLICATIONS

Thus far attention has been concentrated on spectrograms of speech. Other types of signals can be handled as well. The spectrograph is a useful laboratory tool for determining the nature of the time and frequency distributions of energy in sounds other than speech, or in complex waves of any kind whether they exist as sounds or not. Some applications of this type will be illustrated in this section.

Figure 23 shows in Sections (A), (B), and (C) some samples of thermal noise. In Section (A) it was reproduced at a very high level and it shows almost uniform darkness except for occasional light patches randomly spaced. In Section (B) it was reproduced at a lower level and the

characteristic pattern of this type of wave can be clearly seen. Since in thermal noise the energy is concentrated in different frequency regions in different instants of time, the spectrogram shows randomly spaced vertical spindles whose length corresponds roughly to the width of the analyzing filter, which in this case was 300 cycles. In Section (C) the 45-cycle filter was used and the spectrogram shows fuzzier patches due to the slower response of the narrow filter. Many familiar sounds contain such random components. Section (D) for instance shows the sound of striking a match. The dark area at the left portrays the sound generated by the abrasive, the longer portion the roar of the flame. Both of these areas contain random noise as previously illustrated. In addition, sharp vertical lines may be discerned across the whole frequency range. Sharp lines of this type represent clicks or crackling sounds which are characterized by a wide frequency distribution of energy and short duration.

Section (E) shows the sound of filing on a metal plate. Three file strokes are included in the picture, and the actual sound of the file

36 20

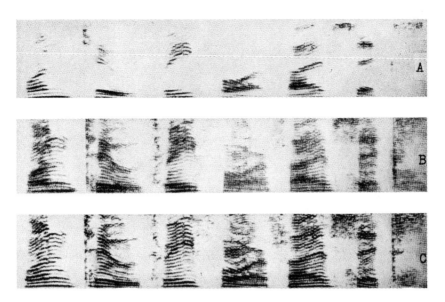

FIG. 22. Illustrating the need for amplitude compression and the action of the narrow band control circuit. Section (A) no compression. (B) compressor in the marking amplifier. (C) narrow band control.

teeth can be seen dimly as rising and falling bands in the lower part of the spectrogram. The dark regions in the upper part of the spectrogram represent resonances in the metal plate which of course remain substantially constant in frequency but vary in amplitude. The definite components can be distinguished from the random components by their more uniform texture. Section (F) shows some machinery noise. There is a low frequency periodicity in the random components, and a dark band across the middle which indicates some discrete components. The small section at the right was made with the narrow filter and shows the four discrete components more plainly.

Whether the wide or narrow analyzing filter should be used depends on the nature of the sound and how far apart in frequency the components are. Figure 24 presents two sounds analyzed with both filters, showing that in some cases the two sets of information from the wide and narrow filters complement each other. Sections (A) and (B) represent the sound of an infant crying. Each cry begins and ends with voiced components of very high pitch. In the middle of each cry the voice breaks down into a very irregular noise. In this example the com-

ponents are far enough apart so that they are easily resolved with the wide filter. However, the narrow filter permits the exact frequencies of the components to be determined. Sections (C) and (D) analyze the sound of snoring. The wide filter shows that the inspiration phase consists of a series of sharp, regularly spaced clicks, with the frequency distribution modified by resonances in two portions of the frequency range. The expiration phase is practically random noise but also shows reenforcement by resonance in definite frequency regions. The narrow filter reveals that the resonances are unexpectedly sharp considering the nature of the oral cavities.

Figure 25 illustrates some bird songs analyzed with the wide and narrow filters. Sections (A) and (B) show the song of the nightingale. There are two distinct types of song in this illustration. One is a rapidly falling note with a double trill at the end. The other is a rising and falling note with an almost linear trend in both directions. It will be seen that each note is accompanied by some noise components. This is recognized with more assurance with the wide filter than with the narrow filter because the narrow filter tends to produce a fuzzy trailing edge when it scans across a component. Since the wide filter has

37

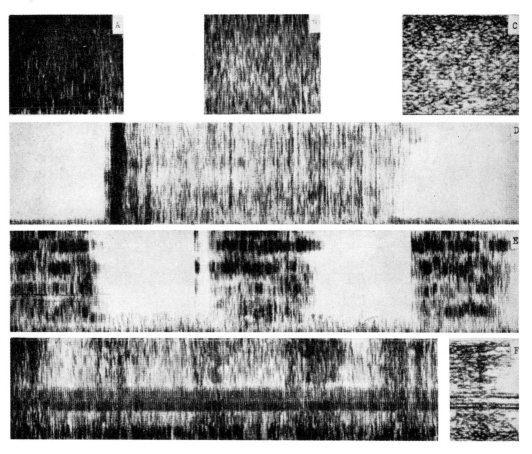

Fig. 23. Some sounds other than speech. Sections (A), (B) random noise at two levels, 300-cycle filter. (C) random noise, 45-cycle filter. (D) sound of striking a match, and the roar of the flame. (E) filing on metal plate. (F) machinery noise.

sharper time resolution, a higher level of signal can be used and thus a wider range of levels can be explored without fuzziness. The noise components in this sample are therefore definitely not a result of the analyzing process.

Sections (C) and (D) represent the song of the wood thrush. Here again a higher level can be used with the wide filter. This song is remarkable for two reasons. The middle portion contains a rapid succession of two distinct notes repeated with great precision. The fainter trace at the top of this section is a second harmonic which was not necessarily generated by the bird but may have been produced in the recording and reproducing processes. The last section of the song however, shows two distinct notes pro-

duced at once, namely an extremely rapid high pitched trill accompanied by a steady note of lower pitch. Since these two notes cannot be multiples or submultiples of each other, they are not harmonically related and must therefore have been produced by the bird with two distinct emitting mechanisms. The rapid trill is almost completely blurred by the narrow filter. Incidentally, these bird songs (and others to be shown later) were taken from phonograph records. They included frequencies above the normal 3500-cycle range of the spectrograph. The phonograph records were therefore played at less than their normal speed so that all frequencies were reduced sufficiently to fall within the range. When this method is used, the actual frequencies can be

38

22

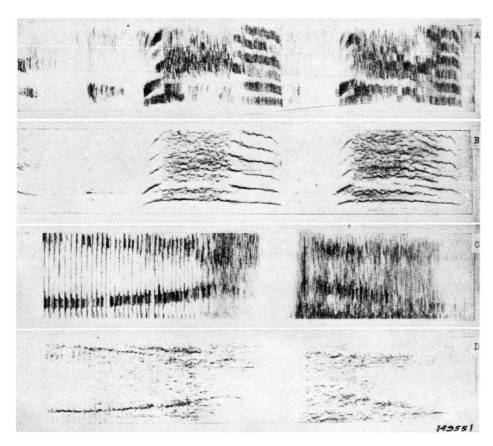

FIG. 24. Comparing the two analyzing filters. Sections (A) and (B) infant crying. (C) and (D) sound of snoring.

computed by dividing the apparent frequencies, as read from the spectrogram, by the speed reduction ratio. The nightingale sample covers about 4500 cycles, and the wood thrush about 6000 cycles.

Figure 26 gives further examples of the behavior of the two filters with signals that vary rapidly in frequency. These are spectrograms of warble tones produced by varying the frequency of a single tone sinusoidally. Sections (A) (narrow filter) and (B) (wide filter) show four different rates of warble from 40 per second to 80 per second. It can be seen that as the frequency of warble is increased, the picture made by the narrow filter tends to exhibit a horizontal structure. In other words, the narrow filter sees this signal as a frequency modulated wave which consists mathematically of side bands around the

average frequency. Sections (C) and (D) show higher frequencies of warble and also somewhat greater excursions. The breaking up into discrete components is complete at 100 cycles with the narrow filter and at higher frequencies even the wide filter shows the same effect. Mathematically, both of these representations are correct; the signal may be regarded either as a set of distinct frequency components or as a rapidly varying single component. The spectrograph therefore does not give a false picture. It is simply a matter of choice which interpretation of the signal is more convenient.

Incidentally, all of the illustrations used in this section were made without any form of compression. In exploring an unknown signal it is generally advantageous to make this kind of analysis first because it gives a better picture of

39

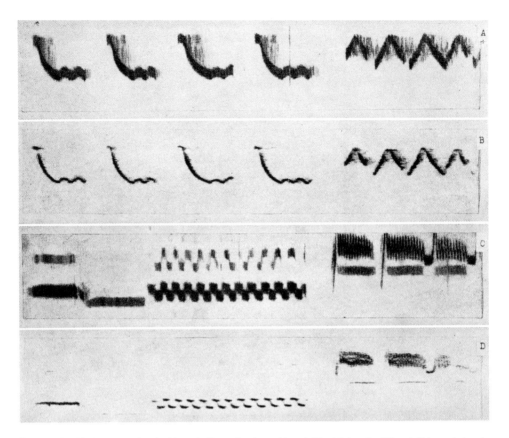

FIG. 25. Two bird songs analyzed with both filters. Sections (A) and (B) nightingale. (C) and (D) wood thrush.

amplitude relations. If the existence of weaker components is suspected, these can be explored with the help of the control circuits if desired.

In Fig. 27 are some spectrograms in which frequency analysis is not the purpose but only the means to an end. Section (A) is the output of an oscillator whose frequency was varied by means of a motor driven condenser. It was desired to determine how the frequency varied with time, and this is immediately apparent from the spectrogram. This type of information could have been obtained by making an oscillogram of the output and determining the frequency *versus* time by counting cycles and making proper interpolations, which would have been an extremely laborious procedure particularly if the determination of slight irregularities were important.

Section (B) portrays the output of a sweep

frequency generator showing that the sweep is substantially linear and the return substantially instantaneous. Section *C* illustrates an experiment in which it was desired to determine the manner of acceleration of a phonograph record when released on a moving turntable. The record contained a single frequency tone and a spectrogram of this tone during release proved that the frequency varied linearly from the time the record was released to the time it reached full speed. The duration of the acceleration period can be measured directly on the time scale.

Incidentally, the spectrograms in Fig. 27 cover an 11,000-cycle range instead of the normal 3500 cycles. This was accomplished by recording the signal at the high speed normally used for reproducing. With this arrangement the time covered by the spectrogram is reduced by a factor of three and the frequency scale is multiplied

40

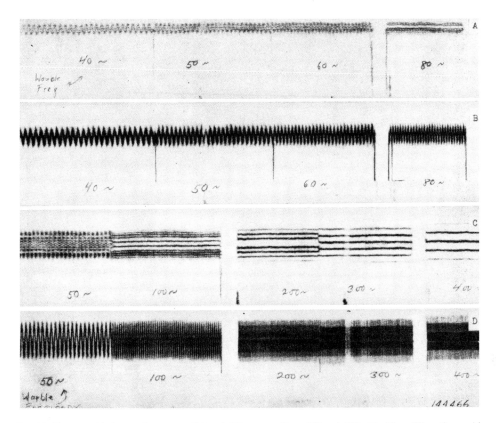

FIG. 26. Tones warbled at various rates. (A) and (C) narrow filter. (B) and (D) wide filter. When the warble rate is comparable to the filter width the warble breaks up into discrete sideband frequencies.

by the same factor. The effective filter width, however, is also multiplied by the same factor, but the apparent width, that is, the width of the trace in the spectrogram, remains the same.

Figure 28 illustrates another application in which the determination of frequency variation rather than analysis was the objective. These spectrograms portray the output of an oscillator whose frequency was governed by a fluctuating d.c. voltage on its grid. The instantaneous frequency can easily be determined at any point with a suitable frequency scale. The fuzziness which is apparent in certain sections results from very rapid amplitude or frequency modulation superposed on the lower frequency modulation. Here the spectrograph takes the place of a string oscillograph, and it avoids the necessity for a d.c. amplifier with sufficiently high output current to drive the low impedance string.

Figure 29 presents another frequency modulation series. In this case a complex wave having both odd and even harmonics was varied in frequency at several rates. The high and low points are marked on the spectrograms. In the uppermost sample the frequency became so low that even the narrow filter resolved the beats. In all these spectrograms "harmonics" will be noted which appear to slope in the opposite direction from the real frequency variation. The effect is due to the fact that the filter, with a rather slow response, is scanning across components at such a rate as to generate a kind of interference pattern. Without attempting to go into the matter thoroughly here, the effect might be compared to the phenomenon of the spokes of a wheel apparently turning backwards in motion pictures. Spurious components like those in Fig. 29 are sometimes visible in analyses

41

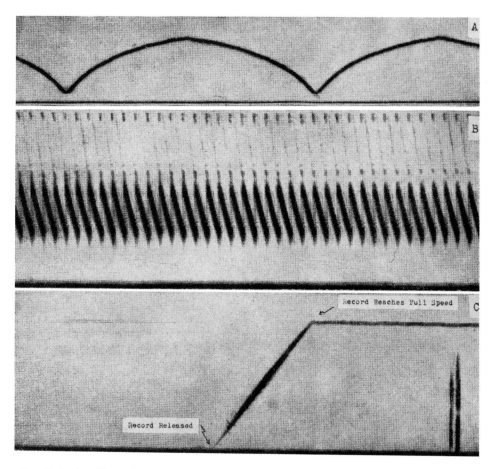

FIG. 27. In these illustrations spectrograms were used to determine frequency *vs.* time rather than energy distribution. Section (A) the output of a motor-driven warbler oscillator. (B) a time base wave. (C) determination of the mode and speed of acceleration of a phonograph disk when released on a moving turntable.

of speech. A good example of this effect can be seen in Fig. 22.

Figure 30 illustrates an interesting application of the spectrograph which should prove very useful. Section (A) shows speech after it has passed through a long loaded line. The line had a cut-off at about 1800 cycles as may be seen by the absence of speech components above that frequency. In addition, however, there is a curious curvature to each syllable. This same curvature can be seen in the small section at the right which represents a click sent over the same line. Ordinarily a click, as mentioned previously, appears as a straight line across the frequency range. The curvature here produced is due to

the fact that different frequencies were delayed by different amounts in transmission over the line. Section (B) shows the same material after a delay correction network had been added to the line. Here the speech and the click are nearly normal. In Section (C) the speech was transmitted through the network alone, resulting in the opposite kind of curvature. This illustrates that the spectrograph may be used to investigate the delay characteristics of filters or other networks which are difficult and sometimes practically impossible to handle mathematically when they include dissipation. These characteristics can be determined by simply measuring the de-

42

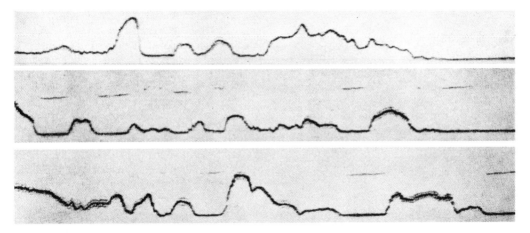

FIG. 28. Another application where spectrograms were used to record frequency *vs.* time. This shows the output of an oscillator whose frequency was governed by a d.c. voltage. The spectrograph here performed the function of a d.c oscillograph.

FIG. 29. Here a complex wave rich in harmonics is varied in frequency at several rates. The maximum and minimum frequencies are marked on the margins. In Section (A) the frequency becomes so low that the narrow filter shows vertical striations due to beats. In all the samples, spurious components may be seen which slope in the opposite direction from the true frequency change.

43

lay *versus* frequency for clicks sent through the networks.

This section will be concluded by presenting a variety of sounds with a wide variety of patterns. First in Fig. 31 are some additional bird songs. Ornithologists have long been trying to analyze and record the songs of various birds accurately. Even after the songs have been slowed down by recording and reproducing at different speeds, it is still difficult for the ear to follow the rapid changes in frequency. Even if the ear were adequate there still remains the problem of a suitable notation for indicating the complex time and frequency relations. With the spectrograph these analyses can be made objectively, and the results recorded unequivocally.

In Fig. 32 are a few additional voice sounds. They require no particular comment except to note that the song in Section (A) is that of a very high pitched voice which is resolved with the wide filter. The amplitude and pitch variations in the vibrato are clearly shown. Presumably the spectrograph will have application in voice training.

Figure 33 contains a variety of animal sounds and Fig. 34 some miscellaneous familiar sounds. The various kinds of components occurring in these sounds have been pointed out in the previous discussion.

VI. SOME VARIABLES

As already indicated above, the general plan of the spectrograph is capable of very wide variations depending upon the application to which it is to be put. For instance, the time scale can be made extremely short for investigating transient phenomena or the like, or it can be made very long for making long spectrograms or for plotting the course of very slowly varying phenomena. The frequency range is also very flexible. Extremely low frequency sounds could be handled by recording very slowly and using a high speed-up ratio. Extremely high frequencies could be handled by recording at high speeds or by the use of modulating processes to bring the high frequencies down to where they could be handled in the normal way.

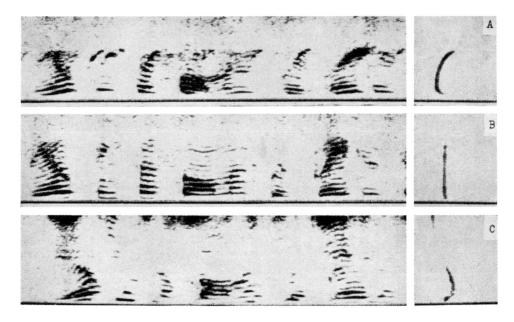

Fig. 30. Illustrating transmission delay in a long loaded line. In Section (A) speech and a click show a cut-off at 1800 cycles, and a curvature which results from the fact that different frequencies were transmitted with different speeds. In Section (B) a delay correction network has been added, restoring the speech and the click to normal. Section (C) shows transmission through the network alone, with the opposite curvature.

44

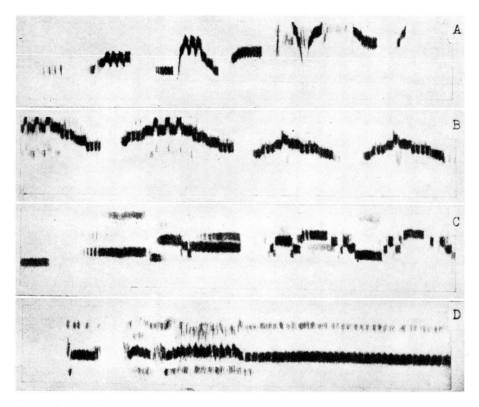

Fig. 31. Some additional bird songs. (A) olive backed thrush. (B) veery. (C) hermit thrush. (D) rooster.

In the present paper all the spectrograms have a linear frequency scale. For some applications, a logarithmic frequency scale would appear to be more logical. In music for instance, the notes are separated by logarithmic intervals. Also, the ear has a natural scale, as shown by differential pitch perception, which is more nearly logarithmic than linear. It might be advantageous to use scales in the spectrograms which approximate those occurring in the ear so that the pictures might be made to look the way they sound. In this connection, the analyzing filters might also be made to simulate more closely the operation of the ear. For instance, a narrow filter might be used in analyzing the low frequencies, with the filter gradually widening towards the high frequencies. The shape of the filter characteristic is also important. In the present spectrograph the narrow filter has extremely steep attenuation characteristics. The wide filter is also very steep with a relatively flat pass band. Different representations can be obtained with filters having different characteristics.

Figure 35 illustrates a few experiments along this line. Sections (A) and (B) were made with the wide and narrow filter, respectively. The subject matter consists of a series of sharp clicks and at the right a calibration tone consisting of all the odd harmonics of 60 cycles. Section (C) was made with a filter which is just about as wide as the one used in Section (B). However, the sides do not slope quite so steeply. It will be noted that in Section (B), the clicks are fuzzy on both the leading and trailing edges. In Section (C), the leading edge is much sharper. In Section (D), the filter is actually narrower than (B) and still retains a sharper leading edge than (B). In Section (E), the pass band is about the same as (B) but the sides slope much more gradually. Here the total width of the clicks is about the

45

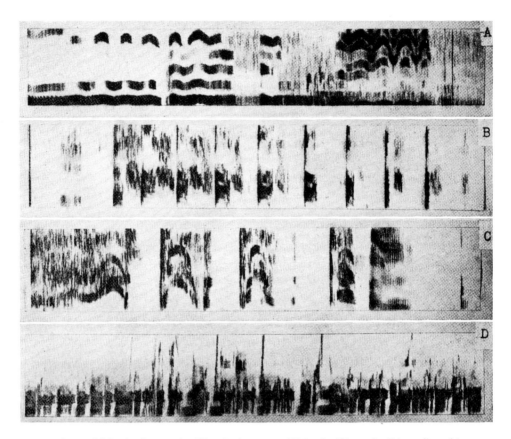

FIG. 32. Some additional voice sounds. (A) trained soprano. (B) laugh. (C) cough. (D) gargling with water.

same as in (B), but the leading edges are about as sharp as with the 300-cycle filter. Obviously, this is a large subject and these illustrations merely indicate the possibilities.

The time requisite for analysis is also subject to wide variation. Time can be saved by reducing the number of lines or by raising the speed-up ratio. If this is carried to sufficiently high frequencies, the patterns might be made substantially instantaneously on a cathode-ray tube.

Various types of signal recording mediums might be used. The magnetic tape seemed desirable because it can be used over and over again. Magnetic recording on wire might be used instead of tape with the advantage that the analyzed samples could be stored. Film recording techniques might be used although this seems

rather slow and expensive. On the whole some of the newer types of magnetic recording look most promising for spectrograph applications.

Similarly, various types of facsimile recording mediums can be used. The particular medium used in the present spectrograph is paper with the trade name Teledeltos. This has the advantage of requiring no processing and is permanent. There are other types of facsimile papers in commercial use, including some which are saturated with a chemical which changes color when current passes through it. These require much less power to mark them and would be adaptable to higher speeds. For a wide range of density, photographic film appears to be best. It has, of course, the disadvantage of requiring processing and is rather expensive.

It might be mentioned that all the variables

46

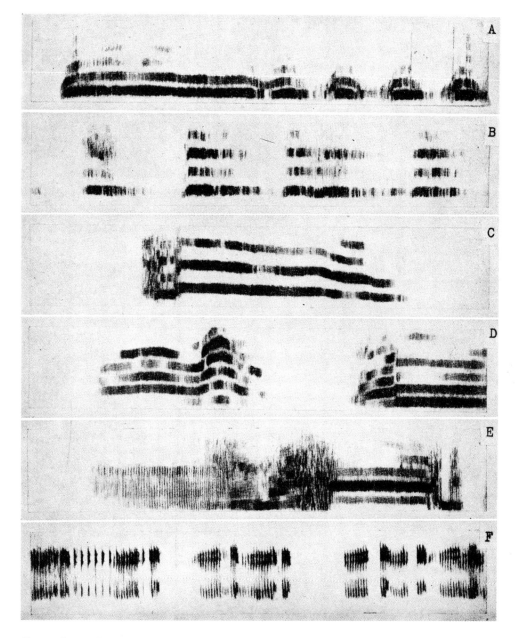

FIG. 33. Some animal sounds. (A) Newfoundland dog. (B) small dog. (C) and (D) wolf. (E) cow. (F) frogs.

47

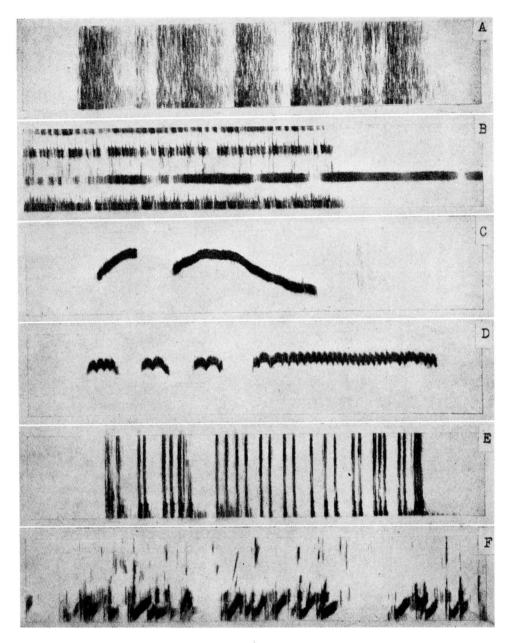

Fig. 34. Some familiar sounds. (A) snare drum. (B) telephone bell. (C) man whistling. (D) police whistle. (E) riffling cards. (F) bubbles blown through water.

48

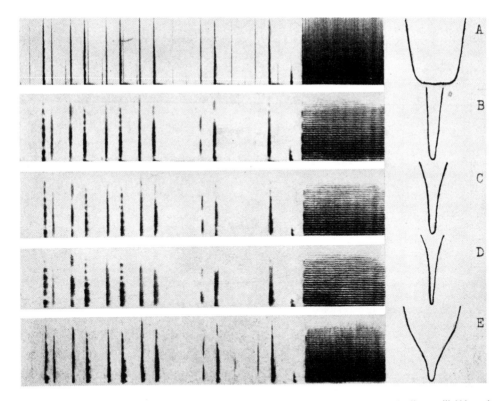

F<small>IG</small>. 35. Illustrating the effect of different filter response characteristics. (A) and (B) the "normal" 300- and 45-cycle filters, respectively. (C), (D), (E) narrow filters with different characteristics. Filters with gradual slopes give sharper pictures of clicks than steep filters.

mentioned in this section have been tried at least in exploratory experiments.

One very important variable should be noted in conclusion. This is the matter of amplitude representation. In the spectrograms presented above, the time and frequency scales are reproducible and subject to precise measurement. The density or amplitude scale, however, is nonlinear and not reproducible. The total range of photometric density is not very great, and furthermore there are many variables such as ambient temperature and humidity, stylus pressure, stylus width, the condition of the drum surface, and so forth, which affect the density scale. In some applications, it is necessary to know the amplitudes of the components quantitatively. Various methods have therefore been devised for representing amplitudes in spectrograms in such a way that they can be interpreted quantitatively. It is planned to cover this subject in a subsequent paper.

49

Reprinted from THE JOURNAL OF THE ACOUSTICAL SOCIETY OF AMERICA, Vol. 27, No. 3, 484–493, May, 1955
Copyright, 1955, by the Acoustical Society of America.
Printed in U. S. A.

Development of a Quantitative Description of Vowel Articulation*

KENNETH N. STEVENS AND ARTHUR S. HOUSE
Acoustics Laboratory, Massachusetts Institute of Technology, Cambridge, Massachusetts
(Received December 13, 1954)

A set of parameters that yield a simple yet reasonably accurate description of the articulation of vowel sounds is developed. The articulatory description is potentially useful in a speech band-width compression system based on the coding of articulatory data. The parameters give information on the position of the tongue constriction, the size of the constriction formed by the tongue, and the dimensions in the vicinity of the mouth opening. An electrical analog of the vocal tract is utilized to obtain experimental relations between the articulatory parameters and the formant frequencies. Contours of vowel articulation are derived from these data. The relation of the contours to classical phonetics is discussed.

IN the past two decades, a considerable amount of speech research has been directed towards the development of a simple description of speech events. This research has been stimulated in part by engineering interest in the problem of band-width compression of speech. To accomplish appreciable reduction of the band width required for speech transmission it is necessary to specify the speech signal by a small number of slowly varying parameters. These parameters must, in turn, be capable of operating on a speech synthesizer to regenerate a signal that is properly interpreted by a listener.

Peterson[1] has outlined the problems confronting the experimenter who endeavors to design an automatic analysis-synthesis system for speech. He points out that the parameters derived from the original signal may represent descriptions of acoustic patterns of speech, or they may represent vocal tract configurations and operations. That is, we may code the acoustic event or the physiological performance. The acoustic data can be derived from a direct analysis of the speech signal. To determine articulatory data from measurements on the speech wave two stages are required: (1) an acoustic analysis of the speech signal must be made, and (2) the probable articulatory configuration that yields this acoustic signal must then be computed. At the receiving end of the system, an automatic speech synthesizer must decode either acoustic data or articulatory data in order to generate a speech output.

In recent years, advances have been made in the development of both *acoustic decoders*[2–9] and *physiological decoders*.[10–12] The synthesizers of the latter type are true electrical (transmission line) analogs of the vocal tract. That is, they consist of a number of variable inductance and capacitance elements, each of which represents a specific section of the actual acoustic vocal tract. The models that now exist are static vocal tract analogs, since their elements are controlled by switches that are operated by hand.

The analog of Stevens *et al.*[12] consists of 35 LC sections, each of which can be varied by a separate switch. Each section represents a $\frac{1}{2}$-cm length of the vocal tract. Consequently the analog can be adjusted to provide an approximation of the area variations in the human vocal tract; many operations are required to make this adjustment, however. Dunn's[10] analog is operated by only three controls that adjust (1) the position of the (lumped) tongue constriction, (2) the degree of constriction of the tongue, and (3) the size of the mouth opening. The accuracy of Dunn's synthesizer is limited, however, since it analogs a vocal tract that has a constant cross-sectional area, with a tongue constriction that is lumped at one point.

The physiological decoder mentioned above is, in effect, a dynamic vocal tract analog in which articulatory dimensions are automatically set by control signals. Such a dynamic vocal tract analog must provide a reasonably accurate representation of the vocal tract profile but at the same time must be controlled by a relatively small number of independent control signals. The simplicity of the control arrangement in Dunn's analog must be combined with the accuracy of the 35-section analog.

In the present study we attempt to develop a set of parameters that yield a simple yet reasonably accurate specification of the articulation of vowel sounds. We establish relations between the parameters that describe the articulatory events and the formant frequencies that describe the acoustic events.

If such specification is feasible it should be of theoretical and practical interest to students of speech in general. Linguists, phoneticians, speech therapists, etc., attempt to utilize articulatory information to specify

* This work was supported by funds from U. S. Air Force contract.

[1] G. E. Peterson, J. Speech Hearing Disorders **17**, 175–188 (1952).

[2] H. Dudley, J. Acoust. Soc. Am. **11**, 169–177 (1939).

[3] C. G. M. Fant, IVA **24**, 331–337 (1953).

[4] K. N. Stevens, Quart. Rept. (Acoustics Laboratory, Massachusetts Institute of Technology, October–December 1952), p. 17.

[5] Doelling, Bastide, and Stevens, Quart. Progr. Rept., Acoustics Laboratory, Massachusetts Institute of Technology, January–March 1953, p. 22.

[6] Stevens, Bastide, and Smith, J. Acoust. Soc. Am. **27**, 207 (A) (1955).

[7] W. Lawrence, "The synthesis of speech from signals which have a low information rate," in *Communication Theory*, edited by W. Jackson (Butterworth Scientific Publications, London, 1953), Chap. 34.

[8] E. S. Weibel, J. Acoust. Soc. Am. **26**, 952 (A) (1954).

[9] Meeks, Borst, and Cooper, J. Acoust. Soc. Am. **26**, 137 (A) (1954).

[10] H. K. Dunn, J. Acoust. Soc. Am. **22**, 740–753 (1950).

[11] C. G. M. Fant, Tech. Rept. No. 12, Acoustics Laboratory, Massachusetts Institute of Technology, January 1952.

[12] Stevens, Kasowski, and Fant, J. Acoust. Soc. Am. **25**, 734–742 (1953).

speech events. Experimental investigations of the anatomy and physiology of speech have, however, been both incomplete and inconclusive. A major deterrent to such investigations has been the inaccessibility of the systems under observation.

DEVELOPMENT OF SIMPLIFIED ARTICULATORY DESCRIPTION

In order to analyze and evaluate the acoustic performance of the human vocal mechanism during the production of vowels it is convenient to view the vocal tract as an acoustic tube of variable cross-sectional dimensions. The tube is excited at one end (the glottis) by an acoustic source, and sound energy is radiated from the mouth opening at the opposite end. In Fig. 1 we show a mid-sagittal section through the vocal tract for the vowel /i/,[13] traced from an x-ray picture. The effective cross-sectional area at each point can be determined from measurements on such a tracing and from direct measurements or estimates of dimensions of the vocal tract in other planes. Such measurements or estimates have been reported by several investigators.[14] In particular, Chiba and Kajiyama[15] have estimated the effective radius of the tract (i.e., radius of the cylindrical tube of the same effective cross-sectional area) for several vowels, and have plotted their data in the form shown in Fig. 1. A representation of this type helps us to visualize the vocal tract as an acoustic tube of variable cross-sectional dimensions.

We usually assume that the cross-sectional dimensions of the vocal tract are small compared with the wavelength of the sound. This assumption is valid in the frequency range below about 4000 cps and implies that only plane waves propagate in the vocal tract. We also assume that there is negligible coupling between the vocal tract and other acoustic resonators such as the nasal cavity or the trachea during the production of vowels. This is probably a reasonable assumption for the vowels of American English.

If we accept both of these assumptions then we can specify the acoustical performance of the vocal tract completely if we know the cross-sectional area at all points along the tube. In principle, a continuous function (like the curve specifying the radius in Fig. 1) which we shall call the area function, is necessary to specify the area at all points. The anatomical structures that shape the vocal tract, however, impose constraints on the area functions, and knowledge of these constraints enables us to simplify our specification of the shape of the vocal tract. We no longer have to specify the cross-sectional area at a large number of points along the length of the tract. Let us examine qualitatively

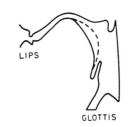

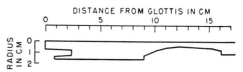

FIG. 1. A mid-sagittal section through the vocal tract during the production of the vowel /i/, and a representation of this vocal tract configuration as an acoustic tube. From Chiba and Kajiyama (see reference 15).

some of the constraints that are imposed by the structures that form the vocal mechanism.

X-ray data[14] have demonstrated that, throughout a major portion of the length of the vocal tract, up to a distance of about 15 cm from the adult male glottis, the cross-sectional dimensions are controlled primarily by the position and shape of the tongue. During the articulation of vowels, the tongue usually forms a constriction or region of minimum cross-sectional area. The cross-sectional area at this constriction may be as small as 0.3 cm². On either side of the constriction there is a gradual increase in area. As the constriction moves forward, the dimensions of the pharynx increase appreciably; as the constriction moves back, the dimensions of the oral portion of the tract increase. In general, the cross-sectional dimensions of the tract at the ends of the tongue remote from the constriction increase if the constriction is narrowed. If the constriction is widened, however, the cross-sectional area along the length of the tongue becomes more uniform. In effect, the x-ray studies indicate that during the articulation of vowels the dimensions of the vocal tract along the length of the tongue are controlled primarily by the position of the tongue constriction and by the degree of tongue constriction. Specification of these two quantities defines within limits the cross-sectional area of the vocal tract at all other points along the length of the tongue.

The x-ray data suggest further that the first few centimeters of the tract above the glottis change through only a restricted range of cross-sectional areas in comparison with other portions of the tract. In the region beyond about 15 cm from the glottis, the mandible and the lips determine the cross-sectional area. This portion of the vocal tract may be short with large cross-sectional area, as in /æ/, or may be long as 3 cm, with small cross-sectional area, as in /u/.

[13] The symbols of the International Phonetic Association are used throughout this paper.

[14] For a review of the x-ray literature pertaining to the vocal tract see A. S. Macmillan and G. Kelemen, Arch. Otolaryngol. **55**, 671–688 (1952).

[15] T. Chiba and M. Kajiyama, *The Vowel, Its Nature and Structure* (Tokyo-Kaiseikan Publishing Company, Ltd., Tokyo, 1941).

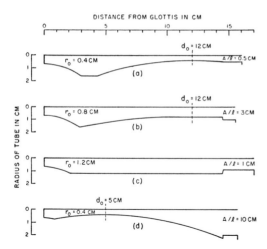

FIG. 2. Idealized vocal tract configurations for typical values of parameters r_0, d_0, and A/l. See discussion in text.

In view of the constraints that are imposed on the profile of the vocal tract it appears that a specification of the approximate shape of the tract can be given in terms of only three numbers. These numbers give information on the position of the tongue constriction, the size of the constriction formed by the tongue, and the dimensions in the vicinity of the mouth opening. We shall outline rules that show how to determine the cross-sectional area at all points along the vocal tract from these three numbers.

Figure 2 indicates the dimensions we use to specify the shape of the vocal tract, and shows examples of four different configurations. The model idealizes the tract as an acoustic tube with no bends, terminated at the left by the glottis and at the right by the mouth opening. The upper boundary of the tube is fixed, and the vertical dimension measured from this boundary at any point along the tube gives the radius r of the tube at that point. The cross-sectional area is, of course, equal to πr^2.

The point of constriction of the tongue is designated by the coordinates d_0 and r_0, representing the distance from the glottis to the constriction and the radius at the constriction respectively. We assume r_0 to vary within the range 0.3 to 1.2 cm since these numbers define the general range of constriction sizes that are measured from x-ray pictures. The radii r at other points along the length of the tongue are given by the equation

$$r - r_0 = 0.25(1.2 - r_0)x^2, \qquad (1)$$

where x is measured horizontally from the point of constriction in cm. Equation (1) represents a parabola with apex at the point of constriction. The parabolic equation provides the model with a range of tongue profiles that are similar to the configurations observed in the x-ray studies of the human vocal tract (see Fig. 1, for example). For values of r_0 approaching 1.2 cm, the coefficient of x^2 in Eq. (1) becomes small, and the parab-

ola is flat. Thus when the constriction is large, the tract is relatively uniform in size along the length of the tongue. Figure 2(b) shows a constriction $r_0 = 0.8$ cm, for which the parabola is relatively flat. The limiting case, $r_0 = 1.2$ cm, is shown in Fig. 2(c). For small r_0, the coefficient of x^2 becomes larger, and the parabola is more peaked. In this case there is an appreciable variation in cross-sectional area along the tract. Figures 2(a) and 2(d) show typical profiles for $r_0 = 0.4$ cm, a relatively narrow constriction.

The parabolic contour defines the radius of the tube up to a point 14.5 cm from the glottis. Beyond this point the size is determined by another parameter, to be discussed below. In the vicinity of the glottis, the radius is determined by the parabolic contour if the constriction position is relatively close to the glottis, as shown by Fig. 2(d). If the constriction is more than 5 or 6 cm from the glottis, however, Eq. (1) would specify a radius that is larger than that expected near the glottis in the human vocal tract. To avoid this discrepancy, a certain maximum radius is specified for points close to the glottis. This radius varies from 0.7 cm adjacent to the glottis to 1.6 cm at a distance of 2.5 cm from the glottis and beyond. The contour indicating this maximum radius is given in Fig. 2(a).

The cross-sectional area and length of the front portion of the vocal tract are controlled primarily by the mandible and the lips. This portion of the tract is usually shorter than 3 cm. As far as the acoustic performance of the tract is concerned (at least for vowel production), this section can be represented by a lumped acoustic element having the proper acoustic impedance. The acoustic impedance of a tube of length l and cross-sectional area A is proportional to l/A, neglecting end corrections. In the case of the mouth opening of the vocal tract, a small correction should be applied to account for the radiation impedance. To a reasonable approximation, however, we can specify the mouth opening by a single number equal to the ratio A/l for this portion of the vocal tract. The ratio A/l is used in preference to its reciprocal l/A since it gives a numerical specification that rank orders the mouth openings according to size. A given value of A/l can be produced in different ways. For example, a mouth opening $A/l = 3$ cm could be 1 cm long with $A = 3$ cm², or could be 3 cm long with $A = 9$ cm². In either case, the acoustic impedance of the mouth opening would be approximately the same. The A/l ratio varies from about 20 cm for the large, short mouth opening (/æ/) to about 0.1 cm for the small, long opening (/u/). Four examples of different mouth openings are shown in Fig. 2.

We have now described a set of rules by which we specify the cross-sectional area at all points along an acoustic tube in terms of three numbers: (1) the distance d_0 from the glottis to a point of maximum constriction of the tube, (2) the radius r_0 of the tube at that constriction, and (3) the ratio of the average cross-sectional area to the length for that portion of the tube that is more than 14.5 cm from the glottis. Each of these three numbers varies through a range of values: 4 to 13 cm for d_0, 0.3 to 1.2 cm for r_0, and 0.1 to 20 cm for the A/l ratio of the mouth opening. As the numbers vary through their ranges of values, they generate a variety of shapes for the acoustic tube.

The three numbers provide a relatively simple specification of a set of tube configurations that are similar in form to those observed in x-ray studies of the human vocal tract, but the detailed shapes are, of course, not identical. If the model can synthesize the range of sounds that human speakers can generate then it probably provides a reasonably accurate representation of the activities of the vocal tract during vowel articulation. The validity of the model can be tested by acoustic and auditory analysis of the sounds generated by appropriate excitation of the tube or of its electrical analog, and

by comparison of the results with similar data on the sounds generated by human speakers.

The remainder of this report is concerned with an experimental study of the relations between the idealized articulatory dimensions and the acoustic properties of the outputs, and an interpretation of the data. Validation of the adequacy of the model by systematic auditory tests is not reported here. Such research is now in progress.

RELATIONS BETWEEN ARTICULATORY AND ACOUSTIC DESCRIPTIONS

In principle, it is possible to compute the acoustic behavior of an acoustic tube of variable cross-sectional area when it is excited by a source with known properties. It is convenient to specify the acoustic behavior of the vocal tract by its transfer function,[11] which is the

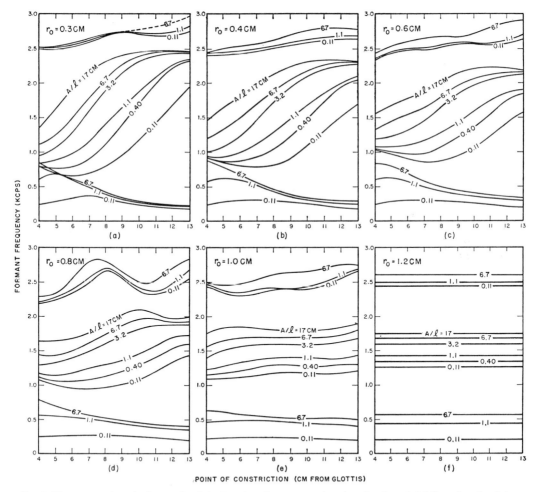

FIG. 3. These curves show the frequencies of the first three formants as a function of r_0, d_0, and A/l. In each section data are presented for a given degree of constriction (r_0) as indicated, with mouth opening (A/l) as the parameter. Three families of curves corresponding to F1, F2, and F3 are plotted in each section. The abscissa is d_0, the distance from the glottis to the point of constriction.

(complex) ratio of the volume velocity at the lips to the volume velocity at the glottis. This transfer function has no zeros, and can be specified (within a constant factor) if the positions of its poles are known, i.e., if the frequency and band width of each resonance or formant is known. Procedures for computing the resonances for various tube configurations have been discussed by Chiba and Kajiyama,[15] Dunn,[10] and Fant.[11] Such calculations are tedious, however, and can be circumvented by the use of an analog of the vocal tract. If a vocal tract analog is adjusted to simulate the desired range of articulatory configurations then measurements on the analog will yield data on the resonances directly. In the present study, relations between the articulatory configurations and the formant frequencies have been obtained by direct electrical measurements on an electrical analog of the vocal tract.

The electrical analog[12] is based on a representation of the vocal tract by an acoustic transmission line. It consists of 35 electrical LC sections connected in cascade, each of which represents a $\frac{1}{2}$-cm section of the vocal tract. Each pair of elements is variable in steps. The effective cross-sectional area of each $\frac{1}{2}$-cm section can be varied through 11 different values from 0.17 to 17 cm² by proper switching of the L and C elements. The total length of the vocal tract analog (VTA) is also variable in $\frac{1}{2}$-cm steps. Thus any articulatory configurations that utilize cross-sectional areas in this range, such as those illustrated in Fig. 2, can be approximated in a step-wise fashion by the VTA with reasonable accuracy.

The VTA was used to simulate the range of articulatory configurations that are generated when d_0, r_0, and A/l are allowed to vary through the ranges of values specified above. Configurations were set up for ten values of d_0(4–13 cm), six values of r_0(0.3–1.2 cm), and six values of mouth opening (A/l=0.11–17 cm), for a total of 306 configurations.[16] For each idealized articulatory shape the frequencies of the first three formants were measured.

An audio oscillator with constant voltage output was connected through a high resistance to the glottis end of the VTA, and a voltmeter was connected across the radiation impedance at the mouth opening. The oscillator was swept through all frequencies up to about 4000 cps, and the frequencies at which there were maxima in the transmission, as indicated by peaks in the voltage output, were noted. These frequencies for which there are peaks in the transmission are the formant frequencies. If the oscillator were replaced by a periodic sawtooth voltage source, the spectrum of the output of the VTA would exhibit peaks at these frequencies. For some of the configurations, such as a "buzz" generator was connected at the VTA input, and the output was amplified and transduced by a loudspeaker. The sounds generated in this manner were judged informally, and appeared to exhibit good vowel quality.

The experimental data presented in the form of graphical relations between the articulatory configurations, as described by three numbers, and the frequencies of the first three formants. One type of presentation is shown in Fig. 3. A separate plot is shown for each constriction size r_0. For example, the data in Fig. 3(b) are for r_0=0.4 cm, i.e., a constriction of cross-sectional area 0.5 cm². In each section, the distance d_0 from the glottis to the point of constriction is plotted as abscissa, with formant frequency as the ordinate.

In each section of the figure three sets of curves are shown, one set for the first formant (F1), a second set for the second formant (F2), and a third set for the third formant (F3). Within each set the parameter is the size of the mouth opening (A/l). For F2, six curves are shown, one for each of the six mouth openings that were set up on the VTA. To avoid confusion with too many closely spaced curves, only three values of mouth openings are shown for F1 and F3.

Before proceeding to other methods of displaying the data, let us examine briefly the trends indicated in Fig. 3:

Formant 1. In general, high first formants are associated with a narrow tongue constriction near the glottis and an unrounded, large mouth opening. The first formant is low when the mouth opening is small and rounded or when there is a narrow tongue constriction near the mouth opening.

Formant 2. Formant 2 generally increases in frequency as the point of constriction moves forward

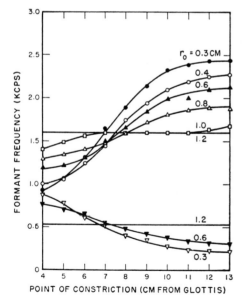

FIG. 4. These curves show the frequencies of the first two formants as a function of d_0 and r_0 for a given mouth opening, A/l =3.2 cm. Experimental points are plotted in this figure to illustrate the degree to which the data are smoothed.

[16] For r_0=1.2 cm, the shape of the tube is independent of d_0, and hence 54 of the 360 possible configurations are identical.

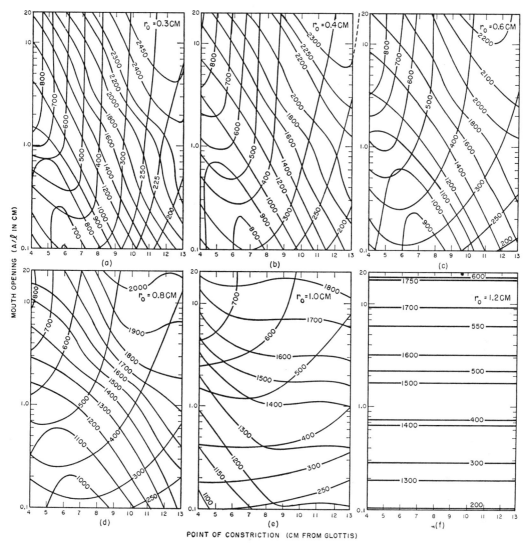

FIG. 5. Contours of constant frequency for F1 and F2. Each section of the figure represents a given degree of constriction. See discussion in text.

from the glottis and as the A/l ratio of the mouth opening increases. This increase in F2 is more pronounced if the tongue constriction is narrow.

Formant 3. There is a small increase in F3 as the constriction moves forward from the glottis and as the mouth opening increases in size and becomes less rounded.

These findings are in agreement with those of Delattre[17] who described relations between measured formant frequencies and cavity configurations used in natural speech.

An alternate method of presenting the data, showing more clearly the effect of constriction size, is illustrated

in Fig. 4. This figure is drawn for a mouth opening with $A/l = 3.2$ cm and shows two sets of curves for the first two formants. The parameter in this case is the constriction size. We observe again that F1 decreases as the constriction moves forward, but the decrease becomes less pronounced as the constriction size increases. Formants 2 and 3 increase as the constriction moves forward, the rate of increase depending markedly on the size of the constriction. At a particular constriction position (near $d_0 = 0.7$ in Fig. 4) there is a crossover point at which the formant frequency is almost independent of constriction size. If the size of the tongue constriction at this point were changed there would be little or no change in the frequencies of the formants.

[17] P. Delattre, PMLA **66**, 864–875 (1951).

A set of curves similar to those shown in Fig. 4 can be plotted for each value of mouth opening. Each set of curves shows the same trend as those in Fig. 4, except the position of the crossover point depends on the mouth opening. This point is rather far forward for a small, rounded mouth opening, and moves back as the mouth opens and becomes less rounded.

In effect, the curves in Figs. 3 and 4 show a graphical transformation between acoustic data (formant frequencies) on one hand and articulatory data on the other. Figure 5 presents this transformation in a different form. In each section of this figure we plot contours of constant F1 and F2 for a specified constriction size. The abscissa represents, as before, the distance d_0 from glottis to constriction, but the ordinate represents the A/l ratio for the mouth opening.

To illustrate the meaning of these contours, let us restrict our attention to Fig. 5(b), for which $r_0 = 0.4$ cm. The data in Fig. 3(b) were used to construct Fig. 5(b). Along the contour labeled 400 cps, for example, we find combinations of constriction position and mouth opening that yield a first formant of 400 cps (when $r_0 = 0.4$ cm). Similarly, along the contour labeled 1800 cps we find combinations of constriction position and mouth opening that yield a second formant of 1800 cps. These two contours intersect at the point where A/l for the mouth opening is 3.0 cm and $d_0 = 8.5$ cm, with $r_0 = 0.4$ cm. This articulatory position will yield, therefore, an F1 of 400 cps and an F2 of 1800 cps. By a similar process we can determine the articulatory positions corresponding to any other combination of F1 and F2, provided the corresponding contours intersect in the figure.

In any one of the sections of Fig. 5 we find, over most of the range, a one-to-one correspondence between articulatory dimensions and the frequencies of F1 and F2. In some of the sections, however, we find limited

regions where there are two intersections of F1 and F2 contours, i.e., there are two combinations of articulatory dimensions that yield the same formant frequencies. An example of such a region appears in the lower left-hand corner of Fig. 5(a), where the constriction is back and the mouth opening is small and rounded.

In Fig. 5(b) we noted the point of intersection of the 400 and 1800 cps contours. We also find intersection of these two contours in Figs. 5(a), 5(c), and 5(d), which represent other constriction sizes, at points somewhat different from the point of intersection in Fig. 5(b). We conclude, therefore, that there is a range of articulatory positions that give rise to the same frequencies for F1 and F2. This point will be discussed further when the data are interpreted in terms of the articulation of specific vowels.

CONTOURS OF VOWEL ARTICULATION

An illustration of the application of the articulatory coordinates is afforded by the use of data reported by Peterson and Barney.[18] These investigators have published acoustical data specifying the frequencies of the first three formants of vowels produced by men, women, and children. The solid lines in Fig. 6, adapted from their paper, delineate the F1-F2 areas for nine common vowels. Within each loop the shaded area represents our estimate of vowels probably produced by adult male speakers. The dashed contours enclosing the estimated areas can now be transposed to the articulatory coordinates previously described.

The results of such a transformation are shown in Fig. 7. This figure presents the ranges of articulatory positions that produce the vowel values indicated by the shaded areas in Fig. 6, when the constraints of the three-number articulatory specification scheme are assumed. Peterson and Barney have computed average values for the formant frequencies of the vowels spoken by their adult male subjects. The solid dots in Fig. 7 represent these values.

In each section of Fig. 7 the degree of constriction is held constant. For example, when the constriction is small ($r_0 = 0.3$ cm), Fig. 7(a) shows that all of the nine vowels of Fig. 6 can be produced by proper manipulation of mouth opening and constriction location. We observe further that the vowel areas vary considerably in size. This variation is a measure of the degree of articulatory precision required for the production of a given vowel. That is, the size and shape of each vowel area indicates the range of variation of mouth opening and constriction position that can be used to generate that vowel.

The remaining sections of Fig. 7 demonstrate the effect of enlarging the constriction introduced into the vocal conduit. As the constriction gets larger the production of extreme or "high" vowels such as /i/ and /u/

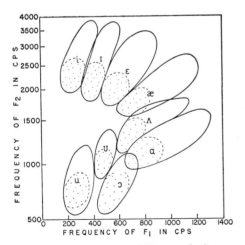

FIG. 6. A plot of the frequency of F2 *versus* the frequency of F1 for nine vowels [after Peterson and Barney (see reference 18)]. The shaded areas enclosed by dashed lines represent estimates of vowels spoken by adult male subjects.

[18] G. E. Peterson and H. L. Barney, J. Acoust. Soc. Am. **24**, 175–184 (1952).

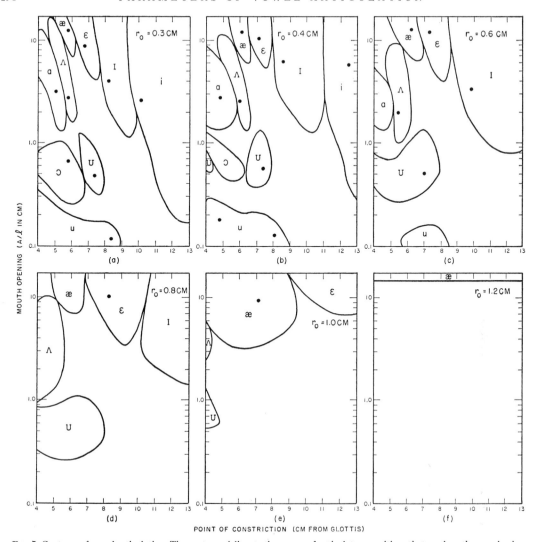

FIG. 7. Contours of vowel articulation. The contours delineate the ranges of articulatory positions that produce the vowel values indicated by the shaded areas in Fig. 6. The solid dots represent average values for adult male speakers (see reference 18).

becomes more restricted and finally impossible. The limiting case, Fig. 7(f), represents the possible vowel vowel output of a uniform tube. In this case there is no point of constriction in the vocal channel, i.e., the lumen is constant, and the mouth opening determines the output.

It is important to note that the formant frequencies, from which Fig. 7 was derived, are not the only determinants of vowel quality. Two vowels that have the same F1 and F2 may differ in quality if there is a difference in the damping or band widths of the formants or in the frequencies of higher formants. The formant band width depends to some extent upon the degree of constriction in the vocal conduit.[19,20] A vowel that is

[19] J. van den Berg, J. Acoust. Soc. Am. **27**, 332-338 (1955).
[20] U. Ingard, J. Acoust. Soc. Am. **25**, 1037-1061 (1953).

produced when the vocal tract is relatively open and unconstricted may have narrower formants than one produced with a constricted tract, even though the articulatory parameters are adjusted to give the same F1 and F2. Simple experiments[7] with synthetic speech have shown, however, that formant band width has only a second-order effect on vowel quality, and that formant frequency is the major influence.

In addition to demonstrating the rather obvious fact that a given vowel can be produced by a variety of articulatory configurations, Fig. 7(b) indicates a more startling finding. The figure shows the articulatory area for /u/ to possess two separate points which will produce the average adult male formants. Examination of Fig. 5 has already revealed that for the smaller constriction values there is a tendency for the extreme formant contours to be double-valued. Thus, the data suggest that a vowel such as /u/ produced at the extremes of certain articulatory ranges, may have a bimodal *articulatory* distribution.

DISCUSSION OF VOWEL CONTOURS

That synthetic speech might be utilized to better understand the phonetics of natural speech has been suggested before.[1,10,12] The fruitfulness of experiments involving the perception of one type of synthetic speech has been demonstrated.[21–23] The present data suggest that at least some of the physiological problems of speech sound production can be approached with profit by means of experiments involving the synthesis of speech.

Peterson[24] has treated at length the definition of the phonetic value of vowels in terms of physiological and acoustic dimensions. He notes that a large number of physiological measurements are required to describe completely the cavity formation of a sustained vowel, but that the various positions can be specified approximately by less than a dozen physiological variables. In addition he points out that more than two dimensions are required to form a consistent physiological vowel diagram when both front (unrounded) and back (rounded) vowels are shown in the same system. The separate front and back series, however, can be described in two dimensions. Peterson also indicates the auditory nature of the conventional vowel diagrams, and demonstrates that they are similar to the vowel diagrams derived from formant plots.

That reconsideration of the so-called vowel triangle is not completely an academic matter has been indicated by others as well. Joos,[25] for example, states that the traditional tongue-height vowel diagrams have an articulatory shape but an "acoustic scale" (sic), and warns phoneticians to be wary of "articulatory" data not known to be based on x-ray or equivalent evidence. In another discussion of vowel diagrams Heffner[26] remarks that a F1-F2 plot becomes a "graph representative of physiological facts rather than a mere juggling of acoustic data if it can be shown that these formant frequencies are correlated with physical resonators which determine the character of the vowel." Although such inferences have been made with some success,[11,17,27–29] a comprehensive physio-acoustic theory of speech has yet to be developed.

The present data are characterized by features that seem to clarify further the physiological description of vowels while providing links to classical phonetics. The well-known progression of front and back vowel series is delineated in articulatory terms in Fig. 7(a), for example. When the central tendencies of the front vowels are connected, a line will run from /i/ to /I/ to /ɛ/ to /æ/. The back vowels seem to be less orderly—a fact pointed out by many phoneticians and supported by x-ray research.[30,31] The figure shows that the two series, front vowels and back vowels, form a vowel diagram highly suggestive of the earlier auditory, acoustic, and physiological varieties.

Some basic differences, however, distinguish the present configurations from traditional vowel diagrams. The various vowel diagrams shown in Fig. 7 represent, in effect, a three-dimensional vowel structure through which six sections are taken. The basic data permit a two-dimensional presentation of the effects of manipulating any two variables while holding a third variable constant. Another obvious difference is the lack of correspondence between the high point of the tongue mass in the oral cavity and the point at which r is smallest, especially for the back vowel series where the smallest constriction may be in the pharynx.

Modern phoneticians,[32,33] while noting the dependence of vowel production on mouth opening, have pointed out that all the common vowels of English can be produced with a pencil clenched between the teeth. This *tour de force*, as well as the popular art of ventriloquism, is suggested by the information in Fig. 7. For example, if the mouth openings (A/l) in the model are restricted to the range 1 to 4 cm instead of the full 200:1 range shown in Fig. 7, we find that all the vowels except /u/ can be produced by proper manipulation of the position and size of the constriction. We should note that values of A/l are not equivalent to such traditional measures of mouth opening as the distance between the upper and lower incisors. Slight variation in lip position with a fixed mandible can produce considerable variation in the value of A/l.

In a recent discussion of the system of symbolization for teaching speech to the deaf, Zaliouk[34] stresses the differences between the manner of production of traditional front and back vowels. While asserting that schematized vowel diagrams based on fixed tongue positions already have been discredited, he points out that the essential characteristics of certain vowels are obscured by over-detailed descriptions of vowel articulation. As an illustration, he states that the vowel /u/ is determined primarily by the rounding of the lips, while

[21] F. S. Cooper *et al.*, J. Acoust. Soc. Am. **24**, 597–606 (1952).
[22] Liberman, Delattre, and Cooper, Am. J. Psychol. **65**, 497–516 (1952).
[23] P. Delattre *et al.*, Word **8**, 195–210 (1952).
[24] G. E. Peterson, Language **27**, 541–553 (1951).
[25] M. Joos, Language 24, Suppl., 1–136 (1948).
[26] R–M. S. Heffner, *General Phonetics* (University of Wisconsin Press, Madison, 1950).
[27] D. Lewis, J. Acoust. Soc. Am. **8**, 91–99 (1936).
[28] H. Dudley, Bell System Tech. J. **19**, 495 (1940).
[29] Potter, Kopp, and Green, *Visible Speech* (D. Van Nostrand Company, Inc., New York, 1947).

[30] J. P. Kelly and L. B. Higley, Arch. Speech **1**, 84–95 (1934).
[31] R. T. Holbrook and F. J. Carmody, U. Calif. Pub. Mod. Philol. **20**, 230 (1937).
[32] D. Jones, *An Outline of English Phonetics* (E. P. Dutton and Company, Inc., New York, 1932).
[33] J. S. Kenyon, *American Pronunciation* (George Wahr, Ann Arbor, Michigan, 1940).
[34] A. Zaliouk, J. Speech Hearing Disorders **19**, 190–207 (1954).

the vowel /i/ is specified primarily by tongue position. The data of Fig. 7 are, in general, in accord with these observations. The figure shows that the production of /i/ is dependent primarily upon the position and size of the tongue constriction. The /i/-area is always more than 9.5 cm from the glottis and moves forward in the vocal tract as the constriction increases; it has disappeared entirely when r_0 equals 0.6 cm. The range of mouth opening values associated with this vowel area, however, is very large. In other words, the vowel /i/ is relatively insensitive to mouth opening changes, but is sensitive to variation in tongue position and height, i.e., place and degree of constriction. Similarly, the figure demonstrates the relative importance of the factors determining the production of /u/. This vowel is produced over a wide range of constriction positions providing the degree of constriction is appropriate, but is restricted to small values of A/l. That is, the production of /u/ is dependent largely on mouth opening characteristics.

The present data, while supporting Zaliouk's clinical observations regarding articulation, do not agree with his point of view pertaining to vowel diagrams in general. It is not being suggested, however, that the present data validate any theory of static positions for vowel production. It is hoped rather, that the articulatory shapes under discussion may specify to a first approximation the "canal shape" that Stetson[35] lists as the first factor of the syllable. Experiments on the dynamics of speech produced synthetically must await the development of a dynamic analog of the vocal tract.

CONCLUSION

The agreement of the present data with the research and observations of others supports the assertion that the proposed three-number articulatory scheme produces idealized vocal tract configurations that are descriptive of human vowel articulation. The effect on the vowels of the variation of the three parameters (r_0, d_0, and A/l) is interpreted as adding to the face validity of this simplified description. We conclude that, in general, the proposed scheme produces configurations of the vocal tract analog that in turn yield formant frequencies appropriate to the end product desired, and that the relationships among the vowels so produced are similar to those regarded by students of speech as characteristic of human speech.

ACKNOWLEDGMENTS

The authors are grateful for the assistance and encouragement of their colleagues at the Massachusetts Institute of Technology, particularly the members of the Acoustics Laboratory Speech Group.

[35] R. H. Stetson, *Motor Phonetics* (North Holland Publishing Company, Amsterdam, 1951).

CHAPTER 3

Reprinted from FOR ROMAN JAKOBSON, M. Halle, H. Lunt, and H. MacLean, eds.
(The Hague: Mouton, 1956).

ON THE PREDICTABILITY

OF FORMANT LEVELS AND SPECTRUM ENVELOPES

FROM FORMANT FREQUENCIES

BY C. GUNNAR M. FANT

INTRODUCTION

THE STUDY OF THE ACOUSTIC nature of speech signals, which in recent years has made great strides, is still in an early stage of development. We are familiar with the general structure of speech waves. This knowledge, however, is largely qualitative and partially incomplete. It has nevertheless made it possible to make a tentative description of the physical correlates of the phonemic oppositions, primarily in terms of general rules for the so-called distinctive features, describing the essential or minimum conditions for the differences in signal structure found in all pairs of phonemes that can be included in a particular distinction category.

We would like to have a more profound knowledge of how a distinction is realized quantitatively within all possible minimally distinct pairs and in all positional variants, including those due to differences among individual speakers as well as to the influence of superimposed denotative and emphatic features. Implementation of this program will require research of great complexity and difficulty, and we may be thus excused for not waiting for a precise mapping of all phonetic details before proceeding to a structural ordering of our knowledge. As research progresses it will be possible to supplement, modify and reformulate more concisely the statements we made in *Preliminaries*(12).

One of our major difficulties lies in the complexity of speech waves. We often observe several concomitant details without being quite sure to what extent they can occur independently. It is evident that before we adjust our methods of specification in order to obtain statements that are optimal with regard to hearing and to the reception of a speech message, it pays to eliminate those redundancies that are due to an interdependence of the parameters of specification. The theory of vocal transmission is of considerable help here since it provides information on the general structure of speech signals, in particular since it reveals the analytical relations between possible variables of specification. We shall make use of this theory in trying to answer, in the remaining pages, the following question: Given the formant frequencies only, to what extent can the relative vowel intensities, the relative intensity levels of the formants, their bandwidths, and the particular shape of the spectrum envelope be predicted?

SPECIFICATION OF VOWEL SPECTRA

A spectrogram (13), (17), (18) of the kind that is obtained with the Sonagraph analyzer has the dimensions time, frequency and intensity. Quantitative measurements of frequency locations and time positions can be made. The intensity of spectral components is portrayed qualitatively only in terms of the blackness of the spectrogram. The spectral energy maxima, i.e., the formants, are visible as dark bands of a certain frequency width and a certain extent in time, covering the duration of the sound and sometimes showing continuity to formants of adjacent sounds. The visible width of such a formant band in the spectrogram of a vowel analyzed with broad filter as in Fig. 1 B or 1 D is determined essentially by the bandwidth of the analyzer, since it is larger than the bandwidth of the vowel formant, to be defined later. If the bandwidth of the analyzer is smaller than the fundamental frequency of the voice as in Fig. 1 A, the recorded pattern is largely different. We still see the formant bands, but they are now carried by a fine structure of essentially horizontal lines instead of the closely spaced vertical lines typical for the broad-band analysis. These horizontal lines are the harmonics of the voice fundamental frequency F_0.

The relative intensities of the harmonics can be determined quantitatively by means of a cross-section, Fig. 1 C or 1 E. This is to be considered as a sample of the vowel, the duration of which is of the order of the inverse value of the bandwidth of the analyzer, i.e., in the case of the narrow band filter of the Sonograph, of the order of 1/40 second. For a detailed description of the vowel sample from the cross-section we need to specify the amplitudes of each of the harmonics within a frequency range up to about 4000 cps. This procedure of tabulating the harmonics is too time-consuming to be of any practical use. All practical experience shows that a detailed specification of all harmonics is unnecessary and that the main vowel quality is correlated with the formants, see ref. (6), (16), (20).

How do we define a formant? When dealing with voiced sounds, the following procedure should be followed: Study the amplitudes of the harmonics within the formant range and its neighborhood, and trace the spectrum envelope, i.e., the curve enclosing the peaks of the harmonics. We define

1. FORMANT FREQUENCY: The frequency of a formant is the position on the frequency scale of the peak of the spectrum envelope drawn to enclose the peaks of the harmonics. When two formants come close or when the formant to be measured is very low in frequency only one side of the formant "mountain" may be visible and the estimate has to be based solely on this information. In such cases it pays to go to the broad band spectrogram and determine the center of the formant band. This method gives more accurate values than may be expected. An experienced investigator may take all his data on formant frequencies form the broad band spectrogram. The inexperienced investigator is advised to use both methods as a control.

In spite of its apparent lack of rigidity, this method for determining formant frequencies is preferable to the center of gravity measurements proposed by Potter and Steinberg (20). The application of their formula may give considerable errors for asymmetrical configurations of harmonics, as in the case of very low frequency formants or when two formants come close. In the latter case it is not possible to assign each harmonic to one formant only.

2. FORMANT LEVEL: The formant level can be defined as the peak value of the formant envelope at the frequency of the formant. The word 'level' here implies a logarithmic measure, i.e., in decibels relative to an arbitrary level or relative to a reference level, preferably 0.0002 dyne/cm².

45

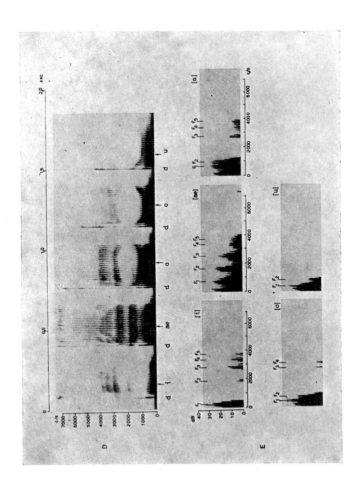

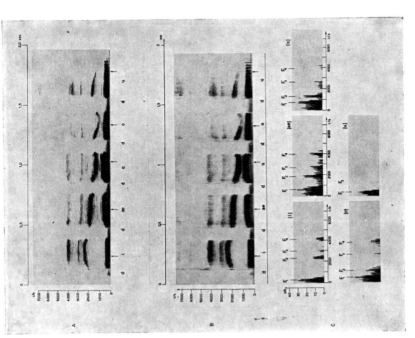

Fig 1. Sonagraph recordings of the nonsense syllable series [di dæ da do du]. A is a narrow-band spectrogram, B and D are broad-band spectrograms, and C and E are cross-sections of vowel spectra sampled at the instant indicated by arrows under the broad-band spectrograms. A B C were uttered by a Texas speaker, D and E by a Swede. — These data show the spectral properties of the 5 vowels but also some individual voice characteristics. The relative weakness of the third formant and the extra formant just below F_1 found in [æ] and [a] of cross-section C and the emphasized second harmonic may be due to slight nasalization or to other factors. e.g. coupling to the subglottal system or peculiarities of the spectrum of the particular voice source. — The differences and similarities of these cross-sections should be compared with the idealized spectra of Fig 5.

46

Any statement of absolute levels, i.e., in decibels relative to the reference level, should be supplemented by a specification of the distance from the microphone to the lips of the speaker. For the case of the formant frequency occurring at the exact frequency of a harmonic, the envelope level equals that of the center harmonic.

3. FORMANT BANDWIDTH: The formant bandwith for an isolated formant that is well defined by harmonics of a low pitch is determined by the following procedure: Determine those points of the spectrum envelope on both sides of the peak where the level of the envelope is 3 db below the peak level. The bandwidth is the frequency difference between the two points. For the case of a high voice fundamental or when two formants come too close or the formant under investigation is too low in frequency, it may not be possible to measure the bandwidth and any estimate would tend to give too large a value. This concept of bandwidth should not be confused with the frequency width of the apparent base of the formant. Also it should not be confused with the width of the bands in the spectrogram which are essentially determined by the properties of the analyzer.

We shall use the following symbols in our descriptions:
  F_n = frequency of formant number n in cps
  B_n = bandwidth of formant number n in cps
  L_n = level of formant number n in db
  F_N = formant number n without special reference to its dimensions. The first formant is thus denoted by Fl and its frequency by F_1 and so on.
  F_0 = the frequency of the voice fundamental in cps.
The natural range of variation (4), (5), (16) of these parameters for non-nasal voiced sounds uttered by an average male speaker is as follows: F_1 150–850 cps, F_2 500–2500 cps, F_3 1700–3500 cps, F_4 2500–4500 cps. For females the formants are on the average about 17% higher and for children even higher. The differences in formant frequencies are thus considerably smaller than the differences in fundamental pitch.

The range of variation of formant bandwidths is not as well known: 40–250 cps are probable limits (1), (14) for the first three formants and 100 cps is a typical average value. The higher the formant number the higher the formant bandwidth. B_1 and B_2 have both an average value of 80 cps.

At an average voice effort the level of the first formant L_1 is of the order of 60–65 db relative to 0.0002 dyne cm^2 at a distance of one meter from the speaker. The relative variations of L_1, L_2 and L_3 for separate vowels are discussed later. The spread in formant levels comparing separate speakers uttering the same vowel is of the order of 4 db. It is higher for L_2 and L_3 than for L_1.

The frequency of the voice fundamental F_0 can be measured either as the frequency spacing between harmonics in a spectrogram or in a cross section taken with narrow band filter, or as $1/T_0$ where T_0 is the spacing between fundamental periods in the time scale. The period time can be measured from broad-band spectrograms for low pitched voices. Each of the successive vertical lines typical for the fine structure of the broad band spectrogram indicates the beginning of a fundamental period.

Typical values of F_0 in speech are 120 cps for male voices, 220 cps for female voices and about 300 cps for children of about 10 years of age. The mean value of pitch within each of the male and female groups varies of course according to voice character. The maximal variations for a single speaker within a sentence are of the order of one octave.

THE MATHEMATICAL THEORY OF VOWEL STRUCTURE

The dependent relationships between formant frequencies and other spectral phenomena such as the relative amplitude values of all harmonics within a cross-section can be conveniently studied from the theory of poles and zeros, i.e., the complex frequency representation of spectral quantities. No proof or derivation will be presented here – just the end results.

A vowel or any voiced sound can be regarded as the response of the vocal tract system to the voice source at the vocal cords. In other words, the vowel has the properties of the voice source modified by the filtering action of the vocal tract. A third factor enters also, and that is the radiation at the lips of the speaker. It can be thought of as a part of the filter function, or it can be handled separately.

Somewhat more specifically, we can decompose the spectrum envelope of the measured sound into constituents originating from each of these stages in the production. If a decibel scale is used, the vowel spectrum is merely the sum of the separate frequency curves. If linear scales are used, the vowel spectrum is the product of each of the frequency curves for the parts. The periodicity of the vowel, i.e., the harmonic structure of the spectrum, originates from the vocal cord source, the formants come from the vocal tract filter function, and the changes in formant levels and the overall slope of the spectrum envelope that occur in cases when formant frequencies and bandwidths are kept constant, depend on the slope of the envelope of the voice source spectrum.

We express these relations by the following formula:

Speech sound = (source) . (filter function) . (radiation)[1]

At this stage the poles and zeros enter the picture. Since mathematical formalism is to be avoided, we shall speak of the pole-zero specification in terms of simple geometrical configurations only.

Theory tells us that the filter-function can be specified completely by the frequencies and the bandwidths of the formants (11). Each formant thus can be given by two numbers, its frequency and bandwidth. This fact makes it possible to represent a formant by points in a two dimensional graph. Such a graphic representation will be seen in the upper portion of Fig. 2. In this figure, the points labelled pole nr 1 and nr 1* are located symmetrically at $f = \pm F_1$ and $b = +B_1/2$. For formant F_n, the conjugate poles would be located at $f = \pm F_n$ and $b = B_n/2$. To determine the contribution of the formant F_n to the envelope level at any frequency f, locate the frequency f on the f-axis, and draw vectors (lines) from this point to the two poles ($f = 400$ cps in the example shown in Fig. 2). It can be easily seen that the length of the vector V_n to the positive pole is by the Pythagorean theorem

$$V_n = \sqrt{(f - F_n)^2 + (\frac{B_n}{2})^2}$$

and that to the negative pole is by the same token

$$V_n^* = \sqrt{(f + F_n)^2 + (\frac{B_n}{2})^2}$$

---

[1] In more rigorous mathematical terminology, the terms in this equation are defined as follows: The *speech sound* is the transform of the sound pressure wave measured at a distance from the speaker's lips; the *source* is the transform of the volume velocity wave at the glottis; the *filter function* is the ratio of the transform of the volume velocity through the lips to the transform of the volume velocity through the glottis; the *radiation* is the ratio of the transforms of the sound pressure measured at a distance from the speaker's lips to the transform of the volume velocity through the lips. If the magnitudes of these ratios are expressed in decibels, then the operations of multiplication in the equation become simple additions.

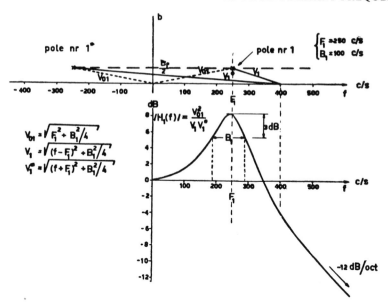

Fig 2. The derivation of the resonance curve of a formant from its frequency and bandwidth, i.e., from the two quantities that determine the formant pole. The particular values utilized in the example, i.e., a formant frequency of 250 cps and a formant bandwidth of 100 cps could pertain to the first formant of a high front vowel. The procedure is begun by plotting the two conjugate poles, i.e., the points $B_1/2$, $\pm F_1$. The resonance curve is then

$$20 \log_{10} \frac{V^2_{01}{}^*}{V_1 V_1}$$

where V_{01} is the length of the vector from the origin to the poles and $V_1{}^*$ and V_1 are the lengths of the vectors drawn from the frequency f on the f-axis to the positive and to the negative pole respectively.

Now draw vectors from the origin to the two poles. Both these vectors have the length

$$V_{On} = V_{On}{}^* = V \sqrt{F_n{}^2 + (\frac{B_n}{2})^2}$$

The contribution of formant F_n to the value of the filter function at frequency f is the product of (V_{On}) $(V_{On}{}^*)$ divided by the product of (V_n) $(V_n{}^*)$, which can be summarized in the following formula

$$H_n (f) = \frac{F_n{}^2 + (\frac{B_n}{2})^1}{V\sqrt{(f - F_n)^2 + (\frac{B_n}{2})^2} \; V\sqrt{(f + F_n)^2 + (\frac{B_n}{2})^2}} \tag{1}$$

If F_n is substantially larger than B_n we can simplify formula (1) by neglecting B_n in those cases where B_n plays a minor role. We then obtain a simplified formula

$$H_n (f) = \frac{F_n{}^2}{(f + F_n) V \sqrt{(f - F_n)^2 + (\frac{B_n}{2})^2}} \tag{2}$$

Repeat the procedure for other values of f and plot the calculated data as a frequency curve, as shown in the lower half of Fig. 2. This is the resonance curve corresponding to formant F_n.

The function $H_n(f)$ is a maximum when the denominator is a minimum, which occurs when $f \cong F_n$. Substituting this in (2) we get

$$H_n\,(F_n) = \frac{F_n{}^2}{\frac{B_n}{2}\cdot 2\,F_n} = \frac{F_n}{B_n} = Q \tag{3}$$

It is to be noted that the quantity Q, which gives the intensity of the formant peak, increases as the formant frequency, provided that the bandwidth remains constant.

Returning again to (2) we observe that $H_n(f)$ goes down to $\frac{1}{\sqrt{2}}$ (i.e. -3db) of the maximum value when $f = F_n - \frac{B_n}{2}$ as can be seen by substituting these values in equation (2) and making the same approximations as above.

When f is substantially larger than F_n and B_n we can further simplify equation (2) as follows

$$H_n\,(f) = \frac{F_n{}^2}{f^2} \tag{4}$$

which tells us that the contribution of the formant F_n beyond a frequency which is large compared with F_n, drops as the square of the frequency or 12 db per octave.

We can calculate in this manner all formants that are of interest (usually F1 to F4) and plot the intensity in db (logarithmic measure) as a function of frequency.

Next the contribution of the glottal source must be evaluated. It varies, of course, with voice effort and individual speaker. Various spectra can be used here without affecting materially the vowel quality. In the following we shall use a voice source with a spectrum dropping at the rate of 12 db per octave.

Finally the effects of radiation at the lips can be accounted for by assuming a rise of 6 db per octave, which is equivalent to postulating a zero at the origin.

It is convenient to have the most variable factors separated from the more constant ones. The constant factors are summarized in Fig. 3. The source spectrum slope, -12 db per octave, modified by the -6 db per octave increase due to radiation, is a new curve of slope -6 db per octave. The influence of the poles higher than nr 4 must also be added. The composite curve for constant factors falls about 6 db per octave at low frequencies. It is level from 1000–2000 cps and has thereafter a steep positive slope. As demonstrated in Fig. 4, the spectrum envelope of a vowel is thus regarded as the superposition of resonance curves, one for each of the first 4 formants, and a curve including the characteristics of the source, the radiation and the higher poles. Even if the latter are not visible as formants they have to be taken into account. This procedure has proved very successful for the synthesis of speech in speaking machines employing resonant circuits in cascade (9).

The systematic decomposition of vowel spectra enables us to make some interesting observations, one of which has been illustrated in Fig. 4. The solid line curves pertain to a vowel with formant frequencies at 500, 1500, 2500, 3500 cps. This is the idealized neutral vowel [ə]. All bandwidths have been assumed to be 100 cps. If the first formant is lowered to 250 cps the vowel quality changes to [u]. The resonance curve for $F_1 = 250$ cps has a level 12 db below the curve for $F_1 = 500$ cps at frequencies above 700 cps. The same difference in the level of the spectrum envelope is found comparing [u] to [ə]. If B_1 is held constant, a lowering of F_1 by one octave will cause a 6 db fall of the envelope peak of the F_1-curve. This effect is partially counteracted by the combined radiation and source characteristics, as in Fig. 4.

Given the frequencies of the formants, their bandwidths may be predicted from statistical data. By means of the analytical procedure above, the whole spectrum envelope of the sound may be calculated. The source characteristics must be known, but the particular data chosen for the

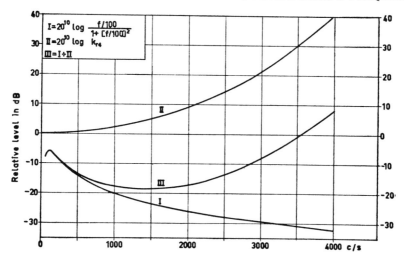

Fig 3. Summation of the "constant"-factors contributing to the spectrum envelope of vowels, including the idealized frequency characteristics of the voice source, of radiation and of the poles higher than number 4.

I. The sum of a +6 db/octave rise for the radiation and an idealized voice source spectrum envelope falling off at a rate of -12 db/octave at frequencies above 100 cps.

II. The contribution from the poles of higher number than 4 to the spectrum level at frequencies below 4000 cps.

III. = I + II is the total frequency correction to be applied to the sum of the resonance curves for the four first formants when calculating the vowel spectrum envelope from the formants or when driving a 4-pole resonance analog of the vocal tract by a source consisting of a series of unit impulses.

source do not influence the main shape of the vowel spectra, at least not if only qualitative statements comparing different vowels are made.

The spectrum envelopes of Fig. 5 are calculated by the same method as shown in Fig. 4. The formant frequencies have been varied systematically in steps of 250 cps and 500 cps in order to show the typical variations in spectrum shape that follow. We may, for instance, state that L_3 and L_4, i.e., the levels of the 3rd and 4th formants, are very low for the vowels [u] and [ɔ] because both F_1 and F_2 are low on the frequency scale. In other vowels with higher frequency positions of F_1 and F_2 these levels, L_3 and L_4, are higher. In general, when two formants approach each other their levels will both increase, e.g., the first and second formants of [a] and [ɔ] and the second and third formants of front vowels. In [i] there is a typical increase in levels L_3 and L_4 since F_3 comes closer to F_4 than to F_2.

CORRABORATIVE MEASUREMENTS

Very little has been reported in the literature on the subject of formant levels. The only available quantitative data of any statistical significance seem to be those of Peterson and Barney (16) on American-English vowels and the data for Swedish vowels measured by the author (4), (5), (6). These two investigations provide very similar data on formant frequencies of English and Swedish sounds that are known to be closely related.

The data on formant levels from the two investigations also compare well as can be seen from Fig. 6, which shows the levels of the three first formants, L_1, L_2, L_3, in decibels for various Swedish and American vowels. The same general observations on formant levels can be made as in Fig. 5. Observe how L_3 increases rapidly with increasing compactness in the grave vowels and that it varies less in the acute vowels. For the Swedish [i₁] L_3 is 3 db higher than L_2. For the American-

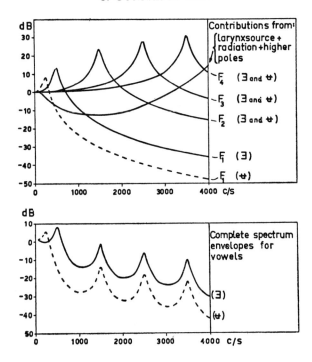

Fig 4. The effect of a shift in frequency of the first formant on the level of the spectrum envelope demonstrated by the composition of two vowel spectra in elementary resonance curves.

[ɜ] denotes the open tube idealized neutral vowel with formant frequencies at 500, 1500, 2500 ... cps. A shift in the frequency of the first formant only from 500 to 250 cps results in a new sound, approximately [u], in which the part of the spectrum envelope above 500 cps is practically identical with that of the original vowel except for a loss of level of 12 db. In general, one octave decrease in F_1 results in -12 db shift of the levels in all parts above the frequency of the first formant. The level of the first formant is also decreased, but to a lesser extent.

English [i] L_3 is 4 db lower than L_2. L_2 is at a maximum for [a₁]. L_1 is highest for [a₁] and varies less than L_2 and L_3. With a few exceptions for L_1, the levels of all three formants increase with increasing compactness, i.e., increasing F_1.

The statistical correlation between phonetic quality and formant levels is thus considerable. It is apparently possible to apply the theory provided in the previous section for an analytical prediction of the systematic trends displayed in Fig. 6.

Two further sets of calculations have been carried out, both on the intensity level of the third formant. One is based on the group of 7 male speakers from the Swedish investigation, the other is based on the data obtained from one speaker only. The object of the calculations was to predict L_3 from the *a priori* reference value of L_3 found experimentally for the vowel [a₁], utilizing the information on the shift in formant frequencies F_1, F_2, F_3, F_4 from [a₁] to the vowel under investigation. Each of the formants was represented by its elementary resonance curve as given by equation (1).

The calculated and measured data compare quite well, see Fig. 7. The deviations are smaller than 3 db for the average data from the 7 male speakers. The agreement is good enough as a proof of the applicability of the theory of poles and zeros for the specification of vowel spectra. Further, it supports the fundamental assumption that the spectrum envelope of the voice source is reasonably independent of the particular vowel.

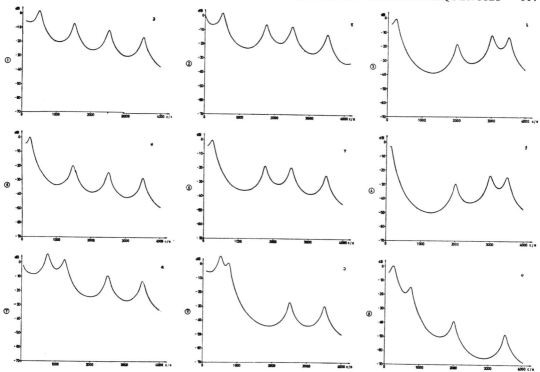

Fig 5. Vowel spectrum envelopes derived from a mathematical synthesis in terms of elementary resonance curves, one for each formant, as in Fig 4. A voice source with a slope of -12 db/octave and constant formant bandwidths of of 100 cps were assumed. Formant frequencies were chosen so as to give vowels that approximate the IPA vowels indicated. These formant configurations must, however, not be interpreted as numerical specifications of the phonetic symbols. The vowels charted are: 1. ɑ, 2. ɛ, 3. i, 4. j, 5. y, 6. ü, 7. a, 8. ɔ, 9. u.

Observe that the spectrum level is emphasized in regions where two formants approach each other and that the levels of all parts of the spectrum as well as as the total energy under the spectrum envelope are primarily determined by F_1. A summation of the total energy under the spectrum envelope yields the following ordering of the sounds in decreasing intensity: [a ɔ ɛ ɑ u i y ü j] which agrees well with published measurements.

CONCLUSIONS

The most complete, and also the most redundant method of describing a vowel spectrum is to specify the amplitude and phase of all harmonics up to 4000 cps. From the acumulated experience on analysis and synthesis of speech it is known that a specification in terms of formant frequencies only, for most purposes, provides a sufficient acoustical correlate to phonetic vowel quality or to phonemic categories. The mathematical analysis carried out in this article indicates that a specification of formant frequencies also conditions the essential physical structure of the vowel.

A formant has the dimensions of frequency, bandwidth, and intensity level. A specification of each formant with these three parameters or with the frequency, rate of decay and initial amplitude of the corresponding damped oscillation as has been suggested by Weibel (24) is highly redundant since formant bandwidths generally are statistically well correlated with the particular pattern of formant frequencies, and since formant levels can be calculated once the frequencies and bandwidths of the three or four first formants and the slope of vocal cord spectrum envelope are given. Such calculations have provided results that check well with experimental data.

In speech analysis for linguistic or technical purposes it can be of some value to verify

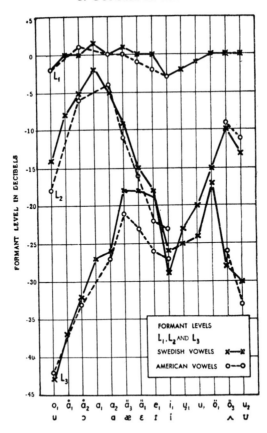

Fig 6. A comparison of formant levels of Swedish (4) and American English (16) vowels. The Swedish vowels are transcribed by symbols of the standard Swedish orthography supplemented by a numerical subscript. Subscript 1 indicates long vowel; 2, short vowel; 3, long vowel before r. Each of the English vowels has been superimposed upon the Swedish vowel differing least in formant frequencies.

Both sets of data show that variations in L_1 are small, no more than 4 db, and that the total range of variation for both L_1 and L_2 is of the order of 25 db.

measurements of formant frequencies from available redundancy in terms of the observed shape of the spectrum, including the relative levels of formants and of the parts between formants. Such observations can aid in minimizing errors in the frequency measurements and they can provide supplementary information on nasality and voice quality. There are, however, practical limitations for the utilization of formant levels alone for specifying distinctive features and other categories of interest since the individual voice characteristics give rise to considerable variations that first must be "normalized" before the relevant information can be extracted. The spread in formant levels is relatively greater than the spread in formant frequencies.

The intimate relation between formant frequencies and formant levels can, in a general sense, be said to remove some of the redundancies in the description of physical correlates to phonetic categories. Two vowels differing in the frequency of the first formant, F_1, i.e., in terms of compactness, are known to differ also in intensity. The greater intensity found with the higher F_1 is not an independent variable. It must occur *because* of the higher F_1, everything else being equal. Similar relations hold for the gravity feature. When the second formant approaches either the first formant, as in grave vowels or the higher formants as in acute vowels there is a summation effect so that the level of the first formant gains from the second formant in grave vowels and the

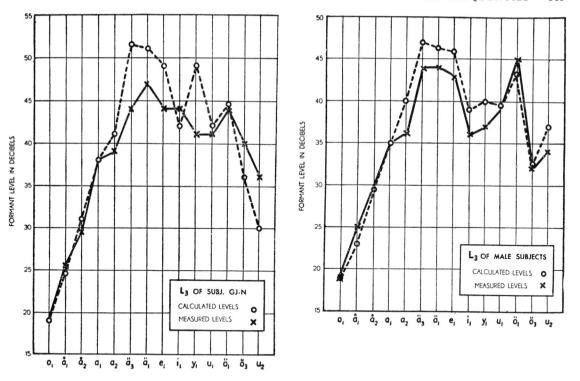

Fig 7. A comparison of measured and calculated levels of the third formant within a series of Swedish vowels. The calculations have been based on the a priori knowledge of L_3 for the vowel [a_1 and the data on the specific shift in formant frequencies from the vowel [a_1] to the vowel under investigation.

For the group of male speakers the agreement is better than 4 db within the whole series. The agreement is especially good for back vowels, i.e., for grave vowels.

evel of the third and higher formants gains from the second formant in acute vowels, thus contributing to shift the balance in the spectrum to the part occupied by the second formant.

The interrelation between formant frequencies and formant levels will be preserved in a speaking machine of the American POVO (21) or Swedish OVE (9) type in which the formants are produced from a cascaded system of resonant circuits. The syllable structure of the sentence "I love you" comes out perfectly well from a synthesis in which the intensity and shape of the vocal cord generator is kept constant and the only intensity variations are those conditioned by the changes in formant frequencies (9). The intensity minima between syllable peaks of the synthesized sentence are entirely due to the lower frequency positions of the first formant in the voiced consonants compared to the higher frequency positions in the intermediate vocalic regions.

ROYAL INSTITUTE OF TECHNOLOGY, STOCKHOLM

LITERATURE

1. B. P. Bogert. "On the Bandwidth of Vowel Formants," *J. Acous. Soc. Am.*, 25, 791–792 (1953).
2. T. Chiba, M. Kajiyama. *The Vowel, Its Nature and Structure*, Tokyo, 1941.
3. H. K. Dunn. "The Calculation of Vocal Resonances, and an Electrical Vocal Tract," *J. Acous. Soc. Am.*, 22, 740–753 (1950).
4. C. G. M. Fant. "Analys av de svenska vokalljuden," L. M. Ericsson protokoll H/P–1035 (1948).
5. C. G. M. Fant. "Analys av de svenska konsonantljuden," L. M. Ericsson protokoll H/P–1064 (1949).
6. C. G. M. Fant. Discussion on the paper of G. E. Peterson: "The information bearing elements of speech," read at the 1952 London symposium on "Applications of Communication theory," published in W. Jackson, *Information Theory*, pp. 421–424, London, 1953.
7. C. G. M. Fant. "Phonetic and Phonemic Basis for the Transcription of Swedish Word Material," *Acta Oto-Laryngolocica, Suppl.* 116 (1954).
8. C. G. M. Fant. "Transmission Properties of the Vocal Tract with Application to the Acoustic Specification of Phonemes," Mass. Inst. of Techn. Acoustics Lab. Technical Report No. 12 (1952).
9. C. G. M. Fant. "Speech communication research," *IVA*, 24, 331–337 (1953). (The Royal Swedish Academy of Engineering Sciences).
10. H. Fletcher. *Speech and Hearing in Communication*, New York, 1953.
11. W. H. Huggins. "A Phase Principle for Complex-frequency Analysis and Its Implications in Auditory Theory," *J. Acous. Soc. Am.*, 24, 582–589 (1952).
12. R. Jakobson, C. G. M. Fant, M. Halle. *Preliminaries to Speech Analysis*, Mass. Inst. of Technology, Acoustics Laboratory, Technical Report, No. 13, May 1952.
13. M. Joos. "Acoustic Phonetics," Supplement to *Language*, 24, pp. 1–136, 1948.
14. D. Lewis. "Vocal Resonance," *J. Acous. Soc. Am.*, 8, 91 (1936).
15. H. Pipping. *Om klangfärgen hos sjungna vokaler.* Helsingfors 1890.
16. G. E. Peterson and H. L. Barney. "Control Methods Used in a Study of the Vowels." *J. Acous. Soc. Am.*, 24, 175–184, (1952).
17. Potter et. al. "Technical aspects of Visible speech," *J. Acous. Soc. Am.*, 17, 1–89 (1946).
18. R. K. Potter, G. A. Kopp and H. C. Green. *Visible Speech*, New York, 1947.
19. R. K. Potter and G. E. Peterson. "The Representation of Vowels and Their Movement," *J. Acous. Soc. Am.*, 20, 528–535 (1948).
20. R. K. Potter and J. C. Steinberg. "Towards the Specification of Speech," *J. Acous. Soc. Am.*, 22, 807–820 (1950).
21. K. N. Stevens, R. P. Bastide and C. P. Smith. "Electrical Synthesizer of Continuous Speech," *J. Acous. Soc. Am.*, 27, 207 (1955).
22. K. N. Stevens, S. Kasowski and C. G. M. Fant. "An Electrical Analog to the Vocal Tract," *J. Acous. Soc. Am.*, 25, 734–742 (1953).
23. F. Trendelenburg. *Einführung in die Akustik*, Berlin, 1950.
24. E. S. Weibel. "Vowel Synthesis by Means of Resonant Circuits," *J. Acous. Soc. Am.*, 22, 858–865 (1955).

ACKNOWLEDGEMENTS

The author is indebted to M. Halle, K. N. Stevens, and H. M. Truby for editorial advice.

CHAPTER 4

Reprinted from the *Journal of Speech and Hearing Research*
March 1959, Vol. 2, No. 1

A Note On Optimal Vocal Frequency

ARTHUR S. HOUSE

In a recent paper Thurman (*4*) reported an investigation of a clinical procedure for estimating a natural, or optimum, vocal frequency. The procedure in question requires subjects to sing or hum the musical scale while an observer locates an involuntary increase in vocal output alleged to coincide with the vocal frequency under search. Thurman's subjects intoned the three vowels /ɛ/, /ɑ/ and /u/ and hummed in approximate musical steps over their vocal ranges. Their productions were recorded and these data subsequently were processed to yield measures of fundamental frequency and relative level. This experimental examination failed to support the clinical technique in question.

Since the validation of clinical concepts and tools is of interest to many, it seems appropriate to offer some further comment on the problem. The comments that follow are in support, essentially, of Thurman's conclusions. They are meant to point out, however, that in addition to his experimental evidence, a consideration of the mechanism of speech production suggests

Arthur S. House (Ph.D., University of Illinois, 1951) is Associate Professor of Audiology and Speech Pathology, Syracuse University. This note was written while the author was a visiting staff member of the Research Laboratory of Electronics, Massachusetts Institute of Technology, and was supported in part by the Air Force Cambridge Research Center under contract AF 19(604)-2061.

strongly that the clinical procedures in question are predestined not to produce an indication of optimum level, at least in those cases where vowel sounds are produced by the subject.

When a search for an optimum pitch level is made by intoning vowel sounds at discrete fundamental frequencies throughout a subject's vocal range there probably is a tacit assumption (a) that some sort of optimal physical relationship among the various components of the vocal mechanism will be found, (b) that when this relationship obtains, the laryngeal output will be maximal and will be reflected in a maximum in vocal output at the lips and (c) that the change in over-all level will be perceptible. It might be assumed, furthermore, that vocal effort is constant during the procedures. Parenthetically, it can be pointed out that no good measure of effort is available; this problem is discussed briefly below.

The description of the clinical procedure leads one to suspect that its proponents intuitively are seeking a condition of optimal 'coupling' (in some undefined sense) between the action of the larynx and the supraglottal system. It has been shown, however, that the volume velocity at the glottis is relatively unaffected by the supraglottal configurations (*5*). A maximum in laryngeal output, therefore, must originate from activity within the

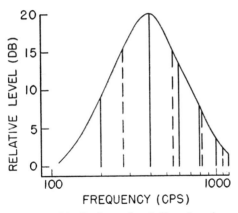

FIGURE 1. Idealized pass-band filter function. Harmonic lines appropriate for two fundamental frequencies are indicated, as follows: solid lines, $F_0=200$ cps; broken line, $F_0=275$ cps.

larynx itself and not from some so-called coupling effects. This note attempts to show that maxima in vocal output can be expected when the laryngeal output is constant. Furthermore, it points out that without elaborate controls it would be difficult to detect maxima in laryngeal activity from observations on the vocal output.

The relative independence of the glottal and supraglottal effects makes possible the mathematical description of speech sounds by specifying the source function and the filter function which together determine the system function (1, 2). Such a specification indicates that the glottal output serves to excite a resonating system whose characteristics help determine the various spectra associated with vowels. The harmonic spectrum of vowels is derived from the glottal impulses and is well known, as is the location of the spectral maxima or formants of vowel sounds. Probably less well understood is the fact that the spacing of the harmonics of a vowel sound is independent

of the center frequencies of the resonances of the vocal tract.

The effect of this independence is exemplified in Figure 1 which shows an idealized filter of known half-power band width (200 cps) excited by a signal with a harmonic spectrum consisting of a fundamental and overtones. When the fundamental frequency is 200 cps, the harmonics are at 400 cps, 600 cps, . . . (the solid spectral lines), and the relative over-all level of this signal is approximately 21.5 db[1]. That is, the over-all level is almost identical with the level of the harmonic situated at the center frequency of the filter. When the fundamental frequency is raised to 275 cps, the harmonics are at 550 cps, 825 cps, . . . (the dashed spectral lines), and the relative over-all level of the signal is reduced to approximately 18.5 db, a level about 3 db greater than the second harmonic. The mechanism is analogous to the excitation of the vocal tract by the glottal source, except that since in natural vowels the band width of the first formant is considerably less than 200 cps, the variation in level could be greater.

To obtain an estimate of the degree of variation in over-all level that can be expected in vowels, idealized first formant functions appropriate to /u/, /ɛ/, /ɑ/ were constructed. These functions were derived primarily from studies of vowel synthesis using resonant circuits and agree well with theoretical expectations. In the analyses that follow only the first formant is considered, since the higher formants

---

[1]In this discussion, over-all levels are computed by adding the squares of the amplitudes of the harmonics and expressing the results in decibels.

are far enough below the level of the first formant to contribute very little to the over-all level of the vowel[2]. To simplify the graphic constructions, the center frequencies of the first formants of the vowels were chosen to be 300 cps, 500 cps and 700 cps for /u/, /ɛ/ and /ɑ/, respectively, and the half-power band widths of the formants were made to be approximately 100 cps. Since these formant values resemble closely those usually attributed to male talkers, 100 cps was taken as the initial fundamental frequency and the harmonics of this fundamental were constructed. The fundamental frequency was then varied systematically and similar graphic constructions were made and the relative over-all levels under the first formant curves were computed for the various line spectra. These procedures were followed for the three 'vowels.'

The results of the measurements are shown in graphic form in Figure 2. In the figure the abscissa shows the fundamental frequency of the glottal source excitation and the ordinate indicates the over-all level of the vocal output. Each curve shows as a function of frequency the levels associated with a specific first formant whose center frequency is constant. The curves were normalized by setting equal the amplitudes of the formants at center frequency.

The data indicate that extensive, and presumably perceptible, changes in over-all level will occur when the articulatory configuration of the vocal

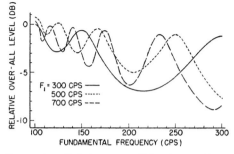

FIGURE 2. Relative over-all levels as a function of frequency for three idealized vowels. Estimates restricted to energy close to first formant (F_1). Center frequencies of F_1 at 300 cps, 500 cps and 700 cps. All formant band widths are approximately 100 cps. Over-all levels normalized by equating amplitudes of first formants. An assumption of constant dc volume velocity at the glottis is made.

tract remains fixed and the fundamental frequency of the voice is changed. The variations, furthermore, are not of the kind sought by the clinician endeavoring to identify optimum level, since a maximum is associated with each subharmonic of the center frequency of the first formant.

If natural speech is to be discussed, it must be pointed out that the curves in Figure 2 embody an assumption about the operation of the glottis, that is, that there is a constant dc volume velocity through the glottis. It is interesting to speculate that this physical condition correlates positively with 'constant effort' on the part of the talker.

Using these assumptions it can be said, for example, that if the glottis generates an impulse of amplitude x every 10 msec (that is, produces a 100-cps signal at a known level), then raising the vocal frequency by one octave, while maintaining constant effort, means producing twice as many impulses per unit time, each impulse having an amplitude of $x/2$. On the other hand,

[2]When the spectral components of an idealized vowel /u/ with F_1=300 cps and F_0=100 cps are examined, it can be shown that the partials higher than the lowest five raise the over-all level considerably less than 0.5 db.

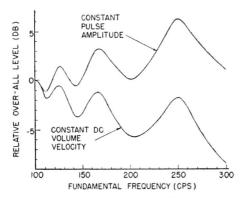

FIGURE 3. Relative over-all levels as a function of frequency for a vowel with F_1 at 500 cps. Upper curve assumes constant pulse amplitude at glottis; lower curve assumes constant dc volume velocity at glottis.

it can be assumed that constant effort is a condition of equal amplitude of glottal impulses. If this is the case there would be a gain proportional to frequency in the level of the harmonics of the output. The major consideration here, however, is whether the latter assumption will change the range of variation in over-all levels predicted by the curves in Figure 2. The curves in Figure 3 demonstrate the effect of changing the assumption and indicate that the question can be answered in the negative.

Each curve in Figure 3 describes the variations in over-all level when the center frequency of the first formant is at 500 cps. The upper curve assumes equal impulse amplitudes (and changes in the amplitudes of harmonics); the lower curve assumes constant dc volume velocity at the glottis or changes in impulse amplitudes (and equal harmonic amplitudes).

It may be of interest to examine this situation in the time domain. Figure 4

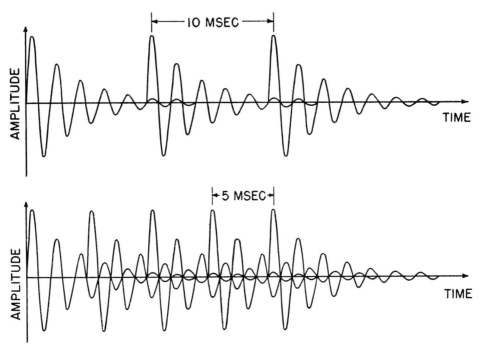

FIGURE 4. Damped exponential wave forms showing phase effects as fundamental frequency is changed.

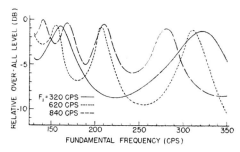

FIGURE 5. Relative over-all levels as a function of frequency for three idealized vowels with first formants appropriate to female talkers. Center frequencies of F_1 at 320 cps, 620 cps and 840 cps. All formant band widths are approximately 100 cps. Over-all levels normalized by equating amplitudes of first formants. An assumption of constant dc volume velocity at the glottis is made.

shows trains of exponentially damped wave forms similar to the supraglottal (vocal) output. In the upper part of the figure the wave forms occur every 10 msec, that is, the fundamental frequency is 100 cps, and the period of the first resonance is 2 msec, that is, the frequency is 500 cps. After the first period of the fundamental the wave forms are in phase and will summate to produce maxima.

In the lower part of the figure the fundamental frequency has been doubled, that is, the wave forms occur every 5 msec, but the first resonant frequency remains at 500 cps. In this case the subsequent wave forms do not summate completely but will tend to reduce the level of the signal.

In the recent experimental attempt to validate the pitch-finding technique, the probability of failure is raised by the presence of both males and females among the experimental subjects. As is well known, on the average the vocal-tract dimensions of females will produce formants with center frequencies displaced upwards from corresponding

male values (3). This systematic difference plus the wider spacing of harmonics in the vocal range of female voices will introduce variation into the experimental results. In Figure 5, for example, are the relative over-all levels of 'vowels' /u/, /ɛ/ and /ɑ/ with center frequencies of their first formants more appropriate to female talkers and with fundamental vocal frequency varying over an appropriate range. Comparison of these curves with those in Figure 2 shows the maxima and minima to be displaced but to recur systematically.

It can be asserted, of course, that the analogy to natural speech processes is not perfect. If the so-called vocal swells are sought by modulating the fundamental vocal frequency continuously in time, the variation in over-all level probably will not be as great as those delineated above. Similarly, during natural speech the center frequencies of the formants would not remain as stationary as in the model—the articulatory configuration is not easy to maintain and the talker might habitually 'tune' the resonators by means of auditory cues—and this presumably could reduce the range of level variation. In addition, neither assumption made here about vocal effort might describe this phenomenon adequately. It is felt strongly, however, that these limitations would not reduce the range of variation sufficiently to obliterate perceptible changes in over-all level that are not attributable to optimal laryngeal operation.

In conclusion, the theoretical considerations outlined above could account for most of the seemingly unlawful variations in the data reported by Thurman. They imply, furthermore, that tests similar to Thurman's will yield indecisive results unless elaborate experimental controls are added. It would seem, however, that at the present time the cost of realizing such controls is so great as to suggest that the most profitable approach to this and similar problems is through a consideration of theoretical models or experiments utilizing synthetic speech.

Summary

The article describes a physical characteristic of vowel production sufficient to account for systematic and presumably perceptible variations in overall vowel level as a function of vocal frequency. The discussion supports the conclusion that certain traditional methods advocated for locating optimum pitch levels are not adequate

References

1. FANT, C. G. M., Transmission properties of the vocal tract with application to the acoustic specification of phonemes. Technical Report 12, Acoustics Laboratory, Massachusetts Institute of Technology, January 1952.

2. HUGGINS, W. H., System-function analysis of speech sounds. *J. acoust. Soc. Amer.*, 22, 1950, 765-767.

3. PETERSON, G. E., and BARNEY, H. L., Control methods used in a study of the vowels. *J. acoust. Soc. Amer.*, 24, 1952, 175-184.

4. THURMAN, W. L., Frequency-intensity relationships and optimum pitch level. *J. Speech Hearing Res.*, 1, 1958, 117-123.

5. VAN DEN BERG, Jw., Ueber die Koppelung bei der Stimmbildung. *Z. Phonet. usw.* 8, 1954, 281-293.

CHAPTER 5

Reprinted from THE JOURNAL OF THE ACOUSTICAL SOCIETY OF AMERICA, Vol. 33, No. 12 (December 1961).
Copyright 1961 by the Acoustical Society of America.

Reduction of Speech Spectra by Analysis-by-Synthesis Techniques

C. G. BELL,* H. FUJISAKI,† J. M. HEINZ, K. N. STEVENS, AND A. S. HOUSE
Research Laboratory of Electronics, Massachusetts Institute of Technology, Cambridge, Massachusetts
(Received September 6, 1961)

Procedures are described for reducing the speech wave to a specification in terms of the time-varying vocal-tract resonances and source characteristics. The basic method, which has been called analysis by synthesis, involves the comparison of speech spectra with a series of spectra that are synthesized within the analyzer. Each comparison spectrum is generated according to a set of rules based on an acoustical theory of speech production. The result of the analysis of each input spectrum is a set of parameters that describes the synthesized spectrum providing the best match. In one version of the method convergence, towards the best match is controlled by the experimenter; in another version convergence to a match is accomplished automatically without the intervention of the experimenter. All the operations have been programmed on a general-purpose digital computer and have been applied to the analysis of vowels and some consonants. The advantages of the analysis techniques are discussed.

THE problem of representing speech events in terms of low-information-rate signals that describe the essential features of the speech wave is one of the central problems in the area of speech communication. To the student of phonemics and phonetics it is important to be able to describe in a simple way the acoustical features associated with the various allophones of the phonemes. For the engineer concerned with problems of communication, an efficient description of speech signals is needed for the development of systems for speech bandwidth compression and for the realization of procedures for machine recognition and generation of speech.

The development of the sound spectrograph[1] represented a significant contribution to speech analysis, since it displays the speech events in a way that brings into clear focus certain of the essential features of the signal such as the formant movements. The three-dimensional intensity-frequency-time representation, together with the procedure for displaying spectral sections, provides a means for isolating significant features for certain classes of sounds, although the techniques are less successful for other classes, particularly certain types of consonants.

During the past few years, there have been two developments which suggest that it is now possible to bring more powerful techniques to bear on problems of speech analysis. The first has been the significant advance that has occurred in our understanding of the acoustics of speech production. The second has been the increasing availability of high-speed digital computers for applications such as speech analysis. Theoretical studies have led to a clearer understanding of the constraints imposed on the speech signal by the vocal mechanism, and have suggested means whereby speech signals can be represented in terms of parameters that have a definite and rigorous relation to articulation. Digital computers have made it possible to use the results of the acoustical studies in such a way that rapid and precise reduction of speech signals can be accomplished.

This paper describes an attempt to utilize the findings of the acoustical theory to develop procedures for the analysis and reduction of speech signals by computer techniques. Since the method is based on an acoustical theory of speech production, it is appropriate to outline the essential features of such a theory before proceeding to a description of the analysis techniques.

ACOUSTICAL THEORY OF SPEECH PRODUCTION

The generally accepted theory of speech production[2-4] views the speech wave as the result of acoustic excitation of the vocal tract by one or more sources. In the case of voiced sounds, there is a source at the glottis, and this glottal source is a quasi-periodic volume-velocity wave whose spectrum envelope decreases with increasing frequency at a rate of about 12 db/octave in the range 300–2500 cps. The characteristics of the glottal source are to a large extent independent of the vocal-tract configuration anterior to the glottis. For some classes of sounds there may be a source of excitation of the vocal tract as a result of a sudden pressure release or as a result of turbulent air flow through a constriction or past the teeth or other obstructions. Such a source can be considered as a differential-pressure source, usually located in the vicinity of a vocal-tract constriction, and this source generally has a relatively broad and smooth spectrum. The spectrum $P(s)$ of the sound pressure measured at a distance from the lips as a result of a source of excitation whose spectrum is given by $S(s)$ can be written

$$P(s) = S(s) \ T(s) \ R(s). \tag{1}$$

In this equation $T(s)$ is the transfer function of the vocal tract; for voiced sounds, $T(s)$ is the ratio of the volume

* Present address: Digital Equipment Corporation, Maynard, Massachusetts.
† Present address: University of Tokyo, Tokyo, Japan.

[1] W. Koenig, H. K. Dunn, and L. Y. Lacy, J. Acoust. Soc. Am. 17, 19 (1946).

[2] H. Dudley, Bell System Tech. J. 19, 495 (1940).
[3] T. Chiba and M. Kajiyama, *The Vowel, Its Nature and Structure* (Tokyo-Kaiseikan Publishing Company, Ltd., Tokyo, 1941).
[4] G. Fant, *Acoustic Theory of Speech Production* (Mouton and Company, 's-Gravenhage, 1960).

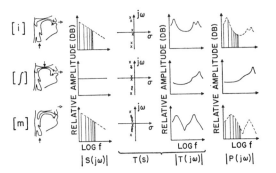

FIG. 1. A nonquantitative representation of the production and acoustic characteristics of speech sounds. In the left column are sketches of articulatory configurations in the midsagittal plane for three phones as indicated, together with source (solid arrows) and output (open arrows) locations. In addition each row of the figure shows the magnitude of the source spectrum $|S(j\omega)|$, the pole and zero locations in the complex frequency plane for the vocal-tract transfer function $T(s)$, the magnitude of the transfer function $|T(j\omega)|$, and the magnitude of the sound pressure at a distance in front of the face $|P(j\omega)|$, respectively, for each representative articulation. In cases with periodic (glottal) excitation, incomplete sets of harmonics are shown together with spectrum-envelope curves.

velocity at the mouth opening (and at the nostrils if there is coupling to the nasal cavities) to the source volume velocity, whereas for a noiselike or transient source at a constriction, $T(s)$ is the ratio of the volume velocity at the mouth opening to the sound pressure of the source. The radiation characteristic $R(s)$ is the ratio of the sound pressure at distance r in front of the talker to the volume velocity at the lips, and in the frequency range up to about 4000 cps is given approximately by the result for a simple source

$$R(s) = (s\rho/4\pi r)e^{-(sr/c)}, \tag{2}$$

where $\rho =$ density of air and $c =$ velocity of sound in air. In all of these relations, s is the complex frequency, and can be replaced by $j\omega$ to obtain Fourier spectra, where ω is the angular frequency.

When the source is at the glottis and when there is no coupling to the nasal cavities, $T(s)$ is characterized by a number of poles, and can be written

$$T(s) = \frac{s_1 s_1^* s_2 s_2^* \cdots}{(s-s_1)(s-s_1^*)(s-s_2)(s-s_2^*)\cdots}, \tag{3}$$

where the asterisks designate complex conjugates and $s_1, s_2, \cdots$ are the poles corresponding to the various vocal-tract resonances or formants. The frequencies and bandwidths for the poles are, of course, dependent on the vocal-tract configuration. For an idealized source spectrum envelope with a decreasing slope of 12 db/octave, i.e., a spectrum envelope proportional to $1/\omega^2$, and for a radiation characteristic proportional to ω [cf. Eq. (2)], the magnitude of the spectrum envelope $|P_E(j\omega)|$ of the sound pressure for a nonnasal vowel

is given by

$$|P_E(j\omega)| \propto (1/\omega)|T(j\omega)|. \tag{4}$$

Thus if the idealized source spectrum is assumed, the envelope $|P_E(j\omega)|$ is characterized by a pole in the vicinity of $\omega = 0$ and by a set of conjugate-complex pairs of poles, corresponding to the poles of $T(s)$ in Eq. (3). Alternatively, if the sound pressure is transduced and passed through a circuit with a frequency characteristic that rises at 6 db/octave, the spectrum envelope of the resulting signal is characterized by the poles of $T(s)$ and only those poles, assuming the idealized shape for the source spectrum envelope.

When there is coupling between the vocal tract and the nasal tract, or when the vocal-tract excitation is at a point other than the glottis, the transfer function $T(s)$ is characterized by zeros as well as poles, and can, in general, be written

$$T(s) = K\frac{(s-s_a)(s-s_a^*)(s-s_b)(s-s_b^*)\cdots}{(s-s_1)(s-s_1^*)(s-s_2)(s-s_2^*)\cdots}, \tag{5}$$

where $s_a, s_a^*, s_b, s_b^*, \cdots$ are the zeros and K is a real quantity independent of frequency. The frequencies and bandwidths for the zeros depend both on the vocal-tract configuration and on the location of the source in the vocal tract, whereas for a given vocal-tract configuration the poles of $T(s)$ are independent of the location of the source.

Relations between the speech spectra and the articulatory processes that produce them are summarized by the sketches in Fig. 1 for three classes of speech sounds. For each class of sounds, the figure shows a typical articulatory configuration and source location, and approximate source spectrum, a representation of the poles and zeros of the transfer function, a plot of the magnitude of the transfer function vs frequency, and the output spectrum. The spectra for the vowel and for the nasal consonant are, of course, line spectra, whereas the fricative has a continuous spectrum. In each case, the output spectrum (in decibels) is obtained by adding the spectra of the source and the transfer function, and then applying a 6 db/octave correction for the radiation characteristic, as explained above.

The acoustical theory may be summarized, therefore, as follows. The spectrum of the vocal-tract output (in decibels) is the sum of a source spectrum, a transfer function and a radiation characteristic. For a given class of speech sounds, the source spectrum and the radiation characteristic are relatively invariant from one talker to another, and are largely independent of the articulatory configuration. The transfer function is determined by the articulatory configuration and the source location, and is completely described in terms of a set of poles in the case of nonnasal vowel and vowel-like sounds, and by a set of poles and zeros for other classes of sounds.

ANALYSIS-BY-SYNTHESIS MODEL

The term *analysis by synthesis* is used to refer to an active analysis process that can be applied to signals that are produced by a generator whose properties are known.[5,6] The heart of an analysis-by-synthesis system is a signal generator capable of synthesizing all and only the signals to be analyzed. The signals synthesized by the generator are compared with the signals to be analyzed, and a measure of error is computed. Different signals are generated until one is found that causes the error to reach some smallest value, at which time the analyzer indicates the properties of the internally generated signal. It has been suggested[6,7] that a scheme of this type has applications in the analysis of linguistic phenomena at various levels of representation: acoustic, graphic, phonological, morphological, and syntactic. Of concern in the present discussion is the analysis of linguistic events at the acoustic level.

The procedure used to accomplish analysis by synthesis at the acoustic level[7] is shown schematically in Fig. 2. The speech is passed first through a peripheral element in this case a *filter set*, the outputs of which are rectified, smoothed, sampled at prescribed time intervals, and then stored. (The techniques used to process the speech by the filter system and to store the spectra in the computer memory are described in the Appendix.) The component labeled *spectrum generator*, when given appropriate instructions, can generate outputs that are compatible with the original stored speech data. In the present case, this component generates speechlike spectra when provided with information on the poles and zeros of the vocal-tract transfer function and on the type of vocal-tract excitation. The *comparator* computes a measure of the difference between the input speech spectra and spectra generated by the model. The order in which different trial spectra are synthesized by the model is prescribed by a control or *strategy* component that makes decisions on the basis of (1) previous error scores for the spectral sample under analysis, (2) the results of analyses of adjacent spectral samples, and (3) possibly the results of preliminary direct measure-

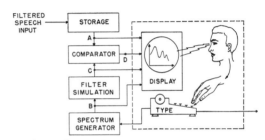

FIG. 3. Paradigm of the mode of the analysis-by-synthesis reduction scheme in which the experimenter controls the selection of parameters of the comparison spectra. The strategy or control element of Fig. 2 is realized by the contents of the dashed box at the right. The nodes A–D show points where functions can be selected and displayed on the cathode-ray tube output. The process is described fully in the text.

ments on the spectral sample. When a synthesized spectrum that provides minimum error is obtained, the analyzer indicates (or stores) the pole-zero locations and source characteristics of that spectrum.

Five operations, therefore, are performed in the analyzer: (a) storage of the speech data processed by the input filter set, (b) generation of speech spectra, (c) instruction of the spectrum generator by a control system, (d) calculation of measures of the difference between the input speech spectra and the spectra computed internally, and (e) display, in some form, of the parameters of the generator that yield minimum error.

The success and utility of the analysis-by-synthesis technique in comparison with other analysis methods depends largely upon the speed and accuracy with which speech spectra can be analyzed, and it is important, therefore, that the number of trial spectra that need to be synthesized in order to obtain a minimum error be kept as small as possible. Thus one of the central problems in the design of an analysis-by-synthesis scheme is that of devising a strategy to be used by the control component to assure rapid convergence to the desired result.

In the analysis procedures described here, two different methods have been used to implement the operations in the strategy component of Fig. 2. In one case, the control function is performed by the experimenter, and hence the problem of specifying a strategy for automatic analysis is circumvented. In the other case a rudimentary strategy that permits automatic analysis of speech spectra is employed. The former method is slower than the automatic procedure, but leads to greater accuracy of analysis, and can be used in the development of strategies that might ultimately be incorporated into a more sophisticated automatic procedure. The two analysis methods will be discussed in detail in the following sections.

EXPERIMENTAL MATCHING OF VOWEL AND CONSONANT SPECTRA

When control of the internal spectrum generator is placed in the hands of the experimenter, the analysis-by-

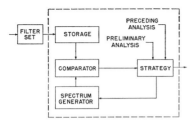

FIG. 2. Paradigm of an analysis-by-synthesis process for the reduction of speech spectra.

[5] D. M. Mackay, Brit. J. Philo. Sci. **2**, 105 (1951).
[6] M. Halle and K. N. Stevens, "Analysis by synthesis," Proc. Sem. Speech Compression and Processing, edited by W. Wathen-Dunn and L. E. Woods, AFCRC–TR–59–198, December 1959, Vol. II, Paper D7.
[7] K. N. Stevens, J. Acoust. Soc. Am. **32**, 47 (1960).

SAMPLING PULSES (120/SEC)

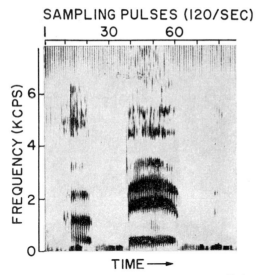

FIG. 4. Sound spectrogram of a nonsense utterance, [hə'bɪb]. The time sampling pulses (high-pass filtered) appear at the top of the spectrogram.

synthesis procedure takes the form shown in Fig. 3. In this figure all operations indicated in the blocks, except the decisions and actions of the operator, are performed within the digital computer or its peripheral equipment. Instructions are communicated to the spectrum generator through a typewriter that is operated by the experimenter. The locations (in the complex frequency plane) of a trial set of poles and zeros are typed, and the spectrum generator and filter simulation portions of the system compute a spectrum to be compared with the input speech spectrum that is under analysis. Measured or computed functions existing at various points in the analysis process can be displayed on a cathode-ray tube, as shown in the figure. The task of the operator is to adjust the positions of the poles and zeros until a "best fit" is obtained between the spectrum under analysis and the internally generated spectrum. The experimenter can use both a set of numerical error scores and visual examination of the displayed functions to determine how to adjust the set of poles and zeros in order to improve the match and to decide when a best fit has been obtained.

As indicated in the Appendix, the speech spectra in the present analysis scheme are obtained by passing the speech signal through a pre-emphasis circuit with a rising characteristic of 6 db/octave and then through a bank of 36 filters. Each filter output is rectified and smoothed by a low-pass filter with a time constant of about 10 msec. The rectified and smoothed outputs are sampled periodically at intervals of 8.3 msec, processed by an analog-to-digital converter, converted to logarithmic values (to the nearest decibel), and stored in the computer memory. The spectral data are also stored on punched tape and are thus available for future analysis.

In order to facilitate analysis of specific components of the utterances, conventional sound spectrograms of the speech materials are made. A spectrogram of a typical dissyllabic utterance used in one experimental study is shown in Fig. 4. Time pulses indicating the instants at which the filter outputs are sampled by the computer are high-pass filtered and mixed with the speech signal before the spectrograms are made, and appear as closely spaced vertical lines across the top of the spectrogram. The numerical identification of the pulses shown on the spectrogram corresponds to the way successive spectra are labeled in the computer memory. Thus the experimenter can, if he wishes, use the spectrogram as a guide in the selection of a particular spectrum or group of spectra from the computer memory. The selection is achieved by a simple instruction to the computer identifying the spectrum to be displayed and analyzed.

The manner in which the speech spectra are displayed is shown by the example in Fig. 5, which was taken from the utterance whose spectrogram is given in Fig. 4. The number at the upper right of the display indicates that the spectrum number is 48, and reference to the spectrogram shows that the spectrum occurred during the stressed vowel [ɪ]. The points along the abscissa represent successive filters in the analyzing bank, and the ordinate is the amplitude in decibels. In terms of the processes portrayed by Fig. 3, this spectrum is found at node A.

As described above, the experimenter specifies the locations of a set of poles and zeros and the internal spectrum generator computes the corresponding spectrum that is to be compared with a speech spectrum such as that shown in Fig. 5. Computation of the synthesized spectrum is carried out in two steps. The first step is to calculate the logarithm of the magnitude of the transfer function as a function of frequency and the second step is to compute the effective spectrum that would be measured if a signal with a spectrum corresponding to this transfer function were processed by the analyzing filter bank. The second step is necessary since the original speech signal itself is, of course, processed by a bank of relatively broad filters, and thus a

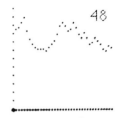

FIG. 5. Photograph of a spectral representation of an input speech sample (at node A in Fig. 3) displayed on the face of the output cathode-ray tube. Each point on the horizontal axis represents one of the 36 filter outputs; the points on the vertical axis represent 5-db steps in amplitude. The input speech has received a 6 db/octave pre-emphasis. The number 48 identifies a sample in the vowel [ɪ] in the word shown in Fig. 4.

valid comparison can be made only if both the inputsignal and the internally generated signal undergo the same sequence of operations.

For a single conjugate pair of poles at frequency F_n with bandwidth ΔF_n the function to be computed in the internal spectrum generator during the first step is[8]

$$20 \log |T_n| = 20 \log \left\{ \frac{F_n{}^2 + (\tfrac{1}{2}\Delta F_n)^2}{[(f-F_n)^2 + (\tfrac{1}{2}\Delta F_n)^2]^{\frac{1}{2}}[(f+F_n)^2 + (\tfrac{1}{2}\Delta F_n)^2]^{\frac{1}{2}}} \right\}, \qquad (10)$$

where f is the frequency variable and T_n is the portion of the system function associated with the nth pair of poles. The logarithm of the magnitude of the system function for a zero is, of course, the negative of that for a pole with the same frequency and bandwidth. For a real-axis pole at a frequency minus F_a, the function to be computed is

$$20 \log\{F_a/(f^2 + F_a{}^2)^{\frac{1}{2}}\}. \qquad (11)$$

These functions are computed to the nearest $\tfrac{1}{8}$ db at 100-cps intervals of f. When more than one pole or zero is specified, the logarithm of the system function is obtained by adding the logarithms of the system functions corresponding to the individual poles and zeros. A result of this calculation for a typical set of poles appropriate for a vowel is shown in Fig. 6, which is a photograph of the cathode-ray tube display obtained from node B in Fig. 3. Although values up to 10 kc are displayed here, usually only the spectrum up to about 3000 cps is of interest for vowels. In this type of display a logarithmic scale is used for the abscissa.

The second step in the computation of comparison spectra is the evaluation of the effect of the filter bank on the computed transfer function. If the magnitude of the transfer function of a filter is designated as $|A_i(f)|$, where i represents the filter number from 1 to 36, then the magnitude of the square-law rectified and smoothed output of the filter when the input spectrum has a magnitude $|H(f)|$ is proportional to

$$\left[\int_0^\infty |H(f)|^2 |A_i(f)|^2 df \right]^{\frac{1}{2}}. \qquad (12)$$

The difference between the result of this computation and the result of processing the data by full-wave rectification can be expected to be less than 1 db. Thirty-six such integrals are evaluated in the computer to obtain the hypothetical rectified filter outputs corresponding to a given input spectrum. These numbers are expressed in decibels to permit direct comparison with the spectra that are under analysis.

The result of the filter calculation for the spectrum given in Fig. 6 is shown as one of the curves in Fig. 7. Figure 7 is an example of the display of the events at nodes A, C, and D in the system schematized previously

in Fig. 3. The original speech spectrum (the one previously given in Fig. 5) and the difference curve (node D) are shown in addition to the internally synthesized spectrum (node C). The numbers at the left are three numerical measures of the error.

In all of the spectrum matching procedures described in this report, three different error scores were computed and were available as measures of the goodness of fit between the speech spectra and the internally synthesized spectra. The error curve is represented by 36 values (corresponding to the 36 filters) that will be designated as a set of numbers e_i. The error curve is always adjusted automatically such that the weighted mean of e_i is zero over the entire range of values of i. The three error measures are the following:

$$\text{Absolute error} = \sum_{i=1}^{36} |w_i e_i| \, ;$$

$$\text{Variation} = \sum_{i=1}^{35} |w_{i+1} e_{i+1} - w_i e_i| \, ;$$

$$\text{Square of error} = \sum_{i=1}^{36} w_i{}^2 e_i{}^2 \, ;$$

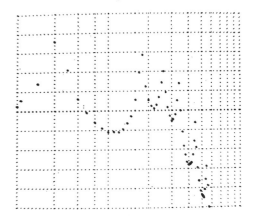

Fig. 6. Photograph of a computed spectrum (at node B in Fig. 3) displayed on the face of the output cathode-ray tube. The horizontal axis is a logarithmic frequency scale from 200 cps to 10 000 cps. The vertical axis represents amplitude in decibels, the small points indicating 1-db steps. The spectrum shown is characterized by resonant frequencies (bandwidths), in cps, of 430 (30), 1770 (80), 2580 (150), plus resonances every 1000 cps from 3500 cps to 9500 cps with bandwidths gradually increasing to 300 cps. Datum points are plotted every 100 cps. For convenience, the datum points at 100 and 200 cps are both plotted close to the 200-cps line.

---

[8] More precisely, ΔF_n is $1/\pi$ times the real part of the complex frequency of the pole (i.e., $1/\pi$ times the distance of the pole from the $j\omega$ axis in the s plane). When ΔF_n is small compared with F_n, then ΔF_n is very nearly equal to the bandwidth.

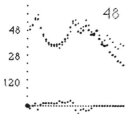

FIG. 7. Photograph of output display showing superposition of input spectrum (upper curve of light points) and comparison spectrum (upper curve of heavy points) obtained at node C of Fig. 3. The lower curve is the difference curve, obtained at node D of Fig. 3. The three numbers at the left show, from top to bottom, the magnitude of the absolute, variation, and squared error scores (see text) over 24 filter points, that is, up to about 3050 cps. The input spectrum is sample 48 shown in Fig. 5; the comparison spectrum is that shown in Fig. 6 after processing by the simulated filters. The error curve is typical of a situation in which a resonance in the comparison spectrum is improperly located.

where w_i represents arbitrary weighting factors which may be assigned depending on the frequency range considered to be important for matching a particular class of spectra. For example, it has been found convenient to match vowel spectra over the values of i from 1 to 24, corresponding to a frequency range of 100 to 3050 cps. A simple way of weighting the error in this case is to put $w_i=1$ over $i=1$ to 24, and $w_i=0$ over $i=25$ to 36. More sophisticated schemes for assigning weighting factors can, of course, be adopted. The variation, being a sum of first differences of the weighted error curve, provides an indication of the amount of fluctuation in the error curve, while the other two numbers provide measures of the amount of deviation of the curve from the zero axis. The significance of the different measures of error will be of particular interest in the discussion of automatic matching procedures in the next section. For experimental matching of various types of speech spectra the square of the error has been used more frequently than the other measures.

For the spectral match shown in Fig. 7, the square of the error, summed over 24 points in frequency, is 120 db². The error curve in this case has an irregularity at frequencies in the vicinity of the second resonance. This irregularity is due, apparently, to an incorrect selection of the frequency position of the second pole. When this frequency is adjusted upwards, the match between the two spectra would be expected to become better.

Some indication of the sensitivity of the error scores to small changes in the resonant frequency in this example is given by the upper curve in Fig. 8. This curve has a reasonably sharp minimum of 30 db² for a resonant frequency of 1870 cps. Evidently this error score is quite sensitive to small changes in the resonant frequency, and an accuracy better than 30 cps is to be expected in this case. The minimum for the variation error score generally is not as sharp as that for the squared error. Figure 8 also shows the squared error as a function of the frequency of $F2$ for a second formant in a lower frequency range, the second formant of the

vowel [ɑ]. Curves of form similar to those of Fig. 8 have been obtained for variations in both bandwidth and resonant frequency in the process of matching a large number of vowel spectra.

When the second resonant frequency of the internally generated spectrum of Fig. 7 is given the value that yields minimum squared error in Fig. 8, the spectral match shown in Fig. 9 is obtained. It is to be noted that a good match to the vowel spectrum shown in Fig. 9 was obtained in the frequency range 100–3050 cps by synthesizing a spectrum characterized by three conjugate pole pairs in this frequency range together with a group of poles at higher frequencies. The high-frequency poles must be included simply to provide the proper levels for the lower resonances.[9] Since the original speech spectrum was pre-emphasized with a slope of 6 db/octave, then, as noted previously, the spectrum envelope of the resulting signal is characterized simply by the set of conjugate pairs of poles of $T(s)$, if an idealized source spectrum envelope with a falling characteristic of 12 db/octave is assumed. As a matter of fact, any significant deviation of the synthesized spectrum from the speech spectrum of Fig. 9 would indicate that the shape of the actual source spectrum differed from this ideal shape. The fact that a good match is obtained in this case indicates that a −12 db/octave slope is a reasonable approximation for the spectrum envelope of the glottal source.[10]

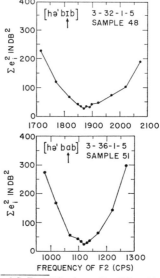

FIG. 8. Examples of the effect on the squared error score of varying the frequency of a single resonance of the comparison spectrum through a range of values in the vicinity of the actual vowel formant frequency. The upper graph refers to a sample taken centrally in a vowel characterized by a high-frequency second formant (sample 48, as in Figs. 4, 5, 7). The lower graph illustrates the same result for a sample from a vowel with a second formant at a lower frequency.

[9] G. Fant, "On the predictability of formant levels and spectrum envelopes from formant frequencies," *For Roman Jakobson*, edited by M. Halle *et al.* (Mouton and Company, 's-Gravenhage, 1956), pp. 109–120.
[10] The matching of a large number of spectral samples in voiced speech sounds has shown the same general results. These analysis procedures, however, are not highly sensitive to local variations in the shape of the glottal spectrum since the analog filters used in processing the speech materials are not very selective. Thus the form of the glottal spectrum derived by this method cannot be compared in detail with that derived from time-domain analyses.

By the procedure discussed above, matches have been obtained for a number of spectra associated with vowel and consonant portions of utterances by several male talkers. Systematic studies of the pole-zero patterns for various time locations through these utterances have been made[11] and detailed reports are in preparation. Examples of the matches obtained for three classes of speech sounds other than nonnasal vowels are shown in Fig. 10. In all cases it was possible to select a set of poles and zeros such that good fits were obtained with the data. In the matching of a spectrum such as one of these, the initial step was to determine the approximate locations of the poles and zeros from theoretical considerations and by examination of the general shape of the spectrum. Convergence to pole and zero locations yielding an optimum fit was achieved through a trial-and-error process, always with the constraint that the locations be consistent with known theoretical relations between vocal-tract configurations and the acoustic signal.

AUTOMATIC MATCHING OF VOWEL SPECTRA; THE STRATEGY PROBLEM

Although application of the spectrum-matching technique described above usually resulted in good agreement between the speech spectra and the synthesized spectra, and, presumably, in reasonably accurate values for spectral poles and zeros, the method has the disadvantage that it is tedious and is not completely automatic. Attempts have been made, therefore, to reduce the time required for the generation of comparison spectra and to program the computer to perform the function of the experimenter in the analysis scheme of Fig. 3. The task of developing an optimum strategy whereby rapid convergence to a best-fitting vowel spectrum is achieved is by no means trivial, and is an example of the hill-climbing problem that has received considerable attention in the field of pattern recognition.[12] The strategy that is used in the present automatic

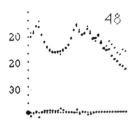

FIG. 9. Photograph of a display such as that described in Fig. 7, showing a good match between the input and comparison spectra. To obtain this match to the vowel [ɪ] the values of the lowest four resonant frequencies (bandwidths), in cps, of the comparison spectrum were 430 (30), 1870 (80), 2580 (150), and 3400 (120); additional resonances were spaced at 1000-cps intervals from 4500 to 9500 cps with gradually increasing bandwidths up to 300 cps.

[11] A. S. House, K. N. Stevens, and H. Fujisaki, J. Acoust. Soc. Am. **32**, 1517 (1960); J. M. Heinz, J. Acoust. Soc. Am. **32**, 1517 (1960); O. Fujimura, J. Acoust. Soc. Am. **32**, 1517 (1960).
[12] M. Minsky, Proc. Inst. Radio Engrs. **49**, 8 (1961).

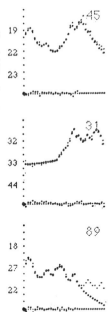

FIG. 10. Photographs of matches similar to that of Fig. 7 for spectra of speech sounds other than nonnasal vowels. The upper photograph shows a match to a (nasalized) vowel [i] occurring in the phonetic environment [m-m]. The comparison curve was constructed from three poles (and their conjugates) up to 3200 cps, a correction for higher poles, and a pole-zero pair in the vicinity of 1200 cps; the error scores were computed over 24 filters.[16] The middle photograph is a match to the fricative [ʃ] in initial position in a stressed syllable. In this case the error score was computed over 36 filters up to 7000 cps and the comparison curve was constructed from seven poles, three zeros, and three real-axis zeros close to zero frequency.[11] In the lower photograph the speech spectrum was sampled from an [n] in word final position and the error score was computed over 24 filters. The comparison curve was constructed from five poles and a zero up to 3000 cps, plus a higher-pole correction.[11]

matching scheme is a rather elementary one; more complex strategies are being developed to obtain more accurate and rapid analyses.[13,14] The automatic method to be described is applicable only to the analysis of the spectra of nonnasal vowels.

Generation of Comparison Spectra

In the experimental analysis procedure described above, each internally generated spectrum is computed as needed, and the integrations to simulate the effect of the filter bank are performed for each trial spectrum. The calculation of each pole factor and the simulation of the filtering of the synthesized spectra are the most time-consuming portions of the above method, however, and automation of the matching procedure would not be practical unless the time required for these operations was reduced. A more rapid (but less precise) procedure for the generation of comparison spectra was therefore adopted. In this procedure the comparison spectra are assembled from a limited set of elemental spectra that are stored within the computer memory.

Five elemental spectra are added to obtain the spectrum envelope of a vowel (in decibels) in the frequency range that includes the first three vocal-tract resonances (up to about 3000 cps for adult male voices). Four of these spectra are simple resonance curves each of which corresponds to a conjugate pair of poles of the vocal-tract transfer function. An inventory of 78 simple resonance curves is stored in the computer memory with resonant frequencies spaced every 20 cps from 160 to

[13] A. Paul, S.M. thesis (unpublished), M.I.T. (1961).
[14] M. V. Mathews (personal communication, 1961).

500 cps, every 50 cps from 500 to 3000 cps, and every 100 cps from 3000 to 4000 cps. The bandwidth of the resonance associated with each of these curves is fixed at a value suggested by measured data on formant bandwidth; it is 60 cps for the low-frequency resonances and increases to 180 cps for the high-frequency resonances. Vowel spectra with various combinations of resonances can be assembled by selection of appropriate groups of four such curves. The fifth elemental spectrum is a curve that, in the frequency range of the first three vocal-tract resonances, accounts for the source spectrum, the radiation characteristic, and poles of the vocal-tract transfer function higher than the fourth. This "correction" spectrum is a relatively smooth curve, and its shape is not expected to change markedly from one adult male speaker to another or from one vowel to another, although some variation in the slope of the curve may occur. An inventory of six such correction spectra is stored in the computer memory, and one of these is always added to the group of four resonance curves to synthesize a complete vowel spectrum.

The 84 elemental spectra that are stored in the computer memory are actually the curves that would be obtained if each of the simple resonance spectra and correction spectra were processed by the filter bank in the manner discussed above [Eq. (12)]. The elimination of the necessity of spectrum calculation and filter simulation greatly reduces the time required for the generation of comparison spectra (by a factor of about 50 in the present case), but it inevitably leads to some error in the synthesized spectra, especially at high frequencies where the filter bandwidths are not constant. Correction for the primary effect of the filter bandwidths can be made, and is actually included in the above procedure. It can be shown, however, that compensation for this error cannot be made exactly, especially for cases in which two resonances are closely spaced. Consequently this procedure for assembling vowel spectra has some inherent error, although this error is usually quite small.

Description of Strategy

From the 84 stored elemental curves, it is possible to assemble about 5×10^5 vowel-like spectra, if reasonable assumptions are made concerning the frequency range for each of the first four formants. Since in the analysis of a given speech spectrum it is impractical to make a comparison with each of these synthesized spectra, it is essential to devise a strategy whereby only a small subset of comparison spectra needs to be assembled and tested before convergence to the best-fitting spectrum is achieved. It is possible to distinguish two situations that require different strategies. One situation arises when no prior information is available concerning the formant frequencies for the vowel spectrum under analysis, and/or when no previous data have been obtained for the talker who generated the utterance in

which this spectrum occurs. Such a case would occur when, in the analysis of the formant frequencies during the vowel portion of a syllable, one spectrum is selected to be examined first. Here the basic task of the analyzer is to establish a good first approximation to the input spectrum. In the second situation, which occurs much more frequently than the first, approximate data concerning the formant frequencies and the appropriate correction spectrum are already available in the analyzer. These data may have been obtained either from analysis of a spectrum sample located adjacent to the spectrum to be analyzed or from a preliminary approximate analysis of the spectrum. In this case, the task of the analyzer is to optimize the match between the input and the synthesized spectra.

When there is no prior knowledge of the locations of the formants, one method that has been used to establish the approximate values of the formant frequencies consists of the following steps: (1) Elemental spectra corresponding to formant frequencies in the expected range of F_1 (plus a standard F_4 curve and a standard correction curve) are each compared with the speech spectrum to be analyzed, and the curve yielding the minimum variation error is selected tentatively as identifying F_1. (2) Elemental spectra corresponding to formant frequencies in the expected range of F_2 are each added in turn to the curve found in (1) and the composite curve yielding the minimum variation error is selected tentatively as identifying F_2. (3) Step (2) is repeated to find tentative values for F_3. (4) After approximate values for the first three formant frequencies are found in this way, elemental spectra corresponding to formant frequencies in the expected range of F_4 are each added in place of the standard F_4 curve adopted in previous steps, and the one yielding the minimum error score is found. (5) Step (4) is repeated to find the correction curve yielding the minimum error score. (6) The set of first four formant frequencies and the correction curve found by the above procedures are then used as starting points for the more exact analysis procedure that is employed when approximate data of this type are available.

It is to be noted that in the first step above, no elemental spectra corresponding to F_2 and F_3 are included in the synthesized spectrum. It can be shown, nevertheless, that the variation error score can serve to locate the approximate position of the lowest resonance in the input spectrum. The squared error score can give reliable results only after a reasonable approximation to the input spectrum is established, and is not a good criterion at this stage of the preliminary analysis. Throughout the automatic procedures pertaining to the analysis of vowels produced by adult male talkers error scores were computed with equal weighting for the 24 filters in the frequency range 100–3050 cps.

In the process of developing the preliminary analysis procedure outlined above, various alternative schemes for obtaining a first approximation to the formant frequencies were tried. In one such scheme the spectrum of a neutral vowel, i.e., $F_1 = 500$ cps with subsequent formants occurring at intervals of 1000 cps, was used as the zero-order approximation, and the frequency positions of the formants were revised successively within appropriate ranges. Another scheme involved the matching of the input spectrum against members of a small stored set of standard vocalic spectra and the selection of the best approximation. A third procedure obtained estimates of approximate values of formant frequencies from direct measurements of certain gross features of the input spectrum.[15] Further studies with a large number of talkers and utterances will be required before the over-all performance of these various preliminary analysis procedures (or possibly combinations of them) can be compared quantitatively.

When approximate values for the formant frequencies and correction spectrum are available, an iterative procedure is employed, and the sequence of operations is the following: (1) With F_2, F_3, F_4, and the correction spectrum fixed at the given values, curves with resonant frequencies in the vicinity of the given F_1 are used to form a series of spectra that are compared with the speech spectrum to be analyzed. The value of F_1 yielding the minimum squared error is selected and used in subsequent steps. (2) Step (1) is repeated but with F_1, F_3, F_4, and the correction spectrum at the given values and F_2 as the variable. (3) Step (1) is repeated to find, in turn, revised values for F_3, F_4 and the correction spectrum. (4) Steps (1)–(3) are repeated. If the results are the same as those obtained after the first set of trials, the analysis of the given spectrum is terminated; otherwise the process is repeated until no improvement in the fit is obtained.

The automatic method for the analysis of vowels has been used to obtain data on the variation with time of the formant frequencies of stressed vowels in a number of dissyllabic utterances. The computer has been programmed to perform the analysis on each spectral sample in turn within a designated region of the utterance. The initial step in the procedure is to prescribe the range of spectral samples over which the analysis is to be performed and to select a sample located centrally within this range. The analysis is first carried out on the centrally located sample, following one of the procedures that require no *a priori* knowledge of the approximate formant frequencies. The more precise iterative procedure is then applied to this sample to locate the formant frequencies and correction spectrum more exactly. These values of formant frequencies and correction spectrum are used as first approximations in the analysis of the following spectral sample. In this manner the analysis is performed on each spectral sample in turn until the end of the designated interval is reached. Then the program returns to the centrally located sample, and uses the results previously obtained

15 F. Poza, S.M. thesis (unpublished), M.I.T. (1959).

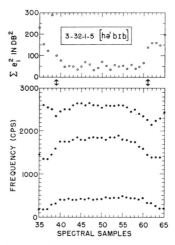

FIG. 11. Display of data on vowel formant frequencies derived by the automatic analysis procedure. The utterance is the same as that shown in Fig. 4. Time is on the horizontal axis and is indicated in terms of samples which occur at 8.3-msec intervals. The solid points represent the lowest three vowel formants in each sample as determined by the automatic procedure. The open points at the top of the figure give a measure of the error of fit between the input and comparison spectra. The arrows indicate points in time where study of the spectrogram of the utterance (see Fig. 4) suggests the locations of vocalic boundaries.

for this sample as first approximations to the next preceding sample. The analysis is carried out on each preceding sample moving toward the beginning of the designated time interval. The results for each spectral sample are stored in the computer memory. After the analysis of all samples is completed, an instruction can be given to the computer to print or punch out the results of the analysis of each sample in order, or to display the results on the oscilloscope in various ways.

Typical Results

Figure 11 displays typical results of the automatic vowel analysis program for a portion of the utterance whose spectrogram is shown in Fig. 4. The first three formant frequencies found by the program are plotted for each spectral sample in the stressed vowel. The squared error score for each sample is also shown in the upper part of the figure. The arrows indicate the "vowel" boundaries suggested by study of the spectrogram. It is noted that the error score increases sharply at these boundaries, since it is not possible, of course, to obtain good matches with consonant spectra by assembling a set of simple resonance curves by a procedure based on a theory of vowel production.

Several limitations of the automatic procedure have already been pointed out, and further studies will be necessary to overcome these limitations. The automatic analysis procedure in its present form requires that many trials be made before convergence to a set of resonant frequencies is achieved, and consequently the analysis takes a considerable amount of time (order of 1000 times real time for the computer and the programs used in these studies). Furthermore, small but systematic errors in formant locations occur as a result of (a) the incomplete correction for the effect of the filters in the construction of the comparison spectrum and (b) the inability to vary the bandwidths of the formants. Both of these types of errors can be eliminated if a more complex and time-consuming procedure is used to assemble the spectra, similar to the procedure used in the experimental method described in connection with Fig. 3. If, however, formant bandwidth were a variable in the matching process, then a more detailed strategy would be necessary to converge to both the frequencies and the bandwidths appropriate to a given spectral sample.[13]

Remarks on Extension of Automatic Analysis Procedure to Other Classes of Speech Spectra

The automatic speech reduction procedure just described is applicable only to spectra of nonnasal vowels or vowel-like sounds for which the vocal-tract transfer function is characterized by a set of conjugate pairs of poles. Thus for the matching of these types of spectra the internal spectrum generator in Fig. 2 need be instructed simply to synthesize spectra corresponding to a product of terms each of which represents a conjugate pair of poles. On the other hand, completely automatic procedures for reduction of spectra other than those of vowels or vowel-like sounds have not yet been developed. This lack of progress stems largely from the fact that the generation of these other classes of sounds is not yet understood in detail. While it is known, for example, that spectra occurring during the production of nasal, stop, and fricative consonants are characterized by zeros as well as poles, the numbers of zeros and poles required and the frequency ranges to be expected for each cannot be specified easily and systematically on the basis of present knowledge.

The spectrum of a nasalized vowel, for example, is characterized by about four poles and one zero in the frequency range up to 3000 cps,[16,17] but the problem of devising a strategy that would lead to automatic matching of such a spectrum is a formidable one. If the positions of the four poles and zero were varied independently, a large number of combinations would have to be tried, but in order to avoid erroneous results these should include only those combinations that could in fact represent outputs of a vocal tract. To meet this requirement constant reference to articulation would have to be made during the process of searching for suitable pole-zero combinations.

In view of these complications it is suggested that the strategy in an automatic analysis-by-synthesis procedure that is applicable to all types of spectra should consist of a search for parameters that are more directly related to articulation than are the pole-zero locations. In effect, the proposed strategy would require a search through a set of articulatory configurations. For each trial configuration the pole-zero locations, and hence the over-all spectrum, would be computed and compared with the spectrum under analysis. Different articulatory configurations would be tried until a spectrum yielding a best fit with the input spectrum was obtained. Thus in the case of matching the spectrum of a nasalized vowel, the strategy would try different vowel configurations and different amounts of coupling to the nasal cavities until an optimum spectral match was obtained.

The realization of this type of analysis scheme requires that a model be developed for specifying articulatory configurations in a simple yet meaningful way. Although various simple models have already been proposed[18-20] it is clear that much must be learned concerning articulatory constraints and the relations between articulation and the acoustic output before a suitable strategy for the automatic reduction of all kinds of speech spectra is developed.

DISCUSSION

Analysis-by-synthesis procedures for the reduction of speech spectra have been used in one form or another by several investigators. Early attempts to use a spectrum matching technique were reported by Steinberg[21] and by Lewis,[22] who matched simple resonance curves to vowel spectra in the vicinity of the spectral peaks. The method was carried much further by Fant,[4,23] who demonstrated how the spectra associated with simple linear circuits can be matched against vowel and consonant spectra. In Fant's studies, the experimenter can be said to have been situated within the feedback loop (as in Fig. 3 above) and the comparison spectra were either computed or measured from simple analog circuits. The goodness of fit was assessed by visual examination of the curves. Similar procedures were used by Heinz and Stevens[24] for the matching of the spectra of fricative consonants. Matching of the spectra of several vowels was achieved by Mathews, Miller, and David,[25] who used digital computer techniques for the analysis

[16] O. Fujimura, "Analysis of nasalized vowels," Quart. Progr. Rept. 62, Research Laboratory of Electronics, M.I.T. (1961). pp. 191–192.
[17] Reference 4, pp. 148 ff.

[18] Reference 4, pp. 71 ff.
[19] K. N. Stevens and A. S. House, J. Acoust. Soc. Am. 27, 484 (1955).
[20] O. Fujimura (personal communication, 1960).
[21] J. C. Steinberg, J. Acoust. Soc. Am. 6, 16 (1934).
[22] D. Lewis, J. Acoust. Soc. Am. 8, 91 (1936).
[23] C. G. M. Fant, "Transmission properties of the vocal tract, II." Quart. Progr. Rept. Acoustics Laboratory, M.I.T. (Oct.–Dec. 1950), pp. 14–19.
[24] J. M. Heinz and K. N. Stevens, J. Acoust. Soc. Am. 33, 589 (1961).
[25] M. V. Mathews, J. E. Miller, and E. E. David, Jr., J. Acoust. Soc. Am. 33, 179 (1961).

of spectra computed from individual periods of the glottal output. They devised procedures for finding a set of poles corresponding to the vocal-tract transfer function and zeros to approximate the detailed form of the glottal spectrum such that best fits were obtained with the spectra under analysis. By performing a "pitch synchronous" analysis, they were able to obtain a rather detailed picture of the characteristics of the glottal excitation as well as the vocal-tract resonances, although the procedure was complicated by the necessity for adjusting a large number of parameters in order to converge to a best fit. The principles of the active speech analysis procedure have also been enunciated by Inomata,[26] who, in connection with a program concerned with automatic speech recognition, has used computer techniques to search for a set of poles that yield a spectrum that matches a given vowel spectrum.

Whereas the methods just summarized, as well as those described in this paper, involve the matching of speech spectra and thus are carried out in the frequency domain, analysis procedures based on the same principle can also be applied in the time domain. The "inverse filtering" techniques described by Miller[27] involve the processing of the vowel sounds by a cascaded set of filters that are characterized by a set of conjugate pairs of zeros. When the frequencies of the zeros are adjusted to coincide with those of the poles that describe the vocal-tract transfer function for the vowel, then the output of the filters represents the waveform of the glottal source. Since the general shape of the glottal pulse is known, then a procedure can be devised for adjusting the zeros until the expected shape is obtained. The processing of the signal by a cascaded sequence of filters in the time domain is analogous to subtracting elemental resonance spectra (in decibels) from the speech spectrum. It would appear difficult, however, to devise an automatic analysis procedure based on time-domain methods, since criteria for optimum cancellation of a pole by a zero might be difficult to devise.

The various versions of analysis-by-synthesis or feedback methods of speech spectrum analysis such as those that have been described here and by others are considered to have important advantages over other analysis schemes. For the feedback analysis method, once a set of parameters is found such that a good replica of the input signal is generated when these parameters are applied as instructions to the internal generative model, then there is little question that this set constitutes an adequate representation of the input. In contrast to this method are the passive or open-loop analysis procedures in which simple attributes of the spectra, such as the major spectral peaks, are measured directly and are used to provide a simple representation of the speech signal. There is no assurance in these cases that important data have not been discarded or that

an error has not been made in the extraction of a particular parameter.

Other potential advantages of the feedback analysis procedure stem from the fact that it permits certain quasi-invariant features of the speech signal to be accounted for in a relatively straightforward manner. Thus, in principle, once certain properties of a given talker, such as the spectrum of the glottal output or the approximate range of variation of his formant frequencies, have been evaluated, then these properties can be assumed to remain relatively unchanged over a period of time, and the strategy during this period is simplified. In a sense, the method is geared to the extraction of features of the signal that are changing, and spends little time on the extraction of features that do not change or that change only slowly.

The similarity between an analysis-by-synthesis procedure and certain aspects of human perception have led several investigators to speculate that man manipulates sensory data such as speech by an active internal replication process.[5–7,26,28,29] If there is any basis for such speculation, then analysis techniques of the type described here would have the additional advantage that they bear at least some resemblance to the process of human speech reception.

ACKNOWLEDGMENTS

The authors have profited from stimulation, counsel and technical assistance contributed by their associates. Discussions with Osamu Fujimura have particularly influenced the course of the research. Ideas contributed by George Rosen and Fausto Poza are also acknowledged with gratitude, as is the criticism and encouragement of Morris Halle, the programming aid of Paul T. Brady and the technical assistance of Jane Arnold. Finally, the work would not have been possible without the availability of the TX-O computer, a facility of the Department of Electrical Engineering, M.I.T., and the cooperation and help of its technical staff.

This work was supported in part by the U. S. Army Signal Corps, the Air Force Office of Scientific Research, and the Office of Naval Research; and in part by the Air Force Cambridge Research Laboratories.

APPENDIX: SPEECH INPUT SYSTEM

Sampled speech data are introduced into the computer in spectral form using equipment the block diagram of which is shown in Fig. 12. Speech is recorded on one channel of a two-channel magnetic tape loop and sampling pulses are recorded on the other channel. The speech is played back through a pre-emphasis network into a

[26] S. Inomata, Bull. Electro-Tech. Lab. (Tokyo) **24**, 597 (1960).
[27] R. L. Miller, J. Acoust. Soc. Am. **31**, 667 (1959).

[28] G. A. Miller, E. Galanter, and K. H. Pribram, *Plans and the Structure of Behavior* (Henry Holt and Company, New York, 1960).
[29] L. A. Chistovich, Soviet Phys.—Acoustics **6**, 393 (1961); [Akust. Zhur. **6**, 392 (1960)].

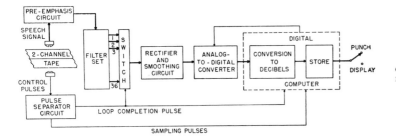

Fig. 12. Block diagram of the procedure used in preparing speech materials for computer analysis.

bank of 36 simple-tuned filters. The pre-emphasis network has a rising frequency characteristic of 6 db/octave. The center frequencies of the filters range from 150 to 7025 cps and are selected so that the half-power points of adjacent filters are coincident. The filter bandwidths are constant at 100 cps for center frequencies up to 1550 cps and then increase gradually until reaching a value of 475 cps for a center frequency of 7025 cps. During the read-in process, the outputs of the filters are selected in sequence by a stepping switch that steps after each cycle of the tape loop. Thus the loop is played 36 times to obtain a complete spectral analysis of the speech sample. The selected filter output is full-wave rectified and smoothed before being converted from analog to digital form. A commercial analog-to-digital encoder performs this conversion.

The second tape channel contains recorded control pulses. A pulse train of positive polarity in which the pulses occur every 8.3 msec is used to indicate times at which the data are to be sampled. A train of opposite polarity marks the end of the tape loop and initiates the stepping switch. These control pulses enter two light-pen flip-flop registers of the computer, so that the sampling can then be controlled by the computer.

The computer is programmed to search the light-pen flip-flop registers for "sample" pulses and to transfer data from the encoder when such a pulse appears. The filter outputs are encoded into 10 bits and are read into the computer, where the data are then converted into decibels, encoded into six bits, and rearranged so that three samples are stored in each 18-bit memory register. Thus each group of 12 registers contains outputs of the 36 filters at one sample time. Successive groups of 12 registers contain speech spectra at successive 8.3-msec intervals. With the present 8192-word memory, 3648 registers are used for data storage, and thus approximately 2.5 seconds of speech can be processed. The program provides routines that allow the data to be displayed on an oscilloscope or punched out on paper tape for later use. In addition, several error-checking routines are built into the program to maintan the accuracy of the read-in process.

CHAPTER **6**

Reprinted from the *Journal of Speech and Hearing Research*
December 1961, Vol. 4, No. 4

An Acoustical Theory of Vowel Production and Some of its Implications

K E N N E T H N . S T E V E N S

A R T H U R S . H O U S E

It is 20 years since the publication of the monograph on the vowel by Chiba and Kajiyama (*3*)—a work that introduces and epitomizes the modern era in the study of speech production and perception. The past two decades have seen a continuous advance in the understanding of the mechanism of speech sound generation, as exemplified by the publication of Fant's treatise (*10*). The fruits of the experimental and theoretical progress, however, have not been universally appreciated and applied. The time may be ripe, therefore, for a concise yet rigorous exposition of current concepts of speech production. The remarks that follow represent an attempt to provide such an exposition on an acoustical theory of vowel production, and to point out its relevance

Kenneth N. Stevens (Sc.D., Massachusetts Institute of Technology, 1952) is Associate Professor of Electrical Engineering, Massachusetts Institute of Technology. Arthur S. House (Ph.D., University of Illinois, 1951) is Research Associate, Department of Electrical Engineering, Massachusetts Institute of Technology. Both authors are on the staff of the Research Laboratory of Electronics, M.I.T.
This work was supported by the U. S. Army Signal Corps, the Air Force Office of Scientific Research, and the Office of Naval Research; and in part by the Air Force Cambridge Research Laboratories under Contract AF 19(604)-6102.

to and compatibility with certain known characteristics of speech.

Theory of Vowel Production

Vowel sounds are produced by acoustic excitation of the vocal tract by a source at the glottis. The vocal tract is viewed as an acoustic circuit, and the acoustic disturbances in this circuit are usually described in terms of sound pressures and volume velocities of vibration of the air at various points in the circuit. In all cases of present interest, the cross-sectional dimensions of the vocal tract may be considered to be small compared with a wavelength. This means that only plane acoustic waves propagate in the vocal tract, and that the sound pressure and volume velocity measured in the vocal tract are functions of only one spatial dimension—the distance measured along the vocal tract from the glottis.

For those who prefer to think in terms of electric rather than acoustic circuits, the following analogous quantities should be noted: sound pressure p is analogous to voltage; volume velocity U is analogous to current. Acoustic impedance is defined by $Z = p/U$, where p and U are complex amplitudes,

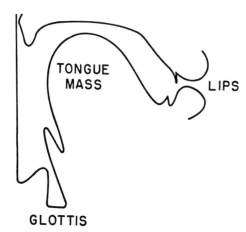

GLOTTIS

FIGURE 1. Schematized midsagittal section through the vocal tract during the production of a vowel. Adapted from Wendahl (43).

from the mouth is approximately that for a 'simple source' (27, pp. 312 ff.):

$$R(j\omega) = p_r(j\omega)/U_o(j\omega) = j\omega\rho/(4\pi r).$$
$$(1)$$

Of particular interest is the factor of ω in the numerator, indicating a radiation characteristic $\left|\dfrac{p_r(j\omega)}{U_o(j\omega)}\right|$ that rises at 6 db per octave.

In Figure 1 is shown a schematized midsagittal section through the vocal tract during the production of a vowel. The excitation of the tract is a quasi-periodic series of pulses of air that pass through the glottis during the open phases of the vocal-fold vibratory cycle. A typical waveform of the volume

following the usual conventions of electric current theory.[1]

When one end of an acoustic tube such as the vocal tract is open, the effect of this open end on the sound in the tube can be represented by a radiation impedance. At low frequencies this radiation impedance may be represented by a resistance $\rho c/A$ in parallel with a small acoustic mass $M_r \cong 0.4\ \rho/\sqrt{A}$, where A is the cross-sectional area, ρ is the density of air, and c is the velocity of sound. In the study of speech sounds, the experimenter usually is interested in the sound pressure p_r measured at some distance r from the mouth. If $U_o(j\omega)$ represents the Fourier spectrum of the volume velocity at the mouth opening, where ω is the radian frequency, then at low frequencies (below, say, 5 000 cps) the relation that describes the radiation of sound

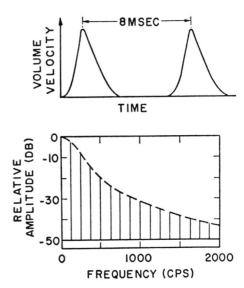

FIGURE 2. A typical waveform of the volume velocity of the glottal output for a fundamental frequency of 125 cps, and a Fourier spectrum corresponding to this type of waveform. The dashed curve describes the envelope of the line spectrum. The slope of the spectrum envelope at low frequencies is derived from Fourier analysis of quasi-triangular waveforms.

[1]See, for example, E. A. Guillemin, *Introductory Circuit Theory*. New York: Wiley, 1953.

velocity as a function of time is shown in Figure 2, along with its corresponding Fourier spectrum. The general shape of the volume velocity waveform is not unlike that of the waveform of the area of the glottis opening as a function of time (*11*). The duration and shape of the pulses shown in Figure 2 are similar to that derived from study of the larynx in action (*33, 39*). It can be demonstrated that this volume velocity waveform $U_s(t)$ is relatively independent of the vocal-tract configuration (*40, 42*), that is, is more or less independent of the acoustic impedance looking into the vocal tract from the glottis, and consequently the internal impedance of the volume velocity source can be considered to be high. The Fourier spectrum of U_s, assuming a periodic waveform, is a line spectrum with components at multiples of the fundamental frequency. At frequencies above about 250 cps (for a typical male voice) the magnitude of these components decreases with increasing frequency at a rate of about 12 db per octave, that is, the spectrum 'envelope' of $|U_s(j\omega)|$ is roughly proportional to ω^{-2}. Below 250 cps, the downward slope of the spectrum envelope is less steep. This low-frequency behavior of the spectrum envelope is predicted from Fourier analysis of triangular waveforms of the type shown in Figure 2.

The shape of the spectrum shown in Figure 2 is typical of the glottal output for conversational speech. The slope of the spectrum envelope at high frequencies can deviate from that of Figure 2 as vocal effort is changed (*24*). Furthermore, irregularities are present in the spectrum shape (*11, 26*), particularly when the spectrum of a single glottal pulse is considered.

As a result of the excitation at the glottis, a volume velocity $U_o(t)$ exists at the mouth opening. If $U_o(j\omega)$ is the Fourier spectrum of the output volume velocity, and $U_s(j\omega)$ the spectrum of the input volume velocity, then a transfer ratio $T(j\omega) = U_o(j\omega)/U_s(j\omega)$ can be defined. In general this transfer function is characterized by a number of resonances or poles, and varies markedly as the configuration of the vocal tract changes.

The above remarks may be summarized by saying that the Fourier spectrum of the sound pressure p_r measured at a distance from the lips during vowel production may be considered as the product of three terms:

$$p_r(j\omega) = U_s(j\omega) \cdot T(j\omega) \cdot R(j\omega) \quad (2)$$

where $R(j\omega)$ is a factor that accounts for radiation from the lips as given in Equation 1. Each term in this product has a phase and an amplitude, each of which is a function of frequency. Usually the experimenter is concerned only with the amplitude spectrum, in which case the magnitude of each term in the product is taken. In general, $U_s(j\omega)$ and $R(j\omega)$ are independent of the articulatory configurations, whereas $T(j\omega)$ is highly dependent upon the vocal-tract shape, and thus varies considerably from vowel to vowel.

Lumped-Circuit Approximation. A rough approximation to $T(j\omega)$ may be obtained if the vocal tract is viewed as a lumped circuit, that is, if the dimensions of the vocal tract are considered to be small compared with a wavelength in the frequency range of interest. Figure 1 shows a typical configuration for which this approximation

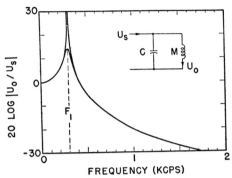

FIGURE 3. A plot of the magnitude of the transfer ratio (in db) as a function of frequency for a one-resonator lumped-circuit approximation of the vocal tract, together with an equivalent lossless circuit. For the ideal lossless case where there is no resistance in the circuit, the curve tends to infinity at the resonant frequency F_1; in realizable circuits with small amounts of dissipation the curve has a finite peak at approximately the same frequency, as shown.

is valid at low frequencies. The assumption of lumped-circuit elements is not unreasonable, since at 300 cps the wavelength is about 100 cm and the length of the vocal tract for an average male is about 17 cm. An equivalent circuit for this configuration is shown in Figure 3, together with a plot of the transfer ratio (in decibels) as a function of frequency. The volume of the tract is represented by C, and the narrow mouth opening (including the radiation impedance) by M. In the ideal lossless case, there is no resistance R in the circuit, and the transfer ratio for this circuit tends to infinity at frequency $F_1 = 1/(2\pi\sqrt{MC})$. Small amounts of dissipation always are present, however, and, consequently, the transfer ratio will have a finite peak at approximately the same frequency. The figure shows curves for the theoretical lossless case and for the case in which the dissipation is typical of that found in the vocal tract.

A typical value for the volume V of the tract between lips and glottis is about 50 cm^3, so that $C = V/\rho c^2 = 3.5 \times 10^{-5}$ cm^5/dyne. For this particular configuration the length l of the mouth opening is about 2 cm and has an average cross-sectional area A of about 0.3 cm^2, so that $M = \rho l/A = 8.0 \times 10^{-3}$ gm/cm^4. Thus $F_1 \cong 300$ cps, a value near the observed frequency of the lowest resonance for the vowel /u/ as spoken by male voices.

If a small amount of dissipation is included in the equivalent circuit of Figure 3, it can be shown from linear circuit theory that the transfer function can be written

$$T_1(j\omega) = \frac{U_o(j\omega)}{U_s(j\omega)} = \frac{s_1 s_1^*}{(j\omega - s_1)(j\omega - s_1^*)}$$
(3)

where $s_1 = \sigma_1 + j\omega_1$, $s_1^* = \sigma_1 - j\omega_1$, $\omega_1 = 2\pi F_1$ and σ_1 is a constant that depends on the amount of dissipation. When the amount of dissipation is small, $\sigma_1 \ll \omega_1$ and the half-power bandwidth of the resonance is σ_1/π cps. The complex numbers s_1 and s_1^* are often called the *poles* of the transfer function. Under the assumption $\sigma_1 \ll \omega_1$, the magnitude of the transfer function is

$$|T_1(j\omega)| = \left|\frac{U_o(j\omega)}{U_s(j\omega)}\right| \cong$$

$$\frac{\omega_1^2}{(\omega + \omega_1)[(\omega - \omega_1)^2 + \sigma_1^2]^{1/2}}.$$
(4)

This relation was used to plot the transfer ratio in Figure 3.

The transfer function of the vocal-tract configuration represented by the equivalent circuit in Figure 3 can be described in any of three equivalent ways: (a) the volume of the tract and the length and area of the lip opening (together with an appropriate damping constant) can be specified; (b) the values of C and M (and the resistance) in the equivalent circuit can be specified; or, (c) the resonant frequency ω_1 and the damping constant σ_1 can be specified. From any one of these specifications the entire resonance curve in Figure 3 can be described at all frequencies for which the approximations stated above are valid. If the previous statement that the spectrum envelope of the source and the radiation characteristic are relatively invariant is accepted, then it can be asserted that specification of the resonant frequency and bandwidth (or damping constant) permits the construction of the entire spectrum envelope for the vowel. This conclusion will be of particular significance when more complicated models for the vocal tract are discussed.

A one-resonator approximation to the vocal tract is rather unrealistic since it is valid only for frequencies below

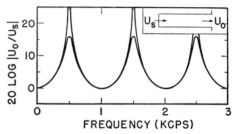

FIGURE 5. A plot of the magnitude of the transfer ratio (in db) as a function of frequency for a distributed (transmission line) representation of an acoustic tube. As shown, the tube is of uniform cross-sectional area and is open at one end; its length is 17 cm. The curve has infinite peaks at resonant frequencies for the ideal lossless case, and peaks of finite amplitude for the slightly dissipative case, as shown. The half-power bandwidth of all resonances was assumed to be 100 cps.

about 300 cps. A vocal-tract model consisting of more than one resonator would be valid over a frequency range for which *each* resonator is small compared to the wavelength. A representation of the vocal tract by two resonators, which might be valid up to a frequency of about 1 000 cps, is shown in Figure 4 along with a plot of the transfer function. The transfer function is now the product of two terms of the type shown in Equations 3 and 4. In this case, the transfer function exhibits two resonances; each resonant frequency is dependent upon the volumes of both resonators and on the dimensions of both constrictions in the model. The extent to which a given resonance is affiliated with a particular cavity depends upon the amount of coupling between the cavities, that is, upon the sizes of the constrictions. For vocal-tract configurations appropriate to vowel production, it is generally not valid to assign resonant frequencies exclusively to particular cavities (*3*, p. 93, *5*, *10*, pp. 284 ff.).

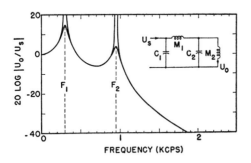

FIGURE 4. A plot of the magnitude of the transfer ratio (in db) as a function of frequency for a two-resonator lumped-circuit approximation of the vocal tract, together with an equivalent lossless circuit. Transfer ratios for the lossless case and the slightly dissipative case are shown (see Figure 3).

Transmission-Line Description. A more general description of the vocal tract that is accurate over a wide frequency range considers the tract as a distributed system or transmission line in which one-dimensional plane waves propagate. In order to explicate this approach it is convenient first to consider a vocal-tract configuration in which the cross-sectional area is constant and in which the radiation impedance is negligible. This provides a uniform acoustic tube driven at one end by a volume velocity U_s and terminated in a short circuit through which volume velocity U_o flows. The situation is illustrated in Figure 5; the articulation of the schwa vowel is similar to this uniform configuration.

Transmission-line theory must be used to compute the transfer function for the uniform configuration, whereas lumped-circuit theory was adequate in the situation where the dimensions of the configuration were small compared with a wavelength. When an acoustic tube is considered as a transmission line, the acoustic disturbances in the tube are viewed as being composed of plane sound waves propagating in both directions. Such a tube has, in theory, an infinite number of resonances, rather than just one resonance as was the case for the simple resonator in Figure 3. The contribution of each resonance to the transfer function of the tube has the same form as that given in Equations 3 and 4. To account for all the resonances it is necessary to take the product of an infinite number of factors like $T_1(j\omega)$ in Equations 3 or 4. Each factor is characterized, however, by a different pair of poles, that is, by a different resonant frequency and a different damping constant. Thus

$$T(j\omega) = \frac{U_o}{U_s} = \frac{s_1 s_1^*}{(j\omega - s_1)(j\omega - s_1^*)} \cdot$$
$$\frac{s_2 s_2^*}{(j\omega - s_2)(j\omega - s_2^*)} \cdot \dots \cdot$$
$$\frac{s_n s_n^*}{(j\omega - s_n)(j\omega - s_n^*)} \cdot \dots \quad (5)$$

where $s_n = \sigma_n + j\omega_n$.

In the case of the uniform-tube model of the vocal tract, if end effects are neglected, the various resonant frequencies $f_n = \omega_n/2\pi$ are odd multiples of a lowest natural frequency, that is, the resonances for the familiar situation of a pipe open at one end and closed at the other. In this case, therefore, $\omega_n = (2n + 1)\omega_1$, where n is an integer. The lowest natural frequency $\omega_1/2\pi$ occurs when the length l of the tube is one-quarter wavelength. Since the wavelength λ is given by $\lambda = c/f$, where f is the frequency and c is the velocity of propagation of sound, then

$$\omega_n = (2n + 1)\frac{\pi c}{2l},$$

or $f_n = (2n + 1)\dfrac{c}{4l}.$

For the case of a uniform vocal tract of length 17 cm, the resonant frequencies occur at about 500, 1 500, 2 500, . . . cps.

A plot of the magnitude of the transfer function in decibels (similar to the plot in Figure 3 for a single resonance) for the uniform tube of length 17 cm can be constructed by *adding* together an infinite number of curves each similar to that in Figure 3, with resonant frequencies at 500, 1 500, 2 500, . . . cps. The result of such a construction, assuming resonance bandwidths of 100 cps, is shown in Figure 5. The important features of this plot are that the value of $|T(j\omega)|$ is the same at each resonant frequency, and that $|T(j\omega)|$ is approximately unity at zero frequency and at frequencies midway between the resonant frequencies, that is, at 1 000, 2 000, 3 000, . . . cps in this case.

The uniform tube is an idealized configuration that may not occur precisely in practice. Several conclusions may be drawn from a discussion of the properties of this configuration, however, and these conclusions will apply, in general, to other configurations. (a) The transfer function $T(j\omega)$ is characterized by an infinite number of resonances; on the average, these resonances occur every $c/2l$ cps (or approximately every 1 000 cps for male voices). (b) Lengthening the vocal tract tends to lower the frequencies of all resonances; shortening the tract increases the frequencies of all resonances.

In order to study resonant frequencies for a particular vowel configuration for which the cross-sectional area of the vocal tract is not uniform, the configuration can be visualized as a perturbation of the uniform tube. (It is assumed throughout the discussion that there is no coupling to the nasal cavities.) Starting with the uniform tube with resonant frequencies at, say, 500, 1 500, 2 500, . . . cps, the shape is distorted gradually until the configuration approaches that of the vowel under study. As this perturbation process is carried out, the resonant frequencies gradually shift their positions and in the limit settle at new values. The number of resonances and their average spacing will not change, how-ever, if the vocal-tract length does not change. For a configuration appropriate for the production of /ɑ/, for example, typical values of the resonant frequencies are 800, 1 200, 2 500, etc. *(19)*. Thus, for a general vowel configuration, Equation 5 can still be used to specify the vocal-tract transfer function, but the values of ω_n and σ_n must be selected to correspond to the resonant frequencies and bandwidths for that particular configuration. The values of ω_1, ω_2, . . . for a particular vocal-tract configuration may be viewed as the natural frequencies of free vibration for that configuration, and they are the same, independent of how the system is excited. Once the values of the resonant frequencies and bandwidths are known, then these values can be used in Equation 5 to compute the *entire* transfer function $T(j\omega) = U_o/U_s$ for *all frequencies*.

The relations between the configuration of the vocal tract and the resonant frequencies and bandwidths have been the subject of study for many years *(3, 4, 5, 10, 36, 41)*. When the cross-sectional area of the vocal tract is known at all points along its length, calculations of the resonant frequencies can be made, but such calculations are complex, and, therefore, computational aids such as electrical analog devices and digital computers have been used to establish the relations *(5, 10, 36)*. While it is not the purpose of this paper to discuss these relations in detail, one general relation will, however, be noted since it has a bearing on the ensuing discussion. This relation is the following: the frequency of the first resonance tends to decrease as the cross-sectional area at some point along the vocal tract decreases, that is, as the vocal tract becomes more constricted (except when the constriction occurs within a few centimeters of the glottis). This result has been discussed in quantitative terms elsewhere (*36*), but can easily be verified if reference is made to the analog circuits shown in Figures 3 or 4, which are reasonably valid representations of the acoustic behavior of the vocal tract at low frequencies. In these circuits a vocal-tract constriction is represented by an acoustic mass M whose magnitude is inversely proportional to the cross-sectional area of the constriction. In the case of Figure 3, therefore, M becomes larger as the area of the constriction decreases, and thus the frequency of the first resonance $F_1 = 1/(2\pi\sqrt{MC})$ decreases. In the case of Figure 4, which corresponds to a two-cavity idealization of the vocal-tract configuration, it can be shown that the frequency F_1 of the first resonance decreases as M_2 becomes large, and also decreases as M_1 becomes large, provided the constriction with which M_1 is associated is not too close to the glottis. An increase in M_1 corresponds to a decrease in the cross-sectional area of the constriction separating the two cavities, whereas an increase in M_2 corresponds to a decrease in the cross-sectional area of the anterior end of the vocal tract.

Properties of the Spectrum Envelope. It has been shown in Equation 2 above that the spectrum of the sound pressure p_r measured at a distance r in front of the lips is the product of three terms (or the sum of three terms if each is expressed in decibels): a source spectrum $U_s(j\omega)$, a radiation characteristic $R(j\omega)$, and a transfer function $T(j\omega)$ The first two terms are both almost independent of the articulatory

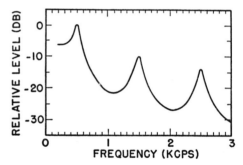

FIGURE 6. A vowel spectrum envelope constructed by adding together the transfer function of Figure 5, the spectrum envelope of the glottal source shown in Figure 2, and a radiation characteristic rising at 6 db/octave.

configuration, while the last is dependent on the configuration and is characterized by a number of resonances or poles. The spectrum envelope of a vowel can be constructed, therefore, simply by adding to the 20 log $|U_o/U_s|$ curve of Figure 5 the spectrum envelope of U_s, which has a form similar to that shown in the lower part of Figure 2, plus the radiation characteristic, which rises at 6 db per octave in the frequency range of interest. An over-all vowel spectrum envelope constructed in this way for the uniform vocal-tract configuration is shown in Figure 6. For a glottal excitation of fixed frequency the spectrum actually is a line spectrum, the spacing between components being equal to the fundamental frequency.

When the vocal-tract configuration differs from the uniform-tube idealization, the frequencies of the resonances and hence the frequencies at which there are peaks in the spectrum envelope, shift to positions different from those shown in Figure 6. If the frequencies and bandwidths of the resonances for the new configuration are known, then the transfer

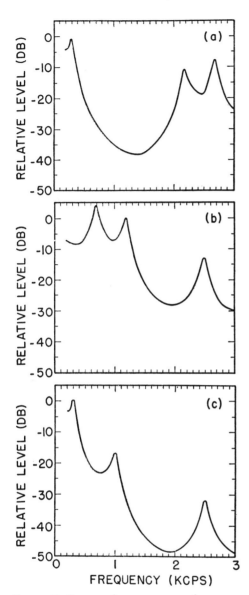

FIGURE 7. Computed spectrum envelopes approximating the vowels /i/, /ɑ/, and /u/. The half-power bandwidths of all resonances were assumed to be 100 cps.

function $T(j\omega)$ can be computed using Equation 5 in the manner discussed above, and the entire spectrum envelope can again be constructed by adding to $T(j\omega)$ (in decibels) the radiation

characteristic and the spectrum envelope of the source. This procedure has been used to construct the three spectrum envelope curves shown in Figure 7. In order to simplify the calculations, the half-power bandwidths of all resonances again were assumed to be 100 cps, a value that is not greatly different from the bandwidths of the first three resonances for spoken vowels (2, *18*, *23*). The three curves correspond roughly to the spectrum envelopes for /i/, /ɑ/, and /u/.

The curves in Figures 6 and 7 demonstrate that the relative amplitudes of the spectral peaks vary markedly depending on the frequencies of the resonances. Consider, for example, spectra (a) and (c) in Figure 7, in which the frequencies of the first and third resonances are roughly the same but the second resonance is at 2 200 cps in one case and 1 000 cps in the other. The amplitude of the third spectral peak is about 24 db higher in spectrum (a) than in spectrum (c) as a result of the difference in the frequencies of the second resonances.

The fact that the amplitudes of the spectral peaks in vowel spectra are predictable when the resonant frequencies are known has been discussed in some detail by Fant (*8*). From theoretical considerations, Fant predicted the amplitudes of the first three spectral peaks of selected vowels and showed that these calculated levels were in good agreement with previously reported measurements of the average levels of the spectral peaks of spoken English and Swedish vowels.

Some insight into the causes for the changes in the amplitudes of the spectral peaks with changes in the resonant frequencies can be gained from re-

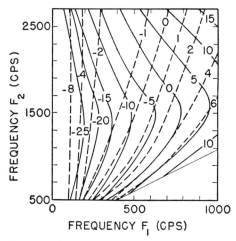

FIGURE 8. Computed isoamplitude contours of the first resonance peak (dashed curves) and second resonance peak (solid curves) for vowel spectrum envelopes as a function of the frequencies of the first and second resonances. Amplitudes are given in decibels relative to the level of the first resonance peak when $F_1 = 500$ cps, $F_2 = 1500$ cps, $F_3 = 2500$ cps, etc. See text for assumptions used in the calculations and for corrections to be applied when the assumptions are not met.

examination of the transfer function for the two-resonator approximation of the vocal tract. It is recalled that the transfer function in Figure 4 was constructed by adding two simple resonance curves of the type shown in Figure 3. In that example the resonant frequency for one component curve was 300 cps and the resonant frequency for the other was 950 cps. If now the frequency F_2 of the second resonance is shifted upwards while the first resonant frequency F_1 is held fixed, then the amplitude of the second peak in the composite curve will decrease. Likewise, if F_2 is held fixed while F_1 is shifted upwards, then the amplitude of the second peak in the composite curve will increase. There will be concomitant changes in the amplitude of the first resonance peak in both these

cases, but these changes will be relatively small. Although the amplitude relations just noted are discussed with reference to the vocal-tract transfer function, the same relations apply to the over-all spectrum envelope, since the source spectrum envelope and the radiation characteristic that are added to the transfer function to obtain the over-all spectrum envelope are independent of changes in the transfer function. Furthermore, these relations apply not only to the two-resonator model but also to the more exact transmission-line model, for which the transfer function is constructed by the addition of many resonance curves.

Calculations of Levels of Resonances. Up to this point it has been assumed tacitly that the spectra under discussion were characterized by resonances, each of which gives rise to a separate peak or prominence at the resonant frequency. When resonant frequencies are sufficiently close, however, they are not necessarily identical with the frequencies of the peaks in the spec-

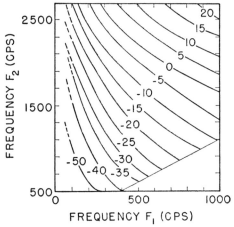

FIGURE 9. Computed isoamplitude contours of the third resonance peak for vowel spectrum envelopes as a function of the frequencies of the first two resonances (see legend Figure 8).

trum. For example, when two resonances with bandwidths of about 100 cps are about 100 cps apart, the spectrum envelope may show only one prominence; the frequency of the peak will be somewhere between the two resonant frequencies. In the discussion that follows, the levels of the resonances will be defined to be the levels of the spectral envelope at the frequencies of the resonances (rather than at the spectral peaks).

The quantitative relations among the levels of the three lowest resonances for a range of values of the frequencies of the first two resonances can be calculated by means of the relations discussed above. Such calculations have been carried out by means of a digital computer, and are depicted by the contour plots shown in Figures 8 and 9. Along any one contour the level of a particular resonance remains constant at the indicated value. In Figure 8, the dashed contours represent loci of constant amplitude of the first resonance, while the other contours represent corresponding loci for the second resonance; the contours in Figure 9 pertain to the third resonance. In both figures the amplitude levels are given in decibels relative to the level of the first resonance when $F_1 = 500$ cps, $F_2 = 1\,500$ cps, $F_3 = 2\,500$ cps, etc.

The following constraints were applied to the generation of the data in Figures 8 and 9. The bandwidths of all resonances were 100 cps. The spectrum envelope of the glottal output was that shown in Figure 2, and the over-all level of the excitation was held constant. The third and higher resonances were held constant at 2 500 cps, 3 500 cps, 4 500 cps, etc., except that $F_3 = F_2 + 500$ cps when F_2 exceeded

2 000 cps and $F_4 = F_3 + 500$ cps when F_3 exceeded 3 000 cps.

The use of the contours is made clear by considering the spectrum envelope associated with the uniform tube, as shown in Figure 6. If the level of the first resonance at 500 cps is the zero db reference, then the level of the second resonance is about -9.5 db and that of the third resonance is about -15 db. In Figure 8, the intersection of $F_1 = 500$ cps and $F_2 = 1\,500$ cps gives levels of zero db and about -9.5 db, respectively; the same operation in Figure 9 provides a level of about -15 db for the third resonance. Similarly the relative levels of the resonances of the three samples in Figure 7 may be read from the contours.

In general the contour plots indicate that the level of a given resonance is influenced strongly by the frequencies of the lower resonances. Thus the level of the second resonance at a given frequency drops sharply when the frequency of the first resonance is decreased; similarly the level of the third resonance is influenced strongly by the frequencies of both the first and second resonances. If the frequencies of two resonances are close together, the levels of both are relatively high, as when F_2 is below 1 500 cps and F_1 is above 500 cps, or when F_2 is above 2 000 cps and F_3 is only 500 cps higher.

Since the contours in Figures 8 and 9 assume that the bandwidths of the various resonances are always 100 cps, a word must be said about the effect of variations from this value. If the bandwidth B of a given resonance differs from 100 cps, then $20 \log_{10} (100/B)$ should be added to the level read from Figure 8 or 9 for that resonance. For example, if the bandwidth of the second resonance of the vowel shown in Figure 6 is narrowed to 70 cps, the correction to be applied is +3 db, and hence the level of the second resonance becomes −6.5 db instead of −9.5 db.

Some Implications of the Theory

A number of measurements pertaining to amplitudes and spectra of speech sounds have been reported in the literature. In particular, studies have been made of frequencies and amplitudes of vowel formants, amplitude relations and formant transitions within syllables, and relative intensities of vowels and consonants. In general, acoustic data of this type have not been organized within a cohesive theoretical framework, except in the technical monograph by Fant which appeared recently (10). The acoustical theory of vowel production outlined above provides such a framework for the discussion of amplitude relations in syllabic nuclei.

Relative Intensities of Vowels. It has long been recognized that different vowels generated with the same vocal effort have different over-all levels (1, 7, 32). The range of over-all levels for the common vowels of American English is roughly 4 to 5 db, with /i/ and /u/ having the lowest levels and /æ/, /ɑ/, and /ɔ/ the highest levels.

An attempt to relate these data to articulation was made by Fairbanks (6), who postulated that vowel intensity should be correlated with the anterior opening of the vocal conduit, and demonstrated such a correlation between two sets of published data. Figure 8 shows that the over-all intensity of a vowel is determined largely by the frequency of the first vowel resonance since the level of that resonance is always greater than that of

TABLE 1. Calculation of the over-all relative intensities of four vowels. The column headings are as follows: *A*, average frequencies of the first and second vowel resonances, in cps (*19*); *B*, relative levels of resonance peaks, in db, derived from Figure 8; *C*, half-power bandwidths of resonances, in cps (*19*); *D*, corrections $10 \log_{10}(100/B)$ db to account for deviation of bandwidths from 100 cps; *E*, relative contributions of resonances to over-all intensity of vowel, in db; *F*, relative intensity of vowels, in db. The assumptions regarding higher formants and glottal spectrum are the same as those used in constructing Figures 8 and 9.

Vowel	A		B	C	D	E	F
i	$F_1 =$	300	− 1.9	50	3.0	1.1	1.3
	$F_2 =$	2 260	−11.0	120	−0.8	−11.8	
æ	$F_1 =$	730	2.0	100		2.0	3.8
	$F_2 =$	1 650	− 1.0	100		− 1.0	
ɑ	$F_1 =$	720	4.2	130	−1.1	3.1	5.6
	$F_2 =$	1 190	1.0	80	1.0	2.0	
u	$F_1 =$	320	− 1.1	60	2.2	1.1	1.2
	$F_2 =$	1 110	−16.0	100		−16.0	

higher resonances. But the frequency of the first resonance is closely related to the size of the mouth opening (see *supra* and *36*), and, therefore, the positive correlation described by Fairbanks can be considered to be a consequence of the acoustical theory.

Quantitative prediction of the overall vowel intensities can be made from the contours of Figure 8. The procedure is first to find the relative levels of the first two resonance peaks, knowing the frequencies of these resonances. For resonance bandwidths of 100 cps, the relative levels given in the contours are identical to the contributions of the individual resonances to the overall vowel intensity. If, however, the bandwidth B of a resonance is different from 100 cps, a correction of 10 $\log_{10}$ (100/B) must be added to determine the contribution of that resonance to the over-all vowel intensity.[2] The over-all relative intensity of the vowel is obtained by summing the contributions of the first two resonances (the contribution of higher resonances will be very small and can be neglected).

Typical calculations for four vowels are shown in Table 1. The values of resonant frequencies and bandwidths represent means for three male talkers who generated the vowels in a large number of consonant contexts. The measurements were made with the aid of a digital computer using spectrum matching techniques, and refer to spectral samples appearing centrally in the

temporal course of the vowel (*19*). The computed values of relative intensity in the right-hand column of the table compare well to previously published measurements of vowel intensity, the range from /u/ to /ɑ/ being 4.4 db. For example, from the data of Sacia and Beck (*32*) a list of these four vowels in order of intensity ('average peak power') would be /uiæɑ/, with 4.8 db difference between the extreme vowels; other experimenters report similar data (*1, 7*).

Amplitude Relations within the Syllable. The motoric description of speech production espoused by Stetson (*35*) defines the so-called releasing and arresting actions of consonants (or of other muscular activity) to constitute the boundaries of the syllable. In a symmetric consonant-vowel-consonant (CVC) syllable, the initial C that releases the syllable is characterized by a vocal-tract constriction that gradually (or abruptly) increases in size, while the final C that arrests the syllable is characterized by a gradual (or abrupt) decrease in the size of a constriction in the vocal tract. During the temporal course of this activity, the vocal tract may be excited by one or more acoustic sources, but typically the central portion of the syllable is characterized by glottal excitation or voice. It has already been noted above that the frequency of the first resonance decreases as the vocal tract becomes more constricted. The amplitude relations depicted in Figure 8 demonstrate, moreover, that the amplitude of the first resonance peak—and consequently the over-all amplitude of the vowel—decreases as F_1 decreases. The rate of decrease becomes more rapid as F_1 falls below 300 cps, that is, as F_1

---

[2] The correction factor to determine the contribution of a resonance to over-all intensity is different from the correction used to find the level of the resonance peak. The over-all intensity is determined by the area under the spectrum envelope, and is a function, therefore, both of the height of the resonance peak and of its width.

assumes values associated with vocal-tract configurations more appropriate to consonant production than vowel production (*37*). In other words, during the course of a typical CVC syllable the acoustical theory predicts that, while the source excitation remains constant, the over-all intensity will build up to a maximum value in a central (vocalic) portion and then decrease.

Stetson and Hudgins (*35*, pp. 179 ff.) have reported data on amplitude fluctuations within the syllable obtained by simultaneous kymographic and spectrographic recordings. These data, together with descriptions of the typical form of oscillographic and graphic level records (*7, 17*), demonstrate that the syllable is characterized by an intensity maximum reached during the central portion of the vowel. The acoustical theory of vowel production, therefore, is compatible both with the motoric point of view regarding syllable production and with the classical statements of inherent and relative sonority and syllabic peaks of prominence (*20*). Hence the so-called 'undulation of prominence' (*20*, p. *55*) that is perceived by the hearer is a reflection both of the acoustic end-product and of the articulatory events responsible for it.

Spectrum Balance in the Vowel. While the over-all vowel intensities discussed above are related primarily to changes in the first vocal-tract resonance, Figures 8 and 9 also demonstrate wide variations in the levels of the second and third resonance peaks as a function of the frequencies of the first two resonances. The variation in the levels of resonance peaks within the vowels of actual speech is well known (*29*), but the dependence of these variations on articulation was not explained adequately until recently (*8*).

The fact that rigorous relations obtain among the levels of the resonance peaks, the frequencies of the resonances, and the articulatory configuration has a bearing on the formulation of theories of vowel perception. The lack of independence among these factors makes it inappropriate to hypothesize that the perception of a vowel is attributable to any one of them to the exclusion of the others. Independent manipulation of these characteristics in experiments using synthetic speech is to be questioned if the results are to be generalized to explain the perception of natural speech.

The attempts made in the past to characterize a vowel in terms of the frequency locations of spectral prominences have focused attention on an aspect of the physical event that may not be clearly observable (*22*), particularly when two resonances are closely spaced in frequency, a resonance has a broad bandwidth, or the amplitude of a resonance is very low. The theoretical discussions above indicate, however, that the presence of a resonance may be signaled not only by spectral prominences but also by amplitude relations within the spectrum envelope. In the spectrum of a vowel /u/, for example, the third resonance is often below the dynamic range of the measuring equipment, while the first two resonances are sometimes not manifested as separate spectral prominences. When it is understood, however, that a low-amplitude third resonance is a consequence of low-frequency first and second resonances the spectrogram is easily interpreted.

On Defining the Formant. The discussions above suggest the need for more precise definitions of some of the traditional terms used by linguists, phoneticians, and other students of speech. One such term, conspicuous because of its almost complete absence in this paper to this point, is the word *formant*.

In the literature the term *formant* has been used principally to indicate a concentration of spectral energy in a narrow frequency region of a speech signal. Futhermore, it generally has been applied only to those portions of the speech signal called voiced, that is, characterized by glottal excitation. When sound spectrograms (intensity-frequency-time displays) are made on an instrument using a broad (300 cps) analyzing filter, the formant structure of continuous speech is displayed as a number of more-or-less horizontal 'bars' (*30*). For any given vocalic sound a number of formants may occur in the frequency range 0 to 4 000 cps, but attention is usually focused on the lowest two or three.

When the term *formant* was proposed originally, it was used to designate a natural frequency (charakteristischer Ton) of the vocal cavities, and a so-called inharmonic theory of vowel production was implied (*15, 16*). Subsequently the term was adopted by the advocates of another theory of production—the harmonic theory—and used to designate the center frequency in a 'tonal domain' contributing to the character of the particular vowel (*38*).

A typical description of a formant was given by Joos (*21*): 'The frequencies corresponding to the centers of the two principal peaks of the [spectrum] profile . . . are called formant 1 and formant 2, respectively.'

Potter and Steinberg (*31*), on the other hand, attempted to specify the measurement procedures used in their investigations as follows: ' . . . we suspect that the ear deals with something akin to effective pitch centers of loudness of the energy concentrations. For our initial work we have adopted as an approximation of such a center, a weighted average of the frequencies of the formant components.'

The problem of defining the formant was confused further by the attempts of investigators to specify variant and invariant formants in speech spectra. Sovijärvi (*34*), for example, reported finding seven variable and 11 fixed formants and attempted to relate each of them to a cavity resonator in the vocal system. More recently, Ochiai and Fukumura (*28*), in an investigation of voice quality, have discussed the probable role of invariant formants. These investigators have complicated the terminological situation still further by using *formant* to refer to a spectral concentration that is manifested when the vowel spectra of a number of subjects are summed graphically.

In view of this historical resumé, the common usage of the term *formant* leaves several questions unanswered. Should the word be applied to energy concentrations in consonant spectra? If so, is it permissible to apply it to both voiced and voiceless consonants? Is it appropriate to refer to the various energy concentrations in the spectrum of a nasalized vowel or a nasal consonant as formants? How can the frequency of a formant be measured precisely? And so on . . . .

It has been recognized (*10, 12, 14*) that the acoustical theory of speech production can provide a precise definition for the term formant. Following Hermann (*15*), it is proposed that a formant be interpreted as a normal mode of vibration of the vocal tract, and formant frequency be defined as the frequency of such a normal mode of vibration. The term formant is applied to the vocal tract in a manner similar to the way in which *pole* is used to characterize an electric network, and implies, therefore, a complex number consisting of a real part (proportional to the formant bandwidth) and an imaginary part (the formant frequency).

This definition of formant means that the vocal tract has formants regardless of its excitation. During the production of certain sounds (notably the vowels) the formants are manifested in the acoustic output as maxima in the spectra. When the formants are reasonably well separated in frequency, and when their bandwidths are not abnormally wide, the frequencies of the spectral maxima are good measures of the formant frequencies. During the production of other sounds (particularly certain consonants) certain normal modes are only weakly excited and will not be immediately apparent in the output spectra. It can be argued, however, that since the vocal tract executes continuous motions during the production of syllables, the formant frequencies are continuous functions of time (*9*).

Defining the formant in terms of articulation raises certain problems of measurement, since usually only the acoustic signal is available for analysis. Traditional spectrographic procedures for measuring formant frequencies of vowels can often lead to reliable data, however, providing that the constraints imposed by the acoustical theory are kept in mind. A more powerful technique should take into account the effect of a given formant on the entire spectrum shape. Such techniques are under development and will provide data relative to consonant as well as vowel production (*10, 13, 14, 19, 25*). It is interesting to note that, as early as 1936, Lewis (*23*) used a technique of matching simple resonance curves to vowel spectra in the vicinity of spectral maxima, thus applying to his measurements some of the constraints imposed by the acoustic theory.

Summary

A contemporary acoustical theory of vowel production is outlined and certain implications of the theory are discussed. The theory considers a vowel sound to be the result of excitation of a linear acoustic system by a quasi-periodic volume velocity source. The transfer function of the acoustic system is completely described by a number of poles whose frequency locations depend on the vocal-tract configuration. It is shown that the theory is compatible with data relevant to the over-all intensity of vowels, amplitude relations within syllables, and questions of balance in the vowel spectrum. Finally it is proposed that the traditional term *formant* be restricted to mean a normal mode of vibration of the vocal system.

Summario in Interlingua

Un contemporaneo acustic theoria de vocal production es contornate e certe implicationes de le theoria esse discutite. Le theoria considera un vocal sono esser le resultato de excitation de un linear acustic systema per un quasi-periodic volumine velocitate fonte. Le transfer function de le acustic systema es describite completemente per un numero de polos cuje frequentia locations depende sur le vocal-tracto configuration. Ille es monstrate que le theoria es compatibile con datos relevante a le supertoto intensitate de vocals, amplitude relations intra syllabas, e questions de balancia in le vocal spectro. Al fin ille es proponite que le traditional vocabulo *forman* esser restringite a significa un normal moda de vibration de le vocal systema.

References

1. BLACK, J. W., Natural frequency, duration, and intensity of vowels in reading. *J. Speech Hearing Dis.*, 14, 1949, 216-221.
2. BOGERT, B. P., On the band width of vowel formants. *J. acoust. Soc. Amer.*, 25, 1953, 791-792.
3. CHIBA, T., and KAJIYAMA, M., *The Vowel, Its Nature and Structure.* Tokyo: Tokyo-Kaiseikan, 1941.
4. DELATTRE, P., The physiological interpretation of sound spectrograms. *Mod. Lang. Ass. Publ.*, 66, 1951, 864-875.
5. DUNN, H. K., The calculation of vowel resonances, and an electrical vocal tract. *J. acoust. Soc. Amer.*, 22, 1950, 740-753.
6. FAIRBANKS, G., A physiological correlative of vowel intensity. *Speech Monogr.*, 17, 1950, 390-395.
7. FAIRBANKS, G., HOUSE, A. S., and STEVENS, E. L., An experimental study of vowel intensities. *J. acoust. Soc. Amer.*, 22, 1950, 457-459.
8. FANT, C. G. M., On the predictability of formant levels and spectrum envelope from formant frequencies. In M. Halle and others, *For Roman Jakobson.* The Hague: Mouton, 1956, pp. 109-120.
9. FANT, C. G. M., Transmission properties of the vocal tract with application to the acoustic specification of phonemes. *Tech. Rep. 12*, Jan. 1952, Acoust. Lab., Mass. Inst. Technol.
10. FANT, G., *Acoustic Theory of Speech Production.* 'S-Gravenhage: Mouton, 1960.
11. FLANAGAN, J. L., Some properties of the glottal sound source. *J. Speech Hearing Res.*, 1, 1958, 99-116.
12. FLANAGAN, J. L., and HOUSE, A. S., Development and testing of a formant-coding speech compression system. *J. acoust. Soc. Amer.*, 28, 1956, 1099-1106.
13. FUJIMURA, O., Spectrum matching of nasal consonants. *J. acoust. Soc. Amer.*, 32, 1960, 1517. Abstract: Analysis of nasal consonants. *Quart. Prog. Rep. 60*, Jan. 15, 1961, pp. 184-188, Res. Lab. Electronics, Mass. Inst. Technol.
14. HEINZ, J. M., and STEVENS, K. N., On the properties of voiceless fricative consonants. *J. acoust. Soc. Amer.*, 33, 1961, 589-596.
15. HERMANN, L., Nachtrag zur Untersuchung der Vocalcurven. *Arch. ges. Physiol.*, 58, 1894, 264-279.
16. HERMANN, L., Weitere Untersuchungen über das Wesen der Vocale. *Arch. ges. Physiol.*, 61, 1895, 169-204.
17. HOUSE, A. S., and FAIRBANKS, G., The influence of consonant environment upon the secondary acoustical characteristics of vowels. *J. acoust. Soc. Amer.*, 25, 1953, 105-113.
18. HOUSE, A. S., and STEVENS, K. N., Estimation of formant band widths from measurements of transient response of the vocal tract. *J. Speech Hearing Res.*, 1, 1958, 309-315.
19. HOUSE, A. S., STEVENS, K. N., and FUJISAKI, H., Automatic measurement of the formants of vowels in diverse consonantal environments. *J. acoust. Soc. Amer.*, 32, 1960, 1517.
20. JONES, D., *An Outline of English Phonetics.* (8th ed.) New York: Dutton, 1956.
21. JOOS, M., Acoustic phonetics. *Language Monogr.*, 23 (suppl. to 24, 1948, 2).
22. LADEFOGED, P., Spectrographic determination of vowel quality. *J. acoust. Soc. Amer.*, 32, 1960, 918-919.
23. LEWIS, D., Vocal resonance. *J. acoust. Soc. Amer.*, 8, 1936, 91-99.
24. LICKLIDER, J. C. R., HAWLEY, M. E., and WALKLING, R. A., Influences of variations in speech intensity and other factors upon the speech spectrum. *J. acoust. Soc. Amer.*, 27, 1955, 207.
25. MATHEWS, M. V., MILLER, JOAN E., and DAVID, E. E., JR., Pitch synchronous analysis of voiced sounds. *J. acoust. Soc. Amer.*, 33, 1961, 179-186.
26. MILLER, R. L., Nature of the vocal cord wave. *J. acoust. Soc. Amer.*, 31, 1959, 667-677.
27. MORSE, P. M., *Vibration and Sound.* (2nd ed.) New York: McGraw-Hill, 1948.
28. OCHIAI, Y., and FUKUMURA, T., Timbre study of vocalic voices. *Mem. Fac. Engng Nagoya*, 5, 2, 1953, 253-280.

29. PETERSON, G. E., and BARNEY, H. L., Control methods used in a study of the vowels. *J. acoust. Soc. Amer.*, 24, 1952, 175-184.

30. POTTER, R. K., KOPP, G. A., and GREEN, HARRIET C., *Visible Speech*. New York: Van Nostrand, 1947.

31. POTTER, R. K., and STEINBERG, J. C., Toward the specification of speech. *J. acoust. Soc. Amer.*, 22, 1950, 807-820.

32. SACIA, C. F., and BECK, C. J., The power of fundamental speech sounds. *Bell Syst. tech. J.*, 5, 1926, 393-403.

33. SONESSON, B., On the anatomy and vibratory pattern of the human vocal folds. *Acta Otolaryng.*, suppl. 156, 1960, 7-80.

34. SOVIJÄRVI, A., Die wechselnden und festen Formanten der Vokale, erklärt durch Spektrogramme und Röntgenogramme der finnischen Vokale. *Proc. Third Cong. Phonet.*, 1939, 407-420.

35. STETSON, R. H., *Motor Phonetics; A Study of Speech Movements in Action*. (2nd ed.) Amsterdam: North-Holland, 1951. (for Oberlin Coll.)

36. STEVENS, K. N., and HOUSE, A. S., Development of a quantitative description of vowel articulation. *J. acoust. Soc. Amer.*, 27, 1955, 484-493.

37. STEVENS, K. N., and HOUSE, A. S., Studies of formant transitions using a vocal tract analog. *J. acoust. Soc. Amer.*, 28, 1956, 578-585.

38. STUMPF, C., *Die Sprachlaute*. Berlin: Springer, 1926.

39. TIMCKE, R., VON LEDEN, H., and MOORE, P., Laryngeal vibrations: Measurements of the glottic wave. Part I. The normal vibratory cycle. *Arch. Otolaryng.*, 68, 1958, 1-19.

40. VAN DEN BERG, JW., Calculations on a model of the vocal tract for vowel /i/ (meat) and on the larynx. *J. acoust. Soc. Amer.*, 27, 1955, 332-338.

41. VAN DEN BERG, JW., Transmission of the vocal cavities. *J. acoust. Soc. Amer.*, 27, 1955, 161-168.

42. VAN DEN BERG, JW., Über die Koppelung bei der Stimmbildung. *Z. Phonet. usw.*, 8, 1954, 281-293.

43. WENDAHL, R. W., Vowel formant frequencies and vocal cavity dimensions. Ph.D. thesis, Univ. Iowa, 1957.

CHAPTER 7

Reprinted from LOGOS, Volume 5, No. 1, Pages 3 to 17, April 1962

DESCRIPTIVE ANALYSIS OF THE ACOUSTIC ASPECTS OF SPEECH[1,2]

C. GUNNAR M. FANT, Sc.D.[3]

Stockholm, Sweden

SPEECH RESEARCH OBJECTIVES

The scientific study of speech is at present in a transitional stage of development. The classical articulatory or rather physiological phonetics dealing mainly with a description of the speech mechanism and with articulatory correlates of phonetic symbols is still the basic source of knowledge in phonetics courses at linguistic faculties, although acoustic phonetics is gaining ground. Acoustic phonetics, dealing with the structure of speech as sound waves and the relations of this structure to any other aspects of the speech communication act, does not lack traditions either. This field is developing rapidly as a result of the last few years' intensified investments in speech research from communication engineering quarters.

One aim of the technical speech research is to lay a foundation for techniques of producing artificial speech and of machine identification of spoken words. Applications such as more efficient speech communication systems, book-reading aids for the blind, and means of visual and tactile recording of speech for communication with the deaf, as well as specific voice controlled automata, are within reach of present technology or may be expected to be so in a not too distant future.

The perfect speech typewriter, representing the engineering criterion of a profound knowledge of the acoustic nature of speech and of dialectal, individual, and contextual variations, is a more distant object — it is rather a symbol of combined efforts in speech research. This profound knowledge does not exist yet.

SPEECH ANALYSIS IN THEORY AND PRACTICE

The techniques of synthesizing speech are already quite advanced. Analysis techniques have not been developed to the same extent, and this is especially true of the analysis directed towards teaching a machine to recognize spoken items. This is not due to lack of research efforts. On the contrary, there is a considerable amount of work undertaken on the use of large digital computers for machine identification of speech, but this work is still in an initial instrumental phase of methodological studies[1]. Phoneme recognizing machines of a simpler analog type have been constructed but their performance has not been very advanced. The possible vocabulary or phoneme inventory has been restricted, and the machines have not responded very well to any one else than "his master's voice"[2,11].

What we really lack is a descriptive study of the visible sound patterns of speech providing an acoustic mapping of the spectrographic correlates to phonetic signs and categories with due regard to particular language, dialectal, individual, and contextual variations. A speech re-

---

1) Paper presented at the Wenner-Gren Foundation for Anthropological Research Symposium on Comparative Aspects of Human Communication at Burg Wartenstein/Austria, September 1960.

2) The research reported in this article has in part been carried out under contract USAF 61(052)-342, and with support by the Swedish State Council of Technical Research.

3) Director of Speech Transmission Laboratory, Royal Institute of Technology, Stockholm, Sweden.

searcher may be well acquainted with the art of synthesizing speech by general rules but the same man is probably not able to decipher the text of a spectrographic record of which he has no a priori information*.

The difficulties may in part be due to technical shortcomings of commercially available spectrographs, but there are other reasons, such as the lack of a rationale for going through the necessary learning process. Small deviations of the visual pattern may be highly significant for phonemic discriminations whereas quite apparent pattern features may be primarily related to accidental voice characteristics of the speaker. A spectrogram provides an over-detailed reference for the formal contents of a speech message. A basic problem in speech analysis is to formulate the complex transforms whereby the phonetically significant aspects may be extracted from the mass of data available. The pioneering work on the establishment of the meta-language of Visible Speech is that of Potter, Kopp, and Green[31]. This is a valuable reference but it has shortcomings such as the restriction of the frequency range to that of telephony, i.e., to approximately 3200 c/s upper limit.

The lack of quantitative data on acoustic correlates of phonetic units is especially great for consonants and the more extensive vowel studies available refer to single stressed test words[2] or to sustained forms[8]. What about the distinctive feature approach by Jakobson, Fant and Halle[18]? Is it not possible to learn to read Visible Speech simply by reference to a maximum of 12 distinctive pattern aspects within any sound? The answer is no. Not without the addition of a considerable amount of linguistically redundant information. The particular choice of features* is supported by the main systematizing principles of classical phonetics. The distinctive features[7,18,19] are described in terms of the articulatory and the corresponding acoustic and perceptual correlates of linguistically relevant spectrographic studies of speech.

The limitations of the preliminary study of Jakobson, Fant and Halle[18] are that the formulations are made for the benefit of linguistic theory rather than for engineering or phonetic applications. Statements of the acoustic correlates to distinctive features have been condensed to an extent where they retain merely a generalized abstraction insufficient as a basis for the quantitative operations needed for practical applications. It should also be remembered that most of the features are relational in character and thus imply comparisons rather than absolute identifications. The absolute references vary with the speaker, his dialect, the context, the stress-pattern, etc., according to normali-

---

*As a matter of fact I have not met one single speech researcher who has claimed he could read speech spectrograms fluently, and I am no exception myself. I only know of the group of subjects at Bell Telephone Laboratories who participated in a Visible Speech learning experiment in 1945. Speech researchers would, however, benefit from going through this learning process. It would, aid them in teaching machines to do the same job.

*A few words may be apropos here to explain the nature of distinctive features. If a minimal difference is found between two phonemes, it is highly probable that the same distinction will recur in several other phoneme pairs. Thus, the difference between /s/ and /f/ is the same as between /z/ and /v/, and between /t/ and /p/, and /d/ and /b/, and between /n/ and /m/. This is the acute/grave distinction according to the terminology of Jakobson, Fant, and Halle. It is similar to and stands in complementary distribution with the distinction between /i/ and /u/, /e/ and /o/, and /ae/ and /a/, which motivates the usage of the same term acute/grave also for vowels. Within the consonants referred to above it is apparent that the relation of /z/ to /s/ is the same as of /v/ to /f/, /b/ to /p/, and /d/ to /t/. The main advantage of the distinctive features approach is that the number of basic signs is minimized. Maximally 12 distinctive features are sufficient for defining any phoneme of most languages.

zation principles which have not been fully investigated.

It should be noted that a specification of speech wave data may be translated to any of an infinite number of alternative forms, each based on a different choice of variables. This is true of instrumental techniques as well as of the technical and conceptual operations performed on the raw material from analysis. A linguist may radically change a specificational system in order to gain a small saving in specificational costs. The minimum redundancy of the system becomes the holy principle and a purpose in itself. The engineer is more interested in the application of the system and will generally accept some redundancy in order to facilitate automatic recognition procedures or to clarify the nature of a distinction. However, in several respects the linguistic and engineering systems should be identical. The more rigidly and unambiguously a linguistic distinction can be correlated to quantitative speech wave data, the more useful it will be for engineering applications. Investigations into the quantitative aspects of formulating distinctive features are much needed. Some experimental work in this direction has been undertaken by Halle and associates[12,15,17].

Speech synthesis is an important tool for testing the relative importance of various aspects of the sound patterns contributing to a distinction. Valuable empirical information on these "cues" and on the general rules for synthesizing speech stems from the well-known work at the Haskins Laboratories[4,24,25]. Similar work is now also under progress at various other places[*].

One of the achievements of acoustic speech research is the study of the analyti-

* Phonetics Department, University of Edinburgh; Massachusetts Institute of Technology, Cambridge/Mass., U.S.A.; Royal Institute of Technology, Stockholm, Sweden.

cal ties between the physiological and the acoustic aspects[7,33,34]. Given the evidence of the dimensions of the vocal cavities, it is possible to calculate the essentials of the spectral properties of the corresponding speech sound. There is also a reverse predictability, though to a lesser extent due to the fact that compensatory forms of articulation can provide rather similar speech wave patterns.

The rules relating speech waves to speech production are in general complex since one articulatory parameter, e.g., tongue height, affects several of the parameters of the spectrogram. Conversely, each of the parameters of the spectrogram is generally influenced by several articulatory variables. However, to establish and learn these analytical ties is by no means a hopeless undertaking. Some elementary knowledge in acoustics is valuable, but the main requirement is a sound knowledge of articulatory phonetics.

TRANSCRIPTION OF SPEECH SPECTROGRAMS

A common observation when spectrograms of ordinary *connected* speech are studied is that modifications and omissions of speech sounds are frequent. Carefully pronounced single testwords and phrases may differ considerably from ordinary speech. These effects may cause transcription difficulties. Shall the investigator transcribe the spectrograms according to the phonemic structure or shall he, according to phonetical principles, write the phonetic symbols of what he hears? A third possibility might be to infer from the spectrogram how the speech has been produced and adapt the transcription thereafter. The latter method is quite feasible in view of the apparent articulatory significance of phonetic symbols, but the technique will have to rely on the use of an extended set of phonetic signs just as the phonetic transcription by ear utilizes a

greater inventory of signs than the phonemic transcription. The choice of system,
phonemic, perceptual, or articulatory, is

primarily a matter of the purpose of the
investigation. The articulatory transcription is a powerful method of checking the

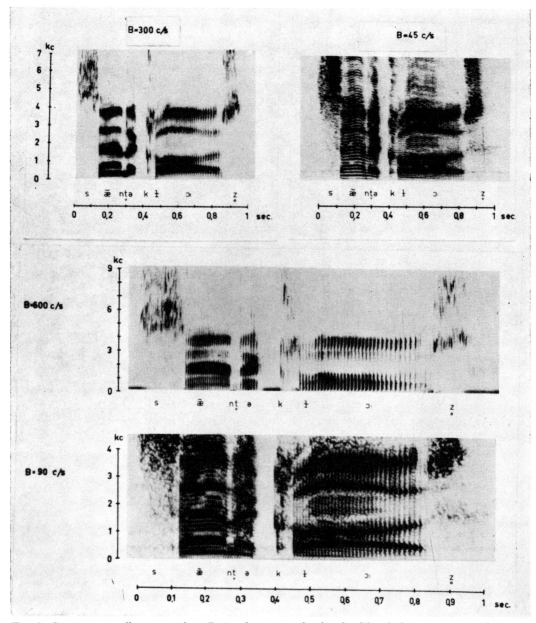

Fig. 1. Spectrograms illustrating the effects of varying the bandwidth of the spectrum analyzer. In
"narrow"-band (B = 45 c/s) analysis (upper right) the harmonics are resolved. In the "broad"-band
(B = 300 c/s) analysis (upper left) the formants are resolved. When the speech material is played
into the analyzer at half speed, the time-scale is stretched by a factor of 2 and all frequencies are
divided by the same factor. The apparent bandwidths of the analyzer then becomes B = 90 c/s and
B = 600 c/s respectively. All spectrograms pertain to one and the same utterance, "Santa Claus".

perceptual transcription and can be utilized once the investigator has become sufficiently accustomed to reading spectrographic patterns.

Fig. 1 exemplifies Visible Speech spectrograms produced with a Sona-Graph analyzer. The text was "Santa Claus" spoken by an American subject*. On the top of the figure there appears the normal broad-band (300 c/s) and the narrow-band (45 c/s) spectrogram. The middle and the bottom spectrograms were made after a speed reduction by a factor of 2 which implies an effective doubling of the filter bandwidths, i.e., 600 c/s and 90 c/s respectively. Normally a broad-band spectrogram shows the formant structure whereas the narrow-band analysis displays a harmonic spectrum. In case of high-pitched voices, however, the 600 c/s-analysis is needed in order to avoid harmonic analysis and retain the formant structure. At a low-pitched interval of speech, on the other hand, the 90 c/s-filter provides an optimal frequency resolution of the formant structure.

The auditive transcription of the utterance was [sǽntə klɔːz]. A segmentation of the spectrum in terms of successive sound intervals, or in other words sound segments, should be performed from the broad-band display and not from the narrow-band display since the latter will tend to smooth out rapid shifts of the spectral composition. The very distinct boundary between the [s] and the [ǽ] in the form of a shift of the spectral energy distribution and the shift from a voiced to an unvoiced sound is typical. Most of the other sound boundaries are also distinct.

As seen from the split first formant the speaker has apparently nasalized the entire [ǽ] in anticipation of the /n/ and there is no separate [t]-segment except for

a weak high frequency burst in the latter part of the [n]-segment. Alternatively, it might be argued that there is no separate [n]-segment, the intended /n/ being signaled by the nasalization of the [ǽ] and of the following voiced nasalized dental stop [ḓ]. Another observation of some interest is that the [z]-segment is devoiced, i.e., no traces of vocal cord vibrations appear within the fricative.

The stop sound [k] of Claus has first a period of silence, the occlusion. Then comes the explosion in the form of a transient and then a continuant noise structure, the latter part of which is merely an unvoiced beginning of the [l]. It has been shown by Truby[35] that the [l] of a cluster [kl] is often fully articulated even before the explosion is released.

The Discrete Versus the Continuous View of Speech

Divergent opinions have been expressed on the nature of speech. The concept of speech as a sequence of discrete units with distinct boundaries joined together as beads on a string is contrasted to the view of speech as a continuous succession of gradually varying and overlapping patterns. This divergency has been discussed by Joos[20], Hockett[16], Halle[13,14], Pike[30], and others. What evidence do we have in favor of one or the other view? Fig. 2 illustrates various concepts. These are from the top:

a) A sequence of ideal non-overlapping phonemes.
b) A sequence of minimal sound segments, the boundaries of which are defined by relative distinct changes in the speech wave structure.
c) One or more of the sound features characterizing a sound segment may extend over several segments.
d) A continuously varying importance function for each phoneme describing the extent of its dependency of particular events within the speech wave. Overlapping curves without sharp boundaries.

The models above may appear to repre-

*General American. The subject was born in Texas.

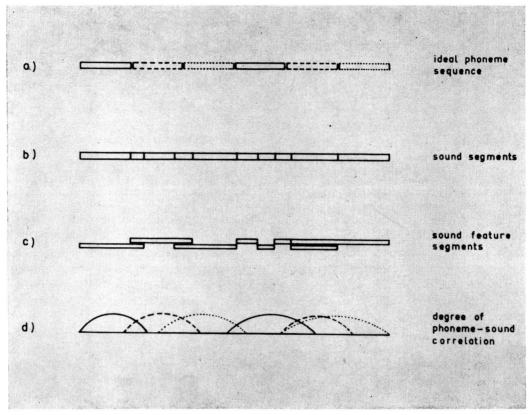

Fig. 2. Schematic representation of sequential elements of speech. a) is the phonemic aspect, b) and c) represent acoustic aspects, and d) shows the degree of phoneme-sound correlation.

sent quite different views of the nature of speech. They are, however, not contradictory in any way. The overlap in the time domain according to d) does not invalidate the concept of the phonemes as discrete and successive in a)[13]. The representation in a) relates to the message aspect of the speech communication whereas representation b) and c) pertain to the speech wave and d) more to the perception of speech.

It is of interest to note that spectrographic pictures of speech often display quite distinct boundaries between successive parts along the time axis. These boundaries are related to switching events in the speech production mechanism such as a shift in the primary sound source, e.g., from voice to noise, or the opening or closing off of a passage within the vocal cavities, the lateral and nasal pathways included. Less distinct sound boundaries may be defined from typical changes in the pattern of formant frequencies. A common aspect of spectrographic records not shown in Fig. 2 is the more or less continuous variation of some of the formants with respect to their frequency locations. Formant frequency patterns may vary within and across sound segment boundaries.

The number of successive sound segments within an utterance is greater than the number of phonemes. Fully developed unvoiced stops, for instance, contain at least two sound segments, the occlusion and the burst, and the latter may be subdivided into an explosion transient and a short fricative. The first part of a vowel following the burst generally assimilates the voicelessness of the preceding sound. It is a matter of convention whether this sound segment is to be assigned to the vowel, or to the preceding "aspirated" consonant.

Sound segments defined from the procedure above may be decomposed into a number of simultaneously present sound features. Boundaries between sound segments are due to the beginning or end of at least one of the sound features but one and the same sound feature may extend over several successive sound segments. One example seen in the spectrogram of Fig. 1 is the nasalization of a vowel adjacent to a nasal consonant. The most common example would be the continuity of vocal cord vibrations over a series of voiced sounds.

Sound segment boundaries should not be confused with phoneme boundaries. Several adjacent sounds of connected speech may carry information on one and the same phoneme, and there is overlapping in so far as one and the same sound segment carries information on several adjacent phonemes. The typical example is the influence exerted by a consonant on a following vowel. The extent to which a phoneme of the message has influenced the physical structure of the speech wave often varies continuously along the sound substance as indicated by Fig. 2 d. One practical method of investigating these dependencies is by means of tape-cutting techniques whereby the removal of a part of the sound substance is correlated with the phonemic discrimination loss*.

---

*See for instance Truby[35] and Öhman[36,37].

POLE-ZERO DESCRIPTIONS OF SPEECH SPECTRA

The engineer's concept of speech is very much influenced by an analytical methodology which has been called analysis-by-synthesis[32]. Any short segment or sample of natural speech may be described in terms of the parameters of a synthesis procedure providing a piece of artificial speech approximating the natural sample with an accuracy which depends on the complexity of the specification.

In one specificational system the spectral energy of a sample is quantitized in terms of the frequency, intensity, and bandwidths of the major energy peaks, the formants. This is the "parallel synthesizer" system in which each formant is fabricated separately and fed in parallel to a mixer. The second system is referred to as the "series synthesizer" scheme in which the output from an electrical analog to the primary sound source is led through a number of consecutive resonance and anti-resonance circuits, the combined filtering effect of which is a good approximation to the filtering of the vocal cavities. Providing the bandwidths of these spectral determinants, in mathematical terminology poles and zeros, are made a unique function of their frequency locations, it follows that formant intensities as well as the intensities at any part of the spectrum will be predictable from the frequency locations of the resonances and the anti-resonances supplemented by the additional information on the intensity and spectral composition of the source[8].

A complete specification thus comprises a statement of the frequencies and bandwidths of each of the poles and zeros of the vocal tract, and the frequencies and bandwidths of each of the poles and zeros of the source. In addition a scale factor representing source-intensity is needed and a statement concerning the nature of the source, whether of voice or noise character and, if voiced, the frequency of the voice fundamental, F_0. Sounds comprising both a noise source and a voice source are regarded as the superposition of two sounds, one voiced and one of noise character.

The filter function of an ideal non-nasalized vowel does not contain any zeros, i.e., anti-resonance effects. The resonance frequencies of the vocal tract, i.e., the pole frequencies, are labeled F_1, F_2, F_3, F_4, etc. The term F-pattern has been suggested as the compound term for a specification of these frequencies[6,7,8].

As viewed from X-ray moving film, articulation is a continuity of movements. The resulting continuous variations in the dimensions of the vocal cavities determine uniquely the variations of the vocal tract resonance frequencies, the F-pattern. There is thus a continuity of F-pattern within any length of utterance and across any sound segment boundary. However, some boundaries are set by a rapid shift of the F-pattern.

The transitional cues whereby a consonant vowel may in part be identified by its influence on an adjacent vowel may thus be described in terms of F-pattern variations. The term "hub" from the book *Visible Speech*[31] is thus identical with F_2.

Only in non-nasalized, non-lateral sounds produced from a source located at a vibrating or a narrow glottis can the F-pattern up to F_3 be seen with optimal clarity. Under these circumstances the vocal tract filter function does not possess any zeros. When the source is located higher up in the vocal tract there will appear zeros at approximately the same frequencies as the poles representing the resonances of the cavities behind the consonantal constriction. The spectral contribution of a pole and a zero of the same complex frequency amounts to nothing,

i.e., the pole-zero pair may be removed from the specification without any effect on the spectrum of the sound to be synthesized. In these instances the pole and the zero are "bound". Those poles which represent the resonance frequencies of the cavities in front of the source, on the other hand, are "free" from adjacent zeros and thus appear as formants in the spectrum of the sound. There are also "free zeros" which depend on the geometry of the back cavities including those parts of the constriction which lie behind the source. The free zeros may under favorable conditions be seen as spectral minima in an amplitude-frequency display.

The alternative condition for the appearance of zeros in the specification of the vocal tract filter function, is that the sound propagated from the vocal cord source to the lips is shunted by the nasal cavities. Similarly, the nasal output of a sound segment of nasal murmur is submitted to the shunting effects of the mouth cavity as a side chamber. A third possibility is in the production of an [l]-sound. The laterally propagated sound is submitted to some degree of frequency selective shunting by the mouth cavity behind the tongue.

The addition of a shunting cavity system introduces not only zeros but also extra poles. The first nasal resonance indicated by FN1 in the spectrogram of Fig. 1 is thus an extra formant. The associated zero probably located between FN1 and F1 causes a marked decrease of the intensities of both these formants. The other pole-zero pairs of the nasalization do not radically change the phonetic value of the vowel.

If the mouth and nose outlets are closed, there is still some sound propagated through the vibrating walls of the vocal cavities. This is the case of the voiced occlusion of stop sounds. The second and third formants of the voiced occlusion are generally very weak and thus below the reproduction threshold of the spectrograph. If the mouth passage is gradually opened from the closed state to a merely constricted state as in voiced fricatives, there is a gradual rise in the intensities of the higher formants. This rise continues with an increasing mouth-opening and is followed by a shift up in frequency of the first formant. An octave increase in F_1 is correlated with $+12$ dB increase in the whole spectrum level above F_1[21].

Spectral descriptions in terms of poles and zeros are the results of a processing of the primary data from spectrum analysis which is performed either by means of a digital computer or by means of a series connected speech synthesizer. A third method would be to perform the matching by paper and pencil and an inventory of resonance and anti-resonance curves.

It should be noted that the analysis-by-synthesis approach even without a detailed matching procedure allows a reader of spectrograms to avoid errors in the identification of the particular type and order number of a formant and increases the accuracy in the estimation of formant frequencies. The mere knowledge of the interrelations between frequencies of formants and the relative levels to be expected within a spectrum is an insurance against errors*.

In most studies for phonetic descriptive purposes, vowels and other zero-free sounds can be described by an F-pattern alone. The source characteristics are generally of very small interest. An exception is F_0, the frequency of the voice fundamental. When zero-functions are to be avoided, the spectra of other sounds are specified in terms of frequencies and intensities of major formants or by some other approximation. The F-pattern should be stated in addition. If the F-pattern formants are not directly observable in the spectrum of the particular sound segment it might be possible to interpolate these frequencies from the F-pattern variations in adjacent sound segments.

A TENTATIVE SYSTEM OF SPEECH SEGMENT CLASSIFICATION

Speech can be divided into a sequence of sound segments the acoustic boundaries of which are definable either from specific articulatory events or from the corresponding time-selective changes in the spectral composition of the speech wave. The following is an attempt to describe the possible structure of these elementary constituents of the speech wave as a basis for phonetic descriptive work and automatic recognition schemes. The classification of sound segments and their sound features should be detailed enough to provide correlates to any category of interest, thus not only to phonemic units. This is the difference of the present approach to that of the earlier work by Jakobson, Fant and Halle[18].

As discussed above, a sound segment is of the dimension of a speech sound or smaller and there may occur several successive sound segments within the time interval of the speech wave traditionally assigned to the phoneme. The number of successive sound segments within an utterance is therefore generally larger than the number of successive phonemes, as conceptually indicated in Fig. 2.

When sound segments are decomposed into bundles of simultaneous sound features it is often seen that a single sound feature carrying a minimal distinction may extend

---

*I know of several vowel studies providing data on formant frequencies which are invalidated by an inability of the investigator to keep track of one and the same formant within a series of vowel sounds. Nasal formants are often confused with the F-pattern formants. Similar difficulties exist in automatic formant-tracking schemes.

over all sound segments of importance for a phoneme, including sound segments which essentially belong to adjacent phonemes. A typical example of this is the GA /r/ phoneme the retroflexion (acoustically low frequency F_3) of which generally modifies neighboring sounds. In other instances, such as the voiced/voiceless distinction, it can be the sound segment of adjacent phonemes that carry the major part of the relevant sound feature (the lengthening of a preceding vowel is a voicing cue of intervocalic consonants).

The acoustic basis for identification of sound features and for the establishment of fine gradations and subdivisions within a sound segment of arbitrary composition can be stated in terms of the following parameters, most of which are time variable within a sound segment.

SPEECH PARAMETERS

1. Segment duration.
2. Source intensity (short-time sample of a specified time location within the segment).
3. Source energy (product of segment duration and the time average of source intensity within the segment).
4. Source spectrum (either a short-time sample or the time average of the source intensity-frequency distribution within the segment).
5. Voice fundamental frequency, F_0.
6. F-pattern (= F_1, F_2, F_3, etc.).
7. Sound intensity (short-time sample of a specified location within the segment).
8. Sound energy (product of segment duration and the time average of sound intensity within the segment).
9. Sound spectrum (either a short-time sample or the time average of sound intensity-frequency distribution within the segment).

It has not been attempted to select a set of independent measures in this list, but rather to exemplify what sort of basic data is made use of in acoustic specifications.

The source characteristics have to be determined by removal of the formant structure from the sound. As indicated in the previous section this is done by spectrum-matching or inverse-filtering techniques, in

more general terminology by means of analysis-by-synthesis techniques.

The first step in the analysis of a sound segment according to the proposed scheme would be a classification in terms of a set of primary features which will be called the *segment type features*. For convenience, these features are referred to by speech production terminology and are to be considered as binary in nature, i.e., expressing presence versus absence of a specific quality. In this respect they reflect the constraints of the human speaking mechanism and correspond to what is commonly referred to as "manner of production". The second step in the analysis of a sound segment is essentially a classification in terms of the "place of articulation". The term *segment pattern features* is adopted here in order to form a more general concept applicable to both articulatory and speech wave phenomena.

LIST OF SEGMENT TYPE FEATURES

Feature number	Feature
	Source features
1	voice
2	noise
3	transient
	Resonator features
4	occlusive
5	fricative
6	lateral
7	nasal
8	vowellike
9	transitional
10	glide*

As indicated in the list of segment type features above, there are three possible sound sources supplying the primary acoustic energy of a speech sound segment. These are *voice* (vocal cord vibrations), *noise* (random noise from turbulent airflow through narrow passages and past sharp obstacles), and *transient* (single shock excitation of the vocal cavities). The

---

*In a recent publication it has been considered desirable to omit feature 10 since it may be included in feature 9. See Fant, Lindblom[10].

transient is due to the sudden release of an over-pressure or a sudden checking of an airflow at any obstruction in the vocal cavities, the vocal cords included. In this sense, voice is identical to quasi-periodically repeated transients. In a broad-band spectrogram of a voiced stop the transient is seen as an additional vertical striation which is non-synchronous with the pitch pulses. Additional noise may also be found in this explosion segment, though of less duration than in an unvoiced stop. In an unvoiced stop the transient precedes a noise interval of fricative or aspirative (vowellike) type. The duration of the interval is not the duration of the transient source, which is very small, but the duration of the damped oscillations excited by the transient. When these extend into the following noise interval there is overlap, i.e., co-occurrence of noise and transient. The typical example of co-occurrence of voice and noise is in voiced fricatives. There is a tendency of the voicing to dominate in the early part and the noise in the later part of the fricative. The extreme case of separate sound segments was pointed out in connection with the [z] of Fig. 1.

The resonator features are on the whole independent of the source features. In one and the same sound segment it is possible to find almost any combination of the segment type features. The possible co-occurrences and their statistics have not been studied in detail yet. The resonator features may be described at the level of speech production as follows.

SPEECH PRODUCTION CORRELATES

4. *Occlusive:* Complete closure in the mouth or in the pharynx.

5. *Fricative:* Very narrow passage for the air stream at an obstructed region of the mouth or the pharynx.

6. *Lateral:* Central closure combined with lateral opening in the mouth cavity.

7. *Nasal:* Nasal passages connected to the rest of the vocal system owing to a lowered velum.

8. *Vowellike:* Free passage for the air stream through the pharynx and the mouth cavities.

9. *Transitional:* The articulators moving at a high speed within the segment.

10. *Glide:* The articulators moving at a moderate speed within the segment.

The speech wave correlates of the resonator features may be described as follows:

4. *Occlusive:* The spectrum of a voiced non-nasal occlusive is dominated by a formant F1 of a very low frequency F_1 (the voice bar). However, with considerable high-frequency pre-emphasis it may be possible to detect F2 and F3.

5. *Fricative:* Spectra of voiced fricatives can display the whole F-pattern up to F4 but with less intensity and a lower frequency F_1 than vowellike sounds. A fricative produced with a supraglottal noise source is recognized by a high-frequency noise area in the spectrum. Compared with an unvoiced vowellike sound of a similar articulation, the fricative spectrum displays a larger high-frequency emphasis. The typical fricative is a noise sound, the spectral energy of which is largely contained in formants from cavities in front of the articulatory narrowing.

6. *Lateral:* Sound segments of lateral articulation produced with a voice source possess the vowellike feature except for a reduction of either second, third, or fourth formant intensity due to the first zero of the shunting mouth cavity behind the tongue. An additional high-frequency formant is generally seen. The oral break provides a typical discontinuity in the connection to a following vowel. The lateral sound segment is generally, but not always, of lower frequency F_1 than a following or preceding vowel.

7. *Nasal:* A voiced occlusive nasal (nasal murmur) is characterized by a spectrum in which F2 is weak or absent. A formant at approximately 250 c/s dominates the spectrum, but several weaker high-frequency formants (not always seen in spectrograms) occur, one typically at 2200 c/s. These higher formants are generally weaker than for laterals. The bandwidths of nasal formants are generally larger than in vowellike sounds. Voiced vowellike nasal sounds (nasalized vowels) possess the nasal characteristics as a distortion superimposed on the vowel spectrum. Typical nasalization cues are addition of the first nasal resonance in the region below the first formant of the vowellike sound and simultaneous weakening and shift up in frequency of the first formant, F_1.

8. *Vowellike:* The F-pattern formants are clearly visible in the spectrogram. In the case of voiced or unvoiced vowellike sounds produced with a glottal source it is required that at least F1 and F2 be detectable. F3 should also be seen providing F_1 and F_2 are not located at their extreme low frequency limits. A specific feature of sounds produced with a glottal source is that the relative formant levels are highly predictable from

the particular F-pattern, i.e., from the formant frequency locations[°]. Vowellike noise sounds produced from a supraglottal source possess a rather weak first formant, F_1. This is especially the case with [h]-segments produced with a tongue articulation of a high front vowel. Unless the fricative feature is superimposed there should not occur a prominent high-frequency noise area in the sound spectrum.

9. *Transitional:* The spectrum changes at a relatively fast rate in the segment. The first part of a vowel following a voiced stop or nasal is characterized by a rapid change in at least one formant frequency, e.g., F_1. The transitional sound segment ends where the major part of the formant transition is completed.

10. *Glide:* The spectrum changes at a relatively slow rate but faster than for a mere combination of two vowels. Variants of [r] [l] [j] [w] sounds occur as glides.

SEGMENT PATTERN FEATURES

ARTICULATION	SPEECH WAVE
11. Tongue fronted	F_2-F_1 large.
a) Prepalatal position	F_2 high, F_3 maximally high.
b) Midpalatal position	F_2 maximally high and close to F_3.
12. Tongue retracted	F_2-F_1 small. F_1 comparatively high.
13. Mouth-opening (including tongue section and lips) narrow	F_1 low.
14. Lips relatively close and protruded (small lip-opening area)	F_1+F_2+F_3 lower than with a larger lip-opening and the same tongue articulation. A progressing lip closure alone causes a decrease in each of F_1, F_2, and F_3 but with varying amounts depending on the particular tongue position. The effect on F_3 is pronounced in case of prepalatal tongue positions.
15. Retroflex modification	
a) Alveolar articulation	F_4 low and close to F_3.
b) Palatal articulation	F_3 low and close to F_2.
16. Bilabial or labiodental closure	F_2 in the region of approximately 500-1500 c/s depending on the tongue location of the associated vowel or vowellike segment. A palatal tongue position favors high F_2. The noise spectrum of the fricative [f] is essentially flat and of low intensity.
17. Interdental articulation	F_2 1400-1800 c/s. Fricative noise of [θ] much weaker than for [s] and with a more continuous spectrum. Center of gravity is higher than for the labiodental fricative [f].
18. Dental or prealveolar articulation	F_2 in the region of 1400-1800 c/s, F_3 high. Fricative noise strong. The main part of the [s]-energy is above 4000 c/s. This cutoff frequency is lower for alveolar than for dentals.
19. a) Palatal retroflex articulation	F_3 low. The fricative noise of [ʂ] is of high intensity and is carried by F_3 and F_4.
b) Palatal articulation with tip of tongue down	F_2 and F_3 high. Strong fricative noise centered on F3 and F4 and also on F2 providing the tongue pass is sufficiently wide. The lower frequency limit of [ç] noise is higher than for retroflex sounds.
20. Velar and pharyngeal articulation	F_2 medium or low. A large part of the fricative noise is carried by F2. The F-pattern except F1 is clearly visible.
21. Glottal source	The entire F-pattern including F1 is visible.

[°]An alternative to the *vowellike* feature would accordingly be *zero-free* which on the speech production level implies non-nasalized, non-lateral, glottis source sound, acoustically correlated to the predictability of formant levels from the F-pattern. An apparent F1 would be one necessary condition. A second alternative would be to retain the term *vowellike* but restrict the feature to glottal sources, in which case the first formant F1 must be present. However, in case of both whispered vowels and [h]-sounds articulated with the tongue in an [i]-position it is highly probable that supraglottal sources exist alone or in addition to glottal sources. This would lead to the classification of some whispered vowels and [h]-sounds as vowellike and other as non-vowellike. The best choice among these alternatives has to be determined from experience.

The existence of *complex articulations* should be kept in mind. The most apparent example referred to above is the freedom of the tongue to take any position during lip closure which makes the F-pattern of labials variable. In dentals the back of the tongue is partially free to approach the back wall of the pharynx which lowers F_2 and increases F_1. This is the case of the "dark 1". The articulatory contrast between a wide unobstructed and a narrow divided pharynx, resulting in a high versus a low F_2, is the counterpart of the hard/soft distinction in Russian consonants.

The Normalization Problem

The phonetic identity of a speech sound is to some extent dependent on the sound context, that is, formant frequencies within a sound segment have to be judged by reference to the average formant frequencies of the speaker and to have his voice fundamental frequency. Variational features are in some respects more essential than the absolute characteristics of the speech wave. This fact is confirmed by experiments with synthetic speech[23].

An international standard of phonetic pronunciation norms could be established by reference to a few selected speakers. For the Cardinal vowels the pronunciation of Daniel Jones has been considered authoritative[21,22]. Another alternative is synthetic speech[3]. The quality of synthetic speech[8] can be made sufficiently high to fulfill the minimum requirements of naturalness. The advantage compared with real speech would be that the acoustic specification could be made more exact.

A more difficult task is to establish a unique code between the measurable parameters of any sample of live speech and its absolute phonetic quality[28]. The analysis-by-synthesis approach[32] would be to specify the sample by the parameters of synthesis providing equal phonetic quality.

We would also like to be able to predict these settings from the available data inherent in the speech wave. However, normalization techniques have not developed far enough yet even for the simpler task of machine identification of the phonemic structure of a spoken message.

One of the most important factors involved in normalization is to take into account the influence of the size of the speaker's vocal tract. The F-pattern frequencies are to a first approximation inversely proportional to the length of the speaker's vocal tract from the glottis to the lips. Children have smaller heads than adults and their formant frequencies are thus on the average higher. The average female-male difference is of the order of 20%. However, normalization is not merely a question of a constant scale factor.

Summary

This article aims at summarizing the present status of speech analysis techniques, specifically spectrographic analysis. Special attention is given to the problems of segmenting speech into successive phonetic elements and to the categorization of such minimal sound segments in terms of segment type (manner of production) and segment pattern (place of articulation). For this purpose the relations between the physiological parameters of speech and corresponding acoustic speech wave characteristics have been summarized in the form of a dictionary.

It is pointed out that segment boundaries are associated with changes in the manner of production (voiced/voiceless, fricative/non-fricative, nasal/non-nasal, etc.) whereas the place of articulation determines acoustic patterns that vary more or less continuously within and across segment boundaries. There are as a rule a larger number of sound segments than phonemes in any utterance. For this reason and because of coarticulation effects any phoneme is generally signalled by several successive sound segments. Conversely, any sound segment is generally influenced by several adjacent phonemes of the speech message transcription.

REFERENCES

1. David, E. E., Jr.: Artificial Auditory Recognition in Telephony. IBM J. 2, 1958, 294-309.
2. Davis, K. H., Biddulph, R. and Balashek, S.: Automatic Recognition of Spoken Digits, in Communication Theory, ed. W. Jackson, London, 1953, 433-441.
3. Delattre, P., Liberman, A. M. and Cooper, F. S.: Voyelles synthétiques a deux formantes et voyelles cardinales. Maître Phonétique, 96, 1951, 30-36.
4. Delattre, P., Liberman, A. M. and Cooper, F. S.: Acoustic Loci and Transitional Cues for Consonants. J. Acoust. Soc. Am. 27, 1955, 769-773.
5. Fant, C. G. M.: On the Predictability of Formant Levels and Spectrum Envelopes from Formant Frequencies. For Roman Jakobson, 's-Gravenhage, 1956, 109-120.
6. Fant, C. G. M.: Modern Instruments and Methods for Acoustic Studies of Speech. Proc. of VIII Internat. Congr. of Linguistics, Oslo. Oslo, 1958, 282-358; and Acta Polytechnica Scandinavica Ph 1 (246/1958).
7. Fant, C. G. M.: Acoustic Theory of Speech Production. 's-Gravenhage, 1960.
8. Fant, C. G. M.: Acoustic Analysis and Synthesis of Speech with Applications to Swedish. Ericsson Technics, 15, No. 1, 1959, 3-108.
9. Fant, C. G. M.: Phonetics and Speech Research, invited paper presented at the International Conference on Research Potentials in Voice Physiology, Syracuse, N. Y., May 29-June 2, 1961; to be publ. in the Proc. from this conference.
10. Fant, C. G. M. and Lindblom, B.: Studies of Minimal Speech Sound Units. Speech Transmission Laboratory, Quarterly Progress and Status Report No. 2/1961, 1-11.
11. Fry, D. B. and Denes, P.: The Solution of Some Fundamental Problems in Mechanical Speech Recognition. Language and Speech, 1, 1958, 35-38.
12. Halle, M.: The Sound Pattern of Russian. 's-Gravenhage, 1959.
13. Halle, M.: The Strategy of Phonemics. Word, 10, 1954, 197-209.
14. Halle, M.: Review of Manual of Phonology by C. F. Hockett. J. Acoust. Soc. Am. 28, 1956, 509-511.
15. Halle, M., Hughes, C. W. and Radley, J. P.: Acoustic Properties of Stop Consonants. J. Acoust. Soc. Am. 29, 1957, 107-116.
16. Hockett, C. F.: Manual of Phonology. Indiana Univ. Publications in Anthropology and Linguistics, No. 11, Bloomington, 1955.
17. Hughes, C. W. and Halle, M.: Spectral Properties of Fricative Consonants. J. Acoust. Soc. Am. 28, 1956, 303-310.
18. Jakobson, R., Fant, C. G. M. and Halle, M.: Preliminaries to Speech Analysis. M.I.T. Acoustics Lab. Tech. Rep. No. 13, 1952; 3rd printing.
19. Jakobson, R. and Halle, M.: Fundamentals of Language. 's-Gravenhage, 1956.
20. Joos, M.: Acoustic Phonetics. Language, 24, 1948, 1-136.
21. Ladefoged, P.: The Classification of Vowels. Lingua, 5, 1956, 113.
22. Ladefoged, P.: The Perception of Vowel Sounds. Edinburgh, 1959, Ph.D. Thesis, Univ. of Edinburgh.
23. Ladefoged, P. and Broadbent, D. E.: Information Conveyed by Vowels. J. Acoust. Soc. Am. 29, 1957, 98-104.
24. Liberman, A. M.: Some Results of Research on Speech Perception. J. Acoust. Soc. Am. 29, 1957, 117-123.
25. Liberman, A. M., Ingemann, F., Lisker, L., Delattre, P. and Cooper, F. S.: Minimal Rules for Synthesizing Speech. J. Acoust. Soc. Am. 31, 1959, 1490-1499.
26. Miller, R. L.: Auditory Tests with Synthetic Vowels. J. Acoust. Soc. Am. 25, 1953, 114-121.
27. Olson, H. F. and Belar, H.: Phonetic Typewriter. J. Acoust. Soc. Am. 28, 1956, 1072-1081.
28. Peterson, G. E.: The Information Bearing Elements of Speech. J. Acoust. Soc. Am. 24, 1952, 629-637.
29. Peterson, G. E. and Barney, H. L.: Control Methods Used in a Study of the Vowels. J. Acoust. Soc. Am. 24, 1952, 175-184.
30. Pike, K. L.: Language as Particle, Wave and Field. The Texas Quarterly II, 1959, 37-54.
31. Potter, R. K., Kopp, A. G. and Green, H. C.: Visible Speech. New York, 1947.
32. Stevens, K. N.: Toward a Model for Speech Recognition. J. Acoust. Soc. Am. 32, 1960, 47-55.
33. Stevens, K. N. and House, A. S.: Development of a Quantitative Description of Vowel Articulation. J. Acoust. Soc. Am. 27, 1955, 484-493.
34. Stevens, K. N. and House, A. S.: Studies of Formant Transitions Using a Vocal Tract Analog. J. Acoust. Soc. Am. 28, 1956, 578-585.
35. Truby, H. M.: Acoustico-Cineradiographic

Analysis Considerations with especial reference to certain consonantal complexes. Acta Radiologica, Suppl. 182, Stockholm, 1959, Ph.D. Thesis, Univ. of Lund.

36. Öhman, S.: On the Contribution of Speech Segments to the Identification of Swedish Consonant Phonemes. Speech Transmission Laboratory, Quarterly Progress and Status Report No. 2, 1961, pp. 12-15.

37. Öhman, S.: Relative Importance of Sound Segments for the Identification of Swedish Stops in VC and CV Syllables. Speech Transmission Laboratory, Quarterly Progress and Status Report No. 3, 1961, pp. 6-14.

Author's address: Kungl. Tekniska Högskolan, Stockholm 70, Sweden.

PART II

Acoustic Structure of Speech

CHAPTER 8

Reprinted from WORD
Vol. 4, No. 2, August, 1948

RESONANCE DATA CONCERNING NASALS, LATERALS AND TRILLS

THOMAS TARNÓCZY

1. The oscillograms of nasals and of sounds like L and R exhibit many traits similar to those of vowels. Thus we see that the curves are periodic and the periods are, usually, typical of the sound in question. Noises are rather rare. The resonant character of these sonants is thus beyond doubt and the methods applied in the investigation of vowels appear to be expedient in this case.

According to *Helmholtz'* theory of formation of vowels, the vibration of the vocal cords rich in harmonics (the *cord-tone*) is altered as to its composition by the resonant effect of the cavities above the vocal cords. The resonator cavities amplify the harmonics vibrating at certain frequencies, the positions of which constitute those of the formants. There are two methods of determining the properties of the formant positions, i.e. the data concerning the resonance of the sound-producing cavities:[1]

(a) the intensity of the harmonics is determined by analyzing the oscillograms of the sounds; if this analysis is performed for different fundamental tones, the extreme points of all harmonic amplitudes will form the resonance curve of the cavities;

(b) by a short sound-pulse (such as knocking at the cheek or electric spark in the mouth) the sound-producing cavities can be made to bring forth their own inherent tone; these 'decaying' vibrations can be fixed with the oscillograph to determine their resonance characteristics.

The value of the data determined according to (b) will depend on the glottis being open or closed during the decay experiment. The values obtained when the glottis is closed will correspond to those obtained by method (a), whereas an open glottis will entail a higher resonance position and a slighter damping. Such data are obtained by the analysis of resonance sounds whispered (or unvoiced).

As far as the sounds analyzed by us are concerned, it is difficult to make the cavities bring forth decaying free vibrations. Only the oscillograms of voiceless R gave good results, whereas the data obtained from decaying L-like sounds were less satisfactory. Therefor I preferred to apply the method described under (a).

2. I photographed the acoustic picture of the sounds from the screen of a cathode-ray oscillograph upon a permanently moving cardiograph paper. Then I analyzed the sound curves by the Fourier method, with certain modifications.[2] Finally I checked the results by examining the distribution of energy among the sounds thru octave filters and by analyzing the curves thus obtained. The formant details could thus be discerned more exactly.

---

[1] For methods and experiments cp. earlier papers by the author.: *Studia 2 Inst. Linguist. et Phonet.* (Budapest 1941); *Akust. Z.* 8.22, 169 (1943); *Arch. Sprach- und Stimmphysiol.* 6.35 (1942-3).

[2] *Akust. Z.* 8.22.

The results were obtained from 120 analyzed curves of spoken and sung voices of altogether six persons.   One of the six persons was a bass, three were baritones

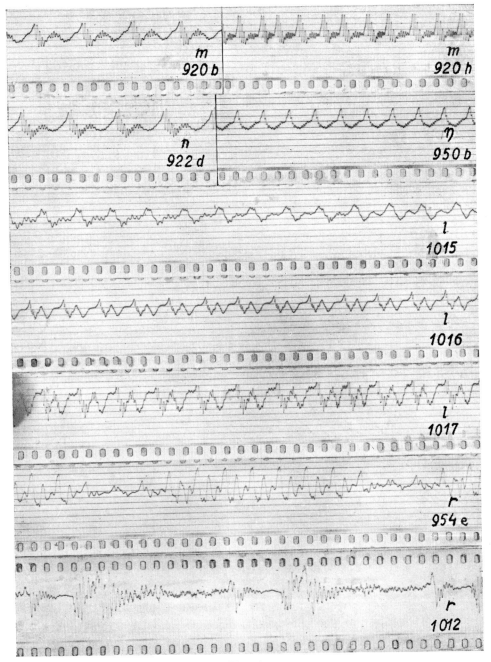

FIG. 1

and two mezzosopranos.   The male singing voices were at 100–260 cps (vibrations per second), the female ones at 200–480 cps.   The spoken text consisted of sequences of sounds repeatedly pronounced (e.g. mama, lili, ruru) and of a few longer words.

3. The results we may expect for the nasals cannot be so clear as those found for the vowels. There are elements in the sound itself that are not of purely

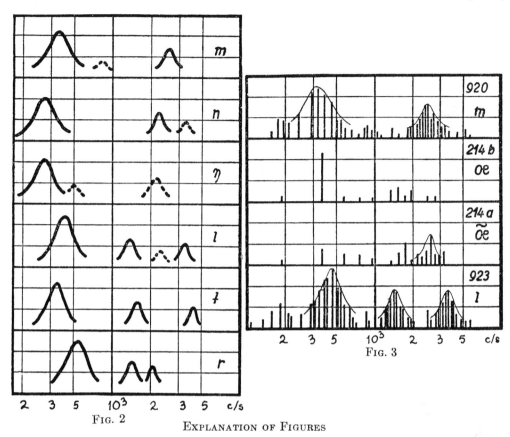

Fig. 2

Fig. 3

EXPLANATION OF FIGURES

Fig. 1. Oscillograms of the sounds studied. The numbers appearing on the oscillograms indicate the sequence of the curves drawn up. Data:

 920b sung *m*, 136 cps, XI male voice
 920h sung *m*, 250 cps, XI male voice
 922d sung *n*, 150 cps, XI male voice
 950b sung *ŋ* 138 cps, VI male voice
 1015–7 spoken *l*, 160 cps, VI male voice in the words *lulu, lala, lili.*
 954e voiced r, 244 cps, VI male voice
 1012 unvoiced r, 244 cps, VI male voice

Fig. 2. General formant curve of all sounds studied. The dotted lines represent the indeterminate formants.

Fig. 3. How the resonance curves really develop from the series of spectra. The resonance curves of *m* and *l* are composed of five series each, *œ* and *œ̃* are the analyses of one fundamental sound. The protuberant formant characteristic of the nasals clearly appears in the *œ̃* curve.

resonant origin. Passing thru complicated and narrow passages, the 'free air'— i.e. the air the current energy of which is not transformed into acoustic energy— will cause noises owing to friction.

The curves obtained during the permanently voiced pronunciation or singing of *m*, *n* and ŋ are represented in Fig. 1. The mere form of the oscillogram reveals a close relation between these sounds; this is confirmed by the results obtained for the formants.   Both *m* and *n* gave rather typical resonance curves, whereas ŋ contained comparatively many noises.   I also took some ɲ curves, but failed in analyzing them.   Controls performed with an octave filter show as a certain *i* character of the ɲ, i.e. a formant over 4000 cps.   We also observe nasality, which, according to the analysis of other nasals, ranks at about 2500 cps.

Fig. 2 summarizes the formants, i.e. the resonance curves of the sound-producing cavities.   The lower formants correspond very well to the particulars given by *Fletcher*.[3]   The 600 cps maximum, which, according to *Fletcher*, is characteristic of the resonance of the nasal cavities, is in my experiments missing or is incomplete, whereas there is a marked upper resonance of *m* and *n*.   According to Sovijärvi,[4] it is these resonances that originate from the nasal cavities.   I share Sovijärvi's opinion—apart from the fact that he has found three different formants of respectively 2000, 2500 and 3000 cps, whereas I have found only one formant—which I have confirmed by speaking certain vowels both in a normal and in a nasalized form into the microphone.   Nasalization called forth the above-mentioned upper formant.   This was confirmed by investigation performed with the octave filter.   The second and third curves on Fig. 3 are the results of the analysis of œ and æ̃ sung at the same pitch.

The damping of the cavities may be expressed with the *logarithmic decrement* (Λ).   I calculated the logarithmic decrement from the breadth of the resonance curves by the vowels in my previously mentioned papers.   Where the resonance curve seemed to be suited for this method, I applied it for the determination of the decrement of the cavities which produce the nasals.   Once the decrement and the resonance frequency are known, we can determine the *decay period* (τ), that is the time during which the amplitude of the free vibration decaying in the cavities is reduced to one thousandth of its original value.   The knowledge of this time is very important in the analysis of the oscillograms.

All resonance particulars concerning the nasals are compiled in Table I. Bracketed data concern formants appearing at indeterminate places.   The resonance frequencies (μ_0) and the other resonance data given in the Table are average values of all cases analyzed.   Regarding the pronunciation of the persons experimented on and the limits of the intelligibility of the sounds, the formants varied ±20 per cent around the value of μ_0 given in Table I.

The Table indicates that the nasals have a formant of an *u*-character.   It is worth particular notice that the resonance data of the lower formants of *m* perfectly agree with the correspondent data of *u*.   The marked third formant is the decisive moment separating *m* from *u*.   This resonance is characteristic of the nasals.

The decay period of the resonance cavity producing the third formant of the vowels required 0.9 hundredths of a second, whereas in the present case the de-

---

[3] *Speech and Hearing* 59 (London 1929).
[4] *Die . . . Vokale und Nasale der finnischen Sprache* 161 (Helsinki 1938).

cay took 0.5–0.6 hundredths of a second. The nasals are thus separated from the *i*-like sounds. Thus, the periods of the oscillograms of nasals exhibit a more tranquil course, because the high harmonics (the higher frequency notchings visible at the beginning of the period) decay more quickly (cf. Fig. 3).

4. The voiced modifications of the *l*-like sounds give fairly clear resonances. Their resonance data may be calculated as those of nasals. The physical investigation of light and dark variants proved interesting in the course of the experiments. The ranges in which the two types are produced cannot be delimited exactly. The results of these experiments will therefor show a wider spread than those of the nasals. The results generally indicate that the darker colour of the back *l* depends not only on a slight displacement of the lower formant, but also on the upper formants' changing position. The resonance data of light *l* remind one of sounds like ε and e, whereas those of dark *l* are closely related to *y* (but not to *u*!). Palatalized *l* has not been investigated.

TABLE I. *The resonance data of nasals*

Resonance frequencies (ν_0) in cps, decrements (Λ) in absolute values, decay periods (τ) in hundredths of a second

	1			2			3			4		
	ν_0	Λ	τ	ν_0	Λ	τ	ν_0	Λ	τ	ν_0	Λ	τ
m	330	1.4	1.8	(800)	—	—	2600	0.5	0.53	—	—	—
n	260	1.3	2.0	—	—	—	2300	0.48	0.63	(3200)	—	—
ŋ	260	—	—	(600)	—	—	(2200)	—	—	—	—	—
ɲ	—	—	—	—	—	—	(2500)	—	—	(4000)	—	—

There are but very few and weak harmonics indicating the occurrence of formants ranking at about 2500 cps and characteristic of nasals. Our experiments therefor by no means confirmed the supposition of the *l* being a 'nasal' *u*.[5]

The considerable variety observed in the acoustic investigation of spoken *l*-like sounds may be explained by the fact that the *l* sounds connected with various vowels reveal different places at which they are produced. Fig. 1. includes three oscillograms representing the *l*-curves cut out of the curves for the combinations *lu*, *la* and *li*.

5. Sounds like ʀ have hitherto not been submitted to thoro acoustic investigation, because the trill seems to deprive the curve of periodicity, thus making analysis by the Fourier method inappropriate, and because lingual *r* (as e.g., in *Scotch* or *Hungarian*) is not quite general in Western European languages. The various kinds of uvular ʀ are not periodic.

The oscillograms indicate that the trill of the tongue interrupts the continuity of the sound, i.e. the periods succeeding each other differ in intensity, but not in

[5] Stumpf, *Die Sprachlaute* 121 (Berlin 1926).

composition. This is also indicated by the analysis of the single periods. The analysis of all periods occurring during one trill shows that the harmonic intensified in the position of the lower formant will appear in all cases. Investigating the change of intensity of the harmonics of higher order, we see that the harmonics of higher order of the weaker periods decrease in intensity. This effect is found in all resonant sounds, including vowels. According to Table II, the three formants found for the lingual voiced r rank at about 550, 1400 and 2000 cps. No vowel shows this position of the formants. The closest acoustical relations to r are shown by l, from which r differs by lacking the high (fourth) formant and by the trill.

The trill is the so-called self-induced vibration of the tongue brought about by the air breathed out. The number of vibrations per second depends on the dimensions and the tension of the tongue. Apart from closing and opening of the resonance cavity, the trill has the function of producing a noise at the very moment of opening. As indicated by the oscillogram, the trill does not entirely eliminate the voicing of the cavity as it is closed, but probably modifies the reso-

TABLE II. *The resonance data of l and r sounds*

	1			2			3			4		
	ν_0	Λ	τ	ν_0	Λ	τ	ν_0	V	τ	ν_0	Λ	τ
l	420	1.0	1.6	1400	0.5	1.0	(2400)	—	—	3200	0.4	0.5
l	350	1.2	1.6	1600	0.45	0.95	?	—	—	(3800)	—	—
r	550	1.3	0.95	1400	0.5	1.0	2000	—	—	—	—	—
R	450	—	—	—	—	—	(2200)	—	—	—	—	—

nances to a certain extent. Owing to a divergence appearing in the experiment for other reasons, we did not succeed in demonstrating such less important displacements of the formants. In the case of voiced pronunciation, the opening noise is hardly significant, because the resonators do not intensify the noises, which have much higher pitch; and, on account of the energy conditions, the harmonics of the voice will prevail. In unvoiced pronunciation, however, the trill causes noise impulses, which induce the decay process on the resonance cavities. One of our oscillograms is that of an unvoiced r, the inherent frequency of which, determined from its curve, is 1550 cps, and its decrement is 0.3. This result seems not to agree with the corresponding data of the voiced variant. We get a different view of the problem when considering the fact that the glottis is entirely open in the case of unvoiced pronunciation, whereas it is periodically closed and opened during voiced pronunciation. It has been demonstrated by experiments that the frequency of the sound producing cavity is increasing and its decrement is decreasing during this process.

The number of trills per second is fairly constant. The over-all range is usually from 25 to 35 in voiced pronunciation, but variation as considerable as this will of course never occur for one person. In the pronunciation of the author, for instance, the number of trills varies between 29 and 33, almost independently of the pitch and the intensity. In unvoiced pronunciation, the trill has somewhat higher speed and the distance between the two extremes grows somewhat greater when the intensity increases.

A few trills are sufficient to produce the *r* and to call forth its acoustic impression. Particularly short *r*-sounds require but one or two trills. The duration of one trill is three or four hundredths of a second.

The oscillogram of unvoiced *r* indicates, apart from the decay data, that the trill of the tongue is not a homogeneous movement, since we observe, apart from the decay figure appearing at the very moment of opening, another, tho less distinct, decay figure returning at regular intervals in the oscillogram. This is also symptomatic of a sudden, pulse-like noise, which, however, is possible only at the moment when the tongue, after being pushed from the palate, starts back to the palate owing to the elastic tension of the tongue. According to the noise figure, the two movements are of different durations.

Uvular ʀ is not suitable for analysis by the Fourier method, because its noise is intensive and appears irregularly, thus disturbing periodicity. Anyhow, we confirm that the lower formant is lowered still more and that there is a third formant too. Since there is no trill, causing interruptions, the variation of intensity, which is characteristic of the *r*, does not appear either.

Budapest.

CHAPTER 9

Reprinted from THE JOURNAL OF THE ACOUSTICAL SOCIETY OF AMERICA, Vol. 24, No. 2, 175–184, March, 1952
Copyright, 1952, by the Acoustical Society of America.
Printed in U. S. A.

Control Methods Used in a Study of the Vowels

GORDON E. PETERSON AND HAROLD L. BARNEY
Bell Telephone Laboratories, Inc., Murray Hill, New Jersey
(Received December 3, 1951)

Relationships between a listener's identification of a spoken vowel and its properties as revealed from acoustic measurement of its sound wave have been a subject of study by many investigators. Both the utterance and the identification of a vowel depend upon the language and dialectal backgrounds and the vocal and auditory characteristics of the individuals concerned. The purpose of this paper is to discuss some of the control methods that have been used in the evaluation of these effects in a vowel study program at Bell Telephone Laboratories. The plan of the study, calibration of recording and measuring equipment, and methods for checking the performance of both speakers and listeners are described. The methods are illustrated from results of tests involving some 76 speakers and 70 listeners.

INTRODUCTION

CONSIDERABLE variation is to be found in the processes of speech production because of their complexity and because they depend upon the past experience of the individual. As in much of human behavior there is a self-correcting, or servomechanism type of feedback involved as the speaker hears his own voice and adjusts his articulatory mechanisms.[1]

In the elementary case of a word containing a consonant-vowel-consonant phoneme[2,3] structure, a speaker's pronunciation of the vowel within the word will be influenced by his particular dialectal background; and his pronunciation of the vowel may differ both in phonetic quality and in measurable characteristics from that produced in the word by speakers with other backgrounds. A listener, likewise, is influenced in his identification of a sound by his past experience.

Variations are observed when a given individual makes repeated utterances of the same phoneme. A very significant property of these variations is that they are not random in a statistical sense, but show trends and sudden breaks or shifts in level, and other types of nonrandom fluctuations.[4] Variations likewise appear in the successive identifications by a listener of the same utterance. It is probable that the identification of repeated sounds is also nonrandom but there is little direct evidence in this work to support such a conclusion.

A study of sustained vowels was undertaken to investigate in a general way the relation between the vowel phoneme intended by a speaker and that identified by a listener, and to relate these in turn to acoustical measurements of the formant or energy concentration positions in the speech waves.

In the plan of the study certain methods and techniques were employed which aided greatly in the collection of significant data. These methods included randomization of test material and repetitions to obtain sequences of observations for the purpose of checking the measurement procedures and the speaker and listener consistency. The acoustic measurements were made with the sound spectrograph; to minimize measurement errors, a method was used for rapid calibration of the recording and analyzing apparatus by means of a complex test tone. Statistical techniques were applied to the results of measurements, both of the calibrating signals and of the vowel sounds.

These methods of measurement and analysis have been found to be precise enough to resolve the effects of different dialectal backgrounds and of the nonrandom trends in speakers' utterances. Some aspects of the vowel study will be presented in the following paragraphs to illustrate the usefulness of the methods employed.

EXPERIMENTAL PROCEDURES

The plan of the study is illustrated in Fig. 1. A list of words (List 1) was presented to the speaker and his utterances of the words were recorded with a magnetic tape recorder. The list contained ten monosyllabic words each beginning with [h] and ending with [d] and differing only in the vowel. The words used were *heed, hid, head, had, hod, hawed, hood, who'd, hud,* and *heard.* The order of the words was randomized in each list, and each speaker was asked to pronounce two different lists. The purpose of randomizing the words in the list was to avoid practice effects which would be associated with an unvarying order.

If a given List 1, recorded by a speaker, were played back to a listener and the listener were asked to write down what he heard on a second list (List 2), a comparison of List 1 and List 2 would reveal occasional

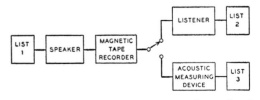

FIG. 1. Recording and measuring arrangements for vowel study.

[1] Bernard S. Lee, J. Acoust. Soc. Am. **22**, 824 (1950).
[2] B. Bloch, Language **24**, 3 (1948).
[3] B. Bloch, Language **26**, 88 (1950).
[4] R. K. Potter and J. C. Steinberg, J. Acoust. Soc. Am. **26**, 807 (1950).

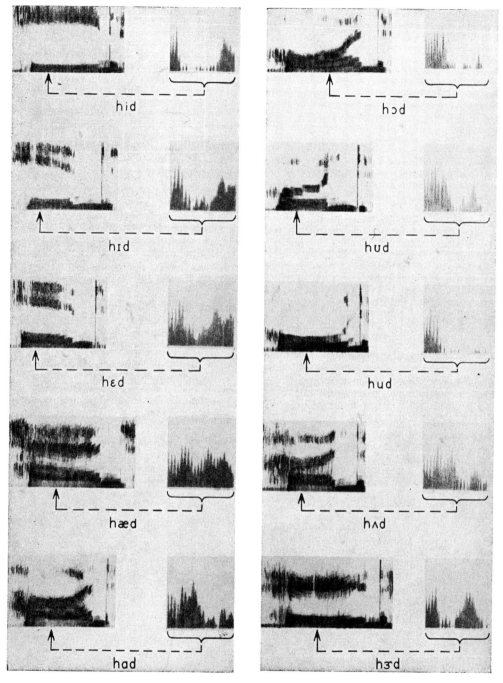

FIG. 2. Broad band spectrograms and amplitude sections of the word list by a female speaker.

differences, or disagreements, between speaker and listener. Instead of being played back to a listener, List 1 might be played into an acoustic measuring device and the outputs classified according to the measured properties of the sounds into a List 3. The three lists will differ in some words depending upon the characteristics of the speaker, the listener, and the measuring device.

A total of 76 speakers, including 33 men, 28 women and 15 children, each recorded two lists of 10 words, making a total of 1520 recorded words. Two of the speakers were born outside the United States and a few others spoke a foreign language before learning English. Most of the women and children grew up in the Middle Atlantic speech area.[5] The male speakers represented a much broader regional sampling of the United States; the majority of them spoke General American.[5]

The words were randomized and were presented to a group of 70 listeners in a series of eight sessions. The listening group contained only men and women, and represented much the same dialectal distribution as did the group of speakers, with the exception that a few observers were included who had spoken a foreign language throughout their youth. Thirty-two of the 76 speakers were also among the 70 observers.

The 1520 words were also analyzed by means of the sound spectrograph.[6,7]

Representative spectrograms and sections of these words by a male speaker are shown in Fig. 3 of the paper by R. K. Potter and J. C. Steinberg;[4] a similar list by a female speaker is shown here as Fig. 2.[8] In the spectrograms, we see the initial [h] followed by the vowel, and then by the final [d]. There is generally a part of the vowel following the influence of the [h] and preceding the influence of the [d] during which a practically steady state is reached. In this interval, a section is made, as shown to the right of the spectrograms. The sections, portraying frequency on a horizontal scale, and amplitude of the voiced harmonics on the vertical side, have been measured with calibrated Plexiglass templates to provide data about the fundamental and formant frequencies and relative formant amplitudes of each of the 1520 recorded sounds.

LISTENING TESTS

The 1520 recorded words were presented to the group of 70 adult observers over a high quality loud speaker system in Arnold Auditorium at the Murray Hill Laboratories. The general purpose of these tests was to obtain an aural classification of each vowel to supplement the speaker's classification. In presenting the words to the observers, the procedure was to reproduce at each of seven sessions, 200 words recorded by 10 speakers. At the eighth session, there remained five men's and one child's recordings to be presented; to these were added three women's and one child's recordings which had been given in previous sessions, making again a total of 200 words. The sound level at the observers' positions was approximately 70 db re 0.0002 dyne/cm², and varied over a range of about 3 db at the different positions.

In selecting the speakers for each of the first seven

[5] C. K. Thomas, *Phonetics of American English*, The Ronald Press Company (New York, 1947).
[6] Koenig, Dunn, and Lacy, J. Acoust. Soc. Am. **17**, 19 (1946).
[7] L. G. Kersta, J. Acoust. Soc. Am. **20**, 796 (1948).
[8] Key words for the vowel symbols are as follows: [i] heed, [ɪ] hid, [ɛ] head, [æ] had, [ɑ] father, [ɔ] ball, [ʊ] hood, [u] who'd, [ʌ] hud, [ɝ] heard.

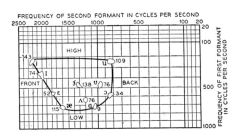

FIG. 3. Vowel loop with numbers of sounds unanimously classified by listeners; each sound was presented 152 times.

sessions, 4 men, 4 women, and 2 children were chosen at random from the respective groups of 33, 28, and 15. The order of occurrence of the 200 words spoken by the 10 speakers for each session was randomized for presentation to the observers.

Each observer was given a pad containing 200 lines having the 10 words on each line. He was asked to draw a line through the one word in each line that he heard. The observers' seating positions in the auditorium were chosen by a randomizing procedure, and each observer took the same position for each of the eight sessions, which were given on eight different days.

The randomizing of the speakers in the listening sessions was designed to facilitate checks of learning effects from one session to another. The randomizing of words in each group of 200 was designed to minimize successful guessing and the learning of a particular speaker's dialect. The seating positions of the listeners were randomized so that it would be possible to determine whether position in the auditorium had an effect on the identification of the sounds.

DISCUSSION OF LISTENING TEST RESULTS

The total of 1520 sounds heard by the observers consisted of the 10 vowels, each presented 152 times. The ease with which the observers classified the various vowels varied greatly. Of the 152 [i] sounds, for instance, 143 were unanimously classified by all observers as [i]. Of the 152 sounds which the speakers intended for [ɑ], on the other hand, only 9 were unanimously classified as [ɑ] by the whole jury.

These data are summarized in Fig. 3. This figure shows the positions of the 10 vowels in a vowel loop in which the frequency of the first formant is plotted against the frequency of the second formant[9] on mel scales;[10] in this plot the origin is at the upper right. The numbers beside each of the phonetic symbols are the numbers of sounds, out of 152, which were unanimously classified as that particular vowel by the jury. It is of interest in passing that in no case did the jury agree unanimously that a sound was something other than what the speaker intended. Figure 3 shows that

[9] R. K. Potter and G. E. Peterson, J. Acoust. Soc. Am. **20**, 528 (1948).
[10] S. S. Stevens and J. Volkman, Am. J. Psychol. 329 (July, 1940).

[i], [ɝ], [æ], and [u] are generally quite well understood.

To obtain the locations of the small areas shown in Fig. 3, the vowels were repeated by a single speaker on twelve different days. A line enclosing all twelve points was drawn for each vowel; the differences in the shapes of these areas probably have little significance.

When the vowels are plotted in the manner shown in Fig. 3, they appear in essentially the same positions as those shown in the tongue hump position diagrams which phoneticians have employed for many years.[11] The terms "high, front, low back" refer to the tongue positions in the mouth. The [i], for instance, is made with the tongue hump high and forward, the [u] with the hump high and back, and the [ɑ] and [æ] with the tongue hump low.

It is of interest that when observers disagreed with speakers on the classification of a vowel, the two classifications were nearly always in adjacent positions of the vowel loop of Fig. 3. This is illustrated by the data shown on Table I. This table shows how the observers classified the vowels, as compared with the vowels intended by the speakers. For instance, on all the 152 sounds intended as [i] by the speakers, there were 10,267 total votes by all observers that they were [i], 4 votes for [ɪ], 6 votes for [ɛ], and 3 votes for [ɔ]. Of the 152 [ɑ] sounds, there was a large fraction of the sounds on which some of the observers voted for [ɔ]. [ɪ] was taken for [ɛ] a sizable percentage of the time, and [ɛ] was called either [ɪ] or [æ] (adjacent sounds on the vowel loop shown in the preceding Fig. 3) quite a large number of times. [ɑ] and [ɔ], and [ʌ] and [ɑ] were also confused to a certain extent. Here again, as in Fig. 2, the [i], [ɝ], [æ], and [u] show high intelligibility scores.

It is of considerable interest that the substitutions shown conform to present dialectal trends in American speech rather well,[12] and in part, to the prevailing vowel shifts observable over long periods of time in most languages.[13] The common tendency is continually to shift toward higher vowels in speech, which correspond to smaller mouth openings.

The listener, on the other hand, would tend to make the opposite substitution. This effect is most simply described in terms of the front vowels. If a speaker produces [ɪ] for [ɛ], for example [mɪn] for [mɛn] as currently heard in some American dialects; then such an individual when serving as a listener will be inclined to write *men* when he hears [mɪn]. Thus it is that in the substitutions shown in Table I, [ɪ] most frequently became [ɛ], and [ɛ] most frequently became [æ]. The explanation of the high intelligibility of [æ] is probably based on this same pattern. It will be noted along the

vowel loop that a wide gap appears between [æ] and [ɑ]. The [a] of the Romance languages appears in this region. Since that vowel was present in neither the lists nor the dialects of most of the speakers and observers the [æ] was usually correctly identified.

The [i] and the [u] are the terminal or end positions in the mouth and on the vowel loop toward which the vowels are normally directed in the prevailing process of pronunciation change. In the formation of [i] the tongue is humped higher and farther forward than for any other vowel; in [u] the tongue hump takes the highest posterior position in the mouth and the lips are more rounded than for any other vowel. The vowels [u] and [i] are thus much more difficult to displace, and a greater stability in the organic formation of these sounds would probably be expected, which in turn should mean that these sounds are recognized more consistently by a listener.

The high intelligibility of [ɝ] probably results from the retroflexion which is present to a marked degree only in the formation of this vowel; that is, in addition to the regular humping of the tongue, the edges of the tongue are turned up against the gum ridge or the hard palate. In the acoustical pattern the third formant is markedly lower than for any other vowel. Thus in both physiological and acoustical phonetics the [ɝ] occupies a singular position among the American vowels.

The very low scores on [ɑ] and [ɔ] in Fig. 3 undoubtedly result primarily from the fact that some members of the speaking group and many members of the listening group speak one of the forms of American dialects in which [ɑ] and [ɔ] are not differentiated.

When the individuals' votes on the sounds are analyzed, marked differences are seen in the way they classified the sounds. Not only did the total numbers of agreements with the speakers vary, but the proportions of agreements for the various vowels was significantly different. Figure 4 will be used to illustrate this point. If we plot total numbers of disagreements for all tests, rather than agreements, the result is shown by the upper chart. This shows that [ɪ], [ɛ], [ɑ], [ɔ], and [ʌ] had the most disagreements. An "average" observer would be expected to have a distribution of disagreements similar in proportions to this graph. The middle graph illustrates the distribution of disagreements given by observer number 06. His chief difficulty was in distinguishing between [ɑ] and [ɔ]. This type of distribution is characteristic of several observers. Observer 013, whose distribution of disagreements is plotted on the bottom graph, shows a tendency to confuse [ɪ] and [ɛ] more than the average.

The distributions of disagreements of all 70 observers differ from each other, depending on their language experience, but the differences are generally less extreme than the two examples shown on Fig. 4. Thirty-two of the 70 observers were also speakers. In cases where an observer such as 06 was also a speaker, the remainder of the jury generally had more disagreements

[11] D. Jones, *An Outline of English Phonetics* (W. Heffer and Sons, Ltd., Cambridge, England, 1947).
[12] G. W. Gray and C. M. Wise, *The Bases of Speech* (Harper Brothers, New York, 1946), pp. 217–302.
[13] L. Bloomfield, *Language* (Henry Holt and Company, New York, 1933), pp. 369–391.

with his [ɑ] and [ɔ] sounds than with the other sounds he spoke. Thus it appears that if a speaker does not differentiate clearly between a pair of sounds in speaking them, he is unlikely to classify them properly when he hears others speak them. His language experience, as would be expected, influences both his speaking and his hearing of sounds.

Since the listening group was not given a series of training sessions for these tests, learning would be expected in the results of the tests.[14] Several pieces of evidence indicate a certain amount of practice effect, but the data are not such as to provide anything more than a very approximate measure of its magnitude.

For one check on practice effect, a ninth test was given the jury, in which all the words having more than 10 disagreements in any of the preceding eight tests were repeated. There was a total of about 175 such words; to these were added 25 words which had no disagreements, picked at random from the first eight tests. On the ninth test, 67 words had more disagreements, 109 had less disagreements, and 24 had the same number of disagreements as in the preceding tests. The probability of getting this result had there been no practice or other effect, but only a random variation of observers' votes, would be about 0.01. When these data are broken down into three groups for the men, women and children speakers, the largest differences in numbers of disagreements for the original and repeated tests was on the childrens' words, indicating a larger practice or learning effect on their sounds. The indicated learning effect on men's and women's speech was nearly the same. When the data are classified according to the vowel sound, the learning effect indicated by the repetitions was least on [i], [ɝ], and [u], and greatest on [ɑ] and [ɔ].

Another indication that there was a practice effect lies in the sequence of total numbers of disagreements by tests. From the second to the seventh test, the total number of disagreements by all observers diminished consistently from test to test, and the first test had considerably more disagreements than the eighth, thus strongly indicating a downward trend. With the speakers randomized in their order of appearance in the eight tests, each test would be expected to have approximately the same number of disagreements. The probability of getting the sequence of numbers of total disagreements which was obtained would be somewhat less than 0.05 if there were no learning trend or other nonrandom effect.

It was also found that the listening position had an effect upon the scores obtained. The observers were arranged in 9 rows in the auditorium, and the listeners in the back 4 rows had a significantly greater number of disagreements with the speakers than did the listeners in the first 5 rows. The effect of a listener's position

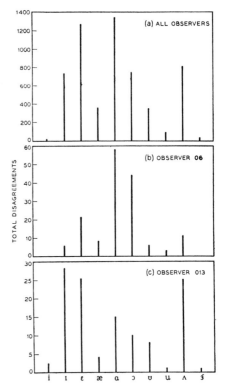

Fig. 4. Observer disagreements in listening tests.

within an auditorium upon intelligibility has been observed previously and is reported in the literature.[15]

ACOUSTIC MEASUREMENTS

Calibrations of Equipment

A rapid calibrating technique was developed for checking the over-all performance of the recording and analyzing systems. This depended on the use of a test tone which had an envelope spectrum that was essentially flat with frequency over the voice band. The circuit used to generate this test tone is shown schematically in Fig. 5. It consists essentially of an overloading amplifier and pulse sharpening circuit. The wave shapes which may be observed at several different points in the test tone generator are indicated in Fig. 5.

The test tone generator may be driven by an input sine wave signal of any frequency between 50 and 2000 cycles. Figure 6(a) shows a section of the test tone with a 100 cycle repetition frequency, which had been recorded on magnetic tape in place of the word lists by the speaker, and then played back into the sound spectrograph. The departure from uniform frequency response of the over-all systems is indicated by the shape of the envelope enclosing the peaks of the 100

[14] H. Fletcher and R. H. Galt, J. Acoust. Soc. Am. 22, 93 (1950).

[15] V. O. Knudsen and C. M. Harris, *Acoustical Designing in Architecture* (John Wiley and Sons, New York, 1950), pp. 180–181.

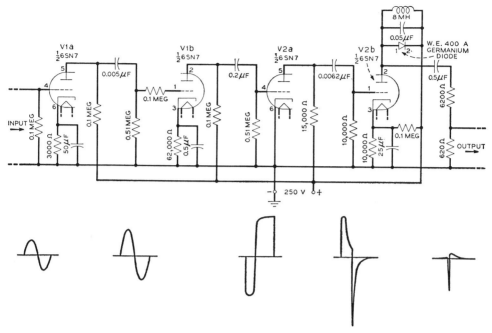

FIG. 5. Schematic of calibrating tone generator.

cycle harmonics. With the 100 cycles from the Laboratories standard frequency oscillator as the drive signal, the frequency calibration of the systems may be checked very readily by comparison of the harmonic spacing on the section with the template scale. The amplitude scale in 6(a) is obtained by inserting a pure tone at the spectrograph in 5 db increments. The frequency scale for spectrograms may also be calibrated as shown in Fig. 6(b). The horizontal lines here are representations of the harmonics of the test tone when the test tone generator is driven by a 500 cycle standard frequency. These lines further afford a means of checking the amount of speed irregularity or wow in the over-all mechanical system. A calibration of the time scale may be obtained by using the test tone generator with 100 cycle drive and making a broad band spectrogram as shown in Fig. 6(c). The spacings between vertical striations in this case correspond to one-hundredth of a second intervals.

In the process of recording some of the word lists, it was arranged to substitute the calibrating test tone circuit for the microphone circuit, and record a few seconds of test tone between the lists of words. When the word lists were analyzed with the spectrograph, the accompanying test tone sections provided a means of checking the over-all frequency response of the recorder and analyzer, and the frequency scale of the sectioner.

The effect of speed variations in either the recorder or the sound spectrograph is to change the frequency scale. A series of measurements with the 100 cycle test tone showed that the tape recorder ran approximately one

percent slower when playing back than it did on recording.

The speed variations on the sound spectrograph were measured with the test tone applied directly, and the maximum short time variations were found to be ±0.3 percent. Such direct calibrations of the frequency scale of the spectrograph, during a period of four weeks when most of the spectrographic analysis was done, showed maximum deviations of ±30 cycles at the 31st harmonic of the 100 cycle test tone. During that period a control chart[16] of the measurements of the 3100 cycle component of the test tone showed a downward trend of about 10 cycles, which was attributed to changes in the electonic circuit components of the spectrograph. As a result of these calibration tests, it was concluded that the frequency scale of the sound spectrograph could be relied upon as being accurate within ±1 percent.

Formant Measurements

Measurements of both the frequency and the amplitude of the formants were made for the 20 words recorded by each of the 76 speakers. The frequency position of each formant was obtained by estimating a weighted average of the frequencies of the principal components in the formant. (See reference 4 for a discussion of this procedure.) When the principal components in the formant were symmetrically distributed about a dominant component, such as the second formant of [ʌ] *hud* in Fig. 2, there is little ambiguity

---

[16] "A.S.T.M. manual on presentation of data," Am. Soc. Testing Materials (Philadelphia, 1945), Appendix B.

in choosing the formant frequency. When the distribution is asymmetrical, however, as in the first formant of [ɜ] *heard* in Fig. 2, the difference between estimated formant frequency and that assigned by the ear may be appreciable.

One of the greatest difficulties in estimating formant frequencies was encountered in those cases where the fundamental frequency was high so that the formant was poorly defined. These factors may account for some, but certainly not all, of the differences discussed later

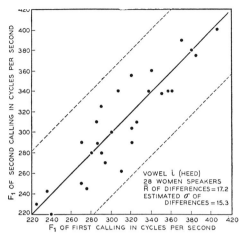

FIG. 7. Accuracy-precision chart of first formant frequencies of [i] as spoken by 28 women.

between vowel classification by ear and by measured values of formant frequencies.

Amplitudes were obtained by assigning a value in decibels to the formant peak. In the case of the amplitude measurements it was then necessary to apply a correction for the over-all frequency response of the system.

The procedure of making duplicate recordings and analyses of the ten words for each of the speakers provided the basis for essential checks on the reliability of the data.

One method by which the duplicate measured values were used is illustrated by Fig. 7. This is a plot of the values for the first formant frequency F_1 of [i] as in *heed*, as spoken by the 28 female subjects. Each point represents, for a single speaker, the value of F_1 measured for the *heed* in the first list, *versus* the value of F_1 for the *heed* in the second list. If the F_1 for the second list or calling was greater than that for the first calling, the point lies above a 45-degree line; if it is less, the point lies below the 45-degree line. The average difference $\bar{R}$ between the paired values of F_1 for first and second callings, was 17.2 cycles. The estimated standard deviation σ derived from the differences between pairs of F_1 values was 15.3 cycles. The dotted lines in Fig. 7 are spaced ± 3 σ cycles from the 45-degree line through the origin. In case a point falls outside the dotted lines, it is generally because of an erroneous measurement.

Each of the three formant frequencies for each of the 10 vowels was plotted in this way. There were 760 such points for each formant, or a total of 2280 points plotted on 90 accuracy-precision charts like Fig. 7. Of these 2280 points, 118 fell outside the ± 3 σ limits. On checking back over the measurements, it was found that 88 of the points were incorrect because of gross measurement errors, typographical errors in transcribing the data, or because the section had been made during the influence period of the consonants instead of in the

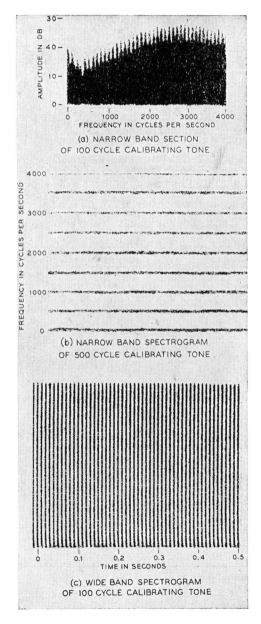

FIG. 6. Spectrograms and section of calibrating tone.

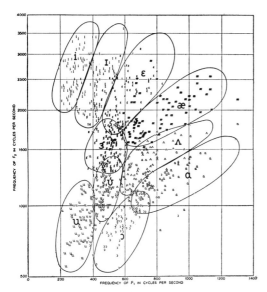

FIG. 8. Frequency of second formant *versus* frequency of first formant for ten vowels by 76 speakers.

steady state period of the vowel. When corrected, these 88 points were within the $\pm 3 \sigma$ limits. Of the remaining 30 points which were still outside the limits, 20 were the result of the individuals' having produced pairs of sounds which were unlike phonetically, as shown by the results of the listening tests.

The duplicate measurements may also be used to show that the difference between successive utterances of the same sound by the same individual is much less significant statistically than the difference between utterances of the same sound by different individuals. An analysis of variance of the data in Fig. 7 shows that the differences between callings of pairs are not significant. However, the value for the variance ratio when comparing speakers is much larger than that corresponding to a 0.1 percent probability. In other words, if the measurements shown in Fig. 7 for all callings by all speakers were assumed to constitute a body of statistically random data, the probability of having a variance ratio as high as that found when comparing speakers would be less than one in a thousand. There-

fore it is assumed that the data are not statistically random, but that there are statistically significant differences between speakers. Since the measurements for pairs of callings were so nearly alike, as contrasted with the measurements on the same sound for different speakers, this indicated that the precision of measurements with the sound spectrograph was sufficient to resolve satisfactorily the differences between the various individuals' pronunciations of the same sounds.

RESULTS OF ACOUSTIC MEASUREMENTS

In Fig. 3, as discussed previously, are plotted areas in the plane of the second formant F_2 *versus* the first formant F_1. These areas enclose points for several repetitions of the sustained vowels by one of the writers. It is clear that here the vowels may be separated readily, simply by plotting F_2 against F_1; that is, on the F_2-F_1 plane, points for each vowel lie in isolated areas, with no overlapping of adjacent areas, even though there exists the variation of the measured values which we have discussed above.

The variation of the measured data for a group of speakers is much larger than the variation encountered in repetitions with the same speaker, however, as may be shown by the data for F_1 and F_2 for the 76 speakers. In Fig. 8 are plotted the points for the second calling by each speaker, with the points identified according to the speaker's word list. The closed loops for each vowel have been drawn arbitrarily to enclose most of the points; the more extreme and isolated points were disregarded so that in general these loops include about 90 percent of the values. The frequency scales on this and Fig. 9 are spaced according to the approximation to an aural scale described by Koenig, which is linear to 1000 cps and logarithmic above.[17]

Considerable overlapping of areas is indicated, particularly between [ɜ] and [ɛ], [ɜ] and [ʊ], [ʊ] and [u], and [ɑ] and [ɔ]. In the case of the [ɜ] sound, it may be easily distinguished from all the others if the third formant frequency is used, as the position of the third formant is very close in frequency to that of the second.

The data of Fig. 8 show that the distribution of points in the F_1-F_2 plane is continuous in going from sound to sound; these distributions doubtless represent

TABLE I. Classifications of vowels by speakers and by listeners. Vowels as classified by listeners.

		i	ɪ	ɛ	æ	ɑ	ɔ	ʊ	u	ʌ	ɝ
	i	10267	4	6	...	...	3	...	...	...	...
	ɪ	6	9549	694	2	1	1	...	...	...	26
	ɛ	...	257	9014	949	1	3	...	...	2	51
	æ	...	1	300	9919	2	2	...	...	15	39
Vowels intended by speakers	ɑ	...	1	...	19	8936	1013	69	...	228	7
	ɔ	...	...	1	2	590	9534	71	5	62	14
	u	...	...	1	1	16	51	9924	96	171	19
	u	...	...	1	...	2	...	78	10196	...	2
	ʌ	...	1	1	8	540	127	103	...	9476	21
	ɝ	...	...	23	6	2	3	...	...	2	10243

[17] W. Koenig, Bell Labs. Record **27**, (August, 1949), pp. 299–301.

TABLE II. Averages of fundamental and formant frequencies and formant amplitudes of vowels by 76 speakers.

		i	ɪ	ɛ	æ	ɑ	ɔ	ʊ	u	ʌ	ɝ
Fundamental frequencies (cps)	M	136	135	130	127	124	129	137	141	130	133
	W	235	232	223	210	212	216	232	231	221	218
	Ch	272	269	260	251	256	263	276	274	261	261
Formant frequencies (cps)											
F_1	M	270	390	530	660	730	570	440	300	640	490
	W	310	430	610	860	850	590	470	370	760	500
	Ch	370	530	690	1010	1030	680	560	430	850	560
F_2	M	2290	1990	1840	1720	1090	840	1020	870	1190	1350
	W	2790	2480	2330	2050	1220	920	1160	950	1400	1640
	Ch	3200	2730	2610	2320	1370	1060	1410	1170	1590	1820
F_3	M	3010	2550	2480	2410	2440	2410	2240	2240	2390	1690
	W	3310	3070	2990	2850	2810	2710	2680	2670	2780	1960
	Ch	3730	3600	3570	3320	3170	3180	3310	3260	3360	2160
Formant amplitudes (db)	L_1	−4	−3	−2	−1	−1	0	−1	−3	−1	−5
	L_2	−24	−23	−17	−12	−5	−7	−12	−19	−10	−15
	L_3	−28	−27	−24	−22	−28	−34	−34	−43	−27	−20

large differences in the way individuals speak the sounds. The values for F_3 and the relative amplitudes of the formants also have correspondingly large variations between individuals. Part of the variations are because of the differences between classes of speakers, that is, men, women and children. In general, the children's formants are highest in frequency, the women's intermediate, and the men's formants are lowest in frequency.

These differences may be observed in the averaged formant frequencies given on Table II. The first formants for the children are seen to be about half an octave higher than those of the men, and the second and third formants are also appreciably higher. The measurements of amplitudes of the formants did not show decided differences between classes of speakers, and so have been averaged all together. The formant amplitudes are all referred to the amplitude of the first formant in [ɔ], when the total phonetic powers of the vowels are corrected so as to be related to each other by the ratios of powers given by Fletcher.[18]

Various methods of correlating the results of the listening tests with the formant measurements have been studied. In terms of the first two formants the nature of the relationship is illustrated in Fig. 9. In this figure measurements for all vowels of both callings are plotted in which all members of the listening group agreed with the speaker. Since the values for the men and the children generally lie at the two ends of the distributions for each vowel, the confusion between vowels is well illustrated by their data; thus the measurements for the women speakers have been omitted.

The lines on Fig. 9 are the same as the boundaries drawn in Fig. 8. As indicated previously, some vowels received 100 percent agreement much more frequently than others.

The plot has also been simplified by the omission of [ɝ]. The [ɝ] produces extensive overlap in the [ʊ] region in a graph involving only the first two formants. As explained previously, however, the [ɝ] may be isolated from the other vowels readily by means of the third formant.

When only vowels which received 100 percent recognition are plotted, the scatter and overlap are somewhat reduced over that for all callings. The scatter is greater, however, than might be expected.

If the first and second formant parameters measured from these words well defined their phonetic values; and if the listening tests were an exact means of classifying the words, then the points for each vowel of

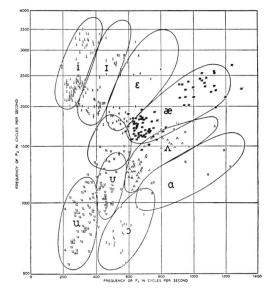

FIG. 9. Frequency of second formant *versus* frequency of first formant for vowels spoken by men and children, which were classified unanimously by all listeners.

[18] H. Fletcher, *Speech and Hearing* (D. Van Nostrand Company, Inc., New York, 1929), p. 74.

Fig. 9 should be well separated. Words judged intermediate in phonetic position should fall at intermediate positions in such a plot. In other words, the distributions of measured formant values in these plots do not correspond closely to the distributions of phonetic values.

It is the present belief that the complex acoustical patterns represented by the words are not adequately represented by a single section, but require a more complex portrayal. The initial and final influences often shown in the bar movements of the spectrograms are of importance here.[19] The evaluation of these changing bar patterns of normal conversational speech is, of course, a problem of major importance in the study of the fundamental information bearing elements of speech.

A further study of the vowel formants is now nearing completion. This study employs sustained vowels, without influences, obtained and measured under controlled conditions. The general objectives are to determine further the most fundamental means of evaluating the formants, and to obtain the relations among the various formants for each of the vowels as produced by difference speakers. When this information has been obtained it is anticipated that it will serve as a basis for determining methods of evaluating and relating the changing formants within words as produced by various speakers.

SUMMARY

The results of our work to date on the development of methods for making acoustic and aural measurements on vowel sounds may be summarized as follows.

1. Calibration and measurement techniques have been developed with the sound spectrograph which make possible its use in a detailed study of the variations that appear in a broad sample of speech.
2. Repeated utterances, repeated measurements at various stages in the vowel study, and randomization in test procedures have made possible the application of powerful statistical methods in the analysis of the data.
3. The data, when so analyzed, reveal that both the production and the identification of vowel sounds by an individual depend on his previous language experience.
4. It is also found that the production of vowel sounds by an individual is not a random process, i.e., the values of the acoustic measurements of the sounds are not distributed in random order. This is probably true of many other processes involving individuals' subjective responses.
5. Finally, the data show that certain of the vowels are generally better understood than others, possibly because they represent "limit" positions of the articulatory mechanisms.

ACKNOWLEDGMENTS

The work which we have discussed has involved the contributions of a number of people. We should like to acknowledge the guidance of Mr. R. K. Potter and Mr. J. C. Steinberg in the plan of the experiment, and the contribution of Dr. W. A. Shewhart who has assisted in the design and interpretation of the study with respect to the application of statistical methods. We are indebted to Miss M. C. Packer for assistance in statistical analyses of the data. We wish to acknowledge also the assistance given by Mr. Anthony Prestigiacomo, Mr. George Blake, and Miss E. T. Leddy in the recording and analysis of the sounds and in the preparation of the data.

---

[19] Potter, Kopp, and Green, *Visible Speech* (D. Van Nostrand Company, Inc., New York, 1947).

CHAPTER 10

Reprinted from The Journal of the Acoustical Society of America, Vol. 25, No. 1 (January 1953).
Copyright 1953 by the Acoustical Society of America.

The Influence of Consonant Environment upon the Secondary Acoustical Characteristics of Vowels

Arthur S. House and Grant Fairbanks

Speech Research Laboratory, University of Illinois, Urbana, Illinois

(Received September 24, 1952)

The consonant environments of vowels were varied by forming nonmeaningful stimulus syllables consisting of 72 combinations of six vowels and 12 consonants. The syllables were spoken by subjects, and the duration, fundamental frequency, and relative power of the vowels were measured. All three factors varied significantly in response to changes of the consonant environment. The variations were systematically related to the attributes of the consonants, the most powerful attribute being the presence or absence of vocal fold vibration, followed by manner of articulation and place of articulation, in that order.

A MONG the acoustical investigations of vowels, experiments employing wave analysis have naturally been most numerous, while studies of the secondary characteristics—duration, fundamental frequency, and intensity—have been relatively few. Especially has this been true of variation in these secondary characteristics which may be systematically related to the widely varying consonantal environments of vowels in words.

Fairbanks, House, and Stevens,[1] reporting the results of an experiment on the relative intensities of vowels, concluded that, "When the same vowel is spoken in different isolated words, its intensity sometimes varies significantly from word to word, and it seems probable that such variations are, in part at least, effects of differing consonantal environments." In that investigation the words spoken by the subjects were monosyllables in which vowels were preceded and followed by consonant elements. All consonants were voiceless and varied unsystematically among stop-plosives, fricatives, and affricates, produced in bilabial, labio-dental, lingua-dental, and velar positions. Since

voicing was held constant and since only 10 words were used for each vowel, such variations were implicitly restricted. The finding that significant variation in intensity obtained even under these conditions was of unusual interest. A few previous studies have shown variation in duration also. Heffner and others[2-5] found the duration of vowels to be longer before voiced consonants than before voiceless consonants. Rositzke[6] also reported consonantal influence upon the duration of vowels, as did Hibbitt[7] for diphthongs. In addition to these results, writers such as Jones,[8] Kenyon,[9] and Thomas[10] assert that the voicing and the manner of production of a consonant following a vowel will in-

---

[1] Fairbanks, House, and Stevens, J. Acoust. Soc. Am. **22**, 457 (1950).

[2] R-M. S. Heffner, Language **16**, 33 (1940).

[3] R-M. S. Heffner, Am. Speech **12**, 128 (1937).

[4] W. P. Lehmann and R-M. S. Heffner, Am. Speech **15**, 377 (1940); **18**, 208 (1943).

[5] W. N. Locke and R-M. S. Heffner, Am. Speech **15**, 74 (1940).

[6] H. A. Rositzke, Language **15**, 99 (1939).

[7] G. W. Hibbitt, *Diphthongs in American Speech* (Columbia University Bookstore, New York, 1948).

[8] D. Jones, *An Outline of English Phonetics* (E. P. Dutton and Company, Inc., New York, 1948), 6th ed.

[9] J. S. Kenyon, *American Pronunciation* (George Wahr, Ann Arbor, 1940).

[10] C. K. Thomas, *An Introduction to the Phonetics of American English* (Ronald Press Company, New York, 1947).

TABLE I. Stimulus items.

	[i]	[e]	[æ]	[ɑ]	[o]	[u]
[p]	hupeep	hupaip	hupap	hupop	hupoap	hupoop
[t]	huteet	hutait	hutat	hutot	hutoat	hutoot
[k]	hukeek	hukaik	hukak	hukok	hukoak	hukook
[f]	hufeef	hufaif	hufaf	hufof	hufoaf	hufoof
[s]	husees	husais	husas	husos	husoas	husoos
[b]	hubeeb	hubaib	hubab	hubob	huboab	huboob
[d]	hudeed	hudaid	hudad	hudod	hudoad	hudood
[g]	hugeeg	hugaig	hugag	hugog	hugoag	hugoog
[v]	huveev	huvaiv	huvav	huvov	huvoav	huvoov
[z]	huzeez	huzaiz	huzaz	huzoz	huzoaz	huzooz
[m]	humeem	humaim	humam	humom	humoam	humoom
[n]	huneen	hunain	hunan	hunon	hunoan	hunoon

fluence its duration. With respect to fundamental frequency, a search of the literature failed to disclose reports of similar variation, although such might be predicted.

The purpose of the present experiment has been to pursue the problem raised by such findings with a more extensive and systematic phonetic design. Its general plan was to place vowels in various consonant environments, to cause them to be spoken by subjects, and to make the appropriate physical measurements. Representative vowels were used, and the following articulatory characteristics of the consonants were controlled: the presence or absence of vocal-fold vibration; variations in the manner of production (fricative, stopplosive, etc.); variations in the characteristic place of articulation (bilabial, velar, etc.).

I. PROCEDURE

Materials

After considerable study of the various alternatives, it was decided to construct stimulus materials in which only one consonant influence was present in each item. Syllables in which the vowel is both preceded and followed by the same consonant, as in the word *cease*, appeared to be suitable. Study of all such symmetrical syllables led to the conclusion that appropriate materials would be provided by restricting these items to 72, involving 12 consonants in combination with six vowels.

The following 12 consonants were selected: [p], [b], [t], [d], [k], [g], [f], [v], [s], [z], [m], [n]. It will be seen that the first 10 sounds are voiceless-voiced cognate pairs, providing direct contrast for the voicing factor. In manner of production, six stop-plosives, four fricatives, and two nasals are available, in that order. Differences in characteristic place of articulation are provided by the bilabials [p], [b], and [m]; the labiodentals [f] and [v]; the post-dentals [t], [d], [s], [z], and [n]; and the velars [k] and [g].

The six vowels chosen were [i], [e], [æ], [ɑ], [o], and [u]. These vowels span the range of tongue, mandible, and lip positions. They also vary in certain of their secondary acoustic characteristics as reported by

Crandall,[11] Parmenter and Treviño,[12] Heffner and others and Black[13] for duration, by Crandall, Black, and Taylor[14] for fundamental frequency, and by Fairbanks, House, and Stevens, Black, and Sacia and Beck[15] for relative intensity.

Combinations of these consonants and vowels resulted in a mixed list of words and nonsense syllables, which appeared to be unsuitable, since control over semantic influences was regarded as important. After various attempts, it was decided to prefix each item by an unstressed syllable, creating bisyllabic nonsense items with iambic stress patterns, and to select orthographic forms that would yield least meaning. Eventually, [hə] was selected as an appropriate initial syllable, since its component sounds are easily pronounced, usually neutral, and seemed likely to have minimal effect upon adjacent sounds. Table I shows the 72 stimulus items in the form used in presentation to the subjects.

Table I may also be regarded as depicting the essentials of the statistical design. With all items produced by all subjects, the triple-classification scheme for analysis of variance was employed to test the significance of the variances attributable to vowels, consonants, subjects, and their first-order interactions, and to enable the other statistical manipulations.[16]

Subjects

Ten male students enrolled in elementary speech courses at the University of Illinois served as subjects. The mean age was 20 years, six months, and the individuals ranged from 18 years, seven months to 26 years, six months. Thirty-five potential subjects were interviewed by two judges trained in phonetics and speech pathology, who screened their speech for aberrations in pitch, loudness, duration, voice quality, articulation, and pronunciation, and questioned them concerning their hearing. The ultimate subjects were without speech disorders, had no history of hearing pathology, and spoke some form of general American dialect. In the case of the intensity data only, 10 additional subjects, selected in the same manner, were added to the basic group.

Apparatus

The procedure involved phonograph recording of the subjects' responses to the stimulus items. Equipment was arranged conventionally in a two-room laboratory, consisting of a sound-treated room and a control room. A General Radio type 759-B sound level meter, with its associated Brush 9898 crystal microphone, was set

[11] J. B. Crandall, Bell System Tech. J. 4, 586 (1925).
[12] C. E. Parmenter and S. N. Treviño, Am. Speech 10, 129 (1935).
[13] J. W. Black, J. Speech Hearing Disorders 14, 216 (1949).
[14] H. C. Taylor, J. Exptl. Psychol. 16, 565 (1933).
[15] C. F. Sacia and C. J. Beck, Bell System Tech. J. 5, 393 (1926).
[16] Q. McNemar, *Psychological Statistics* (John Wiley and Sons, Inc., New York, 1949).

to flat response and 60 db attenuation, and its output fed to a Presto 9ん-A recording amplifier, with equalizer setting out. The recordings were made at 78.26 rpm on a Presto 8D-G turntable with a Presto 1-B cutting head.

The recordings were played for graphic recording of relative power and for simultaneous verification of the presence of the complete set of responses for each subject. The system used included a Presto 64-A turntable with a Lear PA-200 pick-up, a Goodell PRA-1 preamplifier, a Sound Apparatus Company HPL-E high-speed level recorder with 0–50 db potentiometer, and a Goodell ATB-3 power amplifier for the monitor speaker. The level recorder was set for fast stylus speed and 10 mm/sec paper speed. Measurements of duration were made on sound spectrograms recorded on a Kay Electric Company sona-graph. The above reproducing system was employed. Oscillograms used in the measurement of fundamental frequency were obtained through the use of a locally constructed instrument similar to that described by Cowan.[17] The instrument is essentially a special type of oscillograph for the photographing of signals stored on phonograph records. A turntable is mounted on a large drum around which photographic paper is wrapped. During the playing of the record, the turntable and the drum move synchronously, and an optical lever, activated by a crystal pick-up and amplifier, is manually lowered by means of a helical screw mechanism to spiral the trace about the drum.

Experimental Procedures

The phonograph recordings were made with the subject seated comfortably in the sound-treated room and with the microphone, mounted on a boom stand, approximately 12 inches before his mouth in the horizontal plane. An experimenter was seated immediately in front of the subject and presented the stimulus items visually at approximately four-second intervals. Each item was typed in lower case on a 3×5 card. Two judges trained in phonetics independently evaluated the acceptability of each response, using reasonably liberal standards of articulation and stress pattern. When either judge did not accept a response, its stimulus card was displaced backwards in the order of presentation by at least eight items in order to present it to the subject a second time. An auxiliary list was used at the beginning of the recording session to familiarize the subject with the situation and to permit adjustment of equipment. The same auxiliary list was used to displace backwards in time stimulus items so close to the end of the list that they could not otherwise be displaced by at least eight items. The list of 72 items was randomized anew for each subject.

Before actual recordings were made each subject was given a short training period during which he read aloud all items from a standard list arranged as in Table I. He was assured that no premium would be placed on

[17] M. Cowan, Arch. Speech 1, Suppl., 1 (1936).

accuracy of response as such. Instructions pertaining to vocal behavior were kept to a minimum, and no attempt was made to regulate pitch, duration, or intensity. The subject was simply instructed to pronounce each word as if talking to the experimenter.

II. RESULTS
Influence upon Duration of Vowels

The identification of the beginning and end of a vowel surrounded by consonants is an arbitrary act that is both difficult and artificial. Location of these points was aided by the relative clarity with which they are shown in sound spectrograms. In this study, the spectrograms were produced with a narrow, 45-cps, band response at their base and a wide, 300-cps, response in the higher frequencies, and covered a 0–3500-cps range.[18] This procedure simplified the identification of the voice bar without weakening the vowel resonance areas. Identification of specific sounds was facilitated by information presented by Potter, Kopp, and Green[19] and Joos.[20] The preceding and following consonants were used to find the general area of each vowel, but in all instances the vowel limits were established in terms of "vowelness," based on the presence of voice and of resonance areas associated with particular vowels.

Measurements were made in millimeters and multiplied by 0.00754 to yield values in seconds.[21] For purposes of estimating reliability, a number of measurements were also made on the oscillographic films, and comparison of the two methods of measurement showed close agreement. The symmetrical structure of the test syllables greatly simplified the identification of the vowels and tended to create a situation generally favorable to reliability and validity of measurement. Hanley[22]

TABLE II. Duration of vowels in various consonant environments. Vowels pooled. All values in seconds.

Individual consonant environments		Grouped consonant environments	
p	0.159	*Voicing*	
t	0.168	Voiceless (5)	0.174
k	0.157	Voiced (7)	0.253
f	0.188	*Manner of production*	
s	0.197	Stop-plosive (6)	0.203
b	0.237	Fricative (4)	0.239
d	0.258	Nasal (2)	0.232
g	0.239	*Place of production*	
v	0.279	Bilabial (3)	0.205
z	0.291	Labio-dental (2)	0.234
m	0.219	Post-dental (5)	0.232
n	0.245	Velar (2)	0.198

[18] The normal 0–8000-cps range of the sona-graph was modified locally with the advice of the manufacturer. In essence, the slide wire resistor was shunted by an amount determined experimentally and series resistances added to the appropriate leads to keep the total series resistance constant. These modifications resulted in a 0–3500-cps full scale recording.
[19] Potter, Kopp, and Green, *Visible Speech* (D. Van Nostrand Company, Inc., New York, 1947).
[20] M. Joos, Language 24, Suppl., 1 (1948).
[21] The instrument in question records 2.4 sec in 318.5 mm.
[22] T. D. Hanley, Speech Monog. 18, 78 (1951).

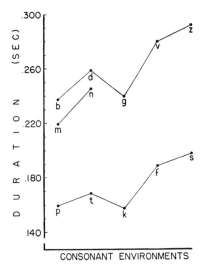

FIG. 1. Mean duration of vowels in various consonant
environments. Vowels pooled.

has shown that even in connected speech durational
measurements from spectrograms have high reliability.

The effect of the consonant environments on the
duration of the vowels is summarized in Table II and
Fig. 1. The left half of Table II shows the mean duration
of all vowels spoken by the 10 subjects in each of the
12 consonant environments. These means vary over a
range of 0.134 sec, and analysis of variance reveals
statistically significant differences between means to
exist at the 1 percent level of confidence. By use of the
t statistic, differences between the various means may
be evaluated with a requirement of 0.011 sec. Of the
total of 66 such intercomparisons, 59 exceed the minimum.

Further study of the duration means shows that they
vary systematically with certain characteristics of
consonant production. A comparison of voiceless environments with their voiced cognate environments,
for example, reveals larger values for the voiced environments in every case. All voiced environments,
furthermore, produced vowels that differed significantly
from all those produced in voiceless environments. When
all responses are pooled with respect to this characteristic, as in the upper right portion of Table II, there is a
statistically significant difference of 0.079 sec between
the two means. The marked effect of voicing on duration is demonstrated in Fig. 1. The baseline shows the
12 consonant environments and is arranged with stop-
plosive consonants to the left of the figure and fricatives
to the right. Cognates and nasal correlatives are shown
in the same vertical plane. Within each manner of
production category sounds are arranged from left to
right according to place of articulation along the antero-
posterior dimension of the oral cavity (e.g., the three
stop-plosives are bilabial, post-dental, and velar in
order).

Attempts to interpret the effect of voicing of the
consonant upon vowel duration have thus far been fruit-
less. It may be, for example, that the voicing of a vowel
in a voiceless environment, in contrast to a voiced
environment, is withheld until the physiological vowel
"target" is more nearly approximated, and terminated
sooner in the transition to the following consonant. The
problem seems to require additional experimentation
with the transition intervals, particularly of a type
employing simultaneous acoustical and physiological
measurements.

Table II also shows that the values for vowels surrounded by stop-plosive, fricative, and nasal classes,
according to manner of production, vary over a 0.036-
sec range, and demonstrate means that differ significantly. The close similarity between the fricative and
nasal means is of interest, since nasal sounds are related
to stop-plosives physiologically and to fricatives dy-
namically. The values suggest a stop-continuant dichotomy, but as the nasal class is composed only of
voiced sounds, which have been shown to increase
the duration of contiguous vowels, this problem cannot
be analyzed definitively with these data.

Reinspection of the 12 individual environment means
in Table II indicates that, voicing constant, consonants
that differ in manner of production produce vowel
durations that usually differ significantly. Figure 1 also
shows, in both voiced and voiceless lines, the trend for
fricative sounds to prolong vowels more than do stop-
plosives. Apparently, the gradual, controlled movements
of continuant consonants favor longer vowel durations
more than do the abrupt, ballistic movements of the
stop-plosives.

The remaining part of Table II shows that the duration of vowels also varies when the responses are sorted
according to place of consonant articulation. The differences reach significance, but this result should be interpreted with caution in view of the findings on voicing
and manner of production. Both velar consonants are
stop-plosives, and both labio-dentals are fricatives,
while the bilabials and post-dentals are weighted with
voiced consonants. The two curves for voiceless and

TABLE III. Fundamental frequency of vowels in various
consonant environments. Vowels pooled. All values in cycles per
second.

Individual consonant environments		Grouped consonant environments	
p	127.86	*Voiced*	
t	127.07	Voiceless (5)	126.46
k	127.17	Voiced (7)	121.99
f	124.32	*Manner of production*	
s	126.06	Stop-plosive (6)	124.36
b	120.86	Fricative (4)	123.80
d	120.58	Nasal (2)	122.47
g	122.77	*Place of production*	
v	122.20	Bilabial (3)	123.90
z	122.62	Labio-dental (2)	123.26
m	123.16	Post-dental (5)	123.62
n	121.77	Velar (2)	124.97

voiced cognates in Fig. 1, however, are remarkably similar in shape, seemingly illustrating characteristic differences between the effects of consonants, voicing constant, for place as well as for manner of articulation.

The three interactions between consonant environment, vowels and subjects were significant at the 1 percent level.

Influence upon Fundamental Frequency of Vowels

The oscillograms described above were synchronized with the spectrograms used in the measurement of duration, and analogous points in the vowel wave forms nearest to the limits of the duration interval were identified. Measurement of this distance was made in centimeters rounded to the nearest quarter of a millimeter and divided by the integral number of cycles which it subtended, yielding mean period in cm. This value, divided into the film speed, 249.3 cm/sec,[23] gave the mean fundamental frequency of the vowel.

The means for the different consonant environments shown in the left column of Table III vary significantly over a range of 7.28 cps. Comparison of these mean values to requirements of 2.40 cps and 1.82 cps at the 1-percent and 5-percent levels, respectively, shows that 41 of the 66 possible differences exceed the minimum at the 5-percent level, and that 35 of these exceed the 1-percent requirement.

Inspection of these means reveals that the fundamental frequencies of vowels in voiceless environments are invariably higher than those in voiced environments. With the exception of [f] compared to [m] and [g], all of these differences are significant at the 5-percent level or better. The means are graphed in Fig. 2, the arrangement being the same as for Fig. 1. Voiceless and voiced groups were formed, with means as shown in the upper right of Table III, and the difference was tested with the expected result. The conclusion is reached that the presence or absence of vocal-fold vibration during consonants has a real effect upon the fundamental frequency of adjacent vowels in the direction mentioned.

In an attempt to explain this effect, frequency curves of a number of complete responses were plotted from the oscillograms, using 0.05-sec sampling intervals. From these curves, and also by ear in the responses generally, it was observed that the pitch inflection of the first, and unstressed, syllable [hə] was usually downward and reached a frequency considerably lower than the dominant level of the vowel in the following stressed syllable. Phonation continued from this low frequency with a rising inflection into the second syllable when the initial consonant of the second syllable was voiced. When that consonant was voiceless, and the characteristic interruption of phonation separated the two syllables, the voicing of the stressed syllable usually started at a higher frequency. It was

[23] Recording paper length × recording speed/sec per min = 191.2×78.26/60 = 249.3.

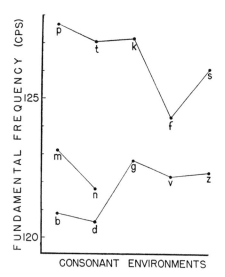

FIG. 2. Mean fundamental frequency of vowels in various consonant environments. Vowels pooled.

suspected, further that the fundamental frequency of voiced consonant environments might influence that of the vowel. Crandall[11] reports lower fundamental frequencies for voiced consonants than for vowels, but his conditions were dissimilar. As it was deemed impractical at this time to make such a comparison with all 720 responses in the present study, one response involving voiced continuant consonants was selected at random from each of the 10 subjects. By chance such selection yielded syllables including four vowels and all four consonants, each of the latter at least twice. For each response the frequencies of the consonants immediately contiguous to the vowel were measured on the oscillogram. A sample of 0.10 sec was used, unless the duration of the consonant was shorter than that interval. For the preceding and following consonants, respectively, the means were three and 10 cps lower than that of the vowels. In other words, the calculations indicated a consonant-vowel-consonant inflection that was circumflex. No definitive explanation can be advanced on the basis of these data, but if the natural fundamental frequency of voiced consonants is lower than that of vowels, it is not implausible to suggest that a vowel surrounded by voiced consonants might have a lower mean fundamental frequency than when these influences are absent. Further study of this problem is in progress.

Comparison of the fundamental frequencies of vowels with respect to the manner of production of adjacent consonants, stop-plosive, fricative, or nasal, is somewhat complex. It may be carried out most readily by studying in conjunction the left column of means in Table II, especially as graphed in Fig. 2, and the right central portion of that same table. The latter measures differ significantly, but the absolute size of the maxi-

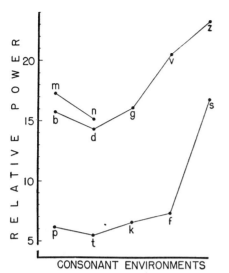

FIG. 3. Mean relative power of vowels in various consonant environments. Vowels pooled.

mum difference is only 1.89 cps. Study of Fig. 2 and evaluation of the statistical significance of the differences there shown discloses that although individual consonant environments may differ in their effects from class to class, the differences are small, often not significant, and variable in direction, when voicing, the predominant factor, is held constant.

The effects of varying the characteristic place of articulation are generally similar. A test of significance of the lower right means in Table III allows the rejection of the hypothesis of no difference at the 5-percent level of confidence, but a close inspection of the variables suggests that most of the differences probably may be attributed to chance.

The interactions involving subjects reached statistical significance, while the vowel-by-consonant interaction failed to reach the 5-percent level. The relative variation of the individual vowels in the differing consonant environments was strikingly similar.

General study of the data presented in this section indicates that the effects of consonants upon fundamental frequency, although significant, are probably less than the variations in fundamental frequency natural to the vowels themselves when consonant environments are constant (see Table V).

Influence upon Relative Power of Vowels

The intensity curves produced by the high speed level recorder showed typical bimodal forms with the second and greater mode corresponding to the stressed syllable. For each such syllable the maximum level was measured. The phonetic structure of the material and the characteristics of the records allow the assumptions that this point was reached during the production of the vowel, that it occurred within the time interval

measured for duration and fundamental frequency, and that it furnished valid data concerning the intensity of the vowel. The measurements for each subject were expressed in db above the lowest value for that subject and in turn converted to relative power to facilitate arithmetic treatment.[24] These manipulations tended to minimize variation in intensity from subject to subject. It will be recalled that this vocal characteristic was not controlled in the original procedure, where each subject was permitted to establish his own general level. The existence of individual differences in vocal output is a well-known phenomenon and was not of interest in this study. It should be noted further that results of analysis of variance indicate that subject variation was not completely obliterated.

Study of the consonant environment means in the left column of Table IV shows them to range from 5.43 to 23.28, and a test of this variation allows the rejection of the null hypothesis at the 1-percent level. If the 66 possible differences between these means are evaluated against a requirement of 4.04, 42 are seen to be significant at the 1-percent level. Further study of these means shows that voicing of the consonant environment was almost uniformly productive of greater mean power. When voiceless and voiced categories are formed, as in the right of the table, this difference is seen to be large on the average and is significant. Statistical evaluation of the differences between the individual consonant means shows that all voiced environments produced significantly greater power than all voiceless environments with the single exception of [s]. The nature of these differences may be visualized in the graphs of these means in Fig. 3. This finding would be an expected one in that the continuation of phonation throughout the consonants as well as the vowel would be likely to favor greater maximum intensity.

The data on the power of vowels in stop-plosive, fricative and nasal environments are presented in Table IV and represent statistically significant differences. These variations may be observed in Fig. 3. In view of the marked effect of voicing, mentioned above, the

TABLE IV. Relative power of vowels in various consonant environments. Vowels pooled. All values in relative power.

Individual consonant environments		Grouped consonant environments	
p	6.11	*Voicing*	
t	5.43	Voiceless (5)	8.40
k	6.48	Voiced (7)	17.46
f	7.21	*Manner of production*	
s	16.78	Stop-plosive (6)	10.68
b	15.72	Fricative (4)	16.94
d	14.28	Nasal (2)	16.19
g	16.08	*Place of production*	
v	20.52	Bilabial (3)	13.03
z	23.28	Labio-dental (2)	13.87
m	17.25	Post-dental (5)	14.98
n	15.13	Velar (2)	11.28

[24] Relative power was taken as equal to antilog$_{10}$ $N/10$, where N was expressed in db.

comparison is probably valid only for the stop-plosive and fricative classes. Voicing constant, differences between the individual fricative and stop-plosive environment means of Table IV generally are significant. An exception is the fricative [f], which did not differ from the voiceless stop-plosives.

The lower right section of Table IV shows that the effect of the place of production of adjacent consonants is small. Although this effect is statistically significant, since the low intensity velar environments are all voiceless, and the post-dental environments at the other extreme are weighted in favor of voicing, the evidence for differences caused by variation in place of articulation is regarded as inconclusive. Nevertheless, the semi-parallel curves of Fig. 3 indicate similarities of consonant effects within a given voicing class.

When relative power is considered, the interaction between vowels and consonants reaches significance barely at the 5-percent level. The interactions involving subjects are significant.

Differences between Vowels

Table V presents the data for the six specific vowels listed in order of the conventional physiological vowel diagram. The general behavior of the three secondary characteristics may be observed in the top row of each section of Table V where the various environments have been pooled, and these data are also graphed in Fig. 4. Analyses of the variances attributable to vowels showed them to be significant beyond the 1-percent level for all three variables.

It will be seen that the duration of vowels is directly related to size of mouth opening and inversely related to tongue height. The conformity of [e] and [o] to the progression is interesting, since they are commonly diphthongized and longer durations would not have been surprising. These trends are in general agreement

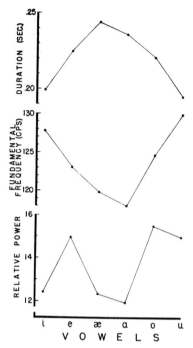

FIG. 4. Mean duration, fundamental frequency, and relative power of vowels. Consonant environments pooled.

with the data reported by Black,[13] by Heffner and others,[2-5] and by Parmenter and Treviño,[12] while Crandall's data[11] show an inversion of the tendency. The results shed considerable doubt upon the classification of [i], [ɑ], and [u] as "long" vowels and of [e], [æ], and [o] as "short" vowels by Jones,[8] and upon the assertion by Thomas[10] that "tense" vowels are generally longer in duration than "lax" vowels. That durational variation should progress as shown is plausible, and probably may be explained on grounds of varying extent of articulatory movement with correspondingly varying time.

In the middle graph of Fig. 4 it will be observed that fundamental frequency varies systematically and directly with the usual vertical location of the high point of the tongue. This finding of a "vowel-pitch triangle" is in general agreement with data reported by Crandall,[11] Black,[13] Peterson and Barney,[25] and Taylor.[14] The concomitant variation of fundamental frequency and tongue position has been explained by the latter author as dynamogenetic radiation from the tongue musculature to the laryngeal muscles controlling the tension of the vocal folds. Thus, in comparison to a "low" vowel, the increase in tongue height of a "high" vowel is accompanied by increased tension of the tongue musculature. Such variations in degree of tension are irradiated to the laryngeal musculature, producing corre-

[25] G. E. Peterson and H. L. Barney, J. Acoust. Soc. Am. 24, 175 (1952).

TABLE V. Acoustic characteristics of specific vowels in various types of consonant environments. Top line of each section shows vowel means when all environments are pooled; remaining lines show vowel means for five mutually exclusive classes of environment. See also Figs. 4 and 5.

	[i]	[e]	[æ]	[ɑ]	[o]	[u]
Duration (sec)						
All environments (12)	0.199	0.225	0.244	0.236	0.221	0.195
Voiceless stops (3)	0.138	0.171	0.184	0.180	0.157	0.138
Voiceless fricatives (2)	0.177	0.199	0.215	0.218	0.187	0.161
Nasals (2)	0.209	0.238	0.253	0.235	0.241	0.217
Voiced stops (3)	0.215	0.251	0.276	0.267	0.244	0.215
Voiced fricatives (2)	0.277	0.283	0.304	0.295	0.293	0.261
Fundamental frequency (cps)						
All environments (12)	127.86	123.03	119.78	118.00	124.64	129.83
Voiceless stops (3)	132.07	126.44	122.00	120.97	128.57	133.79
Voiceless fricatives (2)	129.59	124.05	119.80	119.59	125.86	132.86
Nasals (2)	125.89	119.93	118.75	117.78	122.64	129.83
Voiced stops (3)	125.34	121.02	117.87	115.80	123.13	125.26
Voiced fricatives (2)	125.58	123.00	119.69	116.25	121.22	127.69
Relative power (see text)						
All environments (12)	12.43	14.94	12.35	11.97	15.49	14.94
Voiceless stops (3)	4.16	8.30	5.50	5.78	7.35	4.91
Voiceless fricatives (2)	12.43	12.70	11.39	11.17	12.83	11.48
Nasals (2)	17.05	15.96	17.18	12.14	16.84	17.97
Voiced stops (3)	13.80	16.65	13.66	14.94	18.29	14.78
Voiced fricatives (2)	18.19	23.58	16.74	17.42	24.82	30.67

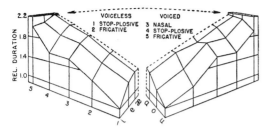

FIG. 5. Three-dimensional graph showing mean duration of specific vowels in various classes of consonant environment. Figure is divided along the median plane and the two halves rotated to show both sides.

sponding variations in vocal-fold tension and in the fundamental frequency of the output.

The group data for relative power are shown in the lowest portion of Fig. 4. With this arrangement of vowels, regularity of progression, as in the case of duration and fundamental frequency, is absent. The curve also differs in certain respects from previous results. While the vowels [æ] and [ɑ] are here seen to be lowest in mean power, Sacia and Beck,[15] Black,[13] and Fairbanks, House and Stevens[1] report reverse findings. These vowels, furthermore, are known to have the largest anterior diameters of the vocal conduit, an aspect which Fairbanks[26] has shown to be closely related to vowel intensity. The vowels fall into two groups of greater and lesser power, and within each group the range is very small. While the general analysis of variance revealed significant differences among the vowels, comparison of the individual means within each of the two groups of vowels mentioned yielded no statistically significant differences.

It would appear that this atypical vowel curve, if not resulting from chance, might be a product of the present experimental design, which differs from those of previous investigations. For one thing, consonant environments were less restricted in the present experiment, which might be important in view of the substantial variance for consonants mentioned above. Investigation of this factor by regrouping according to the three main characteristics of consonant environment, however, showed that similar curves were found under all these conditions. Another difference from previous experiments, although it seems an unlikely source, is that the stimuli in this instance were bisyllabic with the syllable studied being preceded by a common unstressed syllable. A third difference that should be mentioned was that all stimuli were nonmeaningful, although this factor would appear to operate, if at all, in the opposite direction. A more plausible factor is the phonetic symmetry of the present syllables, which required a subject to begin from and return to the same consonant position. It seems reasonable to suggest that this condition might restrict the extent of movement to the vowel position, and that the restriction might be greatest for vowels of

[26] G. Fairbanks, Speech Monog. 17, 390 (1950).

normally large mouth opening such as [æ] and [ɑ]. An additional condition, involving the spelling of stimulus items, should be mentioned. It will be seen in Table I that the vowels [æ] and [ɑ] were represented for the subjects by spellings of one letter while the other vowels were spelled with two letters. Also, it would seem likely that the spoken vowels intended by the four two-letter spellings would, in general, be more clear to the naive subject, and during the course of the experiment it was observed that subjects conditioned more swiftly to them than to the one-letter spellings. It will be recalled that the original recordings included those responses which necessitated repetition because of misarticulation of the vowels. A count of these showed that [æ] and [ɑ] were involved approximately equally in more than two-thirds of the total, or double the chance expectancy. A confident explanation of the atypical findings for relative power cannot be advanced, but both of the latter two possibilities present problems which are themselves worthy of investigation.

It having been shown that the three dependent variables vary significantly among vowels, and that consonant environments also exert significant and systematic influences, it is of interest to determine whether the influence of one is to be felt under the various conditions of the other. The main portions of Table V show means for each of the six vowels in each of five different, mutually exclusive classes of consonant environment. These classes involved voicing and manner of articulation, the two factors demonstrated to be most powerful. Examination of the data will show the influence of both vowel and consonant environment. Thus, the values for any given consonant environment change from vowel to vowel in a manner generally similar to the change when all environments are pooled. The means in any column are observed to progress more

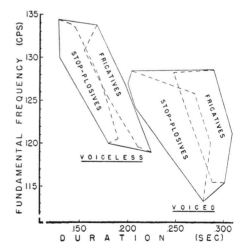

FIG. 6. Frequency-duration ranges of vowels in certain consonant environments.

or less systematically down the column in the direction shown to be generally appropriate for that variable when all vowels are pooled.

The nature of these interactions may best be appreciated by reference to Fig. 5 which displays the values for duration in Table V and is exemplary of the general findings. In this three-dimensional figure, the ordinate is duration while consonant classes and vowels are shown along the horizontal axes. The figure is split and spread to show both sides. The systematic variation of vowel duration in response to changes in both consonant environment and in vowel is clearly seen. It is of considerable interest that the influence of neither factor is obscured by the other, which is a finding of obvious implication for experimental design.

Interrelationships between Acoustical Characteristics

In the above discussion, duration, fundamental frequency, and power have been considered separately. In this section they are brought together for purposes of illustrating their covariation.

Figure 6 shows the effects of voicing and manner of production of consonants on vowels. The figure depicts frequency-duration areas for voiced and voiceless stop-plosives and fricatives. Each area boundary connects the most divergent coordinate values, i.e., the maximally varying vowel means, in each type of consonant environment shown. The characteristic influences of the voiced and voiceless groups upon both duration and frequency, the contrasting effects of cognate environments, and the distinct differences in duration between stop-plosives and fricatives are readily apparent.

A concise illustration of the major findings of the experiment is found in Fig. 7 which shows the means of the pooled vowels for the 12 consonant environments. The ordinate is frequency, the abscissa is duration, and the diameter of the dots is proportional to relative power. Substantial intercorrelations are evident between all dimensions. It will be observed that vowels in voiced environments are, in general, longer in duration, lower in fundamental frequency, and greater in power than are the same vowels when in voiceless environments. Within voicing groups, clusters corresponding to manner of production may also be found.

III. SUMMARY AND CONCLUSIONS

In a study of the influence of consonant environment upon the secondary acoustical characteristics of vowels, the subjects spoke 72 different consonant-vowel-consonant syllables in each of which the vowel was both preceded and followed by the same consonant. Twelve representative consonants were combined with six representative vowels. Acoustical measurements of the duration, fundamental frequency, and intensity of the vowel

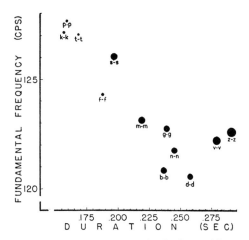

Fig. 7. Relationships between duration, fundamental frequency, and relative power of vowels in various consonant environments. Relative power proportional to dot diameter. Vowels pooled.

of each syllable were made, and analyzed with special reference to variance attributable to the articulatory characteristics of the consonants. Following were the major results.

1. Consonant environment significantly influenced all three acoustical characteristics of the vowels. Of the types of consonant influences studied, the effects of voicing were greatest. In the comparisons of voiced and voiceless consonant environments, vowels in voiced environments, with few exceptions, were longer in duration, lower in fundamental frequency, and greater in relative power.

2. Manner of production was the second most influential consonant characteristic. Its effect upon the duration and relative power of vowels was more consistent than upon fundamental frequency, although all three varied significantly.

3. Place of articulation appeared to be the least important of the consonant characteristics, but its influence may have been obscured by the conditions of the experiment.

4. When all consonant environments were pooled, significant differences between vowels were found in all three acoustical characteristics. From vowel to vowel, duration and fundamental frequency varied in a manner systematically related to the usual conceptions of vowel physiology, while variations in relative power were atypical.

5. When changes in the acoustical characteristics of the vowels were examined in relation to variations of both consonant environment and vowel, the influence of neither factor obliterated that of the other.

6. Variations of the three acoustical characteristics in response to changing consonant environments were substantially intercorrelated.

CHAPTER 11

Reprinted from Miscellenea Phonetica, Vol. II (1954).

Acoustic Analysis of Stop Consonants

ELI FISCHER-JØRGENSEN

(University of Copenhagen)

I. Introduction.

THE main object of this article is to compare the results of a detailed acoustic analysis of Danish stops with the results of the experiments carried out in the Haskins Laboratories in New York [1] on the perception of synthetic stop consonants.

English sounds would have been better for this purpose, since Danish stops show some particularities, but many of the results are of general application, and as far as the influence on vowel formants is concerned, the Danish findings can be compared with American English. The work of Potter, Kopp, and Green [2] has been very important on this point ; but their spectrograms do not allow of an adequate description of the characteristic noise pattern, since the upper limit is 3500 c.p.s.

Swedish stops have been investigated by Gunnar Fant,[3] but only a brief summary of some of the results has been published.[4] The problems have been treated on a more general level by Roman Jakobson, Fant, and Halle.[5]

Danish has six stops : **p t k b d g.** Phonemically, **p:b, t:d, k:g** are only distinguished before (immediately before or as the first member of a cluster preceding) a full vowel (i.e. all vowels except ə) belonging to the same minimal sign—or " morpheme " in the Prague-American sense of this word (with the exception that foreign derivatives in this respect are not treated as separate signs). In all other positions, there

[1] F. S. Cooper, P. C. Delattre, A. M. Liberman, J. M. Borst, and L. Gerstman : *Some Experiments on the Perception of Synthetic Speech Sounds, JASA* 24, 1952, pp. 597–617, and A. M. Liberman, P. Delattre, and F. S. Cooper : *The Role of Selected Stimulus-Variables in the Perception of the Unvoiced Stop Consonants, American Journal of Psychology* 65, 1952, pp. 497–516.

[2] T. C. Potter, G. A. Kopp, and H. C. Green : *Visible Speech*, New York, 1947. Cf. also G. A. Kopp and H. C. Green : *Basic Phonetic Principles of Visible Speech, JASA* 17, 1946, pp. 74–89.

[3] Gunnar M. Fant : *Analys av de svenska Konsonantljuden, L. M. Ericsson protokoll H/P-1064*, 1949, mimeographed.

[4] Gunnar M. Fant : *Transmission Properties of the Vocal Tract, Part II, Acoustics Laboratory, MIT Quarterly Progress Report*, Oct.–Dec., 1950.

[5] R. Jakobson, G. Fant, M. Halle : *Preliminaries to Speech Analysis. Acoustics Laboratory MIT, Technical Report no. 13*, 1952.

are only three stops. In final position, there is free variation between
p and **b, t** and **d, k** and **g.** Before ə, the normal manifestation is
b d g. As the voiced continuants ð and ɣ are found only in the
positions which do not distinguish between **t** and **d, k** and **g,** it is
possible to assume four phonemes which are manifested as **t d k g** in
one position and as **d ð g ɣ** respectively in another position [1] (**p** and **b**
present a different case, because **v** is found in all positions). In this
article we are chiefly concerned with the position initially before a full
vowel. But as regards the distinction between labials, alveolars, and
palato-velars, the stop variants in other positions (here indicated as
B D G) are also considered.

The information about Danish stops given on the following pages [2]
is chiefly based upon the analysis of spectrograms (sonagrams taken
with the Kay Electric Sonagraph) [3] of 1368 stop consonants spoken
by nine different subjects (eight male and one female [EFJ]). Six of
the speakers were from Copenhagen, three from Fyn, but all speak
what may be called Standard Danish without any perceptible
dialectal variations except in the intonation. Seven of the speakers
were trained phoneticians. The material consisted of series of
isolated words (in one of the series, spoken by the three main subjects,
connected by [ʌ] " and "). The sonagrams are the only source of
information about frequency. In a few cases the analysis has been
controlled by " sections ". In most cases this was not possible. The
indications about intensity are based upon intensity curves of 300
stops spoken by the three main subjects and recorded on " Wide
Band " by means of the amplitude display unit which can be combined with the Sonagraph. The results were in conformity with what
might be concluded from the spectrograms, and have been further
controlled by comparison with seventy-two oscillograms of selected

---

[1] As first suggested by H. J. Uldall : *The Phonematics of Danish, Proceedings,
Second International Congress of Phonetic Sciences*, 1935, p. 54.   Cf. also
A. Martinet : *La phonologie du mot en danois*, 1937.

[2] Space has allowed only a very brief summary. A fuller treatment with
detailed documentation will be given later.

[3] Most of the sonagrams were taken in the Modern Language Department
of the MIT, Cambridge, U.S.A., and in the Royal Technical High School in
Stockholm, a small number in the University of Wisconsin. I am indebted to
Professor W. A. Locke, to Mr. Gunnar Fant, and to Professor Martin Joos for
valuable help and for having permitted me to work in their laboratories, and to
the Rockefeller Foundation for having enabled me to undertake studies
in the U.S.

4*

examples.[1] The details given on duration are partly based on the spectrograms (and oscillograms) partly on a kymographic investigation comprising approximately 1450 stops, spoken by five of the same subjects who took part in the spectrographic investigation plus one additional subject. In this case the examples formed part of small sentences. The information on voicing is almost exclusively based on this investigation.

II. Differences between Danish p t k and b d g.

Here we are concerned only with the position in which the two groups are distinguished. The main difference between Danish **p t k** and **b d g** is one of *aspiration* : **p t k** are strongly aspirated, **b d g** are unaspirated or slightly aspirated. In **p t k,** the duration of the aspiration is extremely variable, depending on small differences in rhythm and accent. The extremes in accented syllables are 2 and 14 cs. The average duration of the open interval[2] for all ten subjects is for **p** 6·6 cs. (individual averages from 5·3 to 9·7), for **t** 7·9 (6·4–9·8), and for **k** 7·4 (6·0–9·1). These averages are longer than those found in English and German. The duration amounts to 37–54 per cent (individual averages) of the whole length of the consonant.[3] **b d g** normally have very slight aspiration, which, however, does not exceed the " aspiration " found in languages with so-called unaspirated **p t k.** For the three main subjects, the averages are : **b** 1·4, **d** 1·7, **g** 2·3 (variations from 0 to 4). For the other subjects, the number of examples is not sufficiently safe.

The difference in aspiration is accompanied by a difference in the *duration* of the closure. This is relatively shorter for **p t k** than for **b d g.** The differences are small (under identical conditions 2·8 cs. for **p-b,** 4·5 for **t-d,** and 2·6 for **k-g**) but very stable, and statistically reliable.

These seem to be the only differences between the two groups of sounds. Both are completely voiceless after a pause and after a voiceless sound, and partly voiced by assimilation after a voiced sound (**B D G** are often completely voiced after a voiced sound). There

---

[1] I am indebted to Dr. Svend Smith (Statens Institut for Talelidende, Copenhagen) for helping me to take the oscillograms.

[2] In the sense of explosion + aspiration, which have not been distinguished in these measurements. As the explosion is always very short, its inclusion in the measurement is of little importance.

[3] Duration, aspiration, and voicing of Danish stops have been examined by H. Abrahams : *Études phonétiques sur les tendances évolutives des occlusives germaniques*, 1949. There is great conformity in the results.

does not seem to be any regular correspondence in intensity either : **k** has normally a stronger explosion than **g** ; on the other hand **d** always has a stronger explosion than **t,** and **p-b** do not show any constant differences. There is no physiological evidence either for a stronger tension of **p t k.** Muscular feeling goes in the opposite direction, particularly for **t-d,** and palatograms show identity of contact, or slightly more contact, for **d** and **g.** But there seems to be a difference in the manner of explosion, **p t k** being released by the air current, **b d g** by active movements of lips and tongue.

It is in many ways interesting to note that we have here a case where strong aspiration is combined with weak articulation and short closure.

The Haskins experiments have shown that when listeners hear synthetic vowels with a rise or fall at the beginning of the second formant they tend to hear an initial stop, and " transitions of the first formant appear to contribute to voicing of the stop consonants ".[1] When the first formant has a rising start, the subjects are more inclined to hear **b d g** ; when it is level they are inclined to hear **p t k.** In our spectrograms a movement of the first formant is evident only when it is high, i.e. in open vowels. As all the consonants were said by all the subjects before a short **a** (and twice by one), we possess sixty spectrograms of this type (three could not be used). The number of cases with level, very slightly rising, and clearly rising F1 are for **p t k** 19-5-5, for **b d g** 2-6-20 respectively. There is thus an evident difference, and, as all our stops are unvoiced, it is not simply a question of voicing. It is not difficult to find a physiological explanation of this difference : the height of the first formant has a close relation to the degree of opening.[2] As the distance between the explosion of **b d g** and the beginning of the vowel is short, the maximum opening is not reached until after the beginning of the vowel. After the aspirated consonants **p t k,** there is sufficient time for the opening movement before the vowel starts. Voicing, however, is not without importance. The transition is longer after voiced stops, simply because there is no voiceless pause between the explosion and the vowel, concealing the beginning of the transition (this also appeared from a series of voiced and voiceless **b d g**'s spoken by three of the subjects). The change must therefore be more audible after voiced consonants, and the more so, because

[1] *JASA* 24, p. 600.
[2] Cf. P. Delattre : *The Physiological Interpretation of Sound Spectrograms,* *PMLA* 66, 1951, pp. 864–875.

a low consonant formant precedes. For listeners having voiced **b d g** in their own language, a rising F1 will thus suggest the presence of a preceding voiced consonant. It seems likely, however, that synthetic stops with and without aspiration would give a still better distinction, not only for Danish but also for English listeners.

IIIa. Differences between Danish Labials (p/b), Alveolars (t/d), and Palatovelars (k/g) [1]

A. Explosion.[2]

The *intensity* of the explosion shows characteristic differences for **p t k,** but the relations are complicated by the influence of the subsequent vowel : before the unrounded vowels **i e ɛ a** the explosion of the palatovelars is stronger than before rounded vowels (4–5 db. for **k,** 2–3 for **g**), and in this case the intensity is always decreasing in the order **k > p > t.** Before rounded vowels **k** is stronger than **p** in only half the examples. The unaspirated consonants do not show any constant relationship, but **d** is often relatively strong and **b** relatively weak.

The differences in *duration,* although slight, are more stable. Twenty-seven oscillograms of **b d g** in identical positions show the order **g > d > b** in all nine cases (averages 1·0, 0·68, 0·34 cs.) and forty-five oscillograms of **p t k** show **k > p > t** in thirteen out of fifteen cases (averages 1·12, 0·7, and 0·24 cs.). In addition, spectrograms show that **k** nearly always has a longer explosion than **p** and **t.** Further, it is often found that the explosion of **g** and **k** is double, containing two clicks with approximately 0·5–1 cs. in between. Kymograms also show a slower rise for **k g** than for **p b,** and the same is true for German and English **k g** as compared with **p b t d.** The difference is understandable from a physiological point of view : the bulk of the tongue cannot move as quickly as the tip or the lips.

The *frequency* of the noise cannot be described without considering the vowel that follows. It is necessary, therefore, to say a few words about Danish vowels.

---

[1] We prefer the name " palatovelars " (or " postpalatals ") to the normal term " velars ", because palatograms of **g** and **k** (obtained by the colour method, not with an artificial palate) have not revealed a single pure velar, and predominantly velar **k** and **g** are only found before **r** (Danish **r** is uvular). The back limit of the contact is generally found to be just behind or in front of the borderline between the soft and the hard palate, and the front limit varies according to the vowel.

[2] See the schematic spectrograms on p. 51 illustrating the differences between **p, t, k** before **e** and **o** in respect of duration and frequency of explosion and aspiration, and bending of vowel formants.

Danish has ten vowel phonemes : i e ε a y ø œ u o ɔ (and ə, which may perhaps be dispensed with). All occur long and short with phonemic difference. We hope to be able to give a detailed acoustic description in a later article. For the time being some very rough indications about the frequency of formants for the long vowels of the male subjects may be sufficient. The numbers in the following table give the limits of variation (except for a,[1] where one subject has a particular placement of F1 : 425–525).

		F1	F2	F3
i	. .	225–250	2000–2600	2800–3600
e	. .	275–300	2100–2600	2650–3400
ε	. .	350–400	1900–2250	2500–3000
a	. .	550–650	1650–2100	2400–2850
y	. .	225–275	1800–2100	2000–2400
ø	. .	275–325	1600–1900	2000–2250
œ	. .	350–425	1450–1650	2050–2300
u	. .	225–275	650– 850	2000–2300
o	. .	300–350	625– 750	2000–2600
ɔ	. .	350–400	825–1000	1900–2600

F4 is individually variable. In unrounded vowels it is situated between 3300 and 4100, in rounded vowels between 2900 and 3800.

This rich vowel system is useful for the study of the influence of vowels on contiguous consonants because it permits a distinction between the influence of rounding and of front-back position. The differences between F1 of i y u—e ø o—ε œ ɔ—a are small but very stable. F2 is much more variable. Only two of the eight subjects have the high values 2400–2600 for i and e ; the majority of the subjects have a formant round 2100–2200. F2 of i is in the great majority of cases lower for i than for e, but all have descending F3 in the series i e ε a (long a sounds approximately like English a in *man*). In y ø œ F3 may take the opposite direction. F3 of u o ɔ is weak. In y, the essential point seems to be that F3 is very close to F2. This system supports the recent assumption of the importance of F3, and suggests that distances between formant regions, not simply between formants would seem to be essential (e.g. i and y are similar by having (mostly) narrow regions with great distances : i F1–F2–F3/4, y F1–F2/3–F4). The short vowels have almost the same quality as the long vowels with the exception of ɔ, a and (partly) o.

The explosion of g and k is characterized by having an intensity

[1] In narrow transcription [æː].

maximum of relatively low frequency which varies according to the following (or preceding) vowel, and a high maximum which is independent of the vowel.

The extreme limits of the lower maximum are 600 and 3700 c.p.s. The averages for all subjects taken together are: **i** 2927, **e** 2880, **ε** 2614, **a** 2259, **y** 1708, **œ** 1450, **ø** 1447, **u** 1051, **ɔ** 1018, **o** 969. Long and short vowels have been taken together, since the differences are slight. We have, however, excluded short **ɔ** which is rather like **ʌ** (maximum 1310), and the back variety of long **a** (which is more like German **a** and before which the maximum is 1825). The averages of maxima before the different vowels show the same order for all single subjects except for **u-ɔ** and **ø-œ**. Within the groups **u/o/ɔ**, **y/ø/œ**, **i/e/ε**, and **a**, there is great overlapping of single cases even for the same subject. Between these groups, overlapping is very infrequent and the differences are evidently significant.

Before rounded vowels, the maximum is very concentrated and clear. Before the unrounded vowels, it is broader, and before **e** and **ε** it may be divided into two, with one peak near F2 and one near F3. The strongest of the two has been taken as a basis for the average.

A comparison with the table of the vowel formants will show that the maximum follows F2 of rounded vowels. Before **u o ɔ**, it is normally situated somewhat above F2 (94 cases in all; 72 above, 16 =, and 6 below F2). Before **y ø œ**, it is normally below F2 (65 cases in all; 5 above, 19 =, and 41 below F2).

Before **a**, the maximum is normally found between F2 and F3 (30 out of 47 cases, 9 higher and 9 lower). Before **ε e i**, it is closer to F3 (10 cases at or below F2 (9 of these before **ε**), 44 cases between F2 and F3, and 44 cases at or above F3).

Before rounded vowels, the higher maximum is always clearly separated from the lower maximum by a long distance without any energy. This higher maximum is generally found between 4000 and 5400 (particularly between 4400 and 5000), but two subjects have a much lower position (between 3400 and 3800; these subjects have also a relatively low F4 in the vowels). These two maxima are always present, but there may be a third maximum about 5700–6000 and a fourth about 7000, which with some subjects is rather strong.

Before unrounded vowels, the lower maximum is much closer to the higher maximum, and there is more intensity in between, so that sometimes they are not clearly separated. Moreover, both maxima are broader, and the higher may have two tops, one approximately at 4000 and one at 4800–5000, so that there may be one long stretch of noise from about 2500 to 5000 with two or three not very prominent peaks. The higher maxima at 5700–6000 and 7000 are less prominent and often lacking.

Finally and before ə, **G** is affected by the preceding vowel in much the same way, but the lower maximum is generally 100–200 c.p.s. higher after than before rounded vowels and somewhat lower after than before unrounded vowels, so that there is a certain approximation to a more neutral position.

These findings are in conformity with the results obtained by Fant for Swedish (**g k** in connection with **i a o**) ; and Potter, Kopp, and Green have found similar positions of the lower maximum in English ; it seems, however, to be somewhat higher before back vowels (1200 1700) than in Danish and Swedish. Presumably this is chiefly due to less rounding, but might also raise some doubt as to the velar character of English **k/g**.

The labials and alveolars are less affected by adjacent vowels and, particularly in the case of the labials, the tendency mentioned by Fant [1] towards an average spacing of maxima with approximately 1,000 c.p.s. distance, is very obvious.

Both in labials and alveolars the position of the maxima seems almost unaffected by a following vowel. In the case of the alveolars it is, however, of importance for the relative intensity of the maxima, whether the vowel is rounded or unrounded. The maxima are found approximately at 1950, 3000, 3800, and 4800, and sometimes higher, but before rounded vowels, No. 1 and (particularly) No. 2 of these maxima are relatively strong, and No. 3 and (particularly) No. 4 are relatively weak, so that the main energy is concentrated from about 2000 to 4000 c.p.s., whereas before unrounded vowels, No. 1 and (particularly) No. 2 are relatively weak, and No. 3 and (particularly) No. 4 are relatively strong, and often there is one long stretch of energy from 3500 to 6000. There is no difference between **d** and **t,** except that the maximum at 1950 is weaker and may be absent in **t.** The maxima at 1950 and 3000 correspond to the two maxima at 1500 and 2500 in Fant's figures, explained by him as the neutral resonances of the vocal tract. They are thus somewhat higher in Danish, whereas the higher maxima are somewhat lower. This may perhaps be explained by a somewhat more retracted tongue position in Danish **d t.**—There may be a still lower maximum at 1300–1400, particularly before rounded vowels.

In final position, the maxima are the same. In the case of the alveolars, it is often possible to see the noise of the implosion phase.

---

[1] *Transmission Properties* p. 17 (see p. 42, note 4).

This is almost exclusively concentrated on the high frequencies found at 3800 and 4800.

The labials have approximately the same position of maxima, except that the two first maxima in nearly all cases are slightly lower (approximately 1800 and 2700). A lower maximum (here about 1200–1300) is more often found in labials than in alveolars, and it is often stronger, particularly before rounded vowels. Moreover, there may be a maximum round 400, particularly in case of energetic articulation. It is often absent. But the most predominant characteristic of the labials is an almost even distribution of energy at all frequencies with relative peaks round 1800, 2700, 3800, 4800, and 5800 regardless of the adjacent vowel. The maximum at 2700 is usually relatively weak, and there seems often to be a stretch with weak energy above this maximum and still more definitely between 400 and 1200. This neutral character is also shown by the fact that the maxima are slightly higher for the female subject (averages 1890, 3120, 4090, and approximately 5100), whereas this was not the case for the other consonants.

B. Aspiration.

The *duration* of the aspiration is not the same for all types of stops. g has a longer aspiration than b and d. (The averages for the open interval are g 2·3 cs., d 1·7 cs., and b 1·4 cs.) The difference between g and b/d is statistically significant. It is probably due to the slow explosion. The same tendency is found for k as compared with t and p in German and English, but in Danish t has generally longer aspiration than p and k because of its characteristic affrication (for seven of the ten subjects the order is t > k > p, and the averages for all are 7·9, 7·4, and 6·6).

There may also be differences in *intensity*. The slight aspiration after b d g is often simply a pause, but there may be some noise, particularly after d and g before high vowels. The noise following the explosion of t is much stronger than that following p and k. For the three main subjects, the relations of the peaks measured in db. are: t 24·4, k 14·1, p 12·6.

The noise following the explosion of t has exactly the same *frequency* as a Danish s [1]: 3500/4000 to 9000 before unrounded and 2500/3000 to 9000 before rounded vowels (the upper limit can be found by taking spectrograms from the tape running at half speed), with peaks at 4000–4200 and 4900–5100 before unrounded and at

---

[1] The stops have been compared with spectrograms of 1,412 voiceless fricatives (f s h).

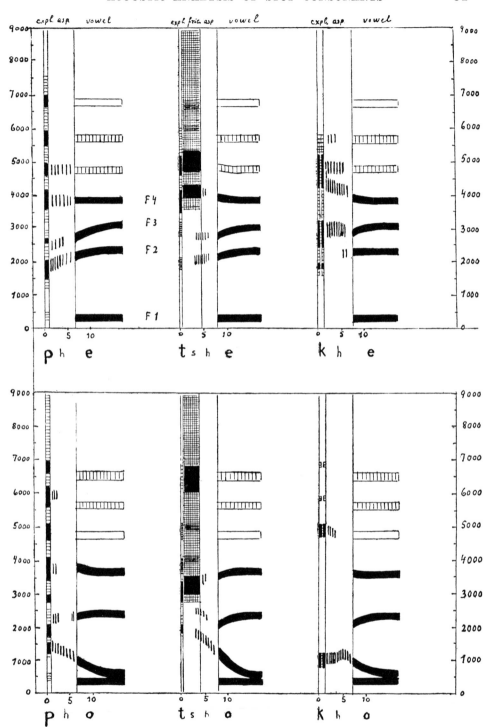

Schematic spectrograms of Danish aspirated **p, t, k** before **e** and **o**. Time is indicated in the horizontal dimension, frequency in the vertical dimension. Dark areas of the explosion and vowel formants represent strong energy, hatched areas weaker energy (which may not be present). The four lower formants of the vowels have been made dark in order to show the bending, although F2, F3, and F4 (particularly F3) of **o** may be weak.

3000–3200 (**u o y ø**), or 3200–3700 (**ɔ œ**) and approximately 6500 before rounded vowels. This high noise is also found in English and German, but it is longer in Danish. The average duration is 4·7 cs. (with variations between 2 and 10 cs.), and it is longer before close vowels than before open vowels. This fricative noise generally exceeds the duration of 2·5–3 cs. indicated by L. G. Jones [1] as the lower limit for an identification as an affricate. (But this would seem to depend on the language of the listeners.) The fricative noise is followed by a real aspiration starting around 1850 and 2700 c.p.s. (somewhat lower before rounded and higher before unrounded vowels) and moving towards F2 and F3 of the vowel. This noise starts 3–4 cs. after the explosion. **s** may have a similar aspiration, but it is always very short (1–3 cs.).

p, on the other hand, does not show any signs of affrication. The aspiration looks like an **h,** i.e. it has no frequency of its own, but moves quickly from a position affected by the **p**-resonance to the positions of the vowel formants. It is particularly strong before F2 of rounded vowels, and of more uniform intensity before F2, 3, 4 (and 5) of unrounded vowels. **f** is characterized by a rather diffuse noise from 2000 upwards, but with predominance of frequencies above 4000. But the **p** aspiration is generally stronger than both **h** and **f.** We have not found a single case of the low aspiration near the baseline mentioned by Potter, Kopp, and Green as being characteristic of **p** and often seen in their spectrograms ; but we have been able to produce a spectrogram of exactly this aspect by talking very close to, and directly into, the microphone.

k may sound slightly affricated. It is difficult to distinguish on the basis of spectrograms between **h** and a **ç/x** sound with frequencies depending on the subsequent vowel. But indications of slight affrication may be seen in the fact that the noise is somewhat stronger than after **p,** and particularly in high frequencies (4000–6000), and perhaps further in the fact that most of the formant bending of **u o ɔ** is accomplished during the aspiration of **p,** but does not take place until the start of the vowel after **k.**

C. Influence on Vowel Formants (and Aspiration).[2]

After *labials*, F2 is rising with decreasing steepness in **e ɛ a** [3] and mostly rising in **y ø œ**, whereas **u o ɔ** have falling F2. This

---

[1] See Jakobson, Fant, Halle : *Preliminaries* p. 24.

[2] After **p t k,** part of the transition movement takes place during the aspiration.

[3] F2 of **i** is not affected by stops or voiceless fricatives in Danish and is not connected with the consonant noise (it is, however, affected by back **r** and

means that vowels which have F2 above 1400 (with a few exceptions in isolated cases) start lower (with starting points from about 1300, for **œ,** to 2200, for **e),** whereas all vowels having F2 below 1000 start higher (with starting points from 1300 to 900).   According to the Visible Speech terminology, Danish labials have a " hub " at approximately 1300.   F3 is rising in **i e ɛ a** (steeply in **i e)** and level in the rounded vowels.   The hub [1] seems to be approximately at 2300.

After *alveolar* stops, F2 of **e** and **ɛ** is rising.   F2 of long **a** [æ:] is rising or level, and the slightly lower F2 of short **a** is level or falling, **y ø œ** have approximately level F2 (it may be falling in **œ),** **u o ɔ** have strongly falling F2.   This means that vowels with F2 above 1800 start lower (but often not quite so low as after labials), and vowels with F2 below 1600 start higher ; this start is definitely higher than after labials (approximately 1300–1800), so that there is often a very steep fall.   The alveolars have thus a hub approximately at 1800. F3 is rising in **i** and **e,** level or falling in **ɛ** and **a,** level or slightly falling in **y ø œ,** and generally rising, but often starting with a short fall in **u o ɔ.**   The hub seems to be at 2700–2800.   Moreover F1 of open vowels seems to start lower after alveolars than after other consonants, and F4 shows a clear tendency to be falling in unrounded, and rising in rounded, vowels.

After *palato-velars,* the formant movement is less pronounced. F2 is normally level in **i e ɛ a** (it may be falling in short **a),** level or rising in **y ø œ,** and falling in **u o ɔ** with a somewhat lower starting point than after labials (800–1200) and, as has been mentioned above, with level or slightly rising-falling aspiration, but falling vowel formant.

F3 is level or (less often) rising in front vowels (but usually rising in **a).**   It is generally rising in **u o ɔ.**   The bending together of F2 and F3 mentioned in *Visible Speech* is obvious only in **a,** and to some extent in **y ø œ.**   F4 may be slightly falling so that it starts near F5 (if such a formant occurs) at the higher intensity peak of **g** and **k.**

The findings concerning formant bendings are for the most part in very good conformity with those described in *Visible Speech,* and

---

connected with F2 of **ð** and **ɣ**).   As has already been mentioned, it is generally lower than F2 of **e.**   We have probably here to do with the case mentioned by H. K. Dunn (*On Vowel Resonances and an Electrical Vocal Tract, JASA* 22, 1950, pp. 740–753) where F2 of a very fronted **i** becomes dependent on the throat cavity and F3 on the mouth cavity.

[1] It may be practical to talk of a " hub ", not only for F2, but also for F3.

also with the findings of Gunnar Fant for Swedish.[1]   There are, however, a few divergencies : front vowels after palato-velars show less bending than in American English. This may, however, mainly be due to the long pause following the explosion of **g,** and to the difficulty of seeing the formants in the long and strong aspiration noise of **k.** When the vowels precede the palato-velars, the bending is very clear in **a ɛ** and **e,** and sometimes in **i.** A real difference is found in the case of labials before back vowels. In the English spectrograms, the formant starts approximately at 800–1000 and is rising in **ɔ:, ɒ,** and mostly **ʊ,** but level or falling in **u:,** whereas the formant starts higher and is falling after the velars. In Danish the relationship is directly reversed. F2 always starts higher after **p/b** than after **k/g** and is always falling.[2] It is possible that this difference has something to do with the intensity of the explosion of **p b** which is definitely stronger in English than in Danish. A strong explosion seems to have more energy at the lowest frequency (about 400). And this is probably not due to a local friction noise but to low resonance.

IIIb. Comparison with the Experiments on Synthetic Sounds

The experiments carried out in the Haskins Laboratories [3] had for their object the examination of the auditory importance of the frequency of the explosion and of the formant bendings.

(*a*) The experiments with artificial explosions comprised schematic bursts of noise of 600 c.p.s. frequency span and 1·5 cs. duration at twelve different frequencies from 360 to 4320 c.p.s., and preceding seven different two-formant vowels (**i e ɛ a ɔ o u**). The result was that an explosion above 3000 was in most cases heard as **t,** and an explosion below 3000 was heard as **k** if it was placed somewhat above the second formant, otherwise as **p.**[4]

The **k-**judgments in particular show very considerable agreement

---

[1] Even such details as the quick fall followed by a rise of F3 after alveolars before rounded back vowels (probably due to the complicated movement of the tongue in this case) is found in our spectrograms as well as in English and Swedish spectrograms. And the slight rise and fall of the aspiration after **k** before the descending vowel formant of **ʊ o ɔ** is found in exactly the same way in Swedish and Danish.

[2] Swedish **p** before **o** looks like Danish, **b** more like English, but this observation is based on only two examples.

[3] See note 1, p. 42.

[4] Cf. now also Carol D. Schatz : *The Role of Context in the Perception of Stops, Language* 30, 1954, pp. 47–56, which appeared after this article had gone to print.

between the subjects. This is natural since real **k**-sounds have a definite maximum above the second formant ; and also, the fact that the maxima of agreement lie definitely above F2 of **i e ɛ,** and only slightly above or at the height of F2 of **a u o ɔ,** is in accordance with the measurements of natural sounds. Only before **i** is the number of **k**-judgments relatively low. The authors suggest two explanations : (1) the lack of formant bendings, (2) less identificability of **k** before **i.** The latter suggestion is the more likely of the two, since the formant bendings of **ɛ** or **a** are usually more pronounced and, in connection with these vowels, the agreement is nevertheless high. And, on the other hand, before **i,** the **k**-explosion comes into the region of **t,** and it is sometimes difficult to distinguish the two on spectrograms.

There is considerable agreement of **t**-judgments from 3000 c.p.s. to 4320 before **i e ɛ a.** Before **u o ɔ** the maximum is lower (about 3200), which is in conformity with the change of relative intensity found in our spectrograms, and the agreement is less pronounced. As **k** has generally no energy in this region, and **p** often less than at other frequencies, we suggest that the reason is the lack of the very characteristic steeply falling F2 after alveolars.

The reason for the maxima of agreement on **p** can hardly be due to the presence of particular energy of natural **p**-sounds in these regions (except that **p** before **i** and **e** may have some concentration of noise below F2). This can be seen by comparing **o** and **a.** At 1440 and 1800 there is a maximum of **p**-judgments before **o,** and a minimum before **a.** This does not reflect a difference of natural **p**-sounds before **a** and **o,** but can only be explained by the fact that **k** has its lower maximum of intensity at these frequencies before **a,** but not before **o.** Thus, if there is no positive reason for hearing **k** or **t,** there will be a majority for **p** since this sound has energy in almost all frequency regions. There is, however, an apparent exception : there is a second, somewhat smaller, maximum of agreement for **k** at 720 before **e** and at 1080 before **ɛ.** And we have never found energy at these frequencies in real **k**-sounds before **e** and **ɛ.** But this is exactly the region where **p** has normally no energy either. This means that no real stops have energy here. That there is a preference for **k** in this case, may be due to the fact that the artificial explosion by its frequency concentration and its duration is more similar to a **k**-explosion than to either **p** or **t.**

(*b*) The experiments with two-formant vowels without explosions but with rising or falling start of the formants have shown that vowels with rising F2 are heard as labial stop + vowel, and vowels with falling F2 as dental or velar + vowel, with the distribution that a steep fall favours **t-d** judgments before **u o ɔ** and **k-g** judgments before **i e ɛ**, and a slight fall has the opposite result. There is a crossing point in **a**.

It is in full agreement with all results of acoustic analysis that **u o ɔ**, with a steeply falling F2, should be heard as preceded by **t** or **d,** and that a slight fall gives the impression of **k** or **g**. But the fact that a rising formant gives the impression of a preceding labial is not in agreement with measurements of the Danish spectrograms, which show falling formants of **u o ɔ** after labials. It is, however, in conformity with most spectrograms of English sounds as found in *Visible Speech*. It would be interesting to discover if Danish listeners would react differently to the artificial vowels. It does not seem likely that they would. The audible difference between Danish and English labials is very slight. And the fact that spectrograms show a somewhat lower resonance in English is hardly of importance for the distinction between labials and velars. A closer inspection of the diagrams of responses [1] will also show that the rising transition of **u** and **o** was interpreted almost equally often as a labial and as a velar stop (although a rising transition after **k/g** has been found neither in English nor in Danish) and that a falling transition was almost exclusively interpreted as a velar stop (although at any rate Danish and Swedish labials, and English labials before **u,** may be followed by a fall). An explanation of these puzzling facts may be found if one considers that it is not legitimate simply to compare the transition of the artificial vowel with the transition of real vowels. The listener does not compare explosion with explosion and transition with transition, but compares artificial syllables comprising either explosion or transition with natural syllables which always contain both. The function of the transition is generally to indicate that something higher or lower precedes. A slight down glide in **u o ɔ** will be interpreted as a preceding **k** or **g** which normally have strong explosion (and aspiration noise) just above the second formant. It is not interpreted as **p** or **b,** for **p/b** have no particularly strong noise at this frequency. A rising transition indicates that something lower precedes. This cannot be a **t,** but it might be **p** or **k,** which both may have some intensity here before **o u ɔ.**

The interpretation is somewhat more difficult in the case of the front vowels and **a** since, in natural vowels of this type, F3 is of importance, and the single higher formant of the artificial vowels will probably act as a representative of F2 + F3. This might explain

---

[1] *JASA* 24, 1952, p. 602.

the very small number of **g /k** responses for **a.** In a real **ga /ka** syllable the explosion would be situated between F2 and F3, which would be falling and rising respectively. In the artificial vowels there is only one formant and, when it is rising, the listeners hear a **p,** when it is falling a **t,** which is in general conformity with spectrograms. And altogether rising transitions are heard as labials. This is understandable since spectrograms show a definite rise in both F2 and F3, very steep in **i** and **e,** rather flat in **a,** and the explosion may show some concentration of energy at any rate below F2 of **i** and **e.** (The rise after labials in this case and the fall after alveolars before back vowels are the most extensive formant movements found in spectrograms and probably of importance even without preceding noise.)

The interpretation of a steep fall as **k /g** may be due to the fact that the explosion is always well above F2, which may be falling. A slight fall should, however, not give **t /d** except in the case of **a.** Both English and Danish have rising F2 and F3 in **i e ɛ** after **t /d.** But the artificial **ɛ** is relatively low, and the judgments for **i** and **e** are rather uncertain and without definite peaks for rise or fall. In natural **t /d** there is high noise and rising formant starting from a lower, relatively weak, maximum of noise. Rising formants are therefore not sufficient for making a good alveolar. A slightly falling formant may be considered as a sort of compromise between the two factors, but it is equally often heard as **k /g.**

The interpretations suggested here are partly of a hypothetical nature ; information about the frequency span of the transitions might have been of help. But, on the whole, it has been possible to find an acoustic explanation of the reactions of the listeners in almost all cases, and the comparison has shown that the differences which seem most apparent from an acoustic point of view are also of importance for the listener.

It might, however, be interesting to extend the experiments at some points. An extension of the explosion experiments to higher frequencies (e.g. up to 6000) might show whether the higher maximum of **k** is of any importance. As **t** before rounded vowels has relatively little energy here, it is possible that higher frequencies would in this case show a decrease of **t**-judgments. (There are some indications of this in the diagrams.) Also experiments with bursts of different frequency-extension and width might be of interest.

IV. General Remarks

Both our acoustic analysis and the Haskins experiments have shown that variants of the same phoneme (e.g. **k**) may be widely different, so that it may be a difficult task to give an acoustic description of a phoneme as such, even if it is kept in mind that we are only looking for a constant relationship between phonemes, not for constant qualities.[1] Cooper, Delattre, and Liberman have suggested that there might be a closer relationship between perception and articulation than between perception and the acoustic domain.[2] This may be true, but opposite conclusions might perhaps be drawn from investigations of r-sounds and vowels. The statement that we perceive speech in larger acoustic units than single sounds[3] is less questionable. From a phonemic point of view we would say that only differences between conditioned variants (or " allophones ") must be phonetically constant, not differences between phonemes[4]; thus the difference between **k** and **t** before **i** must show some constancy if communication by means of speech is to be possible, but even this constancy is of a limited kind, for there may be a bundle of differences which are all present in optimal cases, but which need not all be there. In some cases the frequency of the explosion might perhaps be the same, but the duration might be different, or vice versa. Final **k** and **p** after **u** may have the same formant bendings but different explosion or, if they are unexploded, there must be differences of formant bending, etc. But there has to be some kind of constancy. It is, however, not necessary for communication purposes that the difference between **k** and **t** before **i** and before **u** should be the same. The grouping of variants into phonemes may be more or less arbitrary from a phonetic point of view (and perception is influenced by the phonemic analysis laid down in orthography). But it is, of course, always preferable to find a common denominator, since this gives a simpler phonetic description of phonemes.

In the case of **p-t-k,** Cooper, Delattre, and Liberman suggest (although in the form of " speculations ") the following definitions[5]: **p,** low burst, rising transition ; **k,** low burst, falling transition ; **t,** high burst, falling transition. This is probably an over-simplification. In the first place, we think that the difference in burst between **k** and **p** should not be neglected. It probably constitutes the most important difference between **pu** and **ku.** We should prefer to take both frequency and concentration into account in order to get an adequate description of the explosion : **p,** neutral explosion ;

---

[1] Cf. *Preliminaries* p. 5.
[2] *JASA* 24, p. 605, cf. also Twaddell, ibid. p. 609.
[3] Cooper, etc., ibid. p. 604.
[4] Cf. Twaddell, ibid. p. 609.
[5] *JASA* 24, p. 604.

t, relative concentration at high frequencies ; **k,** strong concentration round a frequency bound to adjacent sounds. This description comes nearer to Jakobsons' formula, **k** compact — **p, t** diffuse ; but **k** has not " one centrally located formant region ".[1] This is true of **k** before **a,** but not before **i** or **u.**

The Cooper-Delattre-Liberman formula concerning transition (**k, t** falling, **p** rising transition) can hardly be sustained, because **t** is generally followed by rising transition of **i e ε,** and **p** may have falling transition. Moreover, the direction of the transition is hardly of fundamental importance. The decisive difference between **p** and **t** in this respect is that **p** has lower resonance than **t,** so that the vowel formants start lower (and may be rising or falling according to the following vowel). Jakobson's distinction acute-grave seems more adequate. **t**'s resonances (approximately 1800 and 2800) are slightly above the neutral resonances found as F2 and F3 in the vowel **ə,** and in the aspiration after final consonant, i.e. the neutral resonances are slightly raised because the tip of the tongue is raised. The subsequent vowels start approximately here, since coarticulation with alveolars is only possible to a slight degree. **p**'s resonances are lower because of the closure or (just after the explosion) small opening of the lips, but they cannot be determined so precisely. 1300 and 2400 are critical values, but not fixed resonances in the same sense as in **t.**[2] The variations may be greater since the tongue is free to take up any position during the labial closure, and the degree of coarticulation will to a certain degree determine the transition movement.[3]—The resonances of **k** are variable, but closer together.

We should therefore prefer the following description[4] : **p/b,** neutral explosion, relatively low resonances ; **t/d,** high explosion, relatively high resonances ; **k/g,** strong concentration of explosion round a frequency bound to adjacent sounds, varying resonances with tendency to mutual attraction. This is a simplified description. The duration of the explosion may also be important ; but further investigations are needed on this point.

---

[1] *Preliminaries* p. 27.

[2] These resonances are also reflected in the explosion noise, but do not constitute the most important differences of the explosion.

[3] It would be tempting to explain the different resonances of English and Danish **p** as a difference in degree of coarticulation, but there does not seem to be any basis for assuming more coarticulation in English.

[4] Based on the explosion and the resonances corresponding to F2 and F3.

Reprinted from THE JOURNAL OF THE ACOUSTICAL SOCIETY OF AMERICA, Vol. 27, No. 4 (July 1955).

Duration and Intensity as Physical Correlates of Linguistic Stress*

D. B. FRY

University College, London, England

(Received November 8, 1954)

The experiments reported in this paper are an attempt to explore the influence of certain physical cues on the perception of linguistic stress patterns. The material chosen was a group of English words in which a change of function from noun to verb is commonly associated with a shift of stress from the first to the second syllable. Spectrograms were used to determine the vowel duration and intensity ratios which occur in these words and this information was applied in making up a test in which listeners' judgments of stress could be correlated with variations in the duration and intensity ratios. The results of the experiments show that duration and intensity ratios are both cues for judgments of stress and that, in the material studied, duration ratio is a more effective cue than intensity ratio.

THE experiments reported in this paper are an attempt to explore the influence of certain physical cues on the perception of linguistic stress patterns. The material chosen was a group of English words in which a change of function from noun to verb is commonly associated with a shift of stress from the first to the second syllable. Spectrograms were used to determine the vowel duration and intensity ratios which occur in these words and this information was applied in making up a test in which listeners' judgments of stress could be correlated with variations in the duration and intensity ratios.

It is not always easy for listeners, especially untrained listeners, to judge where the stress, or accent, falls in a particular word. In this study, the words chosen were all of the type: *object, digest, permit* in which many speakers associate a difference of rhythm with a difference of function; in such words, therefore, the listener can use the criterion of meaning as well as that of sound in deciding where the accent falls. Twelve American speakers were asked to read sentences containing such words and the readings were recorded on tape. There was considerable variation in the behavior of the speakers with respect to the placing of the accent in different words but it was possible to select from the material a set of 5 words which were treated similarly by all, or nearly all, of the speakers. These words were: *object, subject, digest, contract, permit.*

Spectrograms of the selected words were made on a Kay Sonagraph and the duration and intensity were measured for the segments corresponding to the various speech sounds.[1] The duration measurements showed remarkably little variation from speaker to speaker and the effect of a shift in stress was clearly apparent. In all the words, the vowel segments showed a difference in duration ratio between the noun and the verb form. For the two forms of the word *permit*, for example, the mean durations were:

verb form, *er*—0.06 sec, *i*—0.12 sec

noun form, *er*—0.12 sec, *i*—0.09 sec.

The consonant duration ratios, on the other hand, were not materially affected by the shift of stress. For the same word, *permit*, the mean consonant durations were:

p—0.13 and 0.15 sec, *m*—0.08 and 0.08 sec,

t—0.19 and 0.14 sec.

The intensity measurement recorded was the highest intensity level reached in each syllable, and this again occurred in the vowel segments. There was considerable variation in intensity from speaker to speaker, not only in the over-all level but also in the intensity ratio of the two vowels and the difference between the noun and the verb form was in general less clearly marked.

Figure 1 is a summary of the data for the two forms of the word *object*. In the left-hand plot, the duration of vowel 1 is plotted against the duration of vowel 2 for all the speakers; on the right is a similar plot for vowel intensity, with the over-all intensity level brought to the same value for all speakers. The crosses mark the durations or intensities for the noun forms (trochaic, strong-weak rhythmic pattern) and the circles for the verbs (iambic, weak-strong rhythmic pattern). For the word *object* the data for nouns and verbs clearly fall into two well-defined groups. The measurements for the other words show a similar grouping but in some cases the boundary between the groups is more blurred. Figure 2 gives the plots for *contract*, the word in which the grouping was least clear.

Since the data group themselves in this way, we should expect that for duration and intensity ratios which lie between the groups there would be a degree of uncertainty on the listener's part as to where the stress falls. The rest of the experiment was designed to explore this uncertainty range, to obtain a measure of the agreement in listeners' judgments for different parts of the range and to determine the relative effectiveness of duration and intensity as cues for stress judgments. By means of the pattern-playback equipment, different versions of each test-word were synthesised in which the duration and intensity ratios of vowel 1 to vowel 2 were varied over the critical range. The intensity measurements had indicated that for all the words the intensity ratios were symmetrically distributed about a ratio of 1/1 and it was therefore

* Work done at the Haskins Laboratories, New York, New York, and supported in part by the Carnegie Corporation of New York, New York.
[1] See Appendix.

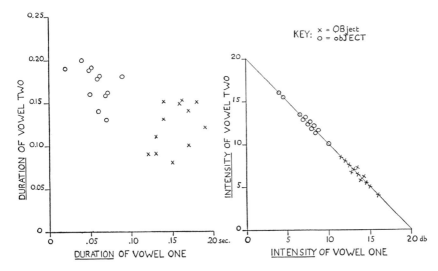

KEY: x = OBject
o = obJECT

Fig. 1. Measured vowel durations and intensities for the word *object*. In the plotting of intensity, the over-all intensity level is brought to the same value for all speakers.

possible to adopt a common range for all five words. The values chosen were: vowel 1/vowel 2, equal; vowel 1, +5 db; +10 db; −5 db; −10 db. The position with respect to duration was not as simple since the probable cross-over point varied from word to word. In *permit*, for example, the vowel 1/vowel 2 ratios ranged from 0.25 to 0.78 for the verb form and from 1.0 to 2.14 for the noun; in *digest* there was considerable overlap between the two forms, the verb giving ratios from 0.53 to 1.5, and the noun from 0.83 to 2.87. It was necessary, therefore, to adopt a slightly different scale for each word; five values of duration ratio were selected which would adequately cover the required range and would include a value close to the cross-over point.[1] For each word, the duration and intensity were varied at the same time so that there were 25 versions of every word and 125 items in the whole test.

In synthesising the test items, the differences in vowel intensity were obtained by painting the patterns with white or grey paint of different shades which had been calibrated for differences in the resulting sound intensity. The duration ratios were adjusted by controlling the distance on the pattern occupied by the vowel segments. The synthesised words were recorded on tape and each one was introduced into a carrier sentence, also in synthesised speech. Each test item came to the listener in the form: "Where is the accent in OBject," "Where is the accent in conTRACT" etc. The 125 test items were placed in random order and the listener was asked to record his judgment of the accent in the following way: he was supplied with a test sheet on which the appropriate word was printed against each item number; capital letters were used to denote the stressed syllable, and each word appeared

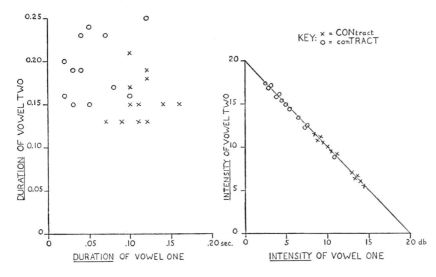

KEY: x = CONtract
o = conTRACT

Fig. 2. Measured vowel durations and intensities for the word *contract*. As in Fig. 1, the over-all intensity level is brought to the same value for all speakers.

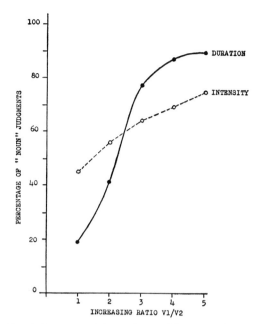

FIG. 3. Percentage of listeners' "noun" judgments for all test words as a function of (a) vowel duration ratio and (b) vowel intensity ratio. See appendix for experimental values of these ratios.

in two versions, one with the first syllable in capitals and the other with the second. The listener was asked to underline one of these forms for each word that he

heard. Altogether 100 subjects listened to the test and recorded responses in this way.

The general pattern of the results was much what one would expect. In words where duration and intensity were operating in the same direction there was excellent agreement between the subjects, that is to say, when the vowel was long and of high intensity, listeners agreed that the vowel was strongly stressed, when it was short and of low intensity, it was judged as weakly stressed. At other points in the range, the degree of agreement varied from word to word but there were several items for each word which divided the listeners about equally.

The most interesting aspect of the results is shown when the effects of duration and intensity are studied separately. It has generally been accepted that variations of intensity are most closely linked with stress differences in English but the results of this experiment indicate that the duration ratio has a stronger influence on judgments of stress than has the intensity ratio. The range of duration and intensity ratios used in the test words was chosen in such a way as to cover the values found in the measurements of actual utterances, and they may therefore be considered, in this sense at least, to be equivalent ranges. Figure 3 shows the increase of "noun" judgments with increase of duration ratio (continuous curve) and with increase of intensity ratio (dotted curve). The whole range of intensity change produces an increase in the number of judgments of only 29 percent whilst the range of duration change

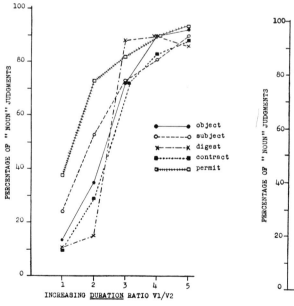

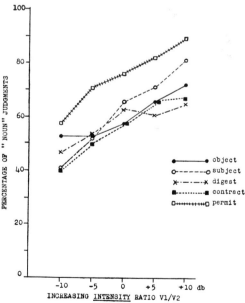

FIG. 4. Percentage of listeners' "noun" judgments for each of the five test words as a function of (a) vowel duration ratio and (b) vowel intensity ratio. See appendix for experimental values of duration ratio.

increases the judgments by 70 percent. The curves of Fig. 4 show the data for each of the five words separately and indicate the scatter of these values about the curves of Fig. 3. The differences from word to word are here evident but a comparison of the duration and intensity curves for each word shows that the same general effect is present. There is therefore a strong indication that the duration ratio is more effective in resolving uncertainty about stress than is the intensity ratio.

The results of these experiments indicate, then, that (1) duration and intensity ratios are both cues for judgments of stress, (2) the vowel segments show the major differences in duration and intensity with a shift of stress, and (3) duration ratio is a more effective cue than intensity ratio.

The author wishes to thank Dr. F. S. Cooper and the staff of Haskins Laboratories for their generous help in carrying out these experiments and preparing this paper.

APPENDIX.

Measured vowel durations				Measured vowel intensities			
obJECT $V1$ $V2$ (seconds)		OBject $V1$ $V2$ (seconds)		obJECT $V1$ $V2$ (decibels)		OBject $V1$ $V2$ (decibels)	
0.05	0.16	0.12	0.09	5	12	15	9
0.07	0.13	0.14	0.13	6	11	20	12
0.07	0.16	0.16	0.15	7	12	16	8
0.05	0.19	0.17	0.10	9	13	16	11
0.04	0.20	0.13	0.11	3	9	15	3
0.06	0.14	0.13	0.09	6	12	18	14
0.09	0.18	0.14	0.15	11	16	18	15
0.05	0.19	0.15	0.08	3	15	15	6
0.02	0.19	0.19	0.12	4	15	18	11
0.06	0.18	0.18	0.15	12	15	14	4
0.06	0.18	0.17	0.14	15	18	12	6
0.07	0.16	0.16	0.15	12	12	13	7

Duration ratios ($V1/V2$)
Observed:
Min	Mean	Max
0.11	0.82	1.87

Intensity ratios ($V1/V2$)
Observed:
Min	Mean	Max
−12 db	0.75 db	12 db

Experimental:
0.25 0.50 0.75 1.25 2.00   −10 db −5 db 0 db 5 db 10 db

Measured vowel durations				Measured vowel intensities			
subJECT $V1$ $V2$ (seconds)		SUBject $V1$ $V2$ (seconds)		subJECT $V1$ $V2$ (decibels)		SUBject $V1$ $V2$ (decibels)	
0.03	0.09	0.09	0.07	7	15	15	7
0.05	0.11	0.10	0.11	14	15	19	7
0.02	0.13	0.12	0.12	6	16	19	9
0.04	0.10	0.09	0.10	9	15	17	10
0.02	0.12	0.10	0.10	3	16	20	5
0.04	0.09	0.08	0.07	12	16	12	9
0.07	0.11	0.12	0.16	13	19	15	16
0.04	0.13	0.11	0.09	9	15	19	6
0.04	0.12	0.10	0.13	9	17	16	14
0.04	0.14	0.10	0.12	10	15	12	3
0.06	0.12	0.08	0.12	15	13	12	4
0.07	0.12	0.10	0.14	14	15	15	6

Duration ratios ($V1/V2$)
Observed:
Min	Mean	Max
0.15	0.66	1.28

Intensity ratios ($V1/V2$)
Observed:
Min	Mean	Max
−13 db	1.2 db	15 db

Experimental:
0.25 0.40 0.60 1.00 1.25   −10 db −5 db 0 db 5 db 10 db

Measured vowel durations				Measured vowel intensities			
diGEST $V1$ $V2$ (seconds)		DIgest $V1$ $V2$ (seconds)		diGEST $V1$ $V2$ (decibels)		DIgest $V1$ $V2$ (decibels)	
0.12	0.13	0.14	0.12	13	12	18	11
0.14	0.12	0.20	0.11	15	15	21	13
0.09	0.17	0.23	0.16	12	20	18	7
0.17	0.21	0.18	0.11	18	18	21	9
0.13	0.17	0.15	0.18	18	20	17	10
0.12	0.17	0.16	0.11	14	19	18	8
0.15	0.18	0.17	0.13	17	15	20	15
0.20	0.21	0.23	0.08	19	14	15	10
0.18	0.12	0.20	0.09	14	15	15	6
0.13	0.14	0.20	0.11	11	14	14	8
0.14	0.19	0.21	0.14	11	12	14	19
0.14	0.18	0.22	0.15	17	17	18	8

Duration ratios ($V1/V2$)
Observed:
Min	Mean	Max
0.53	1.25	2.87

Intensity ratios ($V1/V2$)
Observed:
Min	Mean	Max
−8 db	3 db	12 db

Experimental:
0.25 0.60 1.20 1.75 2.25   −10 db −5 db 0 db 5 db 10 db

Measured vowel durations				Measured vowel intensities			
conTRACT $V1$ $V2$ (seconds)		CONtract $V1$ $V2$ (seconds)		conTRACT $V1$ $V2$ (decibels)		CONtract $V1$ $V2$ (decibels)	
0.11	0.13	0.05	0.15	10	15	23	14
0.10	0.17	0.04	0.19	8	17	15	8
0.12	0.18	0.05	0.24	6	21	20	13
0.12	0.19	0.04	0.23	8	15	18	10
0.07	0.13	0.02	0.20	6	18	10	10
0.10	0.21	0.12	0.25	10	8	10	12
0.12	0.13	0.10	0.16	12	17	12	10
0.11	0.15	0.08	0.17	6	18	12	11
0.10	0.15	0.07	0.23	10	21	16	10
0.09	0.13	0.03	0.15	3	13	7	10
0.14	0.15	0.02	0.16	2	16	16	15
0.16	0.15	0.03	0.19	4	18	17	15

Duration ratios ($V1/V2$)
Observed:
Min	Mean	Max
0.10	0.50	1.06

Intensity ratios ($V1/V2$)
Observed:
Min	Mean	Max
−15 db	−3 db	9 db

Experimental:
0.20 0.40 0.60 0.80 1.00   −10 db −5 db 0 db 5 db 10 db

Measured vowel durations				Measured vowel intensities			
perMIT $V1$ $V2$ (seconds)		PERmit $V1$ $V2$ (seconds)		perMIT $V1$ $V2$ (decibels)		PERmit $V1$ $V2$ (decibels)	
0.04	0.10	0.11	0.10	7	10	13	7
0.06	0.10	0.12	0.08	7	9	10	6
0.04	0.16	0.15	0.13	8	15	17	9
0.05	0.12	0.12	0.08	8	12	15	9
0.05	0.12	0.12	0.12	6	9	11	6
0.05	0.15	0.12	0.08	7	9	11	8
0.06	0.13	0.13	0.09	9	12	10	7
0.05	0.14	0.13	0.07	7	13	12	9
0.05	0.07	0.11	0.07	6	15	14	6
0.05	0.10	0.15	0.07	3	12	9	6
0.11	0.14	0.12	0.10	15	21	15	12
0.08	0.15	0.13	0.10	9	18	21	15

Duration ratios ($V1/V2$)
Observed:
Min	Mean	Max
0.25	0.96	2.14

Intensity ratios ($V1/V2$)
Observed:
Min	Mean	Max
−9 db	−0.25 db	8 db

Experimental:
0.50 0.75 1.00 1.5 2.00   −10 db −5 db 0 db 5 db 10 db

Reprinted from JOURNAL OF EXPERIMENTAL PSYCHOLOGY,
Vol. 52, No. 2, August, 1956

TEMPO OF FREQUENCY CHANGE AS A CUE FOR DISTINGUISHING CLASSES OF SPEECH SOUNDS [1]

ALVIN M. LIBERMAN,[2] PIERRE C. DELATTRE,[3] LOUIS J. GERSTMAN, AND
FRANKLIN S. COOPER

Haskins Laboratories, New York City

In recent experiments with synthetic speech (3, 5, 6, 7) we have isolated many of the acoustic cues by which a listener identifies various consonants of American English. Some of the cues that we have found to be important for the voiced stops (*b, d, g*), the voiceless stops (*p, t, k*), and the nasal consonants (*m, n, ŋ*) are illustrated in the hand-painted spectrograms of Fig. 1. These spectrographic patterns are very highly simplified and schematized by comparison with spectrograms of real speech, yet capable of producing fair approximations to the intended consonant-vowel syllables when converted into sound by an appropriate playback instrument. The vowel, which is *a* in all cases, is given by the two concentrations of acoustic energy, or "formants" as they are called, the one centering at about 720 cps and the other at 1320 cps. The consonant cues, with which we will be more concerned, begin at the left-hand side of each pattern and extend to the point at which the formants assume the steady state that characterizes the vowel.

As can be seen in the hand-painted spectrograms, the acoustic cues that distinguish the columns of the figure (i.e., *b–p–m* from *d–t–n* from *g–k–ŋ*) are the direction and extent of the relatively rapid shifts in the frequency position of the second (higher) formant. These frequency shifts, or "transitions," are typically found in spectrograms of real speech at the junction of consonant and vowel.[4] By converting patterns like those of Fig. 1 into sound, we have found that the second-formant transitions can, in fact, be cues for the perceived distinctions among the three classes,

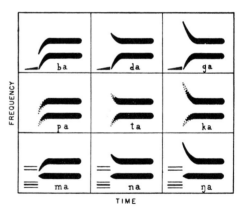

FIG. 1. Hand-painted spectrograms of nine consonant-vowel syllables, showing some of the principal acoustic cues for the perception of the stop and nasal consonants.

b–p–m, *d–t–n*, and *g–k–ŋ*. There are other acoustic cues for these same classes—we have discovered that appropriate transitions of the third formant, for example, contribute to the identification of these sounds— but our results indicate that the second-formant transitions are very nearly sufficient.

[1] This research was supported in part by the Carnegie Corporation of New York and in part by the Department of Defense in connection with Contract DA49-170-sc-1642.

[2] Also at the University of Connecticut.

[3] Also at the University of Colorado.

[4] The transitions presumably reflect the changes in the oral cavities that necessarily occur as the articulators move from the position of the consonant to that of the vowel.

127

We know rather less about the cues that distinguish the patterns that form the rows (i.e., *b–d–g*, *p–t–k*, *m–n–ŋ*). Though we have isolated several cues for the distinction between the voiced (*b–d–g*) and voiceless (*p–t–k*) stops, we have not yet investigated the problem carefully enough to know which of these are most important. That omission need not concern us here, however, since for this paper the most relevant consideration is the evidence that each of these cues is essentially constant within a row (of Fig. 1) and more or less capable of distinguishing that row from others. As shown in the figure, one cue that marks the voiced stops (*b–d–g*) as a class is the low-frequency voice bar that immediately precedes the transitions. The voiceless stops probably depend in part on the presence of aspiration (i.e., noise) in place of harmonics in the first part of the transition. For the distinction between the nasal consonants (*m–n–ŋ*) and stops (*b–d–g*, *p–t–k*) the short, steady-state resonance seen at the beginning of each of the nasal consonants in the bottom row is quite adequate.

The patterns of Fig. 1 provide the basis for a table of acoustic elements out of which many of the sounds of speech can be made.[5] The table is interesting, we think, because it indicates that a small number of cues

on one acoustic dimension (second-formant transition) combine in all possible pairs with various acoustic markers (the constant resonance of the nasal consonants, for example) to produce some of the highly distinctive sounds of speech. Thus, highly identifiable stimuli are created out of the wholly unpatterned combination of simple and discrete elements. We expect that the table of Fig. 1 will ultimately be expanded to include all the consonant sounds. It is one of the purposes of this study to take a step in that direction.[6]

Exploratory work suggested that we might convert the patterns of Fig. 1 into different speech sounds by varying only the tempo of the transitions, thus pointing to time as another of the stimulus dimensions which may be important in the perception of the individual phones of speech. As the transitions are progressively slowed, the pattern for the stop consonant *b* plus the vowel *a* (as in *bottle*) begins to be heard as the semivowel *w* plus *a* (as in *wobble*), and then as a vowel

[5] The 3 × 3 table of Fig. 1, in which the patterns are arranged in terms of the acoustic cues, parallels a commonly accepted phonetic classification according to the articulatory dimensions of *place* and *manner* of articulation. The three columns correspond to three places of production (i.e., points along the oral tract at which the consonant closure is made), *p–b–m* being produced at the lips, *t–d–n* at the alveolar ridge, and *k–g–ŋ* at the velum. Manner of production refers to the particular articulatory features (for example, the presence or absence of voicing or nasality) that are common to the sounds in any given row.

[6] Students of language have long found it useful to describe each consonant as an articulatory event in which one of a small number of places of production is combined with one manner. The specification of place and manner is, then, sufficient to describe a consonant uniquely. To the extent that the relation between articulation and sound is not too complex, we should expect that the categories of place and manner might be equally appropriate for a classification of the acoustic characteristics. That such a classification has utility for a study of speech perception has recently been shown in an important experiment by Miller and Nicely (8). They took account of the confusions that occur when English consonants are heard against progressively increasing amounts of noise and found, for example, that a listener will continue to identify a sound correctly as being a member of a certain manner class even though he does not hear it accurately in regard to its place of production. In general, their results indicated that the place and manner cues, whatever their nature, may be perceived quite independently of each other.

which changes color from *u* to *a* (as in *too odd*). Similarly *ga* (as in *goggle*) goes to *ja* (as in *yacht*), and then to *ia* (as in *theology*). The remaining stop, *d*, goes through comparable transformations, producing (with the vowel *a*) the semivowel ɥ (as in French *nuage*) and then the vowel-of-changing-color *ya* (as in French *cru a*).[7]

The experiments to be reported here were designed to extend our exploratory observations concerning transition tempo as a cue for the perceived distinctions among stop consonants, semivowels, and vowels of changing color.

Experiment I

In this part of the study we have tried to determine whether changing the tempo of first- and second-formant transitions is sufficient to convert the syllables *bɛ* and *gɛ* (stop consonant plus vowel) into *wɛ* and *jɛ* (semivowel plus vowel) and, in the extreme, into *uɛ* and *iɛ* (vowels of changing color). The semivowel (plus vowel) ɥɛ and vowel-of-changing-color *yɛ*, which presumably result from a slowing of the *d* transition, are not familiar to our American listeners and were for that reason excluded from the experiment.

The vowels of changing color are very different linguistically (and perceptually) from stops and semivowels in that they are not single linguistic units and occur only in situations in which one of the vowels belongs to one syllable and the other to the next. We thought it appropriate, therefore,

to deal separately with the two-category distinction between stop and semivowel and the three-category choice among stop, semivowel, and vowel of changing color.

Method

General aspects of procedure and apparatus.— In these experiments hand-painted spectrograms have been used as a basis for creating and controlling speech-like sounds. To convert the spectrograms into sound—an obviously necessary step in this method—we take advantage of a special-purpose instrument called a pattern playback. Descriptions of this instrument, together with discussions of our method, are to be found in earlier papers (1, 2, 4).

The playback employs a variable-density tone wheel to modulate the light from a mercury arc, producing a fundamental of 120 cps and all its harmonics through the fiftieth at 6000 cps. The modulated light beams are imaged on the spectrogram, and are so spread across it as to match its frequency scale. As the hand-painted spectrogram is moved through the light, the white paint reflects beams whose modulation frequencies correspond to the position of the paint on the frequency scale of the spectrogram. The reflected beams are led by plastic light guides to a phototube, the current of which is amplified and converted to sound.

Stimuli.—To vary the tempo of the transitions, we prepared (for conversion into sound) spectrographic patterns like those shown in Fig. 2. The series of patterns illustrated in the top and bottom rows were designed to produce *bɛ*, *wɛ*, *uɛ*, and *gɛ*, *jɛ*, *iɛ*, respectively. In each series, the duration of first- and second-formant transitions was varied from 10 msec. to 300 msec. in steps of 10 msec. When we vary the duration of the transition, we are also, of course, varying the rate of transition (that is to say, the frequency shift per unit time) so long as the frequency extent of the transition remains constant. For convenience, we will present specific values in terms of duration; however, we will continue to speak of this variable generally as tempo.

As can be seen in Fig. 2 the first- and second-formant transitions were varied together, the durations of the two being always equal in any one sound. This approximates what would seem, on the basis of an inspection of spectrograms, to happen in real speech.

The steady-state portion of the pattern has a duration of 300 msec. in all cases, and its formants are so placed as to produce an approximation to the vowel ɛ. By using this vowel, it

---

[7] In articulatory terms *b* and *w* have a common place of production at the lips; *d* and ɥ are both produced at the alveols. The semivowel *j* is normally articulated at a point slightly forward of the velar *g*; however, there is in English no semivowel whose place of articulation is closer to *g*.

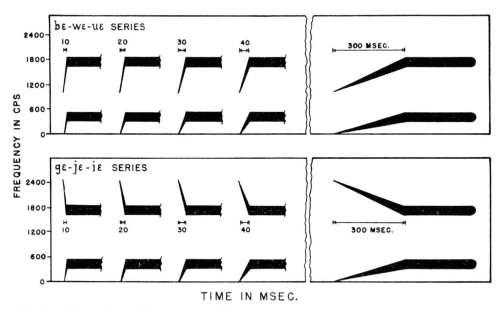

TIME IN MSEC.

FIG. 2. Illustrations of the spectrographic patterns used to produce the stimuli of Exp. I. The first four patterns in each row show how the tempo of the transitions was varied. At the extreme right of each row is a complete stimulus pattern, i.e., transition plus steady-state vowel, for the longest duration of transition tested.

has been possible to make the frequency shifts for the *bɛ–wɛ–uɛ* series exactly equal in extent to those that produce *gɛ–jɛ–iɛ*. The *b* transition begins 720 cps below, and the *g* transition 720 cps above, the steady state of the second formant of the vowel (1800 cps). The first-formant transition begins at 120 cps and rises to the steady state of the first formant at 480 cps.

The transitions of actual speech are not, of course, so angular as those shown in Fig. 2. We have found, however, that drawing the transitions as we have in that figure does not adversely affect the synthetic speech, and it does, for obvious reasons, enable us to control transition durations more precisely. Each formant consisted of a central strong harmonic and two flanking harmonics of lower intensity.

Presentation of stimuli.—As was pointed out in the introduction to Exp. I, we had thought it desirable to experiment separately with the two-category distinction between stop and semivowel and the three-category choice among stop, semivowel, and vowel of changing color. To investigate the distinction between stop and semivowel we assembled two sets of test stimuli. One, which we will call Test B–W, included 12 patterns from the series illustrated in the top row of Fig. 2 (rising second-formant transitions). The transition durations of these 12 patterns ranged from 10 to 120 msec. in steps of 10 msec., and had seemed on the basis of exploratory work to cover quite adequately the range from *bɛ* through *wɛ*. The other set of stimuli, which we

will call Test G–J, included the 12 corresponding patterns from the bottom row of Fig. 2 (falling second-formant transitions). These had appeared in exploratory work to produce sounds that ranged from *gɛ* through *jɛ*.

For the three-category choice among *bɛ*, *wɛ*, and *uɛ*, we used all the patterns of the series illustrated in the top row to make up a set of stimuli that we will refer to as Test B–W–U. The series in the bottom row was used in connection with the distinctions among *gɛ*, *jɛ*, and *iɛ*, and will be referred to as Test G–J–I. For each of these two tests there was a total of 30 stimuli with transition durations that ranged from 10 to 300 msec. in steps of 10 msec.

The spectrographic patterns in each of the four tests were converted into sound and recorded on magnetic tape. By cutting and splicing the magnetic tape we assembled two random orders of stimulus presentation for each test. The signals were arranged on the magnetic tape in such a way that each stimulus would be presented and then repeated after an interval of 1 sec. There was an interval of 6 sec. between successive pairs of stimuli (i.e., a sound and its repetition). This interval provided time for *S* to make and record his judgment. The *S*s heard and identified each stimulus only once in Tests B–W and G–J. Half the *S*s heard the stimuli in one random order, and half in the other. The *S*s who identified the stimuli of Tests B–W–U and G–J–I made two judgments of each stimulus, each of these tests having been given to the Ss once in each random order.

The Ss were told that each stimulus would be a synthetically produced syllable consisting of an initial speech sound followed in all cases by the vowel ɛ. They were asked to identify only the initial sound, and to limit their responses to the choices offered by E. For tests B–W, G–J, B–W–U, and G–J–I these choices were b or w, g or j, b, w, or u, and g, j, or i, respectively. Examples of these sounds, in syllabic contexts with the vowel ɛ, were given. The Ss were urged to make an identification of every stimulus, even though their judgments might in some cases be guesses. Before Ss made judgments in any test they were asked to listen to the first four stimuli of the series in order that they might become familiar with the nature of the sounds and the general method of presentation.

The four tests were variously interspersed among other tests involving synthetic speech (for example, groups of stimuli set up to study the fricative and nasal consonants), and sometimes two tests of the present experiment were given to the same group of Ss at the same session. The only restriction was that Test B–W was never paired with Test B–W–U, and,

similarly, that Test G–J was never paired with Test G–J–I in the same session. An analysis of the results showed essentially no effect of the context in which a particular test was given (or of the random order used), so in reporting the results we have combined all the judgments for each test.

Subjects.—A total of 168 paid volunteers, all of them undergraduate students at the University of Connecticut, served as Ss. Of this group, 59 took Test B–W and 60 took Test G–J. The stimuli of Tests B–W–U and G–J–I were presented to groups of 41 and 49 listeners, respectively. Of the 41 listeners for Test B–W–U, 19 had previously heard and identified the stimuli of Test G–J; 22 of the 49 listeners for Test G–J–I had previously served in Test B–W. Prior to serving in this experiment, none of the Ss had had experience in identifying the synthetic speech sounds produced by the pattern playback.

Results

Figure 3 shows that our listeners were able to use the tempo of first-

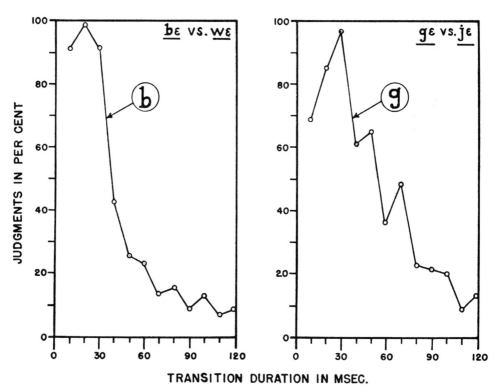

Fig. 3. The distinction between stop consonant and semivowel as a function of the tempo of transition. These curves show the percentage of stop consonant responses, and are based on the judgments of separate groups of 59 and 60 listeners for the *b–w* and *g–j* distinctions, respectively. Tempo is here expressed in terms of duration.

and second-formant transitions as a cue for distinguishing between stop consonant and semivowel. The change from *b* to *w* occurred when the duration of the transitions reached 40 msec., while *g* changed to *j* in the neighborhood of 50–60 msec. It is apparent from both curves that the very shortest duration of transition did not produce the best stop consonant.

Figure 4 shows the judgments we obtained when the range of transition tempos was increased and a third judgment category (*uɛ* or *iɛ*) was added. Apparently, our *Ss* can reliably discriminate the three categories, stop, semivowel, and vowel of changing color on the basis of tempo of transition alone. It is also apparent, however, that the amount of

agreement among our subjects was not so great in the three-category as in the two-category situations (cf. Fig. 3). The expansion of the stimulus range and the inclusion of the third judgment category obviously had the least effect on the responses to the stimuli at the short-duration end of the scale.

Experiment II

All the results of Exp. I, which indicated that transition tempo can distinguish stop consonant from semivowel from vowel of changing color, were obtained with the vowel *ɛ* following the initial transition. In Exp. II we have tried to find out how listeners respond to variations in transition tempo when vowels other than *ɛ* constitute the second part of the syllable. This experiment was

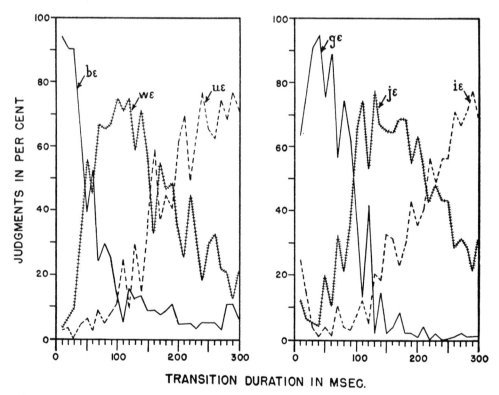

TRANSITION DURATION IN MSEC.

Fig. 4. The distinctions among stop consonant, semivowel, and vowel of changing color as functions of the tempo of transition. The curves representing the *bɛ–wɛ–uɛ* and *gɛ–jɛ–iɛ* responses are based on the judgments of separate groups of 41 and 49 listeners, respectively. Two judgments of all stimuli were obtained from each listener. As in Fig. 3, tempo is expressed in terms of duration.

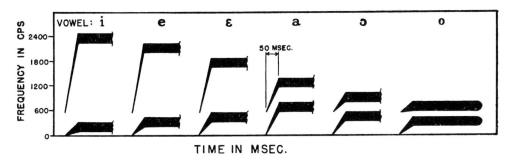

Fig. 5. Illustrations of the spectrographic patterns used to produce the stimuli of Exp. II. One only of the 15 transition durations, viz., 50 msec., is shown with each of the vowels. A complete stimulus pattern is shown at the extreme right.

concerned only with the distinction between the stop consonant *b* and the semivowel *w*. We have omitted the *g–j* distinction because to produce *g* with a variety of vowels requires a radical shift in the frequency level at which the second-formant transition begins, and introduces complications which are largely irrelevant to our present purposes.

In Exp. I rate and duration of transition were varied together. This was unavoidable, of course, because the extent of the transition—that is to say, the frequency range through which the formant moved—remained constant. To produce the various vowels that have been used in Exp. II we have had, necessarily, to put the steady-state formants at several different frequency levels. By starting the transitions from the same point for all these vowels, as can be done with *b*, we have been able to vary the extent of the transitions (from vowel to vowel) and thus to separate the rate and duration aspects of transition tempo. The results of this experiment should, therefore, help to determine which of these variables—rate or duration—is the controlling cue.

Method

Stimuli.—In Fig. 5 are samples of the spectrographic patterns that were used to produce

the stimuli of this experiment. These patterns are the same as those of the B–W test of Exp. I except in three respects. The principal difference concerns the steady-state vowel. In Exp. I the first and second formants of the steady-state portion of the syllable were always set at frequency levels that would produce synthetic approximations to the vowel ε. (See Fig. 2). In Exp. II there are six different steady-state levels of the formants, these levels being appropriate to the vowels *i*, *e*, *ε*, *a*, *ɔ*, and *o*. The second difference is in the frequency at which the second-formant transitions begin—1080 cps in Exp. I and 600 cps in Exp. II. It was necessary in Exp. II to lower the starting point of the second-formant transition in order to produce *b* and *w* with vowels whose second-formant frequencies are as low as those of *ɔ* and *o*. For syllables that contain the other vowels, *i*, *e*, *ε*, and *a*, it is not necessary to start the second formant at so low a frequency, but, as we pointed out above, it is possible to do so.[8] We thought in this case that it would be desirable to start all the second-formant transi-

---

[8] To produce the very best *b*'s we must start the second-formant transition at levels higher than 600 cps, especially when the *b* is followed by a front vowel such as *i*, *e*, or *ε*. When we start this transition from a point as low as 600 cps, we not only produce a somewhat inferior *b*, but we tend in some cases to add at least a suggestion of *bw*. This is to say that starting the second-formant transition at or near the *b–w* locus is itself a cue for the semivowel *w*. For a discussion of "locus" see (4).

The addition of a small amount of *w* is counterbalanced, perhaps, by the fact that starting the first formant at 120 cps, as we do in all the patterns of this experiment, provides a cue for the stop consonant *b* as opposed to the semivowel *w*. To synthesize the best semivowel we must start the first formant at a somewhat higher frequency.

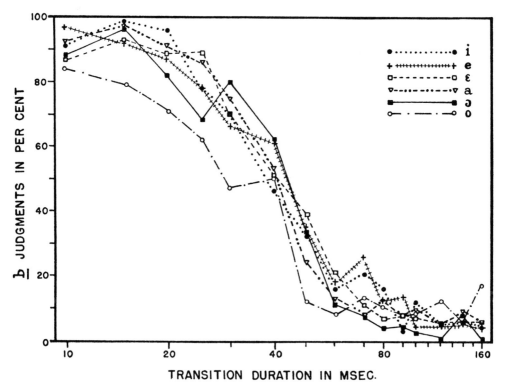

FIG. 6. The distinction between *b* and *w* with various vowels. These curves show the percentage of *b* judgments as a function of transition tempo when tempo is expressed as duration of transition. Each of 38 listeners judged all stimuli twice. Duration is scaled logarithmically to make these curves more directly comparable with those of Fig. 7 and 8.

tions at the same low frequency because in so doing we produced the greatest variation in extent of transition from vowel to vowel and thus obtained the greatest separation of rate and duration. The third difference between the patterns of Exp. I and those of Exp. II concerns the particular transition durations we chose to test. The results of Exp. I (see Fig. 3) had suggested that it would be most appropriate to sample the range 10 to 160 msec., using smaller steps at the short end and larger steps at the long end. Accordingly, we selected for use in Exp. II the following 15 values of transition duration for each vowel: 10, 15, 20, 25, 30, 40, 50, 60, 70, 80, 90, 100, 120, 140, and 160 msec.

Presentation of stimuli.—The 90 stimuli of Exp. II (15 transition durations times six vowels) were converted into sound on the pattern playback and recorded on magnetic tape. By cutting and splicing the magnetic tape we prepared two random orders of these sounds. The presentation of the stimuli was exactly as it had been in the B–W test of Exp. I, except that each *S* heard and judged the stimuli once in each random order. Thus, two judgments of each stimulus were obtained from each *S*.

Subjects.—There were 38 *S*s, all of whom were paid volunteer undergraduates at the University of Connecticut. None of the *S*s had previously served in Exp. I or had any other opportunity to hear the synthetic speech sounds produced by the pattern playback.

Results

We see in Fig. 6 that transition tempo is sufficient to distinguish the stop consonant *b* from the semivowel *w* with each of a wide variety of vowels. A comparison of the curves of Fig. 6 with those obtained for the vowel *ε* alone (see Fig. 3 in Exp. I) shows no very great difference.

When our listeners' judgments are plotted against transition duration, as in Fig. 6, the curves for the various vowels are very nearly superimposed. We may reasonably wonder what these curves will look like when the judgments are plotted against rate of transition, since, as we pointed out earlier, rate and duration can be separated in this experiment. Such plots are shown, separately for second and first formants, in Fig. 7 and 8.

It will be remembered that our stimulus patterns were so drawn as to make the duration of first- and second-formant transitions always equal in any one pattern. Transition rates, on the other hand, are different for first and second formants inasmuch as the transition extents differ. In considering the responses as a function of rate, we must, therefore, deal with first and second formants separately.

We should note in regard to Fig. 8 that duration and rate of first-formant transition covary for the vowels e–o and, also, for ε–ɔ, since, as can be seen in the stimulus patterns of Fig. 5, the extent of first-formant transition is the same

within each of these two pairs. It follows, then, that if the data for e and o, or for ε and ɔ, should yield similar curves when plotted against duration, they would necessarily produce similar curves against rate of first-formant transition.

Clearly the curves for the various vowels are not so nearly coincident for either of the rate plots as they are when the abscissa is laid out in terms of duration. This result would appear to support an assumption that duration of transition is the essential component of what we have been calling "tempo"—that is to say, that duration rather than rate is the controlling cue.

In assessing the relative importance of duration and rate we should take account of the fact that the rates of first- and second-formant transitions move in opposite directions in the vowel series from

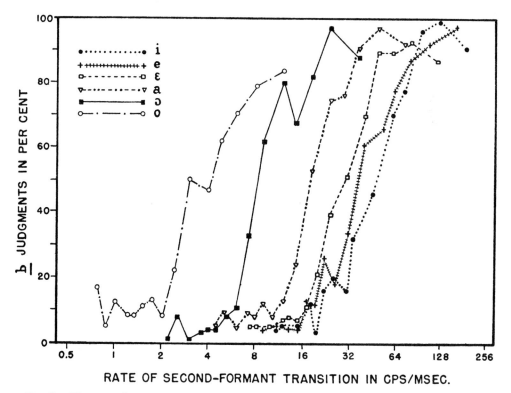

Fig. 7. The same data as shown in Fig 6, here plotted against rate of second-formant transition. Scaling the rates logarithmically serves to equate the distance on the abscissa occupied by the range of rates for each of the vowels.

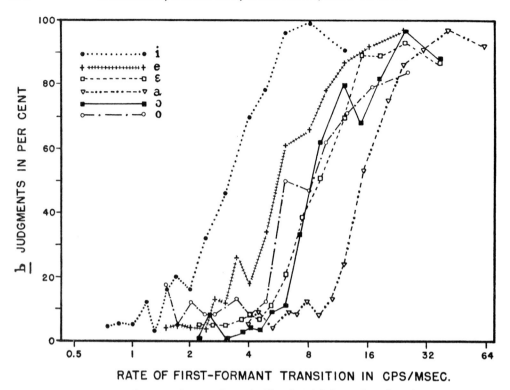

FIG. 8.   The same data as shown in Fig. 6 and 7, here plotted against
rate of first-formant transition.

i through *a*. (The extent of the second-formant transition decreases from 1800 cps for *i* to 720 cps for *a*, while, for the same change in vowel, the extent of the first-formant transition increases from 120 cps to 600 cps. Hence, for a given duration of transition, the rate of the second-formant transition decreases and the rate of the first-formant transition increases as the vowel is changed from *i* through *e* and *ɛ* to *a*.) It is possible, if unlikely, that the rate cues produce effects which cancel each other in such a way as to generate curves that appear to be invariant with duration.

For the vowels *a*, *ɔ*, and *o*, the extents (and hence the rates) of first- and second-formant transitions vary in the same direction, so we ought with these vowels to be able to make a less ambiguous comparison of the roles of duration and rate. If we look at the results for these three vowels, we see that the curves appear to be more closely bunched when plotted against duration than when plotted against rate, though in these

cases the relatively small change in frequency extent of transition provides something less than an ideal basis for comparison.

Obviously, the clearest separation of rate and duration could be made if we were to hold the transition of one formant constant in all respects while varying the rate, duration, and extent of the other. A series of exploratory studies made it clear that for distinguishing stop and semivowel the tempo of the second-formant transition is considerably more important than that of the first. Nevertheless, we failed to produce a highly realistic series from stop to semivowel with one transition fixed, and we have therefore been unable by this means to obtain direct evidence in regard to rate vs. duration.

We have found in exploratory work that the conversion of the stop consonant *b* to the semivowel *w* is most effectively accomplished if, in addition to slowing the transitions, we also make other changes in the spectrographic pattern. The accurate specification of these other cues and an evaluation of their relative contributions have yet to be made. At the present time we can only say that we have so far found no cue that promises to be more important than the time cue we have isolated in the present experiment. In any event, it is clear from the data reported here that the tempo or, more specifically, the duration of transition is a sufficient cue for distinguishing stop from semivowel from vowel of changing color. Thus, duration is to be added to the list of dimensions that are important for the discrimination and identification of individual speech sounds.

SUMMARY

It had been shown in earlier research that the direction and extent of second-formant transitions enable listeners to distinguish speech sounds *within* each of the three classes, voiceless stops (*p–t–k*), voiced stops (*b–d–g*), and nasal consonants (*m–n–ŋ*). In distinguishing *among* these classes, listeners apparently depend on certain other cues, such as the presence of a nasal resonance or voicing, each of which serves as an acoustic marker for its class. In the first part of the present experiment it was found that, with all other things equal, the tempo of the transitions was sufficient to distinguish members of the class of voiced stop consonants from corresponding members of the classes semivowels and vowels of changing color. In the syllable consisting of the stop consonant *b* plus the vowel *ɛ*, the stop *b* was transformed into the semivowel *w* when the duration of first- and second-formant transitions exceeded 40 msec.; the corresponding change from *gɛ* to *jɛ* occurred at 50 or 60 msec. Further increases in the duration of the transitions caused *wɛ* and *jɛ* to become the vowels-of-changing-color *uɛ* and *iɛ*, respectively. The shift from semivowel to vowel of changing color was much less sharp than the change from stop to semivowel.

In the second part of the study it was found that transition tempo served equally well for distinguishing *b* from *w* with many vowels other than the one (*ɛ*) used in obtaining the results just described. By investigating the tempo cue with a variety of vowels, it was possible (as it had not been in the first part of the study) to assess the relative contributions of duration and rate of transition. The results suggest that duration is the significant aspect of the tempo cue.

REFERENCES

1. COOPER, F. S. Spectrum analysis. *J. acoust. Soc. Amer.*, 1950, **22**, 761–762.
2. COOPER, F. S. Some instrumental aids to research on speech. In *Report of the fourth annual round table meeting on linguistics and language teaching.* Washington, D. C.: Institute of Languages and Linguistics, Georgetown University, 1953. Pp. 46–53.
3. COOPER, F. S., DELATTRE, P. C., LIBERMAN, A. M., BORST, J. M., & GERSTMAN, L. J. Some experiments on the perception of synthetic speech sounds. *J. acoust. Soc. Amer.*, 1952, **24**, 597–606.
4. COOPER, F. S., LIBERMAN, A. M., & BORST, J. M. The interconversion of audible and visible patterns as a basis for research in the perception of speech. *Proc. Nat. Acad. Sci.*, 1951, **37**, 318–325.
5. DELATTRE, P. C., LIBERMAN, A. M., & COOPER, F. S. Acoustic loci and transitional cues for consonants. *J. acoust. Soc. Amer.*, 1955, **27**, 769–773.
6. LIBERMAN, A. M., DELATTRE, P. C., & COOPER, F. S. The role of selected stimulus-variables in the perception of the unvoiced stop consonants. *Amer. J. Psychol.*, 1952, **65**, 497–516.
7. LIBERMAN, A. M., DELATTRE, P. C., COOPER, F. S., & GERSTMAN, L. J. The role of consonant-vowel transitions in the perception of the stop and nasal consonants. *Psychol. Monogr.*, 1954, **68**, No. 8 (Whole No. 379).
8. MILLER, G. A., & NICELY, P. E. An analysis of perceptual confusions among some English consonants. *J. acoust. Soc. Amer.*, 1955, **27**, 338–352.

(Received February 20, 1956)

Reprinted from THE JOURNAL OF THE ACOUSTICAL SOCIETY OF AMERICA, Vol. 29, No. 1 (January 1957).
Copyright 1957 by the Acoustical Society of America.

Acoustic Properties of Stop Consonants*

M. HALLE,† G. W. HUGHES,‡ AND J.-P. A. RADLEY§

Research Laboratory of Electronics, Massachusetts Institute of Technology, Cambridge, Massachusetts

(Received September 6, 1956)

The two major cues for stop consonants, the burst of the stop release and the formant transitions in the adjacent vowel, were investigated. Detailed energy density spectra of the bursts were prepared. The transitions were studied by means of sonagrams. Possible criteria for identification were developed and tested. In order to assess the efficacy of the two types of cue, perceptual tests were conducted with isolated segments that contained either stop bursts or vowel transitions alone. Common acoustical properties of bursts and formant transitions are noted; differences as well as similarities are discussed in the light of different varieties of pitch judgments.

THE stop sounds, /p/ /t/ /k/ /b/ /g/, are produced by a complex of movements in the vocal tract. With the nasal cavity closed, a rapid closure and/or opening is effected at some point in the oral cavity. Behind the point of closure a pressure is built up which is suddenly released when the closure is released.

During the period of closure the vocal cords may or may not vibrate; if they do, we have a voiced stop; if they do not, we have a voiceless stop. Although in many instances the presence or absence of voicing serves to distinguish /b/ /d/ /g/ from /p/ /t/ /k/, in English voicing is not crucial to this distinction. The essential difference between these two classes of stops lies in the fact that in the production of the latter more pressure is built up behind the closure than in the production of the former. This difference in pressure results in higher intensity bursts and accounts for the well-known fact that /p/ /t/ /k/ bursts are often followed by an aspiration, which is not present in the case of /b/ /d/ /g/. Differences in the spectra of the bursts of these two classes of stops and in the duration of the preceding vowel can also be observed (see below). Since the role of the vocal-cord vibrations is thus relatively less important, the traditional terms "voiced" and "voiceless" seem somewhat inappropriate and will not be used here. Instead we shall refer to /p/ /t/ /k/ as "tense" and to /b/ /d/ /g/ as "lax" stops.[1]

The acoustic correlates of the complex of movements involved in the production of stops are rapid changes in the short-time energy spectrum preceded or followed by a fairly long period (of the order of at least several centiseconds) during which there is no energy in all bands above the voicing component (above 300 cps).

This "silence" is a necessary cue for the perception of a stop sound: if the "silence" is filled by any other type of sound except voicing, a stop is not perceived.

When the stop is adjacent to a vowel, the movement in the oral cavity to and/or from the closure results in rapid changes in the formant frequencies. These rapid changes in the vowel formants adjacent to a silence are known as *transitions* and they are important cues for the perception of the different classes of stops.[2]

The rapid opening of the oral cavity is commonly accompanied by a short burst of noise. The spectral properties of the burst constitute another set of cues for the perception of the different classes of stops.

When a stop sound is adjacent to a vowel, we usually have all three cues: silence, burst and transition, or transition, silence and burst, as in "tack" in Fig. 1. Of these three, however, only the silence is a necessary cue—the silence with either transition or burst is a sufficient cue for identifying a stop. Thus, for example, in words like "task" (see Fig. 1) the identification of the final stop must evidently be attributed to the spectral properties of the stop burst; since the stop is not adjacent to any vowel, there can be no transition cue. On the other hand, in the ordinary pronunciation of words like "tact" (see Fig. 1), there is only a single silence followed by a single burst, although two stops /k/ and /t/ are perceived. The cue for the stop /k/ must, therefore, be contained in the transitions of the vowel formants preceding the silence.

* This work was supported in part by the U. S. Army (Signal Corps), the U. S. Air Force (Office of Scientific Research, Air Research and Development Command), and the U. S. Navy (Office of Naval Research); and the National Science Foundation.

† Also Department of Modern Languages, Massachusetts Institute of Technology.

‡ Also Department of Electrical Engineering, Massachusetts Institute of Technology.

§ Now at Air Force Cambridge Research Center, Hanscom Field, Bedford, Massachusetts.

[1] Jakobson, Fant, and Halle, Preliminaries to Speech Analysis, Technical Report 13, Acoustics Laboratory, Massachusetts Institute of Technology, May, 1952, pp. 36–39. The phonetic symbols used in this article are those of the International Phonetics Association (IPA).

[2] Ever since it became clear that vowels are products of the resonances of different configurations of the vocal tract, it has also been obvious that these resonances had to change as the geometrical configuration of the vocal tract changed. Not until the development of the sonagraph was it possible to follow these changes easily, although single investigators with unusually acute ears, like the Russian phonetician, A. Thomson, drew attention to these changes more than half a century ago. Thomson wrote: "Depending on the pitch of the proper tone of the mouth cavity ('pitch' refers to the second formant—M. H.) in its articulation of the preceding consonant, the vowel often begins considerably higher or lower, and then continuously and rapidly moves to its characteristic pitch on which it is held for a relatively long time. Towards the end, as it approaches the following consonant, the vowel again rapidly rises or drops, depending on the shape of the resonator characteristic of that consonant . . . even in the central part of the vowel there is no complete constancy in pitch. The same movement from the characteristic pitch of the preceding consonant to that of the following consonant continues here too." A. I. Thomson, Russ. Filol. Vestnik **54**, 231 (1905).

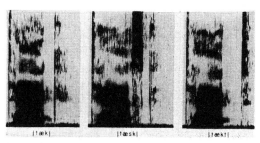

Fig. 1. Sonagrams of the words "tack" "task" "tact" (male speaker *G*) illustrating the role that transitions and bursts play in the perception of stops. In the /k/ of "tack" both transition and burst are present; in that of "task" only the burst is present; while in that of "tact" the transition alone is present.

The objective of the research reported below was to study the burst and transition separately in order to establish ways in which they could be used in a mechanical identification procedure.

SPECTRAL PROPERTIES OF STOP BURSTS

For this phase of the study our corpus consisted of monosyllabic words spoken in isolation by two males and one female. The list of words contained the six stops of English in position before and after the vowels /i/ /ɪ/ /ʌ/ /ɑ/ /u/. In addition, the list contained the voiceless stops in nonvocalic contexts, e.g., in the word "whisk," as well as words ending in the vowels /i/ /u/ /ɑ/.

Since we propose to study the bursts in isolation, the question might well be raised: Is a listener able to identify stop bursts isolated from their context as /p/ /t/ or /k/? We tried to answer this question by performing the following experiment. Words ending in stops produced with a burst and without vocal-cord vibration ("leap," for example) were selected from the corpus. The first 20 msec of each stop burst was gated out and rerecorded. Care was taken not to introduce any perceptible gating transients. The gated stop bursts were presented to listeners with instructions to judge them as /p/ /t/ or /k/. In the initial experiment, we experienced great difficulty in obtaining a reasonable response from our subjects, but with a certain amount of training it was possible to elicit fairly consistent responses. Our five best subjects gave the following percentages of correct responses: 65, 70, 75, 80, and 96. The last three subjects had had a considerable amount of experience with bursts in isolation; the first two subjects had received only a few minutes of instruction before the test. Since the percentages of correct responses of these five subjects were at least twice the percentages that might be obtained by guessing, we concluded that the bursts in isolation are identifiable as particular stops by listeners.

We hypothesized that the clues that make possible the identification of the bursts as different stops, reside in the spectrum. Consequently, we prepared

detailed spectra of the stop bursts of all the words in our corpus. The first 20 msec of each stop burst, or the interval from the onset of the burst to the onset of the vowel—whichever was shorter—was fed into a filter of fixed band width whose center frequency was continuously variable over the range from 250 cps to 10 000 cps. For our filter we used a Hewlett Packard 300 A wave analyzer modified so that its band width was approximately 150 cps. The output of the wave analyzer was amplified, full-wave rectified, and integrated, and the resultant dc voltage was fed to a holding circuit and meter.[3] Samples of spectra are shown in Figs. 2, 3, and 4.

In examining the spectra, we note that the three classes of stops associated with different points of articulation differ from each other as follows:

/p/ and /b/, the labial stops, have a primary concentration of energy in the low frequencies (500–1500 cps).

/t/ and /d/, the postdental stops, have either a flat spectrum or one in which the higher frequencies (above 4000 cps) predominate, aside from an energy concentration in the region of 500 cps.

/k/ and /g/, the palatal and velar stops, show strong concentrations of energy in intermediate frequency regions (1500–4000 cps).

The differences among the various speakers were not very regular or marked. Much greater were the differences in the spectra of tense and lax stops. Since most of our lax stops were pronounced with vocal-cord vibration their spectra contained a strong low-frequency component. This component does not appear in the examples in Figs. 2, 3, and 4, because we passed all lax stops through a 300 cps high-pass filter before measuring them. The lax stops also show a significant drop in level in the high frequencies. This high-frequency loss is a consequence of the lower pressure associated with the production of lax stops and is therefore a crucial cue for this class of stops.

The most striking differences, however, were found in spectra of /k/ and /g/ in position before different vowels. Before front vowels (i.e., vowels having a second formant above 1200–1500 cps) the spectral peak of the bursts was in the region between 2000 and 4000 cps; before back vowels (second formant below 1200 cps) the spectral peaks were at much lower frequencies. These differences are not surprising, since it is well known that in English the phonemes /k/ and /g/ have two distinct contextual variants; one, before front vowels, produced with a closure nearer the front of the vocal cavity, and the other, before back vowels, produced with a closure more to the rear of the oral cavity. In position after vowels these contextual

[3] G. W. Hughes and M. Halle, J. Acoust. Soc. Am. **28**, 303–305 (1956), gives a detailed description of measuring procedure and equipment characteristics.

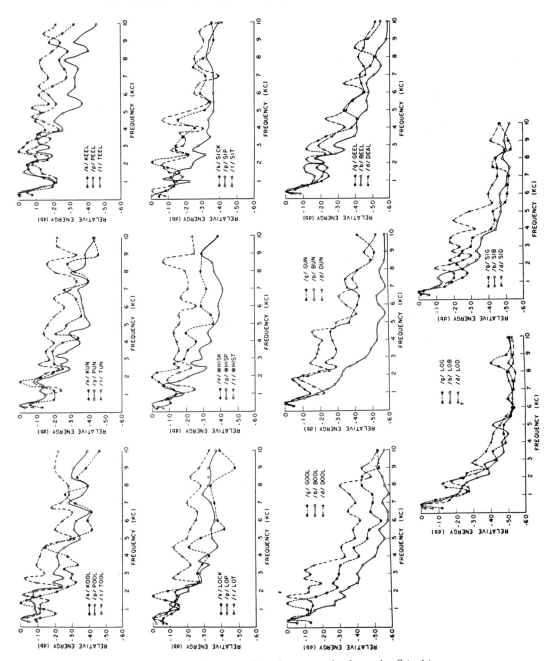

Fig. 2. Energy density spectra of stop bursts as spoken by speaker *G* (male).

differences were much less marked, which is to be expected since the "silence" between the end of the vowel and the burst was of the order of 100 msec.

A number of spectra deviated from the norms described above. Two particularly striking examples are given in Fig. 5; others can be found in Figs. 2, 3, and 4.

In spite of these divergences, the spectra possessed enough uniformity to make possible a statement of criteria that separate the spectra into three classes which are associated with the different points of articulation: First, the intensity in the 700–10 000 cps and 2700–10 000 cps bands was measured for all bursts. When the burst possessed significant energy in

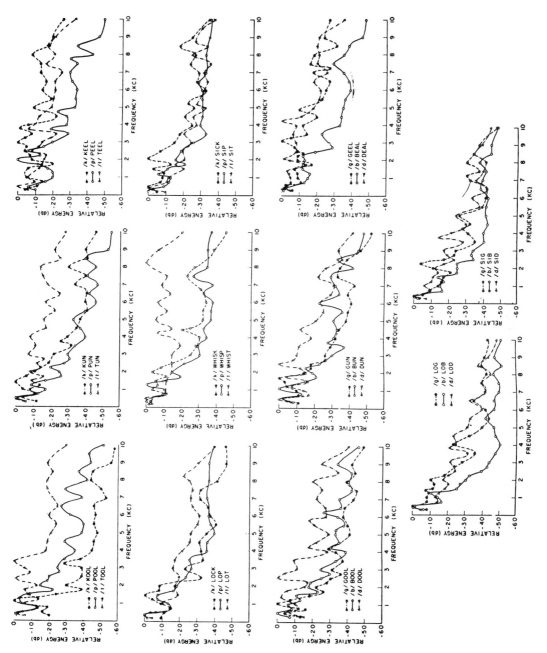

Fig. 3. Energy density spectra of stop bursts as spoken by speaker *A* (male).

the upper frequencies, these two values differed little (5 db for tense stops, 8 db for lax stops). When there was no significant energy in the higher frequencies, the two measurements differed greatly. As we have remarked, significant energy in the high frequencies is a characteristic of /t/ and /d/ and of the front variants of /k/ and /g/, while /p/ and /b/ and the back variants of /k/ and /g/ are characteristically weak in the high frequencies. We subjected our entire catalog of sounds to these two measurements and obtained correct classifications in 95% of the cases.

This step classified all the sounds into two classes; one, which we shall call the *acute* class, contained /t/ /d/ and the front variants of /k/ and /g/; the

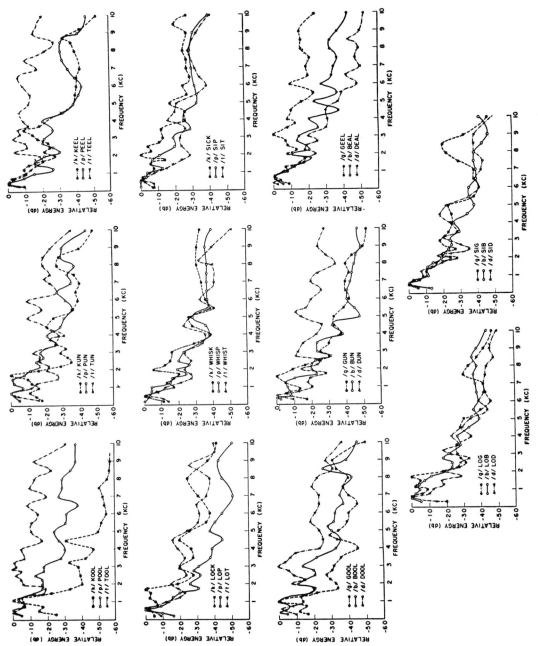

FIG. 4. Energy density spectra of stop bursts as spoken by speaker *R* (female).

other, which we shall call the *grave* class, contained /p/ and /b/ and the back variant of /k/ and /g/.[4] Acute /k/ and /g/ variants were rare in final position due to the "silence" that separates the burst from the preceding vowel. The next task involves subdividing

these two classes again into two; thus obtaining the correct identification of the stops. In order to do this we found it necessary to apply a different procedure for the grave consonants than for the acute.

For the grave consonants, we noted the difference in levels between the two most intense spectral maxima and plotted it as a function of the frequency position

---

[4] See R. Jakobson *et al.*, reference 1, pp. 26–36, for an explanation of the terms "grave" and "acute."

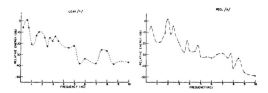

FIG. 5. Deviant spectra of stop bursts /k/ in "leak" (male speaker *G*) and /p/ in "peal" (male speaker *A*).

of the maximum of highest frequency. Such a plot is shown in Fig. 6. By the simple expedient of drawing straight lines across these graphs (the higher line for tense than for lax stops can easily be justified on the grounds of correcting the effects of the high-frequency drop that is characteristic of lax stops), we obtained correct separation of 85% of the tense bursts and approximately 78% of the lax bursts. The only really bad cases are the four low /g/ in final position. No special significance is to be attached to the shape or the position of the line other than that it separates what we know to be different.

We separated the acute stops into /t/ /d/ and /k/ /g/ by measuring graphically the average level of the spectrum between 300 cps and 10 000 cps and comparing it with the average level of the spectrum between 2 kc and 4 kc. Since /k/ and /g/ had an energy concentration in the central frequencies, the spectrum level in these frequencies considerably exceeded (5 db for tense stops, 8 db for lax stops) the average level of the entire spectrum. These values yielded the correct classification in approximately 85% of the cases. This procedure was very efficient in the case of the tense stops; for the lax stops it was not quite as reliable.[5]

TRANSITIONS

The other major class of cue that is important in the identification of the stop consonants is the transitions in the formants of the adjacent vowel. In recent years, a great deal of valuable information concerning this class of cue has been gathered by the researchers at the Haskins Laboratories in their work on the perception of synthetic speech stimuli in which certain features were systematically varied.[6] The problem, as we saw it, was to determine to what extent the uniformities observed with synthetic stimuli were applicable to natural speech.

We approached this problem from two directions: (1) by studying a large number of spectrograms and attempting to correlate the observed formant transitions with the stop that was uttered by the speaker;

and (2) by conducting perceptual tests that were similar to those carried out by the Haskins group except that natural speech was used in place of synthetic stimuli.

Spectrographic Studies[7]

For examining the transitions, the principal tool was a Kay Electric sonagraph. The sonagraph has certain limitations for a study of this kind, the most serious of which are the restricted range of automatic gain control and the fixed band widths of its analyzing filter which make it impossible to obtain clearly defined formants for certain speakers. Nevertheless, in the majority of our samples the presentation was quite satisfactory.

The corpus in this study consisted of words, primarily monosyllables, in which the English vowels /i/ /ɪ/ /e/ /ɛ/ /æ/ /ɑ/ /ʌ/ /ɔ/ /o/ /u/ and /ʊ/ were combined with the six stops in initial and final position. The list was read twice by three males and one female whose dialects varied somewhat.

Our first problem, how to define a transition, illustrates well the difficulties that are encountered in the study of natural speech, but can easily be avoided when one has control over the stimulus.[8] In the sonagrams, shown in Fig. 7, there are a number of stop transitions that differ greatly in duration, rate of change, and their terminal (beginning and end) points. In Fig. 7(a), the final transition is considerably longer than 50 msec. The stop transition cannot be distinguished here from the change in the position of the vowel formants arising from the diphthongal pronounciation of the vowel. In Fig. 7(b), the vowel lasts only 100 msec and it is difficult to find any steady-state

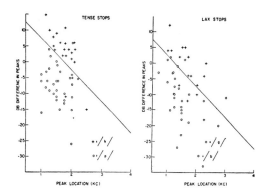

FIG. 6. Plots of the intensity differences of the two most intense spectral maxima as a function of the frequency position of the maximum of highest frequency. The straight lines in each plot divide /k/ and /g/ bursts from /p/ and /b/ bursts.

[5] Attention is drawn to a similar scheme proposed for the identification of Russian stop sounds in a forthcoming book: M. Halle and L. G. Jones, *The Russian Consonants* (Mouton and Company, 'S-Gravenhage, Netherlands, to be published).
[6] Liberman, Delattre, Cooper, and Gerstman, "The role of consonant-vowel transitions in the perception of stop and nasal consonants," Psychological Monographs No. 379, 1954; see also publications cited therein.

[7] For the material (including more than 500 sonagrams) on which the following discussion is based, see J.-P. A. Radley, "The role of transitions in the identification of English stops," S.M. thesis, Department of Electrical Engineering, Massachusetts Institute of Technology, 1955.
[8] Delattre, Liberman, and Cooper, J. Acoust. Soc. Am. 27, 769–773 (1955).

portion or to decide where the transition begins. In Fig. 7(c), the final transitions of the different formants start at different times. Note that here the final $F2$ transition lasts only 20 msec. The initial $F2$ and $F3$ transition can only be discerned with the greatest difficulty even if the aspiration is included with the vowel transition.

All of these difficulties show that it is not easy to decide what segment on a given sonagram constitutes a transition. Specifically, it is often impossible to identify a transition by examining on a single sonagram a fixed time interval before or after a silence or by looking for certain rates of change in the formant center frequency or the formant band width.

We find, however, that by looking at sets of sonagrams of minimally different words, e.g., "seep," "seat," "seek," differences in the formant transitions, if they exist, can be easily pointed out. The transition, like so many other linguistic concepts, must be defined with respect to a set of entities that are otherwise identical.

The regularities that we observed were considerably more complex than the elegant "locus" rules that summarize the results of the Haskins experiments. We found dependencies not only on the steady-state position of the adjacent vowel, but also on the position of the stop with respect to the vowel (preceding or following), and of the feature tense-lax in both the consonant and the vowel.[9]

The least satisfactory group was that of the tense stops in initial position. For these stops, generalizations are only possible about transitions in the lax vowels /ɪ/, /ʌ/, and /ʊ/ and in the tense vowel /u/. Before /ʌ/, $F2$ and $F3$ have neutral or negative transitions for /p/; $F2$ has a positive transition and $F3$ has a negative or neutral transition for /t/; and $F2$ and $F3$ converge for /k/. Before /ɪ/, negative transitions in both $F2$ and $F3$ are associated with /p/, neutral or moderately positive transitions in both $F2$ and $F3$ are correlated with /t/, while /k/ is associated with a positive $F2$ and a neutral $F3$ transition, which can be thought of as a case of convergence. Before /ʊ/ and /u/, the $F3$ transition could not be seen in quite a few instances; in those cases in which it was visible it seemed to us to be neutral. $F2$ had positive transitions for /t/ and neutral or slightly negative transitions for both /p/ and /k/, which, however, could not be separated on the basis of their transitions.

In the case of tense stops in final position, the transitions are considerably more uniform. A partial explanation for this may be that imploded stops are quite common in final position. In these cases, the transition

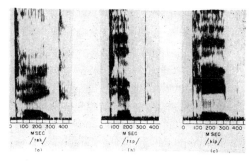

FIG. 7. Sonagrams illustrating the great variety of transitions encountered in actual speech. (a)—"take" (male speaker R); (b)—"tip" (male speaker B); (c)—"keep" (male speaker H).

cue is not supplemented by a burst cue, as it is in initial position. The transitional cues fall into two classes: after /i/ /ɪ/ /ɛ/ /e/ /æ/ /ɑ/ /ɔ/ /ʌ/ and after the rounded back vowels /u/ /ʊ/ /o/. In the former class /p/ induces a markedly negative transition in $F2$, which is absent for /t/ and /k/. The latter two can be distinguished by noting that /k/ has a convergence of $F2$ and $F3$. In the case of /u/ /ʊ/ /o/ the cue for /t/ is a markedly positive $F2$ transition, which sometimes meets a descending $F3$, while the absence of such an $F2$ transition is the cue for /p/ and /k/, which do not differ significantly from each other.

For lax stops in initial position, /b/ has a more negative or less positive $F2$ and $F3$ transition than /d/ for every vowel except /i/, where the transitions may be similar. As we move along the vowel triangle from /i/ to /u/, /d/ gives progressively more positive $F2$ transitions, in conformity with the results obtained in the Haskins perceptual tests; but it was not possible to specify a "locus" frequency. Before the front vowels, /i/ /ɪ/ /e/ /ɛ/ /æ/, /g/ has a more positive $F2$ transition than the other two stops, while before the back vowels, /g/ has a less positive transition than /d/. Convergence of $F2$ and $F3$ is common, though not universal, for /g/ transitions, particularly before back vowels.

In the case of the lax stops in final position, the rules are fairly similar to those stated for tense stops in final position. As with /p/, there is the very marked negative transition before /b/ in all vowels except those with the lowest $F2$: /u/ /o/. Again we find something like a "locus" phenomenon in the behavior of /d/ transitions, which are slightly negative or neutral with vowels having a high second formant and become progressively more positive as $F2$ of the vowels is lower. After front vowels, /g/ has a more positive transition than /d/, and is further distinguished from /d/ by a negative $F3$, thus giving convergence. For the back vowels, however, the $F2$ transition is considerably more positive for /d/ than for /g/. In these instances, /g/ transitions cannot be differentiated consistently from /b/ transitions.

---

[9] See K. N. Stevens and A. S. House, J. Acoust. Soc. Am. **28**, 578–585 (1956). Following common usage, we call a transition "negative" if its terminal (beginning or end) point is of lower frequency than the steady-state or average position of the formant in the vowel; "positive" if it is of higher frequency; and "neutral," if it is of the same frequency.

TABLE I. Responses of the listeners to syllables from which the final stop bursts were gated out. Each box contains the results of tests with syllables beginning with the consonant plus vowel sequence indicated. The vertical columns show the number of different consonant judgments made with respect to a single stimulus.

		Final stop in stimulus syllable /la-/							
		/p/	/t/	/k/	/#/	/b/	/d/	/g/	Total
	/p/	5	0	1	0	3	0	0	9
Number	/t/	9	25	21	0	0	0	0	45
of listener	/k/	5	1	2	0	0	0	0	8
judgments	/#/	9	1	6	25	3	1	0	45
	/b/	2	0	0	4	22	0	3	31
	/d/	0	2	0	0	2	29	20	53
	/g/	0	0	0	1	0	0	7	8
	Total	30	29	30	30	30	30	30	

		Final stop in stimulus syllable /li-/							
		/p/	/t/	/k/	/#/	/b/	/d/	/g/	Total
	/p/	26	14	20	0	3	0	0	63
Number	/t/	3	12	9	0	0	1	1	26
of listener	/k/	0	1	1	0	0	0	5	7
judgments	/#/	0	3	0	20	8	13	19	63
	/b/	0	0	0	6	15	1	5	27
	/d/	1	0	0	3	4	24	4	36
	/g/	0	0	0	1	0	1	1	3
	Total	30	30	30	30	30	40	35	

		Final stop in stimulus syllable /lu-/							
		/p/	/t/	/k/	/#/	/b/	/d/	/g/	Total
	/p/	18	2	11	0	2	0	0	33
Number	/t/	5	24	4	0	0	0	0	33
of listener	/k/	1	1	4	0	0	0	0	6
judgments	/#/	6	1	9	27	30	4	17	94
	/b/	0	2	2	2	7	0	12	25
	/d/	0	0	0	1	1	26	0	28
	/g/	0	0	0	0	0	0	1	1
	Total	30	30	30	30	40	30	30	

		Final stop in stimulus syllable /sʌ-/						
		/p/	/t/	/k/	/b/	/d/	/g/	Total
	/p/	21	0	2	9	0	0	32
Number	/t/	7	27	16	0	0	10	50
of listener	/k/	1	1	11	0	0	0	13
judgments	/b/	1	0	0	11	0	4	16
	/d/	0	2	0	7	19	7	35
	/g/	0	0	1	3	1	19	24
	Total	30	30	30	30	20	40	

		Final stop in stimulus syllable /sɪ-/						
		/p/	/t/	/k/	/b/	/d/	/g/	Total
	/p/	23	5	0	5	0	0	33
Number	/t/	6	23	1	1	7	1	39
of listener	/k/	0	0	27	0	0	2	29
judgments	/b/	1	0	0	24	1	2	28
	/d/	0	2	0	0	22	1	25
	/g/	0	0	2	0	0	23	25
	Total	30	30	30	30	30	29	

Perceptual Tests

It was, unfortunately, impossible to carry out large-scale perceptual tests. The data reported below are, therefore, to be taken as preliminary results.

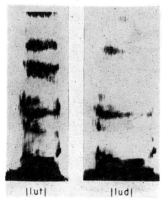

FIG. 8. Sonagrams of the words "lute" "lewd" (male speaker G) illustrating the differences in duration between the vowels preceding tense and lax stops.

In the tests, listeners were presented with mono-syllables recorded by one female and two male speakers. The syllables contained the vowels /i/ /ɑ/ /u/ /ɪ/ /ʌ/ followed by each of the six stops. The first three vowels were also contained in open syllables. Thus, a representative paradigm contained the following stimuli: /lip/ /lit/ /lik/ /lib/ /lid/ /lig/ /li/. By means of an electronic gate each syllable including the open one (i.e., the one ending in a vowel) was terminated immediately after the vowel so that no stop burst appeared in the test. The subjects were asked to identify the end of the syllable as one of the six stops or as "nothing" (#). After the lax vowels, where in English an open syllable is impossible, the judgment "nothing" was omitted. The results of the tests are given in Table I.

Because of the very marked difference in duration of vowels before tense and before lax stops (see Fig. 8), the subjects had little difficulty in distinguishing tense from lax stops. Subjects never confused an open syllable with a syllable ending in a tense stop, but occasionally an open syllable was thought to end in a lax consonant. On the other hand, closed syllables, particularly those ending in lax stops, were rather frequently judged to be open. The "mistakes" are correlated with the position of first formant of the preceding vowel. They seem to indicate that negative transitions of the first formant played a particularly significant role in the identification of stops as class. Where $F1$ was high and, consequently, free to move downward, closed syllables were relatively rarely thought to be open; where $F1$ was low and its downward movement restricted, closed syllables were frequently judged to be open.

Somewhat unexpectedly, in the light of previous studies, but not quite so surprisingly, in view of the transition data reviewed in the preceding section, the greatest differences in response were correlated with the differences between tense and lax vowels. After lax vowels, the transitions seemed, in general, easier to judge correctly than after tense vowels. Especially great difficulties were experienced with stimuli ending in /k/ and /g/ preceded by tense vowels. Here /k/ and /g/ judgments were avoided to such an extent that they constituted only 5% of the responses, although syllables ending in /k/ and /g/ accounted for 28.5% of the stimuli. This compares with 25.5% /k/ and /g/ responses *vs* 36% of the stimuli for the transitions in the lax vowels.

As for individual vowels, we must note the extreme reliability of the judgments for the vowel /ɪ/, which is explained by the very clear transitions of this vowel; see Fig. 9. The other lax vowel in our corpus /ʌ/ was also judged with fair reliability, although not nearly as reliably as /ɪ/. It is significant that /k/ and /g/ judgments are again the least reliable. After /u/ there was a very marked tendency to consider syllables ending in a lax stop as open, which is explained by the total absence of transitions (see Fig. 10). In view of the restricted size of the sample, the tendencies in the /i/ and /a/ transition judgments are not sufficiently marked to warrant specific conclusions.

CONCLUDING REMARKS

The data just reviewed, though fragmentary and in need of further elaboration, give support to the common view that, in the perception of stop sounds, information from the burst as well as from the transition is normally required. This view, however, presents us with the paradoxical situation that what appear to be the two most disparate acoustical phenomena, formant movements and bursts of sound, are perceptually equated. We shall try to account for this by considering some acoustical properties of bursts and transitions and their relation to the perception of speech.

Physically speaking, a formant[10] reflects organization

---

[10] We distinguish between "resonance" and "formant." The former refers to a maximum in the frequency response of a resonator that is computed by taking into consideration only the geometrical properties of the resonator and by specifically neglect-

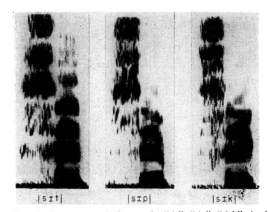

FIG. 9. Sonagrams of the words "sit" "sip" "sick" (male speaker *G*) illustrating the exceptionally unambiguous transitions in the end of the vowel /ɪ/. Note that in "sit" $F2$ and $F3$ transitions are neutral; in "sip" both transitions are negative; while in "sick" $F2$ has a positive transition and $F3$, a negative transition, and the two formants converge.

of the acoustic energy in the frequency domain and no organization in the time domain; while a burst represents organization of acoustic energy in the time domain and no organization in the frequency domain. In the case of an ideal formant, there is no energy outside the infinitely narrow resonance frequency, but the sound lasts forever. An ideal burst (impulse), on the other hand, has an infinitely short duration; i.e., the energy is present only at a given instant, but its band width is infinite.

When a resonance is changing in frequency, the formant band width increases. The more rapid the movement, the broader the band width. In the limiting case of instantaneous movement, the band width is infinite; i.e., we have a phenomenon of strictly limited duration and infinite band width. But these are exactly the terms in which we previously described the burst. The burst can, therefore, be considered as an extreme

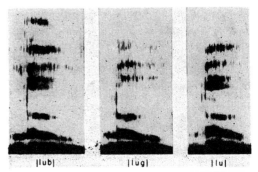

FIG. 10. Sonagrams of the syllables /lub/ /lug/ /lu/ (male speaker *A*) showing almost no differences in the transitions.

---

ing the special effects that are produced when the resonator is excited in a particular manner and its output measured by a particular device and procedure. The term "formant" takes all these factors into consideration; thus it refers to a frequency region of maximal intensity in an actually measured spectrum.

case of transition in which the changes in the short-time energy-density spectrum are very rapid and the organization of the energy in the frequency domain is replaced by organization in the time domain.

It is usually assumed that moving formants are perceived in a manner similar to that of stationary formants. This view seems to be an oversimplification, for no reasons have been advanced that would justify ignoring the fact that when a resonance is changing in frequency the problem of measuring this frequency is complicated by increases in the formant band width. It is obvious that in the case of instantaneous change of resonance frequency, it is meaningless to specify a formant frequency, or formant movement. In intermediate cases, the rate of change (or the formant band width) at which it becomes meaningless to specify a formant frequency depends upon the properties of the measuring apparatus,[11] which, in the case of interest here, are those of the human auditory system.

In experiments with damped sine waves, K. N. Stevens[12] has shown that, as the resonance band width is increased by increasing the damping, it becomes increasingly difficult to match the pitch of such a resonance to that of a pure tone. Although Stevens' experiments were not carried out with enough values of damping to provide conclusive evidence on this point, they indicate that, at some critical band width, which we estimate to be 300 cps, the train of damped sine waves can no longer be matched in pitch to a pure tone. This does not mean that all pitch judgments become impossible; for example, different trains of damped sine waves can still be ordered from high to low with some consistency.

It is interesting that we observe similar facts in judging the pitch of vowels and consonants. On the one hand, the vowels can be matched in pitch to pure tones without much difficulty; such matches have been performed with amazing accuracy ever since the seventeenth century, when Samuel Reyherr, in his book *Mathesis mosaica* (Cologne, 1679), gave in musical notation the "characteristic pitches" (second formant) of German and French vowels.[13] On the other hand, consonants cannot be matched easily in pitch to pure tones; and all "pitch" determinations of consonants are completely unconvincing and usually refer to the terminal stage of the second formant in the adjacent vowel.[14]

One might, therefore, suggest as an hypothesis that the distinction between vowels and consonants, which is the fundamental dichotomy of phonetics, is based on the organism's ability to perform much more elaborate pitch judgments with respect to certain classes of physical stimuli (vowels and undamped or moderately damped sine waves) than with respect to other classes (consonants, tonal masses, noises, and highly damped sine waves). Formant transitions would then be intermediate structures whose assignment to the vowels or to the consonants is a function of their band width, which in turn is dependent on their rate of change.

---

[11] L. L. Beranek, *Acoustic Measurements* (John Wiley and Sons, Inc., New York, 1949), pp. 538–542.

[12] K. N. Stevens, "The perception of sounds shaped by resonance circuits," Sc.D. thesis, Department of Electrical Engineering, Massachusetts Institute of Technology, 1952.

[13] Compare C. Stumpf, *Die Sprachlaute* (Berlin, 1926), p. 148.

[14] Compare the following remark of a nineteenth century English phonetician who attempted to determine the "pitch" of consonants: "When freed from connection with any vowel, the resonance of *f* can be carried a long way both up and down in pitch without at all spoiling the *f* itself. . . . It becomes clear that the essential quality of *f* is but vaguely linked with the actual pitch of its resonance." R. J. Lloyd, Proc. Roy. Soc. (Edinburgh) **22**, 224 (1898).

Reprinted from THE JOURNAL OF THE ACOUSTICAL SOCIETY OF AMERICA, Vol. 29, No. 1 (January 1957).
Copyright 1957 by the Acoustical Society of America.

Realization of Prosodic Features in Whispered Speech*

W. MEYER-EPPLER

Institut für Phonetik und Kommunikationsforschung der Universität, Bonn, Germany

(Received September 26, 1956)

Experiments utilizing a visible-speech analyzer showed that changes of pitch in normal (voiced) speech are replaced in whispered speech by shifts of some formant regions accompanied by added noise between the higher formants.

INTRODUCTION

IT is a well-known fact that people can be understood without any difficulty when they whisper instead of speaking normally. This fact is not very strange if the formant frequencies of the vowels and the envelopes and spectra of the fricative and plosive sounds are considered to be the information-carrying elements of speech. It must be doubtful, however, whether full information can be carried by whispered speech in tonal languages like Chinese or many West-African languages where pitch is used to differentiate the meaning of various lexical items consisting of otherwise identical groups of phons.

Recently, Panconcelli-Calzia[1] and Giet[2] have dealt with the problem of whispering in tone languages. Whereas Panconcelli-Calzia found that it was difficult for Chinese-born subjects to understand whispered Chinese, Giet, who had lived in China for many years as a missionary, states that whispering in Chinese is as effective a means of verbal communication as normally spoken speech. According to Giet's arguments[3] there must exist some substitute for the missing pitch quality in whispered speech within the acoustical range. As

Giet has already pointed out, there is no need to use tone languages for investigating substitutes in whispered speech. Similar results would be achieved by using any language where intonation belongs not to the *phonemic* but to the *prosodic* level, which term refers to features belonging to a sentence as a whole that are expressed by pitch and stress patterns. Intonation, e.g., may differentiate between a question and a statement.

VOWELS "SUNG" WITHOUT VOICE

Some orienting investigations were undertaken with German vowels "sung" without voice. It is not difficult to produce the same whispered vowel on different pitch levels within a range of about a musical fifth (i.e., a frequency ratio of 2:3). Obviously this can only be done by changing the spectral structure of the vowels within the limits of recognizability. The subjects were asked to "sing" the first five tones of a diatonic scale (e.g.: *c*, *d*, *e*, *f*, and *g*) maintaining the quality of a given vowel as well as possible. The sounds were recorded on magnetic tape and analyzed by means of a visible-speech analyzer (Sona-Graph). The spectrograms of a test series using the German vowels [a] (as in *Tal*), [e] (as in *See*), [i] (as in *viel*), [o] (as in *Sohn*), and [u] (as in *Schuh*) are shown in Fig. 1. Whereas in the case of [a], [e], [i] and [o] the position of the first two formants remains unchanged, the third formant of [a] is shifted from its position near 2.5 kc to about 3 kc if higher pitch is intended; a similar shift is found at a weak fifth formant near 5 kc. In the case of [u] the

---

* This work was supported in part by Gesellschaft zur Förderung der Klangforschung, Cologne, and was presented at the Second ICA Congress, June, 1956.

[1] G. Panconcelli-Calzia, Lingua 4, 369–378 (1955).
[2] Franz Giet SVD, *Zur Tonität nordchinesischer Mundarten* (Verlag der Missionsdruckerei St. Gabriel, Wien-Mödling, 1950), pp. 95–97.
[3] Franz Giet, Lingua 5, 372–381 (1956).

main formant itself is raised from 600 cps to 700 cps. This can be seen more easily in Fig. 2 where an enlarged frequency scale together with better spectral resolution is used. The spectrogram of Fig. 2 was achieved by playing back the magnetic tape upon which the vowels had been recorded at a higher than normal speed. The higher formants of [u], however, remain unaffected (Fig. 1). Since in the case of [e], [i], and [o] no very clear shift of formant positions can be observed, the apparent change of pitch must be caused by other spectral properties. Pike already had supposed that differences in intensity might serve as substitute for pitch,[4] and his expectation is confirmed by the spectrograms of Fig. 1. Raising the "pitch" of [e], [i], and [o] means increasing their intensity, thus filling the gaps in the higher spectral regions with noisy com-

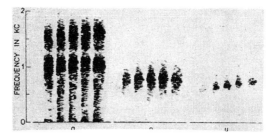

FIG. 2. Three vowels of Fig. 1 with enlarged frequency scale and improved spectral resolution.

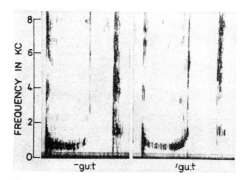

FIG. 3. Examples of different intonation of the word *"gut."*

ponents and eventually broadening the formants above 2 kc to a less-sharply profiled, fricative-like spectrum. The same happens with [a] and [u] in addition to the shift of their formants. Observation of the "singing" subjects reveals their larynx to be raised at the "higher" vowels, indicating a narrowing of the glottal fissure.

ANALYSIS OF SPOKEN SENTENCES

It might seem that singing without voice is a rather unnatural process, and that results obtained in this case need not necessarily be applicable to spoken words or sentences. Visible-speech diagrams of whispered words, however, show that the same effects as with sung vowels occur. Since [u] is an exceptionally good vowel for investigating the influence of intonation, sentences like *"Das ist aber nicht gut"* and *"Ist das etwa nicht gut?"* were whispered by different speakers and analyzed. Figure 3 gives an example of the word *"gut"* spoken with the level tone (-) and with rising tone ('). In the latter case the shift of the formant of [u] towards the likewise raised formant region of [t] is very impressive.

A new phenomenon occurs in the words [-zaen] and ['zaen], taken from sentences like *"Das sollst du sein!"* and *"Wer soll das sein?"* which are shown in Fig. 4. The interrogative intonation causes a new formant to originate at 2 kc belonging to the considerably reinforced [n], whereas the diphthong [ae] shows no clear differences.

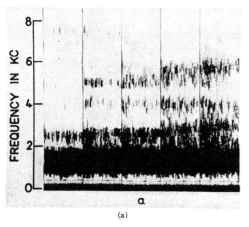

(a)

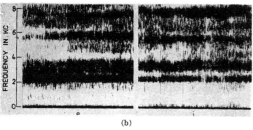

(b)

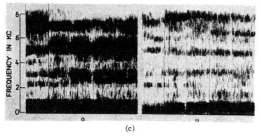

(c)

FIG. 1. German vowels, whispered in a diatonic scale.

[4] Kenneth L. Pike, *Tone Languages* (Edwards Brothers, Ann. Arbor, 1948), p. 34.

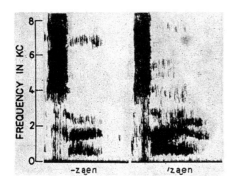

FIG. 4. The whispered words "···*sein!*" and "···*sein?*".

Figure 5 was chosen to give an impression of the reliability of our conclusions concerning the shift of formant positions. The same pair of words having different intonations ("*ja?*" and "*ja!*"), as spoken by two male subjects, shows, despite the unequal length of the individual vowels, the same type of evolution of the third formant.

SUMMARY

Spectrographic analysis of whispered vowels and words shows that there exist two substitutes for pitch

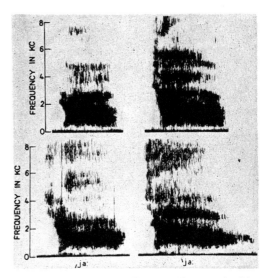

FIG. 5. The words "*ja?*" and "*ja!*" whispered by two male subjects.

movements which in voiced speech are used to indicate different prosodic features. The whispered vowels [e], [i], and [o] substitute spectral noise for pitch, whereas [a] and [u] possess some formants whose position changes with the intended "pitch."

Reprinted from The Journal of the Acoustical Society of America, Vol. 31, No. 4, 428–435, April, 1959
Copyright, 1959 by the Acoustical Society of America.

Vowel Amplitude and Phonemic Stress in American English*

Ilse Lehiste and Gordon E. Peterson

Speech Research Laboratory, University of Michigan, Ann Arbor, Michigan

(Received December 29, 1958)

Many different instrumental techniques for deriving an energy property of the speech wave have been employed in communication studies. There is as yet, however, no satisfactory method of calculating the loudness of the various types of complex quasi-periodic sounds that appear as time functions in speech. This paper does not present a method of making such loudness calculations, but suggests that any such method would be inadequate for deriving physical correlates of accent or stress judgments about speech. The study reports volume indicator and instantaneous amplitude observations on sustained vowels produced under various conditions of speech effort, and on vowels produced in CNC syllables in a carrier phrase with stress held constant. The untested theory is proposed that the perception of linguistic stress is based upon judgments of the physiological effort involved in producing vowels. The relative amplitude and spectrum of the vowel provide the chief basis for judgment of the physiological effort.

SINCE the beginning of the transmission of spoken messages by wire, the measurement of speech levels has been an enduring problem confronting communications engineers. The necessity of the measurement lies in the fact that communication systems are inherently noisy, and that they have limited power capacity. Thus, there is a basic problem of fitting the speech signal within the power capacity limitations of the system and above the noise level.

Speech, however, is not a uniform time function and its spectrum spreads throughout much of the audio-frequency range. As a result, it is necessary to be arbitrary in stating a single number to indicate speech level, and a multitude of instrumental procedures for deriving such a number have been employed.

There are at least three different ways in which amplitude information regarding speech can be derived and recorded.

(a) Perhaps the least useful for research analysis is the meter reading. Because of its convenience, however, the volume indicator, first described in a standard form by Chinn, Gannett, and Morris,[1] has probably been used more extensively than any other type of device in monitoring speech and in estimating speech levels in research studies (such as intelligibility measures).

(b) A number of continuous writing devices have been employed for measuring speech amplitudes. Pen recording instruments and the cathode-ray oscilloscope with associated camera fall within this general category. In general, ink writing devices employ an integrating time constant and usually respond to some function of the power levels of the signal rather than to linear amplitudes. An earlier review of this type of instrumentation was prepared by Stevens, Egan, and Miller.[2]

(c) An interesting and basic approach to obtaining statistical information about energy distributions in speech was developed by Dunn and White,[3] and a more recent instrumental method has been described by Benson and Hirsh.[4] Devices of the latter type employ discrete counting techniques which indicate the percentage of time during which certain amplitude or power values are exceeded in the speech wave.

LINGUISTICALLY SIGNIFICANT STRESS

It is a fundamental assumption of the present paper that the physical properties of speech are organized into a symbolic code. There are several components of this code and these components may be analyzed and described at the physiological, the acoustical, or the perceptual level. It is the intermediate acoustical signal which is primarily available for study. There are, in effect, two directions in which we might go in attempting to interpret this signal. One procedure would be to transform the signal to a series of auditory correlates such as pitch, loudness, and duration. It is not immediately obvious that the psychophysical scales developed for simple stimuli such as pure tones would apply to the interpretation of such a signal. An inverse procedure would be to attempt to derive information about the processes of speech production from the acoustical signal. It is our belief that this latter procedure will provide information which more directly corresponds to the judgments of the listener about speech; i.e., the listener interprets speech according to the properties of the speech production mechanism rather than according to the psychophysical principles of the perception of abstract sounds.

Thus, in the present paper we take the philosophy that the primary information source of speech is the physiological mechanism, and that speech is structured basically in terms of the capabilities and limitations of

* This research was supported by the Information Systems Branch of the Office of Naval Research of the U. S. Navy, under contract Nonr 1224(22), NR 049–122.

[1] Chinn, Gannett, and Morris, "A new standard volume indicator and reference level," Bell Telephone System Tech. Publs. Monograph B–1201 (1940).

[2] Stevens, Egan, and Miller, J. Acoust. Soc. Am. **19**, 771–779 (1947).

[3] H. K. Dunn and S. D. White, "Statistical measurements on conversational speech," Bell Telephone System Tech. Publs. Monograph B–1206 (1940).

[4] R. W. Benson and Ira J. Hirsh, J. Acoust. Soc. Am. **25**, 499–505 (1953).

this system.[5] We assume the acoustical signal to be a representation of the positions and movements of the physiological mechanism relative to the distribution of air pressures within the mechanism. It is easy to show that there is not a complete, one-to-one correspondence between the physiological production and the acoustical result. We assume a further reduction from acoustical patterns to auditory analyses. It is our belief that the interpretation of the speech signal by a listener is based on a very complicated set of auditory parameters by means of which he makes an interpretation of the speech production.

Thus we seek to describe speech in terms of such factors as (a) physiological effort, (b) rate of vocal fold vibration, (c) mode of laryngeal vibration, (d) pharyngeal and oral articulation, (e) palatopharyngeal closure, and (f) duration. While these factors are difficult to quantify, related perceptual terms, such as (a) stress, (b) pitch, (c) vocal quality, (d) segmental phonemes, (e) nasality, and (f) quantity, are even less clearly defined.

Some factors are correlated in the code of any particular language, but the relationships may differ markedly from one language to another. The present paper is primarily concerned with a consideration of those parameters which contribute to the judgment of what has often been called stress in English. These parameters form an important aspect of the code of English, and may form the essential distinction between words or utterances which have very different meanings. Thus they are of considerable interest in research on automatic speech recognition. It is our conclusion that stress is actually physiological stress, and that in English it is reflected in at least four acoustical parameters: speech power, fundamental voice frequency, phonetic quality, and duration. The relative effects of two of these parameters, amplitude and duration, have previously been studied in synthesized speech by Fry.[6] The present paper is primarily concerned with the intereffects of amplitude and phonetic quality.

We suggest that a listener will interpret sounds produced with equal effort as being in some respects similar with regard to stress. In everyday linguistic experience, the words *convict* (noun) and *convict* (verb) appear stressed either on the first syllable (noun) or second syllable (verb), and the degree of stress on the stressed syllable is subjectively felt to be the same. If the acoustical energy of the syllabic sounds is measured, however, the first syllable appears to have considerably more energy in both instances. There must, then, be other factors besides energy which influence our judgments about stress in English. The research of Fry emphasized the effect of duration, and we should like to consider the influence of phonetic quality upon judgments of linguistically significant stress.

Fairbanks[7] and others have previously observed that phonetic changes normally affect vowel amplitudes. Since the human vocal tract is a variable acoustical tube, with a variable radiating orifice, one would not expect to obtain the same pressure or power outputs for identical physiological input energies. Changes of amplitude of the sound wave may thus be caused by two major factors: first, if the phonetic quality of the vowel is held constant, a change in the amount of (input) power used to produce the sound may result in a change in output; second, if input energy is kept constant, a change in the phonetic quality of the vowel may result in a change in the output amplitude. It seems reasonable that in the production of speech, amplitude changes due to changes in phonetic quality should not significantly influence the perception of phonemic stress.

These observations suggest that the listener associates a certain intrinsic relative amplitude (or perhaps average power) with each vowel spectrum, and applies a corresponding "correction factor" to the incoming signal. Assuming that duration and fundamental voice frequency are held constant, this procedure would enable a listener to identify a stressed syllable, even if the average or peak power of that syllable were less than that of an adjacent unstressed syllable containing a more open vowel. If such perceptual corrections are made, an automatic device for identifying linguistically stressed syllables should contain a set of such built-in correction factors.

MEASUREMENT OF AMPLITUDE

The measurement of speech amplitude which will be most closely correlated with physiological effort is not immediately obvious. One of the simplest measurements, of course, is the instantaneous representation of the amplitude of the speech wave as produced on an ordinary cathode-ray oscilloscope. This wave can readily be reduced to instantaneous acoustical power by full wave rectification and the transformation of the wave to a logarithmic scale. Since phase effects within the vocal mechanism may affect the actual amplitudes appearing in the speech wave, there is some question as to whether instantaneous power measurements actually reflect the energy per unit time introduced into the production of speech.

This fact is perhaps the basic reason why integrating circuits of some type have generally been employed in the measurement of average speech powers. If one integrates the area under the instantaneous power curve, he then obtains the total energy represented by the wave. In a continuous recording of integrated speech power, some time constant of integration is required, so that one may obtain, for example, a continuous

[5] G. E. Peterson, Language **31**, 414–427 (1955).
[6] D. B. Fry, J. Acoust. Soc. Am. **27**, 765–768 (1955).

[7] G. Fairbanks, Speech Monographs **17**, 390–395 (1950).

TABLE I. Average values for one speaker of VU meter readings for sustained vowels relative to 0.0002 db/cm². A. Averages for 12 lists recorded on one day. B. Averages for 8 lists recorded four days later. C. Averages for all 20 lists. D. Averages for 2 lists recorded with 130 db masking noise in the ears of the speaker. E. Averages for each vowel for 1263 monosyllables of the CNC type(discussed near the close of the paper).

	i	ɪ	eɪ	ɛ	æ	ə	a	ɔ	ou	ʊ	u	aʊ	aɪ	ɔɪ	r	Average for all vowels
A.	80.2	81.4	81.1	82.9	83.1	85.0	85.5	84.8	83.4	83.4	80.2	84.8	82.7	83.7	81.4	82.91
B.	80.0	81.1	81.1	84.1	82.8	83.7	86.0	86.8	83.6	83.2	80.8	83.9	82.3	84.7	81.5	83.04
C.	80.1	81.3	81.1	83.4	83.0	84.5	85.7	85.6	83.5	83.3	80.4	84.4	82.5	84.1	81.4	83.0
D.	78.8	81.3	81.5	82.0	84.0	85.7	86.0	85.2	83.8	82.3	78.3	85.0	84.2	83.8	80.9	82.85
E.	75.1	78.1	78.6	79.3	79.4	79.7	80.2	80.6	79.7	78.4	78.2	80.1	80.2	80.9	79.0	79.0

trace of "average speech power" as a function of time.

$$\bar{p}(t) \sim \int_{t_1}^{t_2} \frac{e^2(t)dt}{T},$$

where

$$T = t_2 - t_1.$$

We may assume that the physiological effort employed in the production of a sustained vowel is essentially constant. Thus power variations within the fundamental period do not reflect changes in vocal effort and may be eliminated. Since energy variations within the syllable may be of interest, a minimum desirable integrating time is of the order of the fundamental voice period (such as 0.01 sec).

MEASUREMENTS ON SUSTAINED VOWELS

Data about the relative intensities of English vowels have been reported by several investigators.[8] In most of the studies, several speakers have been employed to pronounce test words (or nonsense syllables). In such studies the data are usually collected under controlled conditions, but without the use of monitoring meters, since they obviously would defeat the purpose of the experiment.

Our interests are in understanding the linguistic systems of specific dialects and of specific speakers; thus in order to limit the number of variables in this initial experiment it was decided to study the speech levels produced by one particular speaker. In order to obtain a basic set of data for reference without consonant influences, 20 lists of sustained vowels and diphthongs were recorded by G.E.P. Each list consisted of the following 15 syllable nuclei of English, arranged in random order:

/i ɪ eɪ ɛ æ ə a ɔ oʊ ʊ u ɔɪ aʊ aɪ r/.

The lists were read into a condenser microphone placed 30 cm from the lips of the speaker in an anechoic chamber. The equipment was calibrated so that the amplitudes could be expressed in decibels relative to 0.0002 db/cm². Twelve lists were recorded on one day (late in the afternoon); eight lists were recorded four

days later (in the morning). Each vowel was uttered three times in succession. The pitch was kept constant at 145 cps by using a reference pulse which the speaker heard through a headphone and tried to imitate. Two additional lists were recorded with a masking noise of 130 db in the ears of the speaker. The tapes were then reproduced and the values were read from a VU meter. The levels relative to 0.0002 d/cm² were computed, and the results are presented in Table I. The sound pressure level equivalence is simply the rms value of a pure tone (in SPL) at the diaphragm of the microphone which would cause the same VU meter deflection as that due to the vowel. As it appears from the table, the average difference between the meter readings for the first day and the second day was 0.13 db, which falls well within the range of error probable with this type of procedure.

In Table I, row A contains the average values for one recording day on which 12 lists of 15 syllable nuclei each were recorded. Since every sound in each list was uttered three times, the values in this row represent the averages for 36 utterances. Row B contains the average values for the eight lists which were recorded four days later; these values represent the averages for 24 utterances. Row C contains the average for two lists, six utterances for each value, recorded with a masking noise of 130 db in the ears of the speaker. The relative values shown in Table I are of the same order of magnitude and are approximately similar in distribution to those reported by Fairbanks, House, and Stevens[9] and by Black.[10]

In listening casually to the recorded vowels, they appear to be about equally loud. This observation doubtless represents a confusion in perceptual judgment, however, for the equivalence is probably in physiological stress, not loudness. From what is known about the loudness of sinusoidal complexes, it seems very improbable that the vowels would appear equally loud if judged on that basis.[11]

A preliminary attempt was made to check the casual observation of loudness of the vowels. Another series of lists of randomized vowels was recorded; this time

[8] A. S. House and G. Fairbanks, J. Acoust. Soc. Am. 25, 105–113 (1953).

[9] Fairbanks, House, and Stevens, J. Acoust. Soc. Am. 22, 457–459 (1950).
[10] J. W. Black, J. Speech Hearing Disorders 14, 3–8 (1949).
[11] D. H. Howes, Am. J. Psychol. 63, 1–30 (1950).

TABLE II. Distribution of the initial-final combinations (C—C, vowels pooled) in the list of 1263 CNC words. The initial consonant is shown to the column at the left; the final in the row across the top.

	p	b	t	d	k	g	m	n	ŋ	f	v	θ	ð	s	z	ʃ	ʒ	r	l	č	ǰ	Total
p	8	1	10	3	8	3	1	7	1	1	1	2	···	5	4	1	···	6	10	7	2	81
b	···	3	12	8	8	6	4	10	1	2	···	5	1	5	2	1	1	5	7	2	···	83
t	5	3	8	3	7	2	8	8	2	2	···	2	1	2	1	1	···	7	9	2	···	73
d	3	3	6	5	6	3	8	10	1	2	2	3	···	3	3	2	···	4	7	1	3	75
k	7	4	10	7	6	2	5	10	1	4	3	···	···	4	1	1	···	3	10	4	1	83
g	2	···	8	6	···	2	2	4	2	1	2	1	···	4	4	3	···	2	8	···	2	53
m	3	2	8	8	5	2	2	7	···	1	2	4	···	9	1	3	···	6	7	2	2	74
n	3	1	10	5	5	1	3	7	···	1	2	···	···	4	3	1	···	2	6	2	1	57
f	···	1	6	5	2	3	3	9	1	2	1	1	···	3	1	1	···	5	12	1	1	58
v	···	1	2	1	···	2	···	3	···	···	1	···	···	3	2	···	···	1	5	1	1	23
θ	···	···	1	2	1	···	3	2	2	1	1	···	···	···	···	···	···	1	···	1	···	15
ð	···	···	1	···	···	···	1	3	···	···	···	···	···	2	2	···	···	1	···	···	···	10
s	7	2	8	6	7	1	5	8	4	2	4	2	2	4	2	1	···	5	8	2	4	84
z	···	···	···	···	···	···	···	1	···	···	···	···	···	1	···	···	···	1	1	···	···	4
ʃ	4	···	6	5	7	1	2	5	···	2	2	1	1	···	···	···	···	6	5	···	···	47
r	6	4	10	8	7	4	6	6	4	2	4	2	3	5	2	1	3	3	6	4	2	93
l	6	1	7	8	10	5	6	8	3	4	5	2	3	8	2	3	1	5	2	3	1	93
č	5	1	3	2	6	1	2	3	···	3	···	···	···	3	4	···	···	4	2	1	···	40
ǰ	1	4	4	1	3	4	4	8	···	1	1	···	···	2	1	1	···	2	4	···	1	42
h	6	1	9	8	6	3	6	2	2	2	4	1	···	3	6	2	···	4	8	2	1	76
w	2	1	5	7	6	2	2	6	1	3	3	1	1	1	2	2	···	4	7	2	2	60
hw	1	···	5	···	1	1	1	2	···	1	···	···	···	···	2	···	···	1	4	1	···	20
y	2	···	1	···	1	···	1	4	1	···	···	1	···	2	1	···	···	3	2	···	···	19
Total	71	33	140	98	102	48	75	133	26	39	36	30	11	71	49	25	3	81	130	38	24	1263

the speaker watched a VU meter in the recording room and produced all vowels at the same VU level. Some vowels required considerably greater effort than others. A tape was then prepared, in which various vowels produced with equal effort were mixed at random with vowels produced with unequal effort but which were equal in pressure level as measured by the VU meter. The vowels were arranged in random pairs and were presented to listeners, who were asked to judge the relative loudness of the two paired vowels. The listeners were specifically asked to judge the relative *loudness* of the vowels rather than their relative stress or accentuation. Almost invariably, the listeners identified the vowels that were produced with a greater amount of effort (such as /i/ and /u/ recorded at zero VU) as louder than vowels having greater intrinsic amplitude, but produced with normal effort (such as /ɑ/ and /ɔ/). The results appeared to confirm the basic assumption of this paper.

The listeners often reported changes in vowel quality on those sounds that had been produced with greater subjective effort; the vowels were described as "tense" or "harsh." Thus, it appears that vocal quality may also be a factor in the judgments. From this limited study we cannot determine, of course, whether vocal quality changes have a significant influence upon judgments of stress in American English, but obviously vowel amplitude and vowel quality have a much more predominant influence.

SYLLABLE AMPLITUDES

The study of vowel amplitudes within actual speech presents many problems beyond those involved in the study of the amplitudes of sustained vowels. The next

case in degree of complexity are the amplitudes of monosyllables. Since, by definition, nonsense syllables do not have certain of the distributional properties of actual speech, monosyllabic English words were chosen having the same vowel nuclei as indicated previously. The words were selected from the Thorndike and Lorge[12] list and were all of the CNC type. Both phonetic and phonemic considerations were involved in determining the initial and final C's and the N's. A total of 1263 such words were selected. The consonant distribution is shown in Table II. Since the word list has been described elsewhere, further details of its composition will not be reviewed here.[13]

These monosyllabic words were placed in a constant frame (carrier sentence), "say the word...again," where each word would normally receive the same degree of linguistic stress.

These sentences were recorded in the anechoic chamber with the same apparatus as employed for the sustained vowels; as before, the microphone was at a distance of 30 cm. In the recordings the same intonation contour was applied to each sentence.

The recordings were played into a VU meter and the values for the syllables were tabulated; the readings were recorded to the nearest decimal; repeated readings showed a very high reliability. The meter readings were then referred to 0.0002 db/cm² at the microphone, as were the data for the sustained vowels. The resulting sound pressure levels, based on the VU meter readings, are shown in Tables III and IV. Table III is for each

[12] F. L. Thorndike and I. Lorge, *The Teacher's Word Book of 30,000 Words* (Teachers College, Columbia University Press, New York, 1952).

[13] I. Lehiste and G. E. Peterson, J. Acoust. Soc. Am. **31**, 280 (1959).

TABLE III. Average amplitudes of syllable nuclei following each initial consonant phoneme (final consonants pooled).

Initial consonant	i	ɪ	eɪ	ɛ	æ	ə	ɑ	ɔ	oʊ	ʊ	u	aʊ	aɪ	ɔɪ	r	Average
p	71.3	76.8	77.3	76.5	77.8	77.0	79.5	80.7	78.4	77.5	76.0	78.3	78.5	82.0	77.9	77.3
b	74.9	79.3	78.5	79.9	81.2	80.6	81.0	81.8	80.5	79.4	79.0	82.0	80.5	82.5	79.8	79.7
t	72.2	76.7	77.1	78.2	78.7	78.1	79.3	79.1	77.8	76.6	76.5	80.2	78.3	81.3	78.0	77.7
d	75.3	78.7	79.2	79.3	80.4	80.6	80.4	81.6	79.9	...	79.7	80.3	80.7	...	79.4	79.7
k	74.0	76.4	76.4	78.9	78.3	77.2	79.3	80.0	77.9	76.9	77.5	77.8	78.6	81.0	78.3	77.9
g	71.7	78.2	78.2	78.8	80.3	80.1	80.9	81.2	80.1	80.1	77.5	80.2	81.4	...	80.1	79.7
m	78.1	77.9	78.8	78.4	79.0	80.8	79.8	80.5	79.9	78.5	79.1	80.5	80.9	...	79.0	79.4
n	78.1	76.6	78.8	78.9	78.6	80.2	80.4	79.2	80.0	78.5	79.5	80.1	79.5	80.1	79.0	79.1
f	73.3	78.4	78.4	79.8	80.1	79.8	81.9	80.1	79.7	...	77.7	80.9	80.2	81.3	79.6	79.0
v	74.7	80.7	78.9	...	79.7	...	...	...	79.4	...	...	80.6	80.8	80.5	80.2	79.9
θ	76.9	76.8	77.4	...	78.2	80.5	...	79.0	...	...	...	...	78.7	...	80.7	78.3
ð	75.5	77.5	...	78.9	78.7	80.8	...	...	81.5	77.5	...	...	81.7	...	...	79.1
s	74.7	77.7	78.1	79.2	79.5	79.3	80.1	79.4	79.4	...	76.5	80.2	80.0	78.6	79.1	78.3
z	77.1	...	...	...	...	...	81.5	...	78.5	...	76.5	...	...	...	...	78.4
ʃ	73.7	77.6	77.8	79.5	79.7	79.3	79.7	79.6	79.3	79.1	77.5	79.7	79.4	...	77.9	78.2
r	77.3	80.1	80.2	80.2	81.0	81.6	82.4	81.1	81.4	79.1	80.0	81.8	81.0	83.1	...	80.5
l	77.2	79.7	80.2	81.3	80.5	81.5	81.3	82.1	80.5	79.2	80.5	81.5	81.2	79.6	79.9	80.2
č	73.4	77.3	78.2	78.7	78.7	79.1	79.5	79.3	78.8	...	75.0	...	78.6	81.4	77.7	77.7
ǰ	75.4	78.3	78.2	78.6	79.5	80.0	81.1	81.1	78.9	...	76.6	80.3	81.3	80.1	79.0	79.2
h	73.5	77.2	77.4	79.4	78.4	78.5	77.8	81.4	79.5	77.2	76.8	78.6	79.0	...	78.8	78.1
w	76.4	79.3	80.2	80.7	81.3	81.4	81.4	81.0	79.3	80.4	78.6	...	81.5	...	79.6	79.5
hw	74.1	78.1	81.5	80.2	78.9	...	79.5	...	...	...	...	...	80.7	...	81.1	78.6
y	...	77.7	78.9	79.7	79.4	81.5	79.2	80.7	78.5	80.9	75.2	...	...	...	79.4	79.0
Average	75.1	78.1	78.6	79.3	79.4	79.7	80.2	80.6	79.7	78.4	78.2	80.1	80.2	80.9	79.0	79.0

of the initial consonants and each vowel nucleus (followed by any final consonant); Table IV is for each vowel nucleus (preceded by any initial consonant), followed by each final consonant. These data are summarized in Table V, which shows the initial and final consonants arranged according to the average sound pressure levels (measured by a VU meter) of the vowel nuclei. It appears to the authors to be significant that just as great a decibel range on the vowel nuclei is associated with the initial consonants as with the final consonants. The essential order from strong to weak is (a) semivowels and voiced plosives, (b) glides, nasals, and voiced fricatives, (c) voiceless fricatives, and (d) voiceless plosives.

A matrix was constructed for each syllable nucleus which shows the distribution of pressure levels according to the initial and final consonants. The average value for each syllable nucleus is shown in row E of Table I. A comparison of the total data for sustained vowels and for the 1263 monosyllabic words is shown

TABLE IV. Average amplitudes of syllable nuclei preceding each final consonant phoneme (initial consonants pooled).

Final consonant	i	ɪ	eɪ	ɛ	æ	ə	ɑ	ɔ	oʊ	ʊ	u	aʊ	aɪ	ɔɪ	r	Average
p	72.9	77.0	77.4	76.8	79.7	76.5	79.3	...	79.2	76.3	77.1	...	78.7	...	78.1	77.4
b	...	80.1	...	80.5	79.6	80.1	81.4	81.6	81.0	...	77.3	...	81.3	...	79.7	80.3
t	72.8	76.5	78.0	78.7	78.6	77.3	79.5	78.9	78.9	76.7	76.9	80.4	78.9	...	78.1	77.8
d	75.8	79.0	79.6	80.4	80.8	80.8	80.5	82.1	80.8	79.9	79.6	82.7	80.9	81.0	80.1	79.8
k	74.5	75.9	77.8	77.9	79.1	78.3	79.7	79.8	78.9	77.5	78.1	...	80.1	...	78.3	78.0
g	79.1	78.7	79.1	79.5	80.8	80.4	78.9	81.1	80.5	...	...	...	...	...	80.3	80.1
m	76.9	78.4	77.8	78.8	79.0	80.4	80.3	...	80.5	...	78.5	...	79.7	...	79.4	78.9
n	77.2	77.3	77.9	78.8	79.0	79.9	80.0	80.5	79.1	...	79.6	80.1	80.2	79.7	78.7	79.0
ŋ	...	77.5	...	...	78.8	80.6	...	80.0	...	...	...	...	...	...	...	79.1
f	75.5	78.3	78.9	79.4	79.3	79.7	...	80.2	81.8	...	78.3	...	80.7	81.3	79.1	78.9
v	76.9	80.6	79.5	...	81.3	81.1	...	81.5	80.9	...	80.1	...	80.4	...	78.6	79.8
θ	74.7	76.8	77.1	78.9	80.0	79.9	...	81.9	79.6	...	76.5	81.1	...	...	78.5	78.5
ð	76.0	79.5	80.0	...	...	...	...	...	81.1	...	77.3	...	79.8	...	...	78.7
s	73.3	77.1	78.3	79.7	80.6	79.5	...	80.8	...	76.1	77.6	79.5	81.0	80.9	78.3	78.8
z	74.2	79.5	78.7	...	79.5	81.4	82.1	81.1	80.2	...	79.4	81.4	81.1	81.0	78.9	79.2
ʃ	75.5	77.5	...	80.2	80.2	79.5	81.0	80.9	...	77.8	...	...	...	...	...	79.4
ʒ	77.1	...	79.2	...	...	...	...	...	...	...	79.7	...	...	...	...	78.7
r	...	79.5	81.3	79.3	...	...	81.0	80.6	...	78.8	79.2	80.2	80.3	...	...	80.0
l	76.5	79.8	79.5	80.6	79.6	81.0	80.8	81.1	80.3	80.4	78.1	80.3	81.0	81.3	80.6	79.9
č	73.7	77.5	...	79.0	77.5	78.6	80.5	...	78.2	...	75.5	78.1	...	...	78.6	77.5
ǰ	75.5	80.0	79.3	80.2	...	80.5	80.3	...	80.5	...	...	79.4	...	...	79.7	79.7
Average	75.1	78.1	78.6	79.3	79.4	79.7	80.2	80.6	79.7	78.4	78.2	80.1	80.2	80.9	79.0	79.0

in Fig. 1. While the speaker employed an average level of approximately 3 db less for the vowel nuclei in syllables, it will be noted also that there are some significant shifts in relative level.

MEASUREMENT PROBLEM

While VU meter readings on the sustained vowels are doubtless closely correlated with average power values, the use of a meter with such a time constant and the specification of syllable amplitudes in terms of a single number seems highly arbitrary. For comparison, the syllables (in their sentence contexts) were also processed through a sound apparatus HPL high-speed level recorder. Peak readings of the graphs were obtained for a large sample of the syllables and compared with the VU meter readings. Differences were evident, but in general they were slight, and we have no specific evidence that one number is any more significant than the other. In the past, single numbers have usually been derived from the peaks of such graphs. Since the initial and final levels of the vowel parts of syllables are often considerably influenced by the consonant closures, it seems reasonable that the peak levels (often near the center of the vowel nucleus) best represent the vocal input energy (as modified, of course, by the vowel quality). Relatively short time variations in the speech level become particularly significant, however, when they mark successive stresses within a single vowel; or they may be very significant in other languages such as Estonian where such level variations may mark successive syllable boundaries.[14]

As a practical procedure for speech power measurements, we are considering the use of a circuit which will integrate exactly over one or two fundamental voice frequency periods, with the reading to be taken from the maximum on each syllable nucleus. As a test of the basic hypothesis of this paper, we should like, of course, to correlate such data with physiological measurements. It seems likely that subglottal pressure measurements such as those developed by van den Berg[15] should be most relevant. This hypothesis is based on the assumption that pressures, forces, and muscle tensions are of primary significance in speech. Since speech production involves very small power levels, the actual work done or energy consumed seems secondary. Thus the tensions and forces applied as speech is produced seem to reflect best the degree of physiological effort, and should provide prominant cues in speech perception. Electromyographic techniques for measuring muscular activity in the larynx during phonation, such as those developed by Faaborg-Andersen,[16] might provide some further understanding of the influence of laryngeal quality upon judgments of stress.

TABLE V. Influence of initial and final consonants on the average amplitudes of all vowels.

Amplitude of vowels	Initial consonant	Amplitude of vowels	Final consonant
80.5	r	80.3	b
80.2	l	80.1	g
79.9	v	80.0	r
79.7	b d g	79.9	l
79.5	w	79.8	d v
79.4	m	79.7	j
79.2	j	79.4	ʃ
79.1	ð n	79.2	z
79.0	y f	79.1	ŋ
78.6	w h	79.0	n
78.4	z	78.9	m f
78.3	θ s	78.8	s t
78.2	ʃ	78.7	ð ʒ
78.1	h	78.5	θ
77.9	k	78.0	k
77.7	t č	77.5	č
77.3	p	77.4	p

The data which we have discussed would apply directly to only one condition of stress, the so-called primary stress, which according to one widely accepted theory forms one of four contrastive degrees of stress in English.[17] There are very few data available on the relative amplitudes of the vowel nuclei of English in other stress conditions. In the opinion of the authors the concept of four phonemic levels of stress in English (as distinct from four intonation levels) needs a careful linguistic and experimental examination.

As a rough test of the above described influence of vowel quality upon stress in English, a series of words

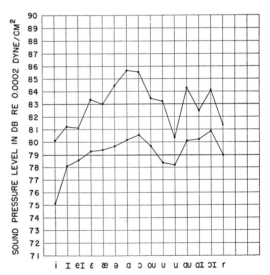

FIG. 1. Averages of equivalent sound pressure levels (as observed with a VU meter) for sustained vowels and diphthongs, and for the vowel nuclei in monosyllables.

14 I. Lehiste, "Segmental and syllabic quantity in Estonian" (to be published).

15 Jw. van den Berg, Folia Phoniatrica 8, 1–24 (1956).

16 K. Faaborg-Andersen, Acta Physiol. Scand. 41, Suppl. 140, 7–148 (1957).

17 George L. Trager and H. L. Smith, Jr., "An outline of English structure," Studies in Linguistics: Occasional Papers (Norman, Oklahoma, 1951), No. 3.

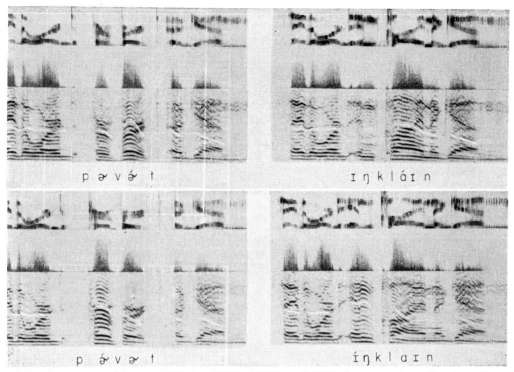

FIG. 2. Sound spectrograms of the words *PERvert-perVERT* and *INcline-inCLINE* in the carrier sentence: "Say the word...again." In each pattern the upper spectrogram was made with a wide filter so that the segmental phonemes may be identified easily; the middle spectrogram is a continuous amplitude display of the over-all wave; and the lower spectrogram was made with a narrow analyzing filter, so that the individual overtones are depicted (the trace is through the tenth harmonic).

that distinguish between the two categories of noun and verb by means of contrastive stress placement were recorded.[18] The same frame as that used with the CNC words was employed, and an attempt was made to retain the same pitch contour. The recording instrumentation was that described in the foregoing. VU meter readings of the words show that in each case the primary stress can be identified by applying a correction factor from row E of Table I.

Figure 2 presents sound spectrograms for two pairs of words from this latter set of recordings. At the left of the figure is the pair *PERvert-perVERT*. As may be seen from the broad-band spectrograms, the segmental patterns are identical within the phonetic limits expected on successive utterances. The narrow-band spectrograms show the characteristic pitch curve associated with stressed syllables. At the right of the figure is the pair *INcline-inCLINE*. The segmental quality and the duration for the two pairs are approximately comparable; in fact, the unstressed [ɪ] in *inCLINE* appears longer than the stressed [ɪ] of *INcline*, although the

opposite might be expected. Also shown in Fig. 2 are continuous amplitude displays for each of these utterances. The amplitude scale is nonlinear; according to the calibration the difference for *PERvert-perVERT* is a little over 2 db; the difference for the two syllables of *INcline* is approximately 0 db. When correction factors for vowel quality are applied, the greater amplitude appears on the linguistically stressed syllable in each case.

It will be evident from the narrow-band spectrograms that the intonations for these two pairs of words are not entirely comparable. We have been considering the hypothesis that phonetic variations in pitch level are due, to a considerable degree, to the intrinsic relative amplitude of the vowel to which the pitch is applied. Each phonemically significant pitch level can, of course, be manifested phonetically by a range of fundamental voice frequencies. The fact that fundamental voice frequency is correlated with vowel quality has been demonstrated by Fairbanks and House,[8] as well as others, in previous research. This rise in fundamental voice frequency for the vowels of higher tongue position has previously been somewhat of a mystery, since from a mechanical viewpoint, when the vocal cavities are more constricted the loading on the larynx should cause the fundamental to lower rather than to rise. It

---

[18] The set of words which we examined is as follows: conDUCT-CONduct, conVERSE-CONverse, conVICT-CONvict, conTENT-CONtent, conVERT-CONvert, diGEST-DIgest, exPORT-EX-port, imPORT-IMport, inCLINE-INcline, inCREASE-INcrease, perMIT-PERmit, perVERT-PERvert, preSENT-PREsent, pro-GRESS-PROgress, subJECT-SUBject.

appears very probable that this phonetic variation in the pitch level associated with a certain phonemic stress may be influenced to a considerable extent by the intrinsic amplitude of the nucleus of the syllable carrying the stress, higher pitch compensating for lower intrinsic amplitude. These observations are made relative to English, of course; we have only some general impressions of how they might apply in other types of languages.

The authors hope to continue this preliminary research with a careful study of the correlations among relative power, vowel quality, fundamental voice frequency, and duration as contributing factors to linguistically significant stress in English, and to extend the study to other speakers and to other degrees of stress beyond the primary stress which has been the topic of the present paper.

SUMMARY

As a result of the considerations presented in this paper, it appears that perceptual judgments of linguistically significant stress may be based on speech power, fundamental voice frequency, vowel quality, and duration; laryngeal quality may also make a very secondary contribution. The data presented in the present paper are based primarily on VU meter readings of vowels and syllables in a controlled context. The data suggest that "correction factors" might be applied for the amplitudes of vowels according to vowel quality. Suggested correction factors are indicated for vowels within syllables. It seems reasonable that similar correction factors might actually be applied for pitch as well as for duration.

Reprinted from THE JOURNAL OF THE ACOUSTICAL SOCIETY OF AMERICA, Vol. 32, No. 6, 693–703, June, 1960
Copyright, 1960 by the Acoustical Society of America.

Duration of Syllable Nuclei in English*

GORDON E. PETERSON AND ILSE LEHISTE

Speech Research Laboratory, University of Michigan, Ann Arbor, Michigan

(Received February 26, 1960)

This study deals with the influence of preceding and following consonants on the duration of stressed vowels and diphthongs in American English. A set of 1263 CNC words, pronounced in an identical frame by the same speaker, was analyzed spectrographically, and the influences of various classes of consonants on the duration of the nucleus were determined. The residual durational differences are analyzed as intrinsic durational characteristics, associated with each syllable nucleus. The theory is tested with a set of 30 minimal pairs of CNC words, uttered by five different speakers.

INTRODUCTION

IN the investigation of the relation of basic speech parameters to their linguistic interpretation, there appear to be two general approaches which may be taken. In one approach speech synthesis is employed, and the parameters under study can be controlled individually and accurately. The limitation of speech synthesis is that it may be necessary to employ incomplete sets of parameters or parameters which do not correspond closely in their properties to those generated in human speech. In the second approach, actual speech is recorded for analysis, and thus the parameters may be procured in their natural form. The limitation of this method is that it is sometimes difficult to measure the parameters accurately, and it is even more difficult to obtain their precise control. It appears that in the present stage of speech technology, useful information can be derived from both techniques of investigation.

The present study involves the latter method, in which samples of actual speech are recorded and analyzed. This paper reports some of the results of a study of stressed syllable nuclei in English, and deals with certain aspects of duration.

Duration may have different linguistic functions in different languages. In certain languages, a meaningful difference may be associated with a change in the duration of a consonant or vowel. In some languages, however, changes in the duration of a sound may be determined by the linguistic environment and may be associated with preceding or following segmental sounds, initial or final position in an utterance, or type and degree of stress. Such durational changes in turn may become cues for the identification of the associated phonemes. In a recent study of acoustical cues to word boundaries,[1] it was found that allophonic variations of sounds at juncture points included significant changes in duration. In order to identify changes in duration which are cues to juncture, it is necessary to isolate such changes from durational features that form an integral part of the distinctive properties characterizing the various English phonemes.

It has been observed before that the duration of the vocalic part of a monosyllabic word may be conditioned to some extent by the class of consonants which follow the syllable nucleus. House and Fairbanks,[2] and more recently Denes,[3] have shown this to be the case for English; Zimmerman and Sapon[4] have examined the problem cross-linguistically and have suggested that such observed variations are a part of the phonetic system of English rather than a general principle applicable to all languages induced by physiological factors.

This paper represents a further examination of some of the characteristics of duration in English. If the factors that condition the duration of syllable nuclei can be isolated and described, and if their influence on the syllable nucleus can be determined, the remaining durational differences, if any, might be defined as intrinsic durational differences associated with each vowel pattern. If such intrinsic durational differences exist, it would be of interest to determine their relation to various types of syllable nuclei, as monophthongs, glides, and diphthongs. Thus durational aspects might contribute to the arrangement of the phonetic data of syllable nuclei into a phonemic pattern.

MATERIALS AND PROCEDURES

Connected speech was used for the experiments. The material studied consisted of two sets of data. The first set involved 1263 words, selected on the basis of frequency of occurrence, and recorded by one speaker in an identical sentence frame, with determined stress and pitch patterns. The words all have the same structure, consisting of one of fifteen common syllable nuclei of English, preceded and followed by a consonant phoneme. The list is described in more detail in a previous publication.[5] The second set involved 70 minimally

---

* This research was supported (under contract) by the Information Systems Branch of the Office of Naval Research.

[1] I. Lehiste, "An acoustic-phonetic study of internal open juncture," Rept. No. 2, Speech Research Laboratory, University of Michigan, Ann Arbor, Michigan (August, 1959).

[2] A. S. House and G. Fairbanks, J. Acoust. Soc. Am. **25**, 105–113 (1953).

[3] P. Denes, J. Acoust. Soc. Am. **27**, 761–764 (1955).

[4] S. A. Zimmerman and S. M. Sapon, J. Acoust. Soc. Am. **30**, 152–153 (1958).

[5] I. Lehiste and G. E. Peterson, J. Acoust. Soc. Am. **31**, 280–286 (1959).

191

different words, including 60 CNC words forming 30 minimal pairs, and 10 disyllabic words constituting five additional minimal pairs; the 70 words were uttered by five different speakers of the same general dialect. These five speakers used the same frame sentence and pitch and stress pattern as the speaker for the larger set of material. The 1263-word CNC list and the 350 items recorded by five speakers were analyzed acoustically by various techniques. Broad-band and narrow-band spectrograms were made of the total set. Analyses were also made of the total set with the Mingograph at the Royal Institute of Technology in Stockholm. These analyses included two intensity curves ·with high-frequency and low-frequency pre-emphasis, a Grützmacher pitch curve, and a duplex oscillogram. The smaller set of 350 items was also processed through the 48-channel spectrograph available at Stockholm.[6] The data measured from the spectrograms form the primary basis for the observations presented in this paper.

SEGMENTATION

An essential problem in the measurement of the duration of syllable nuclei is that of segmentation. Segmentation has long been and continues to be a major problem in speech analysis. Basic difficulties in the concept of segmentation have been discussed previously by one of the present authors.[7] Since vowel and consonant lengths contrast in some languages there can be no question but that duration may be linguistically distinctive. The specification of those cues which are perceptually significant in linguistic judgments of duration is a subject which should receive further study.

Successive speech sounds not only involve physiological targets and controlled movements, but they often involve changes from one sound type to another. These changes often occur at distances far removed from the targets and, for the purposes of this study, were considered the segment boundaries. Such changes obviously represent major points of transition in the activities of the vocal mechanism. If speech perception is closely correlated with these activities, it seems probable that the transitional regions may be of considerable linguistic significance. The perceptual and linguistic significance of such boundaries merit much further investigation. For purposes of automatic speech recognition, it is obviously necessary to employ some procedure for segmentation or quantization.

There are many instances in which the cues signalling the beginning and the end of a syllable nucleus are relatively unambiguous, but there are many other instances where it is very difficult to specify the point of segmentation. An attempt will be made to describe the major cues that were used in the segmentation basic to the measurements of the present study. It should be emphasized that the procedures employed in this study sometimes involved a great deal of human judgment. In several instances, segmental cues of a type not anticipated were observed. We are in no position to consider the universality of these cues, but it appears profitable to investigate some of them further.

In the present study, instrumental accuracy is in general considerably greater than the accuracy with which the segmental boundaries can be determined. It was usually possible to determine segmental boundaries within one or two centiseconds. In some instances, however, the transitions between consonants and vowels involve an overlapping of cues, and in such instances it does not appear meaningful to attempt to determine exact time boundaries.

1. Initial and Final Plosives

The release of a voiceless initial plosive appears as a spike on the spectrogram. The duration of the explosion depends on the bandwidth of the major resonance and is followed by a period of frication and a period of aspiration.[8] Two separate measurements were made for syllable nuclei following aspirated plosives, one from the center of the releasing spike and the other from the onset of voicing immediately after the aspiration. There was usually a measurable concentration of fricative energy in the regions of higher formants throughout the aspiration period, and it was difficult to decide whether at a given moment the pattern in these formants represented breathy phonation or modulated fricative energy. The onset of voicing could be determined relatively accurately, however, by observing the first formant. There was often a weak energy concentration at the frequency of the first formant during the period of aspiration, and the onset of voicing was clearly distinguishable. Thus it was usually possible to determine the frequency of the first formant, both immediately after the release of the plosive and at the onset of voicing after the aspiration. In vowels involving high first formants (particularly /ɑ/, /æ/, and /ɔ/), the energy concentration in the region of the first formant during aspiration was often comparable to that at other formant frequencies, but the onset of voicing was usually clearly distinguishable as the moment in time at which periodic striations started in the first formant frequency.

After voiced initial plosives, the period of aspiration was absent, but the period of frication following the

---

[6] The Mingograph, a recording oscillograph with a relatively high-frequency response, and the 48-channel spectrograph are described by C. G. M. Fant, "Modern instruments and methods for acoustic studies of speech," *Proceedings of the VIII International Congress of Linguists* (Oslo University Press, Oslo, 1958).

[7] G. E. Peterson, Language 31, 414–427 (1955).

[8] The distinction between explosion and frication is a matter of source. Explosion is considered to be the sound produced by the shock excitation of the vocal cavities due to the pressure release, and frication is the sound which originates from turbulence produced by the flow of air through the narrow passage which is formed immediately after the release. Cf. Fant, footnote reference 6, pp. 307–308.

spike was usually more prominent than in the case of voiceless plosives. The measurements were again made from the center of the spike, so that the frication period was included in the duration of the vowel. The duration of the frication varied between about 0.5 and 2.5 csec.

The beginning of final voiceless plosives was determined by the abrupt cessation of all formants. The final voiced plosives were often pronounced with full voicing and a voiced release; under the conditions of recording, a considerable amount of energy was present in the voiced plosives, and up to fifteen harmonics appeared in some of the narrow-band spectrograms. Thus the cessation of voicing was not a proper cue for the termination of the syllable nucleus. Instead, the beginning of final voiced plosives was determined by comparing narrow-band and broad-band spectrograms, from which the moment in time when the energy in the higher harmonics was suddenly greatly diminished could be ascertained. In general, it was possible to specify the boundary with an accuracy of about one vocal-fold period.

Examples of initial and final plosives may be seen on Figs. 1–4. Figures 3 and 4 illustrate initial voiced and voiceless plosives; Figs. 1 and 2 contain examples

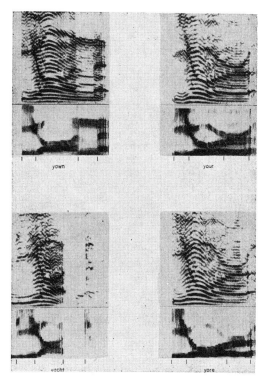

FIG. 2. Broad-band and narrow-band spectrograms of four CNC words spoken by informant GEP. Approximate segmentation points for identifying the boundaries of initial and final consonants have been provided.

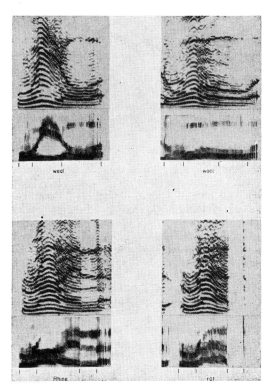

FIG. 1. Broad-band and narrow-band spectrograms of four CNC words spoken by informant GEP. Approximate segmentation points for identifying the boundaries of initial and final consonants have been provided.

of final voiceless plosives, and Fig. 4 contains examples of both voiced and voiceless final plosives.

2. Initial and Final Nasals

In the measurement of syllable nuclei durations, initial nasals offered no difficulty. It was usually possible to identify the vocal-fold period which followed the velar closure by observing the abrupt change from steady formant pattern to rapid onglide movement. Final nasals share the characteristic of steady resonances with initials. In the case of two speakers from the smaller set of data, however, the vowels were nasalized considerably. This had no significant effect upon the identification of the initial boundary of the syllable nucleus, but for these two speakers the nasalization of the vowels obscured the transition from the syllable nucleus to the final nasal consonant on the broad-band spectrograms. The control set of 70 words contained 14 final nasals, but only 3 initial nasals; the relative ease of identifying the boundaries of initial nasals may be due to the very limited data. In the narrow-band spectrograms for these speakers, it was possible to locate the approximate boundaries as the position at which there was a sudden change in the relative marking of the various harmonics. Those

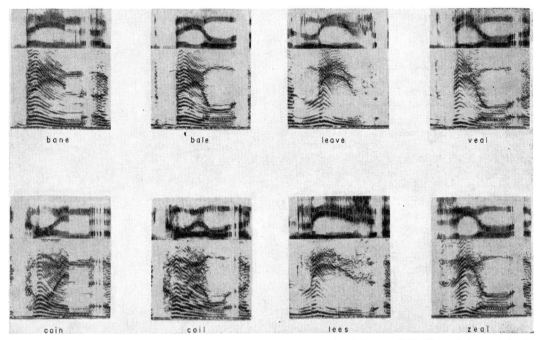

FIG. 3. Broad-band and narrow-band spectrograms of eight CNC words uttered by informant GEP. The tenth harmonic has been traced in white paint on the narrow-band spectrograms; the fifth harmonic has been traced with a dotted white line on some of the spectrograms.

harmonics that were not within the frequency region of either the oral or nasal resonances were marked much more lightly following the vocalic period, and thus a boundary point could be established. Information on relative changes in energy level among the vowel and nasal formants and the minima (or valleys) between is not yet available. Thus the extent to which the marking changes are due to energy-level changes cannot be specified at present. The pattern changes result in part, of course, from the automatic adjustments of the

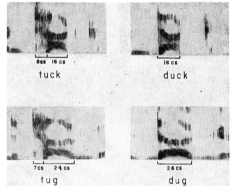

FIG. 4. Broad-band spectrograms of four CNC words spoken by informant GEP. The duration of the aspiration following a voiceless initial plosive has been presented separately from the duration of the voiced part of the syllable nucleus.

narrow-band marking control to the decrease in over-all output energy during the formation of nasals.

Some examples of final nasals may be found on Figs. 1, 2, and 3. The narrow-band patterns in Figs. 1 and 2 are particularly good illustrations of the changes in marking of the harmonics outside the resonances.

3. Initial and Final Fricatives

The beginning of a vowel after an initial voiceless fricative was determined by the onset of voicing in the region of the first formant. This cue was also employed in determining the beginning of the syllable nucleus after an initial /h/, as formant movements were not adequate indications of the points of transition. In such cases, the intensity curves provided a valuable additional reference. There was a period of "breathy" quality for initial /h/ on broad-band spectrograms after the onset of voicing (noise pattern superimposed upon a rather clear formant pattern), but the intensity curves provided a relatively unambiguous cue. Some of the initial voiceless fricatives registered considerable energy on both Mingograph traces and the oscillogram, but there was a cessation of fricative energy before the onset of phonation, and a sharp minimum in the intensity curves provided an appropriate boundary point.

The terminal boundaries of initial voiced fricatives were, in general, rather easily recognized on broad-band spectrograms. The superimposed noise usually ended abruptly. Final voiceless fricatives were recognized by the onset of random noise: The vowel was considered terminated at the point where the noise pattern began, even though voicing in a few low harmonics continued for a few centiseconds in most cases. Final voiced fricatives were more troublesome. In broad-band and narrow-band spectrograms, the transition between vowel and consonant appeared rather gradual, but the onset of high-frequency energy in the case of /z/ and /ʒ/ provided a clear boundary on the intensity curves. The boundaries preceding final /v/ and /ð/ were recognized chiefly by the rapid decrease of energy that could usually be detected on the intensity curves.

Figure 5 presents 4-channel Mingograph tracings of two of the frame utterances spoken by informant Br. Curves *a* and *b* display the sound intensity; low-frequency pre-emphasis was employed in constructing curve *a* and high-frequency pre-emphasis was employed for curve *b*; *c* is a fundamental frequency contour, and *d* a duplex oscillogram.[6] The top utterance represents the sentence "Say the word 'voice' again," and may be compared with "Say the word 'noise' again," presented in the lower half of the illustration. The sharp boundary between initial /s/ and the following vowel in *say* can be observed in both utterances. The boundaries of the voiceless sibilant /s/ in *voice* are more clearly demarcated than the initial boundary of the /z/ in *noise*; curve *b*, which emphasizes energy in the higher frequencies, provides the best clue for isolating final /z/. The initial voiced fricative /v/ in *voice* can be best isolated on curve *a*, with low-frequency pre-emphasis. Initial and final voiced fricatives may also be observed on Fig. 3, which is a good illustration of the difficulty of finding a clear-cut boundary line for final voiced fricatives if only broad-band and narrow-band spectrograms are used for the analysis.

4. Initial /w/ and /y/

Both of these initial consonants involved a steady-state period. Since they were fully voiced and had only a minimal amount of friction, the formant movements from the consonant to the syllable nucleus were uninterrupted. Nevertheless, certain cues appeared with a fair amount of regularity, and together provided reasonably usable criteria for segmentation. For initial /w/ the region in which the slope of the second formant acquired a positive value was considered the boundary. This directional change was often accompanied by a sharp increase in energy, and the energy change was accompanied on the narrow-band spectrogram by a darker marking of the harmonics not in the frequency regions of resonance. Such energy cues were particularly useful in sequences where /w/ was followed by a vowel with a low second formant. Figure 1 contains initial /w/ followed by a front and a back vowel. A steady state for /w/ is followed by a rather sharp upward inflection of the second formant in the sequence /wi/;

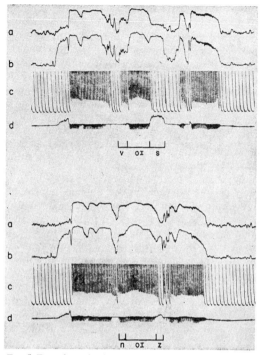

Fig. 5. Four-channel Mingograph tracings of two utterances by informant Br: "Say the word 'voice' again," and "Say the word 'noise' again." Curve *a* is an intensity curve with low-frequency pre-emphasis; curve *b* is an intensity curve with high-frequency pre-emphasis; curve *c* is a pitch curve (modified Grützmacher method); and curve *d* is a duplex oscillogram. The analysis was performed at the Royal Institute of Technology in Stockholm.

there is a noticeable change in the marking of the formants and also in the harmonics not within the resonance regions in the case of the sequence /wu/.

In these data, initial /y/ had a steady state, in which the frequency of the third formant was much greater than that for any simple vowel nucleus. The point, however, at which the transition to the following vowel began was at a considerably lower position in frequency. Thus the third formant of /y/ performs a rapid dip in frequency before rising back to the third-formant position of the vowel. The position in time of the frequency minimum of the third formant was thus considered the point of onset of the following vowel. This cue is most easily determined for vowels with a high third-formant frequency. Figure 2 contains illustrations of initial /y/. The steady state associated with the initial /y/ is characterized by a high third formant and a relatively weak intensity of the harmonics between the resonances; the minimum in the movement of the third formant from the steady state of /y/ to the following vowel serves as the point of segmentation.

5. Initial and Final /l/ and /r/

Both initial /l/ and /r/ had periods of steady resonances. The onset of a vowel after /l/ was usually unambiguously defined on the narrow-band spectrograms by the sudden change in marking of the harmonics between the various resonances at the change from steady formants to onglide. Initial /r/ often had a slight fricative quality. In addition, the frequency movements of the third formants usually provided a clue for the segmentation.

Final /l/ and /r/ presented particularly difficult problems. Very often the formant movements were quite smooth, and the establishment of a boundary on the basis of broad-band spectrograms was questionable. Intensity curves were helpful in instances where the vowel had an intrinsic energy considerably different from that of /l/ or /r/. In the transition from the vowel nucleus to /l/ a frequency minimum or a relatively rapid rise in the frequency of the third formant was sometimes present and was used as the basis of the segmentation. In the total set of data, the third formant of /l/ had an average frequency value of 2635 cps, and the change from the usually lower third-formant position of the vowel to that of /l/ sometimes involved a well-defined change point. But in a rather large number of instances, the formant movements appeared smooth, there was no significant change in the intensity, and the determination of a boundary had to be accomplished by some other criterion.

It was observed that the fundamental voice-frequency curve employed in each utterance had certain characteristic distributional features. The initial consonant of the word in the frame appeared to determine the occurrence of the peak of the fundamental curve. When the initial consonant was voiced, the peak occurred in the middle of the nucleus of the target word, with a rather smooth glide of the fundamental (usually upward but often down on voiced plosives) during the initial voiced consonant. If the consonant was voiceless, and particularly when the consonant was a voiceless fricative, the peak occurred immediately at the onset of voicing, and the fundamental on the syllable nucleus thereafter decreased. The total drop in pitch normally took place during the vocalic part of the syllable. When the final consonant was voiceless, this might have been expected. But when the final consonant was voiced, the fundamental pitch reached its minimum value by the beginning of the consonant and remained almost completely level for the duration of the consonant. This pattern was observed with very great regularity, and we concluded that in this type of utterance the region where the fundamental has become essentially level may be considered the consonant part.

Figure 3 illustrates the parallelism between such words as *coin* and *coil*, where the fundamental voice frequency was used to determine the boundary between the syllable nucleus and final /l/. The tenth harmonic has been traced in white, and provides a visual representation of the fundamental movement associated with this intonation. Some examples of initial /l/ are also included in Fig. 3 to illustrate that in initial position,

the rise in pitch takes place during the pronunciation of the voiced resonant; level fundamental frequency is not a characteristic of all /l/ sounds.

Examples of final /r/ may be found on Fig. 2, where the segmentation has been based on two clues: the steady fundamental frequency associated with final position, and the change in the third-formant frequency. Initial /r/ sounds are represented in Fig. 1. Approximate segmentation may be achieved by comparing the relative markings of the harmonics in the narrow-band spectrogram and by identifying the position at which the third formant begins to rise rapidly in frequency in the broad-band spectrogram.

PROBLEM OF TEMPO

In order to observe the intrinsic duration of syllable nuclei and the influence of preceding and following segmental sounds upon the duration of syllable nuclei, variability in duration due to the suprasegmental features of pitch, stress, and tempo should be eliminated. Since the recorded utterances involved a uniform stress and intonation pattern, it seems reasonable to assume that stress and pitch affected each test word in essentially the same manner. The chief remaining variable to be considered is speaker rate.

There are several different ways in which speaker rate might be defined for such a set of material. For example, speaker rate might be considered constant if the durations of the sentence frames remained constant. In order to study the durations of the sentence frames, the duration of each test word was subtracted from the duration of the entire utterance. It was found that in both sets of data a glottal stop was often inserted following the test word, and the duration of this stop was included in the measurement of the duration of the test frame. The average durations in centiseconds of the frames for the 70 utterances by each of the five speakers were: 122, 130, 144, 150, and 177. Ten samples of 50 sequential frame sentences each were also extracted from the 1263 words of the larger set of data. The average duration of the frame was 174 csec, with a standard deviation of 6.9 csec. The mean for the five speakers was 144, which differs from the average for the speaker of the large set of data by 30 csec. The average durations of the syllable nuclei contained in the test words in the smaller set of data were: 24, 25, 26, 30, and 31 csec, with an average of 27 csec. The average of the nuclei in the same words for GEP was 28 csec. Thus there was much greater relative variation in the average duration of the frame than in the average duration of the stressed syllable nuclei contained in the test words.

The foregoing data imply that differences in tempo may affect stressed and unstressed words in different ways. It has been suggested previously[9] that in English

---

[9] A. Classe, *The Rhythm of English Prose* (Basil Blackwell, Oxford, 1939).

there is a tendency for stress groups to assume approximately the same duration. Such a principle would require that the length of syllables vary, particularly in the case of stress groups containing different numbers of syllables. Thus we might consider whether the speakers spaced the main stresses at regular intervals. If so, the differences in the durations of stressed test words might be compensated by varying the durations of unstressed syllables.

The durations of the intervals between successive test words were measured for the same set of utterances that was used for computing the average duration of the frames. The selection of a time mark, either within the frame or within the test word, is somewhat arbitrary. If the rate of uttering the unstressed syllables of the frame varied according to the duration of the stressed test words, then a recurrent point in the test frames would not provide a satisfactory measure. On the other hand, since the test words all differ, it is obviously difficult to specify a common point within the test words. The selection of the point of maximum stress within the syllable nucleus might seem most appropriate, but it is undoubtedly influenced by both fundamental voice frequency and intensity in a way which is not yet understood, and the peaks for the two are not necessarily concurrent within the stressed syllable. Since the point of release of the initial consonant of the stressed syllable may be physiologically significant, and since it is a point which can be specified fairly accurately, it was chosen as the time mark for the measurements. The duration of the intervals between successive test words was measured accordingly for the same set of utterances that was used for computing the average durations of the frames.

Figure 6 presents a sequence chart for the durations of the time intervals between successive initial consonant releases of the test words (i.e., the total intervals), the durations of the test words, and the durations of the syllable nuclei. In the graph, relatively long pauses for inhalations, irregular breathing patterns, and relatively uniform rate accelerations and decelerations are all evident.

Figure 7(A) shows the duration of the test word versus the total time interval duration, and (B) shows the duration of the syllable nucleus vs the total time interval duration for 100 utterances by GEP. None of these graphs implies a strong relation between the interval duration measure which we chose and the duration of the test word or the syllable nucleus.

In general, the test word represents only a small fraction of the total duration of the interval. Also, the variation in the interval was small relative to the total interval duration, of the order of 3–5%, or approximately 5 to 15 csec. These facts suggest that variations in rate of utterance by any given speaker had little effect upon the duration of the stressed syllables under study.

A further brief experiment was devised to explore

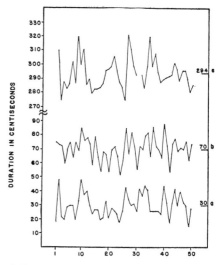

FIG. 6. Utterances 1–50 by informant He. Curve a presents the durations of the syllable nuclei, curve b the durations of the test words (occurring in random order), and curve c the duration of the time intervals between successive initial consonant releases of the test words. The break in curve c between items 30 and 31 represents the turning of the page from which the randomized test words were read.

whether stressed and unstressed syllables are similarly affected by a controlled change in tempo. A selected set of test utterances was recorded by three of the speakers. In one instance the spacing in time between the stressed syllables was controlled to be 2 seconds by asking the subjects to speak in synchronism with a periodic pulse produced over an earphone; in a second similar set of recordings, the spacing between stressed syllables was 1 second. The pulse and the speech were recorded on an SPL recorder and on magnetic tape. The durations of the words spoken at both rates of speech were measured, and the speedup factors were computed. In this experiment, the duration of the syllables with main stress changed less than the duration of the unstressed syllables: When the rate of utterance was increased by a factor of two, the stressed words decreased in duration by a factor of approximately 1.5. Under these conditions the actual durations for the stressed words were very similar for the three speakers.

Further investigations of the relations of tempo and stress to duration appear necessary before this variable can be specified adequately. For the present study, however, it seems reasonable to assume that the duration measurements of the test words were not greatly influenced by variations in tempo during the recording by any given speaker.

INFLUENCE OF PRECEDING AND FOLLOWING CONSONANTS

If the influence of suprasegmental factors is eliminated, the remaining durational differences may be

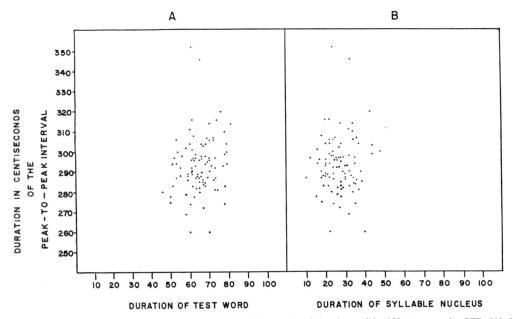

FIG. 7. Durational relationships between test word, syllable nucleus, and total time interval for 100 utterances by GEP. (A) shows the total time interval duration vs the duration of the test word, and (B) shows the total time interval duration vs the duration of the syllable nucleus.

due either to the influence of preceding and/or following consonants, or to intrinsic durational differences. The influence of consonants was considered next. Some of the syllable nuclei are represented by a larger number of words in the CNC list than others. Since we assumed that vowels may have different intrinsic durations, all occurrences of a particular consonant could not be included, as the results would then be weighted according to the predominance of intrinsically short or long syllable nuclei associated with the consonant. Therefore, several smaller subsets, consisting of minimal pairs present in the list, were analyzed. For example, in determining the influence of a following voiced or voiceless consonant on the duration of the preceding syllable nucleus, the durations of the syllable nuclei in such pairs as *beat-bead*, *sight-side*, etc., were compared. There were 118 minimal pairs in the larger set of data, differing in the voicing of the final consonant. The average duration of the syllable nucleus before the voiceless member of the consonant pair was 19.7 csec, and before the voiced member was 29.7 csec. The comparable values for the control group of five speakers were 19.3 csec and 29.1 csec. Thus, for this set of data, the ratio of vowel before voiceless consonant to vowel before voiced consonant is approximately 2:3.

The homorganic nasals influence the preceding vowel in much the same manner as the voiced stops. In 46 instances of triple contrasts, such as *back-bag-bang*, the average values of the syllable nuclei before the voiced stop and nasal were 29.8 csec for the voiced stop and 30.2 for the nasal in the larger set of recordings, and

28.9 csec and 30.0 csec for the stop and nasal, respectively, for the five speakers.

The voiced fricatives appear to have a further lengthening effect. Of the 21 minimal pairs in the set in which the effect of a final voiced plosive could be compared with the effect of the final homorganic voiced fricative, the duration of the syllable nucleus before the voiced plosive was 30.0 csec, whereas the comparable duration before the voiced fricative was 37.9 csec. There were nine sets where four contrasts were represented—sets of such words as *rice-rise-ride-right*. The average durations of the syllable nuclei, in ascending order, were: 18.4 csec before the voiceless plosive, 22.8 csec before the voiceless fricative, 28.0 csec before the voiced plosive, and 37.6 csec before the voiced fricative.

Initial voiced-voiceless contrasts presented no easily discernible pattern. There were 68 minimal pairs in the larger set of data which differed in the voicing of the initial consonant. Figure 8 presents graphically the results of the measurements on these minimal pairs. It appears that there is practically no durational difference associated with an initial /f/−/v/ contrast; in the case of /s/−/z/ and /č/[tʃ]−/j/[dʒ], the effect of voicing appears contradictory, the voiceless member of the pair being followed by a longer syllable nucleus in the case of the /s/−/z/ contrast, but by a shorter syllable nucleus in the case of an initial /č/−/ǰ/ contrast. Initial plosives present a special problem. If aspiration is considered part of the syllable nucleus, then voiceless plosives are regularly associated with longer syllable nuclei than voiced plosives; if, however,

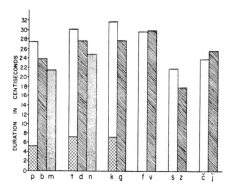

FIG. 8. The duration of syllable nuclei, measured from 68 minimal pairs differing in the voicing of the initial consonant, presented as a function of the initial consonant. The cross-hatched area associated with the columns representing the duration of syllable nuclei following voiceless plosives indicates the duration of aspiration.

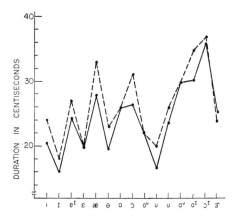

FIG. 9. Average durations of syllable nuclei, measured from minimal pairs differing in the voicing of the final consonant. The solid curve is for a large set of CNC words spoken by GEP; the dotted curve represents the values for 30 minimal pairs uttered by five speakers.

the duration of the aspiration is discounted, the syllable nucleus following a voiceless plosive is usually shorter than that following a voiced plosive. In the phonemic analysis of English, voiceless aspirated plosives are commonly analyzed as single phonemes, although they consist of a sequence of acoustical segments.

The aspiration has also been considered as part of the following vowel.[10] According to this opinion, the voiceless part represents the influence of the voiceless consonant as partial progressive assimilation which extends over a certain portion of the duration of the vowel.

The average duration of the aspiration after an initial |p| was 5.8 csec (for 81 different items); after an initial |t| the aspiration lasted 6.9 csec (in 73 instances), and for initial |k| the duration of the aspiration lasted 7.5 csec (for 83 items). These data suggest that aspiration may become progressively longer as the point of articulation shifts farther back in the mouth, but this observation was not supported by a separate analysis of the two main allophones of /k/, [c] and [k]. The average for the front allophone, [c], followed by front vowels (39 instances), was 7.8 csec, whereas the average for the velar allophone [k], followed by back vowels (44 instances), was 7.2 csec. Nevertheless, the /t/ aspirations were consistently shorter than the aspirations associated with either of the allophones of /k/.

If differences in the duration of the aspiration are conditioned and, therefore, nonsignificant, the question could be raised as to whether the duration of the aspiration is irrelevant to the duration of the syllable nucleus. If it is, then the aspiration may be considered as part of the consonant rather than the vowel. In some instances, this actually seemed to be the case.

[10] E. Fischer-Jørgensen, *Misc. Phonetica* 2, 42–59 (1954).

Figure 4 shows such an instance. In the spectrogram for *duck*, the vowel seems as long as the vowel in *tuck*; if the duration of the aspiration is included in the duration of the syllable nucleus, the total duration is more like the duration of the vowel in *dug*.

If we exclude aspiration, the average duration of the syllable nucleus after a voiceless consonant was 25.1 csec; when aspiration is included, it was 30.8 csec; the average duration after voiced consonants was 27.4 csec. These figures represent the average values for all 68 minimal pairs. Perhaps the most obvious conclusion is that, in our data, the influence of an initial consonant on the duration of the syllable nucleus followed no simple regular pattern.

INTRINSIC DURATIONS OF SYLLABLE NUCLEI IN ENGLISH

If the duration of a syllable nucleus is conditioned by the presence or absence of voicing in the following consonant, the intrinsic duration of the syllable nucleus might be defined as the average duration of the respective minimally contrastive pairs. Such average durations were computed for both the large and the small sets of data. In Fig. 9, the solid curve represents the averages for one speaker, and the dashed curve the averages for five speakers. Table I presents the actual values upon which the graph in Fig. 9 is based. The third row adds, for purposes of comparison, the average durations of the syllable nuclei in all instances in which the syllable nucleus occurred in the CNC list before those final consonants that were involved in the respective minimal pairs. In most instances, there is good agreement between the values computed from minimal pairs and the values averaged from a larger number of occurrences. There is also a considerable similarity between the two curves in Fig. 9.

TABLE I. Intrinsic durations of syllable nuclei
in American English.

Syllable nucleus	Average for five speakers (in csec)	Average for GEP in minimal pairs	Average for all occurrences in CNC list
i	24	20.6	20.7
ɪ	18	16.0	16.1
eɪ	27	24.3	20.0
ɛ	20	20.3	20.4
æ	33	28.0	28.4
ə	23	19.3	18.1
ɑ	26	26.1	26.5
ɔ	31	26.5	25.0
oʊ	22	22.0	22.2
ʊ	20	16.3	16.3
u	26	23.8	23.5
ɑʊ	30	30.2	30.2
ɑɪ	35	30.3	31.0
ɔɪ	37	36.0	36.0
r	24	25.3	25.6

It appears rather clear that the vocalic syllable nuclei may be subdivided into classes according to their durations. As a first approximation, the syllable nuclei may be considered as consisting of four short nuclei, [ɪ], [ɛ], [ʊ], and [ə], and nine long syllable nuclei. The average duration of the nuclei preceding each consonant was next computed, and Fig. 10 presents these durations as a function of the final consonant phoneme. Only minimal pairs were included in constructing the two curves of Fig. 10 and in the accompanying Table II. The top curve is for all long syllable nuclei, and the bottom curve is for the four intrinsically short syllable nuclei. The voiceless-voiced contrasting influence on syllable nucleus duration is clearly evident in the variations of both curves. It is interesting that

TABLE II. Duration of syllable nuclei as a function
of the following consonant.

Following consonant	Duration of short syllable nucleus (in csec)	Duration of long syllable nucleus (in csec)
p	13.8	18.8
b	20.3	30.7
t	14.7	21.0
d	20.6	31.8
k	14.5	20.0
g	24.3	31.4
m	22.0	31.3
n	21.6	32.2
ŋ	21.8	35.0
f	19.2	26.1
v	23.1	37.4
θ	20.8	26.5
ð	26.0	38.1
s	19.9	26.9
z	26.2	39.0
ʃ	21.2	27.8
ʒ	. . .	41.0
r	22.6	29.6
l	21.8	29.3
č	14.5	19.8
ǰ	19.1	30.0

there is durational overlap between the durations of long nucleus plus voiceless consonant and short nucleus plus voiced consonant, for example in such sets as *bead-beat-bit-bid*. A further interesting fact is that the affricates [tʃ] and [dʒ] affect the preceding vowel durations in the same manner as the plosives. There is a possible historical basis for this similarity. Other characteristics of the two durational classes of syllable nuclei will be discussed in a subsequent issue.

CONCLUSION

It appears from the data analyzed during the present study that the durations of all syllable nuclei in English are significantly affected by the nature of the consonants that follow the syllable nuclei; the influence of the initial consonants upon the durations of the syllable nuclei appears to be negligible. In general, the

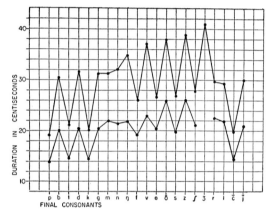

FIG. 10. Duration of syllable nuclei as a function of the final consonant phoneme, computed from minimal pairs of CNC words spoken by GEP. The top curve presents the average durations for all long-syllable nuclei and the bottom curve the averages for four short-syllable nuclei.

syllable nucleus is shorter when followed by a voiceless consonant, and longer when followed by a voiced consonant. In a large number of minimal pairs of CNC words differing in the voicing of the final consonant, the ratio of the durations of the vowels was approximately 2:3, the syllable nucleus before the voiced consonant being longer in every case. As a class, plosives are preceded by the shortest syllable nuclei; nasals had approximately the same influence as voiced plosives. Syllable nuclei were longest before voiced fricatives. Assuming that a voiced consonant has a lengthening influence on a syllable nucleus that is comparable to the shortening influence of a voiceless consonant, the intrinsic duration of syllable nuclei may be defined as the average duration of the syllable nucleus measured from minimal pairs differing in the voicing of the final consonant. Such intrinsic durations were computed for all stressed syllable nuclei in English. Two groups may be established according to this procedure: intrinsically short syllable nuclei, comprising the four vowels [ɪ, ɛ, ə, ʊ], and intrinsically long syllable nuclei, consisting of [i, eᴵ, æ, ɑ, ɔ, oᵁ, u, r, ɑᵁ, ɑᴵ, ɔᴵ].

ACKNOWLEDGMENT

The authors wish to express their appreciation to Dr. C. Gunnar M. Fant of the Royal Institute of Technology in Stockholm for his courtesy in providing mingograph tracings and continuous spectrograms of the data described here.

CHAPTER 18

Reprinted from LANGUAGE AND SPEECH, Vol. 3 (1960).

SPECTRA OF FRICATIVE NOISE IN HUMAN SPEECH*

PETER STREVENS

University of Edinburgh

This paper describes the results of a spectrographic analysis of a number of voiceless fricatives. The sounds are shown to be capable of description in terms of the frequencies of the lower and upper limits of energy present, the presence or absence of formant-like concentrations of energy, and the over-all relative intensity of the sounds.

The sounds investigated fall into three groups: front, mid and back, corresponding to the regions of the vocal tract within which they are produced. Sounds in the front group have a long spectrum, with little patterning of peaks of energy; their relative intensity is low. Sounds in the mid group have a short spectrum, with the main region of energy at a higher frequency than in the other groups; their relative intensity is high. Sounds in the back group have a spectrum of medium length, exhibiting a formant-like patterning of energy; their relative intensity is intermediate between the other groups. Tentative criteria are advanced for distinguishing between members of each group.

Combining this evidence with general phonetic knowledge it is possible to make a number of statements about other categories of sounds which include a component of fricative noise: i.e. voiced fricatives, stops, and affricates.

PRELIMINARY DISCUSSION

The phonetic category of voiceless fricatives comprises speech sounds consisting solely of turbulent noise, or *hiss*.

Nine different voiceless fricatives were selected for analysis in the present study. They are only some of the total members of the class, and were selected to provide a wide coverage of different places of articulation and shapes of orifice. The sounds are those commonly referred to by the following symbols and articulatory labels: —

Φ (bi-labial; f (labio-dental); θ (dental); s (alveolar); ʃ (palato-alveolar); ç (palatal); x (velar); χ (uvular); h (glottal).

It should be made clear that the term *voiceless* is used throughout this paper in its normal, general phonetic sense. Voiceless fricatives are sounds produced with no vibration of the vocal cords. Their spectrum is basically that of aperiodic random noise.

The author has been concerned in the operation for research purposes of PAT, the parametric artificial talking device designed by W. Lawrence. (Lawrence, 1953; Strevens, 1958a, 1958b; Strevens and Anthony, 1958). It was clear from an early stage that the work must include the adequate simulation of at least the voiceless fricatives of English. In practice it was found that the available data were not sufficient

* *This work was undertaken under a contract between the Ministry of Supply and the University of Edinburgh for research into the specification of speech by means of acoustic parameters.*

to programme PAT to do this. The investigation now described was undertaken with a view to providing the basic data for the purpose.

Voiceless fricatives are all produced by turbulent air-flow caused by a constriction in the vocal tract at some point in or above the larynx. The constriction may vary as to position in the tract, degree of constriction, area of constriction, and shape of orifice. Further, although it is customary to think of the vocal tract as if it were a tube having a cylindrical cross-section, it must not be forgotten that the tract is in places highly mobile, and that it may alter its shape to a considerable extent independently of constrictions such as those under discussion. Finally, the air-stream may vary as to pressure or rate of flow. A variation of any combination of these factors can be expected to cause a variation in the physical nature of the resulting sound in any of three ways: by altering the spectrum of the original source of sound ; by altering the filter function of the tract as a whole ; by altering the intensity of the acoustic energy produced.

The spectrum of the sound-source will depend on the degree and the area of constriction, on the shape of the orifice or orifices, and to a minor extent on the rate of air-flow. The chief effect of increased air-flow is to increase the overall acoustic energy. The filter function will depend largely (though not wholly) on the position of the constriction within the vocal tract, since this position will decide what portions of the vocal tract are contributing to the shaping of the source spectrum.

Because of the inter-dependence of the physiological and the physical events it is necessary to consider them both ; the following order will be employed : first, the modifications of the vocal tract which impede the air-stream and give rise to turbulent flow ; secondly, variations in air-pressure and their relation to acoustic intensity ; thirdly, the spectrographic analysis of voiceless fricatives ; fourthly, an extension of the results thus obtained to consideration of other sounds containing a component of noise.

Modifications of the vocal tract

The position of the constriction within the vocal tract is possibly the chief cause of identifiable differences of sound quality in voiceless fricatives. (This is indeed true of all consonants ; a traditional method of defining consonants is in terms of " place of articulation ".) The organs of articulation concerned in the production of the nine selected voiceless fricatives /Φ f θ s ʃ ç x χ h/ and the typical positions within the vocal tract at which the constriction (and hence the turbulent air-flow) occurs, are as follows :

/Φ/ is produced with the constriction at the lips. Its occurrence in British forms of English is limited to certain Scottish and Irish dialects and to the exclamation " Phew ! "

/f/ is produced with the upper teeth close to the inner surface of the lower lip. The air-stream passes between the teeth and the lower lip, and also through some of the interstices between the upper teeth.

/θ/ is produced with the tip of the tongue close to, or touching, the inner edge of the upper incisors. However, there is a good deal of personal variation in the place of articulation of this sound: it has been described as occurring with the tip of the tongue protruding between the upper and lower teeth ; but a tip-teeth articulation is believed to be the commonest one.

/s/ is produced with either the tip or the blade of the tongue raised to approach the alveolar ridge.

/ʃ/ is produced with the blade of the tongue, or the tip and blade, approaching the palate approximately at the part where the alveolar ridge merges into the main body of the hard palate.

/ç/ is produced with the front of the tongue (i.e. roughly that part of its surface which opposes the dome of the palate when the tongue is at rest) approaching the hard palate somewhat forward of its highest point.

/x/ is produced with the back of the tongue approaching the middle of the soft palate.

/χ/ is produced with the back of the tongue approaching the back of the soft palate and the back wall of the pharynx.

/h/ is the subject of some controversy. It is thought by many that the turbulent air-flow is produced somewhere in the larynx ; others believe " cavity-friction " to be generated throughout the vocal tract. The exact mechanism is not clearly understood.

Each of the articulations thus briefly described occurs at a different point in the vocal tract and can therefore be expected to lead to a different shaping of the source spectrum. The source spectrum itself will differ to some extent according to the nature of the orifice formed at the place of constriction. A short description of typical orifices for each of the nine sounds will demonstrate the occurrence of a wide variety of orifice shapes.

/Φ/ is produced with a long narrow slit between the lips.

/f/ is produced with a narrow opening between the upper teeth and the lower lips. There may also be a contribution through slits between the teeth.

/θ/ is produced with a narrow slit between the bottom of the upper teeth and the surface of the tongue ; the configuration of the teeth affects the quality of the sound produced.

/s/ is produced with a narrow slit which may sometimes be accompanied by a deep groove and pit in the tongue.

/ʃ/ is produced with a wider slit or groove than for /s/ (with a greater area of turbulence). Further, the main body of the tongue assumes a different posture for /ʃ/ than for /s/.

In the production of /ç x χ/ the constriction is far back in the mouth. The chief difference between them is the place at which the constriction occurs.

/h/ is produced with increased air-flow through the larynx ; the area of turbulence is probably very extensive.

The above set of statements is to be taken as an approximation and a normalisation, and is not presented as an absolute or final description. Palatographic studies, especially those using the direct photography method (Anthony, 1954 ; Abercrombie, 1956 ; Ladefoged, 1957 ; Way, 1957) show that there are often large variations of the shape of the orifice and even of the place of constriction, within the speech of a single individual as well as between different speakers. Further, the description of these items by no means exhausts even commonly-observed methods of production of hiss. The air-flow in most cases passes over the median line of the tongue, but it may for some voiceless fricatives pass over one or both sides of the tongue ; the tongue may be grooved or flat, or " pitted " ; there may be more than one constriction at one time ; the nasal cavity may be coupled-in with an air-flow sufficient to cause nasal turbulence, and so on.

It is clear that there are available to the speaker compensatory processes which enable him to produce an acceptable quality of voiceless fricative using quite a variety of different articulatory postures. (These processes are familiar to all those who have lost or acquired teeth.) The foregoing descriptions, then, are a catalogue of some configurations that *do* occur, not of those that *must* be used.

VARIATIONS OF AIR-FLOW

A factor which must now be studied is the acoustic *intensity* of these sounds.

Two assumptions underlie this section of the paper ; first, that variations in the air-flow of speech have a major effect upon the *intensity* but only a negligible effect upon the *spectrum* of the sound produced ; secondly, that the amount of acoustic energy produced during a voiceless fricative is closely related to the rate of air-flow involved.

It is common observation that, to put it roughly, all the voiceless fricatives occur sometimes loud and sometimes soft, but some are loud most of the time while others are soft most of the time. It is of importance to discover whether this is because of inherent differences of acoustic energy or because of other factors such as those arising in the initiation and modification of the pulmonic air-streams.

In English (and presumably in all languages using only an egressive pulmonic air-stream) the pressure of the expiratory air is operated upon by two variables: (1) the *affective variations* of pressure ; (2) variations of *phonetic impedance*. These labels need brief explanation : —

(1) During most speech, the mean pulmonic air pressure remains relatively constant. Fig. 1 shows the relation between the sub-glottal pressure and the volume of air in the lungs during a normal conversational utterance. As speech begins the air-pressure rises to an appropriate level (about 3 cms. aq. for normal speech). The pressure-level appropriate to shouting is higher than that for quiet speech. Pressure levels above the minimum for speech are decided by the general degree of loudness at which the speech is to be produced. The monitoring of this factor is entirely subjective and automatic ; the term " affective variations " is proposed, to describe the gross changes in air-pressure level which produce the required loudness.

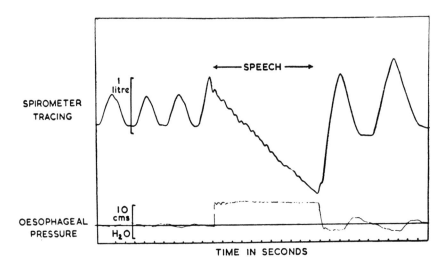

Fig. 1. Two parameters of the air-stream used in respiration and speech. Simultaneous records of volume and pressure. (By courtesy of P. Ladefoged.)

(2) The load on the air-stream varies in complex ways. The air-stream itself above the larynx has two modes of flow ; breath and voice, the former being normally at a higher total rate of flow than the latter. In either mode the flow may be either free or impeded to some extent. Both the extent and the duration of the obstruction will vary from one sound to another. Stops have a momentary but complete obstruction—an infinite phonetic impedance—while fricatives have a lower phonetic impedance of a longer duration. These changes in impedance are added to the changes in pressure brought about by muscular activity in the form of " chest pulses " (Draper, Ladefoged and Whitteridge, 1957, 1959 ; Ladefoged, Draper and Whitteridge, 1958). Between them they produce rapidly fluctuating peaks of pressure super-imposed upon the speech level.

It is now appropriate to describe some preliminary attempts to relate acoustic energy to tracheal air-pressure.

A microphone, set at a distance of 1 ft. from the speaker's mouth, was connected through a pre-amplifier to a valve millivoltmeter. Variations in the acoustic intensity of the nine voiceless fricatives could thus be read as variations in voltage. A nasal catheter tube terminating in a small, lightly-inflated rubber bulb, was passed into the oesophagus of the two subjects, Peter Ladefoged and the author.

Experiments have shown (Draper, Ladefoged and Whitteridge, 1959) that since the oesophagus is separated from the trachea by only a thin membrane, the variations of pressure on the air-filled bulb could be treated as variations in the pressure of the pulmonic air-stream. Further, the oesophagus is on the lung-ward side of all the places of constriction of the nine sounds under investigation. The catheter tube was connected to a transducer incorporating a movable anode whose output was taken to a second voltmeter. The apparatus as a whole can be calibrated by a manometric device.

The subjects spoke a large number of examples of each of the nine voiceless fricatives, using degrees of muscular effort ranging from shouting to little more than a whisper. The two voltages corresponding to acoustic intensity and air-pressure were read simultaneously for each test item. It was found that peristalsis of the alimentary tract interfered increasingly with experimental readings as the next meal-time approached. Nevertheless sufficient readings were taken for the following points to become clear: (a) similar articulations could be made to produce acoustically different sounds; (b) after some little practice, a subject could learn to vary the intensity and pressure readings to some degree independently of each other; (c) a given sound may be produced habitually by a given speaker at a much higher or lower level of intensity than is used by another speaker.

The intensity reading of each item was divided by the pressure reading of each item. In this way it was possible to arrive at a single index for each sound, and a mean for all examples of a given sound by a given subject. There were strong correspondences between the figures of the two subjects; the indications are that the nine sounds as produced by these two subjects in these tests may be arranged as in Table 1:

TABLE 1

1	(lowest)	Φ
2		θ
3		f
4		χ
5		s
6		x
7		ʃ
8		h
9	(highest)	ç

Rank order of intensity per unit air-pressure.

The results of this preliminary experiment should be regarded with reserve, until there has been an opportunity to verify them using a more rigid experimental procedure and a larger number of subjects. When this has been done, it will be possible to establish an order (which may be similar to that given above) representing the relative intensities of the different fricatives when they occur in a sample of speech with a given mean pulmonic air-pressure level, e.g., as shown in Fig. 1.

Spectrographic analysis had not been attempted in the few papers previously published on these sounds. (Halle, Hughes and Radley, 1957 ; Hughes and Halle, 1956 ; Meyer-Eppler, 1956.) A small pilot investigation was undertaken with a view to discovering what the drawbacks would be in using spectrographic analysis, whether adequate data could be obtained, and what procedures should be used.

It was found at once that voiceless fricatives occurring in connected speech rarely gave usable spectral information, for two reasons: first, the over-all acoustic energy of the voiceless fricatives is generally much lower than for the stressed vowels by whose peaks the signal level is usually adjusted, consequently the full spectral pattern of the fricatives is too weak to appear ; secondly the duration of these items is often quite short, so that the quantity of pattern available for study is inadequate. The apparatus available for this study included a Kay Sonagraph ; the first practical task was to find a technique of using the instrument which would overcome these difficulties. A sample of speech was recorded with the aim of studying the voiceless fricatives which occurred in that utterance ; the expedient was tried of setting the recording level by these fricative items, and not by the peaks of energy occurring during vowels. This meant that the stressed vowels and may other voiced sounds were badly overloaded, but it was immediately apparent that greater detail was visible during the voiceless fricatives, and that the patterns for a given fricative were consistent between one utterance and another.

To overcome the problem of the short duration of naturally-occurring fricatives the possibility was considered of using the sounds in isolation and of deliberately lengthening them. Given good listening conditions (e.g., the close proximity of speakers and the low background noise usual for quiet conversation) listeners experienced no difficulty in identifying voiceless fricatives spoken in isolation even when no visual clues were present. Lengthening the sounds in isolation only made their identification more immediate and certain. A scheme of investigation was therefore prepared on the assumption that the spectra of isolated, lengthened utterances of the voiceless fricatives would contain all the clues necessary for their auditory identification, and would not contain any undue quantity of spurious components. (The voiceless fricatives occur more frequently with a short duration, but the additional length used in this investigation is not necessarily an unreal factor. The following occurrences of lengthened voiceless fricatives are relatively common: /ɸɸɸ/ when expressing relief after a narrow escape ; /sss/ expressing disapproval at the theatre ; /fff/ when talking to children (" Pufff, puffff .... " etc.) ; /ʃʃʃ/ asking for silence, etc.)

The list of items was selected, as already mentioned, so as to cover a reasonable range of possible places of production within the vocal tract. Thirteen past and present staff and post-graduate students of the Phonetics Department of Edinburgh University acted as subjects. Each subject spoke each of the items in isolation, lengthened to approximately one second. Using as subjects people with a professional training in phonetics enabled satisfactory recordings to be obtained very quickly with the minimum of

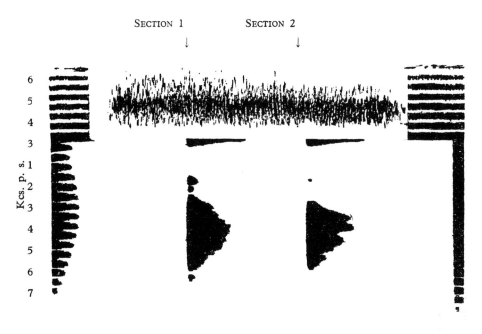

SECTION 1   SECTION 2

Fig. 2. A typical pair of sections: the /s/ of speaker E.

instructions and rehearsal. The utterances were checked both at the time they were made and from the recordings to ensure that the instructions had been carried out. The recordings were made on a Ferrograph tape recorder, with a flat frequency response from 50 to 10,000 cps. ± 2 db, running at 15 inches per second. The recording technique was critical: the subject had to be close enough to the microphone to provide an adequate signal, yet his breath-stream had to be directed in such a direction as not to impinge on the microphone.

Once the recordings were complete the spectrographic analysis was begun. Various displays were tried. The best results compatible with the time and labour involved were obtained from two spectrograms per utterance; (i) a broad-band spectrogram of the normal scale of 0-8000 cps.; (ii) two amplitude sections of each utterance, chosen one from the first half and the other from the second half. A typical pair of spectrograms is shown in Fig. 2.

Each recording was followed by a calibration tone consisting of a short 'pip' of square waves from a signal generator set at a frequency of 500 cps. The display given by this 'pip' has been arranged to provide a calibration scale at each edge of the spectrogram.

Spectrograms of each of these three types were made for each of the nine utterances of each of the thirteen speakers. The spectrograms were then inspected visually. Two things were immediately apparent: first, there were systematic variations of pattern between one item and another in the analysis of a given speaker; secondly, there were similarities of pattern within a given item in the analyses of all speakers.

Many alternative methods were tried in a search for a simple presentation of the patterns which occur in these spectrograms. The least unsatisfactory is to produce an " average line spectrum " for each utterance. These line spectra indicate the range of frequencies within which energy is shown to be present on the spectrograms. The variation of upper and lower limits of frequency within any one spectrogram is surprisingly small, and once it was decided that extremes of variation were to be ignored and only typical frequency limits shown, the preparation of line spectra was easy.

On these lines cross-bars are marked at frequencies when peaks of energy occur. No distinction is made between peaks of different height, or of different breadth: the cross-bars mark simply frequencies at which peaks of some kind occur. The reason for not indicating the magnitude of the peaks is a purely practical one: there is no simple way of describing them. It is arbitrary enough to decide by visual inspection that a peak is or is not present, but distinctions between different sizes or shapes of peak are not feasible, as anyone will confirm who has studied fricative spectra.

Here it may be mentioned that the amplitude cross-sections were considerably less helpful than might have been imagined. One single cross-section per fricative yields apparently helpful information about peaks of energy. A second cross-section from the same utterances, however, almost invariably gives information that conflicts in its details with the previous analysis. The operative point is that the conflict concerns the *details*: the rough outline is generally similar. Presumably the reason for the discrepancies is that we are dealing with the acoustic shaping of aperiodic noise. The general aspect of the cross-section is determined by the shaping which in turn is conferred by the configuration of the vocal tract; but the random nature of the sound is illustrated by variations of detail from one instant to another. To sum up, one cross-section per utterance gave a spurious appearance of firm detail, while two per utterance gave conflicting evidence. The line spectra and the cross-bars indicating frequency were therefore compiled chiefly from the broad-band spectrograms.

These line spectra are shown as Fig. 3, diagrams a to i.

No account can be taken of the upper limits of frequency above 8 Kcs., since the frequency response of the spectrograph dropped away sharply above that point. From rough tests made with recordings played at half speed and then given the same analysis it appears that in the spectra shown as reaching 8 Kcs., some energy is in fact present in most cases up to 10 Kcs., and in a few cases up to at least 12 Kcs. But the evidence is not sufficient to be presented here and no systematic study of the upper limits of frequency has been attempted, where these lie above 8 Kcs.

The averaged line spectra shown in the diagrams must be accompanied by a verbal description of the average spectra of each of the nine voiceless fricatives; this will include a statement of intensity. By this is meant the order of ranking from the investigation of intensity per unit pressure described above. It must be repeated that no general validity is claimed for this figure.

1. /Φ/ (Fig. 3a) Lowest frequency at which energy is visible on the spectrogram is between 1600 and 1650 cps. Low peaks of energy tend to occur around 1800 - 2000 cps., 4000 - 4500 cps., and 5500 cps. Energy rarely above 6500 cps. Intensity ranking: lowest of 9.

2. /f/ (Fig. 3b) Lowest frequency is around 1500 - 1700 cps. Low peaks of energy tend to occur around 1900 cps., 4000 cps., and occasionally 5000 cps. Upper limit of frequency is rarely below 7000 cps., usually around 7500 cps. In general, a higher upper limit than No. 1. Intensity ranking: 3rd in ascending order.

3. /θ/ (Fig. 3c) Lowest frequency varies, but lies between 1400 and 2000 cps. Low peaks of energy tend to occur, the lowest being close to 2000 cps., the upper peaks varying somewhat, but tending to lie about 1000 cycles apart. Upper limit of frequency rarely below 7200 cps.; some speakers reach 8000 cps. In general, a somewhat higher upper limit than No. 2. Intensity ranking: 2nd in ascending order.

4. /s/ (Fig. 3d) Lowest frequency almost always above 3500 cps. Peaks of energy tend to occur with no apparent pattern, except that they do not lie closer to one another than 1000 cycles. Upper limit of frequency exceeds 8000 cps. in most cases. Intensity ranking: 5th in ascending order.

5. /ʃ/ (Fig. 3e) Lowest frequency varies between 1600 and 2500 cps. Peaks of energy tend to occur not less than 1000 cycles apart and the aspect of amplitude cross-sections shows a weighting towards the bottom of the pattern. Upper limit of frequency shows a sharp cut-off around 7000 cps. Intensity ranking: 7th in ascending order.

6. /ç/ (Fig. 3f) Lower limit of frequency varies generally between 2800 and 3600 cps. Peaks of energy tend to appear at roughly 1000 cycle intervals ; these peaks are sharper than those in No. 5. Upper frequency limit very variable, but usually between 6000 and 7200 cps., i.e. lower than for either No. 4 or No. 5. The general shape of the spectrum is like that of No. 4 /s/, but with all values transposed 1000 cps. down. Intensity ranking: greatest of all 9 items.

7. /x/ (Fig. 3g) Lower limit of frequency usually between 1200 cps. and 1500 cps. There is always a strong peak of energy below 2000 cps., with others above about 3500 cps. The aspect of amplitude cross-sections gives a hint of formant-like structure ; the low peak is steeper than the upper peaks, which are often double peaks, some 500 - 600 cycles apart. Upper frequency limit is very variable, usually between 5000 cps. and 7500 cps. A considerable variety of different sound qualities was obtained from the subjects, as was to be expected. Versions judged in phonetic terms to have a more back place of articulation tended to approach more closely to a formant-like structure. Intensity rating: 6th in ascending order.

8. /χ/ (Fig. 3h) Lower limit of frequency varies between 700 cps. and 1200 cps. All spectra bear a marked resemblance to vowels, with a " formant " of one or two

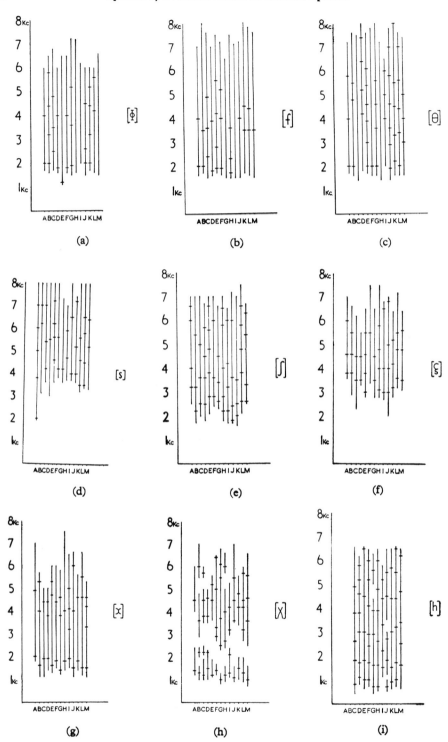

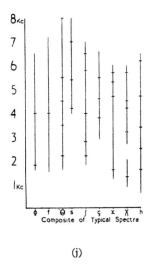

Composite of Typical Spectra

(j)

Fig. 3. Typical line spectra for nine voiceless fricatives. Diagrams (a)-(i) show average line spectra for each item of each speaker; diagram (j) is composed of one typical spectrum of each item, for comparison.

high peaks between 1000 cps. and 2400 cps. Sometimes there are 3 or even 4 " formants " altogether, with 1 or 2 of them having rather high peaks of intensity, in the region from 3000 cps. to 6000 cps. At first glance the spectrographic pattern is that of a vowel rather than a voiceless fricative. Upper limit of frequency variable between 6000 cps. and 7000 cps. Intensity rating: 4th in ascending order.

9. /h/ (Fig. 3i) Lower limit of frequency usually varies between 400 cps. and 700 cps. The peaks of intensity which occur are so marked as to suggest a multi-formant vowel. One major peak occurs around 1000 cps., one around 1700 cps. At least 5 major peaks occur in each pattern; spectra for women subjects exhibit more of these peaks than for men. Upper limit of frequency is usually around 6500 cps. Intensity ranking: 8th in ascending order, but for technical reasons the data (and thus the ranking) for this item are suspect.

A consideration of the data provides a basis for distinguishing three groups of voiceless fricatives, the members of each group sharing certain features. It happens (not surprisingly) that the groupings reflect major differences in place of articulation. The groups may therefore be labelled as follows: *Front* (containing the labial and dental sounds /Φ f θ/); *Mid* (containing the alveolar and palatal sounds /s ʃ ç/) and *Back* (containing the velar, uvular and pharyngal sounds /x χ h/). The groups are distinguished in terms of spectral pattern in the following way:—

Front Group /Φ f θ/ Long spectrum, covering a range of some 5000 to 6000 cycles; a peak of energy frequently occurs below 2000 cps., but in general the peaks

are un-patterned and " spiky " ; the relative intensity is the lowest of the three groups.
Mid Group /s ʃ ç/ Short spectrum, covering a range of some 3000 to 4000 cycles ;
one or more major " humps " around the middle of the pattern ; the relative intensity
is the highest of the three groups.
Back Group /x χ h/ Medium spectrum covering a range of some 4000 to 5500
cycles ; a marked " formant-like " structure with invariably a major peak or " formant " around 1500 cps.; the relative intensity is the middle of the three groups.

The above characteristics identify the groups and can be stated with some confidence.
The factors which distinguish members within a group are not so clear-cut, and are
put forward with some reserve. It is suggested that it is within these groups, rather
than between them, that confusions and misidentifications most frequently occur under
conditions of restricted efficiency of communication (e.g., on poor telephone circuits).
The distinctions between different members of a group may reside in the following
criteria : —

Front Group : " Centre of gravity ". It seems from a study of the amplitude cross-
sections that the sequence /Φ f θ/ (that is, going progressively further back in
place of articulation) displays an increasing weighting of the upper end of the
spectrum, accompanied to some extent by a higher upper limit of frequency.
Mid Group : A combination of upper and lower frequency limits. The sequence
/s ʃ ç/ (that is, going progressively further back in place of articulation) is accompanied by a change of upper limit from highest to lowest ; the lower limit changes
in the same sequence from highest to lowest to intermediate.
Back Group : Doubtful: possibly the frequency of lower limit of frequency, which
becomes progressively lower in the sequence /x χ h/ (that is, progressively further
back in place of articulation). The foregoing features are summarised in Table II.

The sounds with which this investigation has been concerned are well known as
being aperiodic in nature. Unfortunately it has often been assumed that they should
be equated with the classical case of random, aperiodic vibration, known as " white
noise ". It is now quite clear that the randomness of the sound source is greatly
modified by the acoustic shaping characteristics of the vocal tract, and that this shaping
varies in several ways. To extend the " white noise " metaphor it might be said that
voiceless fricative speech sounds consist of " grey noise, streaked with white and black ".

EXTRAPOLATIONS

Once the analysis and classification of voiceless fricatives has been performed on
lengthened, isolated segments, it becomes possible to recognise many or all the features
already described from their occurrence in spectrograms of normal connected speech.
More important, the same sets of features begin to be seen, at least partially, in
spectrograms of voiced fricatives, voiceless and voiced stops, and voiceless and voiced
fricatives.

No detailed analysis of any of these sounds has been attempted by the author but

TABLE 2

Sounds	Articulation Group	Relative Intensity	Spectrum Length	Distinction between Members of the Group
Φ				Φ lowest "centre of gravity"
f	FRONT (Labial & dental)	LOW	LONG (5000-6000 cycles)	f intermediate "centre of gravity"
θ				θ highest "centre of gravity"
s				s highest bottom limit, highest top limit of frequency
ʃ	MID (pre-velar)	HIGH	SHORT (3000-4000 cycles)	ʃ lowest bottom limit, intermediate top limit of frequency
ç				ç intermediate bottom limit, lowest top limit of frequency
x				x highest bottom limit of frequency
χ	BACK	MEDIUM	MEDIUM (4000-5500 cycles) with "formant-like" structure	χ intermediate bottom limit of frequency
h				h lowest bottom limit of frequency

The special characteristics of nine voiceless fricatives.

a combination of general phonetic considerations with extrapolations from the data on voiceless fricatives would lead one to expect with considerable confidence the existence of certain predictable features. The following paragraphs summarise these expectations.

We have seen that when turbulent air-flow occurs its spectrum will be related to the place where it occurs, the shape of the orifice concerned and the flow of air through the constriction. If other sounds containing a component of fricative noise are now considered in the light of the data described above, strong indications may be seen as to the probable nature of the hiss. It is convenient to discuss these sounds in categories according to their method of production.

Voiced fricatives (e.g.: / β v ð z ʒ j ɣ ʁ ɦ /)

These sounds are made up of two components: a component of hiss and a component of "vocal tone" or *voice*. It can reasonably be assumed that the acoustic characteristics of the hiss will correspond in most respects to those of the voiceless fricatives. The major difference in articulation is that in voiced fricatives for a given air-pressure the *air-flow* is less than for the voiceless items, since the breath stream is being interrupted and reduced in flow by the action of the vocal cords. For a given air-pressure the acoustic intensity of the hiss component of voiced fricatives is inherently less than that of the corresponding voiceless items.

Evidence tending to confirm this may be found in spectrograms of ordinary speech. It is instructive to compare two amplitude displays (not cross-sections) of the same utterance, using a flat amplifier response for one and high frequency emphasis for the other. The amplitude of the trace during voiceless fricatives is greatly increased by the high frequency emphasis ; the voiced fricatives, on the other hand, are only slightly higher than in the flat-response condition. The energy present at the higher frequencies is clearly less in the voiced fricatives than in the voiceless ones.

Nevertheless hiss remains comparatively easy to identify, even at low intensities and when accompanied by vocal cord vibration. In teaching general phonetics, there is little difficulty in teaching students to identify the presence of hiss, and the hiss seems not to be masked by voice.

Stops
(i) *Voiceless*

Many languages contain voiceless stops, in the production of which the air-stream is momentarily obstructed, then released with a " burst " of fricative noise, more or less short in duration. The spectrum of the hiss on any given occasion will inevitably be like the spectrum of a closely homorganic fricative. Thus in English when the voiceless stops (/p t k/ are released with a burst of hiss, the spectrum of this affrication must be virtually identical with /Φ s x/ respectively, since /Φ/ and /p/ are homorganic, as are /s/ and /t/ and also /x/ and /k/). This is what one tends to find on close examination of suitable spectrograms. (See also Fischer-Jorgensen, 1954.)

(ii) *Voiced*

Perceptible affrication after voiced stops is much less common, at least in English. The reduced rate of air-flow resulting from vibration of the vocal cords causes a smaller build-up of pressure behind the occlusion, duration for duration, than in the case of voiceless stops. This means that when the stop is released the air-flow may be insufficient to cause audible friction. Even when hiss does occur, it is both short in duration and extremely low in level compared with the voiced components. The spectrum is identical with that of the voiceless counterpart.

Affricates
(i) *Voiceless.* Affricates combine in sequence some of the articulatory features of the stops (e.g., complete but momentary obstruction of the air-stream) with other features characteristic of the fricatives (e.g., partial obstruction of the air-stream). An important additional point is that the place of articulation of the stop release is frequently not the same as the place of the fricative articulation within the same

sound. The relative levels of the stop release and fricative portions may also be different. Consequently the hiss portion of an affricate may consist of two segments having different spectra. Thus /tʃ/ in *church* begins with a short " stop-release " burst having a spectrum closely similar to /s/ and is followed without a break by a longer " fricative " segment having the spectrum of /ʃ/.

(ii) *Voiced*. In voiced affricates (as in *judge*) the considerations for voiced stops and voiced fricatives apply. The stop-release portion will be at a much lower level of intensity, both absolutely and relatively, than in a voiceless plosive. The " fricative " portion will have audible friction with a spectrum appropriate to its place of articulation at a relatively lower level of intensity.

FRICATIVE SOUNDS IN SPEECH SYNTHESIS

Although the foregoing remarks on hiss in sounds other than voiceless fricatives have been presented as a sequel to the discussion of fricatives they also received some practical attention. In the preparation of synthetic speech utterances for Lawrence's PAT, the following observations have been made :

(i) variations of hiss spectrum, in the general direction of simulating the spectra described above, lead to improved acceptability and intelligibility of synthetic speech ;

(ii) even if the transitions have been faithfully simulated, voiced fricatives provided with some hiss of the appropriate spectrum are much more acceptable than the same sounds without hiss or with hiss of some different spectrum ;

(iii) in synthesising affricates a great improvement is obtained by working to a pattern of the appropriate " stop-release " spectrum portion, plus the appropriate fricative spectrum. These *ad hoc* observations are no substitute for a careful series of experiments in the synthesis of hiss sounds, but they provide much empirical confirmation and no refutation of the general validity of the foregoing remarks.

Furthermore, the quality of synthetic speech which PAT can produce is already very greatly improved as a result of this analysis of the acoustic spectra of voiceless fricatives ; it is now at last possible to write some physical specification of the sounds that the machine is to be instructed to simulate.

Experiments on the identification of stops and of fricatives have been described previously by several writers, notably by workers at the Haskins Laboratories (Liberman, Delattre and Cooper, 1952 ; Cooper, Delattre, Liberman and Gerstman, 1952 ; Liberman, Delattre, Cooper and Gerstman, 1957). The fricative noise used in the experiments described consists of white noise of 600 cycles spectrum width ; the only systematic variations reported are variations of the centre frequency of the band of short-spectrum hiss. (The exception is Dr. Harris (1956, 1958) who used wide-band white noise in some experiments and recordings of human fricatives in others, and experimented with variations in the relative intensity of vowel and fricative.)

The question arises whether substantially different results might be expected from these synthetic speech experiments if they were to be repeated using hiss spectra more closely resembling those found in human speech. The conclusions of Schatz (1954) support the contention that the fricative portions of voiceless stops are in many circumstances sufficient clues for identification, without reference to vowel transitions. It seems probable, therefore, that listeners' judgements on any occasion will be influenced in the direction of the naturally-occurring hiss spectrum most closely resembling the synthetic hiss.

ACKNOWLEDGEMENTS

The foregoing spectrographic investigations and the descriptions of articulatory and physiological facts owe a great deal to the co-operation of the author's colleagues at Edinburgh University. The original recordings and 400 spectrograms were produced by Miss Shiona Harkness, M.A., now of the College of Arts, Science and Technology, Zaria, Northern Nigeria. Many facts about articulations, almost the whole of the information about air-pressures, the instrumentation for the preliminary work on intensities and much fruitful discussion were generously given by Dr. Peter Ladefoged ; Dr. Frances Ingemann read the manuscript and made several helpful suggestions ; Mr. David Abercrombie, Head of the Phonetics Department, encouraged the work throughout and contributed much information about articulations. Mr. J. Anthony supervised the technical standards. To all these and to many others who have helped as subjects or with illustrations or secretarial assistance, grateful acknowledgement is made.

REFERENCES

ABERCROMBIE, D. (1956). Direct palatography. *Zeitschr. f. Phonetik,* 10, 21.

ANTHONY, J. (1954). New method for investigating tongue positions of consonants. *Science Technologists Association Bulletin,* 4, 2.

COOPER, F., DELATTRE, P., LIBERMAN, A., and GERSTMAN, L. (1952). Some experiments on the perception of synthetic speech sounds. *J. acoust. Soc. Amer.,* 24, 597.

DRAPER, M., LADEFOGED, P., and WHITTERIDGE, D. (1957). Expiratory muscles involved in speech. *J. Physiol.,* 138, 17.

DRAPER, M., LADEFOGED, P. and WHITTERIDGE, D. (1959). Respiratory muscles in speech. *J. Speech & Hearing Res.,* 2, 1.

FISCHER-JØRGENSEN, E. (1954). Acoustic analysis of stop consonants. *Miscellanea Phonetica II,* 42.

HALLE, M., HUGHES, G. and RADLEY, J. (1957). Acoustic properties of stop consonants. *J. acoust. Soc. Amer.,* 29, 107.

HARRIS, K. (1956). Some acoustic cues for the fricative consonants. (Report from Haskins Laboratories, New York.)

HARRIS, K. (1958). Cues for the discrimination of American English fricatives in spoken syllables. *Language and Speech,* 1, 1.

HUGHES, G., and HALLE, M. (1956). Spectral properties of fricative consonants. *J. acoust. Soc. Amer.,* 28, 303.

LADEFOGED, P. (1957). Use of palatography. *J. Speech & Hearing Disorders,* 22, 764.

LADEFOGED, P., DRAPER, M. and WHITTERIDGE, D. (1958). Syllables and stress. *Miscellanea Phonetica III,* 1.

LAWRENCE, W. (1953). The synthesis of signals having a low information rate. *Communication Theory,* ed. W. Jackson (London).

LIBERMAN, A., DELATTRE, P. and COOPER, F. (1952). The role of selected stimulus variables in the perception of the unvoiced stop consonants. *Amer. J. Psychol.,* 65, 497.

LIBERMAN, A., DELATTRE, P., COOPER, F., and GERSTMAN, L. (1954). The role of consonant-vowel transitions in the perception of the stop and nasal consonants. *Psychol. Mono.,* no. 379, 1.

MEYER-EPPLER, W. (1953). Untersuchungen zur Schallstruktur der stimmhaften und stimmlosen Geräuschlaute. *Zeitschr. f. Phonetik,* 7, 89.

SCHATZ, C. (1954). The role of context in the perception of stops. *Language,* 30, 47.

STREVENS, P. (1958a). The performance of "PAT", the six-parameter speech synthesiser designed by W. Lawrence. *Revista do Laboratório de Fonética Experimental, Coimbra,* IV, 5.

STREVENS, P. (1958b). Edinburgh's artificial talking machine. *University of Edinburgh Gazette,* 20, 4.

STREVENS, P. and ANTHONY, J. (1958). The performance of a six-parameter speech synthesizer. *Proc. 8th Intern. Congr. Linguists* (Oslo), 214.

WAY, R. (1957). The Articulation of Certain "Alveolar" Plosives. Dissertation for University of Edinburgh Diploma in Phonetics, 1957. (Unpublished).

Reprinted from THE JOURNAL OF THE ACOUSTICAL SOCIETY OF AMERICA, Vol. 33, No. 5 (May 1961).
Copyright 1961 by the Acoustical Society of America.

On the Properties of Voiceless Fricative Consonants*

JOHN M. HEINZ AND KENNETH N. STEVENS

Department of Electrical Engineering and Research Laboratory of Electronics,
Massachusetts Institute of Technology, Cambridge, Massachusetts

According to an acoustical theory of speech production, the spectra of voiceless fricatives can be characterized by poles and zeros whose frequency locations are dependent on the vocal-tract configuration and on the location of the source of excitation within the vocal tract. The locations of the important poles and zeros in the spectra of fricatives can be determined by a matching process whereby comparison spectra synthesized by electric circuits are matched against the spectra under analysis. This method has been used to determine the frequencies and bandwidths of the important poles and zeros for several versions of /f/, /s/, and /ʃ/. Based on these findings, a simplified electrical model is developed for the synthesis of voiceless fricatives. The model consists of a noise-excited electric circuit characterized by a pole and a zero whose frequency locations can be varied. Stimuli generated by this model, both in isolation and in syllables, are presented to listeners for identification. The results of the listening tests are consistent with the data from the acoustic analyses and with the findings of other investigators.

A T the present time, the production, the perception, and the acoustical properties of the voiceless fricative consonants are only partially understood. At the level of speech production it is known that the sounds are generated as a result of turbulence and other nonlinear processes in a vocal tract of fairly complicated shape,[1,2] but a satisfactory quantitative theory that describes this situation in detail has yet to be developed. At the level of the acoustical signal, some analyses of fricatives have been made,[2–5] but a detailed discussion of significant acoustic features of fricatives and of their statistical distributions in various contexts has not been given. The perception of fricatives has been studied by various methods, particularly by synthesis techniques,[6–8] but our understanding of the important cues is far from complete.

The study to be reported here reviews the acoustic theory of the production of fricative consonants. This theory is then used as a point of departure for an analysis of the acoustic spectra of a small sample of fricatives and for an experimental investigation of the synthesis and perception of this class of consonants. Thus, the present study represents an attempt to follow a unified approach, based at the articulatory level, for the examination of fricatives at the acoustical and perceptual levels.

ACOUSTICAL PROPERTIES OF FRICATIVE CONSONANTS

A mid-sagittal section through the vocal tract during production of a typical fricative is shown in Fig. 1. The articulatory configuration is characterized by a rather narrow constriction, the position of which depends upon the particular consonant. Air is forced through this constriction at high velocity, and turbulent flow occurs in the vicinity of the constriction and possibly also at the teeth. Noise is generated as a result of the turbulent flow, and this noise acts as excitation for the acoustic tube that forms the constriction and for the cavities anterior to the constriction. There may also be some acoustical coupling through the constriction to the rear cavities.

Experimental studies suggest that the equivalent plane-wave noise source within the vocal tract has a low internal acoustical impedance and a relatively broad spectrum.[2,9,10] Thus, an equivalent-circuit representation of the production of fricative consonants would have the form shown in Fig. 2. This equivalent circuit differs from the usual vowel circuit representation in several respects: (1) the source is a constant-

* This work was supported in part by the U. S. Army (Signal Corps), the U. S. Air Force (Office of Scientific Research, Air Research and Development Command), and the U. S. Navy (Office of Naval Research); and in part by the U. S. Air Force under contract.

[1] W. Meyer-Eppler, Z. Phonetik, usw. **7**, 196 (1953).
[2] G. Fant, *Acoustic Theory of Speech Production* (Mouton and Company, The Hague, 1960); also Tech. Rept. No. 10, Speech Transmission Laboratory, Royal Institute of Technology, Stockholm, Sweden, 1958.
[3] T. Tarnoczy, Acta Linguistica (Budapest) **4**, 313 (1954).
[4] G. W. Hughes and M. Halle, J. Acoust. Soc. Am. **28**, 303 (1956).
[5] P. Strevens, Language and Speech **3**, 32 (1960).
[6] K. S. Harris, Language and Speech **1**, 1 (1958).
[7] G. Rosen, "Dynamic analog speech synthesizer," Sc.D. thesis, Massachusetts Institute of Technology, January, 1960; also Tech. Rept. No. 353, Research Laboratory of Electronics, Massachusetts Institute of Technology, February, 1960.
[8] K. Nakata, J. Radio Research Lab. (Japan) **7**, 319 (1960).
[9] J. M. Heinz, Mass. Inst. Technol. Acoustics Lab., Quart. Rept. (October–December 1956) p. 5.
[10] J. M. Heinz, Mass. Inst. Technol. Research Lab. Electronics, Quart. Progr. Rept. (July 15, 1958), p. 146.

FIG. 1. Midsagittal section illustrating an articulatory configuration appropriate to the fricative consonant /s/ (adapted from Fant[2]).

589

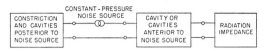

FIG. 2. An equivalent circuit representation of the production of fricative consonants.

pressure noise source rather than a periodic constant-velocity source; (2) the source is located within the vocal tract rather than at the glottis; (3) additional damping is introduced by turbulence losses at the constriction and also by losses at the glottis and below, since the glottis remains somewhat more open than during vowel production in order that air may flow continuously through the tract. These differences indicate that, for fricative consonants, the energy-density spectrum of the acoustic output signal is continuous and is characterized by approximately the same poles (or resonances) as those that characterize a vowel spectrum produced with the same vocal-tract configuration.[11] The poles are simply the natural frequencies of the vocal tract and do not depend on the location of the source.[12] In the case of fricatives, however, usually some of the poles are more heavily damped

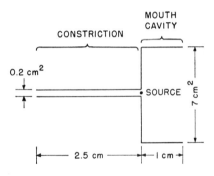

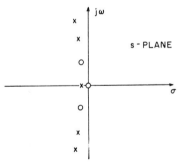

FIG. 3. An idealized model of the vocal tract for the production of the fricative consonant /s/, together with a pole-zero plot of the transfer ratio appropriate to this configuration and source location.

[11] C. G. M. Fant, Mass. Inst. Technol. Acoustics Lab., Tech. Rept. No. 12 (January, 1952).
[12] For a discussion of this property of linear systems, see, for example, E. A. Guillemin, *Synthesis of Passive Networks* (John Wiley & Sons, Inc., New York, 1957), Chap. 1.

because of the additional losses. Zeros (or antiresonances) characterize the output spectra of fricatives at frequencies for which the driving-point impedance of the portion of the vocal tract posterior to the noise source is infinite, i.e., at poles of that impedance. At these frequencies the source is decoupled from the front cavities.

The transfer function relating the sound pressure produced at a distance in front of a speaker to the equivalent source sound pressure (expressed as a function of the complex frequency $s=\sigma+j\omega$) can be described by the product

$$T(s)=[P(s)\cdot R(s)]Z(s), \qquad (1)$$

where $P(s)$ is a function containing the poles that represent the natural frequencies of the vocal tract, $R(s)$ is the radiation characteristic, and $Z(s)$ is a function containing the zeros of the transfer function. The first two factors are approximately the same as those constituting the transfer function for a vowel produced with the same vocal-tract configuration as the fricative. (The vowel transfer function relates the sound pressure at a distance to the volume velocity of the glottal source.) The last factor in Eq. (1), containing the zeros, is dependent on the position of the noise source, and does not occur in the vowel transfer function. Quantitatively, $T(s)$ is of the form

$$T(s) \propto \left[s \cdot \prod_i \frac{s_i s_i^*}{(s-s_i)(s-s_i^*)} \right] \cdot \prod_i \frac{(s-s_j)(s-s_j^*)}{s_j s_j^*}(s-s_g),$$

where $\prod$ denotes a product of terms, s^* denotes the complex conjugate of s, s_i are the poles of the transfer function, s_j are the zeros of the transfer function, and s_g is a real-axis zero dependent upon glottal losses.

A male vocal tract is approximately 17 cm in length, giving rise to resonances spaced, on the average, 1000 cps apart. Since, in a particular example, the source may be posterior to the mouth opening, the average spacing of the antiresonances is more than 1000 cps. If a long narrow constriction is formed in the vocal tract near the mouth opening, some of the resonances and antiresonances tend to move together in pairs in such a way as to cancel any net effect on the spectrum of the output. Since the average spacing of the anti-resonances is greater than that of the resonances, this cancellation cannot obtain throughout the entire frequency range, but is usually effective below the frequency for which the length of the constriction is a quarter wavelength. Above this frequency, there is a region in which there are more poles than zeros and these are sufficiently well separated to permit each to have its individual effect on the spectrum. Thus, a definite formant structure appears, and typically several formants are prominent. In addition, the first formant normally is heavily damped and the bandwidths of the first few formants reflect the presence of losses greater than those typical of vowel production.[2]

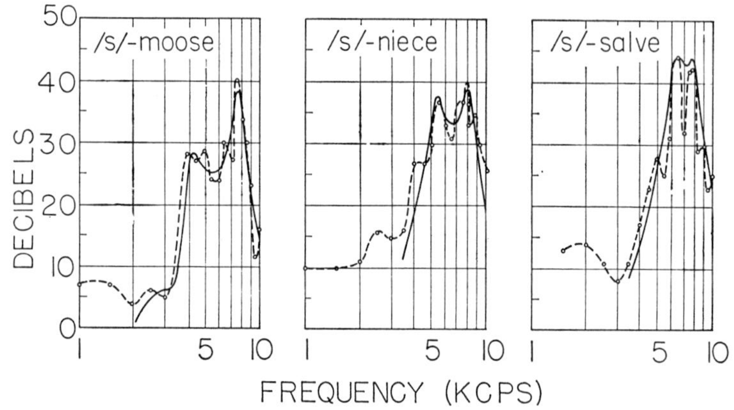

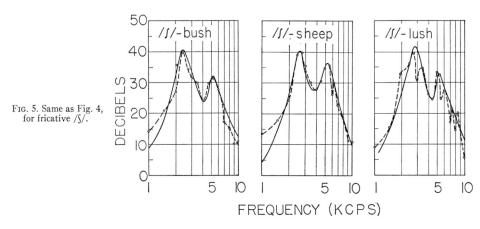

FIG. 4. Comparison of spectra measured by Hughes and Halle[4] for the fricative /s/ as spoken by one subject in different contexts (dashed curves), and spectra obtained as the output of appropriate electric networks (solid curves).

The pole-zero cancellation may also be viewed differently: the cancellation may be considered to occur because the coupling between the source and back cavities is small. Thus, for a vocal-tract configuration with a narrow constriction the output spectrum is approximately unchanged if the back cavities are neglected. The prominent formants in the spectrum are very nearly those arising from the natural frequencies of the front cavities and possibly the constriction. The antiresonances in this approximation are then contributed solely by the constriction. If the constriction is not sufficiently narrow or long, this approximation may not adequately describe the output spectrum.

As an example, consider the highly idealized representation of the /s/ configuration, shown in Fig. 3. The acoustical output of the configuration is characterized by poles whose frequencies are the natural frequencies of the front cavity and of the constriction and by zeros at frequencies for which the impedance looking back from the source is large. For the idealized structure depicted in Fig. 3, there are two poles and one zero in the frequency range below 10 000 cps, at the relative locations shown in the diagram of the s-plane in the figure. The frequency locations for the two poles correspond closely to frequencies for which the length of the constriction

is λ/2 (one-half wavelength) and the length of the front cavity is λ/4, i.e., 6800 and 8600 cps, respectively. The zero is located at a frequency for which the length of the constriction is λ/4, in this case 3400 cps. In this example, it is possible to associate specific resonances with specific cavities because the impedance levels or cross-sectional areas of the two cavities are quite different, and consequently there is relatively little interaction between the two cavities.

Although a model of the type shown in Fig. 3 is highly idealized, it gives results that are in general agreement with measured spectra of spoken fricative consonants. An electrical analog of such a model would be a linear electric circuit whose transfer function is characterized by an appropriate set of poles and zeros.

In Fig. 4 measured spectra[4] for the fricative /s/ as produced by one speaker in several different words are shown as dashed lines. The solid lines show the spectra that were obtained at the output of an appropriate electric circuit when excited by white noise; the transfer function of the circuit from source to output is characterized by two conjugate pairs of poles and by a conjugate pair of zeros. By proper selection of the center frequencies and bandwidths of the poles and zeros, it was possible

FIG. 5. Same as Fig. 4, for fricative /ʃ/.

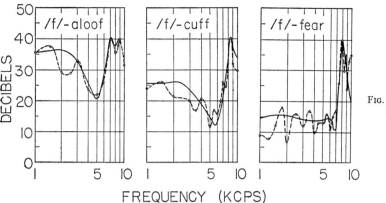

FIG. 6. Same as Fig. 4, for fricative /f/.

to obtain a reasonably good fit to each of the measured spectra, as the figure demonstrates.

Measured spectra for /ʃ/ and /f/ in several contexts are shown as dashed lines in Figs. 5 and 6, respectively. The solid lines are again spectra obtained from simple electric circuits. A circuit having two conjugate pairs of poles and a conjugate pair of zeros was used to generate the /ʃ/ spectra. In addition, the noise source had a spectrum with a slope of +18 db/octave up to 3000 cps and a flat characteristic above 3000 cps. This low-frequency rising characteristic compensates in part for an actual pole-zero pair that occurs in the speech spectrum, typically a zero near 900 cps and a pole (corresponding to the second vowel formant) near 2000 cps. The presence of this pole-zero pair has been verified in close examination of /ʃ/ spectra.[13] The two poles and zero of the circuit for /ʃ/ are located at frequencies higher than the simulated pole-zero pair, but in general they are at lower frequencies than the poles and zero for /s/.

A circuit and source similar to that used for the /s/ spectra was used in the generation of the /f/ spectra in Fig. 6. The frequencies of the principal poles and zeros for /f/ are considerably higher than those for /s/, since the lengths of the constriction and of the cavity anterior to the constriction for /f/ are quite short, of the order of 1 or 2 cm depending to some extent upon whether the adjacent vowel is rounded or unrounded. The half-wavelength resonance (corresponding to a pole in the output spectrum) for a tube of length 2 cm, for example, is about 8000 cps. It was found that some of the /f/ spectra were characterized by broad low-frequency noise in addition to the high-frequency peaks; for these sounds it was necessary to add low-frequency noise electrically in order to obtain good agreement with the measured spectra. A possible source of this low-frequency noise is turbulence at the lips beyond the constriction; this source is relatively uncoupled to the vocal-tract cavities.

[13] J. M. Heinz, J. Acoust. Soc. Am. 32, 1517 (A) (1960).

Table I presents a summary of data for several examples of /ʃ/, /s/, and /f/ in different contexts. The table shows that the variation in pole and zero locations from one version of a fricative to another is often quite large. This variation is evidence of appreciable influence of the adjacent vowel on the articulation of a fricative; additional differences are to be expected from one subject to another. The natural speech spectra shown here were measured with filters having bandwidths of 100 cps, and hence exhibit resonances which have greater bandwidths than do the resonances of actual speech. A more accurate procedure would be to pass the sounds generated by electric circuits through the same filters that are used to measure the speech spectra before comparing the two.

TABLE I. Frequencies and bandwidths (in cps) of poles and zeros of the transfer functions of electric circuits that were used to generate spectra providing good matches with spectra of /ʃ/, /s/, and /f/ spoken in the words shown at the left. The speech spectra are from the data of Hughes and Halle,[4] and are samples of utterances of one speaker. Two poles and one zero were used to match all the spectra. In order to match the spectra of /ʃ/ an additional circuit was added to provide a relatively sharp cut-off for frequencies below 3000 cps, as explained in the text; low-frequency noise was added to the synthesized spectra in order to match some of the /f/ spectra at low frequencies.

Sample	First pole frequency	First pole band width	Second pole frequency	Second pole band width	Zero frequency	Zero band width
/ʃ/-sheep	2400	400	5400	1100	3400	1800
/ʃ/-shack	2200	600	5100	1000	3900	1500
/ʃ/-sure	2500	500	4300	1100	3400	1400
/ʃ/-bush	2200	400	4900	1100	3800	1400
/ʃ/-leash	2400	500	4800	900	3700	1400
/ʃ/-lush	2700	600	5400	900	4400	1600
/s/-sect	6400	900	8000	1400	2900	1100
/s/-soothe	3500	600	8100	700	2700	1100
/s/-salve	5700	800	8000	1200	2900	1100
/s/-moose	4000	600	8000	600	3300	1000
/s/-niece	4900	700	8400	1100	2400	1300
/s/-bus	4600	800	8000	800	2300	1100
/f/-fear	7900	900	8200	900	6800	600
/f/-cuff	8400	1000	12200	1000	5900	1100
/f/-aloof	6800	1000	9000	1100	4600	1000

The general procedure of matching speech spectra with spectra generated by simple linear circuits in order to obtain data on frequency locations of poles and zeros in speech spectra has much to recommend it.[14] Since a match is found over the entire spectrum rather than just at the peaks, it is possible to obtain data that are more accurate than those found by a method that locates spectral peaks or valleys. This is particularly true if the spectrum is noisy so that the formants are not well defined, or if two formants lie close together with the result that the spectrum does not have two separate peaks. In these cases, the additional information gained by considering the effect of a pole or zero over the whole spectrum is quite important.[2] The method also lends itself to an unambiguous definition of a formant frequency as a resonant frequency or pole of the vocal tract which produced the sound.[15,16] A natural frequency of the vocal tract may not always be identical with the frequency of a peak in the spectrum, especially if two formants lie close together. A procedure that takes the entire spectrum shape into account, however, allows a formant frequency to be determined in many cases in which the spectrum does not show an obvious or distinct peak in the vicinity of that frequency.

SYNTHESIS AND PERCEPTION OF FRICATIVE CONSONANTS

Reasonably good approximations to the fricative spectra in Figs. 4–6 could be obtained by white noise excitation of circuits that are characterized by one (conjugate-pair) zero and by only one (conjugate-pair) pole instead of two. The output spectra for such circuits would have the same shapes as the spectra plotted in Figs. 4–6, at least up to a frequency somewhat above the frequency of the first major peak. Examination of a number of spectra from the Hughes-Halle paper[4] suggest that the best simple fit is obtained when the frequency of the zero of the circuit is roughly an octave below the pole frequency. A basic circuit having this property was used for the generation of all stimuli in the perceptual tests to be described here. A typical output spectrum of the circuit when excited by white noise is shown by the solid curve of Fig. 7.

In order to allow for examples of /f/ and /θ/ which may have additional broad low-frequency energy, as mentioned earlier, low-frequency noise was added electrically to some of the basic stimuli that have resonant frequencies above 6500 cps. Typical spectra of the low-frequency noise are shown by the dashed lines in Fig. 7, in which the values 0, −7, and −14 db represent the level of the low-frequency noise relative to the level of the noise in the unmodified stimulus.

<hr />

[14] One of the early attempts to use this technique was reported by D. Lewis [J. Acoust. Soc. Am. 8, 91 (1936)], who matched simple resonance curves to vowel spectra in the vicinity of the spectral peaks.

[15] L. Hermann, Arch. Physiol. 58, 264 (1894).

[16] J. L. Flanagan and A. S. House, J. Acoust. Soc. Am. 28, 1099 (1956).

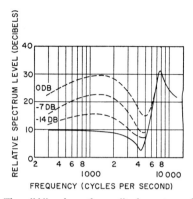

FIG. 7. The solid line shows the amplitude spectrum of a typical stimulus used in the fricative identification tests. When the resonant frequency was 6500 or 8000 cps, some stimuli were modified by the addition of low-frequency noise, yielding spectra like those shown by dashed lines. The parameter is the level of the low-frequency noise relative to the level of the noise in the unmodified stimulus.

The purpose of the perpetual tests to be described here is to determine whether a highly idealized analog circuit characterized by one pole and one zero can generate stimuli that elicit appropriate responses from human listeners, and to establish ranges of pole-zero locations that are associated with particular fricative responses.

Identification of Isolated Synthetic Fricatives

In the first perceptual test, which was an exploratory experiment, sounds of the type described above were generated in isolation. The resonant frequency of the circuit was varied through several values from 2000 to 8000 cps. As noted above, the frequency of the anti-resonance was constrained to lie one octave below the frequency of the resonance. For each resonant frequency, the resonance bandwidth was given three different values that encompassed the range of bandwidths observed in the spectra of fricatives reported by Hughes and Halle. At 2000 cps, the half-power bandwidth values were 170, 300, and 500 cps, and at 8000 cps they were 1000, 1500, and 2000 cps. When the resonant frequency was 6500 or 8000 cps, additional stimuli with three values of low-frequency noise were generated: the levels of low-frequency noise were those shown in Fig. 7.

The stimuli were tape recorded in random order and were presented over a high-quality loudspeaker in a sound-treated studio to a group of six subjects who were asked to identify each by making one of the responses /ʃ,ç,s,θ,f/. Each stimulus was presented four times to each subject in the course of the test. The level of each sound was the same, as measured with a VU meter, and the duration of each sound was fixed at about 200 msec. The subjects were members of the speech research group at the Massachusetts Institute of Technology.

No significant differences in response were obtained over the range of bandwidths used, and consequently

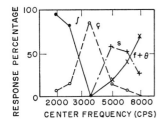

FIG. 8. Results of identification test for isolated synthetic fricative consonants. The abscissa represents the resonant frequency of the electric circuit used to generate the stimuli. Responses of /f/ and /θ/ are combined.

the responses for the three bandwidth values were averaged. In Fig. 8, the response percentages are plotted as a function of the center frequency of the noise for the stimuli that contained no additional low-frequency energy (solid line of Fig. 7, for example). A consistent shift in responses from /ʃ/ to /ç/ to /s/ to /f,θ/ is obtained as the resonant frequency is increased. Distinctions between /f/ and /θ/ could not, apparently, be made for these isolated stimuli, and hence these responses are lumped together. Addition of low-frequency noise to the stimuli with resonant frequencies at 6500 and 8000 cps did not cause an appreciable shift in the pattern of responses; the /f,θ/ responses increased slightly at the expense of /s/ responses.

The results of the exploratory test demonstrate that a consistent pattern of responses is obtained with isolated stimuli. It is reasonable to expect, however, that the identification of a fricative consonant may be dependent not only on the spectrum of the steady-state portion of the sound but also on the formant transitions of the adjacent vowel or vowels and on the intensity of the fricative relative to that of the vowel. In order to examine the role of these cues, it is necessary to generate stimuli consisting of syllables.

Identification of Fricative-Vowel Syllables

The fricative portions of the stimuli in the fricative-vowel syllable test were synthesized in the same manner as those in the test of isolated stimuli. Fricatives with the following five values of resonant frequency were generated: 2500, 3500, 5000, 6500, and 8000 cps. When the resonant frequency was 6500 or 8000 cps, additional stimuli with two levels of low-frequency noise were used, designated 0 and −10 db (cf. Fig. 7). Thus, nine noise spectra were tested, four of which were characterized by additional low-frequency noise. Only one value of bandwidth was selected for each resonant frequency, since the test of isolated fricatives showed that the responses were relatively independent of bandwidth over a 2:1 range in bandwidth. The resonance bandwidths at 2500, 3500, 5000, 6500, and 8000 cps were 400, 600, 800, 1000, and 1500 cps, respectively.

The test syllables consisted of each of the nine noise spectra followed by the synthetic vowel /ɑ/. A schematized intensity-frequency-time pattern of a typical stimulus, together with graphs showing the modulating signals controlling the synthesizer, are shown in Fig. 9.

The vowel was generated by a resonance synthesizer.[17] Timing of fricative onset and decay, vowel onset and decay, and formant transitions was accomplished by a timer and control apparatus designed by Rosen.[7] The over-all level of the fricative relative to the vowel (at the input to the tape recorder) was given three values: −5, −15, and −25 db. The resonant frequencies of the synthesizer were controlled to execute piecewise-linear transitions from a set of starting frequencies or loci[18] to frequencies appropriate to the vowel /ɑ/. The starting frequency for the first-formant transition was 200 cps, and the starting frequency for the second-formant transition was 900, 1700, or 2400 cps; there was no third-formant transition. The time at which the formant frequencies began moving in a piecewise-linear fashion from these starting frequencies was 25 msec prior to the onset of buzz excitation. Stimuli with no vowel transitions were also tested. The 108 stimuli (nine spectra, three levels, four transition values) were tape-recorded in random order and presented twice to a group of listeners. Eight listeners participated, and thus the total number of judgments per stimulus was 16. The stimuli were presented under PDR-8 earphones at a

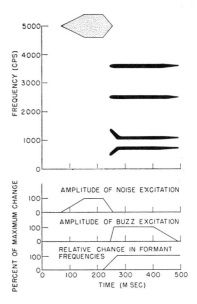

FIG. 9. Schematized description of a typical stimulus used in the identification test for fricative-vowel syllables. The solid bars in the upper part of the figure show how the formant frequencies change as a function of time in the vowel portion of the syllable, including typical transitions at the onset of buzz excitation and the steady formants corresponding to the vowel /ɑ/. The shaded area preceding the vowel depicts the fricative portion of a typical syllable. The lower part of the figure shows the form of the signals used to control the excitation and formant parameters in the synthesizer.

---

[17] K. N. Stevens, J. Audio Eng. Soc. 4, 2 (1956)
[18] P. C. Delattre, A. M. Liberman, and F. S. Cooper, J. Acoust. Soc. Am. 27, 769 (1955).

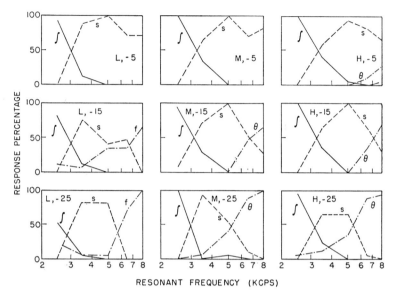

FIG. 10. Results of the identification test for synthetic fricative-vowel syllables. Percentage of responses for eight listeners is plotted as a function of the resonant frequency of the electric circuit used to generate the initial (fricative) portion of the syllable. Three starting frequencies for the transition of the second formant are denoted by *L* (900 cps), *M* (1700 cps), and *H* (2400 cps); the numbers −5, −15, and −25 indicate the over-all level, in decibels, of the fricative portion relative to the vowel portion of the syllable.

comfortable listening level.[19] The subjects were instructed to identify the initial consonant in each syllable as one of /f,θ,s,ʃ/. For the second presentation of the material, they were also instructed to indicate which stimuli they judged to be "natural versions" of the syllables.

The results of the fricative identification test for stimuli with formant transitions are summarized in Fig. 10. The percentages for each consonant response are plotted as a function of the resonant frequency of the synthesizing circuit. For stimuli with no formant transitions the maximum response percentages for each fricative were almost always lower than the best percentages shown in the figure.

Stimuli with resonant frequencies of 6500 or 8000 cps usually yielded /f/ and /θ/ responses, particularly for the lower noise levels. In general, the addition of low-frequency noise to the basic stimuli with these resonant frequencies (see Fig. 7) did not greatly influence the responses, although the response percentages for /f/ and /θ/ were slightly higher when low-frequency noise was present. The points at 6500 and 8000 cps in the curves in Fig. 10 represent data for the 0-db level of low-frequency noise.

Analysis of the "naturalness" responses showed that, in general, stimuli with high response percentages in a particular class were also judged to be "natural" syllables. It may be significant to note, however, that two of the stimuli were judged unanimously to be natural versions of /f/ and /θ/, respectively, whereas no version of /s/ or /ʃ/ received such a unanimous vote.

The data of Fig. 10 for relative fricative levels of −5 and −25 db are replotted and smoothed in Fig. 11. For each fricative level, these response maps indicate regions of resonant frequencies and formant transitions associated with each of the four responses.

Figures 10 and 11 demonstrate that /ʃ/ responses are always associated with resonant frequencies in the vicinity of 2500 cps. These results are in good agreement with the analysis of the Hughes-Halle data in Table I, which shows the frequency of the first major resonance for /ʃ/ to be in the range 2200 to 2700 cps. Responses of /s/ are obtained when the resonant frequency of the stimulus is above 3000 cps, and /f/ and /θ/ responses are obtained for very high frequency resonances,

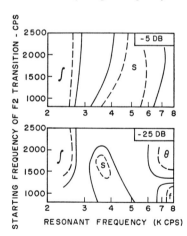

FIG. 11. Results of Fig. 10 are plotted in a different way for over-all levels of the fricative portion relative to the vowel portion of the syllable of −5 and −25 db. The contours show ranges of F2 transitions and resonant frequencies for fricative portions of syllables within which each fricative response is greater than 75% (solid lines) and greater than 90% (dashed lines).

---

[19] Calibration curves of the PDR-8 earphones used in this experiment (measured with a 6-cc coupler) show that there may be fluctuations in the frequency response as great as ±8 db in the frequency range 7000–9000 cps. Since the relative levels described above were measured before the stimuli were transduced, caution should be exercised in applying precise interpretation to certain of the data for stimuli having a resonant frequency of 8000 cps.

especially when the intensity of the fricative is low. The data of Table I are in agreement with these results, since they indicate that the frequency of the first major pole for /s/ is in the range 3500 to 6400 cps and for /f/ is in the range 6800 to 8400 cps. As noted above, the listeners were not unanimous in judging any stimulus to be a "natural" version of /s/ or /ʃ/. It is suggested that a circuit with more than one pole and zero may be necessary if highly natural versions of these fricative consonants are to be synthesized.

The general features of the results shown in Figs. 10 and 11 are similar to those reported by Nakata[8] who studied the synthesis and perception (by Japanese listeners) of the fricative consonants /ʃ,s,f/. The resonant frequencies for greatest /ʃ/ and /s/ responses for Japanese listeners were, however, somewhat higher than the corresponding frequencies in the present experiment, and formant transitions had less influence on the responses of Nakata's listeners.

The effects of the transitions of adjacent vowel formants on the identification of fricative consonants in the present experiment are consistent with the results of fricative identification tests reported by Harris.[6] Harris' stimuli were constructed by combining the noise from one spoken fricative-vowel syllable with the voiced portion of another; the stimuli were presented to listeners for identification as one of the voiceless fricatives of American English. She argued from her results that the important cues for the fricatives /s/ and /ʃ/ are given by the noise, but that differentiation of /f/ and /θ/ is accomplished primarily on the basis of cues contained in the vocalic part of the syllable. The present data lead to similar conclusions: /f/ is distinguished from /θ/ apparently on the basis of the transition of the second formant in the adjacent vowel, whereas formant transitions do not have an appreciable effect on /s/ and /ʃ/ responses, particularly when the intensity of the fricative is high.

It is well known that the locus or apparent starting frequency for the second formant ($F2$) of a vowel preceded by a consonant such as a stop or fricative gives some indication of the articulatory configuration used to generate the consonant.[18,20,21] In general, tests with synthetic speech and studies with vocal-tract analogs have shown that $F2$ loci of low frequency (1000 cps or less) are associated with bilabial or labio-dental configurations; $F2$ loci in the middle frequency range (1500 to 2000 cps) are associated with alveolar configurations; and $F2$ loci above 2000 cps are associated with palatal configurations. These loci are probably influenced to some extent by the adjacent vowel and are only approximate. The present data relating to formant transitions appropriate to the articulation of fricative consonants are in general agreement with these findings, although precise comparisons are, of course, not possible since the scope of the present experiment is rather limited.

SUMMARY AND CONCLUSIONS

In this paper an acoustical theory of the production of voiceless fricative consonants is reviewed, and it is shown that the results of analyses of spectra of these consonants are consistent with the theory. Simplified versions of fricative consonants, generated in accordance with the theory, are demonstrated to elicit responses that are in agreement with the results of the spectral analyses. Although the data presented here are not of sufficient scope to be considered as general descriptions of fricative consonants as they occur in all phonetic contexts and as they are produced by many different talkers, they nevertheless suggest a method of approach for further study of these and other classes of speech sounds.

ACKNOWLEDGMENTS

The authors wish to express their appreciation to Jane Arnold and Kazuo Nakata, who administered the listening tests, and to Arthur House, who provided helpful comment and discussion during the course of the work.

[20] R. K. Potter, G. A. Kopp, and H. C. Green, *Visible Speech* (D. Van Nostrand Company, Inc., Princeton, New Jersey, 1947).
[21] K. N. Stevens and A. S. House, J. Acoust. Soc. Am. **28**, 578 (1956).

Reprinted from THE JOURNAL OF THE ACOUSTICAL SOCIETY OF AMERICA, Vol. 33, No. 3, 268–277, March, 1961
Copyright, 1961 by the Acoustical Society of America.

Transitions, Glides, and Diphthongs*

ILSE LEHISTE AND GORDON E. PETERSON

Communication Sciences Laboratory, The University of Michigan, Ann Arbor, Michigan

The study deals with the formant movements associated with transitions, glides, and diphthongs in spoken American English. The transitional characteristics associated with all initial and final consonant phonemes were studied in a large sample of utterances. The rate of change of the transition from a consonant hub to the steady state vowel formant position and conversely was investigated for vowels which are commonly considered monophthongs. It is assumed that such changes are cues for the perception of the consonants rather than linguistically significant components of the vocalic nucleus. The rate of change associated with syllable nuclei commonly perceived as diphthongs, [aɪ], [ɔɪ], [aʊ] was investigated and compared with the changes due to consonant transitions in monophthongs. Criteria are suggested by which the formant movements due to transitions may be distinguished from movements that have linguistic signalling value within the syllable nucleus.

INTRODUCTION

THE purpose of the present study is to investigate the distinction between formant movements which serve as cues for consonant identification and formant movements which signal the presence of a complex syllable nucleus, such as a glide or a diphthong. The set of material that was analyzed has been described in a previous publication.[1] Briefly, the materials include 1263 monosyllabic CNC words (consonant phoneme—syllable nucleus—consonant phoneme) recorded by one speaker, and a control set of 70 words, uttered by five speakers of the same general dialect. All words were recorded in random order in an identical sentence frame, with determined stress and pitch patterns. The total set was analyzed acoustically by various techniques.

For this present study, the following measurements were made: the frequencies of the first three formants at the beginning of the onglide, measured from the

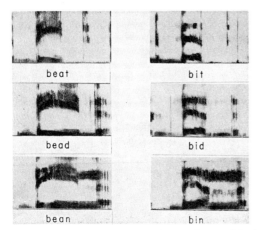

FIG. 1. Broad band spectrograms of six words uttered by informant GEP, illustrating formant transitions associated with the vowels /i/ and /ɪ/ followed by dental-alveolar consonants.

beat | bit
bead | bid
bean | bin

release of the consonant; the duration of the onglide from the consonant release to the steady state of the syllable nucleus; the formant positions at the steady state; the duration of the steady state; the frequencies of the first three formants at the end of the offglide; and the duration of the offglide.[2] We thus have information about the transitional formant movements associated with each initial and final consonant phoneme, information about the formant frequencies associated with the syllable nuclei, and data for calculating the rates of change associated with each formant movement.

If the rate and direction of formant movements are predictable from the combination of the formant positions of the vowel and the consonant loci, it seems that the movements would serve as cues for the identity of the consonant. The influence which such movements have upon the perception of vowel quality in monophthongs is also an interesting question for future study. If two vowel targets appear between the initial and final consonants of the CNC words, the syllable nucleus is a diphthong. It is possible that if only one target is present, the rate of change associated with either the onglide or the offglide may produce a linguistic contrast. The so-called glide phonemes that occur in some languages may fall in this category.

CONSONANT TRANSITIONS

Previous research about the interaction between vowels and consonants has resulted in the "hub"[3] and "locus"[4] theories. The "hub" theory associates with each consonant a relatively fixed frequency position for the second formant transitions; the "locus" theory adds the requirement that the direction of the movement be taken into consideration and extends the concept to all formants. Both theories appear to assume that the steady state position of the vowel formants remains

---

* This research was supported under contract by the Information Systems Branch of the Office of Naval Research of the U. S. Navy.

[1] G. E. Peterson and I. Lehiste, J. Acoust. Soc. Am. **32**, 693 (1960).

[2] For the purposes of this study, we have defined onglide as the initial transition from the consonant to the vowel target, and offglide as the final transition from the vowel target to the consonant.

[3] R. K. Potter, G. A. Kopp, and H. C. Green, *Visible Speech* (D. Van Nostrand Company, Inc., Princeton, New Jersey, 1947).

[4] P. C. Delattre, A. M. Liberman, and F. S. Cooper, J. Acoust. Soc. Am. **27**, 769 (1955).

essentially the same regardless of the preceding and following consonants. The frequency of the beginning of the onglide and the end of the offglide is commonly assumed to remain relatively constant for the different sets of consonants produced at the same point of articulation. In the literature dealing with the loci of different consonants, it appears furthermore that the frequencies of the initial and final terminations of the transitions are considered to be identical. While the "hub" theory may be considered a generalization from observations made from the speech of several informants (two main informants, one male, one female), the "locus" values are essentially based on one idiolect, that of the pattern playback. The "hub" and "locus" concepts are both valuable as attempts to extract a pattern from the great diversity of actually occurring speech events. It should be kept in mind, however, that this diversity exists. A detailed analysis of additional idiolects may yield values that differ considerably from currently accepted "hub" or "locus" values.

Some of our data show considerable divergence from previously published locus positions; we have also observed directional patterns which differ from those used for establishing the loci of consonants. In our materials, the transitions also differ considerably depending upon the position of the consonant relative to the vowel. Some general illustrations of this fact are presented in Figs. 1–3. A more detailed consideration of second formant transitions is given in the discussion of some of the later tables.

Figure 1 illustrates the formant transitions associated with the vowels [i] and [ɪ] followed by [t], [d], and [n]. The second formant of the vowel [i] in the words *beat, bead,* and *bean* moves toward a frequency of approximately 2000 cps; the second formant of [ɪ] in *bit, bid,* and *bin* ends in the frequency range of 1400 cps. Both transitions are negative. The expected second formant locus position for the alveolar consonants is approximately 1800 cps; while this value could be obtained by extending the slope of the second formant in

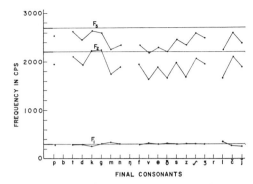

FIG. 2. Positions of the first three formants of the vowel /i/ at the end of the offglide toward all final consonants, based on 105 CNC words uttered by informant GEP.

beat and *bead,* an extension of the falling formant in *bit* and *bid* would yield an even greater difference between the expected value and the measured value.

Given the general direction of the movement, the transition associated with the offglide depends further on whether the following consonant is voiced or voiceless. In the case of voiced final consonants, the preceding syllable nucleus is relatively longer, and the transition proceeds to a frequency value that is greater in a positive transition, or smaller in a negative transition, than the corresponding value before a voiceless consonant. Figure 2 illustrates the formant positions (F_1, F_2, F_3) for the vowel [i] at the end of the offglide toward all final consonants. The values are averaged from the 105 words containing [i] as the syllable nucleus in the larger corpus. Each point represents the average for all occurrences of the [i]+C sequence. The average [i] target positions of the formants are also indicated by the thin horizontal lines, so that the direction of the movement may be inferred. Except for the pair /k/–/g/, the transitions proceed to a lower frequency value when a voiced consonant follows the [i]; the second formant transitions toward both /k/ and /g/ are positive, and

TABLE I. Average formant positions measured at the target.

Syllable nucleus	Averages for 1263 CNC words spoken by GEP			Averages for 350 CNC words spoken by 5 speakers		
	F_1	F_2	F_3	F_1	F_2	F_3
i	315	2200	2700	320	2205	2800
ɪ	415	1750	2470	410	1755	2415
eᴵ	360	2015	2510	335	2105	2630
ɛ	570	1610	2465	540	1705	2415
æ	640	1570	2460	625	1740	2415
ə	610	1185	2565	585	1155	2255
ɑ	645	1110	2540	665	1145	2520
ɔ	505	880	2525	590	985	2365
oᵁ	495	960	2495	435	905	2435
ʊ	450	980	2360	400	1015	2090
u	355	895	2240	350	845	2105
ɑʊ	655–510	1255– 910	2520–2415	655–415	1235– 870	2215–2225
ɑɪ	665–485	1200–1790	2540–2450	700–375	1315–1975	2360–2585
ɔɪ	510–505	900–1610	2510–2425	550–370	950–1830	2255–2485
ɝ	475	1245	1680	430	1255	1575

TABLE II. Frequency ranges of second formant transitions.

F_2 "hub"	Labial Initial	Labial Final		Dental-alveolar Initial	Dental-alveolar Final		Velar Initial	Velar Final		Palatal Initial	Palatal Final
p	1725 ɪ / 1335 / 1075 ʊ	1960 i / 1225 / 720 u	t	1825 i / 1695 / 1600 ɔɪ	2105 i, eᴵ / 1485 / 1065 u	k	1360 oᵁ / 1285 / 1200 ʊ	1045 ʊ / 890 / 680 oᵁ	c	2200 i / 1880 / 1495 ɑ	2245 i / 1785 / 1195 ɑ
b	1780 i / 1205 / 900 ɔ	1300 ɑɪ / 1010 / 750 oᵁ, u	d	1785 i / 1575 / 1535 ɑ	1960 i / 1465 / 1250 ɑᵁ	g	1325 u / 1290 / 1225 ɔ	1055 ɔ / 945 / 830 oᵁ	ɟ	2110 eᴵ / 1875 / 1465 ɝ	2250 i / 1770 / 1100 ɑ
m	1780 i / 1185 / 825 oᵁ	1755 i / 1160 / 705 oᵁ	n	1740 i / 1450 / 1290 ɔ	1900 i / 1430 / 1180 oᵁ	ŋ		950 ɔ	ɲ		2110 ɪ / 1770 / 1130 ə
Average	1240	1130		1575	1460		1285	930		1875	1775
f	1825 i / 1210 / 800 ɔɪ	1960 i / 1355 / 800 oᵁ, u	θ	1625 i / 1385 / 1190 ɔ	1935 i / 1375 / 1100 oᵁ				ʃ	1955 i / 1650 / 1390 ɔ	2100 i / 1700 / 965 ʊ
v	1650 i / 1270 / 960 ɔɪ	1650 i / 1205 / 815 oᵁ	ð	1575 i / 1400 / 1250 oᵁ	1665 i / 1395 / 1200 oᵁ				č	1995 i / 1610 / 1325 ɔ	2140 i / 1455 / 1050 u
			s	1685 i / 1430 / 1290 ɔ, ɝ	2000 i / 1560 / 1400 ʊ				ǰ	1865 ɪ / 1740 / 1600 ɔɪ	1925 i / 1490 / 1175 ɑᵁ
			z	1625 i / 1400 / 1200 oᵁ	1700 i / 1480 / 1300 ɑᵁ						
Average	1240	1280		1405	1455					1665	1550
Combined average	1240	1190		1475	1455		1285	930		1750	1665

the second formant proceeds, on the average, toward a higher frequency for the voiced member of the pair. The over-all curve has a certain resemblance to the duration curve presented in the previously indicated paper.[1]

The average value for [i] was taken from Table I which also contains the average target positions for all syllable nuclei included in the study. The smaller corpus of 350 words does not contain a sufficient number of occurrences of each initial and final consonant to offer a reliable comparison with the 1263-word CNC list;

the target values of the syllable nuclei, however, have been included in Table I.[5]

Figure 2 should be compared with Fig. 3, representing formant positions at the onset of the vowel [i] after all consonants.[6] In Fig. 2 it could be seen that voicing of the final consonant influenced the termination of the off-glide, but voicing or voicelessness appears to have no clearly discernible influence on the beginning of the onglide. It should be noted that for corresponding consonants the initiations of the onglides for formants 2 and 3 are, in general, appreciably different from the terminations of the offglides for these formants. Compare, for example, the points for /t/ in Figs. 2 and 3.

A study of specific transitions associated with each consonant-vowel combination is not the primary purpose of this paper; therefore, only the initial and final transitions of the second formant will be given more detailed consideration. Table II contains a summary of the data for the second formant.

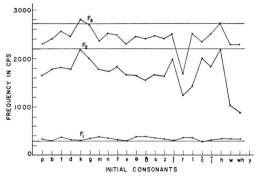

FIG. 3. Positions of the first three formants of the vowel /i/ at the onset of the vowel after all initial consonants, based on 105 CNC words uttered by informant GEP.

[5] The accuracy of formant measurements was within ±25 cps; repeated measurements differed by no more than that amount. The values included in the tables represent averages of these measurements, rounded to the nearest 5 cycles.

[6] The number of actual occurrences of each C+[i] and [i]+C sequence in the CNC list may be seen from Tables II and III of the paper by the present authors on "Transitions, glides, and diphthongs," Studies of Syllable Nuclei, Part II, SRL Rept. No. 4, Ann Arbor (1960). The report contains several additional tables.

The four columns show the average initial and final transitions associated with the labial, dental-alveolar, velar, and palatal consonants. Transitions to and from all vowels were combined in computing the table. Initial transitions will be considered first. It has been suggested that the second formant locus for labials is located at approximately 700 cps, the second formant locus for dental-alveolar consonants at 1800 cps, and that there are two loci for velar consonants, one at a low frequency value, and the other at approximately 3000 cps. If these values are to represent generally applicable locus positions for American English consonants, then in analyzing the speech of various native speakers of standard American English, we should expect to find similar loci with a fairly small range of variation for the combination of each consonant with different vowels. The Table contains both the average beginnings of transitions and the range of average values observed in the corpus. As may be seen from Table II, the average initial transitions for labials began considerably higher than 700 cps for this speaker. The beginning of the onglide from /p/ to a following vowel ranged from 1725 for /pɪ/ to 1075 cps for /pʊ/; similar large variations were observed for all labials. The dental-alveolar series appears to be associated with an initial transition beginning at approximately 1475 cps rather than 1800 cps, as postulated by the locus theory. In this case, the range of fluctuation is somewhat smaller than in the case of labials, but there is a complete overlap of the ranges for the two sets: the highest average initial transition value, associated with /fi/, was 1825 cps, which is identical with the average transition value associated with /ti/, and the lower extreme of the initial hubs associated with the dentals falls within the lower range of the labials. It is difficult to generalize that the palatals and velars are associated with two hubs, considering the very gradual changes in vowel onset frequency associated with the various allophones of the /k/ and /g/ phonemes. The values for velars in Table II were computed for the five syllable nuclei, [ɔ oʊ ʊ u ɔɪ]; the values for palatals are averaged over the ten remaining syllable nuclei, but the range from 2200 cps for [ci] to 1495 cps for [kɑ] is quite extensive. It might be added that there is a similar gradual scale of onset frequencies associated with /ʃ/ and /č/, phonetically realized as [tʃ]; it appears that if two allophones are assumed for /k/ ([k] and [c]), the allophones of /ʃ/ and /č/ should be described in an analogous way.

Even greater fluctuations are found in final position than were observed in connection with initial transitions. The range of final hubs for labials is from an average of 1960 cps for the sequence /ip/ to 705 cps for the sequence /oʊm/; the average value of 1190 cps becomes rather meaningless under such circumstances. The final dental-alveolar consonants have an average hub position at 1455 cps, with a range of from approximately 2100 cps for the sequences /it/ and /eɪt/ to

about 1065 cps characterizing the average final hub that occurred in the sequence /ut/.

The various final allophones of /k/ present a somewhat different picture from the initial allophones. While the initial /k/ followed by /ə/ and /ɑ/ appeared to pattern with the allophones followed by front vowels (i.e., had relatively high hubs), allophones of /k/ appearing in final position after /ə/ and /ɑ/ belong clearly in the group characterized by a low hub position. The range for the velars and palatals together (i.e., the range associated with all allophones of the /k/ phoneme) extends from 2245 cps for /ik/ to 680 cps for /oʊk/, which is quite comparable to the range observed for the labials.

Other consonants exhibit similar fluctuations. It appears from our data, furthermore, that the vowel allophones associated with the different consonants show considerable modifications due to the influence of the consonant. (This part of the data will be discussed in a separate publication.) There seems to be no evidence that in the interaction between two sounds in sequence one will remain constant; however, the locus values seem to have been obtained by keeping the vowels constant and varying the consonant transitions. From a linguistic point of view, an allophone is a variant of a phoneme, whose phonetic shape is determined by its environment. Of two sounds in sequence, each constitutes part of the environment of the other; thus a mutual interaction between them might be expected. It may well be that for purposes of automatic speech recognition, it is necessary to specify the beginning of the onglide and the end of the offglide for each consonant and vowel combination separately. If rules for predicting the extent of the influence of consonants upon vowel formants and conversely can be established, such rules should be incorporated in the instructions.

Detailed tabulations of the frequency positions of the beginning of the onglide and the end of the offglide for the first three formants for each of the syllable nuclei, and for the initial and final consonants for the 1263 CNC words, uttered by one speaker, are presented in Tables V–X of the report referred to in footnote 6.

The values listed in Table II are based on measurements made at the point of transition between vowel and consonant; the locus theory also requires a consideration of the slope of the formant at the point of transition. As mentioned above in connection with Fig. 1, we have observed that in a considerable number of instances, even when the syllable nucleus is a monophthong and the initial and final consonants are the same phoneme (in such words as *bib, did, cease*), both the terminal transition values and the slopes are different for the onglides and offglides. A further complication is that in many instances, particularly in the case of certain final transitions (for example, /k/ and /g/ after front vowels), the second formant has a positive transition, while the third formant has a negative transition. If lines are drawn through the centers of the

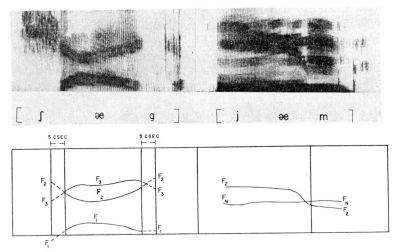

FIG. 4. Broad band spectrograms of the word *shag* uttered by GEP, and the word *yam* uttered by a dysarthric patient. The graphs below the spectrograms represent tracings of the formant positions from the spectrograms.

formants and are continued with their original slopes, they intersect at a value between the two offglide terminal positions. This case is illustrated by the tracing of the spectrogram for [ʃæg] in Fig. 4. For some consonants, previous work with synthesized speech[4] has suggested locus positions for F_2 that are considerably higher than the intersection of the lines drawn as continuations of the two formants. If formants are numbered in ascending order, it appears inconsistent that F_2 should have a locus that is higher than the locus of F_3. The intersection of the lines drawn to represent the continuation of F_2 and F_3 represents a point at which $F_2 = F_3$, and beyond that point the lower in frequency of the two could be called F_2, although the lower line represents a continuation of F_3. If it were possible to assign a single formant to a single cavity resonance, it would seem entirely plausible that the resonance frequencies could overlap. The apparent crossing of formants in the second spectrogram of Fig. 4 indicates that this may occasionally be possible. The spectrogram is for the word *yam* pronounced by a dysarthric patient. A steady nasal resonance may be observed throughout the vowel, and appears to continue into the nasal consonant. The second oral formant of the vowel [æ] apparently crosses this nasal formant during the transition period from the target position of [æ] to [m]. If loci could be defined in terms of specific cavity resonances, perhaps a higher locus for F_2 than for F_3 could be given a satisfactory explanation. From our data it appears that loci established for second formants without considering the directions of the transitions of the third formants are open to question.

DURATION OF TRANSITIONS AND RATE OF CHANGE

In order to compare the relative durations of the onglide, target, and offglide, it appeared necessary to establish a working rule as to what constitutes a target.

The time interval within the syllable nucleus where the formants are parallel to the time axis has been considered the extent of a vowel target. The minimum duration of such a time interval was arbitrarily chosen as 2 csec. There were some instances where no fixed target appeared, but usually somewhere within the syllable nucleus there was a noticeable change in the slope of the moving formant which suggested a target. In addition, the intonation pattern was often helpful in determining the position of the target, since the peak of the intonation contour associated with the CNC word usually coincided with the target of the syllable nucleus. Some uncertainty in determining the actual durations could not be avoided; however, the uncertainty did not appear sufficiently great to affect significantly the general pattern of values which was obtained.

There appear to be many factors which influence the duration of the transition from the release of the initial consonant to the target position of the vowel. To determine whether these durations are used as distinctive characteristics of the vowels, the average durations of initial transitions for all consonant-vowel combinations were computed for the 1263 utterances; these appear in Table III.

This Table shows considerable variation in the durations associated with the different initial consonants and also in the durations associated with the same consonant followed by different vowels. Some generalizations may be made from the variations. It appears that labials usually have shorter initial transitions than lingual consonants. A possible explanation lies in the fact that the tongue does not participate essentially in the articulation of an initial labial consonant but remains free to move toward the articulatory position of the following vowel during the consonant formation. Thus in many instances the transition from a labial consonant to a vowel is shorter than a transition from a lingually articulated consonant to the same vowel. For example,

TABLE III. Average duration of initial transition in centiseconds for 1263 CNC words.

	i	ɪ	eᴵ	ɛ	æ	ə	ɑ	ɔ	oᵁ	ʊ	u	aᵁ	aɪ	ɔɪ	ɝ	Average
p	8.9	4.4	17.5	5.7	8.4	4.4	5.2	8.0	3.2	4.2	4.7	4.3	5.2	10.0	5.7	6.7
b	6.6	4.3	15.8	4.8	4.9	3.7	3.8	3.3	2.2	2.0	3.3	3.0	4.0	4.0	4.0	5.1
t	11.2	2.6	14.0	3.5	8.0	7.3	6.0	8.2	9.3	7.0	9.0	7.0	8.1	10.0	10.0	7.9
d	8.2	4.0	16.2	4.8	6.2	6.2	5.8	6.4	6.7	...	7.5	6.0	5.7	...	7.0	6.8
k	10.0	6.6	18.2	9.0	9.8	8.5	6.6	6.6	6.3	6.7	7.0	6.0	6.0	7.0	9.1	8.8
g	8.0	3.4	14.9	6.0	7.4	7.0	7.0	6.7	6.8	7.0	6.0	8.0	7.0	...	5.3	7.8
m	4.8	3.3	12.7	5.2	4.0	3.2	2.7	3.6	2.3	...	2.2	2.0	2.8	...	5.0	4.5
n	7.3	3.0	13.5	2.8	4.3	4.0	3.7	4.5	4.8	4.0	2.6	4.0	4.2	6.0	9.0	4.9
f	6.0	3.6	15.7	3.8	5.8	3.3	4.0	3.2	2.3	2.0	3.0	4.0	1.8	2.0	2.0	5.3
v	7.0	4.0	15.5	...	8.0	...	...	...	3.5	...	...	4.5	3.4	2.3	6.0	6.4
θ	8.3	2.0	17.0	...	4.0	4.0	...	3.3	...	...	...	...	3.0	...	6.0	5.3
ð	8.0	6.0	14.9	6.3	4.0	...	...	...	3.0	...	...	...	4.0	...	...	5.2
s	6.8	3.1	13.7	4.2	4.5	4.1	5.2	4.0	4.5	4.0	3.6	4.3	3.8	4.0	5.3	5.5
z	6.0	...	...	...	...	6.0	...	7.0	...	4.0	...	...	...	...	...	5.7
ʃ	5.0	2.3	14.0	4.5	6.0	6.8	5.0	7.5	6.0	4.7	5.0	7.0	5.5	...	4.0	6.3
r	5.6	6.3	14.3	7.0	7.1	3.9	5.0	5.0	4.2	2.0	4.1	4.0	3.9	4.0	...	6.2
l	6.3	4.5	12.9	6.6	7.5	2.2	3.0	2.0	2.0	2.0	3.2	3.3	2.9	2.0	4.7	4.9
č	4.2	2.2	12.8	4.3	5.5	5.0	4.5	6.0	5.0	...	3.0	...	6.0	4.0	4.3	5.2
ǰ	6.0	2.3	17.7	6.8	7.5	8.7	7.2	8.0	7.0	...	5.3	8.0	6.0	6.0	7.0	7.0
h	3.4	2.4	12.0	1.6	2.6	3.1	3.0	3.3	3.2	2.5	6.2	3.0	2.4	...	3.8	3.4
w	4.7	6.7	12.5	8.2	10.0	2.0	7.3	3.6	4.0	2.0	2.0	...	4.3	...	5.6	6.4
wh	7.0	7.6	12.0	10.3	8.0	...	6.0	...	...	...	...	...	2.7	...	4.0	7.2
y	...	4.0	8.0	5.3	5.5	8.0	4.5	7.0	6.0	6.0	5.3	...	...	...	8.0	5.8
aver.	6.6	4.2	14.7	5.4	6.2	4.9	5.2	4.9	4.5	4.0	4.4	5.1	4.3	5.0	5.8	

the average duration of the transition in the sequence /pu/ is 4.7 csec, compared to 9.0 csec for the sequence /tu/. It appears also that there is much more variability in the durations associated with the different vowels following the same lingually articulated consonant than there is in the case where the different vowels follow a labial consonant. For example, the duration of the transition in the sequence /tɪ/ is, on the average, 2.6 csec, and for the sequence /tu/ 9.0 csec; /pɪ/ and /pu/ have average transitions of 4.4 and 4.7 csec. The tongue movement for /tu/ is clearly much more extensive than for /tɪ/. Apparently the tongue anticipates the articulatory position to a considerable extent in /pɪ/ and /pu/.

A study of Table III also reveals other facts about the transitions for this particular speaker. For example, there is very little difference in the duration of the transition from /k/ to front and back vowels. The reason may be found in the fact that the point of articulation for /k/ shifts with the vowel. This change is reflected in the continuous range of transition frequencies associated with the various allophones of /k/. Shorter transitions are, in general, more closely associated with voiced initial consonants than with voiceless initial consonants. It may also be noted that in some instances /h/ appears to have a definite articulatory position of its own; in sequences such as /hu/ and /hɝ/, the liprounding and the retroflection seem to occur during the pronunciation of the vowel.

It appears that the duration of the initial transition is essentially physiologically conditioned. Except for the syllable nucleus /eᴵ/, to be discussed later, the differ-ences in rate of change due to differences in the duration of the initial transition are probably not significant in determining the linguistic interpretation of the vowel. The exact relationships between the rate of articulatory change and the corresponding changes in the resonances can probably best be determined by correlating x-ray studies of articulation with acoustic analysis of the produced sequences.[7]

The rate of change of a vowel formant may be specified as the frequency range in cycles per second through which the formant moves in a given time interval. The interpretation of the rate is complicated, however, by the fact that the initial transitions appear conditioned physiologically. The interpretation is also complicated by the fact that the following consonant in the case of a final transition not only conditions the frequency at which the transition terminates, but also the duration of the preceding syllable nucleus. In such pairs as *bit-bid*, there are differences in both duration of the syllable nucleus and the frequency position of the termination of the offglide which influence the rate of formant transition. Such differences, however, do not cause either of these syllable nuclei to be perceived as glides or diphthongs.

The rate of formant change has been investigated extensively with synthetic speech,[8,9] and the contrast

[7] H. M. Truby, *Acta Radiologica, Supplementum* 182 (Stockholm, 1959).

[8] A. M. Liberman, P. C. Delattre, L. J. Gerstman, and F. S. Cooper, J. Exptl. Psychol. **52**, 127 (1956).

[9] J. D. O'Connor, L. J. Gerstman, A. M. Liberman, P. C. Delattre, and F. S. Cooper, Word **13**, 24 (1957).

between such combinations as [u]+[i] and [w]+[i] can be described in terms of rate of change. According to our data, however, such a contrast is not utilized within the linguistic signalling system of the English speech we analyzed. This type of change may be illustrated with examples from Finnish. In that language, a sequence of vowel plus vowel may contrast with a sequence of semivowel plus vowel in such word pairs as *iäinen* "eternal" vs *jäinen* "icy." In the analysis of a number of contrasts of this type the formant frequencies associated with the targets remained constant, but the change in the rate of formant movement produced a meaningful difference. As another illustration, the diphthongs [ui] and [iu] in Estonian may be compared with the semivowel+vowel sequences /wi/ and /yu/ in English. Again, the slopes of the transitions and the durations of the target positions were the only differences, since the formant positions were identical for the same speaker.

It appears that if the target position remains constant, the slope of the transition is a criterion for defining the difference between diphthongs and glides. The movement in frequency of any one formant, however, is not sufficient to describe the characteristic properties of the syllable nuclei. The changes in the total formant pattern reflect changes in the total articulatory configuration. In the next section it is considered that the time taken to produce this total change, relative to the total duration of the syllable nucleus, may be a criterion for defining characteristic differences among syllable nuclei.

CLASSIFICATION OF SYLLABLE NUCLEI

In the preceding paper[1] the data confirmed previous suggestions that, as a first approximation, syllable nuclei

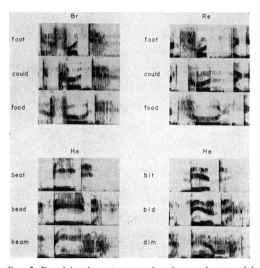

Fig. 5. Broad band spectrograms for nine words uttered by three informants. The words illustrate the difference in the relative durations of the targets and offglides for the tense vowels /u/ and /i/, as compared with the lax vowels /ʊ/ and /ɪ/.

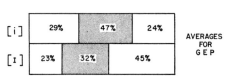

Fig. 6. Relative durations of the onglide, target, and offglide for /i/ and /ɪ/ in CNC words. Averages for the large corpus spoken by GEP are compared with the averages for five speakers of the control set.

may be divided into short and long. The short vowels, [ɪ ɛ ə ʊ], all appear to be monophthongs. An examination of the changes in the formant patterns associated with these vowels shows that they have an additional feature in common. They contrast with the long vowels [i æ ɑ ɔ u] in the relative durations of the two stages we have called target and offglide. The four short vowels have a relatively long offglide and a correspondingly shorter target; the long vowels have a relatively longer target and a shorter offglide.

Figure 5 illustrates the difference in the relative durations of the targets and offglides for two contrasts, /u/−/ʊ/ and /i/−/ɪ/. The contrasts for /u/ and /ʊ/ were uttered by two different speakers, Br and Re; those for /i/−/ɪ/ were spoken by He. The significant difference for the two sets of contrasting vowels is the duration of the offglide relative to the duration of the total syllable nucleus, and not the absolute duration of the transition or the rate of formant change.

Figure 6 compares the relative durations of the three stages for all occurrences of the vowels /i/ and /ɪ/ in both sets of data. The durations are expressed in percentage of total duration to allow for the differences in intrinsic duration. Table IV presents the relative durations in percent of the three formant stages for all syllable nuclei in both sets of data.

Thus it appears that the characteristic difference between the long and short monophthongs may be described as a difference in the articulatory rate of change associated with the movement from target position to the following consonant. The traditional terminology "lax" and "tense" seems appropriate to label this difference. "Lax" vowels, then, are those vowels whose production involves a short target position and a slow relaxation of the hold; for "tense" vowels the target position is maintained for a longer time, and the (articulatory) movement away from the target position is relatively rapid. The relationships of the three stages to the total duration remain approximately constant,

TABLE IV. Relative duration in percent of targets and transitions.

Syllable nucleus	Averages for 1263 CNC words spoken by GEP			Averages for 350 CNC words uttered by five speakers		
	Onglide	Target	Offglide	Onglide	Target	Offglide
i	29	47	24	28	50	22
ɪ	23	32	45	15	36	49
eᴵ	50	30	20	46	39	15
ɛ	23	34	43	17	40	43
æ	20	53	27	22	40	38
ə	24	41	35	31	39	30
ɑ	18	60	22	14	65	21
ɔ	16	59	25	15	56	29
oᵁ	15	25	60	12	42	46
ʊ	19	40	41	28	29	43
u	17	63	20	20	56	24

	Onglide	Target 1	Glide	Target 2	Offglide	Onglide	Target 1	Glide	Target 2	Offglide
ɑʊ	16	26	27	16	15	19	26	27	12	16
ɑɪ	12	26	31	17	14	21	30	28	15	6
ɔɪ	13	25	30	17	15	15	20	33	18	14
ɝ	22	31			47	10	40			50

regardless of the fluctuation in duration produced by the following consonant. The tense-lax opposition becomes particularly significant when the difference in intrinsic duration is neutralized, as for example in such pairs as *beat-bid* shown in Fig. 5.

The remaining syllable nuclei may be classified again into two groups. The first group, /eᴵ/, /oᵁ/, and /ɝ/, have only one steady state each, and therefore should not properly be classed as diphthongs. Phonetically, these single-target complex nuclei are difficult to segment into a sequence of two sounds. There is no steady state for the first element of /eᴵ/, but a slow glide appears toward the target position, the glide being longer than the target. Often the first part of /eᴵ/ has been called the "full vowel" and the second element the glide or semivowel. In the dialect under study, it is actually the second element that has a steady state and the first element that is phonetically a glide—longer than any other onglide. If the second formant onset position for /eᴵ/ is lower than approximately 1800 cps, the movement of the formant is normally smooth. However, if the preceding consonant is characterized by a higher second formant onset frequency, as in the case of /k/, /g/, /ʃ/, /č/, /ǰ/, the second formant performs a movement toward a frequency of approximately 1800 cps and glides from there toward the second formant target position of approximately 2000 cps. The formant movement is continuous, however, in such instances, and no target according to our definition can be located. The duration of the onglide from the consonant toward this minimum is approximately 30% of the total, and the glide from this minimum toward the steady state portion of the syllable nucleus lasts approximately 20% of the total duration.

Unlike /eᴵ/ which has a long glide as the first element, /oᵁ/ involves a short steady state target as the first element, and a long glide as the second element. The second formant of /oᵁ/ may have a minimum at a frequency of approximately 780 cps, after which the formant bends rapidly toward the point in frequency associated with the end of the offglide for the following consonant. When the second formant transition value associated with the final consonant is lower than the frequency of this approximate minimum, the glide is quite smooth, and it is impossible to detect a steady state for the second element. In the case of a higher transition value for F_2, the total duration of the glide (60% of the syllable nucleus) is divided into a glide toward 800 cps and an offglide from that point, with durations of 38 and 22% of the total, respectively.

The /ɝ/ consists of a relatively short steady state followed by a rather long glide. This glide is unique in

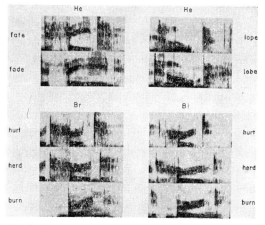

FIG. 7. Broad band spectrograms of seven words, spoken by three informants. The words represent occurrences of single-target complex nuclei.

235

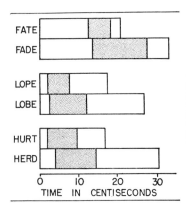

FIG. 8. Average values of the onglide, target, and offglide durations in six words spoken by five informants. The words illustrate single-target complex nuclei.

TABLE V. Average values of rate of change in cps/csec for the glides for five speakers.

	Onglide			Offglide		
	F_1	F_2	F_3	F_1	F_2	F_3
Fate	−8	+52	+31	−8	−62	−54
Fade	−7	+38	+22	−3	−34	−22
Lope	+10	0	−100	−7	−28	0
Lobe	+33	−13	−63	−9	−13	−10
Hurt	0	+19	−63	−8	+29	+29
Herd	0	−3	−26	−3	+15	+13

that it involves parallel movements of the second and third formants. The direction of the movement appears to be determined to a considerable extent by the following consonant. The slow, controlled change in articulatory position appears as the main characteristic of the three sounds, /e$^\text{I}$/, /o$^\text{U}$/, and /ɝ/.

Figure 7 illustrates some occurrences of single-target complex nuclei; the items were recorded by three speakers, He, Br, Bi. Figure 8 presents the average values for the same words for the five speakers; the durations of the targets are shown by the dotted areas, preceded by the onglide durations and followed by those of the offglides. Table V expresses the glides of the single-target complex nuclei in terms of average values of rate of change in cps/csec. Since all our duration measurements are in centiseconds, the rate of change is expressed in cps per centisecond in Table V; the signs indicate the direction of the rate of change. It is seen from Table V that the rate of change of the movement of any single formant is unsatisfactory for the definition of a specific glide.

The second group, /aɪ/, /aʊ/, and /ɔɪ/, is characterized by two target positions. In our data the first target is usually longer than the second, but the transitions between targets are longer than either target

position. Neither of the elements comprising the diphthong is ordinarily phonetically identifiable with any stressed English monophthong; for example, in /aɪ/ the first element is neither /ɑ/ nor /æ/, and the second element is neither /i/ nor /ɪ/. The symbols /aɪ/, /aʊ/, and /ɔɪ/ are adopted tentatively as labels for these syllable nuclei; neither a phonetic nor a phonemic commitment is implied at this moment.

Figure 9 illustrates some of the double-target syllable nuclei. The recordings were made by the three speakers, Br, Re, and He. The significant feature is the appearance of a definite steady state for both elements, but the transitions between the target positions are also quite prominent.

CONCLUSION

It appears that within the rather homogeneous dialect analyzed, and under the restricted conditions of the experiment, the syllabic sounds of American English can be described in terms of fifteen syllable nuclei, subdivided into short and long. The long nuclei are further subdivided into simple and complex nuclei. The four short nuclei are lax monophthongs. The five simple long nuclei are tense monophthongs; the complex long nuclei consist of three single-target nuclei and three double-target nuclei. The single-target nuclei are glides. Only the double-target nuclei are diphthongs. The total inventory of stressed syllable nuclei might then be listed

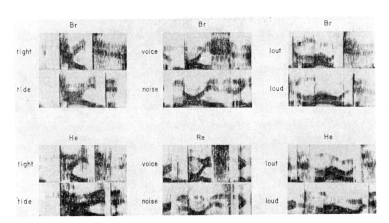

FIG. 9. Broad band spectrograms of six words illustrating double-target complex nuclei, uttered by three informants.

as follows:

Short nuclei: [ɪ] [ɛ] [ə] [ʊ]
Long nuclei:
   (1)   Simple: [i] [æ] [ɑ] [ɔ] [u]
   (2)   Complex:
        (a) Single target: [eᴵ] [oᵁ] [ɝ]
        (b) Double target: [ɑɪ] [ɑʊ] [ɔɪ].

The following phonetic definitions are suggested:

A *formant transition* is a formant movement in frequency from the initiation of the vowel of a consonant-vowel combination to the target position of the vowel; or a movement of a formant from one target position to the next target position; or a movement from the target position of a vowel to the point at which the vowel terminates for a particular vowel-consonant combination.

A *glide* is a vocalic syllable nucleus consisting of one target position, with associated formant transitions to the target, and formant transitions from the target. The duration of either the onglide or the offglide must be comparable to that of the target. Glides are specified only when both the target position and the duration of the significant part of the transitional movement (onglide or offglide) are described.

A *diphthong* is a vocalic syllable nucleus containing two target positions.

Reprinted from THE JOURNAL OF THE ACOUSTICAL SOCIETY OF AMERICA, Vol. 34, No. 12, 1865–1875, December, 1962
Copyright, 1962 by the Acoustical Society of America.
Printed in U. S. A.

Analysis of Nasal Consonants

OSAMU FUJIMURA

University of Electro-Communications, Chofu, Tokyo, Japan

(Received September 5, 1962)

The sound spectra of nasal murmurs in various vowel contexts have been studied by use of an analysis-by-synthesis scheme. The acoustic characteristics are described in terms of format–antiformant distributions (pole–zero locations of the transfer function for the articulatory system) in the frequency domain. It is shown that the location of the antiformant characterizes the murmur of each consonant within the class. The spectral structures are discussed with reference to the articulatory features, and acoustical interpretations of the observed characteristics of the formants and antiformant are given. Also suggested is the existence of certain gross spectral features that are characteristic of nasals as a class.

THE generation of nasal sounds is characterized by two essential features. One is the participation of the nasal passages in the formation of the spectral characteristics of the sound output, and the other is the characteristic condition in the vocal tract proper and its change as a function of time. The latter feature of nasal consonants resembles, to some extent, the feature characterizing the production of stop consonants.[1] The former feature reveals itself most predominantly in the spectral pattern of the nasal murmur, i.e., the sound produced with a complete closure at a point in the oral cavity, and with an appreciable amount of coupling of the nasal passages to the vocal tract.

The present study gives the results of a detailed analysis of a number of samples of nasal murmurs occurring in various vowel contexts. The speech material consisted of natural utterances of nonsense syllables generated by talkers of American English. The experimental data were obtained with a computer, using an analysis–synthesis scheme.[2] An interpretation of the acoustic data is given in terms of the articulation of nasal consonants, following theoretical principles similar to those enunciated by Fant.[3]

I. THEORETICAL CONSIDERATIONS

The entire articulatory system for the production of nasal murmurs, which is shown in the upper part of Fig. 1, consists of three subsystems: (a) the pharynx extending from the glottis to the velum, (b) the oral cavity, with a complete closure at the anterior end, and (c) the nasal tract including the nasopharynx and nasal passages that are terminated by radiation impedances. For discussion of signal components in the frequency range of primary interest, say 200 to 2500 cps, we can assume that these three parts are acoustically coupled to one another only at their ends at the velum. The dimension of the part of the system that serves for this coupling is assumed to be small compared to the wavelengths of the sound components of interest. The transmission through the wall is also assumed to be negligible.

A simplified model for the acoustic system is shown in the lower part of Fig. 1.

Let us represent the volume velocity at the glottis by the time function $u_s(t)$ and the volume velocity at the nostrils by $u_0(t)$. Their Laplace transforms $U_s(s)$ and $U_0(s)$ are related to each other by the transfer function $T(s)$ through the equation

$$U_0(s) = T(s) \cdot U_s(s), \tag{1}$$

where s is the complex frequency. The transfer function $T(s)$ can be expressed in terms of its poles, represented by s_i, and zeros, represented by s_j, as follows:

$$T(s) = \frac{\prod_{j=1}^{n}\left(1 - \frac{s}{s_j}\right)\left(1 - \frac{s}{s_j^*}\right)}{\prod_{i=1}^{m}\left(1 - \frac{s}{s_i}\right)\left(1 - \frac{s}{s_i^*}\right)} H(s), \tag{2}$$

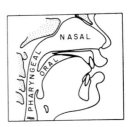

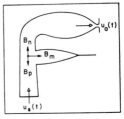

FIG. 1. The upper figure is a tracing from a radiograph showing a midsagittal section of the vocal and nasal tracts during production of the nasal consonant /n/. The structure of the articulatory system is schematized in the lower figure as a joined three-tube model. The figure also indicates the source and output volume velocities $u_s(t)$ and $u_0(t)$, and shows the velopharyngeal coupling point where the susceptances B_p, B_m, and B_n looking into the pharynx, mouth, and nose are defined.

[1] O. Fujimura, J. Speech Hearing Research 4, 233–247 (1961).
[2] C. G. Bell, H. Fujisaki, J. M. Heinz, K. N. Stevens, and A. S. House, J. Acoust. Soc. Am. 33, 1725–1736 (1961).
[3] C. G. M. Fant, *Acoustic Theory of Speech Production* (Mouton and Company, 's-Gravenhage, The Netherlands, 1960).

238

where m and n are appropriately selected numbers, for example five and one, respectively (see *infra*). The correction term $H(s)$ represents the effect of poles and zeros of frequency higher than those accounted for in the products.[3] Except for this correction term, which is considered to be a relatively smooth function of frequency, the characteristics of the transfer function are specified completely within the frequency range of interest by the locations of the limited number of m poles and n zeros.

In order to estimate the essential structure of the transfer function $T(s)$, it is profitable to begin discussion by assuming a nondissipative system. The poles and zeros of the transfer function for the lossless case lie on the imaginary axis of the s plane, and their frequencies can be estimated semiquantitatively by a graphical method.[3] If we assume that the three subsystems—pharyngeal, nasal, and oral—can be approximated by three acoustic tubes that transmit plane waves and in general have varying cross-section areas along the direction of sound transmission, then we can find the locations of the poles and zeros of $T(s)$ by examining the driving-point susceptances looking into the three tubes from the coupling point. These susceptances are defined in Fig. 1 as B_p, B_n, and B_m, as shown. The locations of the poles of $T(s)$, i.e., the formant frequencies, are in general given by the frequencies where the sum of the susceptances looking in all possible directions at any arbitrary point in the system is zero. Thus at the coupling point, in particular, the internal susceptance $B_i = B_p + B_n$ must be equated to the negative of the driving-point susceptance B_m looking into the mouth cavity to obtain the formant frequencies. The zeros of $T(s)$ occur at frequencies for which $B_m = \infty$, since at these frequencies the mouth cavity short-circuits transmission to the nose.

Figure 2 gives sketches of the susceptance curves for articulatory configurations that are considered to represent typical productions of /m/ and /n/. From the general theory of linear lossless networks, a driving-point susceptance is always a monotonically increasing function of frequency except at singularities. The locations of the zero-crossing points and the singularities of the susceptance curves can be estimated grossly from the geometrical configurations of the tracts corresponding to the given articulation. Since the oral cavity is terminated by a complete closure and the nostrils are open for normal articulations of nasal murmurs, the susceptance curve for B_m starts from the origin and the internal susceptance B_i starts from minus infinity.

If the mouth cavity is not coupled to the main tube (viz., the pharyngo-nasal tract), as in the case of /ŋ/ approximately, the axis-crossing points (i.e., the zeros) of the internal susceptance B_i give the formant frequencies. These frequencies are designated by arrows in Fig. 2. When coupling to the mouth cavity is introduced, the normal modes are perturbed and a shift in

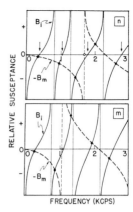

FIG. 2. Frequency characteristics of the susceptances B_i and B_m, assuming the acoustic system to be lossless. The internal susceptance B_i is the sum of the susceptance B_p and B_n shown in Fig. 1. The upper graph was drawn for the /n/ configuration and the lower graph for the /m/ configuration, based on the analysis data of utterances by a male speaker (KS). The arrows in the upper graph indicate the zeros of B_i, which coincide approximately with the formants observed during the production of /ŋ/. The open circles identify the first singularity of B_m and hence show the locations of antiformants. The solid points identify the points of intersection of the curves, corresponding to the resonance condition $B_i + B_m = 0$, and thus predict the frequencies of the formants.

the formant frequencies is observed. The altered formant frequencies are given by the locations of the intersections of the two curves (closed circles in the figure), where the condition $B_m + B_n + B_p = 0$ is satisfied. The density of the zero-crossing points of B_i depends on the acoustical length of the composite main tube extending from the glottis to the nostrils. The average spacing of these formants of the uncoupled system along the frequency axis is about 800 cps for a typical male speaker. This value is appreciably smaller than the average spacing of about 1000 cps for vowels, and the difference is ascribed to the unequal lengths of the nasal and oral cavities.

The location of the first pole of B_m, i.e., the first resonant frequency of the mouth cavity when it is open to a free field at its posterior end, is usually not lower than 700 cps, and is lower for /m/ than for /n/ (see *infra*). This antiresonance observed in the output, or "antiformant" as it may be called, probably constitutes the only zero of $T(s)$ in the low- to middle-frequency ranges. The second singularity of B_m usually seems to occur near 3000 cps or higher for /m/, and is much higher for /n/.

Once we know the essential structure of the transfer function for the lossless case in which the poles and zeros lie on the imaginary axis, we can account for the effect of damping on the output spectrum in an approximate manner by adding appropriate real parts to the poles and zeros. The amount of damping is not necessarily the same for each pole or zero, nor is it well established in the available data reported so far. There are some estimations, however, both from analyses of the spectra of natural utterances and from analog-synthesis experiments.[3-5] The present study supplies further information on the damping factors for the poles and zeros of $T(s)$.

The acoustic output that is of most interest is the sound pressure $P_d(s)$ picked up at a distance d from the speaker's face. If the radiation from the nostrils is approximated by that from a simple spherical source,[6] then the sound pressure is related to the output-volume velocity $U_0(s)$ by

$$P_d(s) = (s\rho/4\pi d) \cdot \exp(-sd/c) \cdot U_0(s), \quad (3)$$

where ρ is the density of air and c is the velocity of sound in air.

In our simplified model of the articulatory system, an assumption is made that the nasal tract consists of a single acoustic tube. In reality, of course, the nasal system at a central point branches into two separate tubes, each of which opens at one of the nostrils. If the system is symmetric with respect to the point at which the sound is measured, this geometrical branching is acoustically immaterial. In this case, we can legitimately interpret the output signal $U_0(s)$ in (1) as representing the total volume velocity from the nostrils, and we can predict the frequency characteristics of the susceptance B_n on the basis of the simple tube model.

When the two nasal passages are appreciably different in their acoustical dimensions, we may define a virtual output-volume velocity $U_0(s)$ by the formula (3), $P_d(s)$ being an observable quantity. In such a case, however, the volume velocity, which may be interpreted as a total output at the nostrils, no longer represents the output from a single nasal tube, and the effective transfer function $T_e(s) = U_0(s)/U_s(s)$ may contain additional pole–zero pairs in a relatively high-frequency region. We can assume, however, that the effect of these pole–zero pairs on the spectrum within the frequency range of interest is small, and can be represented by a smoothly changing function of frequency. This deviation function can be absorbed into the over-all correction term (see *infra*).

By combining (1), (2), and (3), we obtain

$$P_d(s) = (s\rho/4\pi d) \exp(-sd/c)$$

$$\times \frac{\displaystyle\prod_{j=1}^{n}\left(1-\frac{s}{s_j}\right)\left(1-\frac{s}{s_j^*}\right)}{\displaystyle\prod_{i=1}^{m}\left(1-\frac{s}{s_i}\right)\left(1-\frac{s}{s_i^*}\right)} H(s) \cdot U_s(s). \quad (4)$$

Since we are interested in comparing the calculated spectrum to the observed spectrum, we shall take the

absolute value of (4) and put $s = j\omega$, ω being the radian frequency. The amplitude spectrum of the source $|U_s(j\omega)|$ contains the so-called harmonic structure when the system is excited by a periodic glottal source. If we take the envelope of the spectrum, however, the peaks and valleys in the spectrum are consequences of the product terms of the poles and zeros[7] in Eq. (4). Both $|H(j\omega)|$ and the envelope of $|U_s(j\omega)|$ can be represented by slowly varying functions of frequency, and they contribute only to the gross slope of the spectrum. As a first approximation, the envelope of $|U_s(j\omega)|$ can be represented by a constant slope of -12 dB/octave on a logarithmic frequency scale, i.e., by a term proportional to ω^{-2}. The first term of (4), which represents the transfer characteristic of the radiation, is proportional to ω and introduces a constant slope of $+6$ dB/octave. We now transfer these major effects of the source and the radiation to the left-hand side of the formula, and we introduce a new over-all correction term $K(\omega)$, which takes care of the possible deviations of these two functions from the first approximations above as well as the magnitude of the higher-pole correction term $H(j\omega)$. The factor $K(\omega)$ may also contain correction terms representing the effects of the asymmetry of the nasal passages, and possibly the effects of the nonrigid walls of the cavities and the nonrigid termination at the glottis. Thus we obtain the following relation between the spectrum envelope $E(\omega)$ and the poles and zeros of the transfer function:

$$\kappa\omega E(\omega) = K(\omega)\left|\frac{\displaystyle\prod_{j=1}^{n}\left(1-\frac{j\omega}{\sigma_j+j\omega_j}\right)\left(1-\frac{j\omega}{\sigma_j-j\omega_j}\right)}{\displaystyle\prod_{i=1}^{m}\left(1-\frac{j\omega}{\sigma_i+j\omega_i}\right)\left(1-\frac{j\omega}{\sigma_i-j\omega_i}\right)}\right|, \quad (5)$$

where κ is a constant which varies according to the absolute signal level at the point where the sound is observed. In deriving (5) from (4), we have put $s_i = \sigma_i + j\omega_i$ and $s_j = \sigma_j + j\omega_j$.

II. EXPERIMENTAL PROCEDURE

Preparation of the Speech Materials

The speech materials used in the experimental study were drawn from a large group of nonsense utterances generated by three talkers.[8] These utterances were all of the form /hə'CVC/, i.e., a stressed consonant–vowel–consonant syllable preceded by an unstressed syllable. In the case of syllables with /m/ and /n/, the initial and final consonants were identical. The consonant /ŋ/ occurred in final position only, in utterances of the form

[4] K. Nakata, J. Acoust. Soc. Am. **31**, 661–666 (1959).
[5] A. S. House, J. Speech Hearing Disorders **22**, 190–204 (1957).
[6] Experimental evidence supporting this approximation is found in J. L. Flanagan, J. Acoust. Soc. Am. **32**, 1613–1620 (1960).

[7] Furthermore, depending on the particular waveform of the glottal vibration, the envelope of the source spectrum may be represented by a number of zeros which are densely distributed in the frequency domain; cf., M. V. Mathews, J. E. Miller, and E. E. David, Jr., J. Acoust. Soc. Am. **33**, 179–186 (1961).
[8] A. S. House, J. Acoust. Soc. Am. **33**, 1174–1178 (1961).

/həˈrVŋ/. For each of these syllables a variety of vowels was used.

In preparation for further analysis, quantized intensity–frequency–time representations of all of these utterances were obtained in a form suitable for processing by a digital computer.[2] The speech was passed through a bank of 36 filters, covering the frequency range 100 to 7200 cps, the filter outputs were rectified, smoothed, and sampled periodically at 8.3-msec intervals, and the sampled outputs were quantized in 1-dB steps. The "digital spectrogram" for each utterance was stored on punched tape, and these data were then available to be read into the memory of the computer in preparation for further processing by the analysis-by-synthesis techniques.

General Method of Spectrum Reduction

A previous paper has described a procedure utilizing a digital computer for obtaining accurate data on the pole–zero distributions for the vocal-tract transfer function from spectral samples of natural utterances.[2] In the present study this procedure, with minor modifications, has been used for the analysis of spectral samples of nasal murmurs.

The basic steps in the analysis procedure are the following: (a) the operator specifies the locations of a set of poles and zeros in the complex-frequency plane, viz., the poles and zeros of the right-hand side of Eq. (5), including a set of poles and zeros to approximate the

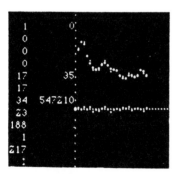

Fig. 3. Photograph of display on the cathode-ray tube of the digital computer when the pole and zero locations have been adjusted to match a spectral sample of /n/. On the graph, the points on the vertical axis represent 5 dB steps in amplitude; each point on the horizontal axis represents one of the 36 filter outputs. These curves are displayed: the input speech spectrum (upper curve of light points), the comparison spectrum (upper curve of heavy points), and the difference curve. The three numbers 17, 34, and 23 at the left show the magnitude of the absolute, variation, and squared-error scores over 24 filter points, that is, up to about 3050 cps. The number 35 appearing near the center of the display represents the sample number (the time location of the sampled spectrum) within the utterance. The other numbers are not relevant to this discussion. The frequencies (bandwidths) in cps of the poles and zeros used to construct the comparison spectrum in this example are: poles at 300 (30), 1050 (120), 1450 (100), 2000 (200), 2650 (100), 3300 (200), 3600 (200); zero at 1600 (450), plus a correction for higher poles. See reference 2 or a discussion of this type of display.

correction factor $K(\omega)$; (b) a trial spectrum corresponding to this configuration of poles and zeros is computed internally in the analyzer; (c) this spectrum is compared with the speech spectrum to be analyzed, and measures of the goodness of fit between the two spectra are computed; (d) the pole and zero locations are modified by the operator until a satisfactory match is obtained between the trial spectrum and the spectrum under analysis. The set of poles and zeros that yields the best-fitting spectrum is then assumed to characterize the input spectrum. The computation of each trial spectrum includes a calculation that takes into account the characteristics of the filters that perform the initial processing of the speech, and the spectrum is then specified at 36 points corresponding to the center frequencies of the 36 filters. The difference between input and trial spectra is thus calculated at each of 36 points. These calculations are performed after the over-all level of the trial spectrum in relation to the input spectrum is adjusted so that the sum of the difference values over the frequency range of interest is zero.

The calculated and input spectra are displayed on the cathode-ray tube of the computer, together with the difference values. An example of such a display is shown in Fig. 3. The display also indicates three measures of the goodness of fit, calculated from the error curve. One of these error scores, to which reference will be made in the later discussions, is the sum of the squares of the difference values (square sum). In the present study, visual inspection of the curves displayed on the cathode-ray tube provided the principal basis for the judgment as to whether the calculated spectrum gave a satisfactory match with the input spectrum. The error scores were also taken into consideration, and these were recorded to provide a quantitative description of the goodness of fit. The frequency range over which the error scores were calculated could be selected by the experimenter; for most of the study, the lowest 24 channels (up to 3100 cps) were used for fitting of spectra of /n/ and /ŋ/, and 20 channels (up to 2300 cps) were used for /m/.

In general, a number of spectral samples at 8.3-msec intervals was analyzed successively for a given nasal consonant. When a satisfactory match for a given spectral sample was obtained, i.e., when no appreciable improvement in the accuracy of the data in terms of the pole–zero distribution was expected for further adjustments of the poles and zero(s), then the locations of the poles and zero(s) that gave the match were recorded, and the next spectral sample was tried. It was sometimes necessary to make many adjustments of the poles and zeros before a reasonable match with a given input spectrum was obtained.

Matching of Spectra of Nasal Murmurs

The strategy that prescribes how to adjust the pole-zero locations in order to find a best match is not necessarily simple or mechanical. Limitations have to be imposed on the choice of the pole–zero distributions, since it is possible that different distributions provide a good fit with a given spectral sample. One constraint governing the selection of pole–zero distributions is imposed by the requirement that the frequencies of the poles and zeros must change continuously with time within the murmur period and cannot perform discontinuous jumps during the few milliseconds between spectral samples. Another requirement is, of course, that the pole–zero distributions must be compatible with the theoretical considerations that are given above and are epitomized in the graphs of Fig. 2.

In order to predict the approximate locations of the poles for spectral samples of /m/ or /n/ it is necessary first to find the approximate frequencies of the zeros of B_i in Fig. 2. These can be determined empirically by examining spectral samples of utterances of /ŋ/. The poles required for matching spectra of /ŋ/ should be almost the same as the zeros of B_i, since the length of the mouth cavity for the /ŋ/ configuration is short, and hence no antiformants are to be expected in the frequency region below 3000 cps. Thus as a preliminary to a study of /m/ and /n/ spectra, matches were obtained for a number of spectral samples of /ŋ/ uttered by three talkers in several vowel contexts. Four conjugate pairs of poles were required below 3000 cps to obtain these matches; the frequency ranges of the poles were 250–400 cps, 950–1150 cps, 1700–2200 cps, and 2300–3000 cps. For a given talker these ranges were more limited. For talker KS, whose utterances were most intensively analyzed in the study, the frequencies of the four formants for /ŋ/ were typically 350, 1050, 1900, and 2750 cps, and the dependence on vowel context was rather small. Since these values are in agreement with previously reported data[3,5,9] and are also reasonable in view of the dimensions of the articulatory system, they were used to indicate the average positions of the zeros of B_i, and hence to determine the approximate shape of the B_i curves.

In addition to the B_i curve in Fig. 2, it is necessary to know roughly the frequency of at least the first pole of B_m for the /m/ and /n/ configurations in order to predict the approximate pole–zero distributions for the spectra of these sounds. Some previous studies have provided data on this antiformant frequency, and it is known that the first singularity of B_m occurs at about 1000 cps or lower for /m/, and in the range of 1500–2000 cps for /n/.[3,5,9,10]

Keeping these values and the graphical structures shown in Fig. 2 in mind, we examined a number of spectral samples of /m/ and /n/ in a preliminary way, in order to gain experience with the matching technique and to determine the approximate frequency ranges to

be expected for the formants and antiformants. Practical representations of the correction curve $K(\omega)$ in terms of distributions of a set of poles and/or zeros in the complex-frequency domain were also tested before proceeding to a systematic collection of data. In matching the spectra of /n/, it was determined that a suitable correction curve could be constructed by locating fixed poles at 4500, 5000, 5500, and 7000 cps and two "buffer poles" in the range 3000–4000 cps. The buffer poles were adjusted, if necessary, to improve the fit in the upper part of the frequency range under consideration. Thus it was necessary to adjust the frequencies and bandwidths of seven poles (the five poles shown in Fig. 2 plus the two buffer poles) and one zero in order to obtain a spectrum that matched a spectral sample of /n/.

In the case of /m/, the frequency range within which a match was to be obtained was restricted to 100–2300 cps, corresponding to 20 filter channels, in order to avoid the necessity of including a second antiformant. Two fixed zeros on the negative real axis, located at 1000 cps and 2000 cps, served to represent the average effect of the higher poles and zeros. This simpler specification of the correction curve was found to be quite appropriate as far as its influence on the pertinent frequency range was concerned. Again the frequencies and bandwidths of seven poles and one zero were adjusted in order to obtain a match for each spectral sample of /m/.

With the practical procedure thus established, the accuracy of the spectral matches in terms of the square sum was typically 20 to 40 dB² for the lowest 20–24 filter channels, although occasionally it was not possible to obtain such a good match. In some utterances, an additional pole–zero pair above the main frequency range was inserted to match the spectrum near the high-frequency end of the pertinent range. Likewise, an auxiliary pole–zero pair (mostly in the frequency range 0 to 500 cps) was inserted in order to improve the match at low frequencies, presumably representing a deviation of the source spectrum from the ideal slope of −12 dB/octave.

III. RESULTS

Examples of intervocalic nasal consonants occurring in 14 different words of the type described previously were closely studied by the matching techniques just outlined. Ten of these words were spoken by KS, and provided versions of /m/ and /n/ before each of the five stressed vowels /iɛæɑu/. The remaining four, spoken by JM, contained /m/ and /n/ followed by /ɛ/ and by /ɑ/. For each of these intervocalic nasal consonants, matches were obtained for every spectral sample throughout the nasal murmur. Many other spectral samples in both intervocalic and final /m/ and /n/ and in final /ŋ/, in various vowel contexts, were matched for portions of the murmur periods. These supplemental materials

[9] S. Hattori, K. Yamamoto, and O. Fujimura, J. Acoust. Soc. Am. **30**, 267–274 (1958).
[10] S. Horiguti, Japan. Z. Oto-Rhino-Laryngol. **49**, 551–575 (1943) (in Japanese).

consisted of utterances by three speakers, two of whom were KS and JM.

Movements of the Formants and Antiformants

Since spectral matches were made throughout the entire duration of the nasal murmurs, it was possible to

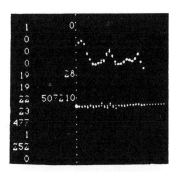
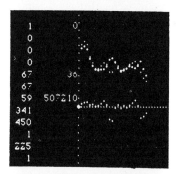
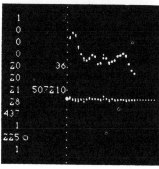

FIG. 4. Three photographs of computer display showing typical changes that occur in the spectrum during an utterance of /m/ in intervocalic position. The upper photograph shows the results of matching a spectral sample (No. 28) near the beginning of the /m/. The frequencies (bandwidths) in cps of the poles and zero at frequencies below 2500 cps are: poles at 280 (60), 940 (30), 1240 (30), 1950 (300), 2560 (50); zero at 980 (50). The middle photograph shows the result obtained when the same comparison spectrum is matched against a spectral sample (No. 36) 67 msec later in the utterance. The square-sum-error score is 341 dB², as compared to 23 dB² in the match above. In the lower photograph the frequencies (bandwidths) of the poles and zero of the comparison spectrum have been adjusted to: poles at 290 (30), 980 (40), 1360 (50), 1950 (300), 2300 (120); zero at 1170 (50). This comparison spectrum provides a better fit (square sum 28 dB²) to spectrum No. 36.

trace the movements of the poles and zeros continuously during these intervals. An example of the changes that occur in the pole–zero configuration is demonstrated in Fig. 4, which gives the cathode-ray tube display for two spectral samples in the intervocalic nasal /m/ in the syllable /həˈmim/. The first sample (No. 28) occurred approximately 35 msec after the beginning of the /m/, and the second sample (No. 36) occurred about 65 msec later, or about 40 msec before the explosion into the front vowel. The poles and zeros were adjusted to give a reasonable match to the first sample, as shown in the upper part of Fig. 4. When the same trial spectrum was compared with the second sample (Fig. 4, middle portion), a large error score (341 dB²) was obtained, indicating that the poles and zero had shifted. When the frequencies and bandwidths of the poles and zero were readjusted, the match shown in the lower portion of Fig. 4 was obtained. It is interesting to note that the two spectra have quite different appearances, particularly in the central frequency region, even though the framework of the pole–zero distribution is not altered (see *infra*).

This variability that is observed in the spectrum for a relatively restricted kind of change in the formant–antiformant structure indicates that it may be difficult to describe the characteristics of individual nasal consonants in terms of their spectra. As a matter of fact, the uppermost sample of /m/ in Fig. 4 apparently resembles the spectral sample from /n/ shown in Fig. 3 more closely than it does the lower /m/ sample of Fig. 4.

The change of the pole–zero distribution throughout the entire intervocalic nasal murmur in the word /həˈmim/ is shown in the upper portion of Fig. 5. The interval from samples 25 to 40 corresponds to the time during which the lips are closed. For the first four samples the zero is located very close to one of the poles, with the result that the effect of this pole–zero pair on the spectrum is minimized. Toward the later part of the murmur period the zero shifts upward and the frequency of the pole immediately above it rises gradually at the same time.

In the lower portion of Fig. 5 similar data are plotted for the intervocalic /n/ in the utterance of /həˈnɑn/ by the same speaker. The most conspicuous change occurs in the portion close to the boundary of the following vowel, where the zero shifts downward in frequency and the pole immediately below it also moves downward. At the last sample, the zero apparently overtakes the pole. The frequency of the second pole gradually increases over the entire interval, and there are slight changes in the first, fourth, and fifth poles.

Comparison of Nasals in Different Vowel Environments

Data for each of the two nasals in five vowel environments for speaker KS are summarized in Fig. 6; similar utterances of words containing the vowel /ɛ/ by the

243

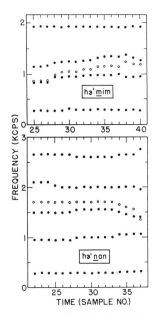

FIG. 5. Frequencies of formants (closed circles) and antiformants (open circles) for typical utterances of intervocalic /m/ (upper graph) and /n/ (lower graph) plotted against time throughout the murmur periods. Time samples are 8.3 msec apart. The data are illustrative of transitions that occur as a result of articulatory movement during the production of nasal murmurs. Sample 35 in the lower portion of the figure corresponds to the spectrum in Fig. 3; samples 28 and 36 in the upper portion correspond to the spectra in Fig. 4.

the third and fourth formants and the antiformant, and the first, second, and fifth formants are relatively stable. The structure of the cluster can change radically, i.e., the order of the two formants and one antiformant on the frequency axis is not always the same (see *infra*).

The variability is, however, limited only to that in local structures, and the location of the antiformant normally falls within a distinctly defined range for the individual consonant, as described above. In other words, the difference between the murmur sounds of the three nasal consonants may be described in the following way: /ŋ/ has four formants in the main frequency range (up to about 3000 cps), /n/ is obtained when the third of the formants is replaced by a cluster consisting of two formants and one antiformant, /m/ is obtained when the second formant is replaced by a similar cluster.

Damping

The damping of the resonance or antiresonance is another important factor that may characterize nasal sounds when compared with oral sounds.[4,5] This study has supplied quantitative data on the bandwidths of the formants and antiformant, but unfortunately the accuracy of the data in this respect is not as high as that of the data on the frequencies of the formants or antiformant. Certain errors can stem in part from the

speaker JM are shown for comparison. In addition, the locations of poles for the uncoupled nasal /ŋ/ are indicated by arrows for each of the two speakers. Of the three points connected by lines, the point at the left corresponds to the second sample within the consonant, the middle point represents the sample at the center of the interval, and the point at the right represents the next-to-last sample within the interval.

When we compare the upper and lower portions of Fig. 6, we see a clear difference in the location of the antiformant (zero) for the two nasals /m/ and /n/. The zero is located between 750 cps and 1250 cps for /m/ and between 1450 cps and 2200 cps for /n/. Since the zero for /ŋ/ is above 3000 cps, it can be said that the nasals /m/, /n/, and /ŋ/ are characterized by low, medium, and high positions of the antiformant, respectively. Furthermore, the antiformant changes its position appreciably from word to word and also within the same utterance, depending on the change in the configuration of the oral cavity. The antiformant seems to have a considerable influence on the formants in its immediate vicinity, but other formants within the frequency range of interest remain relatively constant, at least for the same speaker. Thus for /m/, the first and the fourth formants are almost invariant and the second and third formants with the antiformant form a variable "cluster." For /n/, on the other hand, the variable cluster consists of

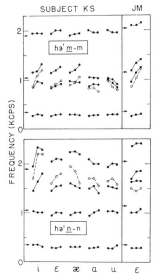

FIG. 6. Data on formant (closed circles) and antiformant (open circles) locations for examples of /m/ (upper graph) and /n/ (lower graph) in intervocalic position preceding the different vowels identified on the abscissa. In each case the three joined points represent samples in a given nasal consonant; from left to right the points represent a spectral sample located close to the beginning of the nasal murmur, a centrally located sample, and a sample close to the end of the nasal murmur. Each right-hand sample, therefore, reflects an immediate influence of the following vowel. Data for two subjects are shown. For each subject the arrows at the left represent the locations of the formants for utterances of /ŋ/ (cf., Fig. 2).

TABLE I. Values of half-power bandwidths in cps of formants and antiformants for various intervocalic nasal consonants. Averages are taken for spectral samples throughout the nasal murmur in five vowel contexts; data for one talker (KS).

	/m/	/n/	/ŋ/
Formant 1	60	40	80
2	60	100	100
3	90	110	230
4	280	170	100
5	170	100	...
Antiformant	80	600	...

approximate method used to calculate the comparison spectrum, in part from the harmonic structure of the observed spectrum, and in part and probably most unpredictably from the lack of precise knowledge concerning the voice–source characteristic $|U_s(\omega)|$. Reliable conclusions can, however, be drawn from some characteristics that are consistently observed in the data. On the average, bandwidths of formants observed in the samples of nasal murmurs are comparable to or greater than those observed in vowels. Individual formants, however, have different amounts of damping, and the bandwidths are not necessarily constant nor monotonically related to the frequency of the formant. Table I shows the average values of the half-power bandwidths corresponding to each of the poles and zeros. The averages were taken for /m/ and /n/ separately over the entire periods of the intervocalic nasals in the five words containing different vowels. In the case of /n/, the second, third, and fifth formants have comparable bandwidth values on the average, and the fourth, which is normally located slightly above 2000 cps, has an appreciably higher damping. The tendency is the same in /m/, but the fourth formant seems to have still wider bandwidths than those of /n/, and the second and third formants have appreciably narrower bandwidths than the corresponding formants of /n/. More notable, however, is the very wide bandwidth of the antiformant of /n/ as compared with the rather sharp antiformant of /m/. In the case of /ŋ/, the third formant, somewhat below 2000 cps, always had a wider bandwidth than the second and the fourth formants.

The tendencies observed above for the frequencies and bandwidths of the formants and antiformant for speaker KS were consistently seen for other speakers also. There seems little doubt, therefore, that the above findings illustrate typical features of the nasal consonants. The present data indicate, however, that certain details, particularly the location of the highest pole within the frequency region considered above, are quite dependent on individual speakers.

IV. DISCUSSION

The data of Figs. 5 and 6, which were obtained by examining the acoustic spectra of nasal murmurs, can be used to infer the nature of the articulatory configurations that gave rise to the sounds. The analysis is made by comparing the data on pole–zero locations with susceptance sketches of the type shown previously in Fig. 2.

Frequency and Bandwidth of Antiformant

Figure 6 shows that the frequency of the antiformant for /m/ is relatively high when the consonant precedes a front vowel such as /i/, and is lower when the context is a back vowel. A simple calculation shows that this antiformant would occur at about 1000 cps if the mouth cavity were a uniform tube of length 8 cm. When /m/ precedes a front vowel, the anterior part of the oral cavity during the /m/ is narrowed in anticipation of the vowel, and acoustical theory would predict a consequent rise in the frequency of the first pole of B_m. In the case of the back vowel context (/ɑ/ and /u/ in Fig. 6), the anticipatory tongue position results in a large mouth cavity with a comparatively narrow neck, with a consequent decrease in the frequency of the antiformant.

Similar effects of the adjacent vowel are noted in the case of /n/, although now the mouth cavity is smaller than for /m/, and the antiformant occurs at a higher frequency. The average value of the antiformant frequency for /n/ in various vowel contexts is about 1700 cps. If a uniform tube were assumed as a crude model of the oral acoustic system, the effective length would be about 5 cm. In a similar fashion, a mouth tube less than 3 cm in length would give rise to an antiformant frequency above 3000 cps, and would correspond to the generation of /ŋ/.

It was mentioned in the preceding section that the antiformant of /n/ has considerably more damping than that of /m/. In the case of /n/, the wedge-shaped termination of the oral cavity causes a gradual change in characteristic impedance and hence results in relatively large absorption of sound energy at the termination. The configuration of the oral cavity for /m/, on the other hand, has a rather abrupt termination, and the mouth cavity has a smaller ratio of surface area to volume. The acoustic losses in the oral cavity are, therefore, less appreciable, and the bandwidth of the antiformant is smaller.

Interpretation of Formants

The interpretation of the poles of the transfer function, viz., the formants of nasal consonants, is more complex than the interpretation of the zeros because, in general, we have to consider the effects of all three of the constituent tracts (see *supra*). The behavior of the formant–antiformant distribution as a consequence of a change in the articulatory conditions can be understood most easily if we interpret the acoustic characteristics of the articulatory system in terms of the singularities of the three driving-point admittances looking into the oral, pharyngeal, and nasal cavities from the velum.

Let us consider a frequency range that lies between two adjacent singularities of the internal admittance B_i, for example, the frequency range 800–1300 cps in the upper portion of Fig. 2. The curve B_i has always one zero-crossing point within such a range, and this point gives the frequency of a formant of the uncoupled system. If the antiformant is not within this range, we can always find one and only one formant of the coupled system, and its frequency is generally different from the formant frequency of the uncoupled system. In particular, if the frequency range is below the frequency of the lowest antiformant, the formant of the coupled system is always lower in frequency than that of the uncoupled system. The amount of the shift is generally small if the formant is located far away from the antiformant, or if the pertinent frequency range is very narrow, i.e., if the two singularities of B_i are closely located. In the present data, in good conformity with the statement above, the first formants of /m/ and /n/ were found to be somewhat lower than that of /ŋ/ in general. The second formant of /n/ also was generally lower than that of /ŋ/.

If an antiformant is located within the frequency range between two singularities of B_i, then two formants as well as the antiformant occur within the region, replacing the formant of the uncoupled system. Their locations and the degree of concentration of the cluster change considerably from case to case. The formants are always located on either side of the antiformant, however, and they also lie on either side of the formant frequency of the uncoupled system. In other words, there cannot be a singularity of B_i immediately next to the antiformant without having a formant in between. (There is always one singularity of B_i between any two adjacent formants when no antiformant lies between the formants.) When the formant and antiformant are located close to each other, the singularity is also close to the formant. If the antiformant shifts continuously toward a singularity of B_i, then the formant–antiformant pair tends toward the latter, and finally the order of the antiformant and the formant is inverted as the antiformant crosses the singularity of B_i. Thus an annihilation of a formant–antiformant pair can occur if and only if the antiformant frequency coincides with the frequency of a singularity of B_i, i.e., coincides with a characteristic frequency of either the pharyngeal or nasal cavity. Therefore, by observing an annihilation or a crossing of such a pair in the output spectrum, we can conclude that a singularity of the internal admittance exists at that frequency. It should be mentioned, however, that the location of this annihilated pair can be determined only when the movement of the pair is traced continuously for a considerable period of an utterance. Examples are seen in Figs. 5 and 6.

In the upper portion of Fig. 5, a superposition of the second formant and the antiformant is observed in the beginning portion of /m/, and hence there is a singularity of B_i at this frequency, i.e., at about 800 cps. For the reasons given below, this lowest (except one at the origin) singularity of B_i is considered to correspond to the lowest short-circuit resonance of the nasal cavity. In the lower portion of Fig. 5, toward the end of /n/, a similar annihilation is observed for the third formant and the antiformant at about 1400 cps. The singularity of B_i at this frequency is probably the lowest short-circuit resonance of the pharynx cavity. The marked descent of the antiformant in this case is caused by the retraction of the tongue in anticipation of the back vowel.

In Fig. 6, the antiformant for /m/ is generally found in the vicinity of the second formant. If we inspect this frequency region in the light of the rules given above, we conclude that the location of the lowest singularity of B_i is relatively constant (just below 1000 cps) regardless of the coarticulation. The next higher singularity of B_i, on the other hand, seems to shift its location considerably depending on the tongue position (probably near 1000 cps before /u/ and around 1500 cps before front vowels). When the tongue is retracted in anticipation of the high back vowel /u/, the pharyngeal cavity must be narrowed significantly at its upper end (near the coupling point), and hence the location of the singularity of B_p (the susceptance looking into the pharynx) must be lowered. Conversely, a higher position of this singularity is expected for an /m/ anticipating a front vowel. The data for /m/ depicted in Fig. 6, therefore, provide evidence that the lowest singularity of B_i is a singularity of B_n, and the next is a singularity of B_p. The singularity of B_n is always around 850–1000 cps for the data of the speaker KS. Other data of different speakers, however, indicate somewhat less stability of this singularity of B_n. It is expected that this frequency generally shifts from utterance to utterance, to some extent randomly depending on the height of the velum, and of course from subject to subject depending on the individual nasal-tract configuration. It is theoretically not impossible, in an extreme case, that the singularity of B_p descends so much (in the case of a coarticulation of a high back vowel) that it becomes lower than the singularity of B_n.

The data of Fig. 6 show in general that there are some formants that remain relatively unaffected by the change of articulatory conditions. The second formant of /n/, for example, is located always around 1000 cps for all samples of /n/. This relatively constant location of the second formant for /n/ is partially explained by the relatively constant location of the next lower singularity, which is a singularity of B_n. Probably the susceptance looking into the pharynx for the articulation of /n/ is comparatively high (and positive) in this frequency range. (Consequently, as seen in the upper diagram of Fig. 2, the curve of B_i rises rapidly from minus infinity, and the formant is bound close to the singularity of B_i.) If this is true, we can regard the second formant for /n/ approximately as a resonance of the nasal-tract proper. Since at this frequency the nasal tract opens into a low impedance at its posterior end, the formant will remain unchanged unless the position of the velum is altered significantly.[11]

Also at a relatively fixed position is the fourth formant of /m/, which for speaker KS is at about 2000 cps. For /n/, on the other hand, the fourth formant varies considerably with the context, being as high as 2300 cps before the vowel /i/, while the fifth formant is relatively fixed at 2600–2700 cps. The particularly wide bandwidth of the fourth formant of /m/ may be interpreted as an indication that this formant is affiliated to the nasal cavity. At this frequency, probably all of the three susceptances have small magnitudes, and consequently the nasal tract may be regarded as having nearly an open-circuit resonance.

V. COMMON CHARACTERISTICS OF NASAL MURMURS

As was discussed in the preceding sections, the appearance of the spectra of nasal murmurs may vary considerably from one sample to another, depending on the individual nasal consonant and its context; the spectra also depend on the individual speaker who utters the sound, or even his temporary physiological state. The spectrum envelope can be altered significantly by a slight modification of the pole–zero pattern. The structure of the cluster, in particular, is of primary importance in determining the relative levels of the local spectral peaks in the middle-frequency range. The variability of the relative levels even within one nasal murmur presumably causes an inherent difficulty for an automatic recognition scheme that is based on a straightforward analysis.

The perceptual impression of nasal sounds is somehow substantially different from that of other speech sounds. It is reasonable, therefore, to assume that there are some gross acoustic features that characterize the nasals as a class. In view of our data concerning the structure of the spectral envelope, it may be said that the following three features characterize the spectra of nasal murmurs in general: (1) the existence of a very low first formant that is located at about 300 cps and is well separated from the upper formant structure; (2) relatively high damping factors of the formants; and (3) high density of the formants in the frequency domain (and the existence of the antiformant).

In gross terms, the latter two characteristics in combination give rise to an even distribution of the sound energy in the middle-frequency range between, say, 800 cps and 2300 cps. There is neither a prominent

energy concentration nor an appreciably wide and deep spectral "valley" in any portion of this frequency range. This feature, when combined with the very low location of the first spectral peak, cannot be found in other vocalics. Diffuse vowels, for example, have similar low first formant frequencies, but there is an apparent concentration of the sound energy either toward the low end or high end of the middle-frequency range depending on the grave-acute distinction.[3,12,13]

The first general feature results in a relatively well-defined low concentration and a consistent lack of energy in the range just above it (around 600 cps). This frequency range in the vicinity of 600 cps can be influenced by a low antiformant of /m/, but it is not likely to have strong components, for the following reason. The location of the lowest singularity of B_i, which is considered to represent the short-circuit resonance of the nasal cavity, is relatively constant regardless of the tongue articulation; it cannot be very low in frequency during the phonation of a nasal murmur because the back opening of the cavity has to be open. When the antiformant frequency is very low, there can be a formant below the singularity of B_n, but, according to the rules stated in the previous section, the antiformant has to be below the formant in this case. Thus, even for the lowest possible antiformant frequency, say 700 cps, there cannot be a predominant influence of the next higher formant upon the frequency range around 600 cps.

This relatively stable spectral characteristic in the low-frequency range may be of some practical value in the formulation of criteria for identifying nasal consonants as a class. A preliminary experiment has suggested that the murmur samples of the nasals in various contexts always give a good match with a standard curve when the comparison of the spectra is made in a limited range such as 200 to 1000 cps. A combination of this feature with the above-mentioned gross feature in the middle-frequency range may constitute a reliable criterion for the automatic recognition of the class of nasal consonants.

VI. CONCLUDING REMARKS

It has been shown that the spectral structure of nasal murmurs can be described in a unified and compact form in terms of the pole–zero distribution of the transfer function of the articulatory system. Through semiquantitative consideration of the admittance curves the task of finding the pole–zero distribution was made feasible, and reconstruction of the spectra using the theory as a guide has resulted in satisfactory fits between the calculated spectra and the measured spectra.

---

[11] This interpretation agrees with the description of the formant given by Fant.[3] The location of the formant also compares very well with Fant's data and with the data reported by House.[5]

[12] R. Jakobson and M. Halle, *Fundamentals of Language* (Mouton and Company, 's-Gravenhage, The Netherlands, 1956).
[13] K. N. Stevens and A. S. House, J. Speech Hearing Research **4**, 303–320 (1961).

The procedure used to achieve the matches is by no means simple or mechanical, however; the strategy of finding better fits is rather involved, and a machine could hardly replace the human operator at the stage of this study. Since the manual operation was so complex and time-consuming, the amount of spoken material which could be examined in this experiment was quite limited.

In order to automatize the matching process, it is desirable to find a set of variables that incorporates some of the constraints imposed on the pole–zero structures of nasal murmurs. One possibility is that the frequencies of the poles and zero(s) be computed from plausible sets of values of the locations of the singularities (and zero crossings) of the susceptances B_p, B_n, and B_m, assuming appropriate relations between the admittance levels. Perhaps even more desirable is a procedure that tracks articulatory rather than acoustic parameters. In such a scheme, the articulation of the sound is specified in terms of several articulatory variables, the output spectrum is computed from the articulatory description, and the computed spectrum is compared with the observed spectrum.[14] In a recognition scheme of the analysis-by-synthesis type, it is very advantageous to control a set of variables that is directly linked to the speech-production mechanism because then we can immediately exploit our knowledge about the physical restrictions of the motor activities and also about the linguistic or phonetic rules that govern the utterance of the language the speaker talks. The principle of continuity of articulatory movements between a vowel and a nasal when they are adjacent

may, for example, be of great help in finding parameter values that yield spectral matches for nasal murmurs.

In the present study we have discussed only one portion of the acoustic continuum that is influenced by a nasal consonant, namely, the nasal murmur. Although it is possible within the class of nasals to separate /m/, /n/, and /ŋ/ on the basis of the location of the antiformant, there is no doubt that the formant transitions of the adjacent vowels often play a more important or even dominant role in the recognition of the individual nasals.[15]

ACKNOWLEDGMENTS

This study was made possible by the use of a computer program for pole–zero matching and of speech material, both prepared by the Speech Communication Group at the Research Laboratory of Electronics, MIT. Thanks are due to the members of the group, in particular to John M. Heinz and Hiroya Fujisaki for their advice and assistance concerning the use and modifications of the program. Many stimulating discussions and helpful suggestions contributed by Kenneth N. Stevens and Arthur S. House, as well as the constant and understanding encouragement of Morris Halle, are most sincerely appreciated. The spectrum matching was performed on the TX-O computer, a facility of the Research Laboratory of Electronics, MIT.

This work was performed while the author was on the staff of the Research Laboratory of Electronics, Massachusetts Institute of Technology. The work was supported in part by the U. S. Army Signal Corps, the Air Force Office of Scientific Research, and the Office of Naval Research; in part by the Air Force Cambridge Research Laboratories under Contract AF 19(604)-6102; and in part by the National Science Foundation under Grant G-7364.

[14] J. M. Heinz, "Reduction of Speech Spectra to Descriptions in Terms of Vocal-Tract Area Functions," Quart. Progr. Rept. 64, Research Laboratory of Electronics, MIT (January 15, 1961), pp. 198–203. Also, J. M. Heinz, "Analysis of Speech Spectra in Terms of a Model of Articulation," Proceedings of the IVth International Congress on Acoustics, Copenhagen, Denmark, August 1962, and Proceedings of the Speech Communication Seminar, Stockholm, Sweden, August 1962.

[15] A. M. Liberman, P. C. Delattre, F. S. Cooper, and L. J. Gerstman, Psychol. Monograph No. 8, 1–13 (1954).

CHAPTER 22

Reprinted from the *Journal of Speech and Hearing Research*
March 1962, Vol. 5, No. 1

Diphthong Formants and their Movements

ANTHONY HOLBROOK

GRANT FAIRBANKS

The experimental work reported here has taken for its main concern the acoustical characteristics of the five common diphthongs. For convenience, these will be symbolized herein as /eɪ/, /aɪ/, /ɔɪ/, /oʊ/, /aʊ/. The dynamic nature of diphthongs has long been recognized by the practice of transcribing them with double symbols such as the foregoing. There has been considerable variation in the symbols, however, and while it is not the purpose of this article to treat symbolic usage, the variation suggests the desirability of more acoustic data.

The methods of formal experimentation have not been applied extensively to the diphthong. *Visible Speech*, the well-known book by Potter, Kopp, and Green (*9*), contains numerous illustrative spectrograms. Potter and Peterson (*10*), in a paper concerned with graphic methods of representing vowels, traced the shifting formants of a single speaker's diphthongs, as also did Joos (*2*). Peterson and Coxe (*8*) measured some utterances of /eɪ/ and /oʊ/ in isolation, using themselves as subjects, while the work of Lehiste and Peter-

son (*3*) included some treatment of diphthongs. In the prespectrographic period Liddell (*4, 5, 6*) performed wave-by-wave Fourier analyses of diphthongs and, noting the extensive shifting of spectrum, suggested (*6*) the term *polyphthong*.

In the present experiment the general procedure has been to collect samples of the diphthongs as spoken in words by General American speakers under laboratory conditions, and to subject these samples to spectrographic analysis. In addition, it was convenient and appropriate to include the diphthong-like /ju/. Since it is generally conceded that the first three formants of vowels contribute the greatest part of the information, these formants, and their frequencies in particular, were of major interest. The amplitude factor, however, which has been given only limited attention in the vowel studies, was also measured. Special consideration has also been given to variations of frequency and amplitude as a function of time. There was further interest in locating the acoustical areas within which diphthongs vary with reference to the vowel system. To support this inquiry samples of vowels were also collected from the same subjects and measured with respect to frequency and amplitude of the first three formants.

Anthony Holbrook (Ph.D., University of Illinois, 1958) is Assistant Professor of Speech, Wayne State University. Grant Fairbanks (Ph.D., University of Iowa, 1936) is Professor of Speech, University of Illinois. This article is based on the first author's Ph.D. thesis.

Procedure

Collection of Samples. Diphthongs and vowels to be analyzed were recorded by 20 male General American speakers, with no obvious dialectal or clinical speech problems, who were volunteers from introductory speech classes at the University of Illinois. The spoken samples were drawn from real words of the language which were as free as possible from the determining effects of adjacent consonants. The consonant /h/, which has negligible influence upon following vowels, was used with both diphthongs and vowels. The diphthong samples were found in the six surnames *Hay, High, Hoy, Hoe, Howe, Hugh.* For the vowels, the words of Peterson and Barney (7) were used, namely, *heed, hid, head, had, hod, hawed, hood, who'd, hud, heard.* Although the effect of the /d/ is real and large it was believed that it might be minimized by analyzing a portion as close to the /h/ as possible after the establishment of the steady state of the vowel. Thus the samples of diphthongs and vowels were roughly comparable, since both were subjected to approximately the same consonant influence.

In the collection of the diphthongs, a method was sought whereby natural utterances of the words would be obtained. After various attempts it was decided to have the subjects speak each of the six surnames as the last word of the sentence 'My name is John Doe' as if responding to the question 'What is your name?' The sentences were typed in random order on a card and numbered. At the time of the experiment the subject was requested to study the card, and it was explained that his task was to read each line after the experimenter spoke its number, and to do so as if answering the question mentioned. Each of the six sentences was repeated three time in a random order of 18 responses that was different for each subject. The responses were elicited one after the other without stopping, at a rate of one every three to five seconds. In the event of a reading error, the number of the sentence in question was repeated immediately.

The vowels were collected in a different manner, for it was desired that the pronunciation of the words be predictable, but that the words be spoken in a brisk and natural manner. To accomplish this, pronunciations were established by placing each word as the fourth member of a series of rhyming words. The subject read from a card showing lines of the rhyming words. The lines were in random order and numbered. As was the case with the diphthongs, the lines were read by number, and each subject read in a different random order of 10. To facilitate brisk utterance, a reading rhythm was established by the use of a light which flashed automatically at intervals of 0.8 sec. This pacing light was placed so as to be in the periphery of the subject's vision. A practice card which did not contain the experimental words was presented to the subject, and he was allowed to practice the rhythm with the pacing light prior to the reading of the vowel card. This procedure caused the words to be spoken at a rate fast enough for naturalness of utterance, but to be, nevertheless, discrete. The words *say* and *end* bounded the four rhyming words and were used to absorb any end-effects upon intonation and stress. For example, the line for /i/ was as follows:

say deed feed need heed end.

The entire procedure was recorded in a sound-treated room by means of an Altec M-11 microphone system and a Magnecord M-90 tape recorder operated at 15 ips, the recorder being situated in a nearby control room.

Selection of Words for Analysis. With few exceptions, any one of the three samples of a diphthong produced by each subject would have served for analysis in the sense of being representative. To eliminate the exceptions and formalize selection of one of the three a modest judgmental procedure was used. This involved three experienced faculty members who listened independently to the samples over high-quality earphones. Each judge first picked the two of the three that he considered most representative, and then chose between these two. The sample preferred by a majority of the three judges was selected. The judges reported difficulty in making the judgments, remarking on the similarity of most sets, and also indicated that the intelligibility of all samples was unquestionable.

Spectrographic Measurements. A Kay Electric Company Sona-Graph was used for the acoustical analysis of the samples. The normal frequency range of 8 000 cps full-scale was modified locally according to instruction received from the manufacturer so that it was reduced to 3 500 cps. The frequency calibration of this apparatus was accomplished by the method and equipment described by Fairbanks and Grubb (*1*). The frequency scale was

calibrated with this equipment for each section. Also, the frequencies of Formants One, Two, and Three were determined by the method outlined in the above article. Essentially, this method consisted of determining the component of greatest amplitude in a formant, or the point midway between two components of equal amplitude.

The amplitude characteristics of the spectrograph were determined by tones which were recorded on the instrument at nine levels and 23 frequencies covering the range of interest. The measurements provided a basis for constructing a transparent template by means of which the amplitudes could be read in decibels directly from the sections. The formant amplitude was defined as that of the strongest component, or the arithmetic mean of two equal components, expressed in decibels above the baseline of the section.

Analysis of Diphthongs. In the spectrographic analysis, the tape recordings were played with the playback gain adjusted to equate the maximum voltage of the diphthongs as determined by the tape recorder VU meter. The record gain of the spectrograph was held constant by means of a constant voltage tone. The output of the tape recorder was connected via a Hewlett-Packard 350A attenuator to a 500 ohm matching transformer on the spectrograph. The combination of 45 cps bandwidth and HS frequency response was used, the HS response imparting a positive slope of about 6 db per octave to the sections.

The conventional spectrograms were made with the playback gain of the spectrograph adjusted to 10 db above the calibrated level. In making the sections, the playback gain was returned to its calibrated level so that amplitude measures could be made. Due to the differences in the two circuits involved, the resolving power of the sections was essentially equal to that of the conventional spectrograms despite the difference in gain setting. At the calibrated level both the maximum and minimum signal-to-noise ratios encountered in the experimental samples were measurable.

Following the making of each spectrogram, before it was removed from the instrument, the display was inspected and the portions to be sectioned were located. The sections were made immediately thereafter. The first section was made at the initial appearance of the formants, and then a section was located at the end of each formant. Following this, additional sections were made as needed to describe all of the significant formant changes.

On all sections, frequency and amplitude measures were made for the fundamental and the three lowest formants. The frequency measures were then plotted on semilogarithmic paper, with frequency on the ordinate and duration on the abscissa, and connected by a smooth line. The result was a characterization of the frequency-time display of the spectrogram.

Analysis of Vowels. The acoustic analysis of the vowels was accomplished in a manner similar to that of the diphthongs. However, the method of locating the portion to be sectioned was somewhat different, since only one section was made per vowel. In order to avoid the effect of the final /d/, the spectrograms were carefully inspected and the location of the section established in the steady state portion of the vowel close to /h/. The spectrogram was then removed, and the section was made immediately thereafter. The sections were then measured in the manner described above with respect to frequency and amplitude of the fundamental and the three lowest formants.

Results

Durations of Diphthong Formants. Although the measurement of the formant durations was limited to the resolving power of the spectrograph, the spectrograms of the diphthongs and the time plots made from the sections showed, in a given utterance, variations in the times of onset and cessation of the formants and in their total durations. In addition to the expected variability between subjects, these differences appeared to be in some respects phoneme-linked. It was observed that in all utterances the onset of the first

TABLE 1. Mean time intervals between first measurements of Formant One in diphthongs and final measurements of each formant. Values in sec.

Diphthong	Formant		
	One	*Two*	*Three*
/eɪ/	0.21	0.22	0.22
/aɪ/	0.25	0.26	0.25
/ɔɪ/	0.24	0.25	0.24
/oʊ/	0.22	0.21	0.12
/aʊ/	0.25	0.23	0.17
/ju/	0.22	0.15	0.13

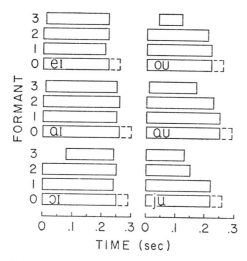

FIGURE 1. Mean durations and time locations of the fundamental and three formants of diphthongs. Fundamental persisted at least 0.04 sec beyond final measurement, as shown by dashed extensions.

formant either coincided with or preceded the onset of the other formants, and this point in time was used as a reference point. The relative starting and ending times for all formants were determined, and the mean ending times are given in Table 1. The mean starting times were all zero except for Formant Three. The mean onset of Formant Three occurred 0.01 sec after the start of Formant One in /eɪ/, /ɑɪ/, and /ɑʊ/; 0.04 sec in /oʊ/; and 0.08 sec in /ɔɪ/. The time measurements are displayed graphically in Figure 1.

The formant durations of /eɪ/ and /oʊ/ are seen to be somewhat shorter than the corresponding ones of /ɑɪ/ and /ɑʊ/. The short durations of /eɪ/ and /oʊ/ correspond to the general conception that they involve less articulatory movement than do /ɑɪ/ and /ɑʊ/. When all three formants are considered, /eɪ/, /oʊ/, and /ju/ had the shortest

durations. For all diphthongs there was simultaneous onset of Formants One and Two and the fundamental, as can be seen by the alignment of the bars at the left of each diphthong. The lowest two formants had about equal total mean duration with the exception of /jul.

It may be seen in Figure 1 that in /eɪ/ and /ɑɪ/ the mean ending times for all three formants were about equal internally. In /oʊ/ and /ɑʊ/ Formant Two is slightly shorter than Formant One, and Formant Three is considerably shorter than Formant Two. The difference in the second vowel elements is, therefore, discernible in the durations of Formants Two and Three, and especially in Formant Three. In /eɪ/, /ɑɪ/, and /ɔɪ/ there is only small variation within the diphthong in the ending times of the formants. Study of /oʊ/, /ɑʊ/, and /ju/ reveals a decreased length of Formant Three. In /ju/ Formant Two was also abbreviated. It should be observed that Formant Three is the most variable in duration. The influence of the back vowel is apparent in the decreased durations of Formant Three. To illustrate the point, a direct comparison of /eɪ/ and /oʊ/ may be made with respect to Formant Three. Its duration equals that of Formant One in /eɪ/, but in /oʊ/ it is only about two-fifths of Formant One. The late start of Formant Three in /ɔɪ/ also reflects the back vowel influence.

In Figure 1 it will be noted that /ju/ has unique features. Although Formant One compares favorably with the durations of /eɪ/ and /oʊ/, Formant Two is exceptionally short, 0.07 sec shorter than Formant One. Formant Three starts early, showing the front vowel

TABLE 2. Median frequencies of diphthong formants at sampling points. Medians based on 20 utterances with exceptions as noted in text. Values in cps.

| Diphthong | Sampling Point | | | | |
	1	*2*	*3*	*4*	*5*
Fundamental					
/eɪ/	110		95		90
/aɪ/	115		98		98
/ɔɪ/	115		100		85
/oʊ/	118		102		95
/aʊ/	115		102		90
/ju/	118		108		92
Formant One					
/eɪ/	550	520	488	418	400
/aɪ/	750	710	735	682	572
/ɔɪ/	552	550	600	570	512
/oʊ/	565	535	505	472	465
/aʊ/	770	740	735	680	610
/ju/	330	342	338	352	400
Formant Two					
/eɪ/	2 032	2 078	2 088	2 125	2 228
/aɪ/	1 280	1 350	1 410	1 648	1 942
/ɔɪ/	835	888	1 062	1 558	1 908
/oʊ/	882	848	820	758	708
/aʊ/	1 400	1 320	1 210	1 062	888
/ju/	2 160	1 962	1 550	1 292	1 240*
Formant Three					
/eɪ/	2 650	2 660	2 650	2 662	2 710
/aɪ/	2 730	2 690	2 515	2 545	2 668
/ɔɪ/	2 525	2 410	2 350	2 290	2 492
/oʊ/	2 385	2 435	2 415	2 460	
/aʊ/	2 695	2 680	2 600	2 500	2 240
/ju/	2 568	2 390	2 275	2 285	

*One utterance.

influence, and ends early, reflecting the back vowel influence.

The fundamental invariably outlasted all formants. In Figure 1 the dashed extension seen at the right of the fundamental bar indicates that it persisted for at least 0.04 sec beyond the longest formant in all utterances. No attempt was made to measure its duration past this point.

Temporal Variations of Diphthong Formants. Formants One and Two essentially coincided throughout their durations, and this common time interval was used as the unit duration of the individual utterance and served as a basis for locating sampling points to characterize the diphthong formants. In the case of /ju/ Formant Two was abbreviated, and the time interval of

Formant One only was taken as the unit duration.

Examination of the individual frequency plots showed that changes of all formants occurred for the most part during this time interval and that three more equally spaced points would follow these interval changes adequately. Three equidistant sampling points were deemed adequate to describe the changes of the frequency and amplitude of the fundamental.

The measures at the five sampling points described above were made in the following manner. The first and last sampling points were taken from the frequency and amplitude measures derived from the sections. If the section was less than 0.02 sec away, the section value was recorded. For the second, third, and fourth sampling points, the frequency was read from the individual frequency-time plots to the nearest 5 cps, and the amplitude

TABLE 3. Median amplitudes of diphthong formants at sampling points. Values in db re baseline of section.

Diphthong	Sampling Point				
	1	2	3	4	5
Fundamental					
/eɪ/	42		38		36
/aɪ/	40		38		36
/ɔɪ/	41		38		36
/oʊ/	42		38		36
/aʊ/	40		38		36
/ju/	42		39		36
Formant One					
/eɪ/	30	34	36	32	26
/aɪ/	32	35	31	30	22
/ɔɪ/	33	37	38	31	24
/oʊ/	34	38	38	32	26
/aʊ/	30	33	33	32	24
/ju/	35	40	36	33	24
Formant Two					
/eɪ/	18	23	21	18	11
/aɪ/	22	26	23	20	13
/ɔɪ/	30	28	26	20	13
/oʊ/	25	28	28	25	20
/aʊ/	24	25	27	26	20
/ju/	14	18	15	11	0
Formant Three					
/eɪ/	14	18	16	14	8
/aɪ/	10	12	14	13	10
/ɔɪ/	0	8	11	14	10
/oʊ/	0	5	7	0	0
/aʊ/	12	12	12	6	0
/ju/	10	16	11	0	0

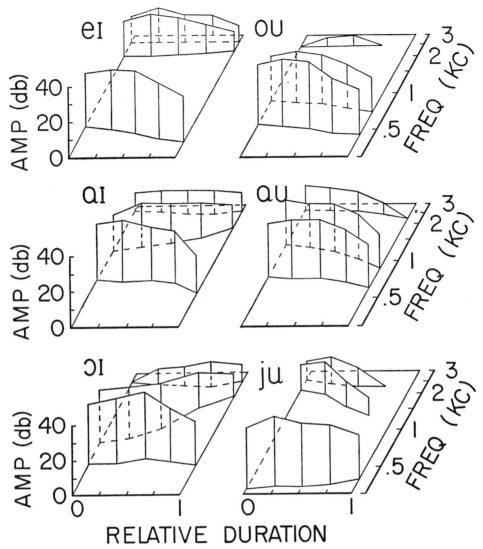

FIGURE 2. Temporal variations of median frequencies and amplitudes of formants during the course of utterance of diphthongs. Amplitude in db re baseline of section.

was determined from the section data. When a sampling point did not coincide with a section, the amplitude value was interpolated from adjacent sections. These procedures resulted in 1 800 sampling points for the three formants, at most of which the amplitude was sufficient for measurement. The median frequencies and amplitudes of the three

formants are tabulated in Tables 2 and 3. Each entry is based on 20 subjects except when the number was reduced by inadequate amplitude. For example, in Formant Two of /ju/ no measures were available at 28 sampling points in the last half of duration; in fact, only one subject yielded a measure for Formant Two at the last sampling point. In Formant Three there was no measurable amplitude at 197 sampling points. Such points tended to occur in those diphthongs having back vowels as one or both elements. As an example, at the first sampling point of Formant Three in /ɔɪ/ the amplitudes of 13 utterances were insufficient for measurement, and at the fifth sampling point of Formant Three there was no measurable energy for /oʊ/ and /ju/ for any subject.

The median frequencies and amplitudes of the three formants are graphed in Figure 2. The base line is relative duration, equal graphically for all diphthongs. Frequency is plotted logarithmically along the diagonal, and the height of the vertical line indicates amplitude in decibels. These lines are connected to show the changes that occurred during the course of the diphthong.

In /eɪ/ it will be observed that the frequencies (F_1 and F_2) of Formants One and Two started at about 550 and 2 000 cps, respectively, and, as the utterance progressed, F_1 decreased to about 400 cps, while F_2 rose to about 2 200 cps. The amplitudes of the formants varied, with the amplitude of Formant One (A_1) increasing about 5 db during the first half of the diphthong, which was followed by a decrease of about 10 db by the end of the last half. The A_2 variation was similar in both location and extent. The changes of both frequency and amplitude occurred at a fairly regular rate in /eɪ/, and F_1 and F_2 diverged during the course of the diphthong.

In a general way, changes similar to those of /eɪ/ may be observed in the other two /ɪ/ diphthongs. The lower two formants in /ɑɪ/ and /ɔɪ/ started at different frequency locations, and the change in frequency accelerated in the last half of utterance. Also, F_1 and F_2 diverged during the course of the diphthong as was the case with /eɪ/. With respect to frequency direction, all three of the /ɪ/ diphthongs were similar. The changes in A_1 and A_2 of /ɑɪ/ were like those in /eɪ/, but the range of amplitude change was considerable, being 13 db in both A_1 and A_2 during the course of the formants. In /ɔɪ/ F_1 started slightly lower than that of /ɑɪ/ and fell only a few cycles, while F_2 showed the largest change of the diphthongs. A_1 increased and then diminished; in contrast, A_2 diminished at a regular rate across a rather large range of 17 db. In /eɪ/, /ɑɪ/, and /ɔɪ/, A_1 started with a relatively high amplitude, increased slightly, and then diminished to a smaller amplitude than that at the start. In /ɔɪ/ A_2 diminished throughout at a steady rate, in contrast to the increase and decrease in /eɪ/ and /ɑɪ/.

The graph for /oʊ/ shows that Formant One was similar to that of /eɪ/ in both frequency and amplitude, but F_2 of /oʊ/ started much lower and went steadily downward, while A_1 and A_2 increased slightly and then decreased, the A_1 range being 12 db while that of A_2 was 8 db. F_1 and F_2 of /oʊ/ maintained about the same ratio since both formants demonstrated a fairly steady rate of decline during the course of the diphthong. The formants of /ɑʊ/ varied similarly to those of /oʊ/. However, F_2 descended more swiftly than did F_1 so that the two formants tended to converge. A_1 and A_2 rose and then fell characteristically in /ɑʊ/.

The time course of /ju/ was unique in that F_1 rose slightly while F_2 fell across a wide frequency range and terminated at the fourth sampling point. The relative convergence of F_1 and F_2 was far greater than in /ɑʊ/. The greatest variation of A_1 and A_2 may be observed in /ju/. The A_1 variation was 16 db, while that of A_2 was 18 db. In addition, it may be seen that /ju/ also had the greatest A_1/A_2 ratio across the sampling points.

Among the six diphthongs F_3 either stayed relatively constant or tended to follow F_2. With respect to amplitude, the largest contrast of A_3 was between /eɪ/ and /oʊ/. In fact, only at the second and third sampling points did the median of A_3 of /oʊ/ exceed zero db. With the exception of /ɔɪ/, the variations of A_3 during the course of the diphthong were quite similar to those of A_2. In /ɔɪ/, however, A_3 started weakly and tended to increase throughout except at the very end. In /eɪ/, /ɑɪ/, and /ɔɪ/ A_3 tended to remain at a fairly high level throughout, but in /oʊ/, /ɑʊ/, and /ju/, it diminished to zero db by the end of utterance. Consequently, it may be seen that the /ɪ/ diphthongs were characterized by a fall of F_1, a rise of F_2, and a strong A_3 for most of the duration. In contrast, the /ʊ/ diphthongs were characterized by a fall of both F_1 and F_2 and by a diminishing of A_3 toward the end of utterance. Finally, /ju/ was characterized by a rising F_1, a falling F_2, and a decrease of A_2 and A_3.

The locations of F_1 and F_2, as would be expected from past research, appear to constitute the main defining features of the six individual phonemes. The data shown in Figure 2 indicate, however, that the amplitudes and amplitude variations of Formant Three are distinctive for each of the phonemes, although

the frequencies of this formant would not appear to be very distinctive for the individual phonemes. With no single exception at any sampling point A_1, A_2, and A_3 decreased progressively in that order. An inspection of the diphthongs in Figure 2 will show that the steepness of the decrease in amplitude varied from phoneme to phoneme at the respective sampling points. The slope of the amplitude across the formants is related to the vowel elements of the diphthong. For example, the slope from A_1 to A_3 was about 15 db steeper in /oʊ/ than in /eɪ/ over about the same frequency range. The slopes remained fairly constant across the duration in both /eɪ/ and /oʊ/. At the final sampling point, the A_1/A_3 slope was about 18 db in /eɪ/ as compared with 26 db in /oʊ/. The slope of /ɑɪ/ is similar to that of /eɪ/, that is, slight. This is in contrast to that of /ɑʊ/, which starts with a slope similar to /ɑɪ/, but ends with a slope of 24 db. This latter fact illustrates the difference in the influences of an open back vowel and a relatively close back vowel. In /ɔɪ/ the change in the slope was large. The A_1/A_3 slope was 33 db at the beginning where the first element is a back vowel, but only 14 db at the end where the second element is a front vowel. In general, with respect to the final sampling points, the A_1/A_3 slope was steep for the /ʊ/ diphthongs and for /ju/, with A_3 not being measurable in all three cases. In contrast, a more gradual slope was seen in the /ɪ/ diphthongs.

Although the fundamental was not of particular interest in the experiment, it will be noted (Tables 2 and 3) that the changes with time are not only regular, but also substantial. In fact, the fundamental frequency typically decreased about two and one-half tones and amplitude about 5 db during the course of the diphthong.

Frequencies of Formants One and Two in Diphthongs. Figure 3 shows a coordinate plot of the frequency measurements of Formants One and Two

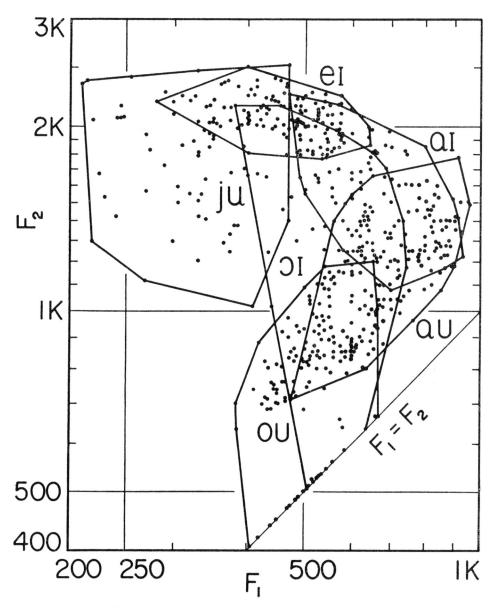

FIGURE 3. Frequencies (F_1 and F_2) of Formants One and Two as measured at all sampling points in the various utterances of diphthongs.

for all of the individual samples. The display is in a manner usual for the vowels with F_2 and F_1 shown logarithmically along the ordinate and abscissa, respectively. The five sampling points have been plotted without regard to their time locations, and the solid lines enclose the total scatters of the points for the various diphthongs. It may be seen that the areas overlap one another

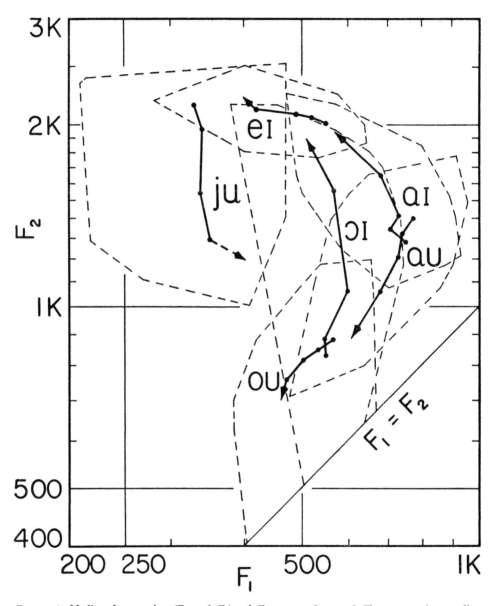

FIGURE 4. Median frequencies (F_1 and F_2) of Formants One and Two at each sampling point in diphthongs (dots), with directions of change shown by arrows. General areas (dashed lines) from Figure 3.

as a rule rather than the exception. The areas reveal the general locations of the diphthongs and their relationships to each other. For instance, the F_1 range for /aɪ/ is similar to that of /aʊ/, while the F_2 ranges of /aɪ/ and /aʊ/ overlap in part and then extend in opposite directions. In /eɪ/ and /oʊ/ the F_2 ranges are widely separated, but they have the F_1 range largely in common. It may be seen that /ɔɪ/ has a very wide F_2 range, and that it occupies a central position in both F_1 and F_2 with respect to the other diphthongs.

In /ɔɪ/ and /oʊ/ F_1 and F_2 could not be distinguished as separate regions in some of the samples. In Figure 3 these values are represented by the points placed along the 45° line at the bottom of the figure. In their study of vowel formants, Fairbanks and Grubb (*1*) found that in some samples of /ɔ/ only one formant could be identified in the lower frequency range. It was reported that such vowels were carefully studied to make certain that the sectioning point was representative; several sections were taken, and the one-formant finding was confirmed in every case. The same one-formant characteristic was found in the present experiment in six utterances of /ɔɪ/ and in four of /oʊ/, the two diphthongs having a portion of their areas in common.

The large size of the /ju/ area suggests that considerable variation is permissible in F_1 and F_2, perhaps because confusion with other phonemes would be unlikely.

In Figure 4 the medians of the sampling points for the several diphthongs are shown against the background of the areas which have been duplicated

from Figure 3. The points have been connected and the directions of change indicated by arrows at the final sampling points. In the right center of the figure, the /aɪ/ and /aʊ/ are seen to start essentially from the same area and travel in opposite directions. The course of /eɪ/ is seen for the most part as a decrease in F_1. On the other hand, /oʊ/ shows a decrease of both F_1 and F_2, the F_1/F_2 ratio being about 1.5 and remaining fairly constant. A long upward shift of F_2 characterizes /ɔɪ/, while /ju/ is seen as essentially a downward shift of F_2. The final measure of /ju/ represents the obtained value of F_1, but F_2 has been extrapolated, as shown by the dashed line since Formant Two had a shorter duration than that of Formant One.

The rate of frequency shift may be estimated since the dots along the lines of Figure 4 indicate equal time intervals. In /aɪ/ it may be seen that the amount of frequency change varied during the four quarters of its duration. In the first two quarters the change was small, but there were large shifts during the last two. A similar acceleration in frequency change was apparent during the last half of utterance in both /aʊ/ and /ɔɪ/. For the three diphthongs above, a basic vowel appears to be firmly established in the first half, whereas the latter half involves continuous and accelerated change. In contrast, the rate of frequency change in /eɪ/ and /oʊ/ is seen to be fairly regular throughout with the exception of the third quarter of /eɪ/. There is a notably small frequency shift during the first quarter of /ju/ with the most rapid rate of change occurring during the second quarter.

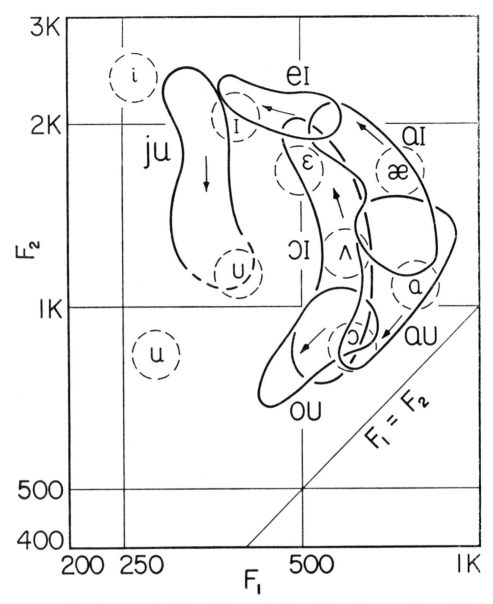

FIGURE 5. Central regions of variation of frequencies (F_1 and F_2) of Formants One and Two in diphthongs (see text). Dashed circles indicate locations of *preferred* vowels (1).

Diphthong Formants Relative to Vowel Formants. In Figure 5 the envelope for each diphthong represents a smoothed enclosure of the 10 samples closest to the median at each sampling point during the utterance. Each of the envelopes may be interpreted as the band within which the middle 50% of the subjects varied during the course of utterance. Except for /ju/, it will be noticed that each envelope narrows as time goes on. The diphthongs give the impression of heading toward target points with variations decreasing as the terminal points are approached. This is particularly true in /eɪ/ where the terminal portion of the envelope is seen to be quite small. In /ju/, a 'rising diphthong,' the glide portion also has the smaller area and the base vowel the larger, but the smaller area is seen at the beginning rather than at the end. The shapes of the envelopes suggest somewhat less individual variability in the glide portion than in the stressed portion.

The small circles shown in Figure 5 indicate the locations of Fairbanks and Grubb's (*1*) *preferred* vowel samples. These circles may be considered as representative of vowel areas since they derive from a rigorous procedure of selection and judgment. In the Fairbanks and Grubb study nine General American vowels were sustained by seven skilled speakers at approximately the same fundamental frequency. The samples were **recorded** and self-approved by each speaker as representative of the intended vowel. The samples were then presented twice to a group of eight trained observers. The observers attempted vowel identification during the first presentation, and they rated the samples on a scale of representativeness, knowing the vowel which each sample was intended to represent during the second presentation. An arbitrary category of *identified* samples consisted of those samples correctly identified by 75% or more of the observers. Within the group of identified samples of each vowel another category of *preferred* samples was defined. This last category was to contain the most representative samples from among the most readily identified

samples. From each set of identified samples of a vowel the four with the highest median ratings were chosen to be the *preferred* samples.

The frequencies of Formants One and Two of the vowels shown in Figure 5 are those of the *preferred* vowel samples. In this figure it may be seen that the starting area of /eɪ/ lies somewhat above and slightly to the right of /ɛ/, and its ending is just above /ɪ/. At the bottom center of the figure, the starting area of /oʊ/ is seen to be slightly above /ɔ/. A starting area between /æ/ and /ɑ/, perhaps in the location of /a/, is common to /ɑɪ/ and /ɑʊ/. It may also be seen that /ɑɪ/ passes through /æ/ and extends into the starting area of /eɪ/. In the opposite direction, /ɑʊ/ passes through /ɑ/ and extends into the starting area of /oʊ/. It should be noted also that /ɑʊ/ ends squarely at the preferred area of /ɔ/. In a general way the ending areas of /ɑɪ/, /eɪ/, and /ɔɪ/ approximate the F_2 value of /ɪ/, whereas the endings of /ɑʊ/ and /oʊ/ approximate the F_2 value of /u/. There is a sort of rudimentary triangle formed by the pathways of /ɑɪ/ and /eɪ/ on the one hand,

TABLE 4. Median frequencies of vowel formants. Values in cps.

Vowel	F_0	F_1	F_2	F_3
/i/	120	272	2 312	2 940
/ɪ/	120	422	2 025	2 710
/ɛ/	125	520	1 925	2 610
/æ/	112	592	1 955	2 615
/ɑ/	125	752	1 245	2 500
/ɔ/	135	630	902	2 580
/ʊ/	130	465	1 132	2 385
/u/	135	342	940	2 302
/ʌ/	120	630	1 322	2 600
/ɝ/	125	475	1 310	1 650

and of /ɑʊ/ and /oʊ/ on the other, which are joined by the curved pathway of /ɔɪ/. The area of /ɔɪ/ starts near /ɔ/, passes through /ʌ/, and extends slightly beyond /ɛ/ toward /ɪ/.

It will be observed that /ju/ starts between /i/ and /ɪ/ and extends to the /ʊ/ area. Again, the dashed portion of the envelope indicates extrapolation of F₂, as was mentioned previously. The results of the experiment show no tendency for the second element of /ju/ to reach the /u/ area in the F₁ and F₂ coordinate plane. In every case

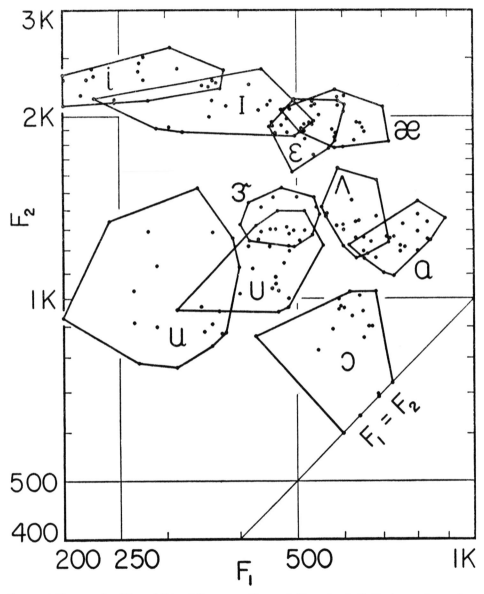

FIGURE 6. Frequencies (F₁ and F₂) of Formants One and Two for individual vowel samples.

Formant Two subsided, and only Formant One was measurable during the final quarter of the utterance.

It is interesting to note that /eɪ/ appears to be essentially an extension of /aɪ/. If one pronounces these two diphthongs with /aɪ/ immediately followed without interruption of phonation by /eɪ/, the articulatory movement may be perceived as being continuous. A similar flowing movement exists with the /aʊ/–/oʊ/ combination.

The major movement of the diphthongs tends to occur during the last

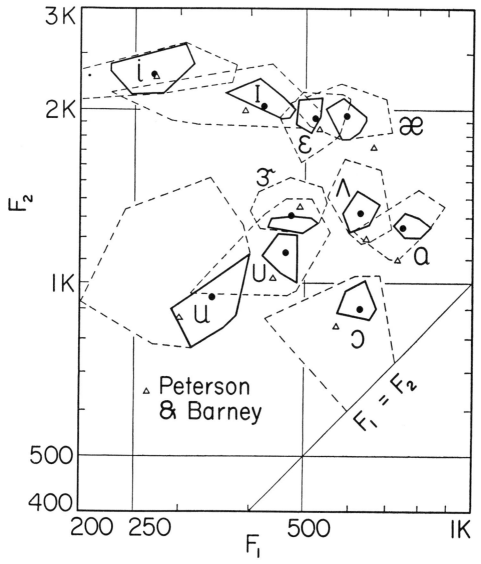

FIGURE 7. Areas of frequencies (F₁ and F₂) of Formants One and Two for middle 50% of vowel samples. Medians of all samples shown by points; means from Peterson and Barney (7) shown by triangular points. General areas (dashed lines) from Figure 6.

half of the utterance, so that the first half of the time is spent on the base vowel. As was seen in Figure 4, one-half of the durations of /aɪ/, /aʊ/, and /ɔɪ/ were devoted to accomplishing the first one-third of the frequency shift.

The off-glide is characterized by shift of frequency which may not achieve any specified combination of F_1 and F_2 in the sense of a steady-state vowel but may perhaps need only to satisfy a general location of F_2 as the utterance subsides. As has been seen in connection with Figure 2, the amplitude of Formant Three is strong at the end of the /ɪ/ diphthongs, weak at the end of the /ʊ/ diphthongs. As will be shown below in the discussion of the vowel samples, the differences in A_3 appear to characterize front and back vowels as classes. Accordingly, since the data on diphthongs show no single terminal vowels to which the different classes of diphthongs glide when both F_1 and F_2 are considered, the use of /i/ and /u/ as glide symbols, as has sometimes been the practice, might be considered to indicate the polar changes of F_2 and A_3.

Frequencies of Formants One and Two in Vowels. In Table 4 the median frequencies of the formants and the fundamental are presented for each of the 10 vowels studied. A graphic display of the vowels may be seen in Figure 6 wherein Formants One and Two are plotted coordinately, with solid boundary lines enclosing the 20 individual samples of each vowel. In the upper left-hand corner the area of /i/ may be seen to extend over a relatively wide range in F_1, but the F_2 range is somewhat restricted. A larger variation of both F_1 and F_2 is

seen for /ɪ/. The areas of both /ɪ/ and /æ/ overlap the /ɛ/ area. In fact, about 50% of the /æ/ area overlaps into that of /ɛ/, whereas the /ɑ/ and /ʌ/ areas overlap only slightly. The /ɔ/ area is the only one which does not overlap any of the other vowel areas. The points located along the 45° line at the bottom of the /ɔ/ area represent samples similar to those mentioned earlier in the discussion of /ɔɪ/ and /oʊ/ in which there was only one low frequency formant. The /ʊ/ area extends into both /ɝ/ and /u/, and the largest vowel area is that of /u/.

In Figure 7 the vowel areas have been reproduced from Figure 6 and are represented by the dashed lines. The smaller areas within each vowel area surround the 10 samples closest to the median. The median vowel is indicated in each area by a round point, and the means of Peterson and Barney (7) are shown by triangular points. It is immediately apparent that these restricted areas are mutually exclusive and generally small. For the most part the differences between the findings of Peterson and Barney and those of this

TABLE 5. Median amplitudes of vowel formants. Values in db re baseline of section.

Vowel	A_0	A_1	A_2	A_3
/i/	40	41	20	18
/ɪ/	40	40	25	22
/ɛ/	40	40	26	23
/æ/	38	37	28	24
/ɑ/	38	38	30	16
/ɔ/	36	40	33	12
/ʊ/	39	42	23	14
/u/	40	41	20	8
/ʌ/	38	41	26	16
/ɝ/	38	40	26	20

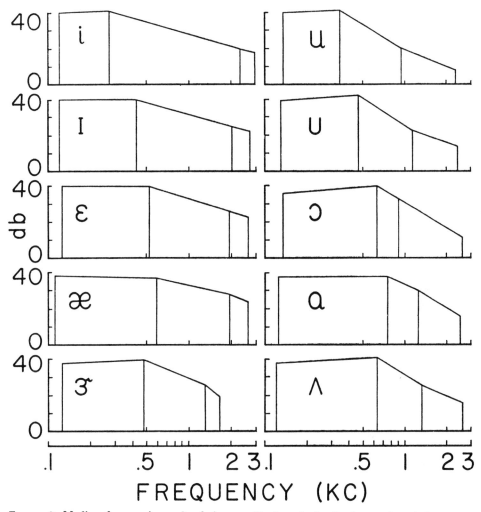

FIGURE 8. Median frequencies and relative amplitudes of the fundamental and first three formants of vowels. Amplitude in db re baseline of section.

experiment were minor. The only difference of consequence is in /æ/, which is closer to /ɛ/ in the present experiment. The explanation of this difference may lie in the method of collecting samples. In Peterson and Barney's experiment the subject read the words one at a time from a list, which may have invited contrasts more marked than those occurring with the procedure of the present study.

Spectra of Vowels. The median amplitudes of Formants One, Two, and Three and the fundamental may be seen in Table 5. In Figure 8 the data in Tables 4 and 5 were utilized for the graphs in which frequency is displayed logarithmically on the abscissa with the amplitude in db on the ordinate. These graphs show the essential features of sections made on the sound spectrograph.

A study of Figure 8 shows that F_3 tends to be higher in the front vowels than in the corresponding back vowels. This finding is in agreement with earlier work. Also, it should be noted that F_3 in /ɚ/ is very low and close to F_2, a finding which also agrees with previous reports. The fundamental frequency does not seem to vary systematically, nor does it vary over a large range. The characteristics of F_1 and F_2 have already been discussed in connection with Figure 7. There is very little difference from vowel to vowel with respect to A_0 and A_1, the range being 5 db over all. It will be observed that A_1 is greater than A_2, which in turn is greater than A_3 in all vowels. It may also be observed that A_2 tends to vary inversely with F_2. In other words the graph suggests that the amplitude of a given formant tends generally to be dependent upon its frequency. With respect to A_3, however, the largest A_3 among the back vowels is of less amplitude than the smallest A_3 of the front vowels. With the exception of /ɔ/ A_3 increases from the high to the low vowels in both the back vowel and the front vowel series. Since A_1 is relatively constant for all vowels, the steepness of the slope of the spectrum is primarily controlled by A_3. As a result the back vowel spectra are steeper than those of the corresponding front vowels. A similar systematic difference was observed in A_3 between the /ɪ/ diphthongs and the /ʊ/ diphthongs. Accordingly, the variations of A_3 during the various diphthongs are seen to be related to the differences in A_3 between the vowels that are pertinent.

Summary

Six diphthongs and 10 vowels were spoken in words by 20 men, all native General American speakers. By means of the sound spectrograph the variations of the frequencies and amplitudes of the lower three formants were measured with the following major findings.

Durations of the formants were relatively short in /eɪ/, /oʊ/, and /ju/, longer in /aɪ/, /ɔɪ/, and /aʊ/. Formants One and Two coincided approximately throughout.

The Formant One and Formant Two frequencies, F_1 and F_2, diverged during their course in /eɪ/, /aɪ/, and /ɔɪ/, tended to maintain a constant ratio as both lowered during /oʊ/, and converged during /aʊ/ and /ju/. The Formant One and Formant Two amplitudes, A_1 and A_2, tended to increase slightly at first and to decrease thereafter, becoming lower at the end than at the beginning. A_3 appeared to be capable of differentiating classes of diphthongs, being prominent in /ɪ/ diphthongs, weak in /ʊ/ diphthongs.

Coordinate plots of F_1 and F_2 showed extensive overlap of vowel areas, but the areas were mutually exclusive when the 10 samples closest to the median were considered. The findings were in general agreement with those of earlier measurements. In some of the /ɔ/ samples only one formant was identified in the lower frequency region. A_3 in front vowels exceeded A_3 in back vowels. Back vowel spectra were steeper than those of corresponding front vowels.

Summario in Interlingua

Sex diphthongos e dece vocals esseva parlate in vocabulos per vinti masculos, toto native General American parlators. Per medio de le sono spectrograph le variationes de le frequentias e amplitudes de le plus basse tres formants esseva mesurate con le sequente major trovantes.

Durations de le formants esseva relativement curte in /eɪ/, /oʊ/, e /ju/, plus longe in /aɪ/, /ɔɪ/, e /aʊ/. Formants Un e Duo coincide approximamente in omne partes.

Le frequentias de Formant Un e Formant Duo, F_1 e F_2, divergite durante lor curso in /eɪ/, /aɪ/, e /ɔɪ/, tendite mantener un constante ration como ambes bassate durante /oʊ/, e convergite durante /aʊ/ e /ju/. Le amplitudes de Formant Un e Formant Duo, A_1 e A_2, tendite augmentar legiermente al principio e discrescer pois, deveniente plus basse a le fin que al entrata. A_3 apparite esser capabile de differentiante classes de diphthongos, essente prominente in /ɪ/ diphthongos, debile in /ʊ/ diphthongos.

Coordinate designantes de F_1 e F_2 monstrate extense duplication de vocal areas, sed le areas esseva mutualmente exclusive quando le dece exemplos le plus proximine a le mediana esseva considerate. Le trovantes esseva in general concordantia con istes de ante mesuration. In alicun de le /ɔ/ exemplos sol un formant esseva identificate in le inferior frequentia region. A_3 in fronte vocals excedite A_3 in post vocals. Post vocal spectra esseva plus precipitose que illes de correspondente fronte vocals.

References

1. FAIRBANKS, G., and GRUBB, PATTI, A psychophysical investigation of vowel formants. *J. Speech Hearing Res.*, 4, 1961, 203-219.
2. JOOS, M., Acoustic phonetics. *Language Monogr.*, 23 (suppl. to 24, 1948).
3. LEHISTE, I., and PETERSON, G. E., Transitions, glides, and diphthongs. *J. acoust. Soc. Amer.*, 33, 1961, 268-277.
4. LIDDELL, M. H., The physical characteristics of speech sound. Bull. No. 16, Eng. Exper. Stat., Purdue Univ., 1924.
5. LIDDELL, M. H., The physical characteristics of speech sound–II. Bull. No. 23, Eng. Exper. Stat., Purdue Univ., 1925.
6. LIDDELL, M. H., The physical characteristics of speech sound–III. Bull. No. 28, Eng. Exper. Stat., Purdue Univ., 1927.
7. PETERSON, G. E., and BARNEY, H. L., Control methods used in a study of the vowels. *J. acoust. Soc. Amer.*, 24, 1952, 175-184.
8. PETERSON, G. E., and COXE, M. S., The vowels /e/ and /o/ in American speech. *Quart. J. Speech*, 39, 1953, 33-41.
9. POTTER, R. K., KOPP, G. A., and GREEN, HARRIET C., *Visible Speech*. New York: Van Nostrand, 1947.
10. POTTER, R. K., and PETERSON, G. E., The representation of vowels and their movements. *J. acoust. Soc. Amer.*, 20, 1948, 528-535.

PART III

Synthesis and Perception

Reprinted from The Journal of the Acoustical Society of America, Vol. 24, No. 6, 597–606, November, 1952
Copyright, 1952, by the Acoustical Society of America.

Some Experiments on the Perception of Synthetic Speech Sounds*

Franklin S. Cooper, Pierre C. Delattre,† Alvin M. Liberman,‡ John M. Borst, and Louis J. Gerstman
Haskins Laboratories, New York, New York
(Received August 4, 1952)

Synthetic methods applied to isolated syllables have permitted a systematic exploration of the acoustic
cues to the perception of some of the consonant sounds. Methods, results, and working hypotheses are
discussed.

THE program of research on which we are engaged was described in general terms at the preceding Speech Communication Conference.[1] As we pointed out there, and in more detail in another paper,[2] our work on the perception of speech was based on the assumption that we would have a flexible and convenient experimental method if we could use a spectrographic display to control or manipulate speech sounds. Workers at the Bell Telephone Laboratories had developed the sound spectrograph, which made it instrumentally feasible to obtain spectrograms of relatively long samples of connected speech, and it had become evident that the spectrographic transform has important advantages over the oscillogram as a way of displaying speech sounds to the eye. We were interested in using the spectrogram, not merely as a representation of speech sounds, but also as a basis for modifying and, in the extreme case, creating them. For that purpose we built a machine called a pattern playback, which converts spectrographic pictures into sound, using either photographic copies of actual spectrograms or, alternatively, "synthetic" patterns which are painted by hand on a cellulose acetate base. Having determined first that the playback would speak quite intelligibly from photographic copies of actual spectrograms, we proceeded to prepare hand-painted patterns of test sentences[3] which were, by comparison with the original spectrograms, very highly simplified (see Fig. 1). In drawing the hand-painted spectrograms we tried, as the first step, to reproduce as well as we could those aspects of the original pattern which were most apparent to the eye, and then, by working back and forth between hand-painted spectrogram and sound, we modified the patterns, usually by trial and error, until the simplified spectrograms were rather highly intelligible.

The work with simplified spectrograms did not provide unequivocal answers to questions about the minimal and invariant patterns for the various sounds of speech, but it did enable us to develop our techniques, and, further, it suggested certain specific problems which appeared to warrant more systematic investigation. In our research on these problems we have departed from the procedure of progressively simplifying the spectrograms of actual speech and have undertaken instead to study the effects on perception of variations in isolated acoustic elements or patterns. Thus, we can hope to determine the separate contributions to the perception of speech of several acoustic variables and, ultimately, to learn how they can be combined to best effect.

STOP CONSONANTS: BURSTS OF NOISE

A careful inspection of actual spectrograms suggests, and our experience with simplified spectrograms seems to confirm, that one of the variables that may enable a listener to differentiate *p*, *t*, and *k* is the position along the frequency scale of the brief burst of noise which constitutes the acoustic counterpart of the articulatory explosion. In an attempt to isolate this variable and determine its role in perception, we prepared a series of schematized burst-plus-vowel patterns in which bursts at each of twelve frequency positions were paired with each of seven cardinal vowels. As can be seen in Fig. 2, the bursts were constant as to size and shape, and the vowels, which maintained a steady state throughout, were composed of two formants only.[4] All of the combinations of burst and vowel—a total of 84 syllable patterns—were converted into sound and presented in random order to 30 college students with instructions to identify the initial component of the syllable as *p*, *t*, or *k*.

Figure 3 shows, for each of the vowels, how the subjects' identifications varied according to the frequency position of the burst. In general, it appears that this one variable—the frequency position of the burst—provides the listener with a basis for distinguishing among *p*, *t*, and *k*. We see that high frequency bursts were heard as *t* for all vowels. Bursts at lower frequencies were heard as *k* when they were on a level with, or slightly above, the second formant of the vowel; otherwise they were heard as *p*. It is clear that for *p* and *k*

---

* This research was made possible in part by funds granted by the Carnegie Corporation of New York and in part through the support of the Department of Defense in connection with Contract DA49-170-sc-274.
† Also at the University of Pennsylvania, Philadelphia, Pennsylvania.
‡ Also at the University of Connecticut, Storrs, Connecticut.

[1] F. S. Cooper, J. Acoust. Soc. Am. 22, 761–762 (1950).
[2] Cooper, Liberman, and Borst, Proc. Natl. Acad. Sci. 37, 318–325 (1951).
[3] We employed sentence lists prepared by Egan and co-workers. See J. Egan, O.S.R.D. Report No. 3802, Psycho-Acoustic Laboratory, Harvard University, November 1, 1944.
[4] For a complete account of the experimental work leading to the choice of the formant frequencies of these vowels, see Delattre, Liberman, and Cooper, Le Maître Phonétique No. 96, 30–36 (July–December, 1951).

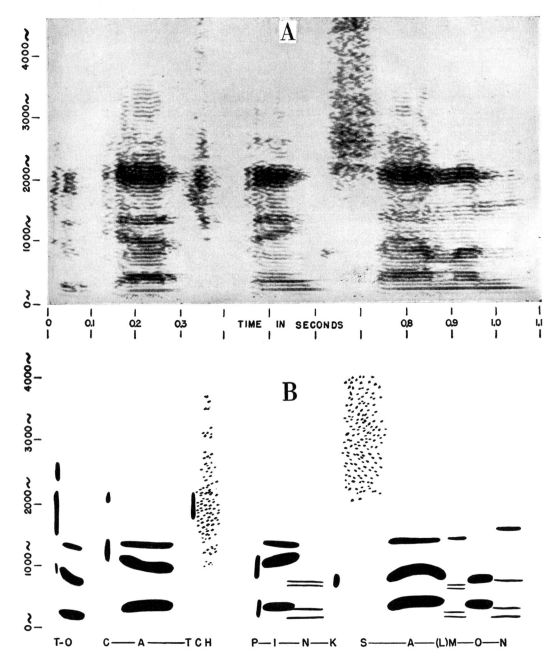

FIG. 1. (A) Sound spectrogram of human speech. (B) Simplified version of the same phrase, painted by hand. Both of these spectrographic patterns are intelligible after conversion into sound by means of the pattern playback. (Reproduced by courtesy of the American Journal of Psychology.)

the identification of the consonant depended, not solely on the frequency position of the burst of noise, but rather on this position in relation to the vowel. In other words, the perception of these stimuli, and also, perhaps, the perception of their spoken counterparts,

requires the consonant-vowel combination as a minimal acoustic unit.[5]

---

[5] For a detailed account of the experiment and a further discussion of the results, see Liberman, Delattre, and Cooper, Am. J. Psychol. (to be published).

STOP CONSONANTS: TRANSITIONS

We turned next in our study of the stop consonants to another aspect of the acoustic pattern which is often evident in spectrograms, namely, the consonant-vowel transitions. These transitions are seen as rapid shifts in the frequency positions of the vowel formants where vowel and consonant join and are typically most marked for the second formant, although they are usually present in some degree for the other formants as well.

The interpretation of these transitions is a major problem. In articulatory terms it is clear that the positions of the speech organs for consonant and vowel are, in general, different and that the rapid movement from one position to the other will usually produce an equally rapid shift in the acoustic output. The parallel interpretation in perceptual terms is that these rapid changes in the sound stream are no more than the necessary transitions (hence, the name) between the sounds that serve to identify successive phonemes; by implication, the transitions are merely nulls which dilute, or even confuse, the acoustic message.

An alternative interpretation is that these rapid changes are heard as important distinguishing characteristics of the sound stream and may indeed serve as a principal acoustic cue for the perception of the consonant-vowel combination—the syllable or "half-syllable," as the case may be.[6] Since a vowel is usually loud and long (hence, identifiable by itself) whereas a consonant is often weak or of very short duration, the practical effect is that the transitional portion of the vowel is transferred to the acoustic counterpart of the consonant. But whether one considers the syllable as separable in this restricted sense or as an indissoluble unit, the second interpretation of transitions gives far more weight to their role in speech perception than the term "transition" would imply. The first step in exploring this question experimentally was to select one vowel and to draw synthetic spectrograms in which a

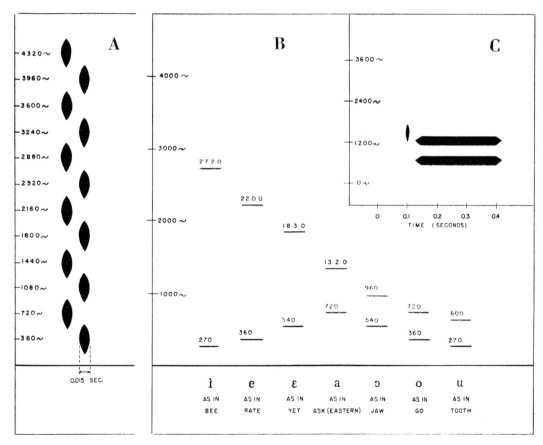

FIG. 2. Stimulus patterns used in determining the effect of burst position on the perception of the unvoiced stop consonants. (A) Frequency positions of the twelve bursts of noise. (B) Frequency positions of the formants of the two-formant vowels with which the bursts were paired. (C) One of the 84 "syllables" formed by pairing a burst of noise and a two-formant vowel. (Reproduced by courtesy of the American Journal of Psychology.)

[6] M. Joos, Language, Suppl. 24, 122, 1948.

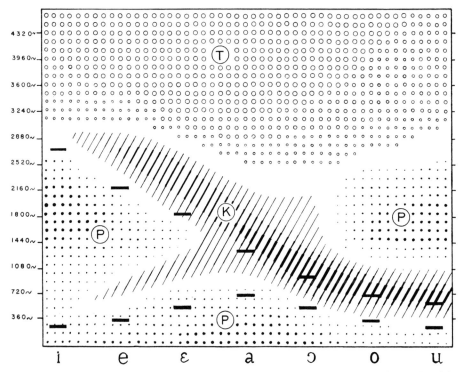

FIG. 3. Preferred identifications by 30 listeners of the stimuli of Fig. 2. The twelve center frequencies of the bursts of noise are shown along the *y* axis; the seven vowels are arranged in the order front-to-back along the *x* axis, with formant positions given. The zones show the burst-vowel combinations for which one of the three responses was dominant and indicate roughly the extent of dominance. (Reproduced by courtesy of the American Journal of Psychology.)

variety of "transitions" were added to the two-formant version of the vowel. Such a series is shown in Fig. 4. In the upper line, the first formant has always the same rising transition, but there is a systematic variation in the transitions of the second formant: rising sharply at the left of the figure, straight in the center, and falling steeply at the right. In the lower line, the same sequence of second-formant transitions is repeated, but the first formant has a very small rising transition. One observation that came from this sort of exploratory work was that the transitions of the first formant appear to contribute to voicing of the stop consonants, while transitions of the second formant provide a basis for distinguishing among *b*, *d*, and *g*, or their cognates *p*, *t*, and *k*. [The sounds corresponding to these painted spectrograms were presented by means of magnetic tape recordings.[7] These sounds were generated by passing the patterns of Fig. 4 through the pattern playback.]

Our first attempts to generalize from the second-formant transitions for *ba*, *da*, and *ga* to the corresponding transitions for a different vowel showed quite clearly that matters would be more complicated—that

we were again dealing with interactions or interrelations between the acoustic counterparts of consonant and vowel when they occur together as a syllable.

This exploratory work was followed by systematic tests of a range of second-formant transitions applied to each of the seven vowels that had previously been used in the *PTK*-burst experiment. The resulting test syllables are very much like those shown in Fig. 4 except that the extent of second-formant transitions was increased by one degree at the left and two at the right, giving a total of eleven different degrees of transition. Thus, with seven vowels, there were seventy-seven consonant-vowel stimuli to be judged. The results are

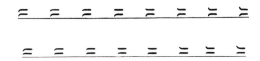

FIG. 4. Variations in the onset of vowel formants used in exploring the role of transitions. When the patterns shown in the upper line are converted into sound by the playback, the syllables *ba*, *da*, and *ga* are heard in succession as the second-formant transitions vary from rising to falling. The upper and lower lines differ only in the extent of the first-formant transitions; this seems to contribute to the voiced (upper) or unvoiced (lower) characteristics of the consonants.

---

[7] The authors will supply, at cost, copies of the sound demonstration on magnetic tape or disk.

shown in the upper left-hand corner of Fig. 5. There are, for each vowel, three bars showing the distribution of judgments among *b*, *d*, and *g* as a function of the direction and extent of the second-formant transition. All first formants had rising transitions similar to those in the upper half of Fig. 4. The length of the bar gives a rough indication of the range of different transitions included within the group judgment for each sound and, hence, some indication of the degree of over-lap or confusion among the sounds. Specifically, the connecting lines pass through the median judgments, and the bars end at the quartile points. Thus, the array shows that most of the subjects heard a rising second-formant transition as *b* and that falling transitions might be heard either as *g* or *d*, depending on the vowel.

In the lower left-hand quadrant of Fig. 5 are the results of a comparable test in which all of the first formants were straight, or "unvoiced." Also, the two right-hand arrays of Fig. 5 give comparable data for the two sets of test stimuli mentioned above when, how-ever, the subjects were instructed to choose among *p*, *t*, and *k*. In a general way, the four arrays are similar. The results agree in the predominance of *b* (or *p*) judgments for rising second-formant transitions and in the existence of a crossover between *d* (or *t*) and *g* (or *k*) judgments for falling transitions. It does appear that the cognate relationships between *ptk* and *bdg* are effectively cued by the second-formant transitions. A problem remains, however, of finding adequate cues for the distinction between voiced and unvoiced stops. Transitions of the first formant make some difference, and, of course, the presence or absence of a "voice bar" at the fundamental frequency plays a role.

The same data are presented somewhat more directly in Fig. 6. Vowel color is now displayed along the *y* axis, and the extent of second-formant transition is the *x* dimension, as shown pictorially at the lower left; the heights of the "mountains" show the percentage distributions of the responses indicated by the column headings (*b*, *d*, *g*, or *p*, *t*, *k*) for the various stimulus

INSTRUCTIONS FOR JUDGING

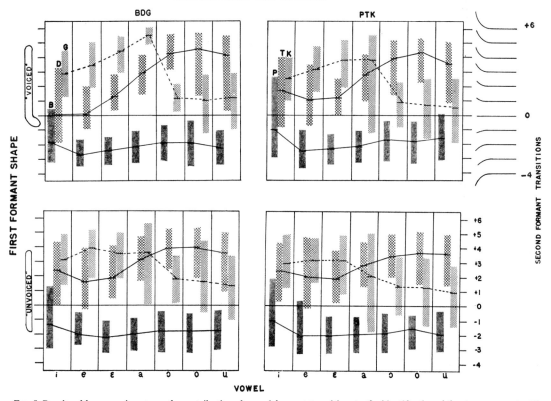

Fig. 5. Results of four experiments on the contribution of second-formant transitions to the identification of the stop consonants. The upper left quadrant is derived from the responses *b*, *d*, or *g* given by 33 subjects to a set of syllables similar to those in the upper row of Fig. 4, that is, syllables characterized by a constant rising transition of the first formant, eleven degrees of transition of the second-formant (*y* axis), and seven vowels (*x* axis). The connecting lines go through the transitions eliciting median responses for each vowel; the lengths of the bars show the quartile ranges. The upper right quadrant indicates the responses of a numerically equal, but different group of subjects to the same stimuli, but with instructions to limit their responses to *p*, *t*, or *k*. The lower two quadrants are based on experiments which differ from the above only in the employment of stimulus patterns similar to those of the lower row of Fig. 4, that is, of patterns with no transitions in the first formants.

combinations of transition plus vowel. One is somewhat reassured, in dealing with experiments of this kind, to find that some of the stimuli do yield unanimous agreement and that the variations, both with degree of transition and with vowel color, seem to be smooth and continuous. At the same time, it is evident that these transitions do not suffice in all cases; there are a few consonant-vowel combinations for which none of the transitions gives an unambiguous cue. However, a comparison of the data on transitions with the previous results for bursts shows that most of the ambiguous cases would possibly be resolved if *both* of these cues were being used.

NASAL RESONANTS: *M* AND *L*

A class of sounds which are cognate to *b*, *d*, *g*, and *p*, *l*, *k* consists of the nasal resonants *m*, *n*, and *ŋ*. Another series of exploratory experiments indicated that each of these consonants involves a vowel transition and also a steady-state resonant sound whose intensity and frequency characteristics are different from those of the vowel. We were interested, in the first instance, in segregating the effects of the transitions, and this seemed to require that we find a neutral position for the resonant portion which would convey the impression of resonant nasal consonants as a class without providing important cues to the identity of the particular consonant. This is probably an oversimplification, but it does permit us to collect data for a comparison of the resonants with the voiced and voiceless stops. We have run a first set of tests in which the previous seven vowels and eleven degrees of transition were paired in all possible combinations in syllables which also contained a neutral nasal resonance portion. The consonant was placed in terminal position since initial ŋ does not occur in English. This work is still in process; hence, no figure will be presented. In a general way, we find about the same distributions that appeared in the *BDG*-transition test. Thus, the second-formant transitions which were regularly heard as *b* (or *p*) in the preceding test now give the cognate *m*, and there is a comparable crossover in which *n* parallels *d* (or *t*) and ŋ parallels *g* (or *k*). There are some indications in the data that we are not dealing with a monovalent stimulus in this case; probably we shall have to explore variations in the supposedly neutral resonance.

The exploratory work that precedes systematic tests of the kind that we have been discussing tends to become divergent almost without limit, but also it turns up interesting leads, such as the example shown in Fig. 7.

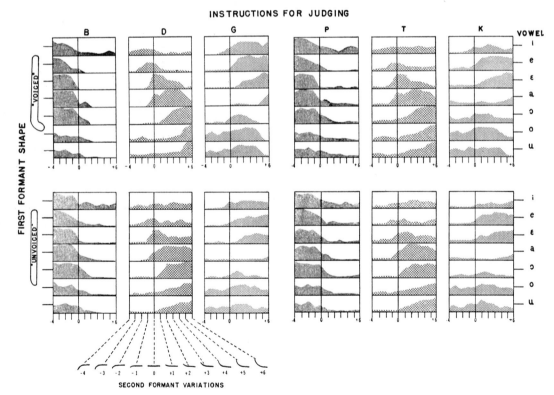

FIG. 6. Distributions of judgments of the stop consonants obtained with variations in second-formant transitions. The percentage of *b*, *d*, and *g* (or *p*, *t*, and *k*) responses is plotted for each vowel as a function of the direction and degree of second-formant transition (*x* axis). The medians and quartiles of these distributions were shown in the corresponding quadrants of Fig. 5.

We find that a transition from higher to lower frequency which is followed by a steady-state resonant sound is often heard as *m* but may at times sound like *l* instead. Our best guess at the moment and on the basis of cut-and-try experiments with only two vowels is that the distinctions between *l* and *m* are multiple, involving (a) the rate of transition of the second formant—a gradual transition favors *l*, a rapid transition favors *m*; (b) the frequency position of the low formant of the resonant portion—*l* is favored by a higher frequency; and (c) the behavior of the second formant in passing from vowel to resonance—if the second formant of the resonant portion forms a plausible continuation of the second formant of the vowel, one tends to hear *l*, whereas a sudden discontinuity contributes to an *m* impression. The first three lines of Fig. 7 illustrate these three pattern differences; the fourth line shows a composite pattern which incorporates all three differences. These are tentative results, but they indicate the kind of thing that one finds in the exploratory phase. [The sounds which correspond to these syllables were demonstrated, line by line, and in both forward and reverse directions.]

VOWELS

In this review we shall pass over a sizable block of work on two-formant and one-formant synthetic vowels, except to say that some of the results are most readily explained on the basis that the ear can, and sometimes does, perform an averaging operation on two formants which lie close together; thus, the first and second formants of the back vowels may at times be replaceable by a single formant, or the second and third formants of *i* by a single high formant. We have not so far found it necessary to use three formants to obtain reasonably good vowel color for the cardinal vowels, but an exploratory investigation has indicated that *transitions* of the third formant may contribute to consonant identification. Of course, the behavior of the third formant in spectrograms of the Midwestern *r* and of nasal vowels is well known.[8]

SOME FUTURE DIRECTIONS

The general directions in which the present work should be extended are fairly obvious. We have studied various acoustic cues in isolation. We can reasonably expect that the synthetic sounds will be identified with greater accuracy if two or three cues are provided *simultaneously*. We can even hope that *not more* than two or three acoustic cues will be required to give high intelligibility, even though the resulting sounds may still not be entirely lifelike. In addition, it is quite possible that such speech will be more resistant to noise than normal speech. As to the effectiveness of multiple cues, we know already that a transition added to a burst

[8] M. Joos, Language, Suppl. **24**, 93 (1948); also, Potter, Kopp, and Green, *Visible Speech* (D. Van Nostrand Company, Inc., New York, 1947), p. 220 ff.

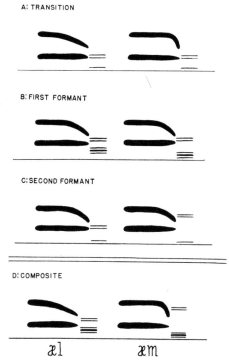

A: TRANSITION

B: FIRST FORMANT

C: SECOND FORMANT

D: COMPOSITE

æl æm

FIG. 7. Spectrographic patterns showing three acoustic cues which contribute to the perceptual differentiation of *l* and *m* following the vowel æ.

of noise improves the stop consonants, but we have yet to investigate what adjustments in burst position and in extent of transition may be required for the best combination of these two cues and just how much improvement will result. Also, while it is clear that bursts and transitions complement each other in the sense that when one cue is weak, the other is usually strong, nevertheless, there may remain some syllables for which both cues together may not suffice, and one must then search for other cues. One such possibility is a transition in the third formant of the vowel, and we do have some exploratory evidence of contributions from this quarter. However, the problem is not merely to find additional acoustic cues which make a contribution, but rather to sift out the two or three most efficient cues; that is, we should like eventually to rank-order the cues in terms of their *relative* contributions to intelligibility. Also, we need to run tests in which a greater variety of stimuli are presented and wider ranges of judgments are allowed, until finally, all of the phonemes of American English have been studied in their usual combinations.

The step from phoneme combinations to connected speech will involve a variety of additional problems, but we ought, eventually, to be able to synthesize connected speech on the sole basis of rules, or principles, of the same general kind that we are beginning to derive for the stops and the resonants. This is not our primary

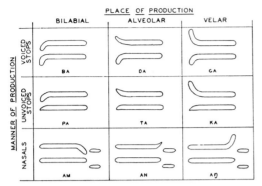

FIG. 8. An arrangement according to articulatory categories of spectrographic patterns which are heard as syllables consisting of the voiced stops, unvoiced stops, and nasal resonants paired in each case with the vowel a.

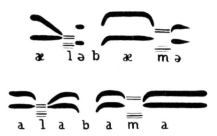

FIG. 9. Simplified spectrograms of the word "Alabama," drawn, in so far as this was possible, according to the rules derived from our research on the component phones and then modified somewhat to mimic a Southern U. S. Pronunciation (upper figure) and a French pronunciation (lower figure).

objective, but it does provide an over-all check on the validity of the acoustic descriptions.

SOME SPECULATIONS

In addition to the pragmatic objective of synthesizing speech and giving simplified acoustic descriptions of the speech sounds, we may hope that eventually an acoustic counterpart of the linguistic structure of the language might emerge—and indeed, that the regularities of the one structure might complement those of the other. Figure 8, for example, shows one attempt to correlate some of our acoustic data with the articulatory and linguistic patterns of English. There the schematic patterns for the voiced and voiceless stops and the nasal resonants (paired with the vowel a) are arranged in a 3-by-3 array based on articulatory features. It does seem that the acoustic data fit naturally into the array, with the distinctions among columns being given by the transitions of the second formant, and, among rows, by three "markers," namely, rising transitions of the first formant for the voiced stops, no transitions of the first formant (also bursts of noise not shown in the figure) for the unvoiced stops, and a steady resonant portion for the nasal resonants. [The playback sounds corresponding to the patterns of Fig. 8 were played, row by row and column by column.] We should probably not try to generalize from these limited data; we have not yet made the corresponding comparisons for a range of vowels, and some changes in interpretation may be necessary when we do.

As a second point, it may be of interest to examine the data from the point of view that perception involves a set of binary choices. You will recall that bursts of noise preceding a vowel were always heard as t when the center frequency of the burst was high, but that low bursts were heard as p or k, depending on the vowel that followed:

$$\text{Bursts:} \quad \frac{\text{High } (+) = \quad t}{\text{Low } \;\; (-) = p \text{ or } k}.$$

You will also recall that transitions of the second formant, if rising, were always heard as p, and if falling as t or k, depending on the vowel that followed:

$$\text{Transitions:} \quad \frac{\text{Falling } (+) = t \text{ or } k}{\text{Rising } \;\; (-) = \quad p}.$$

We have then a basis for deciding among p, t, and k, when both cues are given: $p = - -$ (low burst, rising transition), $t = + +$ (high burst, falling transition), $k = - +$ (low burst, falling transition). It would appear, then, that perceptual distinctions among p, t, and k might conceivably be made on the basis of only two separate binary decisions.[9] If this is correct, we should be able to synthesize satisfactory stop consonants without regard to the exact placement of bursts or to the precise degree of transition, but merely on the basis of "high" or "low" bursts and transitions. We are by no means confident that this can be done.

For a third point, let us return to the general subject of transitions. It seems fairly clear that transitions are important in speech perception, and one could wish for a name that would carry *this* implication rather than its opposite. You have seen how the identification of a particular transition (or burst) seems to depend also on the vowel, so that, apparently, one is perceiving an acoustic unit having the approximate dimensions of a syllable or half-syllable. Now this is not really very surprising if spectrograms are taken at face-value, but we—and perhaps some other workers as well—had undertaken to find the "invariants" of speech, a term which implies, at least in its simplest interpretation, a one-to-one correspondence between something half-hidden in the spectrogram and the successive phonemes of the message. It is precisely this kind of relationship that we do *not* find, at least for these stripped-down stops and nasal resonants. It may be useful to phrase this departure from a one-to-one correspondence between phoneme and sound in the technical jargon of cryptography, thereby borrowing a well-established

[9] We should, perhaps, point out that the kind of binary scheme being considered here differs in several respects from the system put forward by Jakobson, Fant, and Halle, Technical Report No. 13, Acoustics Laboratory, M.I.T. May, 1952.

distinction, and say that we seem to be dealing, at the acoustic level, with an *encoded* message rather than an *enciphered* one—or, more probably, with a mixture of code and cipher. But the important point, however phrased, is a caution that one may not always be able to find the phoneme in the speech wave, because it may not exist there in free form; in other words, one should not expect always to be able to find acoustic invariants for the *individual* phonemes.

The problem of speech perception is then to describe the decoding process either in terms of the decoding mechanism or—as we are trying to do—by compiling the code book, one in which there is one column for acoustic entries and another column for message units, whether these be phonemes, syllables, words, or whatever.

One more bit of speculation, if we may. The results of the *PTK*-burst experiment—and also the results with transitions—provide some extreme cases which suggest that the perceived similarities and differences between speech sounds may correspond more closely to the similarities and differences in the *articulatory* domain than to those in the *acoustic* domain; that is to say, the relation between perception and articulation may be simpler than the relation between perception and the acoustic stimulus. In Fig. 3, the set of bursts which were called *k* differ markedly in acoustic terms, despite the fact that they are heard as the same speech sound and are spoken in about—although not quite—the same way. On the other hand, the bursts at 1440 cps are identical sounds in acoustic terms, but they are heard as different speech sounds when paired with different vowels, e.g., *pi*, *ka*, and *pu*. Here, the perceived *differences* in the consonant are in contrast to the acoustic "*similarities*," but they might very well parallel articulatory differences if it is reasonable to assume that a person, in attempting to duplicate the sound of these bursts, would find it easiest to use his lips when his mouth is set to say *i* or *u* (close vowels) but would find it easiest to use the arch of the tongue with his mouth in position to say *a* (open vowel).

These are examples of what we mean in saying that perception may at times be more closely and simply related to the articulatory movements than to the acoustic stimuli. This is not a new concept—the central idea has been stated in various ways by various workers[10]—but we do believe that these considerations must be taken into account in any theory of speech perception; obviously, they are most directly related to the functioning of the decoding mechanism.

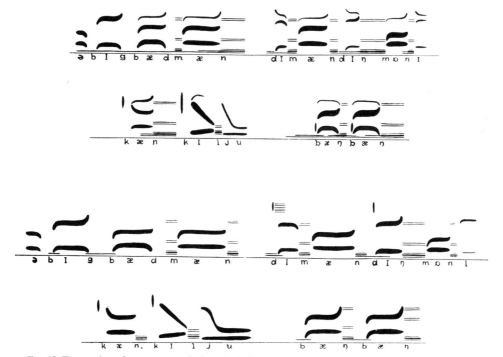

F‌IG. 10. Two versions of a sentence employing principally stop and resonant consonants. The lower version is a first draft which was painted directly from the typewritten text in accordance with the rules derived from our experiments. Revisions by ear (including the use of some third-formant transitions) resulted in the upper version. Both were highly intelligible when converted into sound by the playback.

---

[10] Notably, R. H. Stetson, *Motor Phonetics* (Oberlin College, 1951); also, M. Joos, Language, Suppl. 24, 98 (1948).

SYNTHESIS OF CONNECTED SPEECH

In discussing future directions for the general program of work that has been described here, we mentioned the synthesis of connected speech as a long-range objective. It is possible, of course, to attempt synthesis using only the limited information we now have about only a few of the sounds of speech. We shall play for you some examples of words and sentences which were synthesized on the basis of rules derived from our experiments. It is fairly evident that the rules alone are inadequate at this stage and that these examples do benefit from extrapolations of the cardinal vowels to the vowels of American English and from some hunches about diphthongization, syllable length, and stress. However, in all cases, the words were created *de novo* —without reference to actual spectrograms—and employed bursts and transitions for the production of the stop and resonant consonants. [This portion of the demonstration consisted of the following recordings from the playback: (1) "Alabama," from the patterns of Fig. 9. The upper version yielded a Southern dialect; the lower version gave the word as it might have been pronounced by a Frenchman. (2) Spondees taken from the lists prepared at the Psycho Acoustic Laboratory: "backbone, bonbon, outlaw, pancake, cookbook, cupcake, nutmeg." (3) Sentences: "Oh my aching back." "At M.I.T. meet Lick and Locke." "A playback can talk back." (4) The sentence of Fig. 10, in two versions; the lower is the first draft, painted directly from the typewritten page; the upper version benefited from revisions by ear. Some transitions of the third formant were introduced, in addition to the use "by rule" of second-formant transitions and bursts.]

Apparently most of you understood some, if not all, of the examples; even so, it is clear that much remains to be done to achieve a working mastery of the rules governing the acoustic stimuli by which we perceive speech.

Reprinted from The Journal of the Acoustical Society of America, Vol. 27, No. 4, 769–773, July, 1955
Copyright, 1955, by the Acoustical Society of America.

Acoustic Loci and Transitional Cues for Consonants*

Pierre C. Delattre,† Alvin M. Liberman,‡ and Franklin S. Cooper
Haskins Laboratories, New York, New York
(Received April 8, 1955)

Previous studies with synthetic speech have shown that second-formant transitions are cues for the perception of the stop and nasal consonants. The results of those experiments can be simplified if it is assumed that each consonant has a characteristic and fixed frequency position, or locus, for the second formant, corresponding to the relatively fixed place of production of the consonant. On that basis, the transitions may be regarded as "movements" from the locus to the steady state of the vowel.

The experiments reported in this paper provide additional evidence concerning the existence and positions of these second-formant loci for the voiced stops, b, d, and g. There appears to be a locus for d at 1800 cps and for b at 720 cps. A locus for g can be demonstrated only when the adjoining vowel has its second formant above about 1200 cps; below that level no g locus was found.

The results of these experiments indicate that, for the voiced stops, the transition cannot begin at the locus and go from there to the steady-state level of the vowel. Rather, if we are to hear the appropriate consonant, the first part of the transition must be silent. The voiced stops are best synthesized by making the duration of the silent interval equal to the duration of the transition itself.

An experiment on the first formant revealed that its locus is the same for b, d, and g.

I N an earlier experiment[1,2] we undertook to find out whether the transitions (frequency shifts) of the second formant—often seen in spectrograms in the region where consonant and vowel join—can be cues for the identification of the voiced stop consonants. For that purpose we prepared a series of simplified, hand-painted spectrograms of transition-plus-vowel, then converted these patterns into sound and played the recordings to naive listeners for judgment as b, d, or g. The agreement among the listeners was, in general, sufficient to show that transitions of the second formant can serve as cues for the identification of the stops and, also, to enable us to select, for each vowel, the particular transitions that best produced each of the stop consonant phones. These transitions are shown in Fig. 1.

We found in further experiments[2] that these same second-formant transitions can serve as cues for the unvoiced stops (p-t-k) and the nasal consonants (m-n-η), provided, of course, that the synthetic patterns are otherwise changed to contain appropriate acoustic cues for the voiceless and nasal manners of production. Moreover, and more important for the purposes of this paper, the results of these experiments plainly indicated a relationship between second-formant transition and articulatory place of production. Thus, the same second-formant transitions that had been found to produce b proved to be appropriate also for the synthesis of p and m, which, like b, are articulated at the lips; the second-formant transitions that produced d produced the consonants t and n, which have in

common with d an articulatory place of production at the alveols; and, similarly, the second-formant transitions were found to be essentially the same for g, k, and η, which are all produced at the velum.

It is an obvious assumption that the transitions seen in spectrograms reflect the changes in cavity size and shape caused by the movements of the articulators, and if we further assume that the relation between articulation and sound is not too complex, we should suppose, on the basis of the evidence of the preceding paragraph, that the second-formant transitions rather directly represent the articulatory movements *from* the place of production of the consonant *to* the position for the following vowel. Since the articulatory place of production of each consonant is, for the most part, fixed, we might expect to find that there is correspondingly a fixed frequency position—or "locus"—for its second formant; we could then rather simply describe the various second-formant transitions as movements from this acoustic locus to the steady-state level of the vowel, wherever that might be.[3] As may be seen in Fig. 1, the various transitions that produce the best d with each of the seven vowels do, in fact, appear to be coming from the same general region, and on the assumption that the first part of the acoustic transition is somehow missing, one may suppose that the transitions originate from precisely the same point. Clearly, d is the best case. For b the transitions all appear to be coming from some point low on the frequency scale, but an exact position for the b locus is not evident. In the case of g,

* This work was supported, in part, by the Carnegie Corporation of New York and, in part, by Department of Defense Contract. Some of the results of this research were reported in a paper read before the Acoustical Society of America on October 15, 1953.
† Also at the University of Colorado, Boulder, Colorado.
‡ Also at the University of Connecticut, Storrs, Connecticut.
[1] Cooper, Delattre, Liberman, Borst, and Gerstman, J. Acoust. Soc. Am. 24, 597–606 (1952).
[2] Liberman, Delattre, Cooper, and Gerstman, Psychol. Monogr. 68, No. 8, 1–13 (1954).

[3] We do not wish to restrict the concept of locus to the second formant, nor do we mean to relate it exclusively, on the articulatory side, to place of production. By "locus" we mean simply a place on the frequency scale at which a transition begins or to which it may be assumed to "point." We have found this to be a useful concept, since, for first and second formants, there appear to be many fewer loci than there are transitions.

The locus is in certain respects similar to the concept of the "hub" as developed by Potter, Kopp, and Green. See Potter, Kopp, and Green, *Visible Speech* (D. Van Nostrand Company, Inc., New York, 1947), pp. 39–51.

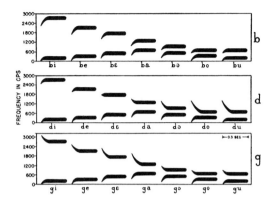

FIG. 1. Synthetic spectrograms showing second-formant transitions that produce the voiced stops before various vowels.

there would appear to be a single high-frequency locus for the front vowels i, e, ε, and the mid-vowel a; but for the back vowels $ɔ$, o, and u the acoustic pattern breaks sharply, and it is obvious that the same g locus cannot serve for all vowels. In this connection it is known that the articulatory place of production of g is displaced somewhat according to the vowel that follows it, but there is no evidence that there is in this displacement the kind of discontinuity that occurs at the acoustic level in the sudden and large shift of the g transition. It would appear, then, that in this particular instance the relationship between place of production and sound has become rather complex, and a simple correspondence between this articulatory variable and a second-formant acoustic locus is not found.

In the series of experiments to be reported here we have, first, undertaken to collect additional evidence concerning the existence and position of the second-formant loci for b, d, and g, and, in particular, to determine whether these loci are independent of vowel color as, indeed, they must be if the concept is to have any utility; second, we have tried to determine whether, in the case of the stops, the locus can be the actual starting point for the transition, or whether, alternatively, the locus is a place to which the transition may only point; and, third, we have collected evidence concerning a first-formant locus.

APPARATUS AND GENERAL PROCEDURE

All the acoustic stimuli used in this study were produced by converting hand-painted spectrograms into sound. The special-purpose playback that accomplishes this conversion has been described in earlier papers.[4,5] It produces 50 beams of light, separately modulated at each of the first 50 harmonics of a 120-cycle fundamental, and spreads them across the hand-painted spectrogram in such manner that the frequency of the modulated light at any point corresponds approximately

[4] F. S. Cooper, J. Acoust. Soc. Am. **22**, 761–762 (1950).
[5] Cooper, Liberman, and Borst, Proc. Natl. Acad. Sci. **37**, 318–325 (1951).

to the frequency level of the place at which it strikes the spectrogram. The painted portions of the spectrogram reflect the appropriately modulated beams of light to a phototube whose current is amplified and fed to a loudspeaker.

As shown in Fig. 2, the hand-painted patterns consisted of two formants, each of which included three contiguous harmonics of the 120-cycle fundamental. The intensity of the central harmonic of the formant was 6 db more than the two outlying ones; the frequency of that harmonic is used in specifying the frequency position of the formant. All transitions of either formant were always painted and heard in initial position in the syllable. A transition is called "rising" or "falling" according to whether it originates at a frequency lower than (rising) or higher than (falling) the steady state of the corresponding formant of the vowel.

SECOND-FORMANT LOCI

The purposes of this part of the investigation were to find the positions of the second-formant loci of the

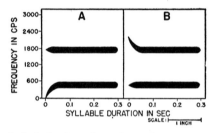

FIG. 2. Scale drawings of sample two-formant patterns used in this study. (A) A rising transition in the first formant and a straight transition in the second. (B) A straight transition in the first formant and a falling transition in the second.

stop consonants, and to test whether their existence and position are independent of vowel color and, also, of the extent of first-formant transition. Accordingly, we prepared the series of patterns shown schematically in Fig. 3, and converted them to sound for evaluation by ear.

As shown in the figure, each stimulus pattern had a straight transition of the second formant and some degree of rising transition of the first formant. This arrangement was dictated by two considerations: first, the possibility that the initial part of the transition is not sounded, in which case we should suppose that only a straight second formant can "point" precisely to the frequency position of the locus[6]; and, second, the fact

[6] Potter, Kopp, and Green (pp. 81–103 of reference given in footnote 3) located the "hub" of each of the stop consonants by a technique which obviously takes account of the same consideration. They made spectrograms of each of the stops paired with a variety of vowels and then looked for those patterns in which the second formant was straight. The syllables *d*æ (as in "dad") and *b*ʊ (as in "book") yielded straight second formants, and they concluded that the hub of d is in the same position as the hub of æ and that, in similar fashion, b goes with ʊ. The hub of g was found to be variable.

that with zero transition of the second formant, a consonant will be heard, if at all, only when the first formant is curved.

When the first and second formants of Fig. 3 are paired in all combinations, 65 vowels are produced, comprising a wide variety of colors and including many that do not correspond to known speech sounds. The extent of first-formant transitions was varied as shown in the figure. Each of the two-formant patterns was converted into sound and listened to carefully by the authors of this paper, who identified and evaluated each sound as *b*, *d*, or *g*. When the judgments thus obtained are appropriately tabulated, the following conclusions emerge:

(1) Rather clear stop consonants are heard at particular positions of the second formant. The best *g* is produced by a second formant at 3000 cps, the best *d* at 1800 cps, and the best *b* at 720 cps.[7,8] We shall suppose that these three frequencies represent the

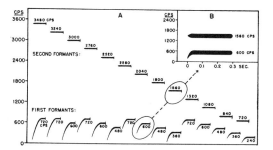

FIG. 3. Schematic display of the stimuli used in finding the second-formant loci of *b*, *d*, and *g*. (A) Frequency positions of the straight second formants and the various first formants with which each was paired. When first and second formants were less than 240 cps apart they were permitted to overlap. (B) A typical test pattern, made up of the first and second formants circled in (A).

acoustic loci of *g*, *d*, and *b*, respectively. At other frequency levels of the straight second formant a stop-like sound is heard, the identity of which is more or less clear depending on its nearness to one of the three frequencies given above. At about 1320 cps the sound is indifferently *b*, *d*, or *g*.

---

[7] One would infer from the graphs of Fig. 1 that the locus of *b* must be somewhere below the second formant of *u* (720 cps), since the best *bu*, as indicated by the amount of agreement among our naive listeners in the earlier transition study, was formed when the second formant had a rising transition. We believe that the discrepancy between that result and the present one is to be attributed to differences of detail in the patterns used in the two studies.

[8] As is indicated in Fig. 3, the straight second formants were spaced at intervals of 240 cps. After it had begun to appear that the stop consonant loci were in the vicinity of 3000, 1800, and 720 cps, we experimented, on an exploratory basis, with straight second formants 120 cps on either side of each of these three values, and found that none of the stops was significantly improved by these adjustments.

Of the three stops that are produced when the straight second formants are at the loci, the *d* (at 1800 cps) is the most compelling, the *b* (at 720 cps) is slightly less so, and *g* (at 3000 cps) is, perhaps, the least satisfying.

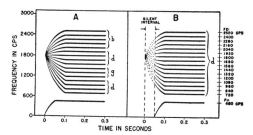

FIG. 4. Stimulus patterns (shown schematically) and identifications with and without a silent interval between the second-formant locus and the onset of the transition. (A) Second-formant transitions that originate at the *d* locus and go to various steady-state levels, together with the first formant with which each was paired. (B) The same patterns, except that a silent interval of 50 msec has been introduced between the locus and the start of the transition. Note that there is no silent interval in the first formant, but that it has been displaced along the time scale so that its onset is, as in (A), simultaneous with that of the second formant. Similar adjustments in time of onset were made for all the silent intervals tested in this experiment. The introduction of a silent interval into the first formant always weakened the consonant, but did not affect its identity.

(2) The steady-state level of the first formant has essentially no effect on either the strength or identity of the consonant impression, with the exception that when the straight second formant is about midway between the *g* locus (at 3000 cps) and the *d* locus (at 1800 cps), raising or lowering the level of the first formant tends to push the sound toward *d* or *g*. Otherwise, it appears that the second-formant loci are independent of the changes in vowel color that are produced by varying the position of the first formant.

(3) The extent of the first-formant transition has little or no effect on the identity of the stop consonant. Such variations do, however, affect the strength of the consonant impression. As was pointed out earlier, the first formant must have some degree of rising transition if a consonant is to be heard at all when the second formant is straight. Our observations in this experiment point additionally to the conclusion that in the case of the voiced stops the consonant impression is stronger as the first-formant transition is larger. The strongest stop is obtained when the first formant starts at the lowest frequency (120 cps) and rises from that point to the steady-state level appropriate for the following vowel.

THE LOCUS AND THE START OF THE TRANSITION

This part of the investigation was designed to determine whether the transitions can start from the locus and move to the steady-state level of the vowel, or whether the transitions must only point to this locus, as they appeared to do in Fig. 1. For that purpose we used the locus values that had been found in the first part of this investigation, and, making the assumption that the transition can actually originate at the locus, we prepared a series of patterns like those shown schematically in A of Fig. 4. There we have, with a fixed lower formant, a choice of second formants which all originate at the *d* locus, i.e., at 1800 cps, and move from that point to their respective steady-state positions. When these patterns are sounded—the fixed first formant with each of the second formants in turn—we do not hear *d* in every case. Rather, we hear *b* when the steady state of the second formant is in the range 2520 cps through 2040 cps, then *d* from 1920 cps through 1560 cps. With second-formant levels from 1440 cps through 1200 cps, *g* is heard, and then *d* again when the second-formant level goes below about 1200 cps.

We find, however, that if we erase the first 50 msec of the transition, creating a silent interval between the locus and the start of the transition, as shown in *B* of the figure, then reasonably good *d*'s are heard in all cases. A silent interval less than 50 msec does not produce *d* at all steady-state levels of the second formant, and intervals greater than 50 msec also fail, at least at some second-formant levels, to give *d*. At we pointed out earlier in this paper, the second-formant locus of a consonant presumably reflects the articulatory place of production, and the transition can be assumed to show the movement from that place to the articulatory position appropriate for the following vowel. The fact that the transition serves best if it does not begin at the locus might be taken as an indication that no appreciable sound is produced until at least part of the articulatory movement has been completed.

In all the patterns of Fig. 4, the time interval between the locus and the steady state of the second formant was 100 msec. We should suppose that this corresponds to some particular rate of articulation. To find out what might happen at other articulatory rates we have repeated the procedures described above with sets of patterns in which the total interval between locus and steady state of the vowel was 40, 60, 80, and 120 msec; that is, for these additional total intervals we prepared and listened to patterns in which the transition went all the way to the locus, and also to patterns in which various amounts of the initial part of the transition had been erased. For total intervals of 80 and 120 msec the results are almost identical with those that were obtained with a total interval of 100 msec, except that the "best" silent intervals (that is, the ones at which *d* is most clearly heard at all steady-state levels of the second formant) are about 40 and 60 msec, respectively. From these values (together with that of 50 msec which was best for a total interval of 100 msec) it would appear that the best silent interval is approximately half the total interval. When the total interval is 60 msec or less, we do not get good *d*'s at any silent intervals.

We have repeated these procedures with the *b* locus (at 720 cps) and with the *g* locus (at 3000 cps). It is reasonably clear in these cases, as it was with *d*, that the transition cannot start at the locus and go all the

way to the steady state. The length of the silent interval that gives the best results seems to depend on the total duration of the interval (from locus to steady state), the best silent interval, as with *d*, is approximately half the total interval. With *b* and *g* the best results are obtained (with the appropriate silent intervals) when the total interval is 80 or 100 msec. Both these sounds are relatively poor (at all silent intervals) with a total duration of 120 msec; at total durations of 60 and 40 msec, *g* suffers rather more loss in clarity than *b*.

The results obtained with *b* and *g* are in certain other respects different from those that were found with *d*, and they are also, perhaps, somewhat less definite. When the transition started at the *d* locus, consonants having other than the *d* (alveolar) place of production were clearly heard at some levels of the second-formant steady state. (Thus, as shown in A of Fig. 4, *b* was heard at relatively high levels of the second formant, and *g* was heard when the steady-state level of the second formant was in the range 1440 cps to 1200 cps.) When the transition starts at the *b* locus, however, we hear *bw* (which has the same place of production as *b*) for steady-state levels from 2520 cps through 1440 cps, and then from 1220 cps through 960 cps we hear something that sounds very vaguely like *gw*. The alveolar consonant (*d*) is not heard at all in the *b* series, and the *g* in the *gw* cluster is very weak. Thus, the impossibility of starting the transition at the locus is less strikingly demonstrated for *b* than it was for *d*, and the improvement in the *b* which results from the introduction of a silent interval is, accordingly, less dramatic than the effects that are produced when a silent interval precedes the *d* transitions.

The results obtained with the *g* locus were different from those with *b* and *d* in that there is, apparently, no silent interval that will produce *g* at all steady-state levels of the second formant. In the best case—that is, with the best silent interval—one hears *g* from a steady state of 2520 to one of approximately 1200 cps. Below the latter value we hear *d*. This result is not surprising, since it was quite clear from our earlier data on transitions as cues that the same *g* locus could hardly apply to all vowels.

FIRST-FORMANT LOCUS

In the first part of this investigation, which was concerned primarily with finding the second-formant loci, it appeared that the best stop consonants were produced when the curved first formant started at the lowest possible frequency. The purpose of the third part of the study was to explore further the problem of the first formant, using straight first formants and curved second formants. The straight first formant will presumably serve here, as the straight second formant did in the first part of the investigation, to avoid the problems introduced by the possibility that the transition does not reach all the way to the locus; the transition in the second formant will be necessary, as was the first-formant transition of the earlier experiment, to produce a consonant effect.

The experimental patterns are shown schematically in Fig. 5. Four first formants were used having frequencies appropriate for the first formants of the cardinal vowels *i*, *e*, *ɛ*, and *a*. These were paired with various second formants as shown in the figure and explained in the legend. The second formants always had transitions that rose or fell through four harmonics (of the 120-cycle fundamental). These patterns were converted into sound by the playback and judged by the authors of this paper.

As we should have expected from the results we had previously obtained in our work on second-formant transitions, the listeners heard *g* or *d* when the transition of the second formant was falling, and *b* when it was rising. (With falling transitions of the second formant, *g* was heard for steady-state levels from 3000 to 2280 cps; between 2280 and 1320 cps the sound could be identified either as *g* or *d*; and below about 1320 cps it was clearly *d*.) It will be remembered, however, that our primary interest was not in the second formant, but rather in the first, and, more particularly, in the effects of its frequency level. In this connection we found that the stop consonant—whether *b*, *d*, or *g*—was best when the first formant was at the lowest position (240 cps). When the first formant was raised from 240 cps, there was, apart from the change in vowel color, a weakening of the stop consonant; however, the identification of the stop as *b*, *d*, or *g* was not affected by the frequency level of the first formant. It would appear, then, that the locus of the first formant is at 240 cps for all the voiced stops, but inasmuch as we did not, and, indeed, with our playback could not, center the first formant much lower than 240 cps, we should rather conclude that the first-formant locus is somewhere between that value and zero.

DISCUSSION

The experiments reported here were concerned only with the voiced stops, *b*, *d*, and *g*. We know, however, that the same second-formant transition that produces *b*, for example, will also produce other consonants, such as *p* and *m*, which have the same articulatory place of production. From some experiments now in progress it appears, further, that with an appropriate lengthening of its duration, this same transition will produce the semivowel *w*. We should suppose, then, that *b*, *p*, *m*, and *w* might have the same second-formant locus, which would correspond, as it were, to their common place of production, and that we might generalize the results of this study by assuming that the second-formant loci we found here are appropriate not only for *b*, *d*, and *g*,

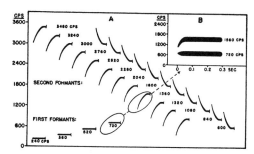

FIG. 5. Schematic display of the stimuli used in finding the first-formant locus of *b*, *d*, and *g*. (A) Frequency positions of the straight first formants and the various second formants with which they were paired. All combinations of first and second formants were used, except for eight cases in which the two formants were so close together as to overlap. The formant shown at 520 cps is composed, in slightly unequal parts, of the fourth harmonic at 480 cps and the fifth harmonic at 600 cps; 520 cps is an estimate of its equivalent frequency.

but, more broadly, for the three places of production (bilabial, alveolar, and velar) that these stop consonants represent.

Although we expect that consonants with the same place of production will be found to have the same second-formant locus, we do not think that they will necessarily have the same best silent interval. In the case of the stops it is clear that approximately the first half of the total interval from locus to steady state must be silent. With a semivowel like *w*, on the other hand, it appears on the basis of exploratory work that the second-formant transition can be made to go all the way from the locus to the steady state of the vowel without adversely affecting the identifiability of the sound—indeed, it may well be that the best semivowel is made in this way.

The results of these experiments indicate that the locus of the first formant is not different for *b*, *d*, and *g*. We might guess, then, that the first-formant locus has little or nothing to do with *place* of production. Evidence from experiments now in progress suggests rather that it is closely related to the articulatory dimensions of *manner*.

We know from earlier experiments that third-formant transitions are cues for the identification of the stop consonants according to place of production, and we might expect, therefore, that there would be a third-formant locus for each of the stops. We have been trying to find these loci by procedures analogous to those used in the present study, that is, by varying the frequency position of a straight third formant. These procedures have yielded some evidence that the third-formant loci do exist. The results are less clear than for the second-formant loci, however, and it appears that additional and more sensitive techniques will be required.

Reprinted from THE JOURNAL OF THE ACOUSTICAL SOCIETY OF AMERICA, Vol. 27, No. 3 (May 1955).
Copyright 1955 by the Acoustical Society of America.

A Difference Limen for Vowel Formant Frequency*

JAMES L. FLANAGAN

*Acoustics Laboratory, Massachusetts Institute of Technology, Cambridge,
Massachusetts, and Air Force Cambridge Research Center,
Cambridge, Massachusetts*

Experiments have been conducted to determine difference limens (DL's)
for vowel formant frequency. The DL's are obtained from quality judgments
on synthetic vowel sounds. The results indicate the maximum accuracy
necessary in analyzing the formant structure of spoken vowels and in
synthesizing the sounds from the resulting formant data.

VOWEL sounds have been synthesized successfully with resonance analog types of speech synthesizers which require only a knowledge of the spectral energy concentrations or formant frequencies.[1-4] In a band-width compression system utilizing such a synthesizer the question arises as to what accuracy is necessary in the derivation, coding, and utilization of the formant frequency data. Since it is not necessary to analyze and synthesize vowels with formant frequency accuracy exceeding that which man can detect, some experiments were conducted to determine frequency difference limens (DL's) for vowel formants. The DL's (or just noticeable differences in formant frequency) determined in these tests represent essentially the maximum accuracy necessary in analyzing the formant structure of spoken vowels and in synthesizing the sounds from the resulting formant data.

The test stimuli employed were synthetic vowels generated by the M.I.T. POVO speech synthesizer.[1] For vowel production the synthesizer utilizes four independent, cascaded, simple series resonant circuits, excited by a repetitive impulse voltage source. The output from each successive resonator is taken across the capacitive element; hence the transfer function of the synthesizer has four poles and no zeros in the finite complex frequency plane. The output wave is therefore a superposition of four damped sinusoids with frequencies corresponding to the first four formants. The first three resonators can be continuously tuned by capacitive reactance modulators and cover frequency ranges corresponding to those of the first three formants. The fourth resonator is fixed and tuned at 3550 cps. The half-power band width of each resonant circuit is set to a value corresponding to averaged measured formant band widths for spoken vowels.[5] These band widths are approximately 130 cps, 150 cps, and 185 cps for the first (F1), the second (F2), and the third (F3) formants, respectively.

Test procedure.—Tests were set up to determine frequency DL's for F1 and F2. A synthetic vowel sound with prescribed formant pattern was chosen as a standard. Variations in this standard were established by varying the frequency of either the first or second formant in discrete steps.

The DL's for F1 were determined for three different standard sounds having first formant frequencies of 300, 500, and 700 cps. The second, third, and fourth formants for all three F1 test sounds were 1500, 2500, and 3550 cps, respectively. The spectral envelopes of the F1 test sounds are shown in Fig. 1. The frequency variations used in determining the DL's for F1 were: ±10, ±20, ±30, ±40, ±50, ±60, and ±70 cps.

The DL's for F2 were determined for three different standard sounds having second formant frequencies of 1000, 1500, and 2000 cps. The first, third, and fourth formants for all three F2 test sounds were 500, 2500, and 3550 cps, respectively. The spectral envelopes of the F2 test sounds are shown in Fig. 2. The frequency variations used in determining the DL's for F2 were: ±25, ±50, ±75, ±100, ±125, ±150, and ±175 cps.

The synthesizer was excited in all cases by a repetitive impulse source having a fundamental frequency of 120 cps and harmonics of equal amplitude up to 3500 cps.

The standard sound and its variations were programed in random order into the relay storage of the synthesizer and an

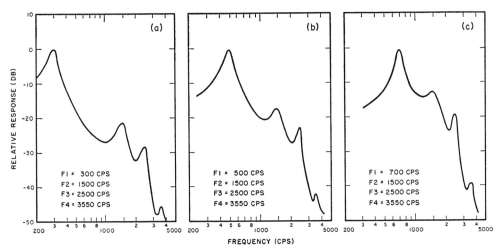

Fig. 1. Spectral envelopes of standard sounds used in F1 tests.

AB listening test was performed. Subjects were presented a $\frac{3}{4}$-second sample of the standard (A) followed by a $\frac{3}{4}$-second sample of one of the variations (B), or by the standard (A) repeated. Time spacing between samples was approximately $\frac{1}{2}$-second and between pairs was approximately five seconds. A test consisted of 20 randomized pairs, of which 14 pairs involved physical differences (AB) and six pairs were identical (AA). Four adult male subjects with normal hearing listened to five tests for each standard sound. The subjects listened binaurally on PDR–8 headphones while seated in an anechoic room. The sound pressure level at the phones was approximately 70 db re 0.002 dyne/cm² and was constant for all samples. The subjects were instructed to judge whether the quality of B was the same as or different from the quality of A. Each subject recorded his judgment as "same" or "different" on a score sheet.

Result.—For each stimulus condition the total percent "different" votes was determined from the twenty judgments of that stimulus. Ogives were plotted showing the percent "different" votes *versus* the formant frequently deviation for all F1 and F2 standard conditions. The ogives resulting from the F1 tests are shown in Fig. 3. Those resulting from the F2 tests are shown in Fig. 4. Taking the 50 percent point as the DL we tabulate the results shown in Table I.

Ogives for individual subjects were plotted in some of the cases where the variability between subjects seemed the greatest. The variability of the individual DL's obtained from these plots did not appear excessive and pooling of the data seemed justified. For example, in the case of greatest subject variability the standard deviation of the individual DL's about the mean DL was, in terms of percent of varied formant frequency: 1.3 percent for negative DL's and 0.9 percent for positive DL's. This was a case in which the mean DL was approximately 5 percent of the formant frequency.

Discussion.—The above values for F1 and F2 frequency DL's agree in order of magnitude with related data. Stevens[6] has obtained data on the frequency DL for trains of single damped sinusoidal waves for a number of values of frequency and damping. These stimuli were generated by repetitive impulse excitation at 125 cps of a single resonant circuit, the band width and resonant frequency of which were known. We may use Bogert's data[5] on the band widths of vowel formants to compute damping factors to be applied to such trains of single damped waves. (The damping constant for the wave is approximately π times the half-power

band width in cps of the resonance.) Using these computed damping factors, together with the knowledge of the formant frequency ranges,[7] we may derive from Stevens' data frequency DL's for trains of single damped waves which damp in a manner analogous to vowel formants. Such damped waves might be thought of as corresponding to individual formants. Representative values for damped wave DL's obtained in this fashion are shown in Table II.

The values of the F1 frequency DL's determined from Fig. 3 correspond closely to the above derived DL for a damped wave in the F1 frequency range. This might be expected since the first formant is usually the most intense component in the vowel sound and to a very crude approximation the vowel is simply a repeated single damped wave. The F2 DL's determined from Fig. 4 are from one to four and one-half times as large as the derived DL's for the repeated single damped wave. It may also be noted from the tabulation of the F1 and F2 DL's that, except in a couple of extreme cases, the frequency DL's for both F1 and F2 are approximately three to five percent of the formant frequency.

TABLE I.

For the F1 tests:			
	F1 of standard (cps)	−DL (cps)	+DL (cps)
(a)	300	17	12
(b)	500	25	27
(c)	700	27	19
For the F2 tests:			
	F2 of standard (cps)	−DL (cps)	+DL (cps)
(a)	1000	20	50
(b)	1500	45	75
(c)	2000	90	20

TABLE II.

Frequency of damped wave (cps)	Frequency DL (cps)	Formant range containing damped wave frequency
500	20	F1
1000	20	F2
2000	20	F2
3000	35	F3

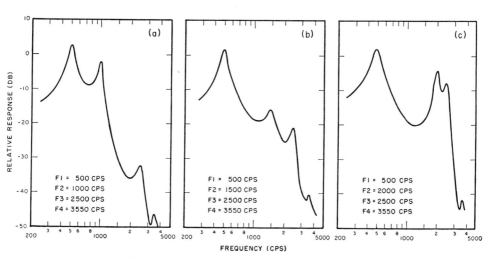

Fig. 2. Spectral envelopes of standard sounds used in F2 tests.

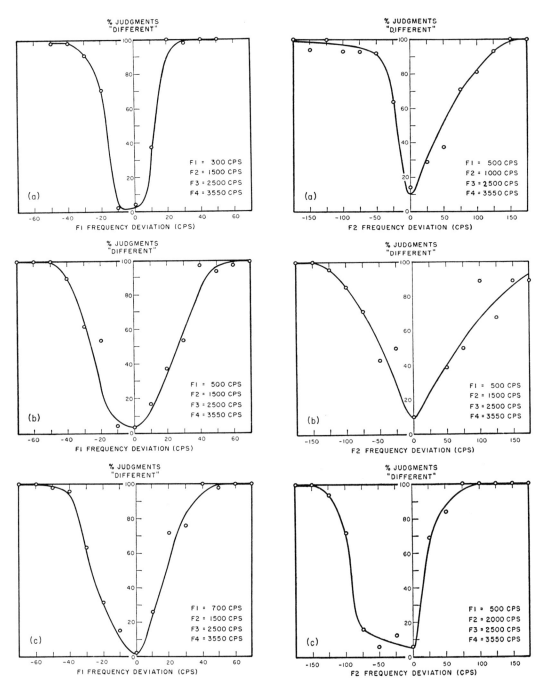

FIG. 3. F1 test ogives showing percent of judgments called different.

FIG. 4. F2 Test ogives showing percent of judgments called different.
FIG. 4a: F3 should read 2500.

290

Certain of the ogives in Figs. 3 and 4 exhibit marked asymmetry. The asymmetry is most pronounced for the cases shown in Figs. 4(a) and 4(c). These two cases correspond to standard sounds having two formants in close proximity, as shown in Figs. 2(a) and 2(c), respectively. In these cases it appears that changes in relative amplitude of the spectral peaks, occasioned by small frequency shifts of one formant in close proximity to a higher or lower formant, may be playing a considerable role in determining just noticeable differences in formant frequency. The fact that the frequency and amplitude of the formants of the synthesized sound are not independent is a constraint characteristic of the synthesizer. The synthesizer is a cascade of four independent, fixed band-width resonators, three of which may be tuned. Therefore, as any two resonators are tuned to nearly the same frequency, the amplitude of response is greatly enhanced in this frequency range, and small frequency shifts in either resonance result in relatively large changes in the amplitudes of the resonances. When these resonances are not in close proximity, small frequency shifts result in negligible changes in amplitudes. This same situation obtains approximately in human production of vowels. Man in effect tunes his cascade of acoustic resonators by properly constricting the vocal tract, and formant frequency and amplitude are not adjusted independently. (The vocal resonators, however, cannot be considered as uncoupled nor strictly as lumped elements.) This nonindependence of formant amplitude and frequency in spoken vowels is evident if one compares the spectrum of a spoken vowel having essentially equi-spaced formants (i.e., a sound corresponding to an unconstricted tract) to the spectrum of one having F1 and F2 in close proximity and also to the spectrum of one having F2 and F3 in close proximity. Good examples of these respective situations are the sounds /æ/, /ɔ/, and /ɝ/.

In Fig. 2(a) the first and second formants of the synthetic vowel are relatively close. Negative deviations of F2 result in comparatively large increases in amplitudes of F1 and F2 and hence a small negative frequency DL. Similarly, in Fig. 2(c) the second and third formants are in close proximity and positive deviations of F2 result in comparatively large increases in F2 and F3 amplitudes and hence a small positive frequency DL. These effects obtain, of course, in spite of the fact that over-all intensity levels are maintained constant. Intensity DL experiments seem to be indicated to explain quantitatively some of these asymmetrical conditions.

Concluding Remarks.—The formant frequency DL's obtained from the tests indicate the greatest degree of formant frequency resolution necessary in vowel sound analysis and synthesis. These results may be taken as essentially the maximum values of formant frequency accuracy because the criterion employed in the judgments was one of detecting a change in quality. A criterion involving identification of the phoneme would in general lead to much larger formant DL's. This is made evident if one considers the area on an F1–F2 plot corresponding to the identification of a given vowel phoneme.[7] It is known that quality differences exist within such an area, that is, quality differences exist within the phoneme. Therefore, the formant DL's associated with quality distinctions must correspond to an area smaller than the phoneme area. More particularly, if one selects a sound which is highly representative of a vowel phoneme, and if it is assumed that such a sound is located centrally in its F1–F2 phoneme area, then the DL's for detecting a quality difference correspond to a small area lying within the phoneme area. In topological terms, the DL's for detecting a quality difference in such a sound represent a small subset of the DL's for detecting a phonemic difference. If the sound selected happens to lie near or on a phoneme boundary which is relatively well defined (say for example the boundary between /i/ and /I/) then the quality DL's must still be less than, or at most equal to, the DL's for phoneme identification. This follows from the fact that the quality DL's determined here are simply a "detection of something different" and therefore represent a minimum perceptible change.

The tests reported here were prompted by an immediate need for order-of-magnitude design data and do not represent an exhaustive experiment. Additional data are needed to permit the mapping of quality DL *areas* on the F1–F2 plane. The present tests have determined DL's only along the F1 and F3 axes while a mapping of DL areas requires the simultaneous variation of F1 and F2. Similarly, the question of formant amplitude-proximity relations has not been fully investigated. Further quantitative observations on the asymmetrical situations could have been made by bypassing one of the two adjacent resonators. This, however, would have necessitated modification of the existing equipment and in the interest of expediency was not included in the present tests.

In an experiment dealing with complex stimuli one is always faced with the problem of ascertaining what the subject is judging. In regard to the present tests it might be argued that one is dealing with at least two phenomena: one due to phonemic boundaries and the other simply due to relative formant position. The writer believes that in the type of experiment reported here the fact that phoneme areas are associated with certain formant patterns is of no real consequence. Quality DL's can be determined for standard sounds placed anywhere in the F1–F2 plane and not necessarily corresponding to any English vowel phoneme at all. Determining the DL's for phoneme identification, however, is certainly a different story.

The data presented here represent a pilot study for a more complete investigation which is in the planning stage. It is anticipated that some of the questions left unanswered here will be explained by further tests.

The writer gratefully acknowledges the assistance of Mr. R. P. Bastide of the M.I.T. Acoustics Laboratory in performing the tests.

* This work was supported by funds from U. S. Air Force contract No. AF–19(604)–626.

[1] Stevens, Bastide, and Smith, J. Acoust. Soc. Am. **27**, 207(A), (1955).
[2] Meeks, Borst, and Cooper, J. Acoust. Soc. Am. **26**, 137(A) (1954).
[3] W. Lawrence, "The synthesis of speech from signals which have a low information rate," in *Communication Theory*, edited by W. Jackson (Butterworth Scientific Publications, London, 1953), Chap. 34.
[4] C. G. M. Fant, "Speech communication research," IVA **24**, 331–337 (1953).
[5] B. P. Bogert, J. Acoust. Soc. Am. **25**, 791–792 (1953).
[6] K. N. Stevens, "The perception of sounds shaped by resonant circuits," Sc.D. Dissertation (Electrical Engineering Department, M.I.T., January, 1952).
[7] G. E. Peterson and H. L. Barney, J. Acoust. Soc. Am. **24**, 175–184 (1952).

CHAPTER 26

Reprinted from Studia Linguistica, Vol. 9 (Lund, Sweden: C.W.K. Gleerup, 1955).

BERTIL MALMBERG

THE PHONETIC BASIS FOR SYLLABLE DIVISION

In *Proceedings of the Second International Congress of Phonetic Sciences* (Cambridge 1936, p. 30—33), Alf Sommerfelt discusses the problem whether syllable divisions can have phonological importance. He quotes interesting examples from Norwegian and Gaelic. It would be easy to mention other languages where a type [a|pa] can be opposed phonemically to a type [ap|a]. It is a well-known fact that many languages favour — or even use exclusively — open syllables, whereas others accept closed syllables or even seem to favour implosive [1] consonants and heavy implosive clusters (such as *-tskt*, *-mskt*, etc. in Swedish). French and Ibero-Romance are examples of the first type, most Germanic languages of the second.[2] The French and Spanish habit of carrying over any final consonant to a following initial vowel is well-known (Spanish: *lo|s(h)ombres*). In English, the *n* in *an aim* remains implosive, and the group [ən|eim] can be opposed phonemically to [ə|neim] (vz. *a name*).[3] Swedish children often pronounce a final consonant as explosive before a following vowel, which seems incorrect to an adult. Frenchmen speaking Swedish often use the same faulty pronunciation. The examples quoted may be sufficient to remind the reader of the fact that the syllable frontier is a phonetic phenomenon which may be utilized in a phonemic system. The difference [a|pa] ~ [ap|a] may be a distinctive feature.[4] In a language

---

[1] The terms *implosive* and *explosive* are used here in Saussure's sense and mean consequently "following" respectively "preceding the vowel of the syllable".

[2] See my papers *La structure syllabique de l'espagnol* (*Boletim de filologia* IX, 1949, p. 99—120), *Notes sur les groupes de consonnes en espagnol* (*Zeitschrift für Phonetik* II, 1948, p. 239—255), and G. von Proschwitz, *Etude sur la répartition des syllabes ouvertes et fermées en français moderne*, Göteborg 1953.

[3] Cp. Stetson, *Bases of Phonology*, p. 46.

[4] I just mention these linguistic phenomena without entering here into a detailed discussion which will appear in a later, more comprehensive study of the whole of the syllabic problem.

80

where this is not the case, the predilection for either of the two types is often a feature which characterizes the phonetic habits of the language (its so-called articulatory basis). It is an important task for instrumental phonetics to try and solve all the problems related to the physical reality behind this phonetic distinction.

I am not going to discuss in detail the different theories presented so far as regards the physiological or acoustic basis for the phonemic and/or auditive distinction mentioned (muscular tension, breathing rhythm, jaw opening, "sonority", acoustical intensity, etc.).[5] At least some of these phenomena are probably of importance for the opposition under discussion. I consequently cannot accept the opinion of those scholars who deny the existence of the syllable and/or of the syllabic frontier. Jespersen believed in the existence of the syllable but refuted the idea of fixed limits between the syllables (*Lehrbuch*, § 13). To Panconcelli-Calzia and von Essen, the syllable is only a psychological, traditional, or phonemic unit without any physical (acoustic or articulatory) counterpart.[6] According to Panconcelli-Calzia, there are only longer and shorter groups of sounds, but no phonetically delimited units within these groups ("die Silbe ist überhaupt kein phonetisches Element"; von Essen, *Zeitschrift für Phonetik*, V, 1951, p. 200). The reason for this negative attitude is of course the difficulty for phoneticians to discover, in the acoustic or physiological speech curves registered, any objective factor which could be interpreted as the physical counterpart of the distinction subjectively perceived or linguistically utilized. No instrumental data obtained so far have been quite convincing.

The present investigation was made in order to examine whether a certain factor in the sound wave as reflected in a sound spectrogram, i. e. the modification which the wovel formants undergo in combination with consonants, could be considered responsible for the subjectively perceived syllabic division. The method used at the Haskins Laboratories (New York) for producing synthetic sound groups seemed to me the ideal procedure for examining this

---

[5] See Malmberg, *La phonétique*, Paris 1954, p. 78—83, *Kort lärobok i fonetik*, 3:rd ed., Lund 1955, p. 135—142, and works quoted there. For further documentation, see e. g. Sa Nogueira, *O problema da sílaba*, Lisboa 1942.

[6] See von Essen, *Allgemeine und angewandte Phonetik*, p. 87 ff.

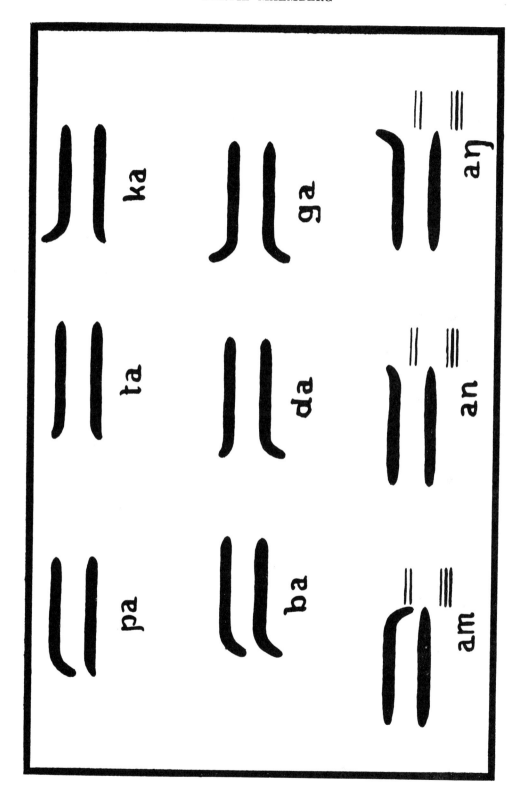

Fig. 1.

problem, since, in this way, the factors involved could be reduced to the minimum wanted.

The inflections of the vowel formants due to the surrounding consonants have been studied in detail by members of the Haskins group and certain results are already fairly well known.[7] We know, thanks to their experiments, that in many cases the form of these inflections are the only necessary cues to the identification of the consonants (as was already supposed by Joos, *Acoustic Phonetics*, p. 122; cp. the spectrograms reproduced by Potter, Kopp, Green, *Visible Speech*, pp. 90, 97, 98, etc., and Malmberg, *Studia linguistica* VI, 1952, pp. 14—15). The above hand-painted spectrograms taken from the Haskins material already published, may serve as examples of initial and final stops+a following and a preceding vowel, respectively (fig. 1).

When working on synthetic vowels and consonants at the Haskins Laboratories May—June 1955, I asked myself if a difference of the type illustrated by the hand-painted spectrograms seen in fig. 2 could possibly be interpreted by the ear as a difference of syllabic division, the consonant in the first case being heard as explosive, in the second as implosive. If such was the case, this difference in the spectrum of the group could be supposed to be the missing physical factor — or at least one of the factors — behind the distinction subjectively perceived. The experiment was carried out in the following manner.

I chose three types of dissyllabic nonsense groups: [*i p i*], [*o d o*], and [*a g a*], and painted spectrograms of them with three formants (1, 2 and 3) and with the inflections typical of the three stops in question in combination with the vowels [*i*], [*o*], and [*a*].

---

[7] See Liberman, Delattre, Cooper, Gerstman, *The rôle of Consonant-Vowel Transitions in the Perception of the Stop and Nasal Consonants* (*Psychological Monographs*, no. 379, 1954), Cooper, Delattre, Liberman, Borst, Gerstman, *Some Experiments on the Perception of Synthetic Speech Sounds* (*Journal of the Acoustical Society of America* XXIV, no. 6, 1952, pp. 597—606), Liberman, Delattre, Cooper, *The Rôle of Selected Stimulus-Variables in the Perception of the Unvoiced Stop Consonants* (*The American Journal of Psychology* LXV, 1952, pp. 497—516), Delattre, Liberman, Cooper, *Acoustic Loci and Transitional Cues for Consonants* (*Journal of the Acoustical Society of America* XXVII, no. 4, 1955, pp. 769—773), and Marguerite Durand, *La perception des consonnes occlusives; problèmes de palatalisation et de changements consonantiques* (*Studia linguistica* VIII, 1954, pp. 110—122).

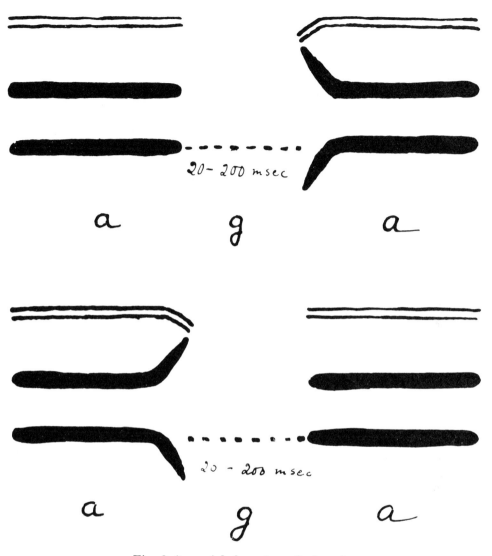

Fig. 2 (type 1 below, type 2 above).

I made two variants of each type according to the above example, one variant with inflections only in the first vowel, and one with inflections only in the second. They will be called types number 1 and 2. The distance between the formants — i. e. the phase corresponding to the occlusion in articulatory phonetics — was varied in ten steps, from 200 to 20 milliseconds (fig. 2). I consequently made 20 spectrograms of each "word". These spectrograms were transferred into sound on a playback[8] and the sound was registered by a tape recorder. The different variants of each of the two types

[8] For the description, see e. g. Liberman, Delattre, Cooper in *The American Journal of Psychology* LXV, 1952, pp. 501—502.

84

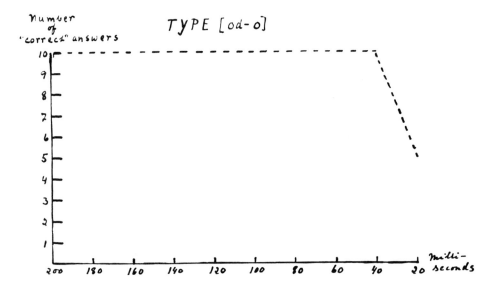

Fig. 3. Number of "correct" answers plotted against the variation in distance between the formants (the silent phase). The number of "correct" answers should be understood as the number of subjects interpreting the type *od-o* etc. (type 1) as if the consonant belonged to the first syllable (implosive). It should be noticed that in this case, only the smallest distance between the formants (20 milliseconds) caused disagreement in the judgements.

(fig. 2), i. e. 20 different [*ipi*]- "words" and 20 different [*odo*]- "words", were presented in random order to a group of ten listeners who had to answer the question if they had the impression that the consonant belonged to the first or to the second vowel (by putting just 1 or 2). The [*ipi*]-series and the [*odo*]-series were examined in New York. The listeners were persons working in the Haskins Laboratories, all of them phonetically trained and accustomed to synthetic speech sounds. Eight of them had American-English, one French and one Swedish as their mother tongues. The [*aga*]-series was examined in Sweden. The ten listeners were, with one exception, more or less trained phonetically, but nobody was accustomed to synthetic speech sounds. One of the listeners was a Norwegian, one of German origin, the others Swedes.

The result appears from the following tables, for brevity's sake including only the figures obtained for type 1 (the one which was supposed to be interpreted as [*ipi*] etc.). See fig. 3—5.

These results seem to prove that a difference in inflections of the kind examined here is perceived as a difference in syllabic

85

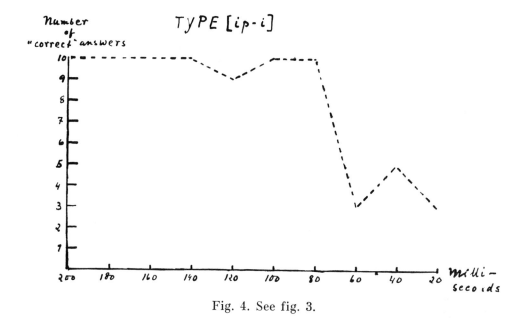

Fig. 4. See fig. 3.

division. Inflections only in the preceding vowel spectrum are interpreted as if the consonant was implosive, whereas inflections only in the following vowel are heard as if the consonant was explosive. One important condition for type 1 to be heard as implosive was, however, that the distance between the formants — i. e. in traditional terms the stop phase of the consonant — ex-

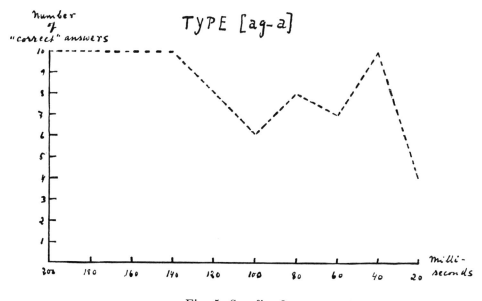

Fig. 5. See fig. 3.

86

ceeded a certain minimum of duration. If not, both types were heard as explosives, which implies that the distinction in question can be perceived auditively only under favourable conditions.[9]

The result obtained from the experiment described above means that, for the first time, a possible physical basis for the syllabic division has been found. This, of course, does not mean that the acoustic difference examined here is the only cue to the phonetic distinction in question. It does not even mean that it is necessarily the most important one. But the above results are sufficient to prove the impossibility of the entirely negative attitude taken e. g. by the Hamburg school as regards the notions of syllable and syllabic frontier. I pretend to have found one factor capable of functioning as physical correlate to the linguistically important distinction of syllabic division (and, consequently, of implosive and explosive consonants). There are probably other such factors. Further investigations will prove which of them is the most important.

Institute of Phonetics, Lund.
Haskins Laboratories, New York.

---

[9] Cp. Stetson's important remark that an increased speed of articulation tends to open the syllables (*Bases of Phonology*, Oberlin, Ohio, 1945, p. 54).

Reprinted from THE JOURNAL OF THE ACOUSTICAL SOCIETY OF AMERICA, Vol. 27, No. 2 (March 1955).
Copyright 1955 by the Acoustical Society of America.

An Analysis of Perceptual Confusions Among Some English Consonants

GEORGE A. MILLER AND PATRICIA E. NICELY
Lincoln Laboratory, Massachusetts Institute of Technology, Cambridge, Massachusetts
(Received December 1, 1954)

Sixteen English consonants were spoken over voice communication systems with frequency distortion and with random masking noise. The listeners were forced to guess at every sound and a count was made of all the different errors that resulted when one sound was confused with another. With noise or low-pass filtering the confusions fall into consistent patterns, but with high-pass filtering the errors are scattered quite randomly. An articulatory analysis of these 16 consonants provides a system of five articulatory features or "dimensions" that serve to characterize and distinguish the different phonemes: voicing, nasality, affrication, duration, and place of articulation. The data indicate that voicing and nasality are little affected and that place is severely affected by low-pass and noisy systems. The indications are that the perception of any one of these five features is relatively independent of the perception of the others, so that it is as if five separate, simple channels were involved rather than a single complex channel.

THE over-all effects of noise and of frequency distortion upon the average intelligibility of human speech are by now rather well understood. One limitation of the existing studies, however, is that results are given almost exclusively in terms of the articulation score, the percentage of the spoken words that the listener hears correctly. By implication, therefore, all of the listener's errors are treated as equivalent and no knowledge of the perceptual confusions is available. The fact is, however, that mistakes are often far from random. A closer look at the problem suggests that we might learn something about speech perception and might even improve communication if we knew what kinds of errors occur and how to avoid the most frequent ones. Such was the reasoning that led to the present study.

Perhaps the major reason that confusion data are not already available is the cost of collecting them. Every phoneme must have a chance to be confused with every other phoneme and that large number of potential confusions must be tested repeatedly until statistically reliable estimates of all the probabilities are obtained. Such data are obtained from testing programs far more extensive than would be required to evaluate some specific system.

In order to reduce the magnitude of the problem to more manageable size, we decided to study a smaller set of phonemes and to explore the potential value of such data within that smaller universe. Since the consonants are notoriously confusable and are quite important for intelligibility, we decided to begin with a comparison of 16 consonants: $|p|$, $|t|$, $|k|$, $|f|$, $|\theta|$, $|s|$, $|\int|$, $|b|$, $|d|$, $|g|$, $|v|$, $|\delta|$, $|z|$, $|3|$, $|m|$, and $|n|$. These 16 make up almost three quarters of the consonants we utter in normal speech and about 40 percent of all phonemes, vowels included. It was our suspicion that when errors begin to occur in articulation tests, the culprits would usually be found among this set of 16 phonemes. A further reason for being interested in consonants is that the information-bearing aspects of these sounds are less well understood than is the case for vowels; we hoped to pick up some clues as to what the important features of these phonemes might be.

The major portion of the work to be reported here was done with the aforementioned 16 consonants. However, a number of other, even smaller, experiments were conducted with subsets of those 16. In general, the results of the smaller studies agree with and support the conclusions of the larger study. These results will be introduced into the discussion where appropriate, but the major emphasis will be placed on the 16-consonant data.

EXPERIMENTAL PROCEDURES

Five female subjects served as talkers and listening crew; when one talked, the other four listened. Since the tests lasted several months, some of the original crew members departed and were replaced; care was taken to train new members adequately before their data were used. The subjects were, with one Canadian exception, citizens of the United States. None had defects of speech or hearing and all were able to pronounce the 16 nonsense syllables without any noticeable dialect. Since rhythm, intonation, and vowel differences were not involved, we have assumed that regional differences in speech habits were not a significant source of variability in the data.

The 16 consonants were spoken initially before the vowel |a| (father). The list of 200 nonsense syllables spoken by the talker was prepared in advance so that the probability of each syllable was 1 in 16 and so that their order was quite random within the list and from one list to the next. The syllables were spoken at an average rate of one every 2.1 seconds and the listeners were forced to respond—to guess, if necessary—for every syllable. When the speech was near the threshold of hearing, the listeners were kept in synchrony with the talker by a tone that was turned on at fixed intervals. Otherwise, a 2.1-second pause was inserted after every block of five syllables. With four listeners, there were 800 syllable-response events per talker for which confusions could be studied. Pooling the five talkers gives us 4000 observations at each condition tested.

At the completion of each test of 200 syllables, the talker went from the control room back to the test room and the crew proceeded to tabulate their responses. Each listener had a table showing what syllable was spoken and what syllable she had written in response; each cell of the table represented one of the $16 \times 16 = 256$ possible syllable-response pairs, and the number entered in that cell was the frequency with which that syllable-response pair occurred. We shall refer to such tables as "confusion matrices."

A headrest on the talker's chair insured that the distance to the WE-633A microphone was constant at 15 inches. The speech 15 inches from the talker's lips was about 60 db re 0.0002 dyne/cm². The speech voltage was amplified, then filtered (if frequency distortion was to be used), then mixed with noise, then amplified again and presented to the listeners by PDR-8 earphones. In all tests the noise voltage was fixed at -32 db below one volt across the earphones and the signal-to-noise ratio was varied by changing the gain in the speech channel. A separate amplifier was used to drive a monitoring VU-meter with the output of the microphone. The gain to the VU-meter was fixed so that the talker could maintain her speech level at a constant value. The talkers did succeed rather well in keeping a constant level; several hundred sample readings of peak deflections gave an average of $+0.18$ VU with a standard deviation of 1.04. However, it should be noted that with this system, the signal-to-noise ratios are set by the peak deflection of the VU needle and that peak occurs during the vowel. The consonants, which are consistently weaker than the vowel, were actually presented at much less favorable signal-to-noise ratios than such a vowel-to-noise ratio would seem to indicate. It was, therefore, especially important to keep the same speech level for all tests since otherwise the vowel-to-consonant ratio might have changed significantly and the data would not be comparable.

The frequency response of the system was essentially that of the earphones, which are reasonably uniform between 200 and 6500 cps. A low-pass filter at 7000 cps in the random noise generator insured that noise voltages could be converted directly to sound pressure levels according to the earphone calibration. A Krohn-Hite 310-A variable band-pass filter was used to introduce frequency distortion into the speech channel; the skirts dropped off at a rate of 24 db per octave and the cutoff frequency was taken as the frequency 3 db below the peak in the pass band.

RESULTS

The results of these tests are confusion matrices. Since these matrices represent a considerable investment and since other workers may wish to apply summary statistics differing from those which we have chosen, the complete confusion matrices are presented in Tables I–XVII. Data for all listeners and all talkers have been pooled so that 4000 observations are summarized in each matrix; on the average, each syllable was judged 250 times under every test condition.

Tables I–VI summarize the data obtained when the speech-to-noise ratio was -18, -12, -6, 0, $+6$, and $+12$ db and the band width was 200–6500 cps. Tables VII–XII summarize the data when the high-pass cutoff was fixed at 200 cps and the low-pass cutoff was 300, 400, 600, 1200, 2500, and 5000 cps with a speech-to-noise ratio corresponding to $+12$ db for unfiltered speech. Tables XII–XVII summarize the data when the low-pass cutoff was fixed at 5000 cps and the high-pass cutoff was 200, 1000, 2000, 2500, 3000, and 4500 cps with a speech-to-noise ratio that would have been $+12$ db if the speech had not been filtered.

In these tables the syllables that were spoken are indicated by the consonants listed vertically in the first column on the left. The syllables that were written by the listener are indicated horizontally across the top of the table. The number in each cell is the frequency that each stimulus-response pair was observed. The number of correct responses can be obtained by totalling the frequencies along the main diagonal. Row sums would give the frequencies that each syllable was written by the listeners.

A GENERALIZATION OF THE ARTICULATION SCORE

The standard articulation score is obtained from Tables I–XVII by summing the frequencies along the main diagonal and dividing the total by n, the number of observations. Although this score is useful, it tells us nothing about the distribution of errors among the off-diagonal cells. If we wanted to reconstruct an adequate picture of the confusion matrix, we would need other scores to supplement the usual articulation score.

In order to generalize the articulation score, we can combine stimuli (and their corresponding responses) into groups in such a way that confusions within groups are more likely than confusions between groups. Combining stimuli creates a smaller confusion matrix that shows the confusions between groups, and the sum along the diagonal gives a new articulation score for this new, smaller matrix. The new score will be greater than the original score, since all the responses that were originally correct remain so and in addition all the confusions within each group are now considered to be "correct" in the new score. If the original score, A, is supplemented with such an additional score, A', we would reconstruct the data matrix by spreading the fraction A along the main diagonal. Then $A' - A$ would go off the diagonal but within groups, and $1 - A'$ would be distributed off the diagonal between groups. This general strategy can be repeated quite simply if the several groupings used form a monotonic increasing sequence of sets: $A \leq A' \leq A''$, etc.

A simple example will illustrate this technique. A test was conducted at $S/N = -12$ db over a 200–6500-cps channel using six stop consonants in front of the vowel $|a|$. The confusion matrix for 2000 observations

TABLE I. Confusion matrix for $S/N = -18$ db and frequency response of 200–6500 cps.

	p	t	k	f	θ	s	ʃ	b	d	g	v	ð	z	ʒ	m	n
p	14	27	22	23	25	22	14	15	16	7	17	11	12	11	16	12
t	16	26	21	15	15	18	14	7	10	6	17	9	13	11	9	13
k	20	22	24	15	14	29	12	4	11	9	12	10	16	11	17	14
f	27	22	27	23	13	12	10	19	20	14	16	16	15	3	13	18
θ	17	18	18	13	15	21	12	14	20	14	23	6	14	9	12	14
s	18	17	23	11	18	21	17	11	24	15	15	16	11	13	17	5
ʃ	16	20	27	17	13	37	14	10	21	7	20	18	9	8	16	15
b	12	11	24	15	19	15	12	24	20	19	24	12	15	11	18	17
d	16	24	18	13	15	15	14	22	25	21	25	17	18	13	15	25
g	11	20	29	9	18	18	15	26	30	14	18	14	16	20	24	22
v	9	17	18	11	7	12	9	25	14	13	15	15	19	11	12	17
ð	16	11	10	7	6	14	10	20	17	18	15	7	17	12	18	18
z	18	18	15	9	13	19	7	22	14	9	21	12	23	10	22	12
ʒ	8	16	17	14	12	15	7	22	18	8	15	11	15	11	18	13
m	19	24	15	14	14	14	8	14	15	12	13	8	11	6	25	28
n	11	18	20	6	9	18	9	14	14	13	9	8	10	12	33	32

TABLE II. Confusion matrix for $S/N = -12$ db and frequency response 200–6500 cps.

	p	t	k	f	θ	s	ʃ	b	d	g	v	ð	z	ʒ	m	n
p	51	53	65	22	19	6	11	2		2	3	3	1	5	8	5
t	64	57	74	20	24	22	14	2	3	1	1	2	1	1	5	1
k	50	42	62	22	18	16	11	4	1	1	1	2			4	2
f	31	22	28	85	34	15	11	3	5		8	8	3		3	
θ	26	22	25	63	45	27	12	6	9	3	11	9	3	2	7	2
s	16	15	16	33	24	53	48	3	5	6	3	1	6	2		1
ʃ	23	32	20	14	27	25	115	1	4	5	3		6	3	4	2
b	4	2	2	18	7	7	1	60	18	18	44	25	14	6	20	10
d	3		1	4	7	4	11	18	48	35	16	24	26	14	9	12
g	3	1	1	1	4	5	7	20	38	29	16	29	29	38	10	9
v		1	1	12	5	4	5	37	20	23	71	16	14	4	14	9
ð		1	4	17	2	3	2	53	31	25	50	33	23	5	13	6
z	6	1	2	2	6	14	8	23	29	27	24	19	40	26	3	6
ʒ	3	2	2	1		6	7	7	30	23	9	7	39	77	5	14
m		1			1	1		11	3	6	8	11		1	109	60
n	1			1		1		2	2	6	7	1	1	9	84	145

TABLE III. Confusion matrix for $S/N = -6$ db and frequency response of 200–6500 cps.

	p	t	k	f	θ	s	ʃ	b	d	g	v	ð	z	ʒ	m	n
p	80	43	64	17	14	6	2	1	1		1	1			2	
t	71	84	55	5	9	3	8	1				1	2		2	3
k	66	76	107	12	8	9	4				1				1	
f	18	12	9	175	48	11	1	7	2	1	2	2				
θ	19	17	16	104	64	32	7	5	4	5	6	4	5			
s	8	5	4	23	39	107	45	4	2	3	1	1	3	2		1
ʃ	1	6	3	4	6	29	195	3								1
b	1			5	4	4		136	10	9	47	16	6	1	5	4
d							8	5	80	45	11	20	20	26	1	
g					2			3	63	66	3	19	37	56		3
v				2		2		48	5	5	145	45	12		4	
ð					6			31	6	17	86	58	21	5	6	4
z				1	1	1		7	20	27	16	28	94	44		1
ʒ								1	26	18	3	8	45	129		2
m	1							4			4	1	3		177	46
n				4				1	5	2		7	1	6	47	163

TABLE IV. Confusion matrix for $S/N = 0$ db and frequency response of 200–6500 cps.

	p	t	k	f	θ	s	ʃ	b	d	g	v	ð	z	ʒ	m	n
p	150	38	88	7	13											
t	30	193	28	1												1
k	86	45	138	4	1		1									
f	4	3	5	199	46	4		1				1			1	
θ	11	6	4	85	114	10					2					
s		2	1	5	38	170	10			2						
ʃ		3	3			3	267									
b				7	4			235	4		34	27	1			
d									189	48		4	8	11		
g									74	161		4	8	25		
v				3	1			19		2	177	29	4	1		
ð								7		10	64	105	18			
z									17	23	4	22	132	26		
ʒ									2	3	1	1	9	191		
m								1							201	6
n												3		1	8	240

TABLE V. Confusion matrix for $S/N = +6$ db and frequency response of 200–6500 cps.

	p	t	k	f	θ	s	ʃ	b	d	g	v	ð	z	ʒ	m	n
p	162	10	55	5	3							1				
t	8	270	14													
k	38	6	171	1												
f	5	1	2	207	57			3			1					
θ	5	1	2	71	142	3					2	2				
s			1	1	7	232	2			1						
ʃ						1	239									
b				1	2			214			31	12				
d									206	14		9	1	2		
g								11	64	194		4	2	1		
v				1	1			14		2	205	39	5			1
ð								2		4	55	179	22	2		
z									3	10	2	20	198	3		
ʒ									3	4			2	215		
m															217	3
n							1								2	285

TABLE VI. Confusion matrix for $S/N = +12$ db and frequency response of 200–6500 cps.

	p	t	k	f	θ	s	ʃ	b	d	g	v	ð	z	ʒ	m	n
p	240		41	2	1											
t	1	252	1	1						1						
k	18	3	219													
f				225	24			5			2					
θ	9		1	69	185			3				1				
s						232										
ʃ							236									
b				1				242			24	12	1			
d									213	22		1				
g				1					33	203		3				
v								6			171	30			1	
ð				1				1		3	22	208	4			1
z									2	4	1	7	238			
ʒ														244		
m												1			274	1
n																252

TABLE VII. Confusion matrix for $S/N = +12$ db and frequency response of 200–300 cps.

	p	t	k	f	θ	s	ʃ	b	d	g	v	ð	z	ʒ	m	n
p	47	61	68	15	11	17	9	3	3	1		1	2	2	3	1
t	59	63	64	19	15	14	13	3	4	1		5	2	2	2	2
k	37	47	56	10	13	15	10	1	2	1		2		1		1
f	21	29	21	38	37	47	19	2	2	1		2	2	3	3	1
θ	13	23	25	23	39	54	39	2	2	1		5	1		4	5
s	16	25	10	29	52	65	34	1	4	2	4	5	1	1	1	2
ʃ	15	33	23	18	28	70	41	1	1			7	3	1	1	2
b		1	1	8	8	5	3	98	28	17	38	19	9	2	8	7
d	1		1	11	7	12	5	70	84	33	12	10	24	9	1	
g	4	1	2	7	5	13	8	56	74	33	13	15	21	13	6	1
v		2	1	1	2	1	1	44	34	18	77	34	36	14	2	1
ð	1				3		1	22	16	19	45	46	45	23	11	8
z	2	3	2	2	4	3	2	15	15	20	46	35	64	21	2	
ʒ	1	1		1	2		1	11	15	24	54	42	70	39	2	5
m			1	1	2	2		1	3	3	4	5	1	4	161	60
n	1	3	2	1	1	1	2	1	3	2	2	4	2	2	133	108

TABLE VIII. Confusion matrix for $S/N = +12$ db and frequency response of 200–400 cps.

	p	t	k	f	θ	s	ʃ	b	d	g	v	ð	z	ʒ	m	n
p	72	68	90	20	15	4	1	2	4	1		1				2
t	73	72	74	20	8	6	3	1	2	2		2		1		
k	63	74	127	9	7	5	2			1		1	1	1		1
f	7	7	10	63	69	41	8	3	1	1	1	3		1	1	
θ	5	8	11	60	85	45	14	2	4	2	6	5	1			
s	1	6	5	19	49	125	60	5	2	1	2	9	4			
ʃ	2	6	8	8	22	69	89	2	4	1		3	5	1		
b		1	1	19	14	5		134	20	13	14	11	4	1	2	1
d			2		1	6	4	19	120	23	2	3	11	3		2
g			2	1		5	1	11	116	59	8	7	11	4	1	2
v		1		1	1	2		25	4	8	111	55	18	2	2	2
ð		1	1	6	5	1		43	16	15	75	66	23	11	1	4
z	2		2	1	5	5	2	21	20	17	18	33	91	25	1	1
ʒ				4		2	2	1	27	29	11	16	83	78		1
m								12	3		1				219	57
n				1	1			12	3	1	1	2			99	120

TABLE IX. Confusion matrix for $S/N = +12$ db and frequency response of 200–600 cps.

	p	t	k	f	θ	s	ʃ	b	d	g	v	ð	z	ʒ	m	n
p	115	43	70	10	3	2						1				
t	69	63	71	4	4							1				
k	59	49	134	4	1						1					
f	2	3	2	126	89	11	1	2			1	8	1		1	1
θ	2	1	1	103	97	35	7	2	1		5	1				1
s	3	3		34	88	93	26	4	1			7		1		
ʃ	3	6	12	7	31	98	87	1	2	1	2	1	1			
b			1	10	5	1		201	13	39	13	4				
d		1		1	1	6	1	29	169	39	3	3	6	5		
g				1		7		12	99	97		4	8	11		1
v				5	2			14	1	2	141	57	9	4	1	
ð								10	6	10	109	90	31	7	1	
z						1	2	3	15	30	17	42	116	22		
ʒ			1				1		10	21	8	17	110	116		
m						1							1		215	39
n				1											119	120

TABLE X. Confusion matrix for $S/N = +12$ db and frequency response of 200–1200 cps.

	p	t	k	f	θ	s	ʃ	b	d	g	v	ð	z	ʒ	m	n
p	165	46	31	3	1			1						1		
t	91	83	68	4	1	2		1				2				
k	48	55	147	2	3							1				
f	16	4	3	146	60	3	2	11			1	2				
θ	4	3		109	76	17	2	12	1			2	1	1		
s	2	1	1	43	83	83	11	3		1	1	7				
ʃ	1	6	2	12	41	86	90		6	4		4				
b				14	5			223	4		5	1				
d	1				1	3	4	4	173	37		2	1	2		
g	1					1			102	107	1	2	7	7		
v	2	2		2	1			23	1	2	163	62	14	3	1	
ð				1		3	2	27	6	32	87	107	36	7		
z	1							4	12	48	10	15	114	39	2	1
ʒ							1		3	35	1	16	60	134		
m	1											1			229	9
n															5	247

TABLE XI. Confusion matrix for $S/N = +12$ db and frequency response of 200–2500 cps.

	p	t	k	f	θ	s	ʃ	b	d	g	v	ð	z	ʒ	m	n
p	215	29	26	5	1											
t	74	91	47													
k	15	16	201													
f	6		1	186	31	2		3				7				
θ	1	5	1	93	81	25	1	1		2	2	4				
s	1	3	1	31	78	142	9	1	1			5				
ʃ		1	1			23	210			1						
b				11	6	1		206	4		11	1				
d							1	1	217	30			1	6		
g				2		1	1	1	54	169		1		3		
v				1	2	1		36		1	178	39	9	1	1	
ð				3	6	2		14		17	58	146	45	1		
z						2			17	40	7	24	122	20		
ʒ				1			5		5	9		11		265		
m															242	18
n															2	242

TABLE XII. Confusion matrix for $S/N = +12$ db and frequency response of 200–5000 cps.

	p	t	k	f	θ	s	ʃ	b	d	g	v	ð	z	ʒ	m	n
p	228	7	7	1			1									
t		236	8													
k	26	5	213													
f	6	1	1	194	35			3			1	3				
θ		2	2	96	146	2		2	1		1	8				
s		2		1	31	204	1	1	9	4		7				
ʃ						1	243									
b				13	12			207	2	3	19	8				
d									240	9				3		
g								1	41	199			2	1		
v				3	3			20		2	182	47	2			1
ð					7			10	3	22	49	170	19			
z				1				3	8	24	2	22	145	3		
ʒ							1		2			13		264		
m															213	11
n																248

TABLE XIII. Confusion matrix for $S/N = +12$ db and frequency response of 1000–5000 cps.

	p	t	k	f	θ	s	ʃ	b	d	g	v	ð	z	ʒ	m	n
p	179	9	44	6	3					2	1					
t		272	3					1								
k	15	1	227					1	1		2					1
f	12	1		162	28	3	1	34			6		1		4	
θ	8	2	7	39	125	13	2	6	2	1	4	19	3		1	
s				3	28	200		2	1	1	4	6	9	1		1
ʃ						1	221							2		
b	2			9	10	1		130		6	74	24			16	
d		2					1		195	35	6	2	2	8		5
g				2					48	151		3	4	5		11
v	1			28	8			48	1	3	145	33	3		17	1
ð	1	1		1	14			8	11	12	31	116	26	5	21	6
z			1	2		24	2	1	19	7	3	31	163	4	2	1
ʒ				1			20		2	2				207		
m	3		2	5	4	1		10			6				224	1
n			1	1	1			1	8	4	2	1	1	1		207

TABLE XIV. Confusion matrix for $S/N = +12$ db and frequency response of 2000–5000 cps.

	p	t	k	f	θ	s	ʃ	b	d	g	v	ð	z	ʒ	m	n
p	94	32	26	15	6	3	1	10	4	4	13	12	1	5	3	3
t	7	223	3	3	1		3		7	1	1	1		5	1	
k	24	25	126	4	7	4	2	3	6	15	1	3	1	2	7	2
f	38	7	19	72	24	5	2	24	3	12	28	11	4	3	12	4
θ	22	7	11	20	63	27		19	8	13	22	26	16		12	10
s	2	9	1	5	23	148			4	3	3	4	44	6		8
ʃ	1	1					208	1					1	28		
b	15	5	5	37	12	2		72	7	8	40	30	4		40	7
d	2	6	7		2			4	192	19	4	6	3	2	2	23
g	2	1	3	1	8	4	1	8	44	122	10	6	6	1	3	20
v	17	1	12	13	7		1	39	5	14	42	23	2	4	32	12
ð	5		6	9	20	5		17	16	19	17	64	20	1	36	25
z	3	2	2	5	8	44		5	22	7	1	13	99	5	7	9
ʒ						37				4				199	4	
m	10	4	3	8	7		1	9	5	10	10	16	2		113	26
n	2		2		3	2		1	20	11	3	7	6	3	4	192

TABLE XV. Confusion matrix for $S/N = +12$ db and frequency response of 2500–5000 cps.

	p	t	k	f	θ	s	ʃ	b	d	g	v	ð	z	ʒ	m	n
p	69	30	37	26	16	4	4	21	9	18	13	12	9	3	7	10
t	4	164	9	2	2	2		1	4	4	1	2	2		3	
k	20	35	76	9	11	5	6	3	5	25	5	3	15	11	7	4
f	27	8	7	24	28	7	8	15	8	14	34	14	6	2	11	11
θ	15	19	7	20	49	10	8	12	16	16	13	20	10	5	16	16
s	6	8	2	1	19	160	4		16	10	8	11	27	2	7	11
ʃ	1	1	2	1	5	1	204	1				1	2	44		1
b	23	4	10	13	17		2	48	17	17	34	28	10	1	28	12
d	1	7	6	5	4	2	1	1	128	16	8	6	5	13	5	16
g	6	3	16	5	6	5	2	17	39	85	11	13	6	7	6	13
v	22	6	6	26	18	3	3	33	12	9	32	28	7	2	18	7
ð	21	11	9	16	28	4	2	35	14	22	20	44	10	2	24	22
z	4	5	1	2	9	60	5	1	27	21		12	86	6	2	3
ʒ	2	4	2			3	49	1	7	1	2	1	5	167		
m	18	3	7	11	16	8	2	13	16	12	16	21	3	1	68	37
n	8	4	12	7	9	2		10	22	17	13	8	5	4	16	119

TABLE XVI. Confusion matrix for $S/N = +12$ db and frequency response of 3000–5000 cps.

	p	t	k	f	θ	s	ʃ	b	d	g	v	ð	z	ʒ	m	n
p	31	15	15	15	14	11	6	19	11	8	15	15	5	9	12	19
t	11	184	16	6	5	5	5	8	9	3	4	2	5	3	6	4
k	15	35	50	7	16	7	2	14	14	24	7	9	8	9	8	7
f	19	12	12	15	19	8	2	25	16	25	15	12	6	2	17	11
θ	15	14	13	13	30	15	3	15	24	12	14	17	10	3	14	20
s	4	4	8	11	8	140	4	7	8	6	6	11	35	7	2	7
ʃ		6	2	3	1	4	177	1	2	2	1	6	1	23	7	
b	17	13	11	25	23	8	1	27	13	19	25	13	5	6	17	13
d	14	23	15	11	11	4	3	15	63	25	14	10	13	6	19	14
g	14	15	17	17	12	8	1	23	39	45	14	10	13	7	17	16
v	19	19	22	18	20	8	10	35	18	16	19	21	7		28	16
ð	19	13	12	12	24	8	6	22	24	15	24	21	10	5	33	16
z	9	21	9	7	17	59	6	6	11	13	10	15	41	4	10	14
ʒ	4	6	1	5	1	11	51	3	3	7	1	10	9	128	7	5
m	16	7	14	11	19	5	4	31	16	17	17	10	10	6	58	19
n	16	7	12	6	16	7	6	14	29	16	13	22	7	4	19	58

TABLE XVII. Confusion matrix for $S/N = +12$ db and frequency response of 4500–5000 cps.

	p	t	k	f	θ	s	ʃ	b	d	g	v	ð	z	ʒ	m	n
p	26	21	23	16	24	20	4	15	16	14	20	9	10	9	16	9
t	10	141	12	3	4	4	3	5	11	5	7	11	4	5	8	3
k	16	34	25	14	11	13	8	20	20	8	18	13	20	10	12	22
f	9	9	22	18	18	6	6	18	17	9	17	19	9	3	27	13
θ	16	21	25	5	20	10	2	29	23	24	27	28	11	5	16	10
s	8	5	15	7	11	138	7	6	4	11	13	7	34	5	6	7
ʃ	3	3	7	1	1	12	190	1	4	2	2	4	6	26	6	4
b	12	8	23	11	18	13	9	26	14	18	21	14	11	6	16	16
d	24	26	28	16	19	8	4	19	18	19	13	11	6	3	16	14
g	12	16	17	14	21	11	10	12	17	21	18	19	7	10	22	13
v	21	11	17	15	24	12	8	19	15	14	33	23	6	3	23	16
ð	18	19	15	16	20	7	5	24	16	16	22	28	9	11	24	10
z	8	12	8	8	7	64	5	12	10	9	12	17	51	11	6	8
ʒ	5	18	10	8	9	11	57	5	4	5	9	11	15	85	9	7
m	8	13	20	13	15	14	7	18	8	16	16	17	12	2	15	18
n	20	15	15	18	15	7	6	19	20	12	17	15	12	4	21	16

TABLE XVIII. Confusion matrix at $S/N = -12$ db
with a 200–6500-cps channel.

	p	t	k	b	d	g	Sum
p	117	58	115	14	10	2	316
t	74	101	103	8	4	6	296
k	105	109	153	5	8	4	384
b	13	9	10	217	45	26	320
d	3	4	5	47	200	117	376
g	3	11	8	45	147	94	308
							2000

is given in Table XVIII. There are 882 entries on the main diagonal, so $A = 0.441$. If we group the consonants $|pk|$, $|t|$, $|b|$, and $|dg|$, there are 1366 correct responses, so $A' = 0.683$. If we again group $|ptk|$ and $|bdg|$, there are 1873 correct responses, so $A'' = 0.9365$. Now if we wish to reconstruct the matrix from these three articulation scores, we would first divide the 882 correct responses equally among the six diagonal cells, which gives 147 observations per cell. When we add the four cells for $|pk|$ and $|dg|$ to the diagonal cells, the count increases from 882 to 1366, so the additional 484 observations must be divided equally among the four additional cells, which gives 121 per cell for $|pk|$ and $|dg|$ confusions. When we add the eight remaining cells for the $|ptk|$ and $|bdg|$ groups, the count increases from 1366 to 1873, so the additional 507 observations must be divided evenly among those eight cells, which gives 63.4 per cell. The remaining 127 observations are then divided equally among the 18 cells remaining in the lower left and upper right quadrants, which gives 7.1 per cell. In this way the generalized, three-valued articulation score gives a reasonably clear picture of the distribution of errors.

The procedure just described can lead to serious errors if the stimulus frequencies are quite disparate. For example, if one stimulus is presented much more often than any other, it will contribute more to the total number of correct responses and then the equipartition of correct responses among the diagonal cells will be in error. In such cases the original data matrix should first be corrected to the frequencies that would presumably have been obtained if the stimuli had been equally frequent. This correction is made by multiplying the entries in each row by n/kn_i, where n_i is the frequency of occurrence of the ith stimulus ($i = 1, 2, \cdots, k$) in a sample of n observations. Then the "articulation scores corrected for stimulus frequencies" are calculated for the revised matrix. To reconstruct the data matrix, the corrected frequencies should be partitioned as before and then each row multiplied by kn_i/n in order to remove the correction and regain the original stimulus frequencies. Whenever an experimenter employs some unusual (nonuniform) distribution of stimulus frequencies, this fact should be stated explicitly in order to avoid misinterpretations of the articulation scores so obtained.

Some such generalization of the articulation score seems essential in order to preserve the data on clustering of errors. In our own analysis of the data, however, we have preferred a somewhat more elaborate statistical analysis. We have presented this simpler technique for the reader who feels that the information measures we have employed are too abstract or do not permit a simple reconstruction of the original matrix. Having pointed out this simpler technique, however, we shall make little use of it in the following discussion.

LINGUISTIC FEATURES

For many years linguists and phoneticians have classified phonemes according to features of the articulation process used to generate the sounds. These features of speech production are reflected in certain acoustic characteristics which are presumably discriminated by the listener. When we begin to look for reasonable ways to group the stimuli in order to summarize the pattern of confusions, it is natural to turn first to these articulatory features for guidance. In order to describe the 16 consonants used in this study we adopted the following set of features as a basis for classification.

(1) *Voicing.* In articulatory terms, the vocal cords do not vibrate when the consonants $|ptkf\theta s\mathint|$ are produced, and they do vibrate for $|bdgv\eth z\mathyogh mn|$. Acoustically, this means that the voiceless consonants are aperiodic or noisy in character, whereas a periodic or line-spectrum component is superimposed on the noise for voiced consonants. In addition, in English the voiceless consonants seem to be more intense and the voiceless stops have considerable aspiration, a sort of breathy noise between the release of pressure and the beginning of the following vowels, and may be somewhat briefer than the voiced stops. Thus the articulatory difference is reflected in a variety of acoustic differences.

(2) *Nasality.* To articulate $|m|$ and $|n|$ the lips are closed and the pressure is released through the nose by lowering the soft palate at the back of the mouth. The nasal resonance introduced in this way provides an acoustic difference. In addition, $|mn|$ seem slightly longer in duration than their stop or fricative counterparts and somewhat more intense. Also, the two nasals are the only consonants in this study lacking the aperiodic component of noisiness.

(3) *Affrication.* If the articulators close completely, the consonant may be a stop or a nasal, but if they are brought close together and air is forced between them, the result is a kind of turbulence or friction noise that distinguishes $|f\theta s\mathint v\eth z\mathyogh|$ from $|ptkbdgmn|$. The acoustic turbulence is in contrast to the silence followed by a pop that characterizes the stops and to the periodic, almost vowel-like resonance of the nasals.

(4) *Duration.* This is the name we have arbitrarily adopted to designate the difference between $|s\mathint z\mathyogh|$ and the other 12 consonants. These four consonants are

long, intense, high-frequency noises, but in our opinion it is their extra duration that is most effective in setting them apart.

(5) *Place of Articulation.* This feature has to do with where in the mouth the major constriction of the vocal passage occurs. Usually three positions, front, middle, and back, are distinguished, so that we have grouped $|pbfvm|$ as front, $|td\theta s\eth zn|$ as middle, and $|kg\int\Im|$ as back consonants. Although these three positions are easy to recognize in the production of these sounds, the acoustic consequences of differences in place are most complex. Of the various accounts of the positional feature that have been given, the work done by the Haskins Laboratory[1,2] seems to provide the best basis for an interpretation of our data. For the voiced stops $|bdg|$ the most important acoustic clue to position seems to be in the initial portion of the second formant

TABLE XIX. Classification of consonants used to analyze confusions.

Consonant	Voicing	Nasality	Affrication	Duration	Place
p	0	0	0	0	0
t	0	0	0	0	1
k	0	0	0	0	2
f	0	0	1	0	0
θ	0	0	1	0	1
s	0	0	1	1	1
$\int$	0	0	1	1	2
b	1	0	0	0	0
d	1	0	0	0	1
g	1	0	0	0	2
v	1	0	1	0	0
$\eth$	1	0	1	0	1
z	1	0	1	1	1
$\Im$	1	0	1	1	2
m	1	1	0	0	0
n	1	1	0	0	1

of the vowel $|a|$ that follows; if this formant frequency rises initially, it is a $|b|$, but if it falls it is $|d|$ or $|g|$. Since the vowel formant is relatively audible, the front $|b|$ is easily distinguished from the middle $|d|$ and the back $|g|$. The latter two positions are much harder to distinguish and probably cannot be differentiated until their aperiodic, noisy components become sufficiently audible so that high-frequency noise can be assigned to middle $|d|$ and low-frequency noise to back $|g|$. For the voiceless stops $|ptk|$, however, the story is different because the transitional portion of the second formant occurs during the period of aspiration, before vocalization has begun, and is correspondingly much harder to hear. The plosive part of the voiceless stops is relatively intense, however, so that the high-fre-

[1] Liberman, Delattre, and Cooper, Am. J. Psychol. **65**, 497–516 (1952).
[2] Liberman, Delattre, Cooper, and Gerstman, Psychol. Monographs 68, No. 8, 1–13 (1954).

quency noise of middle $|t|$ distinguishes it from the low-frequency noise of front $|p|$ and back $|k|$. The distinction between $|p|$ and $|k|$ is slightly harder to hear because it seems to depend upon hearing the aspirated transition into the second vowel resonance. What acoustic representation there is for place of articulation of the fricative sounds is even more obscure. Probably the middle $|sz|$ are distinguished from the back $|\int\Im|$ on the basis of the high-frequency energy in $|sz|$. The distinction between front $|fv|$ and middle $|\theta\eth|$, however is uncertainly attributable to slight differences in the transition to the following vowel. The distinctions between $|f|$ and $|\theta|$ and between $|v|$ and $|\eth|$ are among the most difficult for listeners to hear and it seems likely that in most natural situations the differentiation depends more on verbal context and on visual observation of the talker's lips than it does on the acoustic difference. In any event, when we summarily assign these consonants into three classes on the basis of "articulatory position," we are thereby concealing a host of difficult problems. The positional feature is by all odds the most superficial and unsatisfactory of the five features we have employed.

In Table XIX a digital notation is used to summarize the classification of these 16 consonants on the basis of these five features. From Table XIX it is easy to see in what ways any two of the consonants differ.

Now if we apply the groupings given in Table XIX to the data matrices in Tables I–XVII, we can obtain a set of articulation scores, one score for each feature. For example, we can group the voiceless consonants together *versus* the voiced consonants and so estimate the probability that the voicing feature will be perceived correctly—the articulation score for voicing. The necessary summations for each feature for every table have been made and are given in Table XX.

A COVARIANCE MEASURE OF INTELLIGIBILITY

The recent development of a mathematical theory of communication has made considerable use of a measure

TABLE XX. Frequencies of correct responses in Tables I–XVII.

Condition	S/N	Band	All	Voice	Nasal	Frict	Durat	Place
1	−18	200–6500	313	2286	3200	2032	2600	1439
2	−12	200–6500	1080	3586	3742	2610	3095	1842
3	−6	200–6500	1860	3877	3921	3202	3429	2386
4	0	200–6500	2862	3977	3992	3706	3780	3099
5	6	200–6500	3336	3985	3998	3861	3910	3472
6	12	200–6500	3634	3985	3997	3916	3980	3691
7	12	200–300	1059	3725	3864	2922	2905	1717
8	12	200–400	1631	3801	3939	3402	3388	2088
9	12	200–600	1980	3903	3991	3696	3475	2341
10	12	200–1200	2287	3891	3994	3641	3526	2616
11	12	200–2500	2913	3927	3999	3778	3673	3224
12	12	200–5000	3332	3920	3999	3811	3853	3522
13	12	1000–5000	2924	3735	3861	3566	3801	3476
14	12	2000–5000	2029	3208	3573	3087	3689	2992
15	12	2500–5000	1523	2857	3472	2871	3552	2587
16	12	3000–5000	1087	2527	3283	2601	3390	2227
17	12	4500–5000	851	2283	3267	2463	3260	1927
Random guessing			250	2031	3125	2000	2500	1406

of covariance between input and output. This measure has been defined in terms of the mean logarithmic probability (MLP). If the input variable is x, which can assume the discrete values $i=1,2,\cdots,k$ with probability p_i, then the measure of the input is

$$\mathrm{MLP}(x)=E(-\log p_i)=-\sum_i p_i \log p_i.$$

If the logarithm is taken to the base 2, then the measure can be called the number of binary decisions needed on the average to specify the input, or the number of bits of information per stimulus. A similar expression holds for the output variable y, which can assume the values $j=1,2,\cdots,m$. Similarly, the number of decisions needed to specify the particular stimulus-response pair is $\mathrm{MLP}(xy)$, where p_{ij} is the probability of the joint occurrence of input i and output j. A measure of covariance of input with output is given by

$$T(x;y)=\mathrm{MLP}(x)+\mathrm{MLP}(y)-\mathrm{MLP}(xy)$$
$$=-\sum_{i,j} p_{ij} \log \frac{p_i p_j}{p_{ij}}.$$

$T(x;y)$ is often referred to as the transmission from x to y in bits per stimulus. The relative transmission is given by

$$T_{\mathrm{rel}}(x;y)=T(x;y)/H(x).$$

Since $H(x)\geq T(x;y)\geq 0$, the ratio varies from 0 to 1; if the transmission is poor and the response is not closely correlated to the stimulus, then $T_{\mathrm{rel}}(x;y)$ will be near zero, but if the response can be predicted with considerable accuracy from the stimulus, then $T_{\mathrm{rel}}(x;y)$ will be near unity.

In practice the true probabilities are not known and must be estimated from the relative frequencies

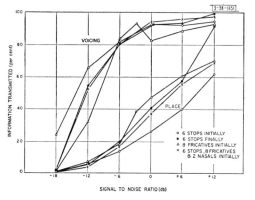

SIGNAL TO NOISE RATIO (db)

FIG. 1. The relative information transmitted about voicing (top four curves) and place (bottom four curves) is plotted as a function of signal-to-noise ratio in decibels. The four curves for each feature were obtained from four independent experiments using different test vocabularies. Voicing information is transmitted at signal-to-noise levels 18 db below those needed for place information.

obtained in a finite sample taken during the experiment. The maximum likelihood estimate of $T(x;y)$ is obtained by using n_i/n, n_j/n, and n_{ij}/n in place of p_i, p_j, and p_{ij}, respectively, where n_i is the frequency of stimulus i, n_j is the frequency of response j, and n_{ij} is the frequency of the joint occurrence of stimulus i and response j in a sample of n observations. In Tables I–XVII the cell entries are the n_{ij}, row sums give n_i, column sums give n_j, and n is 4000. Like most maximum likelihood estimates, this estimate will be biased to overestimate $T(x;y)$ for small samples; in the present case, however, the sample is large enough that the bias can safely be ignored.

The covariance measure of intelligibility can be applied to the several linguistic features separately in just the same way that the articulation score for each feature was obtained for Table XX. For example, we can construct a fourfold confusion matrix by grouping the voiceless sounds together as one stimulus and the voiced sounds as the other and then tabulating the frequency of voiceless responses to voiceless stimuli, of voiced responses to voiceless stimuli, of voiceless responses to voiced stimuli, and of voiced responses to voiced stimuli. For this 2 by 2 confusion matrix we can calculate the covariance of response with stimulus in the same way as described above and so measure the transmission of information about voicing. Similar measures can be calculated for nasality, affrication, duration, and position.

This breakdown of the confusion matrix into five smaller matrices and the measurement of transmission for each one of these five separately is equivalent to considering that we are actually testing five different communication channels simultaneously.[3] Of course, the five channels will probably not be independent. Some interaction or "cross talk" is to be expected, in the sense that knowing one feature may make some other feature easier to hear. However, the impressive thing to us was that this cross talk was so small and that the features were perceived almost independently of one another.

At first thought one might expect that if all five channels were independent, then the sum of the information transmitted by the separate channels should equal approximately the transmission calculated for all five taken together in the whole 16 by 16 matrix. This first thought would be true except for one fact; the inputs to the five channels are not independent and, therefore, even if the channels themselves are independent, the amounts transmitted through each channel will be related.

In Table XXI the average amounts of information in bits per stimulus that the listeners received are presented for the composite channel and for the five sub-channels individually for all 17 conditions of masking and filtering. The last row in the table gives the amounts

---

[3] W. J. McGill, Psychometrika **19**, 97–116 (1954).

TABLE XXI. Amounts of information transmitted in bits per stimulus in Tables I–XVII for composite channel and for each feature separately.

Condition	S/N	Band	All	Voice	Nasal	Frict	Durat	Place
1	−18	200–6500	0.061	0.021	0.008	0.000	0.001	0.001
2	−12	200–6500	0.959	0.516	0.264	0.069	0.087	0.058
3	−6	200–6500	1.834	0.797	0.397	0.279	0.249	0.249
4	0	200–6500	2.797	0.944	0.495	0.620	0.483	0.578
5	6	200–6500	3.226	0.951	0.543	0.782	0.636	0.856
6	12	200–6500	3.546	0.956	0.555	0.853	0.751	1.090
7	12	200–300	1.155	0.623	0.371	0.159	0.042	0.025
8	12	200–400	1.686	0.709	0.457	0.393	0.218	0.125
9	12	200–600	2.159	0.821	0.520	0.614	0.272	0.231
10	12	200–1200	2.379	0.805	0.523	0.583	0.281	0.359
11	12	200–2500	2.828	0.852	0.544	0.702	0.419	0.721
12	12	200–5000	3.185	0.847	0.521	0.730	0.581	0.936
13	12	1000–5000	2.643	0.638	0.350	0.506	0.520	0.872
14	12	2000–5000	1.582	0.273	0.160	0.229	0.426	0.499
15	12	2500–5000	1.053	0.130	0.083	0.143	0.348	0.296
16	12	3000–5000	0.624	0.048	0.023	0.067	0.235	0.143
17	12	4500–5000	0.455	0.014	0.002	0.045	0.193	0.068
Maximum possible			4.000	0.989	0.544	1.000	0.811	1.546

that would be transmitted if no mistakes at all occurred (on the assumption that all 16 syllables occurred equally often). The degree of redundancy in the input is indicated by the fact that the sum of the transmissions for the five channels is 4.890 bits, whereas the composite channel can transmit only 4 bits. This difference means that some of the input information is going through more than one channel. However, for the conditions and phonemes tested, the sum for the five channels can be used to give a rough approximation for the composite channel if the sum is corrected by the factor 4/4.89. If all of the features were transmitted equally well, this correction factor would be exact, but in most cases it is only an approximation.

The fact that the measures for the separate channels can be summed in a simple manner to give an approximate value for the total transmission is of considerable practical significance. This perceptual independence of the several features implies that all we need to know about a system is how well it transmits the necessary clues for each feature; measurements for the individual features can be made much more quickly and easily than can a measurement for the composite channel, and the correction factor for the input redundancy depends entirely on the input vocabulary and not upon an experimental test.

In the following we shall discuss the relative transmission measures. The relative measure is computed from Table XXI by dividing each entry in that table by the maximum value given at the bottom of each column. The advantage of the relative measure is that it permits an easy comparison of one channel with another. Differences in transmission due simply to the fact that the input to one channel was greater than the input to another channel are removed when we examine the relative efficiency of the two channels. We ask simply, what fraction of its input did each channel transmit? The ratio of transmitted to input information

provides us with a normalized measure of stimulus-response covariation.

DISCUSSION

In Fig. 1 the normalized covariance measure—relative transmission in percent—is plotted as a function of the signal-to-noise ratio for two linguistic features, voicing and place of articulation, for the data presented in Tables I–VI. In Fig. 2 a similar plot is shown for the features of nasality, affrication, and duration. In addition to the data in Tables I–VI, the results of three smaller studies are also plotted on the same graph. In one of these smaller studies only the six stop consonants $|p|$, $|t|$, $|k|$, $|b|$, $|d|$, and $|g|$, were used initially before the vowel $|a|$. In a second study these same six stop consonants occurred finally after the phonemes $|ta|$. And in the third study only the eight fricative consonants $|f|$, $|\theta|$, $|s|$, $|\int|$, $|v|$, $|\eth|$, $|z|$, and $|\mathfrak{z}|$ were used initially before the vowel $|a|$. Both voicing and place of articulation are involved in these three smaller test vocabularies, so the relative transmission for these two features can be compared in Fig. 1 with the results obtained from the complete set of 16 consonants. Duration was also tested with fricative sounds and this function is added in Fig. 2. The comparisons show a gratifying degree of agreement from one study to the next.

The glaringly obvious statement that must be made about Figs. 1 and 2 is that voicing and nasality are much less affected by a random masking noise than are the other features. Affrication and duration, which are so similar that a single function could represent them both, are somewhat superior to place but far inferior to voicing and nasality. Voicing and nasality are discriminable at signal-to-noise ratios as poor as −12 db whereas the place of articulation is hard to distinguish at ratios less than 6 db, a difference of some 18 db in efficiency.

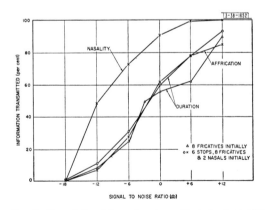

FIG. 2. The relative information transmitted about nasality, affrication, and duration is plotted as a function of signal-to-noise ratio in decibels. The two curves for duration were obtained from independent experiments using different test vocabularies. Nasality and voicing are equally discriminable.

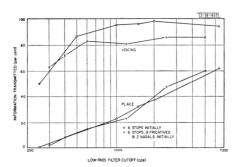

FIG. 3. The relative information transmitted about voicing and place is plotted as a function of the cutoff frequency of the low-pass filter. The two curves for each feature were obtained from independent experiments. The relation between voicing and place is the same for low-pass filtering as for masking with random noise (see Fig. 1).

In Figs. 3 and 4 similar functions are drawn for the results given in Tables VII–XII for low-pass filters. An additional small study with just the six stop consonants is also represented in Fig. 3. Figure 3 looks much like Fig. 1; voicing is greatly superior to place of articulation. Figure 4 is similar to Fig. 2, except that the results for affrication and duration are now somewhat different. These comparisons show that there is a considerable correspondence between masking by random noise and filtering by low-pass filters. This correspondence seems reasonable if we think of the high-frequency components of speech as relatively weak and therefore most susceptible to masking by the uniform spectrum of the noise. That is to say, the uniform noise spectrum should mask high frequencies more than low, so it is in effect a kind of low-pass system.

Whereas low-pass filtering and noise have much the same effect on speech perception, high-pass filtering presents a totally different picture. In Fig. 5 the relative transmissions calculated from Tables XII–XVII are plotted for all five features as a function of the filter cutoff frequency. With a minor exception for duration, all features deteriorate in about the same way as the low frequencies are removed. Duration holds up some-

what better, probably because $|s|$, $|\int|$, $|z|$, and $|3|$ are characterized in part by considerable high-frequency energy. This homogeneity reflects a fact that can be seen from visual inspection of Tables XIII–XVII; the errors do not cluster or fall into obvious patterns in the confusion matrix, but seem to distribute almost randomly over the matrix. When an error occurs with high-pass filtering, there is little chance of predicting what the error will be. Thus we find an important difference between high- and low-pass filtering; low-pass filters affect the several linguistic features differentially, leaving the phonemes audible but similar in predictable ways, whereas high-pass filters remove most of the acoustic power in the consonants, leaving them inaudible and, consequently, producing quite random confusions. Of course, this difference must be tempered by the fact that a random noise was used along with the filters, so that the noise acted "with" the low-pass filter to eliminate high frequencies but "against" the high-pass filter in such a way as to produce a narrow band-pass system. However, casual observations made since these tests were completed convince us that the difference cannot be explained entirely in this way and that, even without noise, audibility is the problem for high-pass systems and confusibility is the problem for low-pass systems.

An important application of data on filtered speech has been to divide the frequency scale into segments making equal contributions to intelligibility. The high-pass and low-pass functions are plotted on the same graph and the frequency at which the two functions cross is said to divide the frequency scale into two equivalent parts; the frequencies above the crossover are exactly as important as the frequencies below the crossover frequency. We have observed this traditional method of analysis in Fig. 6 where the solid functions are the articulation scores and they are seen to cross at about 1550 cps. This frequency is somewhat lower than one would expect for female talkers, but the test vocabulary used here may not permit valid comparisons with other research.

We would like to argue that the meaning of these crossover points is apt to be a bit tricky. In the first place, the point depends crucially upon the test materials, in the sense that we can obtain very different crossover points for the different linguistic features: 450 cps for nasality, 500 cps for voicing, 750 cps for affrication, 1900 cps for place of articulation, and 2200 cps for duration. What crossover point we get depends on how we load the test vocabulary with these different features. In the second place, high- and low-pass filters do different things to speech perception, as we pointed out previously. If we plot the relative amount of information transmitted, instead of the articulation score, we obtain the dashed functions shown in Fig. 6. The crossover point for the information measure is about 1250 cps, a good 300 cps lower than for the articulation score.

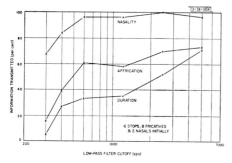

FIG. 4. The relative information transmitted about nasality, affrication, and duration is plotted as a function of the cutoff frequency of the low-pass filter. Nasality is somewhat more discriminable than voicing.

By the same argument as before, there is as much information above 1250 cps as there is below. Why do these two measures give different divisions of the frequency scale? The answer lies in the fact that low-pass errors are more predictable and so carry some information, whereas high-pass errors are more random and contain no hint about what the true message might have been. Relative to the articulation scores, therefore, the high-pass information is smaller and the low-pass information is greater; the relative shifts move the crossover point downward in frequency. Which of these two crossover points is the more meaningful? Here the answer depends upon what use is to be made of the voice communication system. If isolated words, numerals, station call letters, etc. are the only messages, then a miss is as good as a mile; there is no redundancy in the message to enable the listener to correct an error, so the percentage of messages correctly received is what we want to know. On the other hand, if connected discourse in all its notorious redundancy is sent over the system, a listener can detect perceptual errors on the basis of context and can correct them more easily if they are consistent and predictable; then the transmission measure is what we want to know. However, if we arrive at a position where we must weight the frequency scale one way for isolated words and another way for conversational speech, the beautiful simplicity that makes the traditional crossover argument so attractive seems spurious. Our own intuitions would lead us to search for a different line of attack on the problem.

It may be possible to evaluate voice communication systems more adequately if we explore the implications of the multiple-channel argument used to analyze our data. It is not obvious that things will be any simpler if we must replace a single complicated channel with a dozen simpler channels in our theoretical model of speech perception. However, transmission of the separate features may be easier to relate to the system parameters. Even if a completely automatic computational procedure cannot be developed along multiple-channel lines, a short series of relatively simple articulation tests may suffice to determine the necessary parameters. In any event, the development and standardization of tests for the individual features would seem to have considerable value for the diagnosis both of inefficient equipments and of hard-of-hearing people.

One advantage of a multichannel approach to speech perception is that the message, as well as the equipment, is included in the analysis. Given any specific vocabulary of speech signals, we can calculate the relative importance of each feature for distinguishing the alternative signals and so derive a weighting factor for each channel. If the messages are coded properly into those channels or features that the system handles well, considerable advantage may be gained. For ex-

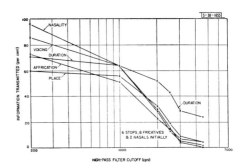

FIG. 5. The relative information transmitted about all five features is plotted as a function of the cutoff frequency of the high-pass filter. The effect of eliminating the low frequencies is the same on all features except duration.

ample, a low-pass system would perform best for speech signals that were distinguishable on the basis of voicing and nasality.

A set of rules for developing an optimally distinguishable vocabulary for a given communication system would be rather complex and involved. There is, however, a very simple procedure for testing any given vocabulary. If the relative efficiencies of the system for the several features are known, we may know that some features will not be transmitted and cannot be used to distinguish two signals. Any two phonemes that differ only with respect to such missing features can be regarded as equivalent stimuli for the listener. Now suppose that we take any one of such a set of equivalent stimuli and use it wherever any of the set occurs; for example, if $|p|$, $|t|$, and $|k|$ are indistinguishable, we might use $|t|$ for all three. When all the speech signals are rewritten with $|t|$ wherever $|p|$, $|t|$, or $|k|$ occurred and similar substitutions are made for all other sets of equivalent stimuli, the rewritten signals will approximate what the listener will hear. If we now alphabetize the rewritten signals, we will probably find some that are identical. These are the signals that will be confused and we can then take steps to eliminate such confusions.

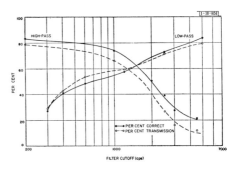

FIG. 6. Both the articulation score and relative information transmitted are plotted as a function of the frequency cutoff for both high-pass and low-pass filters. The crossover points are different for the two measures.

For example, if we look at Figs. 3 and 4 to see what happens when frequencies above 1000 cps are filtered out of the speech, we find that the features of place and duration are effectively absent and that voicing, nasality, and affrication are doing all the work. In other words, the filter has effectively deleted the last two columns in Table XIX. With those two columns gone there are really just five distinguishable phonemes left: $|ptk|$, $|f\theta s\int|$, $|bdg|$, $|v\delta z\mathbf{3}|$, and $|mn|$. Replace these by, say, $|t|$, $|s|$, $|d|$, $|z|$, and $|n|$, respectively. Now when we rewrite the vocabulary of speech signals with just these five consonants instead of the original 16, we will discover which signals are transformed into indistinguishable forms by the filter. Insofar as possible, no two signals should be the same in their rewritten versions. The basic idea behind this procedure is that redundancy in the input signals will be most effective in reducing errors if we insure that frequent confusions do not transform one permissable signal into another permissable signal.

We have explored the validity of this substitution scheme for just those conditions described in the preceding example. Sentences and longer texts were rewritten with the indicated substitution of five for 16 phonemes. Such rewritten passages are appropriately called "elliptic" English, the ellipsis referring to the omission of two features, place and duration. With a little practice it was possible to speak the elliptic passages at normal rates and with normal intonation. Over a high quality communication system the elliptic speech was intelligible but sounded a little as though the talker had a marked dialect or speech defect. Then the low-pass filters were introduced. When all the frequencies

above 1000 cps were removed (the conditions for which the substitutions were designed), the ellipsis could no longer be detected. Elliptic speech sounded just the same as normal speech under these conditions of distortion. A similar result was obtained with a masking noise at signal-to-noise ratios of about 0 db. The illusion is quite compelling and this demonstration that we could duplicate the effects of noise or distortion by deleting certain features of the speech increased our confidence in a multichannel model of speech perception.

An interesting sidelight on elliptic speech is provided by the art of ventriloquism. A ventriloquist talks without moving his lips. The consonants $|p|$, $|f|$, $|b|$, $|v|$, $|m|$, and $|w|$ are normally produced with lip movements and so pose a problem. A variety of solutions are possible; these sounds are avoided or omitted or produced out of the side of the mouth, or made in alternative ways (especially $|f|$ and $|v|$). In most of the older books on ventriloquism, however, a system of substitutions is proposed; $|k|$ for $|p|$, $|g|$ for $|b|$, and $|n|$ for $|m|$ are common suggestions. These substitutions should be especially satisfactory for the "voice in a box" trick, where the high frequencies should be attenuated in passing through the walls of the box and the confusion of sounds would be expected to occur naturally.

The place of articulation, which was hardest to hear correctly in our tests, is the easiest of the features to see on a talker's lips. The other features are hard to see but easy to hear. Lip reading, therefore, is a valuable skill for listeners who are partially deafened because it provides just the information that the noise or deafness removes.

CHAPTER 28

Reprinted from THE JOURNAL OF SPEECH AND HEARING DISORDERS, Vol. 22 (1957).

Difference Limen
For Formant Amplitude

James L. Flanagan

Recent work on systems for narrow-bandwidth transmission of speech indicates that signals representing the relative amplitudes of vowel formants might be utilized as information-bearing quantities (5, 6). In order to carry out computations of the channel capacity required for the transmission of such signals, it is necessary to know the precision with which the signals must be transmitted (4). This article describes a pilot experiment which was designed to provide an estimate of the maximum precision necessary in transmitting data on the amplitude of the second formant of vowels.

A human listener usually is the ultimate recipient of the information transmitted by a speech compression system, and consequently his ability to discriminate changes in the transmitted signals determines the precision with which they must be transmitted. It is probable that the perception of speech by a human subject corresponds more nearly to an absolute judgment of acoustic stimuli than to a differential discrimination. If this is in fact the case, it would appear that differential discrimination tests should provide conservative estimates of the maximum precision necessary in the transmission of speech data.

A psycho-acoustic experiment was conducted, therefore, to determine the just-discriminable differences (or difference limens) for the amplitude of the second formant (F2) of a synthetic vowel sound. The experiment was greatly restricted in scope, treating only the second formant of the vowel [æ] for one sound pressure level and for two patterns of fundamental frequency inflection. However, the results permit quantitative approximation of the precision necessary in transmitting data specifying second formant amplitude.

Procedure

A lumped-constant, 'terminal-analog' electrical synthesizer was used to produce the synthetic vowel sound. The synthesizer arrangement used in the experiment is shown in block diagram form in Figure 1. The synthesizer was composed of three simple series resistance - inductance - capaci-

James L. Flanagan (Sc.D., Massachusetts Institute of Technology, 1955) is Electronic Scientist at the Air Force Cambridge Research Center, Bedford, Massachusetts, and is on the research staff of the Acoustics Laboratory, Massachusetts Institute of Technology.

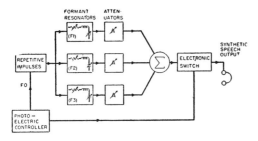

FIGURE 1. Block diagram of a circuit for producing synthetic vowel sounds.

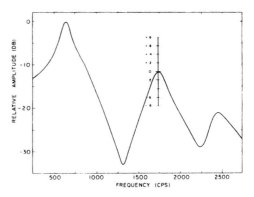

FIGURE 2. Spectral envelope of the synthetic vowel [æ] produced by the electrical synthesizer. The amplitude of the second formant may be increased or decreased in steps of two db by adjustment of the second formant attenuator in the synthesizer.

tance (RLC) resonant circuits connected in parallel.[1] Each formant resonator was driven from a voltage source (a cathode follower) and the output voltage taken across the capacitive element. The output voltage from each resonator was sent through an isolating amplifier and a precision attenuator to a common electronic summing circuit. The voltage response of the synthesizer to a unit impulse of excitation was, therefore:

$$f(t) =$$

$$\sum_{k=1}^{3} \left[A_k \left(\frac{\sigma_k^2 + \omega_k^2}{\omega_k} \right) e^{-\sigma_k t} \sin \omega_k t \right],$$

where $\sigma = R/2L$

$\omega = [(1/LC) - (R^2/4L)]^{1/2}$

$(\sigma^2 + \omega^2) = 1/LC,$

and the A_k's are positive real constants determined by the attenuator settings.

The frequencies of the three vowel formants were set by tuning the resonators with variable capacitive elements, and the relative amplitudes of the formants were set by approximately adjusting the attenuators on the outputs of the resonators.[2] The half-power bandwidths of the resonators were set by adjusting the resistive elements of the resonant circuits.

The resonators of the synthesizer were excited from a voltage source of repetitive impulses, the repetition frequency (FO) of which was arranged to be varied by an electrical voltage. The output of the synthesizer was sent through an electronic switch having a buildup and decay time of about

---

[1] Although a cascade connection of simple, uncoupled series resonators is the best analog of the vocal system, it is not possible in the cascade connection to adjust the amplitude of one formant independently of the others. The parallel connection introduces inappropriate zeros into the spectrum of the synthesized vowel. For the purpose of the present test, however, this effect was deemed of secondary importance.

---

[2] It can be shown that for the parallel connection of the synthesizer, the relative amplitude of a formant is related approximately linearly to the relative amplitude of the output of its resonator.

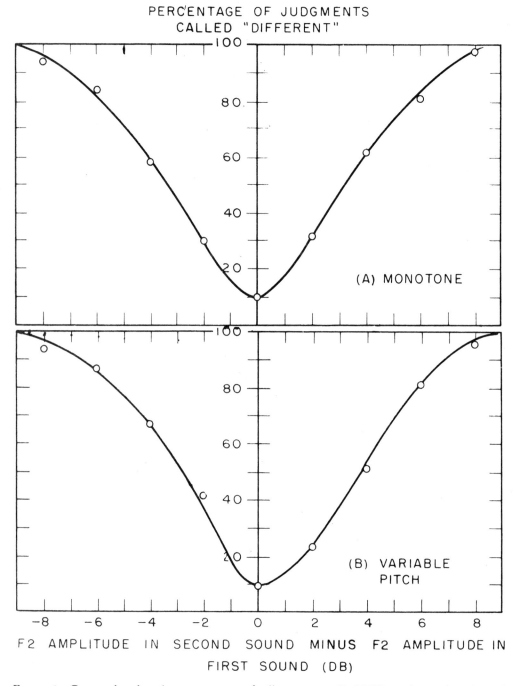

FIGURE 3. Curves showing the percentages of adjustments called 'different' as a function of F2 amplitude in the second sound minus F2 amplitude in the first sound. (A) shows the results of the monotone tests and (B) shows the results of the variable pitch tests. The data are for four subjects, and each plotted point represents the mean of 112 judgments of that experimental condition.

50 ms, and was transduced by PDR-10 headphones located in a sound-treated room. The opening and closing of the electronic switch and the repetition frequency ('pitch') of the impulse source were controlled by an automatic photoelectric device which read the control data from a transparent loop of film.

Formant frequencies, amplitudes, and bandwidths appropriate to the vowel [æ], as produced by an adult male speaker, were set in the synthesizer (1, 7). The spectrum of the vowel sound generated by the synthesizer was measured with a wave analyzer and the spectral envelope is shown in Figure 2. (The spectrum of the repetitive impulses used to excite the synthesizer was flat to beyond 3000 cps. Figure 2, therefore, also represents the frequency response of the synthesizer resonators.) The photoelectric controller was arranged to provide continuously the following cycle of opening and closing of the electronic switch: 0.5 sec closed (stimulus presentation), 1.0 sec open (inter-stimuli silence), 0.5 sec closed (stimulus presentation), and 4.0 sec open (judgment time). The 1.0 sec open time between the 0.5 sec closed times was sufficient to adjust manually the setting of the F2 amplitude attenuator. The sound pressure level in the headphones was set to approximately 70 db *re* 0.0002 dyne/cm².

Four adult male listeners who were experienced in psychoacoustic testing and who had normal hearing were presented pairs of vowel sounds for judgment. One sound of each pair was the standard sound shown in Figure 2, and the other was the same sound with the amplitude of F2 either increased or decreased in steps that were multiples of two db. The steps in which the F2 amplitude was changed are indicated in Figure 2, and were 0, ± 2, ± 4, ± 6, and ± 8 db. The listeners were asked to judge whether the quality of the second sound of each pair was the same as or different from the quality of the first sound. The changes in F2 amplitudes were made in random order, and the standard sound of each pair was presented in the initial position as many times as it was presented in the final position. After several practice runs, each subject made 28 judgments on each experimental pair.

Two different tests were performed: one in which the fundamental frequency (FO) of the vowel sounds was a constant 120 cps monotone, and another in which the fundamental frequency of the sounds was inflected linearly from 95 to 105 cps.

Results

Plots were made for individual subjects of the percentages of the judgments called 'different' as a function of the change in F2 amplitude. Cumulative distribution curves (ogives) were sketched through the plotted points. The variability of the data for different subjects was found to be relatively small, and pooling of the data seemed justified. In the interest of brevity, only the pooled data will be presented here.

The percentages of the judgments called 'different' by the four subjects are plotted in Figure 3 as a function of the F2 amplitude in the second sound minus the F2 amplitude in the first sound. The results of the monotone tests are shown in Figure 3 (A) and the results of the variable pitch tests are shown in Figure 3 (B). Each plotted point on these curves repre-

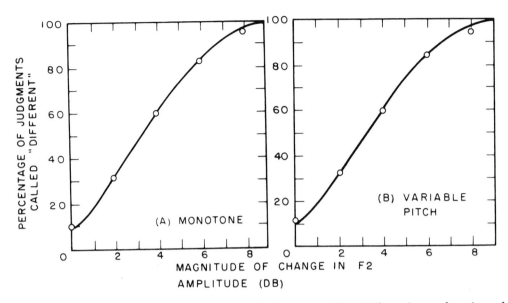

FIGURE 4. Curves showing the percentages of judgments called 'different' as a function of the magnitude of the change in F2 amplitude. (A) shows the results of the monotone tests and (B) shows the results of the variable pitch tests. The data are for four subjects, and each plotted point represents the mean of 224 judgments of that experimental condition.

sents the mean of 112 judgments of that experimental condition.

When the percentages of the 'different' judgments for the four subjects are plotted as a function of the magnitude of the change in F2 amplitude (*i.e.*, without regard to whether the F2 amplitude in the second sound was greater than or less than the F2 amplitude in the first sound), the data appear as shown in Figure 4. Each plotted point on these curves represents the mean of 224 judgments of that magnitude of change in the amplitude of F2.

Discussion

The curves shown in Figure 3 are reasonably symmetrical and are approximately of the same shape. The symmetry of the curves indicates that the percentages of 'different' judg-

ments were not much influenced by the 'polarity' of the change in the amplitude of F2 from the first to the second sound (*i.e.*, whether it increased or decreased), but were mainly dependent upon the magnitude of the change. The differences between the data for the monotone and variable pitch tests are relatively small, suggesting that the just-discriminable changes in formant amplitude are relatively independent of fundamental frequency, at least for the range of fundamental frequencies examined here.

The two curves in Figure 4 showing the percentages of 'different' judgments as a function of the magnitude of the change in F2 amplitude also are similar, suggesting again that the discriminable changes in formant amplitude are not appreciably dependent upon the value of the fundamental frequency, at least for the range investigated. If the difference limen (DL) is taken as the change in formant frequency that is noticed just 50 percent of the time, then both curves of Figure 4 yield values of approximately 3 db as the DL for the amplitude of F2.

The ogive curves obtained in this experiment never quite go to zero, even for the zero-difference stimuli. This effect is one of the troublesome features of the 'same or different' test, and is dependent to a great extent upon the manner in which the subjects are instructed. For example, in an earlier exploratory experiment with different subjects the same effect was noted. It was found that by emphatically instructing the subjects not to call a sound-pair different unless they were absolutely certain they could perceive a difference, the curves could almost always be made to go to zero for the zero-difference condition. In the present experiment, however, the subjects were asked simply to judge whether the quality of the second sound was the same as or different from the quality of the first sound, and no attempt was made to bias the subjects toward being either hyper-sensitive or insensitive to the changes. It was left for each subject more or less to establish his own 'sensitivity' criterion.

In examining the data for individual subjects, it was found that two of the subjects called the zero-difference pair 'different' less than five percent of the time, whereas the other two subjects called the zero-difference stimuli 'different' close to 15 percent of the time. As might be expected, the change in F2 amplitude called 'different' 50 percent of the time by the two more sensitive subjects was slightly less than the change noticed 50 percent of the

time by the two less sensitive subjects. The root-mean-square variance (standard deviation) of the DLs for individual subjects, however, was only about 0.4 db for the monotone tests and about 0.6 db for the variable pitch tests.

One would expect the value of the DL for formant amplitude to be a function of the particular vowel sound as well as of other parameters, such as sound pressure level. The vowel sound [æ], used in these tests, has formants that are nearly equi-spaced in frequency, and its second formant lies near the center of the frequency range usually containing second formants. In most other vowels, the second formant is in closer proximity to one of its adjacent formants than it is in the vowel [æ]. Considering the possible masking of one formant by an adjacent formant, it is conceivable that the just-discriminable changes in the amplitude of a given formant might be larger when that formant is in close proximity to an adjacent formant than when it is farther removed from the adjacent formant. It would seem, therefore, that the vowel [æ] probably represents one of the more favorable conditions for detecting small changes in the amplitude of F2. If this speculation is correct, one might expect the amplitude DLs for the second formants of other vowels to be not much smaller than the F2 amplitude DL for [æ], and, in general, probably larger.

All of the data in the present experiment were taken at one sound pressure level, namely, 70 db *re* 0.0002 dyne/cm², which is reasonably representative of a conversational speech level. It was beyond the scope of this pilot experiment to investigate other sound pressure levels and other vowels, and it is expected that these parameters will be examined in subsequent work.

As suggested at the outset, the results of these differential discrimination tests may be used to estimate the precision necessary in transmitting data specifying the amplitude of F2. If the just-discriminable change in formant amplitude obtained from the tests is expressed as a percentage, then:

$$3 \text{ db} = 20 \log_{10} \frac{A \pm \triangle A}{A},$$

or $\triangle A/A = \pm 40\%$

It appears, therefore, that it should not be necessary to transmit data specifying the amplitude of F2 with an accuracy exceeding ± 40 percent.

In terms of percentage change in amplitude, this DL is relatively large, and it is interesting to compare it to perceptual data on other 'dimensions' of vowel sounds. Similar differential discrimination tests have been used to determine frequency DLs for the first and second formants of several vowel sounds (2), and a DL for the over-all amplitude of a vowel sound (3). Measured by tests similar to the one employed here, the DL for formant frequency is found to be equal approximately to ± 3 percent of the formant frequency, and the DL for over-all vowel amplitude is found to be approximately ± 1 db, or about ± 12 percent. The spectral distribution of the energy contained in vowel sounds is such that most of the energy usually is contained in the low-frequency, high-amplitude first formant. The over-all amplitude DL, therefore, might be used as a very crude estimate of the DL for the amplitude of the first formant.

It might be asked whether, in the present experiment, the changes in F2 amplitude are not reflected as changes in the over-all level of the stimulus. If such were the case, the responses conceivably might be responses to changes in over-all level rather than responses to changes in the relative distribution of spectral energy in the stimulus. In the present experiment, the over-all level of the stimulus was dependent upon the amplitude of F2, but only to an extremely small extent. Measurements of the over-all amplitude of the stimulus were made for all values of the amplitude of F2. It was found that for even the most extreme changes in the amplitude of F2 (i.e., ± 8 db), the over-all level of the stimulus changed by less than 0.5 db. For changes in F2 amplitude of ± 4 db, the change in over-all level was less than 0.2 db. It is apparent, therefore, that the changes in over-all amplitude of the stimulus occasioned by changes in F2 amplitude were considerably less than the DL for over-all amplitude. Consequently, the results of the experiment can be confidently attributed to responses to changes in the relative distribution of spectral energy rather than to responses to changes in the over-all amplitude of the stimulus.

Summary

Listening tests were conducted to determine the just-discriminable change in the amplitude of the second formant of a synthetic vowel sound. The stimulus was the vowel [æ], transduced by headphones at a level of approximately 70 db *re* 0.0002 dyne/cm². Two patterns of fundamental frequency inflection were examined: 120 cps monotone, and linear inflection from 95 to 105 cps. The results indicate that a change of 3 db in the amplitude of the second formant is detected approximately 50 percent of the time for both inflection patterns.

Acknowledgments

This experiment was conducted while the author was a guest in the Speech Transmission Laboratory, Department of Telegraphy and Telephony, Royal Institute of Technology, Stockholm, Sweden. All of the work was done in collaboration with Mr. Arne Risberg, who designed and calibrated the experimental apparatus. The author is greatly indebted to Dr. C. Gunnar M. Fant, Director of the Speech Transmission Laboratory, for making available his laboratory facilities, and to Messrs. H. Truby and S. Ericsson for participating in the tests.

References

1. BOGERT, B. P. On the bandwidth of vowel formants. *J. acoust. Soc. Amer.*, 25, 1953, 791-792.
2. FLANAGAN, J. L. Difference limen for vowel formant frequency. *J. acoust. Soc. Amer.*, 27, 1955, 613-617.
3. FLANAGAN, J. L. Difference limen for the intensity of a vowel sound. *J. acoust. Soc. Amer.*, 27, 1955, 1223-1225.
4. FLANAGAN, J. L. Bandwidth and channel capacity necessary to transmit the formant information of speech. *J. acoust. Soc. Amer.*, 28, 1956, 592-596.
5. FLANAGAN, J. L. and HOUSE, A. S. Development and testing of a formant-coding speech compression system. *J. acoust. Soc. Amer.*, 28, 1956, 1099-1106.
6. HOWARD, C. R., *et al.* Analysis and synthesis of formants and moments of speech spectra. *J. acoust. Soc. Amer.*, 28, 1956, 768.
7. PETERSON, G. E. and BARNEY, H. L. Control methods used in a study of the vowels. *J. acoust. Soc. Amer.*, 24, 1952, 175-184.

CHAPTER 29

Reprinted from
THE JOURNAL OF THE ACOUSTICAL SOCIETY OF AMERICA,
Vol. 29, No. 4 (April 1957).
Copyright 1957 by the Acoustical Society of America.

Estimates of the Maximum Precision Necessary in Quantizing Certain "Dimensions" of Vowel Sounds

JAMES L. FLANAGAN
Air Force Cambridge Research Center, Cambridge, Massachusetts
(Received February 7, 1957)

Results of psychoacoustic experiments are used to estimate the greatest precision necessary in quantizing narrow band-width data specifying the vowel sounds of speech.

RECENT developments in the theory and application of digital techniques have stimulated interest in applying these techniques to certain systems for reducing the band-width and channel capacity necessary to transmit speech. Such an application raises questions concerning the resolution necessary in quantizing (or digitalizing) the "compressed" speech data. It is apparent that employing a resolution in excess of that required would serve to nullify the saving in band-width and channel capacity that the compression system might afford, while, on the other hand, insufficient precision would obviously impair the usefulness of the communication link.

In a voice communication system the speech information usually originates and terminates with a human operator. The perceptual abilities of man, therefore, determine the precision with which the data must be transmitted and processed. It is the purpose of this note to summarize some experimental findings which permit quantitative estimates of the maximum precision necessary in quantizing certain useful "dimensions" of vowel sounds.

"Dimensions" of vowel sounds.—Experimental and theoretical investigations in speech production[1-3] have shown that the acoustic output of a speaker during vowel production can be specified reasonably accurately in a relatively simple fashion;

namely, by specifying the frequencies of the normal modes of vibration of the vocal tract and the fundamental frequency of vibration of the glottis. In the production of vowel sounds the natural frequencies of the tract always are manifested as gross maxima, or formants, in the amplitude spectrum of the acoustic output. The relative amplitudes of the spectral maxima bear specific relationships to one another, uniquely determined by the values of the formant frequencies.[4] During speech the formant frequencies and the fundamental vocal frequency change relatively slowly with time and hence constitute a narrow band-width specification of vowel sounds. For this reason these quantities are useful as information-bearing signals in certain band-width compression systems, sometimes referred to as "formant-coding" system.[5]

In some types of formant-coding systems,[6] it has been found expedient not to make use of the fact that the relative amplitudes of the vowel formants are uniquely determined by the formant frequencies. In these cases additional narrow band-width signals representing the relative amplitudes of the formants usually are transmitted.

If the formant concept is extended to consonant sounds it is no longer true that the formant frequencies uniquely determine the formant amplitudes. For consonant sounds, therefore, data on the relative amplitudes of the spectral maxima are more important than for vowel sounds.

For the purpose of the following discussion let it be assumed that electrical signals representing the formant frequencies, formant amplitudes, and fundamental vocal frequency are to be used as information-bearing quantities in a compression system. In order to compute the channel capacity required for the transmission of such signals it is necessary to know the precision with which the signals must be transmitted.

Perception of speech sounds: differential versus absolute discrimination.—It is probable that the perception of speech by man corresponds more nearly to an absolute judgment of acoustic stimuli than to a differential discrimination. Furthermore, it also is probable that the differences which are differentially discriminable in the vowel dimensions are smaller when the sound exists in an isolated quasi-steady state than when it exists in the more dynamic state characterizing connected speech. If these assumptions are in fact true, it would appear that differential discrimination tests performed with relatively steady-state stimuli should lead to estimates of necessary precision that essentially represent maximum values or upper bounds. Such estimates based upon differential discriminations should be very conservative figures when compared to the accuracies necessary for proper identification of vowel sounds. Experimental evidence on absolute discriminations performed along frequency and amplitude dimensions[7,8] indicates that the ability of man to make absolute discriminations is considerably less acute than his ability to make differential discriminations.

Results of psychoacoustic experiments.—On the basis of the foregoing assumptions, psychoacoustic experiments have been conducted to determine just discriminable differences (or difference limens) for certain of the vowel "dimensions." Most of the experiments have been pilot studies, considerably restricted in scope. In no respect can they be considered exhaustive. The experiments do provide, however, some quantitative data, albeit meager, in an area where none previously existed.

More specifically, experiments have been conducted on synthetic vowel sounds produced at conversational levels to determine difference limens (DL's) for the frequencies of the first and second formants[9]; the fundamental vocal frequency[10]; the amplitude of the second formant[11]; and the over-all vowel amplitude.[12] The gross results of these experiments are summarized as follows: (1) The DL's for formant frequency are of the order of ±3% of the formant frequency; (2) The DL for fundamental frequency (or "pitch") is of the order of ±0.5 to ±1.0% for a vowel having a fundamental frequency in the neighborhood of 120 cps; (3.) The DL for second formant amplitude is of the order of ±3 db, or

TABLE I. Maximum number of levels of quantization and bits of information necessary to specify vowel parameters.

Parameter	Frequency			Amplitude		
	Size of levels (cps)	No. or levels	Bits	Size of levels (db)	No. of levels	Bits
F1	40	14	3.8	2	3	1.6
F2	100	14	3.8	6	3	1.6
F3	150	9	3.2	10	2	1.0
F0	2	40	5.3	...	...	...

±40% of the formant amplitude; (4.) The DL for over-all vowel amplitude is approximately ±1 db, or about ±12% of the over-all amplitude.

Since most of the sound energy of a vowel usually is contained in the first formant, the over-all amplitude DL might be used as a crude estimate of the DL for the amplitude of the first formant.

Quantization of vowel "dimensions".—Considerable data on the formant frequencies and amplitudes of natural vowels are available in the literature.[3] These data indicate that for adult male voices the average ranges occupied by the first three formants ($F1$, $F2$, and $F3$) are approximately: 250–800 cps for $F1$; 800–2300 cps for $F2$; and 1700–3000 cps for $F3$. The data also indicate that if the over-all amplitudes of the vowels in continuous speech are normalized approximately to the same value, the ranges of amplitudes covered by the formants of different vowels are about: 5 db for $F1$; 20 db for $F2$; and 20 db for $F3$.

Data also have been reported in the literature on the range of fundamental vocal frequency.[13] These data indicate that for adult males reading factual material the fundamental vocal frequency ($F0$) usually falls within the one octave frequency range 80–160 cps.

Assuming that the original hypothesis concerning differential discriminations is tenable and knowing the ranges associated with the vowel "dimensions" and the changes which are just discriminable, it is possible to make rough estimates of the maximum precision necessary in quantizing the "dimensions." The results of the psychoacoustic tests indicate that, to a first approximation, it should not be necessary to quantize formant frequency in steps smaller than about ±20 cps for $F1$, ±50 cps for $F2$, and ±75 cps for $F3$. Similarly, it should not be necessary to quantize formant amplitude in steps smaller than about ±1 db for $F1$, ±3 db for $F2$, and possibly ±5 db for $F3$. In a like manner it probably should not be necessary to quantize fundamental vocal frequency in steps smaller than about ±1 cps in the octave range 80–160 cps.

On the basis of these estimates, therefore, the maximum number of levels of quantization and bits of information (assuming uniform probability distributions) necessary to specify the frequencies and amplitudes of the first three formants and the fundamental frequency should not exceed the values shown in Table I.

For adult male voices the first three formants usually lie in the frequency range below 3000 cps and provide a reasonably accurate description of the acoustic output. Assuming, therefore, that vowels can be described and identified from a knowledge of the first three formant frequencies and the fundamental vocal frequency, the amount of information necessary to specify a vowel sound from an ensemble in which both phonemic and vowel-quality distinctions can be made should not exceed the sum of the bits associated with these frequency parameters, i.e., about 16 bits. If, however, in the development of automatic speech analysis and synthesis apparatus (such as a spectrum correlation or pattern-matching apparatus, or a speech compression system employing formant-coding principles) use is not made of the formant amplitude relations implicit in the formant frequency data, an additional amount of information of about· 4 bits is necessary to specify the relative amplitudes of the formants, bringing the total to about 20 bits.

In normal conversational speech vowel sounds persist in a relatively "steady state" for durations of the order of 0.25 sec. However, the vowel formant transitions that occur between constants and vowels, or between two successive vowels, can take place in times as short as 50 msec, and sometimes shorter. If one wishes to resolve in time the transitions of the vowel formants, data on these "dimensions" should be specified at least 20 or 30 times per second.

Assuming that the vowel parameters are sampled once every 50 msec (i.e., 20 times per second) then the information rates connected with specification of the parameters are approximately the values shown in Table II. As the data in Table II show, the

TABLE II. Information rates associated with specification of vowel parameters.

Parameter	Bits/sec	
	Frequency	Amplitude
F1	76	32
F2	76	32
F3	64	20
F0	106	...

information rate associated with specification of the three formant frequencies is of the order of 200 bits/sec, while all of the frequency parameters are specified by a rate slightly greater than 300 bits/sec. The information rate for the formant amplitude data is of the order of 80 bits/sec, bringing the total rate for all the parameters to approximately 400 bits/sec.

It is interesting to note that the estimates of the information rates for the formant frequency parameters made here are in reasonably good agreement with estimates of these quantities that have been made from band-width and signal-to-noise ratio considerations.[14] Calculations of the band-widths and signal-to-noise ratios necessary for the transmission of analog signals representing the frequencies of the first three formants have been made using a criterion of accuracy based upon the formant frequency DL's discussed above. The information rate associated with these computed values of band-width and signal-to-noise ratio has been found to be of the order of 200 bits/sec.

[1] H. K. Dunn, J. Acoust. Soc. Am. 22, 740–753 (1950).
[2] C. G. M. Fant, "Transmission properties of the vocal tract," Technical Report No. 12, Acoustics Laboratory, Massachusetts Institute of Technology (1952).
[3] G. E. Peterson and H. L. Barney, J. Acoust. Soc. Am. 24, 175–184 (1952).
[4] J. L. Flanagan, J. Acoust. Soc. Am. 29, 306–310 (1957).
[5] J. L. Flanagan and A. S. House, J. Acoust. Soc. Am. 28, 1099–1106 (1956).
[6] C. R. Howard, J. Acoust. Soc. Am. 28, 1091–1098 (1956).
[7] I. Pollack, J. Acoust. Soc. Am. 24, 745–749 (1952).
[8] I. Pollack, and L. Ficks, J. Acoust. Soc. Am. 26, 155–158 (1954).
[9] J. L. Flanagan, J. Acoust. Soc. Am. 27, 613–617 (1953).
[10] J. L. Flanagan and M. L. Saslow, "Difference limen for the fundamental frequency of vowel sounds," Quarterly Reports, Acoustics Laboratory, Massachusetts Institute of Technology, (March, September, and December, 1956).
[11] J. L. Flanagan, "Difference limen for formant amplitude," Quarterly Report, Acoustics Laboratory, Massachusetts Institute of Technology, (September, 1956).
[12] J. L. Flanagan, J. Acoust. Soc. Am. 27, 1223–1225 (1955).
[13] G. Fairbanks, J. Acoust. Soc. Am. 11, 457–466 (1940).
[14] J. L. Flanagan, J. Acoust. Soc. Am. 28, 592–596 (1956).

Reprinted from THE JOURNAL OF THE ACOUSTICAL SOCIETY OF AMERICA, Vol. 29, No. 1, 98–104, January, 1957
Copyright, 1957 by the Acoustical Society of America.

Information Conveyed by Vowels

PETER LADEFOGED, *Phonetics Department, University of Edinburgh, Scotland*

AND

D. E. BROADBENT, *Medical Research Council Applied Psychology Unit, Cambridge, England*
(Received June 12, 1956)

Most speech sounds may be said to convey three kinds of information: linguistic information which enables the listener to identify the words that are being used; socio-linguistic information, which enables him to appreciate something about the background of the speaker; and personal information which helps to identify the speaker. An experiment has been carried out which shows that the linguistic information conveyed by a vowel sound does not depend on the absolute values of its formant frequencies, but on the relationship between the formant frequencies for that vowel and the formant frequencies of other vowels pronounced by that speaker. Six versions of the sentence *Please say what this word is* were synthesized on a Parametric Artificial Talking device. Four test words of the form *b*-(vowel)-*t* were also synthesized. It is shown that the identification of the test word depends on the formant structure of the introductory sentence. Some psychological implications of this experiment are discussed, and hypotheses are put forward concerning the ways in which all three kinds of information are conveyed by vowels.

I N recent years a great deal of research has been directed towards the specification of the "information-bearing elements of speech."[1] It seems that at the moment much of this research is hampered through lack of consideration of the kinds of information that are conveyed by speech. For the sake of convenience in exposition we may consider this information to be of three kinds. Firstly, when we listen to a person talking, we can receive information about what he is saying; in other words, we can appreciate the linguistic significance of the utterance. Secondly, in addition to the information we receive as a result of considering an utterance in terms of a linguistic system, we also receive information of a different kind about the general background of the speaker; thus we can usually infer something about a speaker's place of origin and his social status from his accent. This kind of information may be termed socio-linguistic; it is conveyed by the features of a person's speech which he acquires through the influence of the particular groups of which he is (or was) a member. Lastly there is the kind of information conveyed by the idiosyncratic features of a person's speech. These, like the group and linguistic features, may be part of an individual's learned speech behavior; but, unlike the other features, idiosyncratic features may also be due to anatomical and physiological considerations, such as the particular shape of the vocal

cavities. The information which these features convey may be termed personal information. The relations between these three kinds of information are summarized in Fig. 1.

It is possible to arrange experimental situations which will elicit responses with respect to each of these three kinds of information. Thus one can ask a subject: Were these two sounds pronounced by the same speaker? (personal information); or: Is there any difference of accent between these two speakers? (socio-linguistic information); or: Do these two utterances consist of the same words used in the same way? (linguistic information). It is also possible to arrange a situation where the socio-linguistic information and the linguistic information will be assessed concurrently. These two kinds of information taken together are sometimes said to be equivalent to the phonetic value of a sound.[2] This point of view, however, is disputed by others who believe that "The phonetic

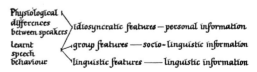

FIG. 1. Differences in utterances and the information that they convey.

---

[1] G. E. Peterson, J. Acoust. Soc. Am. 24, 629–637 (1952).

[2] Peter Ladefoged, Lingua 5, 113–127 (1956).

value of a speech sound is independent of language and meaning."[1]

In this article an experiment is discussed which is concerned with those features of vowel quality which convey linguistic information. This has led to some consideration of both the group and the idiosyncratic features of vowel quality, and tentative conclusions are reached concerning the ways in which all three kinds of information are conveyed.

DEVELOPMENT OF EXPERIMENTAL MATERIAL

It has been supposed for almost a century now that the variations in the formants, or regions of the auditory spectrum in which there is a relatively large amount of spectral energy, are responsible for most of the information conveyed by vowels. However, there is as yet no general agreement on the precise properties of the formants which convey the information. There are differences of opinion as to whether the value of a given vowel depends on the absolute values of certain properties of its formants, or whether it depends on the relation between these values and the values for other vowels pronounced by the same speaker. As a proponent of the first view, we may instance G. E. Peterson, who analyzed a group of matched vowels obtained by recording the sounds produced by speakers trying to imitate the phonetic quality of the vowels in two reference words. He came to the general conclusion that "front vowels could be rather readily identified by observing the positions in frequency of the peaks of the first three formants."[1] Contrasting with this view is the theory propounded by M. Joos,[3] to the effect that the phonetic quality of a vowel depends on the relationship between the formant frequencies for that vowel and the formant frequencies of other vowels pronounced by that speaker.

A necessary part of Joos' theory is that whenever a listener to speech has to identify a vowel without the benefit of any clues from the context, he utilizes whatever knowledge he has of the speaker's formant frequencies in other words. Even when the vowel which the listener is considering is quite unlike any that he has ever heard that speaker produce before, he nevertheless focuses his attention not on the absolute values of the frequencies of the formants, but on the relations between those frequencies and the general ranges of frequencies which seem to be characteristic of the speaker. Thus unknown vowels are identified in terms of the way in which their acoustic structure fits into the pattern of sounds that the listener has been able to observe.

This part of the theorem has now been verified in an experimental situation. It has been found that subjects hearing a test word immediately after hearing a specified introductory sentence are greatly influenced in their identification of the test word by the range of the formant frequencies in the introductory sentence.

In order to carry out this experiment it was first of all necessary to obtain introductory sentences which were identical except in the ranges of their formants. This cannot of course be done by recording different people saying the same sentence, because the utterances are bound to differ in many ways. Accordingly it was decided to use synthesized speech, which can be precisely controlled in all respects. The particular instrument used for the purpose was the Edinburgh University Phonetics Department's copy of the Parametric Artificial Talking Device[4] developed at the Ministry of Supply Signals Research and Development Establishment. The essential parts of the device are a generator producing a pulse corresponding to the larynx pulse which serves to excite the vocal tract; four formant generators which respond to the pulse excitation; and a generator which will produce noise corresponding to the excitation in fricative sounds. This instrument will synthesize speech which can be specified in terms of six variables, but which nevertheless sounds so natural that recordings of some sentences are always confused with recordings of normal speech. The six variables which are normally specified are the intensity and frequency of the pulse excitation, the frequencies of the lowest three formants, and the intensity of the fricative noise. In order to set up the synthesizer so that it will produce an utterance, information depicting these variables as functions of time is painted on a glass slide. The slide is then scanned by a mechanism which produces six controlling voltages which vary with time. The voltages control the appropriate generators of the synthesizer so that a sequence of speech-like sounds is produced.

As well as the factors which are specified by the information painted on the glass slide, it is also possible to vary other factors, such as the frequency of the fourth formant, and the amplitudes and damping constants of all four formants; but no provision is made for controlling these factors as functions of time, and they were not in fact varied in the course of the experiment. In addition, it is possible to alter the frequency range over which each of the formant generators is operating. It was this facility that was used to produce the necessary variations in the introductory sentences.

Six versions of the sentence *please say what this word is* were synthesized with the PAT device. This sentence was chosen as a suitable introductory context because the formant frequencies of the sounds vary over a wide range. Formant one varies between the low value necessary to produce the /i/ in *Please* to the high value required for the /æ/ in *what*; and formant two varies

---

[3] M. Joos, *Acoustic Phonetics*, Supplement to Language 24 (1948).

[4] W. Lawrence, "The synthesis of speech from signals which have a low information rate," in *Communication Theory*, W. Jackson, editor (Butterworths Scientific Publications, London, 1955), Chap. 34.

TABLE I. Differences in the six versions of the introductory sentence: *Please say what this word is.*

Sentence version	Differences from sentence 1	Frequency range in cps Formant 1	Formant 2
1	...	275–500	600–2500
2	F. 1. down	200–380	600–2500
3	F. 1. up	380–660	600–2500
4	F. 2. down	275–500	400–2100
5	F. 2. up	275–500	800–2900
6	F. 1. down F. 2. up	200–380	800–2900

between the high value in the /i/ of *please* and the low value at the beginning of the /w/ in *word*.

In making all six versions of the introductory sentence the synthesizer was controlled by a single slide. Consequently the versions were identical with one another except for the variations which were introduced in the ranges over which the formant generators operated. The variations are summarized in Table I, which shows the highest and lowest values both of formant one and of formant two that actually occurred in each version of this sentence.

It is interesting to note at this point that despite the great acoustic differences between the versions they were all readily identifiable as the same sentence. Moreover, all the trained phoneticians who listened to the different versions agreed that the variations which had been introduced did not appear to make any significant difference in either the linguistic or the socio-linguistic information which was being conveyed. With the exception of version six, which did sound rather unnatural and could not be judged as a sample of normal speech, all the different versions sounded like the same sentence pronounced by people who had the same accent but differed in their personal characteristics.

In addition to these introductory sentences, four test words were synthesized. Each of these was of the form *b*-(vowel)-*t*. The formant frequencies for the middle of the vowel in each of these words are shown in Table II. The vowels in each of these test words were of comparatively short duration.

TEST PROCEDURE

A short listening test was devised with the aid of recordings of the material which has been described in the previous section. This test was taken by sixty

TABLE II. The frequencies of the first two formants in the four test words.

Test word	Frequency in cps Formant one	Formant two
A	375	1700
B	450	1700
C	575	1700
D	600	1300

subjects. The first part of the test consisted of recordings of the test words *A*, *B*, *C*, and *D* arranged in a random order. There were ten items in this part of the test. Subjects were told that they would hear ten words, each of which might be either *bit*, *bet*, *bat* or *but*. They were instructed to tick the appropriate word on the answer sheets with which they had been provided. The means of the responses in respect of each test word are shown in Table III.

Between each of the first five words in the listening test there was a short pause during which subjects were requested to count aloud from one to ten. This was done in an attempt to prevent the identification of a test word being unduly influenced by the auditory memory of the preceding word. The efficacy of this procedure is discussed in a subsequent section.

In the second part of the recording the test words occurred immediately after the various versions of the introductory sentence. Subjects were given the following written instructions:

You will now hear a voice saying *Please say what this word is.* This will be followed immediately by one of the words: *bit, bet, bat, but.* Please tick the

TABLE III. Means of the responses of 60 subjects for the ten words in the first part of the listening test.

Test word	Number of subjects identified as: bit	bet	bat	but
A	52	8	...	...
B	14	46	...	...
C	...	27	33	...
D	...	1	14	45

appropriate word on the answer sheet below. There are twelve test sentences in this part of the recording; after answering in respect of each, there will be a short pause, during which you will be requested to count aloud, slowly, from one to ten.

The twelve items were arranged so that the predicted responses occurred in a random order. The results of this part of the test are shown in Fig. 2.

DISCUSSION OF RESULTS

It will be seen from Fig. 2 that subjects are undoubtedly influenced in their identification of the test word by the auditory context in which it occurs. Thus word *A* is identified as *bit* by 87% of the subjects when it is preceded by version one of the introductory sentence; but as *bet* by 90% of the subjects when it is preceded by version two in which the first formant varies over a lower range. All that remains to be shown is that the influence of the introductory sentence is in accordance with the theory put forward by Joos concerning the relative nature of this aspect of vowel quality.

The relations between the formant structures of the

vowels in a number of words can be conveniently represented by means of a formant chart which shows the frequency of the first formant at a time in the word when the formant structure is changing at a minimum rate plotted against the frequency of the second formant at the same time. In order to provide a basis for discussion, some of the vowels of one of the authors (P.L.) are shown in this form in Fig. 3. The symbols used are /ɪ/ as in *bit*, /ɛ/ as in *bet*, /a/ as in *bat*, /ʌ/ as *but*, /i/ as in *please*, /e/ as in *say*, /ɒ/ as in *what*, and /ɜ/ as in *word*. The axes in this and the subsequent diagrams have been arranged so that these acoustic charts can be easily compared with the vowel diagrams used by phoneticians. The scale used throughout is the Koenig scale.

The pattern formed by the vowels shown in Fig. 3 may be taken as a representation of one of the kinds of relationships which can occur. Bearing this in mind, we may now consider the relationships between the vowels in each of the six versions of the introductory sentence and the test words with which they were designed to be associated. Figure 4 presents these data; solid points lettered *A*, *B*, *C*, and *D* represent the test words, and the open circles indicate the vowels in the different versions of the introductory sentence.

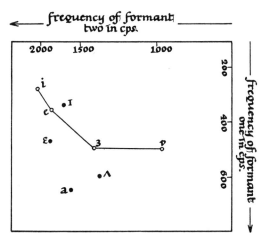

FIG. 3. The formant structure of some of the vowels of one of the authors (P.L.).

It will be seen from a comparison of Figs. 3 and 4 that when the test word *A* is associated with version one of the introductory sentence its relative position is similar to that of P.L.'s *bit*; and, in fact 87.5% of the subjects did identify it as *bit*. But when this word occurs in association with version two its relative position is more like that of P.L.'s *bet*; which accounts for the shift in identification whereby 90% of the subjects now consider it to be *bet*. Similar reasoning explains the change in identification of word *B* when it is associated with version one (92% *bet*) as opposed to version three (97% *bit*). But we must also note in connection with word *B* that when it was associated with versions two and six of the introductory sentence by far the majority of the subjects still identified it in the same way (i.e., as *bet*) as when it was associated with version one. The probable reason for this is that the relative position of the vowel /ɛ/ as in *bet* can be anywhere in a comparatively large area. As Daniel Jones[5] has noted: "The vowel (sc. /ɛ/) varies a good deal with different speakers." Presumably, therefore, the shifts in its relative position due to its being associated with versions two and six were not great enough to move it out of the part of the vowel pattern in which it is reasonable to expect to find a vowel of the /ɛ/ type.

The results shown in Fig. 2 indicate that there is a considerable amount of disagreement concerning the identification of word *C*. Some of the reasons for this can be appreciated from a comparison of the data presented in Figs. 3 and 4. Only when it is associated with version three of the introductory sentence does the vowel in this word have a relative position which is comparable with any of the relative positions of P.L.'s vowels. In these circumstances 80% of the subjects did identify it as the same word, *bet*. But when it occurs in

Test Word	Intro. Version	Relative Formant	Number of subjects identified as			
			bit	bet	bat	but
A	1	=	53	7		
	2	F.1. down	4	54	2	
B	1	=	5	55		
	2	F.1. down	1	57	2	
	3	F.1. up	58	2		
	6	F.1. down F.2 up	7	46	6	1
C	1			25	35	
	3	F.1. up		48	12	
	5	F.2. up		23	37	
D	1	=			11	49
	4	F.2. down		1	36	23

FIG. 2. Means of the responses of sixty subjects identifying the test words *A*, *B*, *C*, and *D* preceded by different versions of the introductory sentence.

[5] Daniel Jones, *An Outline of English Phonetics* (W. Heffer, Cambridge, England, 1956).

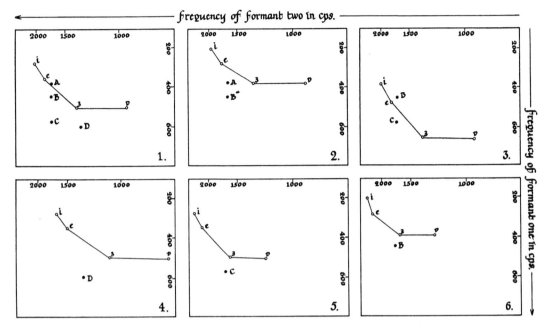

FIG. 4. The formant structure of the six versions of the introductory sentence and the test words that they were each designed to be associated with.

association with version one, where it occupies a relative position only slightly nearer the point in the pattern occupied by P.L.'s *bat* than his *bet*, it is not surprising that 58% of the subjects identify it as *bat* and 42% as *bet*. The results obtained from the association of this word with version five, however, are not so readily understandable. It might be expected that at least a small proportion of the subjects would identify this word as *but* in these circumstances. But in fact this did not happen, perhaps because this simplified treatment in terms of the frequencies of only two formants is not sufficient to account for the differences between these two words. On the other hand, tests with word *D* show that it is possible for the auditory context to influence the identification of a given test word so that it can be taken to be either *bat* or *but*. When this word was associated with version one, the majority of the subjects identified it as *but* (82%) as opposed to *bat* (18%); but in association with version four, in which the second formant was comparatively lower, then the results were *bet* (2%) *bat* (60%), and *but* (38%). Thus word *D* illustrates the fact that shifts in the range of the second formant in the introductory sentence can produce alterations in the identification of the test word which are of the same order as those produced by variations in the range of the first formant.

Taken all together, the results of this test seem to shown quite conclusively that, as Joos has said, the linguistic information conveyed by a given vowel is largely dependent on the relations between the frequencies of its formants and the frequencies of the formants of other vowels occurring in the same auditory context. It is, therefore, only of limited service to look for common points in the acoustic structure of equivalent vowels spoken by different speakers.

PSYCHOLOGICAL IMPLICATIONS

It is obvious that this experiment provides a demonstration of perceptual constancy in the auditory field; that is an auditory phenomenon somewhat parallel to the visual case in which the response evoked by a stimulus is influenced by the stimuli with which it is closely associated. An example is the correct identification of the color of an object in widely differing illuminations. Consequently it is hoped that further investigation of the auditory phenomenon will provide data which are of general psychological interest.

There are many factors which have not been considered in any way in the course of the present experiment. For example, at the moment nothing is known about the length of the introductory sentence which is necessary in order to influence the identification of the test word. Nor do we know to what extent it is necessary to use an introductory sentence containing a wide variety of vowels which may serve as reference points. In addition, further evidence is required concerning the necessary degree of proximity between the auditory context and the stimulus word. A preliminary experiment has been reported[6] in which it is shown that if there is a ten-second silent interval

[6] Broadbent, Ladefoged, and Lawrence, Nature, **178**, 815–816 (1956).

between the introductory sentence and the test word, then the influence of the introductory sentence is significantly less. But the precise temporal limitations of the phenomenon have not yet been established.

Further research is also needed to determine the value of the procedure of counting between items in a test in order to weaken the auditory memory of the preceding words. Subjects were requested to count aloud between the first five items presented in the test. But despite this they were probably influenced in their identifications of the fifth word presented to them by their memory of the previous items. Both the first and fifth items were word *A*. When they first heard this word 45 subjects identified it as *bit* and 15 as *bet*; but when it occurred as the fifth item (i.e., after they had heard other test words) all 60 subjects identified word *A* as *bit*. On the other hand, counting items had a significant effect on some occasions. Word *C* was identified as *bet* by 37 subjects and as *bat* by 23 subjects when it occurred as the fourth item in the test, and could not directly be compared with word *B*; but when word *C* occurred immediately after word *B* it seems likely that the two words were judged together, since in these circumstances 10 subjects identified word *B* as *bit* and 50 as *bet*, and 8 subjects identified word *C* as *bet* and 52 as *bat*.

SOCIO-LINGUISTIC AND PERSONAL INFORMATION

All the responses demanded by the listening test which has been described above are specifically related to linguistic information. But, on the basis of this test, two points may be noted concerning the socio-linguistic and personal information conveyed by vowels. Firstly, as we have mentioned, there do not appear to be any differences in the socio-linguistic information conveyed by the different versions of the introductory sentence. It therefore seems to be a plausible hypothesis that socio-linguistic information does not depend on the absolute values of the formant frequencies, but is, like linguistic information, a matter of the relative formant structure of vowels. Secondly, there is tentative evidence that subjects belonging to different socio-linguistic groups gave different responses to some of the test material. Consideration of the precise criteria that were used in dividing subjects into groups in accordance with their accents is, unfortunately, outside the scope of this article. It must suffice to state that there were three main groups: in one there were seven subjects who had what is known as a Basic Scots vowel system[7]; in the second there were nineteen Scottish speakers who had vowel systems that had been slightly modified due to the influence of the English of England: and in the third there were nineteen subjects who were speakers of the form of English of England known as R.P. Table IV shows the responses of each of these three groups in respect of test word *D* preceded by

TABLE IV. Identifications of test word *D* in association with version one of the introductory sentence by different groups of subjects.

Number in group	Character of group	Identified as:	
		bat	*but*
7	Scots	3	4
19	English influenced Scots	4	15
19	English (R.P.)	1	18

version one of the introductory sentence. It can be seen that there is a greater tendency among the Scottish speakers to favor the identification of this word as *bat*, presumably because in their speech the relative position of the vowel in *bat* is similar to that of the vowel in the test word. The relation between accent and type of response is only just statistically significant, using tau,[8] $p=0.05$, and further confirmation is desirable.

On this basis it seems at least possible that both the linguistic and the socio-linguistic information conveyed by vowels depend largely on the relative positions of the formants. When we consider that a speaker has vowel sounds which are typical of a Scottish speaker (i.e., when we interpret the socio-linguistic information conveyed by his vowels), we probably do so by appreciating the relative formant structure of the vowels.

On the other hand, the personal information conveyed by vowels does seem to depend partly on the absolute values of the formant frequencies. Thus all the versions of the introductory sentence sounded as if they had been spoken by different voices. The reasons for this are best understood by reference to the articulatory processes involved in speech. The formants of a sound are essentially properties of the shape of the vocal tract. Consequently the ranges over which a speaker's formants can vary depend to a great extent on the size of his head. Because the ranges cannot be altered at will, they are not part of a speaker's learned speech behavior, and can therefore convey only personal information. Additional personal information is, of course, conveyed by the relative positions of some of a speaker's vowels, insofar as these are idiosyncratic features of his speech and not aspects which identify him as belonging to a particular group.

Finally, it is interesting to consider the current usages of the term "phonetic quality" in the light of the hypotheses that have been put forward above in connection with the ways in which all three kinds of information are conveyed. It seems that when phoneticians talk about the quality of a speech sound they do not always mean the same thing. When teaching the pronunciation of the vowels of a foreign language, for instance, they assess their pupils' utterances in terms of the linguistic and socio-linguistic information that they convey; they are therefore concerned with the relative formant structure only.

[7] D. Abercrombie and A. J. Aitken, *A Scots Phonetic Reader*, (to be published).

[8] J. W. Whitfield, Biometrika **34**, 292–296 (1947).

But on other occasions when observing utterances, particularly in field-work situations, phoneticians seem to imply that vowel quality can be judged in relation to certain absolute standards. Many phoneticians believe that it is possible to describe the quality of a vowel in an isolated monosyllable spoken by an informant, even if they have no other information concerning the speaker.

It is not yet known whether the cardinal vowels which serve as reference points for phoneticians are really precise points with fixed acoustic specifications, or whether they are only a set of vowels which have the same relative formant structure when pronounced by different phoneticians. But whatever their nature, it seems that the whole theory underlying the methods which are used in practice for describing vowels needs restating, so that it is made clear whether linguistic and socio-linguistic criteria are being used in making assessments of quality, or whether an attempt is being made to classify speech sounds in terms of purely auditory criteria.

ACKNOWLEDGMENTS

The authors would like to acknowledge the help of many of their colleagues. In particular, W. Lawrence, D. Abercrombie, and J. Anthony have been of great assistance.

Reprinted from The Journal of the Acoustical Society of America, Vol. 31, No. 11, 1490–1499, November, 1959
Copyright, 1959 by the Acoustical Society of America.

Minimal Rules for Synthesizing Speech*

A. M. Liberman,† Frances Ingemann,‡ Leigh Lisker,§ Pierre Delattre,‖ and F. S. Cooper
Haskins Laboratories, New York, New York
(Received July 23, 1959)

It has been found to be extremely difficult to isolate phonemic elements from recorded utterances or to synthesize speech by assembling prerecorded phonemic segments. One reason for the difficulty lies in the fact that the perceptually discrete phonemes are typically combined, and in some cases encoded, into units of essentially syllabic dimensions. As a result, prerecorded elements must, in many cases, approximate syllables, and the synthesis of speech by this means will require a large inventory of recordings. By taking advantage of knowledge about the acoustic cues for speech perception, however, it is possible to write rules for synthesis in terms of phonemes (rather than syllables) and thus reduce considerably the number of separate rules or items needed. Indeed, one can reduce the number of rules still further by writing them at the level of subphonemic dimensions, *viz.*, place and manner of articulation. Several complicating factors make it impossible to achieve an ideal minimum. First, rules or rule modifiers must be added to take care of certain prosodic and positional variations. Failure to do so not only affects naturalness, but also impairs intelligibility, even at the level of segmental phonemes. Second, it is necessary in a few special cases to have different rules for a single consonant phoneme (or a dimension of that phoneme) before different vowels. This reflects the occasionally complex relation between phoneme and articulation on the one hand and sound output on the other; presumably, this complication would not affect the rules of synthesis for an articulatory model.

A system of rules for synthesis framed largely in terms of subphonemic dimensions is described with reference to an example. Words and sentences of rather high intelligibility have been synthesized by such rules.

INTRODUCTION

DURING the past ten years a series of studies has been carried out at Haskins Laboratories in an attempt to uncover the acoustic cues that underlie the perception of speech. Many different aspects of the problem have been investigated. Some of the results have been published in acoustical, linguistic, and psychological journals, and some have been quietly entombed in the files of the Laboratory. A few members of the staff have been close to all stages of the work, and so, with all the published and unpublished information quite literally at their fingertips, they have been able for some time to paint spectrographic patterns appropriate for the synthesis of almost any utterance. That is, they can paint to order, as it were, simple, schematized spectrograms which, when run through the Pattern Playback or the Voback,[1] produce speech at rather respectable levels of intelligibility. These spectrograms are prepared largely on the basis of research results and without looking at a real speech spectrogram of the utterance being synthesized. To that extent we have for a rather long time now been synthesizing speech by rule. At least in a sense. But not in the sense that the phrase "rules for synthesizing speech" is used in the title of this paper. In the ideal case, and that is what we want to talk about here, the rules would be together in one place, written down for all to see, and they would be perfectly explicit in all particulars, so that a person with no knowledge of speech or spectrograms could, by reference to the rules, synthesize speech as well as anyone else.

Recently, one of the authors of this paper, Frances Ingemann, undertook to prepare just such a set of rules. For this purpose she combed, winnowed, refined, and distilled the material in our files. Her first set of rules for synthesis was described to this Society at the Ann Arbor meeting in 1957,[2] and recorded samples of the results were played.

We do not propose in this paper to set forth all of the rules in detail or to consider the improvements that have been made since Dr. Ingemann's earlier report to the Society. Rather, we intend to talk about rules for synthesis in relation to some general aspects of the processes of speech production and perception. We shall try, then, to organize some relatively familiar data and concepts in terms of their relevance to a somewhat less familiar problem.

It may help in setting the problem to think in terms of a machine that will process a discrete phonemic input in such a way as to produce a speech output. We shall suppose that the information available at the input is in the form of a succession of phonemes such as would result from an analysis of a series of utterances by a competent linguist. Fortunately, we need not be concerned here with the precise nature of the phonemic system that was assumed in making this analysis. For our present purposes it is sufficient to know that these phonemes represent discrete elements of the kind

* This paper was read by invitation before the Fifty-Sixth Meeting of the Acoustical Society of America in November, 1958. The work described here was supported in part by the Carnegie Corporation of New York, in part by the Prosthetic and Sensory Aids Service of the Veterans Administration in connection with Contract No. V1005M1253, and in part by the Department of Defense in connection with Contract No. DA49-170-sc-2564.
† Also at the University of Connecticut.
‡ Also at the University of Kansas.
§ Also at the University of Pennsylvania.
‖ Also at the University of Colorado.
[1] For accounts of these research tools, see: F. S. Cooper, J. Acoust. Soc. Am. **22**, 761–762 (1950); Cooper, Liberman, and Borst, Proc. Natl. Acad. Sci. **37**, 318–325 (1951); F. S. Cooper, ome instrumental aids to research on speech, in "Report of the fourth annual round table meeting on linguistics and language teaching," pp. 46–53 (Washington, D. C., Institute of Languages and Linguistics, Georgetown University, 1953); J. M. Borst and F. S. Cooper, J. Acoust. Soc. Am. **29**, 777 (A) (1957).

[2] F. Ingemann, J. Acoust. Soc. Am. **29**, 1255 (A) (1957).

everyone knows as consonants and vowels. So far as the output is concerned, we ask simply that it be easily intelligible at normal rates of production.

This exercise may be considered to have any one or all of several purposes. On the one hand it may be practical. One thinks, for example, of the synthesizer end of a speech-recognizer band width compression system or, perhaps, of a reading machine for the blind. On the other hand, the aim may be quite academic, and, in a rather specific sense, not too different from that which motivates the linguist. Given that we know something about the acoustic cues for the various phonemes, we should like to systematize the data by deriving from them an orderly set of rules for synthesis, and, ideally, we should like to produce rules that are few in number, simple in structure, and susceptible of mechanization.

SYNTHESIS FROM PRERECORDED ELEMENTS

For the purposes of this paper it will be helpful to begin by assuming that we know nothing about the acoustic patterns that underlie language, and that we are going to try nevertheless to convert a phonemic input to speech. In that case we are likely to consider, as the simplest solution, a system in which an inventory of prerecorded sounds is assigned in one-to-one fashion to the phonemic signals at the input end. In this system the incoming phonemes simply key the prerecorded sounds. If we instrument such an arrangement, we will almost surely find it quite unsatisfactory. Of all the various difficulties that one will ultimately experience with this system, the most immediately obvious will be a noticeable bumpiness and roughness in the output. One thinks, then, of setting up various smoothing operations, and, indeed, it is surely possible to improve the output by such means. But no amount of smoothing will solve what is here a very fundamental, and, by now, familiar problem. One has only to look at spectrograms to see that speech tends to vary more or less continuously over stretches of greater than phonemic length. The patterns rarely break at what might be considered to be phoneme boundaries, and those who have tried to find the acoustic limits of the phoneme have come to know this as the problem of segmentation.

Now none of this should be taken to deny the existence of the phoneme, either as a convenient linguistic abstraction or as a perceptual unit. It indicates merely that the perceptually and linguistically discrete phonemes are often combined and, indeed, in some cases encoded, into units that are more than one phoneme in length. They are not strung together like beads on a string. It is for this reason that one encounters difficulties when he tries to snip phonemes out of a magnetic tape recording, or when, conversely, he tries to synthesize speech from prerecorded phonemic elements.[3]

If one insists, nevertheless, on trying to produce speech from prerecorded phonemes, he is likely to be forced into one of two undesirable courses. One possibility is to employ different recordings, or allophonic variants, of most of the phonemes for most of the combinations in which they occur. This obviously requires a formidable inventory of prerecorded elements. The number of elements can be reduced by creating classes of variants, each class being represented by a single typical form. But this reduction in the number of items is only to be had by severely compromising the quality of the output; in short, the rougher the approximation to proper junctions, the rougher and less intelligible the speech.

An alternative is to try to record, or recover, the speech sounds in very brief form as, for example, in a rapid recitation of the alphabet (plus a baker's dozen of additional sounds). The difficulty, of course, is that the phonemes have now become syllables and the intended synthetic speech has become a kind of "spelling bee." Nor is this difficulty avoidable: a shift from spelling to phonetic pronunciation only shortens and centralizes the vowel that clings to almost every consonant; indeed, it is difficult to imagine how a voiced stop, for example, could possibly be produced or heard without some vowel-like sound preceding or following it. Thus, we see that this alternative does violence to the speech process; moreover, it has but limited practical utility, since the spelling-bee output will not be so readily or rapidly comprehended as ordinary speech with its phonemes in syllabic combination.

What has been said so far does not mean that one cannot work from prerecorded elements. Rather, it suggests that if one wants by this technique to produce speech rather than spelling, and if he prefers not to deal with allophonic variants, then he has got to include among the prerecorded elements a number of units which exceed one phoneme in length. An inevitable result is that the inventory must be very large (as it was found, above, to be for the method of allophonic variants when high-quality speech was desired). Thus, in a recent attempt to synthesize speech from discrete segments, Peterson, Wang, and Sivertsen[4] have used what they call "dyads," a dyad being a segment which contains "parts of two phones with their mutual influence in the middle of the segment." To produce one idiolect by this technique Peterson, Wang, and Sivertsen estimate that some 8000 dyads are necessary. (It should be noted that this number includes provision for three levels of intonation for many of the dyads.)

---

[3] For the purposes of this discussion it does not matter greatly whether the elements are pronounced and recorded in isolation

or, alternatively, cut out of recordings of connected speech and then reassembled into new combinations. Some of the difficulties that arise in connection with the latter procedure are illustrated in Harris' account of his attempt to isolate the "building blocks of speech." See C. M. Harris, J. Acoust. Soc. Am. **25**, 962–969 (1953).

[4] Peterson, Wang, and Sivertsen, J. Acoust. Soc. Am. **30**, 739–742 (1958).

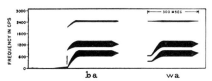

Fig. 1. Hand-drawn spectrographic patterns illustrating some of the acoustic cues for the stop consonant /b/ and the semivowel /w/.

For some purposes such a system may well represent a practical solution. It is not the only solution, however, and from one standpoint not the most interesting. We have in mind here that one may quite properly regard a set of rules for synthesis as a description of the acoustic basis for the perception of language.[5] If so, it must be concluded that discrete segments provide an uneconomical description, since, as has been seen, the number of segments or entries in the system is extremely large.[6]

SYNTHESIS BY PHONEMIC RULES

Although it is very difficult to produce speech from prerecorded phonemic segments, it is nevertheless possible to generate speech from discrete phonemic instructions. That is, rules for synthesis *can* be written which make it possible to go from phonemic units to speech, and thus reduce by a very large factor the total number of rules needed.[7] This can be done by taking advantage of what is known about the cues for speech perception.

The patterns of Fig. 1 illustrate some of these cues and also point to one of the reasons why it is so very difficult to cut and re-assemble phonemic segments. When converted into sound by the Pattern Playback, the hand-drawn spectrograms seen in the figure produce reasonably close approximations to the consonant-vowel syllables indicated. All that we can say about these particular spectrograms that is relevant to the present discussion has been said at other times in talks before this Society and in published papers.[8] Therefore, we ask the indulgence of the reader and, in return, promise to be brief.

Research with patterns such as those shown in Fig. 1 has shown that a primary cue for the perception of these and certain other consonants is the relatively rapid shift in the formant frequencies seen at the left of

each pattern. These shifts have been named "transitions," which is unfortunate because this designation implies that they are mere incidents in the process of going from phoneme to phoneme. Far from being incidental links between phonemes, these transitions are themselves among the most important cues to the perception of many of the consonants. It cannot be too strongly emphasized that the perceptual function of the transitions is not to avoid clicks and thumps, but rather to provide important and sometimes essential information for phoneme identification. This is to say that the essential perceptual cue is sometimes given by information concerning the change from one frequency position to another. For the consonant phonemes of Fig. 1, and for others too, it is unqualifiedly true that there is no position in the pattern that will be perceived as the intended consonant, or, indeed, as any consonant, when it is in steady state. Sounding the initial steady-state portion of /w/ will cause the listener to hear the vowel /u/. Every point on the transition leading into the steady-state vowel will, if prolonged, produce a vowel-like sound.[9,10] The listener will perceive /w/ only if he is given information about where the formant begins, where it ends, and how long it takes to move from the one frequency to the other. Normally, this information is conveyed continuously by the transitions. It is always possible, of course, to degrade the patterns to some degree, as for example by erasing parts of the transitions, without utterly destroying the phoneme as perceived. Indeed, in the case of /w/ one can synthesize it reasonably well by moving from the initial steady state to the steady state of the vowel without actually sounding the transition at all, provided the normal time relationships are preserved.[11] This is a rather extreme case—one cannot remove nearly so much of the transition for the /b/ of Fig. 1 or, indeed, for any of the stop or nasal consonants—and even so it is clear that some indication of the /w/ transitions, as given by the abrupt shift from the initial steady state

[5] We are here concerned only with those aspects of the acoustic pattern that carry the linguistic information.

[6] A description of the acoustic basis of language in these terms is, of course, also incomplete unless the patterns present in each segment are fully described in acoustic terms.

[7] As used in this paper a "rule" will refer to all the statements that must be made in order to specify whatever unit (e.g., phoneme, subphonemic feature, syllable) of the language is being used as a basis for synthesis.

[8] Cooper, Delattre, Liberman, Borst, and Gerstman, J. Acoust. Soc. Am. **24**, 597–606 (1952); Liberman, Delattre, Cooper, and Gerstman, Psychol. Monogr. **68**, No. 8, 1–13 (1954); Liberman, Delattre, Gerstman, and Cooper, J. Exptl. Psychol. **52**, 127–137 (1956); O'Connor, Gerstman, Liberman, Delattre, and Cooper, Word **13**, 24–43 (1957).

[9] It was found in an earlier study (see O'Connor *et al.*, reference 8) that in the case of /w/ in initial position a brief steady-state segment at the onset helps to avoid a stop consonant effect, but it is not really essential. One must be careful, however, not to have the steady-state segment exceed about 30 msec, because at longer durations the listener hears a vowel preceding the /w/. It is not always clear in spectrograms of real speech whether or not there is an initial steady-state segment and, if so, how long the segment is.

[10] With the Pattern Playback it is possible to stop the pattern at any point and determine what that part of the pattern sounds like in steady state.

[11] For the purposes of producing speech by recombining prerecorded phonemic segments, one might take advantage of this possibility with /w/ by isolating something approximating the initial steady state of /w/ which, when spliced in the proper temporal relationship to any of several vowels would, perhaps, produce a fair impression of /w/ plus vowel. This technique would almost certainly not work nearly so well with other consonants, and it will in any case probably be harder to do with real speech than with the idealized, schematized, hand-drawn patterns described in the text. In general, we should expect the application of this technique to be somewhat limited and to produce something less than ideal results, for at best it represents a way to force speech into a wholly unnatural mold.

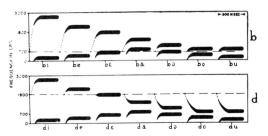

FIG. 2. Second-formant transitions appropriate for /b/
and /d/ before various vowels.

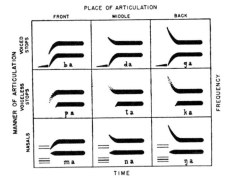

FIG. 3. Patterns illustrating some of the acoustic cues
for the stop and nasal consonants.

to the vowel, is a necessary condition for the perception of the /w/ phoneme. These considerations lead us to disagree with an assumption that Peterson, Wang, and Sivertsen took as basic to their segmentation technique, namely, that "the intelligibility of speech is carried by the more sustained or target positions of the vowels, consonants, and other phonetic features."[4] We would rather say that for many of the consonants an important and sometimes necessary condition for intelligibility is that the listener be provided with information concerning the direction, extent, and duration of formant "movement." When we consider that this information is normally present in formant transitions, and that it cannot really be dispensed with, we see one of the reasons why it is so difficult, starting with recorded utterances, to isolate and recombine phonemic segments.

Now to arrive at "phonemic" rules for the generation of syllables like those of Fig. 1, we begin by taking into account that all the transitions for a given consonant have a common feature. This is illustrated in Fig. 2, where we see in the bottom row that, although the extent and direction of the transitions are different for /d/ before different vowels, it is nevertheless clear that the transitions have originated from approximately the same place. This common origin has been called the locus,[12] and it has been possible to define characteristic loci for essentially all the consonants.

Knowing the first-, second-, and third-formant loci for all the consonants is the key that unlocks the syllable and makes it feasible to write rules at the phoneme level. For example, we may say of /d/ that its second formant should start at about 1800 cps and proceed then at a certain rate to the steady-state level appropriate for the second formant of the following vowel. If, alternatively, we want to synthesize a syllable consisting of /b/ plus vowel, we see from the patterns in the top row of the figure that we should start the

second formant at about 700 cps and proceed to the vowel level from there. In fact, the situation is somewhat more complicated than this in several ways. For example, the stops must not actually start at the loci—rather, they should only "point" to them. In the patterns of the figure the dashed lines represent non-explicit portions of the complete transition specified by the locus hypothesis. This characteristic of the locus is one of the class markers for the stops,[13] as it is also for the nasals. For these and other classes of consonants it is, of course, necessary to add other acoustic cues, such as the noises that occur with stops, affricates, and fricatives,[14] and the relatively brief steady-state resonances that mark the nasals, liquids, and semivowels.[15]

At a different level of complication it is, as we have already implied, necessary that the application of a phoneme rule be made in relation to the phonemes on either side. Thus, in the example used, the second-formant transition for /d/ led to the second-formant level appropriate for the next vowel, wherever that might have been. This means that contextual information must be used in *applying* the rules for successive phonemes, but only to the extent that one must know—as he must in any case—the appropriate formant levels for the next phoneme so that the transitions may be properly connected. Given that the situation is even approximately this simple, we can see how, in principle, the number of rules can approximate the number of phonemes.

SYNTHESIS BY SUBPHONEMIC RULES

But if economy in terms of number of rules is our aim—and it would appear to be a reasonable one—we can go further by setting up the rules in terms of subphonemic dimensions. Figure 3 contains hand-drawn

[12] For a detailed treatment of the "locus," see Delattre, Liberman, and Cooper, J. Acoust. Soc. Am. **27**, 769–773 (1955); Harris, Hoffman, Liberman, Delattre, and Cooper, J. Acoust. Soc. Am. **30**, 122–126 (1958). A rationalization in terms of articulatory-acoustic considerations is contained in a paper by Stevens and House [see K. N. Stevens and A. S. House, J. Acoust. Soc. Am. **28**, 578–585 (1956)]. In certain ways the locus is similar to the "hub" [see Potter, Kopp, and Green, *Visible Speech* (D. Van Nostrand Company, Inc., New York, 1947)].

[13] See Delattre *et al.*, reference 13; O'Connor *et al.*, reference 8.
[14] Liberman, Delattre, and Cooper, Am. J. Psychol. **65**, 497–516 (1952); C. Schatz, Language **30**, 47–56 (1954); G. W. Hughes and M. Halle, J. Acoust. Soc. Am. **28**, 303–310 (1956); Halle, Hughes, and Radley, J. Acoust. Soc. Am. **29**, 107–116 (1957); K. S. Harris, Language and Speech **1**, 1–7 (1958).
[15] Liberman *et al.*, reference 8; O'Connor *et al.*, reference 8.

FIG. 4. Patterns illustrating some of the cues for /m/ in different positions.

spectrographic patterns that illustrate how this can be done. Here we see hand-painted spectrograms that will produce reasonable approximations to the syllables /ba, da, ga, pa, ta, ka, ma, na, ŋa/. All the sounds having the same place of articulation—that is, all the sounds in a given column—have the same second-formant transition. Similarly, all the sounds having the same manner of articulation—that is, those in a given row—have the same first-formant transition, and, in some cases, additional markers, as for the nasality of /m, n, ŋ/. Thus, it is possible to set up a rule for a front place of articulation, a middle place of articulation, and a back place of articulation. Similarly, there is a rule for the class of voiced stops, one for the voiceless stops, and one for nasality. In this way we obtain nine phonemes with six rules.

It should be noted here that when the rules are written at a subphonemic level, arrangements must be made for simultaneous (as well as sequential) combination. Thus, for the consonant phoneme of a syllable, for example, we must put together, at the very least, the appropriate rule for place of articulation and the appropriate rule for manner; these, in turn, must be "meshed" with the rules for the vowel or other consonants of the syllable.

As we have seen, the number of rules is considerably reduced by operating at a subphonemic level. In the ideal case we would, of course, have only as many rules as there are subphonemic features, and this would be in the neighborhood of ten. However, for reasons which will be given below, it is not possible to achieve this ideal.

ADDITIONAL RULES FOR POSITION

One complication at either the phonemic or subphonemic level is that we must sometimes make special provision for positional variations. The few simple examples so far have been of consonants in initial position. Now in most cases it is possible to produce patterns suitable for other positions from the same basic rules.[16] That is, it is usually possible to frame a basic rule for a phoneme or a subphonemic dimension and then derive the particular patterns for each of several positions. As an example, let us take the patterns for the nasal labial consonant /m/ in initial, intervocalic, and final positions, as shown in Fig. 4. The basic rules for /m/ require that there be steady-state

[16] L. Lisker, Word 13, 256–267 (1957); L. Lisker, Language 33, 42–49 (1957).

formants of specified duration, intensities, and frequencies. Furthermore, they require that any adjacent formants have transitions of a specified duration which are discontinuous with the nasal formants and which point to certain locus frequencies. As we see from Fig. 4, the differences among the initial, intervocalic, and final patterns for /m/ involve only the presence or absence of transitions on either side of the nasal formants. Whether or not a transition is to be drawn depends on whether adjacent formants are specified, and that depends, of course, on the rules appropriate for the immediate neighbors of /m/ in the sequence of input phonemes. In other words, before we can have a transition we must have, at the input, two contiguous phonemes both of whose rules call for this acoustic feature.

The preceding example illustrates the most common type of positional variation that must be accommodated by our rules of synthesis. As we have elected to handle them, such positional variations follow from the different ways in which rules for adjacent phonemes "mesh" to specify the transitional portions of our patterns; therefore, additional "connection" rules are not necessary.

In certain cases, however, it is not possible to derive a desired pattern entirely from the basic rules for the constituent phonemes, although we are never forced to the extreme of having to write an entirely new rule for such a case. Rather, we find that an appropriate pattern can be produced simply by applying a qualification or "position modifier" to the basic rule. An example of this is the pattern for the syllable /glu/ shown in Fig. 5. The basic rule for /g/ calls for an interval that is silent except for a voice bar, followed by a burst, and it further stipulates that adjacent formants have transitions which point to particular locus frequencies. The rule for /l/ calls for steady-state formants of a certain duration and specified intensities and frequencies, and it further requires that these /l/ formants be continuous with transitions to any adjacent formants. The rule for the vowel /u/ specifies the duration, intensity, and frequency of each of three formants which are steady state, except as rules for neighboring phonemes prescribe transitions. Now a rigid application of the basic rules for the phonemes constituting the syllable /glu/ yields an ultimate acoustic output of less than tolerable intelligibility. A marked improvement is achieved if the basic rule for each phoneme is modified as follows: /g/ before /l/ requires only a burst of specified frequency; /l/ before /u/ has the frequency of its second formant lowered somewhat; /u/ following /l/ has a second formant which first rises from the second-formant frequency of /l/, and then, after a specified duration, shifts at a given rate to the normal steady-state frequency for /u/. At this point it should be remarked that these position modifiers operate on classes of phonemes; thus, the modification for /g/ applies also to the other stops, the modifier for /l/

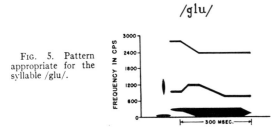

/glu/

FREQUENCY IN CPS

FIG. 5. Pattern appropriate for the syllable /glu/.

←— 300 MSEC. —→

applies also to /w, r, j/, and the modifier for /u/ applies also to /o/ and /ɔ/. In other words, the kind of economy gained by going from phoneme rules to subphonemic rules extends to the position modifiers as well.

Similar problems occur and similarly general solutions are found for other positional variations, as, for example, in the neighborhood of juncture.

LINGUISTIC DIGRESSION

We should like to digress here to discuss briefly the implications of what has been said for the problem of how to define the phoneme. As you remember, we began by referring to a machine that would process a discrete phonemic input so as to produce a speech-like output. The phonemic input would be furnished by linguistic analysis. We might soon discover on consulting several equally competent linguists that they were of divided opinion on two subjects at least. First, they might have different ideas on the best way to define the phoneme; and second, they would not agree entirely on what the phonemes of a particular language are. Now the first point may be dismissed as a bit of academic quibbling, for we observe that two linguists with conflicting definitions of the phoneme can come out with phonemic analyses that are remarkably alike. It is of interest, nevertheless, that at least one linguist, Zellig Harris,[17] has proposed an operational definition of the phoneme which would require for its application that we synthesize speech from prerecorded utterances cut up into segments of phoneme length. For example, if the question were whether two sounds in different environments were or were not the same phoneme, one would interchange the appropriate snippets of tape, play back, and listen to determine whether the resulting utterance, as perceived, was reasonably satisfactory. Now we know that in many cases this operation cannot really be performed satisfactorily, and therefore has very little utility as a tool for phonemic analysis. However, the linguist may be able to do a roughly equivalent thing in terms of our rules and their modifiers. For the case of the sounds in different environments, the question would be whether one could satisfactorily synthesize them by using the same rule in both cases,

provided only he applied the appropriate positional modifier.

The second point of dispute among the linguists is more important to us, since it actually affects what is to go into the input of the synthesizer. For example, one linguist will transcribe the vocalic part of the word *cake* with a single symbol where another will write it as a sequence of two. Then again, they may have differences of opinion about where to put the phonemes that sometimes mark boundaries between words. Instead of waiting for the linguists to resolve these conflicts among themselves, we might try each of the alternative analyses they provide, and then select that one which yields the most intelligible and natural-sounding speech output. Of course, if two alternatives yield the same kind of results by this test, then we may conclude that the problem is phonetically irrelevant and hand it back to the linguists.

ADDITIONAL RULES FOR STRESS AND SYLLABIC ENCODING

Before this digression into linguistics, we were considering the necessity of adding rules beyond the ideal minimum, and had discussed the matter of positional variations.

There remain two other types of complication that deserve mention. The first of these arises in connection with prosodic features, particularly stress.[18] We might have supposed that the basic rules, derived as they are largely from experiments with isolated syllables, would, if anything, yield connected speech that is "over-intelligible" to the point of sounding stilted. Now the speech we get certainly sounds stilted if differences in stress are not provided for, but it is also often markedly less intelligible than would be predicted from the levels of intelligibility achieved for its constituent vowels and consonants when these are tested in nonsense syllables. The quality of the synthetic speech is significantly improved, both in intelligibility and in naturalness, if at least two degrees of stress are provided for in the rules. The stress differences can be specified by one or more acoustic features, such as fundamental frequency, intensity, and duration. (Fundamental frequency is also, of course, the basis for variations in intonation, but no attempt has yet been made to include this feature in the rules.) At the present time only duration is actually being used in the rules for stress.

In order to achieve the greatest gain from adjusting vowel durations for two degrees of stress it is necessary to reduce the durations of some vowels, specifically those in medial unstressed syllables, to such an extent that no steady-state remains. By the rules for stressed syllables, a simple consonant-vowel-consonant pattern consists at the very least of an initial transition, a

[17] Z. S. Harris, *Methods in Structural Linguistics* (University of Chicago Press, Chicago, Illinois, 1951).

[18] D. B. Fry, J. Acoust. Soc. Am. **27**, 765–768 (1955); D. L. Bolinger and L. J. Gerstman, Word **13**, 246–255 (1957); D. L. Bolinger, Lingua **7**, 175–182 (1958); D. B. Fry, Language and Speech **1**, 126–152 (1958); D. L. Bolinger, Word **14**, 109–149 (1958); L. Lisker, J. Acoust. Soc. Am. **30**, 682 (A) (1958).

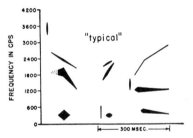

FIG. 6. Pattern appropriate for the word "typical."

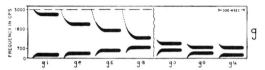

FIG. 7. Patterns illustrating second-formant transitions appropriate for /g/ before various vowels.

steady-state segment, and a final transition. The steady-state segment has formant frequencies characteristic of the vowel alone; the transitions have durations and end points fixed according to the place and manner rules for the consonants. To convert such a syllable into a form appropriate for the unstressed condition, we must effectively omit the steady-state segment, as pointed out above. This means that the second and third formants are in fact drawn as straight lines connecting the end-point frequencies given by the place rules for the adjacent consonants. (It is necessary that the second formant pass through the 1000–2000 cps region. Where the straight line rule would violate this restriction—as, for example, in the case of a vowel between two labials—the second formant must be curved to bring it up or down into the required frequency range.) The configuration of the first formant will depend on whether the adjacent consonants are voiced or voiceless: if voiced, the first formant will move from its initial frequency to 500 cps and then to its final frequency; if voiceless, it will remain at a steady-state frequency of 500 cps. In Fig. 6 the pattern for the word "typical" shows an unstressed vowel between voiceless stops drawn according to this rule.

The other kind of complication is infrequent enough to be of no great practical consequence, perhaps, but is of some interest nevertheless. This difficulty arises because there is occasionally a rather complex relation between the phoneme as a perceptual unit and the sound that elicits it. An example is given in Fig. 7. Here we see a single locus for /g/ before the vowels /i, e, ɛ, a/, but between /a/ and /ɔ/ there is a large and sudden jump to a new locus. It is of more than passing interest that there is no corresponding break in the articulation of the consonant. Between /a/ and /ɔ/ there is a change from unrounded to rounded in the articulation of the vowel, and we may suppose that some rounding of the vowel concomitant with consonant articulation produces the sudden shift in consonant locus. It remains true, however, that so far as the consonant articulation itself is concerned, there is no discontinuity. This is to say, then, that the relation between articulation and phoneme is more nearly one-to-one than that between phoneme and sound. We have in other papers discussed the reason for and

the possible significance of this fact.[19] Here we will simply note, first, that this requires an addition to the acoustic rules; second, that it must occasionally wreak havoc with attempts to work from prerecorded phonemic segments; and third, that this complication would not affect the rules of synthesis for an articulatory model. We should also stress the point, so clearly evident in this instance, that very often phonemes are literally *encoded* into syllables at the acoustic level; in such cases the syllable becomes, in a very real sense, the irreducible acoustic unit.

COMPLEXITY *VS* NUMBER OF RULES; RESULTANT INTELLIGIBILITY

We have so far talked about the number of rules required to do the job as if the matter of number were the only significant dimension of this problem. It is not. Obviously, we must consider not only the number of rules but also their simplicity. A rule, as we have been using the term, includes all the statements that must be made in order to specify a given unit of the system. Thus, at the subphonemic level, a rule includes all the specifications for a bilabial place of production, for example, or a stop consonant manner. A given rule may require many specifications or only a few. Simplicity or complexity is largely independent of the number of rules, and becomes, therefore, a separate consideration.

In the discussion so far we have also, perhaps, given the impression that there is a single, ideal, and final set of rules. It is, we suppose, obvious that beyond a certain point reduction in the number of rules, or an increase in their simplicity, will be accomplished only at the cost of naturalness and intelligibility. It remains to be determined just how and within what limits intelligibility and naturalness will vary as a function of the number of rules. In this paper we have more or less implicitly assumed some particular and reasonable level of intelligibility, and have considered the *minimum* set of rules for that level. At present there are nine rules for place of consonant articulation, five for manner of consonant articulation, and three rules for voicing. For the vowels we have two manner and twelve place rules. In addition, we have one stress modifier and about twelve position modifiers. We should emphasize that there is nothing hard and fast about the numbers cited; they serve only to indicate roughly how large an inventory we are currently dealing with.

[19] See Liberman, Delattre, and Cooper, reference 14; A. M. Liberman, J. Acoust. Soc. Am. **29**, 117–123 (1957).

We have made no comprehensive attempt as yet to measure the intelligibility of the speech produced by such rules. This is not because we are uninterested in intelligibility, but rather because the rules have been changing rapidly, and the data on a really long test are likely to be out of date by the time they have been tabulated. We think it is safe to say that the intelligibility is of a fairly high order. In a few short and rather informal tests, sentence intelligibility has ranged between 60% and 100% depending on the nature of the sentences and the extent to which the listeners are accustomed to hearing this kind of synthetic speech.

EXAMPLE OF THE RULES AND THEIR APPLICATION

To illustrate just how the various categories of rules are combined to specify a pattern let us derive the pattern for the word "labs" as shown in Fig. 8. This word is represented in the input language by the sequence of phonemes: /læbz/.

/l/: The first phoneme is a member of the class of resonant consonants, i.e., /w, r, l, j/. The *manner* rule for the resonants calls for three formants to be maintained (with specified intensities) at appropriate locus frequencies for 30 msec. The manner rule further specifies that adjacent formants shall have transitions of 75 msec drawn so as to be continuous with the locus formants. (This manner characteristic is referred to in the table of Fig. 8 as an "explicit locus.") The manner rule for the resonants also fixes the first-formant locus at 360 cps. Lastly, the resonant manner rule specifies a sound of the harmonic or "buzz" type. The *place* rule for /l/ specifies locus frequencies of 360, 1260, and 2880 cps.

/æ/: The next phoneme of the input is a member of the class of long vowels. The manner rule for this class calls for three formants of the buzz variety, having a duration of 150 msec. The place rule for /æ/ fixes formant frequencies at 750, 1650, and 2460 cps, and also specifies formant intensities.

/b/: The next phoneme shares its manner rule with all the other stops, /b, d, g, p, t, k/; this rule calls for an interval of "silence" (an interval devoid of acoustic energy at all frequencies above the fundamental of the buzz) followed by a burst, and further specifies that adjacent formants have 50-msec transitions pointing toward locus frequencies given by the place rule appropriate to the particular stop. ("Pointing to" means that the end-point frequencies of the actual transitions are midway between the locus frequencies and the formant frequencies of the next phoneme. This characteristic of the stop consonant manner is referred to in the table of Fig. 8 as a "virtual locus.") The manner rule also fixes the locus of the first formant at the frequency of the voice bar. The labial place rule, which serves equally for /b, p, m, f, v/, specifies that adjacent second- and third-formant transitions point to frequencies of 720 and 2100 cps, respectively. The

voicing rule for stops (applicable equally to /b, d, g/) requires that the duration of the "silent" interval be 70 msec and that this interval be filled by a "voice bar," that is, acoustic energy at the buzz fundamental frequency.

/z/: For the final phoneme, the manner rule is that appropriate for the fricatives, /f, v, θ, ð, s, z, ʃ, ʒ/, and it calls for an interval of band-limited noise (that is, a "hiss" rather than a buzz sound). The fricative manner rule also specifies that adjacent formants have 50-msec transitions pointing toward virtual loci given by the place rule for the particular fricative; further by the manner rule, the first-formant locus is at 240 cps. The alveolar place rule for either /z/ or /s/ specifies that the noise (required by the fricative manner rule) have a lower cutoff frequency of 3600 cps, and that adjacent second- and third-formant transitions point to frequencies of 1800 and 2700 cps, respectively. The voicing rule states that the noise should be of low intensity, have a duration of 100 msec and be accompanied by a voice bar.

Finally, we apply a *position modifier* for syllables immediately before silence or juncture which doubles the duration of the vowel, making the over-all duration of /æ/ 300 msec.

At this point we have completely specified a pattern that is directly convertible to an acoustic stimulus which the naive listener will readily identify as the word "labs."

RULES *VS* PRERECORDED ELEMENTS: FURTHER DISCUSSION

Instead of trying now merely to summarize what has already been said, we would rather try to bring into the open a few considerations that have been only implicit in the discussion so far. In particular we should like to call attention to the fact that we have casually mixed two rather different aspects of the problem. The first has to do with the size of the unit in terms of which the rules are written, the second with the difference between assembling prerecorded elements on the one hand and the real honest-to-goodness fabrication of speech on the other. When we introduced the matter of prerecorded elements earlier, it was primarily to make a point about speech. This was somewhat unfair. Although the use of prerecorded elements is synthesis only in the most sweeping sense of the word,[20] it is sufficiently interesting both in practice and in principle that we ought to deal with it in its own right. The practical advantages of such a system are obvious enough. The difficulty, as we tried to point out earlier, is largely in the matter of linkage. As we have seen, linkage presents great difficulties at the level of phonemes. Indeed, the difficulties are likely to be so great

---

[20] The speech sounds in the prerecorded elements are of course produced by human articulatory apparatus and recorded just as any other utterances can be. The synthetic aspect of this process consists only of entering these elements into combinations different from those in which they were originally recorded.

SYNTHESIS BY RULES: /læbz/.

	Resonants /wrly/:	Long Vowels /ieɛæɑɔo/:	Stops /pbtdkg/:	Fricatives /fvθðszʃʒ/:
Manner	Periodic sound (buzz); formant intensities and durations are specified. F1 locus is high. Formants have explicit loci.	Periodic sound (buzz); formant intensities and durations are specified.	No sound at formant frequencies; i.e., "silence." Burst of specified frequency and band width follows "silence." F1 locus is low. F2 and F3 have virtual loci.	Aperiodic sound (hiss); intensity and band width are specified. F1 locus is intermediate. F2 and F3 have virtual loci.
Place	/l/: F2 and F3 loci are specified.	/æ/: Formants frequencies specified.	Labials /pbfvm/: F2 and F3 loci are specified. Frequencies of buzz and hiss are specified.	Alveolars /tdsz/: F2 and F3 loci are specified. Frequencies of buzz and hiss are specified.
Voicing	(The voicing rules are only applied to those phonemes for which the condition of voicing has differential value. For the resonants and vowels, which are invariably voiced, the acoustic features correlated with voicing are specified under Manner.)		Voiced /bdg/: Voice bar. Duration of "silence" is specified. F1 onset is not delayed.	Voiced /vðzʒ/: Voice bar. Duration of hiss is specified. F1 onset is not delayed.
Position		Vowels in final syllable: Duration is double that specified under Manner.		

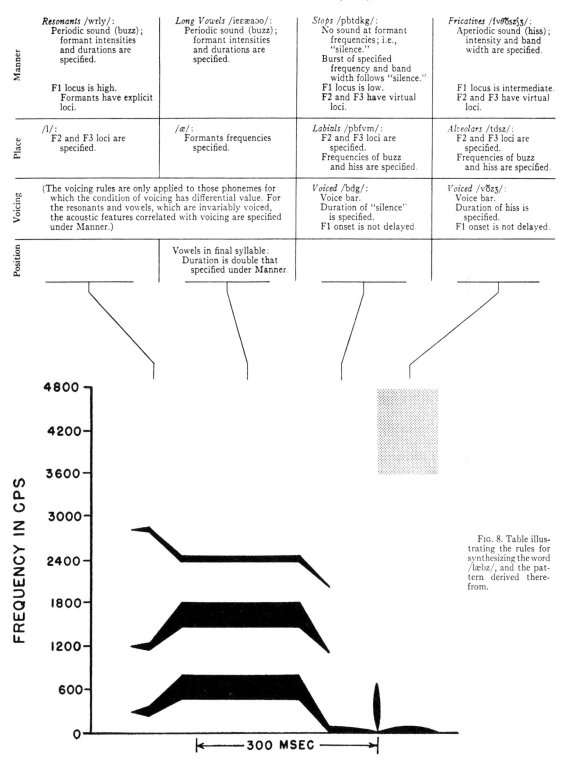

FIG. 8. Table illustrating the rules for synthesizing the word /læbz/, and the pattern derived therefrom.

that one will be driven to use elements which are of essentially syllabic dimensions, and even here problems will occur in the matter of joining the syllables. With units the size of words one will, of course, have much less difficulty about linkages, though he may not, even so, be completely out of the woods.

If we have seemed earlier in this discussion to be unenthusiastic about synthesis from prerecorded elements, we should say now that we have been sufficiently interested ourselves to have begun to explore the possibilities of such a system, at least at the level of words.[21] We have been particularly interested in trying to find the minimum number of versions of each word which will produce appropriate stresses and intonations when the words are arranged in various combinations. This has proved to be a challenging and interesting problem in the sense that its solution will either depend on the application of already known linguistic principles, or, alternatively, will provide information basic to the formulation of such principles.

To return to the point about linkages, the obvious generalization is that the problem grows less severe as the size of the prerecorded unit increases. There is, presumably, a function relating intelligibility or maximum speed of communication to size of the prerecorded units, and this function must certainly rise, though at an ever decreasing rate, as we go from smaller to larger units. At present, we know that with prerecorded phoneme units we are way down on the intelligibility or speed scale, if, indeed, we are on it at all. With prerecorded words we may be within shouting distance of the asymptote. We strongly suspect, without benefit of evidence, that syllables will be marginally useful if we want to communicate at normal speech rates.

It may well be that, for some purposes, prerecorded elements will turn out to be the method of choice. In principle, the system is interesting because when the

[21] "Summary of fourth technical session on reading machines for the blind," Veterans Administration Washington, D. C., August 23–24, 1956; prepared by the Prosthetic and Sensory Aids Service, Veterans Administration, 252 Seventh Avenue, New York 1, New York.

units are of phonemic dimensions the difficulties one encounters illustrate some important truths about speech, and when the units are the size of words, we encounter some partially soluble and therefore challenging problems of stress and intonation—as well as of instrumentation.

We have already dealt at length with true synthesis as opposed to the use of prerecorded elements. With true synthesis the linkage problem is soluble at all levels, and has to a large extent been solved. The rules for synthesis can be written at various levels. Indeed, this system is inherently flexible in all respects. Its limits are set primarily by the limits of our knowledge about speech and, from a practical standpoint, by the difficulties of instrumenting true synthesis rather than random access.

We saw that with prerecorded elements the total inventory of segments (or rules) will likely approximate the number of syllables at the very least. By using true synthesis we can considerably reduce the number of rules by writing them either at the phoneme or subphoneme level. In either case some rules must be added to take care of positional variations, essential prosodic features, and the special cases in which the acoustic encoding of the phonemes into syllables makes it impossible to get along with only one rule for a single phoneme or subphonemic feature. When the rules are written at the phoneme level there must, of course, be provision for connecting the formant transitions or formants of successive phonemes, and at the subphonemic level additional arrangements must be made for simultaneous combination of the rules pertaining to the several features that constitute the phoneme.

Exactly how and where one might wish to make practical use of the rules for true synthesis depends on a large number of considerations that lie far outside the scope of this paper. In this account, we have been interested in such rules primarily because they constitute a description of the acoustic basis of speech perception. The kind of information contained in that description will, we think, prove useful for a variety of practical and theoretical purposes.

CHAPTER 32

Reprinted from the *Journal of Speech and Hearing Research*
March 1959, Vol. 2, No. 1

Transition And Release As Perceptual Cues For Final Plosives

WILLIAM S-Y. WANG

The perception of speech in its everyday form involves at least two sets of variables (*8*): the physical information present in the acoustical wave and the linguistic code with which the listener interprets the physical information.

In the perception of final, postvocalic plosive consonants in noncontextual monosyllables, the physical information includes: (a) the duration of the preceding vowels (*3*), (b) the formant transitions (*6*) and (c) the duration of the voicing that may follow the formant transitions. When a plosive is released, or when there is a cluster of two plosives, additional cues may be found in (a) the duration of the gap (7) and (b) the duration, (c) the intensity and (d) the spectral properties of the release (*2*). In English, the first plosive of a cluster is frequently not released but is signalled by the formant transitions alone and the second plosive is signalled by the release.

The linguistic code, with which the listener interprets the physical information, conditions him to perceive the consonants in the following cases with varying degrees of proficiency: (a) when the consonants do not occur in his native language; (b) when the consonants are in a sequence that does not occur in his language (*1*); (c) when a syllable containing the consonants conforms to the phonotactic (phonetic sequence) rules of his linguistic code but is not a word to him; (d) when the syllable is a word of low frequency of occurrence in his language; and (e) when the syllable is a high frequency word (*9*).

If the native language of the listener is English, the above mentioned cases can be exemplified by the five syllables [sɪq], [sɪtp], [sɪg], [sɪkt], [sɪt]. These syllables are in the order of increasing familiarity to the English-speaking listener. It would appear probable that he will find them increasingly easy to perceive correctly.

Methods in Studying Speech Perception. Within the last decade, investigations on the perception of speech have been rather intensively pursued by means of electronically synthesized speech (*6, 11*). An advantage of generating speech electronically is that, in certain respects, greater precision and ease of control in the production of sounds can be achieved with calibrated

William S-Y. Wang (M.A., University of Michigan, 1956) is Research Associate in the Speech Research Laboratory at the University of Michigan. This article is based on a paper presented at the July, 1958, meeting of the Linguistic Society of America, Ann Arbor. The investigation was supported by the Information Systems Branch of the Office of Naval Research under contract Nonr 1224(22), NR 049-122.

TABLE 1. Monosyllabic words used as the basic corpus. The left column lists the initial consonants for each row; the top row lists the final consonants for each column.

	p	t	k	b	d	g
p	pip	pit	pick			pig
b		bit		bib	bid	big
s	sip	sit	sick	sib	Sid	
r	rip		rick	rib	rid	rig

instruments than with the human speech mechanism. Studies with electronic speech usually simplify the acoustical pattern of actual speech by deleting certain parameters and isolating and varying certain others. Listeners' responses are then correlated with the systematic changes made in the synthesized speech.

Experiments also have been carried out using samples of normal speech, usually in the form of intelligibility tests. While there are more variables to control in natural speech, it yields results whose direct relevance to actual speech need not be justified. Various types of masking noise, clipping, phase shifts and time and frequency distortion have been used to study the perceptual properties of speech sounds.

Procedure

The present study used human speech and systematic modifications of it as the test stimuli. It attempts to investigate the relative significance of various acoustical cues in the perception of final plosive consonants. The method involved deleting or interchanging these cues.

Test Materials. Table 1 lists the monosyllabic words which were selected. Each contained the vowel [ɪ] and ended in a plosive. These words

were recorded with all the plosives released and with what was believed to be uniform prosodic features. The words were then copied four times onto new magnetic tape at a speed of 30 in./sec. These four sets of monosyllables are hereafter referred to as Sets A, B, C and D.

Set A was unmodified. The releases of Set B were removed by cutting away the tape approximately seven centiseconds after the termination of the formants. The voiceless releases of Set C were replaced by voiced releases of the same articulatory positions and vice versa. In Set D the natural releases were replaced by releases from other articulatory positions, without changing the feature of voicing. For Sets C and D, an attempt was made to maintain the tape junction midway between the termination of the formants and the spike of the release. The syllables which

TABLE 2. The four sets of syllables used in listening tests. Set A contains unmodified monosyllabic words. The hyphens indicate the places of tape junction where the releases were deleted or interchanged.

Set A	Set B	Set C	Set D
[pɪpp]	[pɪp-]		[pɪp-k]
[sɪpp]	[sɪp-]	[sɪp-b]	[sɪp-t]
[rɪpp]	[rɪp-]	[rɪp-b]	[rɪp-k]
[pɪtt]	[pɪt-]		[pɪt-p]
[bɪtt]	[bɪt-]	[bɪt-d]	[bɪt-t]
[sɪtt]	[sɪt-]	[sɪt-d]	[sɪt-p]
[pɪkk]	[pɪk-]	[pɪk-g]	[pɪk-p]
[sɪkk]	[sɪk-]		[sɪk-t]
[rɪkk]	[rɪk-]	[rɪk-g]	[rɪk-k]
[bɪbb]	[bɪb-]		[bɪb-d]
[sɪbb]	[sɪb-]	[sɪb-p]	[sɪb-d]
[rɪbb]	[rɪb-]	[rɪb-p]	[rɪb-g]
[bɪdd]	[bɪd-]	[bɪd-t]	[bɪd-b]
[sɪdd]	[sɪd-]	[sɪd-t]	[sɪd-b]
]rɪdd]	[rɪd-]		[rɪd-g]
[pɪgg]	[pɪg-]	[pɪg-k]	[pɪg-g]
[bɪgg]	[bɪg-]		[bɪg-d]
[rɪgg]	[rɪg-]	[rɪg-k]	[rɪg-b]

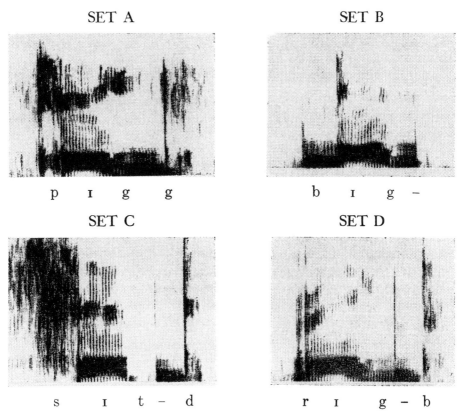

SET A

SET B

p   ɪ   g   g

b   ɪ   g   –

SET C

SET D

s   ɪ   t   –   d

r   ɪ   g   –   b

FIGURE 1. Broad band spectrograms of one syllable from each of the four test sets. The hyphens indicate the places of tape junction.

were used in Sets A, B, C and D were English words if they were considered to end in the plosive signalled by the cues either before or after the tape junction. However, when these syllables are considered as ending in clusters, then only those syllables which end in a non-geminated [t] or [d] conform to the phonotactic patterns of English. Due to a mistake in tape-splicing, the syllables [rɪg-] and [pɪk-] of set B were eliminated from the test materials. The remaining 64 syllables are listed in Table 2.

Spectrograms of one syllable from each set are shown in Figure 1. The first letter after the vowel represents the consonant cues present before the tape junction and the second letter represents the consonant cues present after the tape junction. The hyphens indicate the places of the tape junction.

The 64 syllables were mixed and recorded in random order onto a test tape with approximately four seconds between syllables.

Subjects. The test tape was played to two groups of listeners. Listeners of Group I all had had rather intensive training in phonetics. All but one either had field experience in linguistics or had taught courses in language or phonetics. Listeners of Group II had virtually no background in phonetics but were all native speakers of American English. Most of the listeners in both groups were graduate students at the University of Michigan. The test tape was played to each listener individually through a pair of PDR-8 earphones at a constant setting. Listeners of Group I were informed of the make-up of the syllables, as described in the preceding paragraphs here, and were asked to transcribe the syllables phonetically. Listeners of Group II were given multiple-choice answer sheets which did not permit clusters as possible responses. For example, for a test-tape syllable which begins with [p] the choices on the answer sheet were the words in the top row of Table 1, *pip, pit, pick,* and *pig.* Group II subjects were asked to circle the word which they believed the syllable to be. In most cases, five syllables were played for the listener (in either group) from the latter part of the test tape in order to orient him to the test conditions.

The two groups consisted of 20 listeners each. Multiplied by 64 syllables the total number of elicited responses would have been 2560. There were nine question marks and seven alternative identifications, most of which were volunteered by the listeners of Group I. (To facilitate comparison, the results of the listening test are presented on a percentage scale in all the graphs.)

Results

Measurement of Duration. Spectrograms of the 64 syllables were made for the measurement of the durations of the various vowels and gaps. It was found that although no extra effort was made to control the vowel lengths in recording the syllables, 57 of the 66 vowels were approximately 12 csec in duration (within 1 csec of this value). It is interesting to note in passing that the five short vowels at 9 and 10 csec were all before voiceless consonants

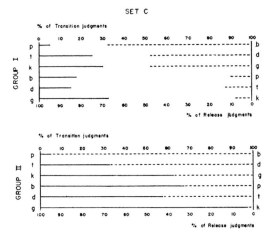

FIGURE 2. The percentage of judgments based on either transitions or releases for the Set C syllables. The solid lines are to be read from left to right and the broken lines from right to left.

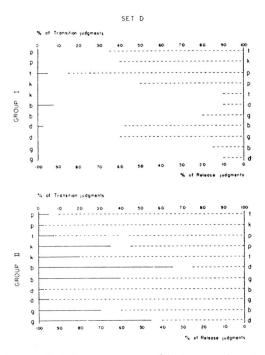

FIGURE 3. The percentage of judgments based on either transitions or releases for the Set D syllables.

(3) and that the four vowels at 14 csec were all before voiced consonants.

For Set B the cuts were made mostly at 7 and 8 csec from the termination of the formants. The lengths of the gap of Set A ranged from 14 to 28 csec. The tape junctions for Sets C and D occurred approximately midway between the termination of the formants and the spike of the release.

In the examination of the data no significant correlation was found between the perception of the plosives and the duration of the gaps.

Transition Versus Release. In Figures 2 and 3 the plosive cues before the tape junction are listed in the column at the left of the graphs and the corresponding plosive cues after the tape junction are listed in the columns at the right. The solid lines, to be read from left to right, indicate the percentage of judgments based on the cues of the left columns; the corresponding broken lines, from right to left, indicate the percentage of judgments based on the cues of the right columns. The intermediate spaces between the solid and the broken lines represent the judgments based on neither of these two types of cues.

To illustrate, the top row in Figure 2 shows the Group I responses to Set C syllables which end with [p-b]. Here 5% of the listeners identified the syllables to end in [p] and 67½% in [b] while 27½% transcribed clusters or single consonants except for [p] and [b].

The general pattern of Figure 2 suggests that the homorganic clusters of Set C were judged more as voiced plosives in both the voiced-voiceless and the voiceless-voiced sequences. This can perhaps be explained by the fact that Set C syllables all had voicing through half the duration of the gaps. The listeners were apparently reacting more to the presence of this cue than

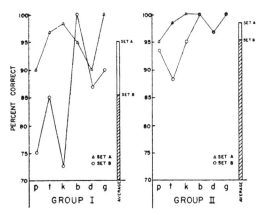

FIGURE 4. The percentage of correct judgments for Sets A and B.

to the significant lack of it in the other half of the gap.

Another fact to be observed was the high percentage of judgments based on the pre-junction cues of the velar plosives. Spectrograms made of these syllables showed maximum movement in the formants for the [k] and [g] transitions. This suggests that the value of formant transitions as perceptual cues for consonants depends on the magnitude of the formant movements, which, in turn, depends on the articulatory positions of the particular vowel and consonant involved.

The combined effect of the above two parameters is best seen in the bottom row. Here, the formant transitions for the voiced velar plosive dominated 97.5% of the responses.

Set D syllables in Figure 3 also showed a high percentage of judgments based on the velar transitions for Group II listeners. For Group I, the clusters which began with velar transitions had a high percentage of correct cluster identification.

It appears that the clusters of the Set D syllables were identified more frequently by the cues present in the releases than they were by cues present in the formant transitions, whereas the Set C clusters were more evenly divided in this respect.

Correct Identifications. In Figure 4, the numerals along the ordinate indicate the percentage of correct identifications for the respective plosives listed along the abscissa. The upper curves in the two graphs represent the scores of the two groups of listeners for Set A syllables, the lower curves for Set B syllables. With respect to both Set A and Set B, the phonetically untrained listeners made more correct identifications than those phonetically trained. This can perhaps be partly explained by the fact that there was greater difficulty in transcribing the syllables than there was in simply selecting an answer. Also, the Group II listeners, all of whom were native speakers of English, were little handicapped by their lack of phonetic training since these two sets or syllables were all normal English words.

Although the released plosives were almost always better identified, the releases made a greater difference in reinforcing the identity of the voiceless plosives for both groups of listeners. This observation seems to be explainable by the fact that before terminal junctures in informal American English, voiced plosives are released less frequently than are voiceless plosives. Consequently, although the releases were additional cues for identifying the plosives, the voiceless ones were more helpful.

In recent years, there has been much interest in relating speech perception to the influence of language background. (One listener from Group I, in whose native language final plosives are always released, made 40% of her errors in identifying the unreleased plosives.) To test such cross-language influences on perception, it would be preferable to use test items which are less conditioned to a particular linguistic code than the ones used here.

The average percentages of correct identifications for Set C and Set D clusters fell to 36% and 32%, respectively. For Set C, clusters of the voiced-voiceless sequence were correctly identified much more frequently than the voiceless-voiced clusters. This seems to check with the previous observation that voiceless releases are more helpful as identificational cues and appears to follow the general tendency in American English to devoice a sound in the final position. This evidence seems to suggest that the sequence of occurrence of the members of a cluster affects the identifiability of the cluster. An analysis of the wrong cluster identifications revealed that more than 70% of these errors contained the correct members but in reversed sequence. Perhaps this evidence can be explained eventually by the effects of time smear.

The four curves for Set D syllables were grouped partly according to 'units of difference in distinctive features' (*10*). The members of the first three clusters were different from each

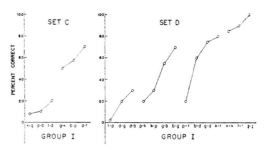

FIGURE 5. The percentage of correct judgments for Sets C and D.

other by three units. The members of the next four clusters were different by four units. The next four clusters conformed to the phonotactic rules of English, although the members were different by only three units. In English, two plosives cluster before junctures when only the second is as an alveolar plosive, which frequently occurs as the past tense morpheme. The last curve shows that the tape-splicing had not significantly decreased the intelligibility of the syllables (Figure 5).

Although the curves for Set D syllables overlap, the clusters whose members were four units different from each other were more correctly identified than the clusters with three units of difference on the left of the graph. But the clusters which are phonotactically permissible in English were better identified than both of the above, even though the members are also different by three units.

Discussion

With respect to the last two graphs, an interesting question can be raised concerning a recent hypothesis on the frequency of consonant clusters (4, 10). This hypothesis assumes that the clusters whose members differ from each other by more units of distinctive features would be more identifiable than those with less units of difference. Clusters differing from each other by the same number of units would be approximately equally perceptible.

However, in the Set D syllables, the English clusters with three units of difference were better identified than the non-English clusters with four units of difference. And, in the Set C syllables, the members of the six clusters

presumably differed from each other by the same number of units of distinctive features. But one sequence of occurrence was decidedly more identifiable than the other sequence. Consequently, the data for the Set C and Set D syllables in general do not support the assumption of the above hypothesis.

Theoretically, the question might be asked whether perception of linguistic units can be adequately specified by a set of physical parameters, such as the distinctive features. It has been previously demonstrated that the phonemic recognition of synthesized vowels partly depends on the physical parameters of neighboring synthesized vowels (5). The evidence of the present exploratory study also seems to suggest that correct identification of consonant clusters depends on the sequence of occurrence within the cluster and on the relationship between the consonants and the contiguous vowels.

Some interesting questions which have been raised previously are concerned with whether perceptibility can be predicted better by describing the units of difference between the particular allophones involved in the cluster than it can be by describing the units of difference between the phonemes so involved. Should these units of difference be weighted somehow as to their relative strength as perceptual cues?

These questions perhaps can lead to the development of an absolute scale of measurement for phonetic differences between speech sounds. Ideally, the developmental process would be based on experimental data and the procedure would be independent of linguistic codes. It is reasonable to believe that such a scale would tend to improve the testing of the perceptual properties of speech sounds and of their distribution in various languages.

Summary

The relative significance of various acoustical cues in the perception of final plosive consonants was investigated. Human speech and systematic modifications of it were used as the test stimuli. Suggestions were made in the direction of an absolute scale of measurement for phonetic differences between speech sounds regardless of linguistic code.

Acknowledgment

The author wishes to thank Prof. G. E. Peterson for his generous guidance, and Mr. Harwood Hess for assistance in tape splicing.

References

1. BROWN, R. W., and HILDUM, D. C., Expectancy and the perception of syllables. *Language*, 32, 1956, 411-419.

2. HALLE, M., HUGHES, G. W., and RADLEY, J.-P. A., Acoustic properties of stop consonants. *J. acoust. Soc. Amer.*, 29, 1957, 107-116.

3. HOUSE, A. S., and FAIRBANKS, G., The influence of consonant environment upon the secondary acoustical characteristics of vowels. *J. acoust. Soc. Amer.*, 25, 1953, 105-113.

4. KELLER, KATHRYN C., and SAPORTA, S., The frequency of consonant clusters in Chontal. *IJAL*, 23, 1957, 28-35.

5. LADEFOGED, P., and BROADBENT, D. E., Information conveyed by vowels. *J. acoust. Soc. Amer.*, 29, 1957, 98-104.

6. LIBERMAN, A. M., Some results of research on speech perception. *J. acoust. Soc. Amer.*, 29, 1957, 117-123.

7. LISKER, L., Closure duration and the intervocalic voiced-voiceless distinction in English. *Language*, 33, 1957, 42-49.

8. PETERSON, G. E., An oral communication model. *Language*, 31, 1955, 414-427.

9. ROSENZWEIG, M. R., and POSTMAN, L., Intelligibility as a function of frequency of usage. *J. exp. Psychol.*, 54, 1957, 412-422.

10. SAPORTA, S., Frequency of consonant clusters. *Language*, 31, 1955, 25-30.

11. STEVENS, K. N., and HOUSE, A. S., Studies of formant transitions using a vocal tract analog. *J. acoust. Soc. Amer.*, 28, 1956, 578-585.

REFERENCES

Chiba, T., and M. Kajiyama, *The Vowel: Its Nature and Structure* (Tokyo: Kaiseikan Publishing Company, Ltd., 1941; 2nd ed., 1958).

Elert, Claes-Christian, *Phonologic Studies of Quantity in Swedish* (Uppsala: Almqvist and Wiksell, 1964).

Fant, C. Gunnar M., *Acoustic Theory of Speech Production* (The Hague: Mouton and Company, 1960).

Flanagan, J. L., *Speech Analysis, Synthesis, and Perception* (New York: Academic Press, Inc., Publishers, 1965).

Hadding-Koch, Kerstin, *Acoustico-Phonetic Studies in the Intonation of Southern Swedish*, Travaux de l'Institut de Phonétique de Lund III (Lund: C. W. K. Gleerup, 1961).

Halle, Morris, *The Sound Pattern of Russian* (The Hague: Mouton and Company, 1959).

Jakobson, Roman, C. Gunnar M. Fant, and Morris Halle, *Preliminaries to Speech Analysis: The Distinctive Features and Their Correlates* (Technical Report No. 13, May 1952, Acoustics Laboratory, M.I.T., Cambridge, Mass., 1952; 3rd ed., The M.I.T. Press, Cambridge, Mass., 1963).

Joos, Martin, *Acoustic Phonetics* (Baltimore: Linguistic Society of America, Language Monograph No. 23, Waverly Press, Inc., 1948).

Ladefoged, Peter, *Elements of Acoustic Phonetics* (Chicago: The University of Chicago Press, 1962).

Lehiste, Ilse, *An Acoustic-Phonetic Study of Internal Open Juncture*, Supplement to *Phonetica*, Vol. 5 (Basel: S. Karger, 1960).

Lehiste, Ilse, *Acoustical Characteristics of Selected English Consonants*, Publication 34 of Indiana University Research Center in Anthropology, Folklore, and Linguistics (Bloomington: Indiana University, 1964).

Meyer-Eppler, W., *Grundlagen und Anwendungen der Informationstheorie* (Berlin-Göttingen-Heidelberg: Springer, 1959).

Potter, R. K., G. A. Kopp, and H. C. Green, *Visible Speech* (New York: Van Nostrand Co., 1947).

Pulgram, Ernst, *Introduction to the Spectrography of Speech* (The Hague: Mouton and Company, 1959).

Ungeheuer, Gerold, *Elemente einer akustischen Theorie der Vokalartikulation* (Berlin-Göttingen-Heidelberg: Springer, 1962).

AUTHOR INDEX

SUBJECT INDEX

Hiss, 202
Hub, 100, 148, 228, 283, 284, 336

Incisors, 42
Intelligibility, 301
Intensity, 44–45, 102, 155, 205
  of harmonics, 111
Intonation, 180
Inverse filtering, 102

Juncture, 191

Labial, 147
Larynx, 57, 58, 77
Lateral, 102, 103, 111, 115
Locus, 176, 227, 228, 283, 336
Loudness, 185

Mandible, 35, 36, 42
Manner of production, 105, 132, 160
Mingograph, 192

Nasal, 102, 103, 111, 193, 238, 278
Nasality, 54, 309
Nasalization, 46
Noise, 20, 21, 22, 102
Normalization, 105

Occlusive, 102, 103
Offglide, 228
Ogive, 319
Onglide, 228
Oscillogram, 3-7, 24, 111
Oscillograph, 4, 25, 27
Overtones, 58

Palatography, 205
Palato-velar, 148
Parameter, 34–41, 102
PAT (parametric artificial talking device), 202, 217, 327
Pattern playback, 155, 161, 273, 333
Period, 3, 47, 61
Periodicity, 21, 48
Pharynx, 35, 42, 103, 238
Phase, 53, 56, 60, 61
Phone, 64
Phoneme, 44, 56, 98, 153, 333
Pitch, 57, 62, 180
  perception of, 29
Place of articulation, 105, 133, 160, 310
Plosive, 192, 343
Pole-zero specification, 48, 66, 99, 220, 239
POVO synthesizer, 289
Prosodic features, 180

Radiation, 48, 82
Release, 343
Resonance, 3–8, 15–16, 49–53, 178, 224
  bar, 19
  level, 84
Resonator, 35, 42, 61
  features, 102
Retroflexion, 102, 121

Scots, 331
Segmentation, 97, 192
Segment duration, 102
Segment type features, 102
Servomechanism, 118
Sonagram, 138
Sonagraph, 45, 46, 130, 208
Sound pressure, 48, 63, 64
Source characteristic, 63, 65, 102
  features, 102
  function, 58
  intensity, 102
  spectrum, 50, 64, 82, 102
Spectrogram, 30–36, 95, 209
Spectrograph, 21–30
Spectrum envelope, 44, 82
  Fourier, 64, 76
  generator, 65, 66, 67
  matching, 102, 241
Speech, information-bearing elements of, 326
  perception, 301, 343
  production, acoustical theory of, 63–64, 220
  recognition, 63
  segment classification, 101
  synthesis, rules for, 333
Spike, 192
Stop consonant, 137, 170, 273, 285
Stress, 155, 183, 338
Striation, vertical, 16, 27, 103, 123
Subglottal system, 46
Supraglottal system, 57
Swedish, 51, 52, 54, 55, 56, 83
Syllable, 26, 43, 46, 55, 87, 186, 225
  division, 293
  nucleus, 191, 228
Synthesizer, 34, 56, 316
  parallel, 99
  series, 99
Synthetic sounds, experiments with, 149, 159, 224, 273, 316, 328

Teledeltos paper, 30
Tempo, 159, 196